The Essential Rudolf Steiner

Theosophy, an Introduction
An Esoteric Cosmology
Intuitive Thinking as a Spiritual Path
An Introduction to Waldorf Education and
Other Essays
How to Know Higher Worlds

The Essential Rudolf Steiner

by Rudolf Steiner

Wilder Publications, LLC.
PO Box 3005
Radford VA 24143-3005

ISBN 13: 978-1-5154-3606-5

Theosophy, an Introduction

Introduction

When in the autumn of 1813, Johann Gottlieb Fichte gave to the world as the ripe fruit of a life wholly devoted to the service of truth, his Introduction to the Science of Knowledge, he said at the very outset, "This doctrine presupposes an entirely new inner sense organ or instrument through which a new world is revealed having no existence for the ordinary man." He then showed by a simile how incomprehensible this doctrine must be when judged by conception of the ordinary senses. "Think of a world of people born blind who, therefore, know only those objects and relations that exist through the sense of touch. Go among them, and speak to them of colors and the other relations that exist only through light and for the sense of sight. You will convey nothing to their minds, and this will be the more fortunate if they tell you so, for you will then quickly notice your mistake and, if unable to open their eyes, you will cease talking in vain . . . ."

Now those who speak about such things as Fichte does in this instance, often find themselves in the position of a normal man among those born blind. Yet these are things that relate to a man's true being and highest goal, and to believe it necessary "to cease talking in vain" would be to despair of humanity. We ought not to doubt for one moment the possibility of opening the eyes of every earnest person to these things. On this supposition all those have written and spoken who have felt within themselves that the inner sense-instrument had developed, thereby enabling them to know the true nature and being of man, which is generally hidden from the outer senses. Hence from the most ancient times such a hidden wisdom has been spoken of again and again. Those who have grasped some understanding of it feel just as sure of their possession as people with normal eyes feel sure of their ability to visualize color. For them this hidden wisdom requires no proof. They know also that this hidden wisdom requires no proof for anyone else to whom the "higher sense" has unfolded itself. They can speak to such a person as a traveler can speak about America to people who have themselves never seen that country but who can visualize it, for they would see all that he has seen were the opportunity to present itself to them.

It is not, however, only to researchers into the spiritual world that the observer of the supersensible has to speak. He must address his words to all men, because he has to give an account of things that concern all men. Indeed, he knows that without a knowledge of these things no one can, in the true sense of the word, be a human being. Thus, he speaks to all men because he knows there are different degrees of understanding for what he has to say. The feeling for truth and the power of understanding it are inherent in everyone, and he knows that even those who are still far from the moment in which they will acquire the ability to make their own spiritual research can bring a measure of understanding to meet him. He addresses himself first to this understanding that can flash forth in every healthy soul. He knows that in this understanding there is a force that must slowly lead to the higher degrees of knowledge. This feeling, which perhaps at first perceives nothing at all of what it is told, is itself the magician that opens the "eye of the spirit." In darkness this feeling stirs. The soul sees nothing, but through this feeling it is seized by the power of truth. The truth then gradually draws nearer to the soul and opens the higher sense in it. In one person it may take a longer, in another a shorter time. Everyone, however, who has patience and endurance reaches this goal, for although not every physical eye can be operated on, every spiritual eye can be opened. When it will be opened is only a question of time.

Erudition and scientific training are not prerequisite conditions for the unfolding of this higher sense. It can develop in the unsophisticated person just as in the renowned scientist. Indeed, what is often called at the present time the only true science can, for the attainment of this goal, be frequently a hindrance rather than a help because this science considers real only what is accessible to the ordinary senses. Its merits in regard to the knowledge of that reality may be ever so great, yet when science declares that what is necessary and a blessing for itself shall also be authoritative for all human knowledge, it thereby creates a mass of prejudices that close the approach to higher realities.

The objection is often made to what has just been said that insurmountable limits have been once and forever set to man's knowledge, and since a man cannot overstep these limits, all knowledge must be rejected that does not take them into account. Furthermore, the one who presumes to make assertions about things, which for many stand proved as lying beyond the limits of man's capacity for knowledge, is looked upon as being highly immodest. In making such objections the fact is entirely disregarded that a development of the human powers of knowledge must precede the higher knowledge. What lies beyond the limits of knowledge before such a development takes place is, after the awakening of faculties slumbering in every man, entirely within the realm of knowledge.

One point in this connection must not be neglected. It might be said, "Of what use is it to speak to people about things for which their powers of knowledge are not yet awakened and are therefore still closed to them?" This is really the wrong way to view the matter. Certain powers are required to discover the things referred to, but if after having been discovered they are made known, every person can understand them who is willing to bring to them unprejudiced logic and a healthy sense of truth. In this book the things made known are wholly of a kind that must produce the impression that through them the riddles of human life and the phenomena of the world can be satisfactorily approached. This impression will be produced upon everyone who permits thought, unclouded by prejudice, and a feeling for truth, free and without reservation, to work within him. Put yourself for a moment in the position of asking, "If the things asserted here are true, do they afford a satisfying explanation of life?" You will find that the life of every man supplied a confirmation.

In order to be a teacher in these higher regions of existence it is by no means sufficient to have simply developed the sense for them. To that end science is just as necessary as it is for the teacher's calling in the world of ordinary reality. Higher seeing alone does not make a knower in the spiritual any more than healthy sense organs make a scholar in the ream of sensible realities. Because in truth all reality, the lower as well as the higher spiritual, are only two sides of one and the same fundamental being, anyone who is ignorant in the lower branches of knowledge will as a rule remain ignorant in the higher. This fact creates a feeling of immeasurable responsibility in the person who, through a spiritual call, feels himself summoned to speak about the spiritual regions of existence. It imposes upon him humility and reserve. This should deter no one — not even those whose other circumstances of life afford them no opportunity for the study of ordinary science — from occupying himself with the higher truths. Everyone can fulfill his task as a man without understanding anything of botany, zoology, mathematics and the other sciences. He cannot, however, in the full sense of the word, be a human being without having come in some way or other nearer to an understanding of the nature and destination of man as revealed through the knowledge of the supersensible.

The highest to which a man is able to look, he calls the Divine, and he somehow must think of the highest destiny as being in connection with this Divinity. The wisdom, therefore, that reaches out beyond the sensible and reveals to him his own being and with it his final goal, may well be called divine wisdom or theosophy. To the study of the spiritual process in human life and in the cosmos, the term spiritual science may be given. When, as in this book, one extracts from this spiritual science those special results that have reference to the spiritual core of man's being then the expression theosophy may be employed to designate this domain because it has been employed for centuries in this way.

From this point of view there will be sketched in this book an outline of the theosophical conception of the universe. The writer of it will bring forward nothing that is not a fact for him in the same sense that an experience of the outer world is a fact for eyes and ears and the ordinary intelligence. The concern here is with experiences that become accessible to everyone who is determined to tread the path of knowledge described in a later chapter of this book. We take the right attitude towards the things of the supersensible world when we assume that sound thinking and feeling are capable of understanding everything of true knowledge that emerges from the higher worlds. Further, when we start from this understanding and therewith lay down a firm foundation, we have also made a great step forward towards, "seeing" for ourselves, even though in order to attain this, other things must be added also. We lock and bolt the door to the true higher knowledge, however, when we despise this road and are determined to penetrate the higher worlds only in some other way. To have decided to recognize higher worlds only when we have seen them is a hindrance in the way of this very seeing itself. The determination to understand first through sound thinking what later can be seen, furthers that seeing. It conjures forth important powers of the soul that lead to this seeing of the seer.

The Essential Nature of Man

The following words of Goethe point beautifully to the beginning of one way by which the essential nature of man can be known. "As soon as a person becomes aware of the objects around him, he considers them in relation to himself, and rightly so, because his whole fate depends on whether they please or displease him, attract or repel, help or harm him. This quite natural way of looking at or judging things appears to be as easy as it is necessary. A person is, nevertheless, exposed through it to a thousand errors that often make him ashamed and embitter his life.

"A far more difficult task is undertaken by those whose keen desire for knowledge urges them to strive to observe the objects of nature as such and in their relationship to each other. These individuals soon feel the lack of the test that helped them when they, as men, regarded the objects in reference to themselves personally. They lack the test of pleasure and displeasure, attraction and repulsion, usefulness and harmfulness. Yet this test must be renounced entirely. They ought as dispassionate and, so to speak, divine beings, to seek and examine what is, not what gratifies. Thus the true botanist should not be moved either by the beauty or by the usefulness of the plants. He must study their formation and their relation to the rest of the plant kingdom. They are one and all enticed forth and shone upon by the sun without distinction, and so he should, equably and quietly, look at and survey them all and obtain the test for this knowledge, the data for his deductions, not out of himself, but from within the circle of the things he observes."

This thought thus expressed by Goethe directs man's attention to three divisions of things. First, the objects concerning which information continually flows to him through the doors of his senses — the objects he touches, smells, tastes, hears and sees. Second, the impressions that these make on him, characterizing themselves through the fact that he finds the one sympathetic, the other abhorrent, the one useful, another harmful. Third, the knowledge that he, as a "so to speak divine being," acquires concerning the objects, that is, the secrets of their activities and their being as they unveil themselves to him.

These three divisions are distinctly separate in human life, and man thereby becomes aware that he is interwoven with the world in a threefold way. The first division is one that he finds present, that he accepts as a given fact. Through the second he makes the world into his own affair, into something that has a meaning for him. The third he regards as a goal towards which he ought unceasingly to strive.

Why does the world appear to man in this threefold way? A simple consideration will explain it. I cross a meadow covered with flowers. The flowers make their colors known to me through my eyes. That is the fact I accept as given. Having accepted the fact, I rejoice in the splendor of the colors. Through this I turn the fact into an affair of my own. Through my feelings I connect the flowers with my own existence. Then, a year later I go again over the same meadow. Other flowers are there. Through them new joys arise in me. My joy of the former year will appear as a memory. This is in me. The object that aroused it in me is gone, but the flowers I now see are of the same kind as those I saw the year before. They have grown in accordance with the same laws as have the others. If I have informed myself regarding this species and these laws, I then find them again in the flowers of this year, just as I found them in those of last year. So I shall perhaps muse, "The flowers of last year are gone and my joy in them remains only in my memory. It is bound up with my existence alone. What I recognized in the flowers of last year and recognize again this year, however, will remain as long as such flowers grow. That is something that revealed itself to me, but it is not dependent on my existence in the same way as my joy is. My feelings of joy remain in me. The laws, the being of the flowers, remain outside of me in the world."

By these means man continually links himself in this threefold way with the things of the world. One should not, for the present, read anything into this fact, but merely take it as it stands. From this it can be seen that man has three sides to his nature. This and nothing else will, for the present, be indicated here by the three words, body, soul and spirit. Whoever connects any preconceived opinions or even hypotheses with these three words will necessarily misunderstand the following explanations. By body is here meant that through which the things in the environment of a man reveal themselves to him, as in the above example, the flowers in the meadow. By the word soul is signified that by which he links the things to his own being, through which he experiences pleasure and displeasure, desire and aversion, joy and sorrow in connection with them. By spirit is meant what becomes manifest in him when as Goethe expressed it, he looks at things as a "so to speak divine being." In this sense man consists of body, soul and spirit.

Through his body man is able to place himself for the time being in connection with things; through his soul he retains in himself the impressions they make on him; through his spirit there reveals itself to him what the things retain for themselves. Only when we observe man in these three aspects can we hope to throw light on his whole being, because they show him to be related in a threefold way to the rest of the world.

Through his body man is related to the objects that present themselves to his senses from without. The materials from the outer world compose his body, and the forces of the outer world work also in it. He observes the things of the outer world with his senses, and he also is able to observe his own bodily existence. It is impossible, however, for him to observe his soul existence in the same way. Everything in him that is bodily process can be perceived with his bodily senses. His likes and dislikes, his joy and pain, neither he nor anyone else can perceive with bodily senses. The region of the soul is inaccessible to bodily perception. The bodily existence of a man is manifest to all eyes; the soul existence he carries within himself as his world. Through the spirit, however, the outer world is revealed to him in a higher way. The mysteries of the outer world, indeed, unveil themselves in his inner being. He steps in spirit out of himself and lets the things speak about themselves, about what has significance not for him but for them. For example, man looks up at the starry heavens. The delight his soul experiences belongs to him. The eternal laws of the stars that he comprehends in thought, in spirit, belong not to him but to the stars themselves.

In this way, man is a citizen of three worlds. Through his body he belongs to the world that he also perceives through his body; through his soul he constructs for himself his own world; through his spirit a world reveals itself to him that is exalted above both the others.

It seems obvious that because of the essential difference of these three worlds, a clear understanding of them and of man's share in them can only be obtained by means of three different modes of observation.

The Corporeal Nature of Man

We learn to know man's body through bodily senses, and the manner of observing it cannot differ from the way in which we learn to know other objects perceived by the senses. As we observe minerals, plants and animals, so can we also observe man. He is related to these three forms of existence. Like the minerals, he builds his body out of natural substances; like the plants, he grows and propagates his species; like the animals, he perceives the objects around him and builds up his inner experiences on the basis of the impressions they make on him. Thus, a mineral, a plant and an animal existence may be ascribed to man.

The differences in structure of minerals, plants and animals correspond with the three forms of their existence. It is this structure — the shape — that is perceived through the senses, and that alone can be called body. Now the human body is different from that of the animal. This difference must be recognized, whatever may otherwise be thought of the relationship of man to animals. Even the most extreme materialist who denies all soul cannot but admit the truth of this passage uttered by Carus in his Oragnon der Natur und des Geistes. "The finer, inner construction of the nervous system and especially of the brain remains still an unsolved problem for the physiologist and the anatomist. That this concentration of structures ever increases in the animal kingdom and reaches in man a stage unequalled in any other being is a fully established fact — a fact that is of the deepest significance in regard to the mental evolution of man. Indeed, we may go so far as to say it is really a sufficient explanation of that evolution. Where, therefore, the structure of the brain has not developed properly, where its smallness and poverty are in evidence as in the case of microcephali and idiots, it goes without saying that we can no more expect the appearance of original ideas and of knowledge than we can expect the propagation of the species from persons with completely stunted reproductive organs. On the other hand, a strong and beautifully developed build of the whole man, and especially of the brain, will certainly not in itself take the place of genius but it will at any rate supply the first and indispensable condition for higher knowledge."

Just as one ascribes to the human body the three forms of existence, mineral, plant and animal, so one must ascribe to it a fourth — the distinctively human form. Through his mineral existence man is related to everything visible; through his plantlike existence to all beings that grow and propagate their species; through his animal existence to all those that perceive their surroundings and by means of external impressions have inner experiences; through his human form of existence he constitutes, even in regard to his body alone, a kingdom by himself.

The Soul Nature of Man

Man's soul nature as his own inner world is different from his bodily nature. When attention is turned to even the simplest sensation, what is personally his own comes at once to the fore. Thus no one can know whether one person perceives even a simple sensation in exactly the same way as another. It is known that there are people who are color-blind. They see things only in various shades of grey. Others are only partially color-blind. Because of this they are unable to distinguish between certain shades of color. The picture of the world that their eyes gives them is different from that of so-called normal persons. The same holds good more or less in regard to the other senses. Thus it will seem without further elaboration that even simple sensations belong to the inner world. I can perceive with my bodily senses the red table that another person perceives but I cannot perceive his sensation of red. We must, therefore, describe sensation as belonging to the soul. If this single fact is grasped quite clearly, we shall soon cease to regard inner experiences as mere brain processes or something similar. Feeling must link itself with sensation. One sensation causes us pleasure, another displeasure. These are stirrings of our inner life, our soul life. In our feelings we create a second world in addition to the one working on us from without. A third is added to this — the world of the will. Through the will we react on the outer world thereby stamping the impress of our inner being upon it. The soul of man, as it were, flows outwards in the activities of his will.

The actions of man differ from the occurrences of outer nature in that they bear the impress of his inner life. Thus the soul as man's own possession stands confronting the outer world. He receives from the outer world the incitements, but he creates in response to these incitements a world of his own. The body becomes the foundation of the soul being of man.

The Spiritual Nature of Man

The soul nature of man is not determined by the body alone. Man does not wander aimlessly and without purpose from one sensation to another, nor does he act under the influence of every casual incitement that plays upon him either from without or through the processes of his body. He thinks about his perceptions and his acts. By thinking about his perceptions he gains knowledge of things. By thinking about his acts he introduces a reasonable coherence into his life. He knows that he will worthily fulfill his duty as a man only when he lets himself be guided by correct thoughts in knowing as well as in acting. The soul of man, therefore, is confronted by a twofold necessity. By the laws of the body it is governed by natural necessity. It allows itself also to be governed by the laws that guide it to exact thinking because it voluntarily acknowledges their necessity. Nature subjects man to the laws of changing matter, but he subjects himself to the laws of thought. By this means he makes himself a member of a higher order than the one to which he belongs through his body. This order is the spiritual. The spiritual is as different from the soul as the soul is from the body. As long as only the particles of carbon, hydrogen, nitrogen and oxygen that are in motion in the body are spoken of, we do not have the soul in view. Soul life begins only when within the motion of these particles the feeling arises, `I taste sweetness," or, "I feel pleasure." Likewise, we do not have the spirit in view as long as merely those soul experiences are considered that course through anyone who gives himself over entirely to the outer world and his bodily life. This soul life is rather the basis of the spiritual just as the body is the basis of the soul life. The biologist is concerned with the body, the investigator of the soul — the psychologist — with the soul, and the investigator of the spirit with the spirit. It is incumbent on those who would understand the nature of man by means of thinking, first to make clear to themselves through self-reflection the difference between body, soul and spirit.

Body, Soul and Spirit

Man can only come to a true understanding of himself when he grasps clearly the significance of thinking within his being. The brain is the bodily instrument of thinking. A properly constructed eye serves us for seeing colors, and the suitably constructed brain serves us for thinking. The whole body of man is so formed that it receives its crown in the physical organ of the spirit, the brain. The construction of the human brain can only be understood by considering it in relation to its task — that of being the bodily basis for the thinking spirit. This is borne out by a comparative survey of the animal world. Among the amphibians the brain is small in comparison with the spinal cord; in mammals it is proportionately larger; in man it is largest in comparison with the rest of the body.

There are many prejudices prevalent regarding such statements about thinking as are presented here. Many people are inclined to under-value thinking and to place higher value on the warm life of feeling or emotion. Some even say it is not by sober thinking but by warmth of feeling and the immediate power of the emotions that we raise ourselves to higher knowledge. People who talk in this way are afraid they will blunt the feelings by clear thinking. This certainly does result from ordinary thinking that refers only to matters of utility. In the case of thoughts that lead to higher regions of existence, what happens is just the opposite. There is no feeling and no enthusiasm to be compared with the sentiments of warmth, beauty and exaltation that are enkindled through the pure, crystal-clear thoughts that refer to the higher worlds. The highest feelings are, as a matter of fact, not those that come of themselves, but those that are achieved by energetic and persevering thinking.

The human body is so constructed that it is adapted to thinking. The same materials and forces that are present in the mineral kingdom are so combined in the human body that thought can manifest itself by means of this combination. This mineral structure built up in accordance with its function will be called in the following pages the physical body of man.

Organized with reference to the brain as its central point, this mineral structure comes into existence by propagation and reaches its fully developed form through growth. Man shares propagation and growth in common with plants and animals. Through propagation and growth what is living differentiates itself from the lifeless mineral. Life gives rise to life by means of the germ. Descendant follows forefather from one living generation to another. The forces through which a mineral originates are directed upon the substances of which it is composed. A quartz crystal is formed through the forces inherent in the silicon and oxygen that are combined in the crystal. The forces that shape an oak tree must be sought for indirectly in the germ-cells of the mother and father plants. The form of the oak is preserved through propagation from forefather to descendent. Thus, there are inner determining conditions innate in living things, and it was a crude view of nature that held lower animals, even fishes, to have evolved out of mud. The form of the living passes itself on by means of heredity. How a living being develops depends on what father and mother it has sprung from — in other words, on the species to which it belongs. The materials it is composed of are continually changing but the species remains constant during life and is transmitted to the descendants. Therefore, it is the species that determines the combination of the materials. This force that determines species will here be called life-force. Mineral forces express themselves in crystals, and the formative life-force expresses itself in the species or forms of plant and animal life.

The mineral forces are perceived by man by means of his bodily senses, and he can only perceive things for which he has such senses. Without the eye there is no perception of light; without the ear no perception of sound. The lowest organisms have only one of the senses belonging to man — a kind of sense of touch. These organisms have no awareness of the world perceptible to man with the exception of those mineral forces that they perceive by the sense of touch. In proportion to the development of the other senses in the higher animals does their surrounding world, which man also perceives, become richer and more varied. It depends, therefore, on the organs of a being whether what exists in the outer world exists also for the being itself as something perceptible. What is present in the air as a certain motion becomes in man the sensation of hearing. Man, however, does not perceive the manifestations of the life-force through the ordinary senses. He sees the colors of the plants; he smells their perfume. The life-force, however, remains hidden from this form of observation. Even so, those with ordinary senses have just as little right to deny that there is a life-force as the man born blind has to deny that colors exist. Colors are there for the person born blind as soon as he has undergone an operation. In the same way, the various species of plants and animals created by the life-force — not merely the individual plants and animals — are present for man as objects of perception as soon as the necessary organ unfolds within him. An entirely new world opens out to him through the unfolding of this organ. He now perceives not merely the colors, the odors and other characteristics of living beings, but the life itself of these beings. In each plant and animal he perceives, besides the physical form, the life-filled spirit-form. In order to have a name for this spirit-form, let it be called the ether body or life body.

To the investigator of spiritual life this ether body is for him not merely a product of the materials and forces of the physical body, but a real independent entity that first calls forth into life these physical materials and forces. We speak in accordance with spiritual science when we say that a purely physical body derives its form — a crystal, for example — through the action of the physical formative forces innate in the lifeless. A living body does not receive its form through the action of these forces because in the moment life has departed from it and it is given over to the physical forces only, it falls to pieces. The ether body is an organism that preserves the physical body from dissolution every moment during life. In order to see this body, to perceive it in another being, the awakened spiritual eye is required. Without this ability its existence as a fact can still be accepted on logical grounds, but it can be seen with the spiritual eye just as color can be seen with the physical eye.

We should not take offense at the expression "ether body." "Ether" here designates something different from the hypothetical ether of the physicist. We should regard it simply as a name for what is described here. The structure of the physical body of the human being is a kind of reflection of its purpose, and this is also the case with the human etheric body. It can be understood only when it is considered in relation to the thinking spirit. The human etheric body differs from that of plants and animals through being organized to serve the purposes of the thinking spirit. Man belongs to the mineral world through his physical body, and he belongs through this etheric body to the life-world. After death the physical body dissolves into the mineral world, the ether body into the life-world. By the word "body" is meant whatever gives a being shape or form. The term body must not be confused with a bodily form perceptible to the physical senses. Used in the sense implied in this book, the term body can also be applied to such forms as soul and spirit may assume.

The life-body is still something external to man. With the first stirrings of sensation the inner self responds to the stimuli of the outer world. You may search forever in what is called the outer world but you will be unable to find sensation in it. Rays of light stream into the eye, penetrating it until they reach the retina. There they cause chemical processes in the so-called visual-purple. The effect of these stimuli is passed on through the optic nerve to the brain. There further physical processes arise. Could these be observed, we would simply see more physical processes just as elsewhere in the physical world. If I am able also to observe the ether body, I shall see how the physical brain process is at the same time a life-process. The sensation of blue color that the recipient of the rays of light experiences, however, I can find nowhere in this manner. It arises only within the soul of the recipient. If, therefore, the being of this recipient consisted only of the physical and ether bodies, sensation could not exist. The activity by which sensation becomes a fact differs essentially from the operations of the formative life-force. By that activity an inner experience is called forth from these operations. Without this activity there would be a mere life-process such as we observe in plants. Imagine a man receiving impressions from all sides. Think of him as the source of the activity mentioned above, flowing out in all directions from which he is receiving these impressions. In all directions sensations arise in response to the stimuli. This fountain of activity is to be called the sentient soul. This sentient soul is just as real as the physical body. If a man stands before me and I disregard his sentient soul by thinking of him as merely a physical body, it is exactly as if, instead of a painting, I were to call up in memory merely the canvas.

A statement similar to the one previously made in reference to the ether body must be made here about perceiving the sentient soul. The bodily organs are blind to it. The organ by which life can be perceived as life is also blind to it. The ether body is seen by means of this organ, and so through a still higher organ the inner world of sensation can become a special kind of supersensible perception. Then a man not only senses the impressions of the physical and life world, but he beholds the sensations themselves. The sensation world of another being is spread out before a man with such an organ like an external reality. One must distinguish between experiencing one's own sensation world, and looking at the sensation world of another person. Every man, of course, can see into his own sensation world. Only the seer with the opened spiritual eye can see the sensation world of another. Unless a man is a seer, he knows the world of sensation only as an inner one, only as the peculiar hidden experiences of his own soul. With the opened spiritual eye there shines out before the outward-turned spiritual gaze what otherwise lives only in the inner nature of another being.

*   *   *

In order to prevent misunderstanding, it may be expressly stated here that the seer does not experience in himself what the other being experiences as the content of his world of sensation. The other being experiences the sensations in question from the point of view of his own inner nature. The seer, however, becomes aware of a manifestation or expression of the sentient world.

The sentient soul's activity depends entirely on the ether body. The sentient soul draws from the ether body what it in turn causes to gleam forth as sensation. Since the ether body is the life within the physical body, the sentient soul is also directly dependent on the physical body. Only with correctly functioning and well-constructed eyes are correct color sensations possible. It is in this way that the nature of the body affects the sentient soul, and it is thus determined and limited in its activity by the body. It lives within the limitations fixed for it by the nature of the body. The body accordingly is built up of mineral substances, is vitalized by the ether body, and itself limits the sentient soul. A man, therefore, who has the organ mentioned above for seeing the sentient soul sees it limited by the body, but its limits do not coincide with those of the physical body. This soul extends somewhat beyond the physical body and proves itself to be greater than the physical body. The force through which its limits are set, however, proceeds from the physical body. Thus, between the physical body and the ether body on the one hand, and the sentient soul on the other, another distinct member of the human constitution inserts itself. This is the soul body or sentient body. It may also be said that one part of the ether body is finer than the rest and this finer part forms a unity with the sentient soul, whereas the coarser part forms a kind of unity with the physical body. The sentient soul, nevertheless, extends, as has been said, beyond the soul body.

What is here called sensation is only a part of the soul nature. (The expression sentient soul is chosen for the sake of simplicity.) Connected with sensations are the feelings of desire and aversion, impulses, instincts, passions. All these bear the same character of individual life as do the sensations, and are, like them, dependent on the bodily nature.

*   *   *

The sentient soul enters into mutual action and reaction with the body, and also with thinking, with the spirit. In the first place, thinking serves the sentient soul. Man forms thoughts about his sensations and thus enlightens himself regarding the outside world. The child that has burnt itself thinks it over and reaches the thought, "Fire burns." Man does not follow his impulses, instincts, and passions blindly but his reflection upon them brings about the opportunity for him to gratify them. What one calls material civilization is motivated entirely in this direction. It consists in the services that thinking renders to the sentient soul. Immeasurable quantities of thought-power are directed to this end. It is thought-power that has built ships, railways, telegraphs and telephones, and by far the greatest proportion of these conveniences serves only to satisfy the needs of sentient souls. Thought-force permeates the sentient soul similarly to the way the formative life-force permeates the physical body. The formative life-force connects the physical body with forefathers and descendants and thus brings it under a system of laws with which the purely mineral body is in no way concerned. In the same way thought-force brings the soul under a system of laws to which it does not belong as mere sentient soul. Through the sentient soul man is related to the animals. In animals also we observe the presence of sensations, impulses, instincts and passions. The animal, however, obeys these immediately and they do not become interwoven with independent thoughts thereby transcending the immediate experiences. This is also the case to a certain extent with undeveloped human beings. The mere sentient soul, therefore, differs from the evolved higher member of the soul that brings thinking into its service. This soul that is served by thought will be termed the intellectual soul. It could also be called the mind soul.

The intellectual soul permeates the sentient soul. The one who possesses the organ for seeing the soul sees the intellectual soul as a separate entity in contrast to the mere sentient soul.

*   *   *

By thinking, the human being is led above and beyond his own personal life. He acquires something that extends beyond his soul. He comes to take for granted his conviction that the laws of thought are in conformity with the laws of the universe, and he feels at home in the universe because this conformity exists. This conformity is one of the weighty facts through which he learns to know his own nature. He searches in his soul for truth and through this truth it is not only the soul that speaks but also the things of the world. What is recognized as truth by means of thought has an independent significance that refers to the things of the world, and not merely to one's own soul. In my delight at the starry heavens I live in my own inner being. The thoughts I form for myself about the paths of heavenly bodies have the same significance for the thinking of every other person as they have for mine. It would be absurd to speak of my delight were I not in existence. It is not in the same way absurd, however, to speak of my thoughts, even without reference to myself, because the truth that I think today was true also yesterday and will be true tomorrow, although I concern myself with it only today. If a fragment of knowledge gives me joy, the joy has significance just as long as it lives in me, whereas the truth of the knowledge has its significance quite independently of this joy.

By grasping the truth, the soul connects itself with something that carries its value in itself. This value does not vanish with the feeling in the soul any more than it arose with it. What is really truth neither arises nor passes away. It has a significance that cannot be destroyed. This is not contradicted by the fact that certain human truths have a value that is transitory inasmuch as they are recognized after a certain period as partial or complete errors. Man must say to himself that truth after all exists in itself, although his conceptions are only transient forms of manifestation of the eternal truths. Even someone who says, like Lessing, that he contents himself with the eternal striving for truth because the full pure truth can only exist for a god, does not deny the eternity of truth but establishes it by such an utterance. Only what has an eternal significance in itself can call forth an eternal striving for it. Were truth not in itself independent, if it acquired its value and significance through the feelings of the human soul, it could not be the one unique goal for all mankind. By the very fact of our striving for truth, we concede its independent being.

As it is with the true, so is it with the truly good. Moral goodness is independent of inclinations and passions inasmuch as it does not allow itself to be commanded by them but commands them. Likes and dislikes, desire and loathing belong to the personal soul of a man. Duty stands higher than likes and dislikes. Duty may stand so high in the eyes of a man that he will sacrifice his life for its sake. A man stands the higher the more he has ennobled his inclinations, his likes and dislikes, so that without compulsion or subjection they themselves obey what is recognized as duty. The morally good has, like truth, its eternal value in itself and does not receive it from the sentient soul.

By causing the self-existent true and good to come to life in his inner being, man raises himself above the mere sentient soul. An imperishable light is kindled in it. In so far as the soul lives in this light, it is a participant in the eternal and unites its existence with it. What the soul carries within itself of the true and the good is immortal in it. Let us call what shines forth in the soul as eternal, the consciousness soul. We can speak of consciousness even in connection with the lower soul stirrings. The most ordinary everyday sensation is a matter of consciousness. To this extent animals also have consciousness. The kernel of human consciousness, that is, the soul within the soul, is what is here meant by consciousness soul. The consciousness soul is thus distinguished as a member of the soul distinct from the intellectual soul, which is still entangled in the sensations, impulses and passions. Everyone knows how a man at first counts as true what he prefers in his feelings and desires. Only that truth is permanent, however, that has freed itself from all flavor of such sympathy and antipathy of feeling. The truth is true even if all personal feelings revolt against it. That part of the soul in which this truth lives will be called consciousness soul.

Thus three members must be distinguished in the soul as in the body, namely, sentient soul, intellectual soul and consciousness soul. As the body works from below upwards with a limiting effect on the soul, so the spiritual works from above downwards into it, expanding it. The more the soul fills itself with the true and the good, the wider and the more comprehensive becomes the eternal in it. To him who is able to see the soul, the splendor radiating forth from a man in whom the eternal is expanding is just as much a reality as the light that streams out from a flame is real to the physical eye.   For the seer, the corporeal man counts as only part of the whole man. The physical body as the coarsest structure lies within others that mutually interpenetrate it and each other. The ether body fills the physical body as a life-form. The soul body (astral shape) can be perceived extending beyond this on all sides. Beyond this, again, extends the sentient soul, and then the intellectual soul, which grows the larger the more of the true and the good it receives into itself. This true and good causes the expansion of the intellectual soul. On the other hand, a man living only and entirely according to his inclinations, likes and dislikes, would have an intellectual soul whose limits coincide with those of his sentient soul. These organizations, in the midst of which the physical body appears as if in a cloud, may be called the human aura.

The perception of this aura, when seen as this book endeavors to present it, indicates an enrichment of man's soul nature.

*   *   *

In the course of his development as a child, there comes a moment in the life of a man when for the first time he feels himself to be an independent being distinct from all the rest of the world. For sensitive natures, it is a significant experience. The poet, Jean Paul, says in his autobiography, "I shall never forget the event that took place within me, hitherto narrated to no one and of which I can give place and time, when I stood present at the birth of my self-consciousness. As a small child I stood one morning at the door of the house looking towards the wood-pile on my left, when suddenly the inner vision, I am an I, came upon me like a flash of lightning from heaven and has remained shining ever since. In that moment my ego had seen itself for the first time and forever. Any deception of memory is hardly to be conceived as possible here, for no narrations by outsiders could have introduced additions to an occurrence that took place in the holy of holies of a human being, and of which the novelty alone gave permanence to such everyday surroundings." It is known that little children say of themselves, "Charles is good." "Mary wants to have this." One feels it is to be right that they speak of themselves as if of others because they have not yet become conscious of their independent existence, and the consciousness of the self is not yet born in them.

Through self-consciousness man describes himself as an independent being separate from all others, as "I." In his "I" he brings together all that he experiences as a being with body and soul. Body and soul are the carriers of the ego or "I," and in them it acts. Just as the physical body has its center in the brain, so has the soul its center in the ego. Man is aroused to sensations by impacts from without; feelings manifest themselves as effects of the outer world; the will relates itself to the outside world, realizing itself in external actions. The "I" as the particular and essential being of man remains quite invisible. With excellent judgment, therefore, does Jean Paul call a man's recognition of his ego an "occurrence taking place only in the veiled holy of holies of a human being," for with his "I" man is quite alone. This "I" is the very man himself. That justifies him in regarding his ego as his true being. He may, therefore, describe his body and his soul as the sheaths or veils within which he lives, and he may describe them as bodily conditions through which he acts. In the course of his evolution he learns to regard these tools ever more as instruments of service to his ego. The little word "I" is a name which differs from all others. Anyone who reflects in an appropriate manner on the nature of this name will find that in so doing an avenue opens itself to the understanding of the human being in the deeper sense. Any other name can be applied to its corresponding object by all men in the same way. Anybody can call a table, table, or a chair, chair. This is not so with the name "I." No one can use it in referring to another person. Each one can call only himself "I." Never can the name "I" reach my ears from outside when it refers to me. Only from within, only through itself, can the soul refer to itself as "I." When man therefore says "I" to himself, something begins to speak in him that has to do with none of the worlds from which the sheaths so far mentioned are taken. The "I" becomes increasingly the ruler of body and soul.

This also expresses itself in the aura. The more the "I" is lord over body and soul, the more definitely organized, the more varied and the more richly colored is the aura. The effect of the "I" on the aura can be seen by the seer. The "I" itself is invisible even to him. This remains truly within the "veiled holy of holies of a human being." The "I" absorbs into itself the rays of the light that flame forth in him as eternal light. As he gathers together the experiences of body and soul in the "I," so too he causes the thoughts of truth and goodness to stream into the "I." The phenomena of the senses reveal themselves to the "I" from the one side, the spirit reveals itself from the other. Body and soul yield themselves up to the "I" in order to serve it, but the "I" yields itself up to the spirit in order that the spirit may fill it to overflowing. The "I" lives in body and soul, but the spirit lives in the "I". What there is of spirit in it is eternal, for the "I" receives its nature and significance from that with which it is bound up. In so far as it lives in the physical body, it is subject to the laws of the mineral world; through its ether body to the laws of propagation and growth; by virtue of the sentient and intellectual souls, to the laws of the soul world; in so far as it receives the spiritual into itself it is subject to the laws of the spirit. What the laws of mineral and of life construct, come into being and vanishes. The spirit has nothing to do with becoming and perishing.

*   *   *

The "I" lives in the soul. Although the highest manifestation of the "I" belongs to the consciousness soul, one must, nevertheless, say that this "I" raying out from it fills the whole soul, and through it exerts its action upon the body. In the "I" the spirit is alive. The spirit sends its rays into the "I" and lives in it as in a sheath or veil, just as the "I" lives in its sheaths, the body and soul. The spirit develops the "I" from within, outwards; the mineral world develops it from without, inwards. The spirit forming and living as "I" will be called spirit self because it manifests as the "I," or ego, or self of man. The difference between the spirit self and the consciousness soul can be made clear in the following way. The consciousness soul is in touch with the self-existent truth that is independent of all antipathy and sympathy. The spirit self bears within it the same truth, but taken up into and enclosed by the "I," individualized by it, and absorbed into the independent being of the individual. It is through the eternal truth becoming thus individualized and bound up into one being with the "I" that the "I" itself attains to the eternal.

The spirit self is a revelation of the spiritual world within the "I," just as from the other side sensations are a revelation of the physical world within the "I." In what is red, green, light, dark, hard, soft, warm, cold one recognizes the revelations of the corporeal world. In what is true and good are to be found the revelations of the spiritual world. In the same sense in which the revelation of the corporeal world is called sensation, let the revelation of the spiritual be called intuition. Even the most simple thought contains intuition because one cannot touch thought with the hands or see it with the eyes. Its revelation must be received from the spirit through the "I." If an undeveloped and a developed man look at a plant, there lives in the ego of the one something quite different from what exists in the ego of the other. Yet the sensation of both are called forth by the same object. The difference lies in this, that the one can form far more perfect thoughts about the object than the other. If objects revealed themselves through sensation only, there could be no progress in spiritual development. Even the savage is affected by nature, but the laws of nature reveal themselves only to the thoughts fructified by intuition of the more highly developed man. The stimuli from the outer world are felt also by the child as incentives to the will, but the commandments of the morally good disclose themselves to him in the course of his development in proportion as he learns to live in the spirit and understand its revelations.

There could be no color sensations without physical eyes, and there could be no intuitions without the higher thinking of the spirit self. As little as sensation creates the plant in which color appears does intuition create the spiritual realities about which it is merely giving knowledge.

The ego of a man that comes to life in the soul draws into itself messages from above, from the spirit world, through intuitions, and through sensations it draws in messages from the spiritual [physical –e.Ed] world. In so doing it makes the spirit world into the individualized life of its own soul, even as it does the physical world by means of the senses. The soul, or rather the "I" flaming forth in it, opens its portals on two sides — towards the corporeal and towards the spiritual.

Now the physical world can only give information about itself to the ego by building out of physical materials and forces a body in which the conscious soul can live and possess within its organs for perceiving the corporeal world outside itself. The spiritual world, on the other hand, with its spiritual substances, and spiritual forces, builds a spirit body in which the `I" can live and, through intuitions, perceive the spiritual. (It is evident that the expressions spirit substance, spirit body, contain contradictions according to the literal meaning of the words. They are only used to direct attention to what, in the spiritual region, corresponds to the physical substance, the physical body of man.)

Within the physical world each human body is built up as a separate being, and within the spirit world the spirit body is also built up separately. For man there is an inner and an outer in the spirit world just as in the physical world there is an inner and an outer. Man takes in the materials of the physical world around him and assimilates them in his physical body, and he also takes up the spiritual from the spiritual environment and makes it into his own. The spiritual is the eternal nourishment of man. Man is born of the physical world, and he is also born of the spirit through the eternal laws of the true and the good. He is separated as an independent being from the spirit world outside him, and he is separated in the same manner from the whole physical world. This independent spiritual being will be called the spirit man.

If we investigate the human physical body, it is found to contain the same materials and forces as are to be found outside in the rest of the physical world. It is the same with the spirit man. In it pulsate the elements of the external spirit world. In it the forces of the rest of the spirit world are active. Within the physical skin a being is enclosed and limited that is alive and feels. It is the same in the spirit world. The spiritual skin that separates the spirit man from the unitary spirit world makes him an independent being within it, living a life within himself and perceiving intuitively the spiritual content of the world. Let us call this "spiritual skin" (auric sheath) the spirit sheath. Only it must be kept clearly in mind that the spiritual skin expands continually with advancing human evolution so that the spiritual individuality of man (his auric sheath) is capable of enlargement to an unlimited extent.

The spirit man lives within this spirit sheath. It is built up by the spiritual life force in the same way as the physical body is by the physical life force. In a similar way to that in which one speaks of an ether body, one must speak of an ether spirit in reference to the spirit man. Let his ether spirit be called life spirit. The spiritual nature of man is thus composed of three parts, spirit man, life spirit and spirit self.

For one who is a seer in the spiritual regions, this spiritual nature of man is, as the higher, truly spiritual part of the aura, a perceptible reality. He sees the spirit man as life spirit within the spirit sheath, and he sees how this life spirit grows continually larger by taking in spiritual nourishment from the spiritual external world. Further, he sees how the spirit sheath continually increases, widens out through what is brought into it, and how the spirit man becomes ever larger and larger. In so far as this becoming larger is seen spatially, it is of course only a picture of the reality. This fact notwithstanding, the human soul is directed towards the corresponding spiritual reality in conceiving this picture because the difference between the spiritual and the physical nature of man is that the physical nature has a limited size while the spiritual nature can grow to an unlimited extent.

Whatever of spiritual nourishment is absorbed has an eternal value. The human aura is accordingly composed of two interpenetrating parts. Color and form are given to the one by the physical existence of a man, and to the other by his spiritual existence. The ego marks the separation between them in such wise that the physical element after its own manner surrenders itself and builds up a body that allows a soul to live within it. The "I" surrenders itself and allows the spirit to develop in it, which now for its part permeates the soul and gives the soul its goal in the spirit world. Through the body the soul is enclosed in the physical. Through the spirit man there grow wings for movement in the spiritual world.

* * *

In order to comprehend the whole man one must think of him as put together out of the components mentioned above. The body builds itself up out of the world of physical matter in such a way that this structure is adapted to the requirements of the thinking ego. It is permeated with life force and becomes thereby the etheric or life body. As such it opens itself through the sense organs towards the outer world and becomes the soul body. The sentient soul permeates this and becomes a unity with it. The sentient soul does not merely receive the impacts of the outer world as sensations. It has its own inner life, fertilized through thinking on the one hand and through sensations on the other. The sentient soul thus becomes the intellectual soul. It is able to do this by opening itself to the intuitions from above as it does to sensations from below. Thus it becomes the consciousness soul. This is possible because the spirit world builds into it the organ of intuition, just as the physical body builds for it the sense organs. The senses transmit sensations by means of the soul body, and the spirit transmits to it intuitions through the organ of intuition. The spiritual human being is thereby linked into a unity with the consciousness soul, just as the physical body is linked with the sentient soul in the soul body. Consciousness soul and spirit self form a unity. In this unity the spirit man lives as life spirit in the same way that the ether body forms the bodily life basis for the soul body. Thus, as the physical body is enclosed in the physical skin, so is the spirit man in the spirit sheath. The members of the whole man are therefore as follows:

A. Physical Body

B. Ether or life body

C. Soul body

D. Sentient soul

E. Intellectual soul

F. Consciousness soul

G. Spirit self

H. Life spirit

I. Spirit man
Soul body (C) and sentient soul (D) are a unity in the earthly human being. In the same way consciousness soul (F) and spirit self (G) are a unity. Thus there come to be seven members in earthly man.
1. Physical body

2. Etheric or life body

3. Sentient soul body

4. Intellectual soul

5. Spirit-filled consciousness soul

6. Life spirit

7. Spirit man
In the soul the "I" flashes forth, receives the impulse from the spirit, and thereby becomes the bearer of the spiritual human being. Thus man participates in the three worlds, the physical, the soul and the spiritual. He is rooted in the physical world through his physical body, ether body and soul body, and through the spirit self, life spirit and spirit man he comes to flower in the spiritual world. The stalk, however, that takes root in the one and flowers in the other is the soul itself.

This arrangement of the members of man can be expressed in a simplified way, but one entirely consistent with the above. Although the human "I" flashes forth in the consciousness soul, it nevertheless penetrates the whole soul being. The parts of this soul being are not at all as distinctly separate as are the members of the bodily nature. They interpenetrate each other in a higher sense. If then one regards the intellectual soul and the consciousness soul as the two sheaths of the "I" that belong together, with the "I" itself as their kernel, then one can divide man into physical body, life body, astral body and "I." The expression astral body designates what is formed by considering the soul body and sentient soul as a unity. This expression is found in the older literature, and may be applied here in a somewhat broad sense to what lies beyond the sensibly perceptible in the constitution of man. Although the sentient soul is in certain respects energized by the "I," it is still so intimately connected with the soul body that a single expression is justified when united. When now the "I" saturates itself with the spirit self, this spirit self makes its appearance in such a way that the astral body is transmuted from within the soul. In the astral body the impulses, desires and passions of man are primarily active in so far as they are felt by him. Sense perceptions also are active therein. Sense perceptions arise through the soul body as a member in man that comes to him from the external world. Impulses, desires and passions arise in the sentient soul in so far as it is energized from within, before this inner part has yielded itself to the spirit self. This expresses itself in the illumination of the impulses, desires and passions by what the "I" has received from the spirit. The "I" has then, through its participation in the spiritual world, become ruler in the world of impulses and desires. To the extent to which it has become this, the spirit self manifests in the astral body, and the astral body is transmuted thereby. The astral body itself then appears as a two-fold body — partly untransmuted and partly transmuted. We can, therefore, designate the spirit self manifesting itself in man as the transmuted astral body.

A similar process takes place in the human individual when he receives the life spirit into his "I." The life body then becomes transmuted, penetrated with life spirit. The life spirit manifests itself in such a way that the life body becomes quite different from what it was. For this reason it can also be said that the life spirit is the transmuted life body. If the "I" receives the spirit man, it thereby receives the necessary force to penetrate the physical body. Naturally, that part of the physical body thus transmuted is not perceptible to the physical senses, because it is just this spiritualized part of the physical body that has become the spirit man. It is then present to the physical senses as physical, and insofar as this physical is spiritualized, it has to be beheld by spiritual perceptive faculties, because to the external senses the physical, even when penetrated by the spiritual, appears to be merely sensible.

Taking all this as basis, the following arrangement may also be given of the members of man:

1. Physical body

2. Life body

3. Astral body

4. I, as soul kernel

5. Spirit self as transmuted astral body

6. Life spirit as transmuted life body

7. Spirit man as transmuted physical body

Re-Embodiment of the Spirit and Destiny

The soul lives between body and spirit. The impressions coming to it through the body are transitory, enduring only as long as the body opens its organs to the things of the outer world. Only while the rose is in my line of vision can my open eye perceive its color. The presence of the things of the outer world as well as of the bodily organs is necessary in order that an impression, a sensation or a perception can occur. But what I have recognized in my mind as truth concerning the rose does not pass with the present moment, and as regards its truth, it is not in the least dependent on me. It would be true even though I had never stood before the rose. What I know through the spirit is rooted in an element of the soul life through which the soul is linked with a world-content that manifests itself in the soul independent of its bodily basis. The point here is not whether what manifests itself is essentially imperishable, but whether the manifestation occurs for the soul in such a way that its perishable bodily basis plays no part, and only that plays a part in it that is independent of this perishable body. The enduring element in the soul comes under observation at the moment we become aware that the soul has experiences not limited by its perishable factor. Again the important point is not whether these experiences come to consciousness primarily through perishable processes of the bodily organization, but the fact that they contain something that does indeed live in the soul, yet is independent of the transient process of perception. The soul is placed between the present and duration in that it holds the middle place between body and spirit. It also mediates between the present and duration. It preserves the present for remembrance, thus rescuing it from impermanence by taking it up into the duration of its own spiritual being. It also stamps what endures upon the temporal and impermanent by not merely yielding itself up in its own life to the transitory incitements, but by determining things out of its own initiative and embodying its own nature in them in the shape of the actions it performs. By remembrance the soul preserves the yesterday; by action it prepares the tomorrow.

If my soul could not retain the red of the rose through remembrance, it would always have to perceive it anew to be conscious of it. What can be retained by the soul after an external impression can become a mental image, independent of the external impression. Through this power of forming visualizations the soul makes the outer world so much its own inner world that it can then retain the latter in memory for remembrance and, independent of the impressions acquired, lead a life of its own with it. The soul life thus becomes the enduring effect of the transitory impressions of the external world.

Action also receives permanence when once it is stamped on the outer world. If I cut a twig from a tree, something has taken place through my soul that completely changes the course of events in the outer world. Something quite different would have happened to the branch of the tree had I not interfered by my action. I have called into life a series of effects that, without my existence, would not have been present. What I have done today endures for tomorrow. Through the deed it acquires permanence just as my impressions of yesterday have become permanent for my soul through memory.

For this fact of creating permanence through action we do not, in our ordinary consciousness form a definite visualization such as we have for memory, or as the result of a perception of an experience made permanent. Is not the ego of a man, however, linked just as much to the alteration in the world resulting from the deed as it is to a memory resulting from an impression? The ego judges new impressions differently depending upon whether or not it has one or another recollection. It has also as an "I" entered into a different relation to the world according to whether or not it has performed one deed or another. Whether, in the relation between the world and my "I," a certain new quality is present or not depends upon whether or not I have made an impression on another person through my action. I am quite a different person in my relationship to the world after having made an impression on my surroundings.

The fact that what is meant here is not so generally noticed as is the change taking place in the ego through its having acquired a recollection, is solely due to the circumstances that the moment a recollection is formed it unites itself with the soul life that man has always felt to be his own. The external effects of the deed, detached from this soul life, produce consequences that are again something quite different from what the memory retains of this deed. Apart from this, it must be admitted that after a deed has been accomplished, there is something in the world upon which the ego has stamped its character. If we really think out what is here being considered, the question must arise as to whether the results of a deed, on which the "I" has stamped its own nature, retain a tendency to return to the "I" just as an impression preserved in the memory is revived in response to some external inducement. Is it not possible that what has retained the imprint of the ego in the external world waits also to approach the human soul from without, just as memory, in response to a given inducement, approaches it from within? This matter is only put forward here as a question because it certainly might happen that the occasion would never arise on which the consequences of a deed, bearing the impress of the ego, could take effect in the human soul. That these consequences are present as such, and that through their presence they determine the relation of the world to the "I," is seen at once to be a possibility when we really follow out in thought the matter before us. In the following considerations we shall inquire whether there is anything in human life that, starting from this possibility, points to a reality.

*   *   *

Let us first consider memory. How does it originate? Evidently in quite a different way from sensation or perception. Without the eye I cannot have the sensation blue, but by means of the eye alone I do not have the remembrance of blue. If the eye is to give me this sensation now, a blue object must stand before it. The body would allow all impressions to sink back again into oblivion were it not for the fact that while the present image is being formed through the act of perception, something is also taking place in the relationship between the outer world and the soul. This activity brings about certain results within man enabling him through processes within himself to form a new image of what, in the first place, was brought about by an image from outside. Anyone who has acquired practice in observing the life of the soul will see the opinion to be quite erroneous that holds that the perception a man has today is the same he recalls tomorrow through memory, it having meanwhile remained somewhere or other within him. No, the perception I now have is a phenomenon that passes away with the "now." When recollection occurs, a process takes place in me that is the result of something that happened in the relation between the external world and me quite apart from the arousing of the present visualization. The mental image called forth through remembrance is not an old preserved visualization, but a new one. Recollection consists in the fact, not that a visualization can be revived, but that we can present to ourselves again and again what has been perceived. What reappears is something different from the original visualization. This remark is made here because in the domain of spiritual science it is necessary that more accurate conceptions should be formed than is the case in ordinary life, and indeed, also in ordinary science.

I remember; that is, I experience something that is itself no longer present. I unite a past experience with my present life. This is the case with every remembrance. Let us say, for instance, that I meet a man and, because I met him yesterday, recognize him. He would be a complete stranger to me if I were unable to unite the picture that I made yesterday through my perception with my impression of him today. Today's image of him is given me through my perception, that is to say, through my sense organs. Who, then, conjures up yesterday's picture in my soul? It is conjured up by the same being in me that was present during my experience yesterday, and that is also present today. In the previous explanations this being has been called soul. Were it not for this faithful preserver of the past, each external impression would always be new to us. It is certain that the soul imprints upon the body, as though by means of a sign, the process through which something becomes a recollection. Yet it is the soul itself that must make this impression and then perceive what it has made, just as it perceives something external. Thus the soul is the preserver of memory.

As preserver of the past, the soul continually gathers treasures for the spirit. That I can distinguish between what is correct or incorrect depends on the fact that I, as a man, am a thinking being able to grasp the truth in my spirit. Truth is eternal, and it could always reveal itself to me again in things even if I were to lose sight of the past and each impression were to be a new one to me. The spirit within me, however, is not restricted to the impressions of the present alone. The soul extends the spirit's horizon over the past, and the more the soul is able to bring to the spirit out of the past, the more does it enrich the spirit. The soul thus hands on to the spirit what it has received from the body. The spirit of man, therefore, carries at each moment of its life a twofold possession within itself. Firstly, the eternal laws of the good and the true, and secondly, the remembrance of the experiences of the past. What the human spirit does is accompanied under the influence of these two factors. If we want to understand a human spirit we must, therefore, know two different things about it. Firstly, how much of the eternal has been revealed to it, and secondly, how much treasure from the past lies stored up within it.

These treasures by no means remain in the spirit in an unchanged shape. The impressions that man acquires from his experiences fade gradually from memory. Not so, however, their fruits. We do not remember all the experiences lived through during childhood while acquiring the arts of reading and writing. Yet we could not read or write had we not had such experiences, and had not their fruits been preserved in the form of abilities. Such is the transmutation that the spirit effects in the treasures of memory. The spirit consigns to its fate whatever can lead to pictures of the separate experiences, and extracts therefrom only the force necessary for enhancing its abilities. Thus not a single experience passes by unutilized. The soul preserves each one as memory, and from each the spirit draws forth all that can enrich its abilities and the whole content of its life. The human spirit grows through assimilated experiences, and although one cannot find past experiences in the spirit as if in a storeroom, one nevertheless finds their effects in the abilities that man has acquired.

*　　*　　*

Thus far spirit and soul have been considered only within the period lying between birth and death. We cannot stop there. Anyone wishing to do so would be like the man who would observe the human body only within these same limits. Much can certainly be discovered within these limits, but the human form can never be explained by what lies between birth and death. It cannot build itself up directly out of mere physical substances and forces. It can only descend from a form like its own that arises as the result of what has handed itself on by heredity. The physical materials and forces build up the body during life. The forces of propagation enable another body, a body with a like form, to proceed from it — that is to say, one able to be the bearer of the same life body. Each life body is a repetition of its forebear. Only because it is such does it appear, not in any chance form, but in that passed on to it by heredity. The forces that make possible my human form lay in my forefathers.

The spirit of a man also appears in a definite form, and these forms of spiritual man are the most varied imaginable. In saying this, the word form is naturally used in a spiritual sense. No two human beings have the same spiritual form. Observations should be made in this region in a manner just as quietly and matter-of-factly as they would be made in the physical world. It cannot be said that the differences in man in spiritual respects arise only from the differences in their environment and their upbringing. No, this is by no means the case because two people under similar influences of environment and upbringing develop in quite different ways. We are, therefore, forced to admit that they have entered on their paths of life with quite different dispositions. Here we are brought face to face with an important fact that sheds light on the nature of man when its full bearing is recognized.

Anyone who is set upon directing his outlook exclusively towards the side of material happenings could, indeed, assert that the individual differences of human personalities arise from differences in the constitution of the material germs. In view of the laws of heredity discovered by Gregor Mendel and developed further by others, such a claim can offer much that gives it the appearance of justification even in scientific judgments. Such judgment only shows, however, that these people have no insight into the real relation of man to his experiences. Careful observation shows that external circumstances affect different people in different ways because of something that by no means enters immediately into mutual relations with material development. To the really accurate researcher in this domain it becomes apparent that what proceeds from the material basis can be distinguished from what arises through the mutual interaction between a man and his experiences, although these experiences can only take shape and form through the participation of the soul itself in this mutual interaction. The soul stands there clearly in relation to something within the external world that, by virtue of its very nature, cannot be connected with the material germinal basis.

Men differ from their animal fellow-creatures on earth through their physical form, but regarding this form they are, within certain limits, like one another. There is only one human species. However great may be the differences between races, people, tribes and personalities, as regards the physical body, the resemblance between man and man is greater than between man and any animal species. All that finds expression in the human species is conditioned by the inheritance of descendants from forebears, and the human form is bound to this heredity. As the lion can inherit its physical bodily form from lion forebears only, so can man inherit his physical bodily form only from human forebears.

The physical similarity of men is apparent to our physical eyes, and the differences of their spiritual forms lie revealed to our unbiased spiritual gaze. There is one fact that shows this clearly — the existence of a man's biography. Were a man merely a member of a species, no biography could exist. A lion or a dove are interesting insofar as they belong to the lion or the dove species. The separate being in all its essentials has been understood when the species has been described. It matters little whether one has to do with father, son or grandson. What they have of interest in them, father, son and grandson have in common. What a man signifies, however, is found only in his individuality, not in his being merely a member of a species. I have not in the least understood the nature of Mr. Smith of Hoboken if I have described his son or his father. I must know his own biography. Anyone who reflects on the nature of biography realizes that regarding the spiritual each man is himself a species.

To be sure, those people who regard a biography merely as a collection of external incidents in the life of an individual may claim they can write the biography of a dog in the same way they can that of a man. But anyone who depicts in a biography the real individuality of a man grasps the fact that he has in the biography of a single man something that corresponds to the description of a whole species in the animal kingdom. The point is obviously not that we can say something in the nature of a biography about an animal — especially clever ones. The point is that the human biography does not correspond to a biography of an animal, but to the description of the animal species. Of course, there will always be people who will seek to refute this by urging that owners of menageries, for instance, know how single animals of the same species differ individually from one another. The man who judges in this way, however shows only that he is unable to distinguish individual difference from difference that is acquired only through individuality.

Now if genus or species in the physical sense becomes intelligible only when we understand it as conditioned by heredity, so, too, the spiritual being can be understood only through a similar spiritual heredity. I have received my physical human form because of my descent from human forebears, but whence have I received what finds expression in my biography? As physical man, I repeat the shape of my forbears. What do I repeat as spiritual man? Anyone who claims that what comprises my biography needs no further explanation but must be accepted just as it stands, is also forced to maintain that he has seen an earth-mound somewhere on which lumps of matter have integrated themselves quite unaided into a living man.

As physical man I spring from other physical men because I have the same shape as the whole human species. The qualities of the species, accordingly, could thus be acquired only within the species. As spiritual man I have my own shape just as I have my own biography. I can have obtained this shape, therefore, from no one but myself. I did not enter the world with undefined, but with defined soul-predispositions, and since the course of my life as it comes to expression in my biography is determined by these predispositions, my work upon myself cannot have begun with my birth. That is to say, I must have existed as spiritual man before my birth. I certainly did not exist in my forebears because as spiritual human beings, they differ from me. My biography is not explainable through theirs. On the contrary, as a spiritual being I must be the repetition of someone through whose biography mine can be explained. The only conceivable alternative at the moment would be that I owe the character of the content of my biography to a spiritual life in which I existed prior to birth or, more correctly, to conception. We should, however, only be allowed to hold this opinion if we are willing to assume that what acts upon the human soul from its physical surroundings is of the same nature as that which affects the soul from a purely spiritual world. Such an assumption contradicts really accurate observation because the effect of its physical environment on the human soul is like the impression made by a new experience on a similar past experience in the same life.

In order to observe these relations correctly, one must acquire a perception of the impressions operating in human life, whose influence upon the predispositions of the soul is like that of standing before a deed that has to be done, and that is related to what has already been experienced in physical life. But the soul does not bring faculties gained in this immediate life to meet these impressions, but predispositions, which receive the impressions in the same way as do the faculties acquired through practice. He who has insight into these matters arrives at the conception of earth-lives that must have preceded this present one. In his thinking he cannot stop at purely spiritual experiences that preceded this present earth-life. The physical form that Schiller bore was inherited from his forebears. In the same way that it was impossible for Schiller's physical form to have grown out of the earth, it was also impossible for his spiritual being to have originated from it. He must have been the repetition of another spiritual being through whose biography his own becomes explicable as his physical human form is explicable through human propagation. In the same way, therefore, that the physical human form is again and again a repetition, a reincarnation of a being of the human species, so too the spiritual man must be a reincarnation of the same spiritual man, since, as spiritual man, each individual is, in fact, his own species.

The objection might be made that what has been stated here is a mere spinning of thoughts, and external proofs might be demanded as are customary in ordinary natural science. The reply to this is that the re-embodiment of the spiritual man is, naturally, a process that does not belong to the domain of external physical facts, but is one that takes place entirely in the spiritual region. No other of our ordinary powers of intelligence has entrance to this region save that of thinking. A person who will not trust the power of thinking cannot in fact enlighten himself regarding higher spiritual facts. For the one whose spiritual eye is opened, the above trains of thought act with exactly the same force as does an event that takes place before his physical eyes. The individual who ascribes to a so-called "proof," constructed according to the methods of natural science, greater power to convince than the above observations concerning the significance of biography, may be in the ordinary sense of the word a great scientist, but he is far from the paths of true spiritual research.

One of the most dangerous assumptions at present consists in trying to explain the spiritual qualities of a man by hereditary transmission from father, mother or other ancestors. Anyone who holds the opinion, for example, that Goethe inherited what constitutes his essential being from his father or mother will at first be hardly accessible to argument because there lies within such a one a deep antipathy to unprejudiced observation. A materialistic spell prevents him from seeing the mutual connections of phenomena in their true light.

In such observations as the above, the presuppositions are supplied for following man beyond birth and death. Within the boundaries formed by birth and death, man belongs to the worlds of physical body, of soul, and of spirit. The soul forms the intermediate link between body and spirit, inasmuch as it endows the third member of the body, the soul body, with the capacity for sensation, and inasmuch as it permeates the first member of the spirit, the spirit self, as consciousness soul. Thus it takes part and lot during life with the body as well as with the spirit. This comes to expression in its whole existence. How the sentient soul can unfold its capabilities will depend on the organization of the soul body. On the other hand, the extent to which the spirit self can develop itself within the consciousness soul will depend on the life of that soul. The more highly organized the soul body, the more complete the intercourse that the sentient soul can develop with the outer world. The spirit self will become that much richer and more powerful the more the consciousness soul brings nourishment to it. It has been shown that during life this nourishment is supplied to the spirit self through assimilated experiences and the fruits of these experiences. The interaction of the soul and spirit described above can, of course, only take place where soul and spirit are within each other, interpenetrating each other, that is, within the union of spirit self with consciousness soul.

Let us consider first the interaction of the soul body and the sentient soul. It is evident that the soul body is the most finely elaborated part of the body. Nevertheless, the soul body belongs to it and is dependent upon it. In a certain sense, physical body, ether body and soul body compose a single whole. Hence the soul body is also drawn within the laws of physical heredity that give the body its shape. Since it is the most mobile and volatile form of body, it must also exhibit the most mobile and volatile manifestations of heredity. Therefore, while the difference in the physical body corresponding to races, peoples and tribes is the smallest, and while in general the ether body presents a preponderating likeness and in single individuals a greater divergence, in the soul body the difference is already a considerable one. In it is expressed what is felt to be the external, personal uniqueness of an individual. Thus, it is also the bearer of that part of this personal uniqueness that is passed on from parents, grandparents, and so forth, to their descendants. As has been explained, it is true that the soul as such leads a completely self-contained life of its own in shutting itself up with its inclinations and disinclinations, its feelings and passions. It is nevertheless active as a whole and this whole comes to expression also in the sentient soul. Because the sentient soul interpenetrates and fills up the soul body, the latter forms itself according to the nature of the soul and can in this way, as the bearer of heredity, pass on tendencies, passions and other qualities from forefathers to children.

On this fact rests the statement of Goethe, "From my father I have stature and the serious manner of life; from my mother, a joyous disposition and the love of romance." Genius, of course, he did not receive from either. In this way we are shown what part of a man's soul qualities he hands over, as it were, to the line of physical heredity. The substances and forces of the physical body are in like manner present in the whole sphere of external physical nature. They are continually being taken up from it and given back to it. In the space of a few years the matter that composes our physical body is entirely renewed. That this matter takes the form of the human body, and that it always renews itself again within this body, depends upon the fact that it is held together by the ether body. The form of the ether body is not determined by events between birth or conception, and death alone, but is dependent on the laws of heredity that extend beyond birth and death. That soul qualities also can be transmitted by heredity — that the process of physical heredity receives an infusion from the soul — is due to the fact that the soul body can be influenced by the sentient soul.

Now, how does the interaction between soul and spirit proceed? During life, the spirit is bound up with the soul in the way shown above. The soul receives from the spirit the gift of living within the good and the true, and thereby of bringing the spirit itself to expression within its own life, within its tendencies, impulses and passions. From the world of the spirit, the spirit self brings to the "I" the eternal laws of the true and the good. These link themselves through the consciousness soul with the experiences of the soul's own life. These experiences themselves pass away, but their fruits remain. The spirit self receives an abiding impression by having been linked with them. When the human spirit encounters an experience similar to one to which it has already been linked, it sees therein something familiar, and is able to take up an attitude towards it quite different from what would be the case were the spirit facing it for the first time. This is the basis of all learning. The fruits of learning are acquired capacities. The fruits of the transitory life are in this way graven on the eternal spirit. Do we not see these fruits? Whence spring the innate predispositions and talents described above as characteristic of the spiritual man? Surely only from capacities of one kind or another that a man brings with him when he begins his earthly life. In certain respects, these capacities resemble exactly those that we can also acquire for ourselves during life.

Take the case of a genius. It is known that the boy Mozart could write out from memory a long musical work after only one hearing. He was able to do this because he could survey the whole at once. Within certain limits a man is also able during life to increase his capacity of rapid survey, of grasping connections, so that he then possesses new faculties. Indeed, Lessing has said of himself that through a talent for critical observation, he had acquired for himself something that came near to genius. We have either to regard such abilities, founded on innate capacities, with wonder, or to consider them as fruits of experiences that the spirit self has had through the medium of a soul. They have been graven on this spirit self, and since they have not been implanted in this life, they must have been in a former one. The human spirit is its own species. Just as man as a physical being belonging to a species bequeaths his qualities within the species, so does the spirit bequeath its qualities within its species, that is, within itself. In each life, the human spirit appears as a repetition of itself with the fruits of its former experiences in previous lives. This life is consequently the repetition of others and brings with it what the spirit self has, by work, acquired for itself in the previous life. When the spirit self absorbs something that can develop into fruit, it permeates itself with the life spirit. Just as the life body reproduces the form from species to species, so does the life spirit reproduce the soul from personal existence to personal existence.

Through the preceding considerations the thought that seeks the reason for certain life processes of man in repeated earth lives is raised into the sphere of validity. This idea can receive its full significance only by means of observations that spring from spiritual insight as it is acquired by following the path of knowledge described at the close of this book. Here it was only intended to show that ordinary observation rightly oriented by thinking already leads to this idea. Observation of this kind, it is true, will at first perceive the idea something like a silhouette, and it will not be possible to defend the idea entirely against the objections advanced by observation that is neither accurate nor guided aright by thinking. On the other hand, it is true that anyone who acquires such an idea through ordinary thoughtful observation, makes himself ready for supersensible observation. To a certain extent, he develops something that, of necessity, he must possess prior to this supersensible observation, just as one must have eyes prior to observing through the senses. Anyone who objects that through the formation of such an idea he can readily suggest to himself the supersensible observation proves only that he is incapable of entering into reality by means of free thinking and that it is just he who thus suggests to himself his own objections.

*   *   *

The experiences of the soul become lasting not only within the boundaries of birth and death, but beyond death. The soul, however, does not stamp its experiences only on the spirit that flashes up within it. It impresses them, as has been shown, on the outer world also through its deeds. What a man did yesterday is today still present in its effects. A picture of the connection between cause and effect is given in the simile of sleep and death. Sleep has often been called the younger brother of death. I get up in the morning. My consecutive activity has been interrupted by the night. Now, under ordinary circumstances it is not possible for me to begin my activity again just as I please. I must connect it with my doings of yesterday if there is to be order and coherence in my life. My actions of yesterday are the conditions predetermining those actions that fall to me today. I have created my destiny of today by what I did yesterday. I have separated myself for awhile from my activity, but this activity belongs to me and draws me again to itself after I have withdrawn myself from it for awhile. My past remains bound up with me; it lives on in my present and will follow me into my future. If the effects of my deeds of yesterday were not to be my destiny of today, I should not have had to awake this morning, but to be newly created out of nothing. In the same way it would be absurd if under ordinary circumstances I were not to occupy a house that I have had built for me.

The human spirit is no more created anew when it begins its earthly life than a man is newly created every morning. Let us try to make clear to ourselves what happens when entrance into this life takes place. A physical body, receiving its form through the laws of heredity, makes its appearance. This body becomes the bearer of a spirit that repeats a previous life in a new form. Between the two stands the soul that leads a self-contained life of its own. Its inclinations and disinclinations, wishes and desires, minister to it. It presses thought into its service. As sentient soul, it receives the impressions of the outer world and caries them to the spirit in order that the spirit may extract from them the fruits that are permanent. It plays, as it were, the part of intermediary, and its task is fulfilled when it is adequate to this part. The body forms impressions for the sentient soul that transforms them into sensations, retains them in the memory as thought images, and surrenders them to the spirit to hold throughout duration. The soul is really that part of a man through which he belongs to his earthly life. Through his body he belongs to the physical human species; through it he is a member of this species. With his spirit he lives in a higher world. The soul binds the two worlds together for a time.

The physical world into which the human spirit enters, however, is no strange field of action to it. On it the traces of the spirit's actions are imprinted. Something in this field of action belongs to the spirit. It bears the impress of, and is related to, the spirit's being. Just as the soul formerly transmitted the impressions from the outer world to the spirit in order that they might become enduring in it, so now the soul, as the spirit's organ, has converted the capacities bestowed upon it by the spirit into deeds that are also enduring in their effects. Thus the soul has actually flowed into these actions. In the effects of his actions, a man's soul lives a second independent life. This statement provides us with a motive for examining life in order to see how the processes of destiny enter into it. Something happens to a man. He is probably at first inclined to regard such a happening as something coming into his life by chance, but he can become aware of how he himself is the outcome of such chances. Anyone who studies himself in his fortieth year, and in the search for his soul nature refuses to be content with an unreal, abstract conception of the "I," may well say to himself, "I am, indeed, nothing more nor less than what I have become through life's experiences, through what has happened to me by reason of destiny up to the present. Would I not be a different man today had I, for example, gone through a set of experiences different from those through which I actually went when I was twenty years of age?" The man will then seek his "I" not only in those impulses of development that come to him from within outwards, but also in what has formatively thrust itself into his life from without. He will recognize his own "I" in what happens to him. If we give ourselves up unreservedly to such a perception, then only one more really intimate observation of life is needed to show us that in what comes to us through certain experiences of destiny there is something that lays hold on the ego from without, just as memory, working from within, lays hold on us in order to make a past experience flash up again. Thus we can make ourselves fitted to perceive in the experiences of destiny, how a former action of the soul finds its way to the ego, just as in memory an earlier experience, if called forth by an external cause, finds its way into the mind as a thought.

It has already been alluded to as a possible subject of consideration that the consequences of a deed may meet the human soul again. Regarding the consequences of some deeds, such a meeting is out of the question in the course of one earth life because that earth life was arranged especially for the carrying out of the deed. Experience lies in its fulfillment. In that case, a definite consequence of that action can no more re-act upon the soul than can someone remember an experience while still in the midst of it. It can only be a question here of the experience of the results of actions that do not meet the ego while it has the same disposition it had during the earth life in which the deed was done. Our gaze can only be directed to the consequences of action from another earth life. If an experience of destiny "befalls" us, and we feel that it is connected with the ego like something that has fashioned itself out of the ego's inner nature, then we can only think we have to do with the consequences of the actions of former earth lives. We see that we are led through an intimate thoughtful comprehension of life to the supposition — paradoxical to ordinary consciousness — that the experiences of destiny of one earth life are connected with the deeds of previous earth lives. This idea again can only receive its full content through supersensible knowledge; lacking this, it remains like a mere silhouette. Once more, however, this thought, this idea, gained by ordinary consciousness, prepares the soul so that it is enabled to behold its truth in actual supersensible observation.

Only one part of my deed is in the outer world; the other is in myself. Let us make this relation of the ego to the deed clear by a simple example from natural science. Animals that once could see migrated to the caves of Kentucky and, as a result of their life there, lost their power of sight. Existence in darkness deprived the eyes of their function. Consequently today the physical and chemical activity that normally occurs when seeing takes place is no longer carried on in these eyes. The stream of nourishment formerly expended on this activity now flows to other organs. These animals are now able to live only in these caves. They have by their act, by their immigration, created the conditions of their later life. The immigration has become a part of their destiny. A being that once acted has united itself with the results of its action. This is also true of the human spirit. The soul was only able to impart certain capacities to the spirit by performing actions, and these capacities correspond to the actions. Through an action that the soul has performed, there lives in the soul the energetic predisposition to perform another action that is the fruit of the first action. The soul carries this as a necessity within itself until the subsequent action has taken place. One might also say that through an action there has been imprinted upon the soul the necessity of carrying out the consequences of that action.

By means of its actions the human spirit has really brought about its own destiny. In a new life it finds itself linked to what it did in a former one. It may be asked, "How can that be, when the human spirit on reincarnating finds itself in an entirely different world from the one it left at an earlier time?" This question is based on a superficial notion of the connections of destiny. If I change my scene of action from Europe to America, I also find myself in entirely new surroundings.

Nevertheless, my life in America depends entirely on my previous life in Europe. If I have been a mechanic in Europe, my life in America will shape itself in quite a different way from what would have been the case had I been a bank clerk. In the one instance, I should probably be surrounded in America by machinery, in the other, by banking paraphernalia. In each case my previous life decides my environment. It attracts to itself, as it were, out of the whole surrounding world, those things that are related to it. So it is with the spirit self. It inevitably surrounds itself in a new life with what it is related to from previous lives. On that account sleep is an apt image of death because a man during sleep is withdrawn from the field of action in which his destiny awaits him. While we sleep, events in this field of action pursue their course. We have for a certain time no influence on this course of events. Our life on a new day depends, nevertheless, on the effects of the deeds of the previous day. Our personality actually embodies or incarnates itself anew every morning in our world of action. What was separated from us during the night is spread out around us, as it were, during the day. So it is with the actions of former human embodiments or incarnations. They are bound up with a man as his destiny, just as life in the dark Kentucky caves remains bound up with the animals that, by migrating into them, have lost their power of sight. Just as these animals can only live in the surroundings in which they have placed themselves, so the human spirit is able to live only in the surroundings that it has created for itself by its acts. That I find in the morning a certain state of affairs, created by me on the previous day, is brought about by the immediate course of events. That I find surroundings when I reincarnate corresponding to the results of my deeds in a previous life, is brought about by the relationship of my reincarnated spirit with the things in the surrounding world. From this we can form an idea of how the soul is set into the human constitution. The physical body is subject to the laws of heredity. The human spirit, on the contrary, has to incarnate over and over again, and its law consists in its bringing over the fruits of the former lives into the following ones. The soul lives in the present, but this life in the present is not independent of the previous lives because the incarnating spirit brings its destiny with it from its previous incarnations. This destiny determines life. What impressions the soul will be able to have, what wishes it will be able to have gratified, what sorrows and joys shall develop for it, with what men and women it shall come into contact — all this depends upon the nature of the actions in the past incarnations of the spirit. The soul must meet those people again in a subsequent life with whom it was bound up in a previous life because the actions that have taken place between them must have their consequences. When this soul seeks re-embodiment, those other souls that are bound up with it will also strive towards their incarnation at the same time. The life of the soul is, therefore, the result of the self-created destiny of the human spirit. The course of man's life between birth and death is determined in a threefold way. In consequence, he is dependent in a threefold way on factors that lie on the other side of birth and death. The body is subject to the law of heredity; the soul is subject to its self-created destiny. We call this destiny, created by man himself, his karma. The spirit is under the law of re-embodiment, repeated earth lives. One can accordingly also express the relationship between spirit, soul and body in the following way. The spirit is immortal; birth and death reign over the body according of the laws of the physical world; the soul life, which is subject to destiny, mediates the connection of both during an earthly life. All further knowledge about the being of man presupposes acquaintance with the three worlds to which he belongs. These three worlds are dealt with in the following pages.   Thinking that frankly faces the phenomena of life and is not afraid to follow out to their final consequences the thoughts resulting from a living, vivid contemplation of life can, by pure logic, arrive at the conception of the law of karma and repeated incarnations. Just as it is true that for the seer with the opened spiritual eye, past lives lie like an open book before him as experience, so it is true that the truth of these things can become obvious to the unbiased reason that reflects upon it.

The Three Worlds
The Soul World

Our study of man has shown that he belongs to three worlds. The materials and forces that build up his body are taken from the world of physical bodies. He has knowledge of this world through the perceptions of his outer physical senses. Anyone trusting to these senses alone and developing only their perceptive capacities can gain no enlightenment for himself concerning the two other worlds, the soul world and the world of the spirit. A man's ability to convince himself of the reality of a thing or a being depends on whether he has an organ of perception, a sense for it. It may, of course, easily lead to misunderstanding if we call the higher organs of perception spiritual senses as is done here because in speaking of senses we involuntarily connect the thought of the physical with them. The physical world is, in fact, designated the sensory, in contradistinction to the spiritual. In order to avoid this misunderstanding, we must take into account the fact that higher senses are spoken of here only in a comparative or metaphorical sense. Just as the physical senses perceive the physical, so do the soul and spiritual senses perceive the soul and spiritual worlds. The expression, sense, will be used as meaning simply organ of perception. A man would have no knowledge of light and color had he no eye sensitive to light; he would know nothing of sound had he no ear sensitive to sound. In this connection the German philosopher, Lotze, says rightly, "Without a light-sensitive eye and a sound-sensitive ear, the whole world would be dark and silent. There would be in it just as little light or sound as there could be toothache without the pain-sensitive nerve of the tooth."

In order to see what is said here in the proper way, one need only think how entirely differently the world must reveal itself to man from the way it does to the lower forms of animal life that have only a kind of sense of touch or feeling spread over the whole surface of their bodies. Light, color and sound certainly cannot exist for them in the same way they do for beings gifted with ears and eyes. The vibrations caused by the firing of a gun may have an effect on them also if, as a result, sensitive areas are excited, but in order that these vibrations of the air exhibit themselves to the soul as a shot, an ear is necessary. An eye is necessary in order that certain processes in the fine matter called ether reveal themselves as light and color. We only know something about a being or thing because we are affected by it through one of our organs.

This relationship of man with the world of realities is brought out extremely well by Goethe when he says, "It is really in vain that we try to express the nature of a thing We become aware of effects and a complete history of these effects would indeed embrace the nature of that thing. We endeavor in vain to describe the character of a man. If instead we put together his actions and deeds, a picture of his character will present itself to us. Colors are the deeds of light — deeds and sufferings . . . Colors and light are, to be sure, linked in the most precise relationship, but we must think of them both as belonging to the whole of nature, because through them the whole of nature is engaged in revealing itself especially to the eye. In like manner, nature reveals itself to another sense.

. . . Nature thus speaks downwards to the other senses — to known, unknown, and unrecognized senses. It thus speaks to itself and to us through a thousand phenomena. To the attentive, nature is nowhere either dead or silent."

It would not be correct were one to interpret this saying of Goethe as though the possibility of knowing the essential nature of things were denied by it. Goethe does not mean that we perceive only the effects of a thing, and that the being thereof hides itself behind them. He means rather that one should not speak at all of a "hidden being." The being is not behind its manifestation. On the contrary, it comes into view through the manifestation. This being, however, is in many respects so rich that it can manifest itself to other senses in still other forms. What reveals itself does belong to the being, but because of the limitations of the senses, it is not the whole being. This thought of Goethe corresponds entirely with the views of spiritual science set forth here.

Just as in the body, eye and ear develop as organs of perception, as senses for bodily processes, so does a man develop in himself soul and spiritual organs of perception through which the soul and spiritual worlds are opened to him. For those who do not have such higher senses, these worlds are dark and silent, just as the bodily world is dark and silent for a being without eyes and ears. It is true that the relation of man to these higher senses is rather different from his relation to the bodily senses. It is good Mother Nature who sees to it, as a rule, that these latter are fully developed in him. They come into existence without his help. For the development of his higher senses, however, he must work himself. If he wishes to perceive the soul and spirit worlds, he must develop soul and spirit, just as nature has developed his body so that the might perceive the corporeal world around him and guide himself in it. Such a development of the higher organs not yet developed for us by nature itself is not unnatural because in the higher sense all that man accomplishes belongs also to nature.

Only the person who is ready to maintain that man should remain standing at the stage at which he left the hand of nature, could call the development of the higher senses unnatural. By him the significances of these organs is misunderstood, "unrecognized," as indicated in the quotation of Goethe. Such a person might just as well oppose all human education because it also develops further the work of nature. He would also have to oppose operations upon those born blind, because almost the same thing that happens to the person born blind when operated upon happens to the man who awakens the higher sense in himself in the manner set forth in the last part of this book. The world appears to him with new qualities, events and facts, about which the physical senses reveal nothing. It is clear to him that through these higher organs he adds nothing arbitrarily to reality, but that without them the essential part of this reality would have remained hidden from him. The soul and spirit worlds are not to be thought of as being alongside or outside the physical world. They are not separated in space from it. Just as for persons born blind and operated upon, the previously dark world flashes out in light and colors, so do things that previously were only corporeal phenomena reveal their soul and spirit qualities to anyone who is awakened in soul and spirit. It is true, moreover, that this world then becomes filled with other occurrences and beings that remain completely unknown to those whose soul and spirit senses are unawakened. (The development of the soul and spirit senses will be spoken of in a more detailed way farther on in this book. Here these higher worlds themselves will be first described. Anyone who denies their existence says nothing more than that he has not yet developed his higher organs. The evolution of humanity is not terminated at any one stage; it must always progress.)

The higher organs are often involuntarily pictured as too similar to the physical organs. It should be understood that these organs are spiritual or soul formations. It ought not to be expected, therefore, that what is perceived in the higher worlds should be only something like a cloudy, attenuated form of matter. As long as something is expected of this kind, no clear idea can be formed of what is really meant here by higher worlds. For many persons it would not be nearly as difficult as it actually is to know something about these higher worlds — of course, at first only about the elementary regions — if they did not form the idea that what they are to see is again merely rarefied physical matter. Since they take for granted something of this kind, they are not at all willing, as a rule, to recognize what they are really dealing with. They look upon it as unreal, and refuse to acknowledge it as something satisfactory. True, the higher stages of spiritual development are accessible only with difficulty. Those stages, however, that suffice for the perception of the nature of the spiritual world — and that is already a great deal — should not be at all difficult to reach if people would first free themselves from the misconception that consists in picturing to themselves the soul and spiritual merely as a finer physical.

Just as we do not know a man entirely when we have only visualized his physical exterior, so also do we not know the world around us if we only know what the physical senses reveal to us about it. Just as a photograph grows intelligible and living to us when we have become so intimately acquainted with the person photographed that we know his soul, so can we really understand the corporeal world only when we gain a knowledge of its soul and spiritual basis. For this reason it is advisable to speak here first about the higher worlds, the worlds of soul and spirit, and only then judge the physical from the viewpoint of spiritual science.

At this present stage of civilization certain difficulties are encountered by anyone speaking about the higher worlds because this age is great above all things in its knowledge and conquest of the physical world. Our words have, in fact, received their stamp and significance in relation to this physical world. We must, nevertheless, make use of these current words in order to form a link with something known. This, however, opens the door to many misunderstanding on the part of those who are willing to trust only their external senses. Much can at first be expressed and indicated only by means of similes and comparisons. This must be so, for such similes are a means by which the seeker is at first directed to these higher worlds, and through which his own ascent to them is furthered. Of this ascent I shall speak in a later chapter, in which the development of the soul and spiritual organs of perception will be dealt with. To begin with, man must gain knowledge of the higher worlds by means of similes. Only then is he ready to acquire for himself the power to see into them.

Just as the matter and forces that compose and govern our stomach, heart, brain, lungs, and so forth, come from the physical world, so do our soul qualities, our impulses, desires, feelings, passions, wishes and sensations, come from the soul world. The soul of man is a member of this soul world, just as his body is part of the world of physical bodies. If we want at the outset to indicate a difference between the corporeal and soul worlds, we could say that the soul world is in all objects and entities much finer, more mobile and plastic than the former. It must be kept clearly in mind, however, that on entering the soul world we enter a world entirely different from the physical. If therefore, the words "coarser" and "finer" are used in this respect, readers must be fully aware that something is suggested by way of comparison that is, nevertheless, actually fundamentally different. This is true in regard to all that is said about the soul world in words borrowed from the world of physical corporeality. Taking this into account, we can say that the formations and beings of the soul world consist in the same way of soul substances, and are directed by soul forces in much the same way as is the case in the physical world with physical substances and physical forces.

Just as spatial extension and spatial movement are peculiar to corporeal formations, so are excitability and impelling desire peculiar to the things and beings of the soul world. For this reason the soul world is described as the world of desires or wishes, or as the world of longing. These expressions are borrowed from the human soul world. We must, therefore, hold fast to the idea that the things in those parts of the soul world that lie outside the human soul are just as different from the soul forces within it as the physical matter and forces of the external corporeal world are different from those parts that compose the physical human body. Impulse, wish, longing are names for the substantiality of the soul world. To this substantiality let us give the name astral. If we pay more attention specifically to the forces of the soul world, we can speak of desire-being, but it must not be forgotten that the distinction between substance and force cannot be as sharply drawn as in the physical world. An impulse can just as well be called force as substance.

The differences between the soul world and the physical have a bewildering effect on anyone who obtains a view of the soul world for the first time, but that is also the case when a previously inactive physical sense is opened. The man born blind has first to learn after an operation how to guide himself through the world he has previously known only by means of the sense of touch. Such a person, for example, sees the objects at first in his eyes, then outside himself, but they appear to him as though painted on a flat surface. Only gradually does he grasp perspective and the spatial distance between things. In the soul world entirely different laws prevail from those in the physical. To be sure, many soul formations are bound to those of the other worlds. The human soul, for instance, is bound to the human body and to the human spirit. The occurrences we can observe in it are, therefore, influenced at the same time by the corporeal and spiritual worlds. We have to take this into account in observing the soul world, and we must take care not to claim as a law of the soul world occurrences due to the influence of another world. When, for example, a man sends out a wish, that wish is brought to birth by a thought, by a conception of the spirit whose laws it accordingly follows. Just as we can formulate the laws of the physical world by disregarding, for example, the influence of man on its processes, so the same thing is possible with regard to the soul world.

An important difference between soul and physical processes can be expressed by saying that the reciprocal action in the processes of the soul is much more inward than in the physical. In physical space there reigns, for example, the law of impact. When an ivory ball strikes a ball at rest, the resting ball will move in a direction that can be calculated from the motion and elasticity of the first. In soul space the reciprocal action of two forms that encounter each other depends on their inner qualities. If they are in affinity they mutually interpenetrate and, as it were, grow together. They repel each other if their natures are in conflict. In physical space there are also definite laws of vision. We see distant objects perspectively diminishing. When we look down an avenue, the distant trees appear closer together than those nearby. In the soul space, on the contrary, all objects near or far appear to the clairvoyant at distances apart that are in accordance with their inner nature. This is naturally a source of the most manifold errors for those who enter the soul world and wish to be at home there with the help of the rules they bring from the physical world.

One of the first things a man must acquire in order to make his way about the soul world is the ability to distinguish the various kinds of forms found there in much the same way he distinguishes solid, liquid, or air or gaseous bodies in the physical world. In order to do this, he must know the two most important basic forces to be found in the soul world. They may be called sympathy and antipathy. The nature of any soul formation is determined according to the way these basic forces operate in it. The force with which one soul formation attracts others, seeks to fuse with them and to make its affinity with them effective, must be designated as sympathy. Antipathy is the force with which soul formations repel, exclude each other in the soul world. It is the force with which they assert their separate identities. The part played by a soul formation in the soul world depends upon the proportion in which these basic forces are present in it. In the first place, we must distinguish three kinds of soul formations that are determined by the way sympathy and antipathy work in them. That these formations differ from each other is due to the fact that sympathy and antipathy have in them definitely fixed mutual relationships. In all three both basic forces are present.

To begin with, let us consider the first of these soul formations. It attracts other formations in its neighborhood by means of the sympathy ruling it. Besides this sympathy, there is at the same time antipathy present by which it repels certain things in its surroundings. From the outside such a formation appears to be endowed only with the forces of antipathy. That, however, is not the case. Both sympathy and antipathy are present in it, but the latter predominates. It has the upper hand over the former. Such formations play a self-seeking role in soul space. They repel much that surrounds them, and lovingly attract but little to themselves. They therefore move through the soul space as unchangeable forms. The force of sympathy that they possess appears greedy. This greed appears at the same time insatiable, as if it could not be satisfied, because the predominating antipathy repels so much of what approaches that no satisfaction is possible. This kind of soul formation corresponds with the solid physical bodies of the physical world. This region of soul matter may be called Burning Desire. The part of Burning Desire that is mingled with the souls of animals and men determines in them what we call their lower sensual impulses, their dominating selfish instincts.

In the second kind of soul formations the two basic forces preserve a balance. Accordingly, antipathy and sympathy act in them with equal strength. They approach other formations with a certain neutrality. They act on them as though related, but without especially attracting or repelling. They erect, as it were, no solid barrier between themselves and their surroundings. They constantly allow other formations in their surroundings to act on them. We can, therefore, compare them with the liquids of the physical world. There is nothing of greed in the way such formations attract others to themselves. The activity meant here may be recognized, for example, when the human soul receives the sensation of a certain color. If I have the sensation of a red color, I receive, to begin with, a neutral stimulus from my surroundings. Only when pleasure in the red color is added to this stimulus does another soul activity come into play. What effects the neutral stimulus is the action of soul formations standing in such reciprocal relationship that sympathy and antipathy preserve an equal balance. The soul substance considered here must be described as a perfectly plastic and mobile substance. It does not move through soul space in a self-seeking way like the first, but by such means that its being receives impressions everywhere, and shows itself to have affinity with much that approaches it. An expression that might be applied to it is Mobile Sensitivity.

The third variety of soul formations is that in which sympathy has the upper hand over antipathy. Antipathy produces self-seeking self-assertion. This, however, retires into the background when inclination towards the things in the surrounding world takes its place. Let us picture such a formation within the soul space. It appears as the center of an attracting sphere that spreads over the objects surrounding it. Such formations must be specially designated as Wish Substance. This designation appears to be the right one because through the existing antipathy, although relatively weaker than the sympathy, the attraction works in such a way that it endeavors to bring the attracted objects within the soul formation's own sphere. The sympathy thus receives an underlying tone of selfishness. This wish substance may be likened to the air or gaseous bodies of the physical world. Just as a gas strives to expand on all sides, so does the wish substance spread itself out in all directions.

Higher levels of soul substance characterize themselves in that one of the basic forces, antipathy, retires completely into the background and sympathy alone shows itself to be really effective. Now this sympathy is able to make its power felt primarily within the various parts of the soul formation itself. These parts act with reciprocal attraction upon each other. The force of sympathy within a soul formation comes to expression in what one calls Liking, and each lessening of this sympathy is Disliking. Disliking is only lessened liking, as cold is only a lessened warmth. Liking and disliking is what lives in man as the world of feelings in the more restricted sense of the word. Feeling is the life and activity of the soul within itself. What is called the comfort of the soul depends on the way the feelings of liking and disliking, attraction and repulsion, interact within the soul.

A still higher stage is represented by those soul formations in which sympathy does not remain shut up within the region of their own life. They, and also the fourth stage, differ from the three lower stages by virtue of the fact that in them the force of sympathy has no antipathy opposing it to overcome. It is only through these higher orders of soul substance that the manifold variety of soul formations can unite and form a common soul world. To the degree that antipathy comes into play, the soul formation strives toward some other thing for the sake of its own life, and in order to strengthen and enrich itself by means of the other. Where antipathy is inactive, the other thing is received as revelation, as information. This higher form of soul substance plays a similar role in the soul space to that played by light in physical space. It causes one soul formation to suck in as it were, the being or essence of others for their own sakes; one could also say, to let itself by shone upon by them. Only by drawing upon these higher regions are the soul beings awakened to the true soul life. Their dull life in the darkness opens outwards and begins to shine and ray out into soul space. The sluggish, dull weaving within itself that seeks to shut itself off through antipathy when the substances of the lower regions alone are present, becomes force and mobility that goes forth from within and pours itself outwards in streams. The Mobile Sensitivity of the second region is only effective when formations meet each other. Then, indeed, the one streams over into the other, but contact is here necessary. In the higher regions there prevails a free out-raying and out-pouring. The essential nature of this region is quite rightly described as an "outraying," because the sympathy that is developed acts in such a way that this expression, taken from the action of light, can be used as a symbol for it. Just as plants degenerate in a dark cellar, so do the soul formations degenerate without the life-giving soul substances of the higher regions. Soul Light, Active Soul Force and the true Soul Life in the narrower sense, belong to these regions and thence pour themselves into the soul beings.

Thus one has to distinguish between three lower and three higher regions of the soul world. These two are linked together by a fourth, so that there results the following division of the soul world.

1. Region of Burning Desire

2. Region of Mobile Sensitivity

3. Region of Wishes

4. Region of Liking and Disliking

5. Region of Soul Light

6. Region of Active Soul Force

7. Region of Soul Life

Throughout the first three regions, the soul formations receive their qualities from the relative proportions of sympathy and antipathy. Throughout the fourth region sympathy weaves its web within the soul formations themselves.

Throughout the three highest, the power of sympathy becomes ever more free. Illumining and quickening, the soul substances of this region flow through the soul space, awakening what, if left to itself, would lose itself in its own separate existence.

Though it should be superfluous, for the sake of clarity it must be emphasized that these seven divisions of the soul world do not represent regions separated one from another. Just as in the physical world, solid, liquid and air or gaseous substances interpenetrate, so in the soul world do Burning Desire, Mobile Sensitivity and the forces of the World of Wishes. Just as in the physical world warmth penetrates bodies and light illumines them, so it is also the case in the soul world with Liking and Disliking, and with the Soul Light. Something similar takes place with regard to the Active Soul Force and the true Soul Life.

The Soul in the Soul World After Death

The soul is the connecting link between the spirit of man and his body. Its forces of sympathy and antipathy that, owing to their mutual relationship, bring about soul manifestations such as desire, sensitivity, wish, liking and aversion, and so forth, are not only active between soul formation and soul formation, but they manifest themselves also in relation to the beings of the other worlds, the physical and the spiritual. While the soul lives in the body, it participates, so to speak, in all that takes place in the body. When the physical functions of the body proceed with regularity, pleasure and comfort arise in the soul. If these functions are disturbed, discomfort and pain arise. The soul, however, has its share in the activities of the spirit also. One thought fills it with joy, another with abhorrence; a correct judgment has the approval of the soul, a false one its disapproval. The stage of evolution of a man depends, in fact, on whether the inclinations of his soul move more in one direction or in another. A man is the more perfect, the more his soul sympathizes with the manifestations of the spirit. He is the more imperfect the more the inclinations of his soul are satisfied by the functions of his body.   The spirit is the central point of man, the body the intermediary by which the spirit observes and learns to understand the physical world, and through which it acts in that world. The soul is the intermediary between the two. It liberates the sensation of sound from the physical impression that the vibrations of the air make on the ear. It experiences pleasure in this sound. All this it communicates to the spirit, which thereby attains to the understanding of the physical world. A thought, which arises in the spirit, is transformed by the soul into the wish to realize it, and only through this can be the thought become a deed with the help of the body as an instrument. Now man can fulfill his destiny only by allowing his spirit to direct the course of all his activity. The soul can by its own power direct its inclinations just as readily to the physical as to the spiritual. It sends, as it were, its feelers down into the physical as well as up into the spiritual. By sinking them into the physical world, the soul's own being becomes saturated and colored by the nature of the physical. Since the spirit is able to act in the physical world only through the soul as intermediary, this spirit itself is thus given the direction towards the physical. Its formations are drawn toward the physical by the forces of the soul. Observe, for example, the undeveloped human being. The inclinations of his soul cling to the functions of his body. He feels pleasure only in the impressions made by the physical world on his senses. His intellectual life also is thereby completely drawn down into this region. His thoughts serve only to satisfy his physical needs. Since the spiritual self lives from incarnation to incarnation, it is intended to receive its direction ever increasingly from the spiritual. Its knowledge should be determined by the spirit of eternal truth; its action by eternal goodness.

Death, regarded as a fact in the physical world, signifies a change in the functions of the body. At death the body ceases to function as the intermediary between the soul and the spirit. In its processes it shows itself henceforth entirely subject to the physical world and its laws, and it passes over into it in order to dissolve therein. Only these physical processes of the body can be observed after death by the physical senses. What happens to the soul and spirit, however, escapes these senses because even during life, soul and spirit cannot be observed by the senses except insofar as they attain to external expression in physical process. After death this kind of expression is no longer possible. For this reason, observation by means of the physical senses and the science based on it does not come under consideration in reference to the fate of the soul and spirit after death. Here a higher knowledge steps in that is based on observation of what takes place in the soul and spirit worlds.

After the spirit has released itself from the body, it still continues to be united with the soul. Just as during physical life the body chained it to the physical world, so now the soul chains the spirit to the soul world. It is not in this soul world, however, that the spirit's true, primordial being is to be found. The soul world is intended to serve merely as its connecting link with the scene of its actions, the physical world. In order to appear in a new incarnation with a more perfect form, the spirit must draw force and renewed strength from the spiritual world. Through the soul it has become entangled in the physical world. It is bound to a soul being, which is saturated and colored by the nature of the physical, and through this has acquired a tendency in that direction. After death the soul is no longer bound to the body, but only to the spirit. It lives now within soul surroundings. Only the forces of this soul world can, therefore, have an effect on it. At first the spirit also is bound to this life of the soul in the soul world. It is bound to it in the same way it is bound to the body during physical incarnation. When the body shall die is determined by the laws of the body. Speaking generally, it must be said that it is not the soul and spirit that forsake the body, but they are set free by the body when its forces are no longer able to fulfill the purpose of the human soul organism.

The relationship between soul and spirit is just the same. The soul will set the spirit free to pass into the higher, spiritual world, when its forces are no longer able to fulfill the purpose of the human soul organism. The spirit is set free the moment the soul has handed over to dissolution what it can experience only in the body, retaining only what can live on with the spirit. This remainder, although experienced in the body, can nevertheless be impressed on the spirit as fruit. It connects the soul with the spirit in the purely spiritual world. In order to learn the fate of the soul after death, the process of dissolution must be observed. It had the task of giving the spirit its direction toward the physical. The moment it has fulfilled this task, the soul takes the direction toward the spiritual. In fact, the nature of its task would cause it henceforth to be only spiritually active when the body falls away from it, that is, when it can no longer be a connecting link. So it would be, had it not, owing to its life in the body, been influenced by the body and in its inclinations been attracted to it. Without this coloring received through the body, it would at once on being disembodied follow the laws of the spirit-soul world only and manifest no further inclination toward the sense world. This would be the case if a man on dying lost completely all interest in the earthly world, if all desires and wishes attaching him to the existence he has left had been completely satisfied. To the extent that this is not the case, all that remains of his interest clings to the soul.

To avoid confusion we must carefully distinguish here between what chains man to the world in such a way that it can be adjusted in a subsequent incarnation, and what chains him to one particular incarnation, that is, to the one just passed. The first is made good by means of the law of destiny, karma. The second can only be got rid of by the soul after death.

After death there follows for the human spirit a time during which the soul is shaking off its inclinations toward physical existence in order to follow once more the laws of the spirit-soul world only and thus set the spirit free. The more the soul was bound to the physical, the longer, naturally, will this time last. It will be short for the man who has clung but little to physical life, and long for the one whose interests are completely bound up with it, who at death has many desires, wishes and impulses still living in the soul.

The easiest way to gain an idea of this condition in which the soul lives during the time immediately after death is afforded by the following consideration. Let us take a somewhat crass example — the pleasure of the bon vivant. His pleasure is derived from food. The pleasure is naturally not bodily but belongs to the soul. The pleasure lives in the soul as does the desire for the pleasure. To satisfy the desire, however, the corresponding bodily organs, the palate, etc., are necessary. After death the soul has not immediately lost such a desire, but it no longer possesses the bodily organ that provides the means for satisfying it. For another reason, but one that acts far more strongly in the same way, the human soul now experiences all the suffering of burning thirst that one would undergo in a waterless waste. The soul thus suffers burning pain by being deprived of the pleasure because it has laid aside the bodily organ through which it can experience that pleasure. It is the same with all that the soul yearns for and that can only be satisfied through the bodily organs. This condition of burning privation lasts until the soul has learned to cease longing for what can only be satisfied through the body. The time passed in this condition may be called the region of desires, although it has of course nothing to do with a "locality."

When the soul enters the soul world after death it becomes subject to the laws of that world. The laws act on it and the manner in which the soul's inclinations towards the physical are destroyed depends upon their actions. The way these laws act on the soul must differ depending upon the kinds of soul substances and soul forces in whose domain it is placed at the time. Each of these according to the its kind will make its purifying, cleansing influence felt. The process that takes place here is such that all antipathy in the soul is gradually overcome by the forces of sympathy. This sympathy itself is brought to its highest pitch because, through this highest degree of sympathy with the rest of the soul world, the soul will, as it were, merge into and become one with it. Then will it be utterly emptied of self-seeking. It ceases to exist as a being inclined to physically sensible existence, and the spirit is set free by it. The soul, therefore, purifies itself through all the regions of the soul world described above until, in the region of perfect sympathy, it becomes one with the general soul world. That the spirit itself is in bondage until this last moment of the liberation of its soul is due to the fact that through its life the spirit has become most intimately related to the soul. This relationship is much closer than the one with the body because the spirit is only indirectly bound to the body through the soul, whereas it is bound directly to the soul. The soul is, in fact, the spirit's own life. For this reason the spirit is not bound to the decaying body, although it is bound to the soul that is gradually freeing itself. On account of the immediate bond between the spirit and the soul, the spirit can feel free of the soul only when the soul has itself become one with the general soul world.

To the extent the soul world is the abode of man immediately after death, it is called the region of desires. The various religious systems that have embodied in their doctrines a knowledge of these conditions are acquainted with this region of desire under the name "purgatory," "cleansing fire," and the like.

The lowest region of the soul world is that of Burning Desire. Everything in the soul that has to do with the coarsest, lowest, most selfish desires of the physical life is purged from the soul after death by it, because through such desires it is exposed to the effects of the forces of this soul region. The unsatisfied desires that have remained over from physical life furnish the points of attack. The sympathy of such souls only extends to what can nourish their selfish natures. It is greatly exceeded by the antipathy that floods everything else. Now the desires aim at physical enjoyments that cannot be satisfied in the soul world. The craving is intensified to the highest degree by the impossibility of satisfaction. Owing to this impossibility, at the same time it is forced to die out gradually. The burning lusts gradually exhaust themselves and the soul learns by experience that the only means of preventing the suffering that must come from such longings lies in extirpating them. During physical life satisfaction is ever and again attained. By this means the pain of the burning lusts is covered over by a kind of illusion. After death in the "cleansing fire" the pain comes into evidence quite unveiled. The corresponding experiences of privation are passed through. It is a dark, gloomy state indeed in which the soul thus finds itself. Of course, only those persons whose desires are directed during physical life to the coarsest things can fall into this condition. Natures with few lusts go through it without noticing it because they have no affinity with it. It must be stated that souls are the longer influenced by burning desire the more closely they have become related to that fire through their physical life. On that account there is more need for them to be purified in it. Such purification should not be described as suffering in the sense of this expression as it is used in the sense world. The soul after death demands its purification since an existing imperfection can only thus be purged away.

In the second region of the soul world there are processes in which sympathy and antipathy preserve an equal balance. Insofar as a human soul is in that condition after death it will be influenced by what takes place in this region for a time. The losing of oneself in the external glitter of life, the joy in the swiftly succeeding impressions of the senses, bring about this condition. People live in it to the extent it is brought about by the soul inclinations just indicated. They allow themselves to be influenced by each worthless trifle of everyday life, but since their sympathy is attached to no one thing in particular, the influences pass quickly. Everything that does not belong to this region of empty nothings is repellent to such persons. When the soul experiences this condition after death without the presence of the physical objects that are necessary for its satisfaction, the condition must ultimately die out. Naturally, the privation that precedes its complete extinction in the soul is full of suffering. This state of suffering is the school for the destruction of the illusion a man is wrapped up in during physical life.

Then a third region of the soul world is to be considered in which the phenomena of sympathy, of the wish nature, predominate. Souls experience the effects of these phenomena from everything that preserves an atmosphere of wishes after death. These wishes also gradually die out because of the impossibility of satisfying them.

The region of Liking and Disliking in the soul world that has been described above as the fourth region imposes special trials on the soul. As long as the soul dwells in the body it shares all that concerns the body. The inner surge of liking and disliking is bound up with the body. The body causes the soul's feeling of well-being and comfort, dislike and discomfort. During his physical life man feels that his body is himself. What is called the feeling of self is based upon this fact, and the more people are inclined to be sensuous, the more does their feeling of self take on this character. After death the body, the object of the feeling of self, is lacking. On this account the soul, which still retains such a feeling, has the sensation of being emptied out as it were. A feeling as if it had lost itself overcomes the soul. This continues until it has been recognized that the true human being does not lie in the physical. The impressions made by this fourth region on the soul accordingly destroy the illusion of the bodily self. The soul learns to feel this corporeality no longer as an essential reality. It is cured and purified of its attachment to the body. In this way it has conquered what previously chained it strongly to the physical world, and it can now unfold fully the forces of sympathy that flow outwards. It has, so to speak, broken free from itself and is ready to pour itself into the common soul world with full sympathy.

It should not pass unnoted that the experiences of this region are suffered to an especial degree by suicides. Such a one leaves his physical body in an artificial way, although all the feelings connected with it remain unchanged. In the case of natural death, the decay of the body is accompanied by a partial dying out of the feelings of attachment to it. In the case of suicides there are, in addition to the torment caused by the feeling of having been suddenly emptied out, the unsatisfied desires and wishes because of which they have deprived themselves of their bodies.

The fifth stage of the soul world is that of Soul Light. In it sympathy with others has already reached a high degree of importance. Souls are connected with this stage insofar as they did not lose themselves in the satisfaction of lower necessities during their physical lives, but had joy and pleasure in their surroundings. Over-enthusiasm for nature, for example, in that it has borne something of a sensuous character, undergoes purifying here. It is necessary, however, to distinguish clearly this kind of love of nature from the higher living in nature that is of the spiritual kind that seeks for the spirit revealing itself in the things and events of nature. This kind of feeling for nature is one of the things that develop the spirit itself and establishes something permanent in it! One must distinguish, however, between such a feeling for nature, and a pleasure in nature that is based on the senses. In regard to this, the soul requires purification just as well as in regard to other inclinations based on mere physical existence. Many people see a kind of ideal in the arrangements of civilization that serve sensuous well-being, and in a system of education that, above all, brings about sensuous comfort. One cannot say that they seek to further only their selfish impulses. Their souls are, nevertheless, directed toward the physical world and must be cured of this by the force of sympathy that rules in the fifth region of the soul world and lacks these external means of gratification. Here the soul gradually recognizes that this sympathy must take other directions. These are found in the outpouring of the soul into the soul region, which is brought about by sympathy with the soul surroundings. Those souls also are purified here that mainly seek an enhancement of their sensuous welfare from their religious observances, whether it be that their longing goes out to an earthly or to a heavenly paradise. They, indeed, find this paradise in the "soul-land," but only for the purpose of seeing through its worthlessness. These are, of course, merely a few detached examples of purifications that take place in this fifth region They could be multiplied indefinitely.

By means of the sixth region, that of Active Soul Force, the purification of the part of the soul that thirsts for action takes place in souls whose activity does not bear an egotistical character but spring, nevertheless, from the sensuous satisfaction that action affords them. Viewed superficially, natures that develop such a desire for action convey the impression of being idealists; they show themselves to be persons capable of self-sacrifice. In a deeper sense, however, the chief thing with them is the enhancement of a sensuous feeling of pleasure. Many artistic natures and those who give themselves up to scientific activity because it pleases them belong to this class. These people are bound to the physical world by the belief that art and science exist for the sake of such pleasure.

The seventh region, that of the real Soul Life, frees man from his last inclinations to the sensory physical world. Each preceding region takes up from the soul whatever has affinity with it. The part of the soul still enveloping the spirit is the belief that its activity should be entirely devoted to the physical world. There are highly gifted individuals whose thoughts, however, are occupied with scarcely anything but the occurrences of the physical world. This belief can be called materialistic. It must be destroyed, and this is done in the seventh region. There the souls see that in true reality there exists no objects for materialistic thinking. Like ice in the sun, this belief of the soul melts away. The soul being is now absorbed into its own world. Now free of all fetters the spirit rises to the regions where it lives entirely in surroundings of its own nature. The soul had completed its previous earthly task, and after death any traces of this task that remained fettering the spirit have dissolved. By overcoming the last trace of the earthly, the soul is itself given back to its own element.

One sees from this description that the experiences in the soul world, and also the conditions of soul life after death, take on an ever less repellent character the more a man has stripped off those elements adhering to him from his earthly union with the physical corporeality and that were directly related to his body. The soul will belong for a longer or shorter time to one or another region according to the conditions created during its physical life. Wherever the soul feels affinity, there it remains until the affinity is extinguished. Where no relation exists, it goes on its way without feeling the possible effects.

It was intended that only the fundamental characteristics of the soul world and the outstanding features of the life of the soul in this world should be described here. This applies also to the following descriptions of the spiritland. It would exceed the prescribed limits of this book were further descriptions of the characteristics of these higher worlds attempted. The spatial relationships and the time lapses — terms that can only be used by way of comparison because the conditions are quite different there from those obtaining in the physical world — can only be discussed intelligibly when one is prepared to deal with then adequately and in full detail. References of importance in this connection will be found in my Occult Science, an Outline.

The Spiritland

Before the spirit can be observed on its further pilgrimage, the region it enters must first be examined. It is the world of the spirit. This world is so unlike the physical that all that is said about it will appear fantastic to anyone who is only willing to trust his physical senses. What has already been said in regard to the world of the soul — that is, that we have to use analogies to describe it — also holds good here to a still higher degree. Our language, which for the most part serves only for the realities of the senses, is not richly blessed with expressions applicable directly to the spiritland. It is, therefore, especially necessary to ask the reader to understand much that is said as an indication only because everything that is described here is so unlike the physical world that only in this way can it be depicted. The author is ever conscious of how little this account can really resemble the experiences of this region owing to the imperfection of our language, calculated as it is to be our medium of expression for the physical world.

It must above all things be emphasized that this world is woven out of the substance of which human thought consists. The word "substance," too is here used in a far from strict or accurate sense. Thought, however, as it lives in man, is only a shadow picture, a phantom of its true nature. Just as the shadow of an object on the wall is related to the real object that throws this shadow, so is the thought that makes its appearance through a human brain related to the being in the spiritland that corresponds to this thought. Now, when his spiritual sense is awakened, man really perceives this thought being, just as the eye of the senses perceives a table or a chair. He goes about in a region of thought beings. The corporeal eye perceives the lion, and the thinking directed to the sensibly perceptible thinks merely the thought, "lion" as a shadow, a shadowy picture. The spiritual eye sees in spiritland the thought "lion" as really and actually as the corporeal eye sees the physical lion. Here we may again refer to the analogy already used regarding the land of the soul. Just as the surroundings of a man born blind operated upon appear suddenly with the new qualities of color and light, so do the surroundings of the person who learns to use his spiritual eye appear as a new world, the world of living thoughts or spirit beings. In this world there are to be seen, first, the spiritual archetypes of all things and beings that are present in the physical and soul worlds. Imagine a painter's picture existing in his mind before it is painted. This gives an analogy to what is meant by the expression archetype. It does not concern us here that the painter has perhaps not had such an archetype in his mind before he paints and that it only gradually develops and becomes complete during the execution of the picture. In the real world of spirit there exist such archetypes for all things, and the physical things and beings are copies of these archetypes. It is quite understandable when anyone who only trusts his outer senses denies this archetypal world and holds that archetypes are merely abstractions gained by an intellectual comparison of sense objects. Such a person simply cannot see in this higher world. He knows the thought world only in its shadowy abstraction. He does not know that the person with spiritual vision is as familiar with spirit beings as he himself is with his dog or his cat, and that the archetypal world has a far more intense reality than the world of the physical senses.

True, the first look into this spiritland is still more bewildering than the first glimpse into the soul world because the archetypes in their true form are very unlike their sensory reflections. They are, however, just as unlike their shadows, the abstract thoughts. In the spiritual world all is in perpetual, mobile activity in the process of ceaseless creating. A state of rest, a remaining in one place such as we find in the physical world, does not exist here because the archetypes are creative beings. They are the master builders of all that comes into being in the physical and soul worlds. Their forms change rapidly and in each archetype lies the possibility of assuming myriads of specialized forms. They let the different shapes well up out of them, as it were, and no sooner is one produced than the archetype sets about pouring forth the next one from itself. Moreover, the archetypes stand in more or less intimate relationships to each other. They do not work singly. The one requires the help of the other in its creating Often innumerable archetypes work together in order that this or that being in the soul or physical world may arise.

Besides what is to be perceived by "spiritual sight" in this spiritland, there is something else experienced that is to be regarded as "spiritual hearing." As soon as the clairvoyant rises out of the soul world into the spirit world, the archetypes that are perceptible become "sounding" as well. This sounding, this emission of a tone, is a purely spiritual process. It must be conceived without any accompanying thought of a physical sound. The observer feels as if he were in an ocean of tones, and in these tones, in this spiritual chiming, the beings of the spirit world express themselves. The primordial laws of their existence, their mutual relationships and affinities, express themselves in the intermingling of these sounds, in their harmonies, melodies and rhythms. What the intellect perceives in the physical world as law, as idea, reveals itself to the spiritual ear as spiritual music. Hence, the Pythagoreans called this perception of the spiritual world the "music of the spheres." To the possessor of a spiritual ear this music of the spheres is not something merely figurative or allegorical, but a spiritual reality well-known to him. If we wish to gain a conception of this spiritual music, however, we must lay aside all ideas of the music of the senses as perceived by the material ear because in spiritual music we are concerned with a spiritual perception, that is, with perception of a kind that must remain silent to the ear of the senses.

In the following descriptions of spiritland reference to this spiritual music will be omitted for the sake of simplicity. We have only to realize that everything described as picture, as shining with light, is at the same time sounding. Each color, each perception of light represents a spiritual tone, and every combination of colors corresponds with a harmony, a melody. Thus we must hold clearly in mind that even where the sounding prevails, perception by means of the spiritual eye by no means ceases. The sounding is merely added to the shining. Therefore, where archetypes are spoken of in the following pages, the primal tones are to be thought of as also present. Other perceptions make their appearance as well, which by way of comparison may be termed spiritual tasting and the like, but it is not proposed to go into these processes here since we are concerned with awakening a conception of spiritland through some few isolated modes of perception selected out of the whole.

Now it is necessary at the outset to distinguish the different species of archetypes from each other. In spiritland also it is necessary to distinguish between a number of degrees or regions in order to find one's way among them. Here also, as in the soul world, the different regions are not to be thought of as laid one above the other like strata, but as mutually interpenetrating and permeating each other.

The First Region. This region contains the archetypes of the physical world insofar as it is devoid of life. The archetypes of the minerals and plants are to be found here, but the archetypes of plants are found only to the extent that they are purely physical, that is, insofar as any life content they may possess is disregarded. In the same way we find here the physical forms of the animals and of men. This by no means exhausts all that is to be found in this region, but merely illustrates it by the most obvious examples. This region forms the basic structure of spiritland. It can be likened to the solid land masses of the physical earth. It forms the continental masses of spiritland. Its relationship with the physical corporeal world can only be described by means of an illustration. Some idea of it can be gained in the following way. Picture a limited space filled with physical bodies of the most varied kind. Then think these bodies away and conceive in their stead hollow spaces having their forms. The intervening spaces that were previously empty must be thought of as filled with the most varied forms having manifold relationships with the physical bodies spoken of above. In appearance this is somewhat like the lowest region of the archetypal world. In it the things and beings that become embodied in the physical world are present as hollow spaces, and in the intervening spaces the mobile activity of the archetypes and of the spiritual music takes place. During their formation into physical forms the hollow spaces become, as it were, filled with physical matter. If anyone were to look into space with both physical and spiritual eyes, he would see the physical bodies and between them the mobile activity of the creative archetypes.

The Second Region. This region of spiritland contains the archetypes of life, but this life forms here a perfect unity. It streams through the world of spirit as a fluid element, like blood, pulsating through everything. It may be likened to the sea and the water systems of the physical earth. Its distribution, however, is more like the distribution of the blood in the animal body than that of the seas and rivers. One could describe this second stage of the spiritland as flowing life composed of thought substance. In this element are the creative primal forces producing everything that appears in physical reality as living beings. Here it becomes evident that all life is a unity, that the life in man is related to the life of all his fellow creatures.

The Third Region. The archetypes of all soul formations must be designated as the third region of the spiritland. Here we find ourselves in a much finer and rarer element than in the first two regions. To use a comparison it can be called the air or atmosphere of spiritland. Everything that goes on in the souls of both the other worlds — the physical and the soul worlds — has here its spiritual counterpart. Here all feelings, sensations, instincts and passions are again present, but spiritually present. The atmospheric events in this aerial region correspond to the sorrows and joys of the creatures in the other worlds. The longing of the human soul appears here as a gentle zephyr; an outbreak of passion is like a stormy blast. He who can visualize what is here under consideration pierces deep into the sighing of every creature if he directs his attention to the matter. We can, for example, speak here of a loud storm with flashing lightning and rolling thunder. If we investigate the matter further, we find that the passions of a battle waged on earth are expressed in spiritland in a storm of spirit beings.   The Fourth Region. The archetypes of the fourth region are not immediately related to the other worlds. They are in certain respects beings who govern the archetypes of the three lower regions and mediate their working together. They are accordingly occupied with the ordering and grouping of these subordinate archetypes. Therefore, a more comprehensive activity proceeds from this region than from the lower ones.

The Fifth, Sixth and Seventh Regions. These regions differ essentially from the preceding ones because the beings to be found in them supply the archetypes of the lower regions with the impulses to their activity. In them we find the creative forces of the archetypes themselves. Whoever is able to rise to these regions makes acquaintance with purposes that underlie our world. Like living germ-points, the archetypes still lie here ready to assume the most manifold forms of thought beings. If these germ-points are projected into the lower regions, they well up, as it were, and manifest themselves in the most varied shapes. The ideas through which the human spirit manifests itself creatively in the physical world are the reflection, the shadow, of these germinal thought beings of the higher spiritual world. The observer with the spiritual ear who rises from the lower regions of spiritland to these higher ranges becomes aware that sounds and tones are transformed into a spiritual language. He begins to perceive the Spiritual Word through which the things and beings no longer make known to him their nature in music alone, but now express it in words. They utter what can be called in spiritual science their eternal names.

We must visualize these thought germ-beings as possessing a composite nature. Only the germ-sheath is taken out of the element of the thought world, and this surrounds the true life kernel. With it we have reached the confines of the three worlds because the kernel has its origin in still higher worlds. When man was described in the preceding pages according to his components were called life spirit and spirit man. There are similar life kernels for other beings in the cosmos. They originate in higher worlds and are placed in the three that have been described in order to accomplish their tasks in them.

The human spirit will now be followed on its further pilgrimage through spiritland between two embodiments or incarnations. While doing this the conditions and distinguishing characteristics of this "land" will once more come clearly into view.

The Spirit in Spiritland after Death

When the human spirit has passed through the worlds of souls on its way between two incarnations, it enters the land of spirits to remain there until it is ripe for a new bodily existence. One can only understand the meaning of this sojourn in spiritland when one is able to interpret in the right way the aim and end of the pilgrimage of man through his incarnation. While man is incarnated in the physical body he works and creates in the physical world as a spiritual being. He imprints on the physical forms, on corporeal materials and forces what his spirit thinks out and develops. As a messenger of the spiritual world he has, therefore, to embody the spirit in the corporeal world. Only by being embodied, incarnated, can man work in the world of bodies. He must take on the physical body as his tool so that through the body he can act on other bodies and they on him. What acts through this physical corporeality of man is the spirit. From this spirit flow the purposes, the direction its work is to take in the physical world.

Now as long as the spirit works in the physical body, it cannot as spirit live in its true form. It can, as it were, only shine through the veil of physical existence because as a matter of fact, the thought life of man really belongs to the spiritual world. As it appears in physical existence its true form is veiled. It can also be said that the thought life of the physical man is a shadow, a reflection of the true, spiritual being to whom it belongs. Thus, during physical life, the spirit working through the physical body interacts with the earthly corporeal world. Although one of the tasks of the human spirit, as long as it proceeds from incarnation to incarnation, is to work upon the physical corporeal world, it could by no means fulfill this task in a proper manner if it lived merely in embodied existence. The purposes and goals of the earthly task are just as little developed and determined within the earthly incarnation, as the plan of a house comes into existence on the site where the laborers work. Just as this plan is worked out in the office of the architect, so are the aims and purposes of earthly creative activities worked out and developed in the land of spirits. The spirit of man has to live again and again in this land between two incarnations in order to be able, equipped with what he takes with him on his departure, to approach the work in the physical life. Just as the architect, without working with brick and mortar, works out the plan of the house in his drafting room in accordance with architectural and other laws, so too does the architect of human creation, the spirit or higher self, develop its capacities and aims in spiritland in accordance with the laws of that land, in order to bring them over into the earthly world. Only when the human spirit sojourns again and again in its own region, will it also be able by means of the physical corporeal instruments to bring the spirit into the earthly world.

On the physical scene of action man learns to know the qualities and forces of the physical world. During his creative activity he gathers experiences regarding the demands made by the physical world on anyone wishing to work on it. He learns to know there, as it were, the qualities of the matter in which he wishes to embody his thoughts and ideas. The thoughts and ideas themselves he cannot extract from matter. Thus the physical world is both the scene of his creating and of his learning. In the spiritland, what has been learned is then transformed into living faculties of the spirit. One can carry the above comparison farther in order to make the matter clearer. The architect designs a house. His plans are carried out. In doing this he gains the most varied experiences. All of these experiences enhance his capacities. When he works out his next design, all these experiences flow into it, and this next design, when compared to the first, is seen to be enriched with all that was learned through the first.

It is the same with the successive human lives. In the intervals between incarnations, the spirit lives in its own sphere. It can give itself up entirely to the requirements of the spirit life. Freed from the physical body, it develops itself in every direction and works into this development the fruits of its experiences in former earthly careers. Thus its attention is always directed to the scene of its earthly tasks. Thus it works continually at following the earth insofar as that is its field of action, through its necessary development. It works upon itself in order to be able in each incarnation to carry out its service during that life in accordance with the condition of the earth at that time. This is, of course, only a general outline of successive human lives. Reality will never quite correspond with it, but only to a certain degree. Circumstances may decree that a man's subsequent life be much less perfect than a previous one, but taken as a whole such irregularities equalize themselves in the succession of lives within definite limits.

The development of the spirit in spiritland takes place in consequence of man's entering completely into the life of the various regions of this land. His own life dissolves, as it were, into these regions successively and he takes on, for the time being, their characteristics. Through this they penetrate his being with theirs in order that the may be able to work, strengthened by theirs, in his earthly life.

In the first region of spiritland man is surrounded by the spiritual archetypes of earthly beings. During life on earth he learns to know only the shadows of these archetypes that he grasps in his thoughts. What is merely thought on earth is in this region experienced, lived. Man moves among thoughts, but these thoughts are real beings. What he has perceived with his senses during life on earth acts on him now in its thought form. The thought, however, does not appear as the shadow hiding itself behind the things. It is, on the contrary, the life-filled reality producing the things. Man is, as it were, in the thought workshop in which earthly things are formed and fashioned, because in the land of spirit all is vital activity and mobility. Here the thought world is at work as a world of living beings, creative and constructive. We see how what we have experienced during the earthly existence is constructed. Just as in the physical body we experience the things of the senses as reality, so now, as spirit, we experience the spiritual, constructive forces as real.

Among the thought beings to be found in spiritland is also the thought of our own physical corporeality. We feel removed from the latter. We feel only the spiritual being as belonging to ourselves, and when we perceive the discarded body as if in memory, no longer as physical but as thought being, then its relation to the external world becomes a matter of direct perception. We learn to look at it as something belonging to the external world, as a member of this external world. We consequently no longer distinguish our own corporeality from the rest of the external world as something more closely related to ourselves. We feel the unity in the whole external world including our own bodily incarnations. Our own embodiments dissolve here into a unity with the rest of the world. Thus man here looks upon the archetypes of the physical corporeal reality as a unity to which he has belonged himself. He learns, therefore, gradually to know his relationship, his unity with the surrounding world by observation. He learns to say to it, "What is here spread out around thee, thou wert that." This is one of the fundamental thoughts of ancient Indian Vedanta wisdom. The sage acquires, even during his earthly life, what others experience after death, namely, the ability to grasp the thought that he himself is related to all things — the thought, "Thou art that." In earthly life this is an ideal to which the thought life can be devoted. In the land of the spirit it is an immediate fact, one that grows ever clearer to us through spiritual experience, and man himself comes to know ever more clearly in this land that in his own inner being he belongs to the spirit world. He perceives himself to be a spirit among spirits, a member of the primordial spirits, feeling within himself the word of the primordial spirit, "I am the Primal Spirit." The wisdom of the Vedanta says, "I am Brahman," that is, I belong as a member to the primordial being in whom all beings have their origin. We see that what is grasped during earthly life as a shadowy thought towards which all wisdom strives is in spiritland an immediate experience. Indeed it is only thought during earth life because it is a fact in spiritual existence.

Thus man during his spiritual existence sees as if from outside from a high watch tower the relationships and facts in the midst of which he stands during his earthly life. During his life in the lowest region of spiritland, he lives in regard to the earthly relationships immediately connected with physical corporeal reality. On earth man is born into a family, a folk; he lives in a certain country. His earthly existence is determined by all these relationships. He finds this or that friend because relationships within the physical world bring it about. He carries on this or that business. All this decides the conditions of his earthly life. All this presents itself to him during his life in the first region of spiritland as living thought being. He lives it all through again in a certain way, but he lives it through from the active spiritual side. The family love he has exercised, the friendship he has produced, become alive and quick from within, and his capacities in this direction are enhanced. That element in the spirit of man that acts as the force of love of family and friend is strengthened. He later enters on his earthly existence again as a more perfect man in these respects. It is to a certain extent the everyday relationships of earth life that ripen as the fruit of this lowest region of spiritland. That element in man, which in its interests is wholly absorbed by these everyday relationships, will feel itself in affinity with this region for the greater part of its life between two incarnations. We find again in the spiritual world the people with whom we have lived in the physical world. Just as everything loosens and falls away from the soul that was peculiarly its own through the physical body, so also does the bond that in physical life linked soul with soul loosen itself from those conditions that have meaning and effectiveness only in the physical world. Yet all that soul was to soul in physical life is carried over beyond death into the spiritual world. It is natural that words coined for physical conditions can only reproduce inaccurately what takes place in the spiritual world. If this is taken into account, it must be described as quite correct when it is said that those souls that belong together in physical life find each other again in order to continue in a corresponding manner their joint lives in the spiritual world.

In the second region the common life of the earth world flows as thought being, as a fluid element, so to speak, of spiritland. As long as one observes the world during physical embodiment, life appears to be confined within separate living beings. In spiritland it is liberated from them and, like life-blood, flows as it were through the whole land. It exists there as the living unity that is present in all things. Of this also only a reflection appears to man during earthly life, and this reflection expresses itself in every form of reverence that he pays to the whole, to the unity and harmony of the universe. The religious life of man is derived from this reflection. He becomes aware of how far the all-embracing meaning of existence does not lie in what is transitory and separate. He regards the transitory as a similitude, a likeness of an eternal, harmonious unity. He looks up to this unity in a mood of reverence and worship. He performs before it religious rites and ceremonies. In spiritland, not the reflection but the real form appears as living thought being. Here man can really join himself to the unity that he has reverenced on earth. The fruits of religious life and all connected with it make their appearance in this region. Man now learns through spiritual experience to recognize that his individual destiny is not to be separated from the community to which he belongs. The capacity to know oneself as a member of a whole develops here. The religious feelings, all that has already during life striven after a pure and noble morality, will draw strength out of this region during a great part of the spiritual life between incarnations, and a man will reincarnate with enhanced capacities in this direction.

While in the first region we are in company of those souls with whom we have been linked by the closest ties of the physical world during the preceding physical life, in the second region we enter the domain of all those things with whom we felt united in a wider sense, that is, through a common reverence, through a common religious confession, and so on. It must be emphasized that the spiritual experiences of the preceding regions continue to persist through the subsequent ones. Thus man is not all torn away from the ties knitted by family, friendship, and so on, when he enters upon the life of the second and following regions. Moreover, the regions of spiritland do not lie like sections one beside the other. They interpenetrate each other, and man experiences himself in a new region not because he has externally entered upon it in any form whatever, but because he has attained in himself the inner capacities for now perceiving what he previously lived within, but without perceiving it.

The third region of spiritland contains the archetypes of the soul world. All that lives in this world is here present as living thought being. We find in it the archetypes of desires, wishes and feelings, but here in the spirit world nothing self-seeking clings to the soul. Just as all life forms a unity in the second region, so in this third region all longings, wishes, all likes and dislikes form a unity. The desire and wish of others are not separable from my desire and wish. The sensations and feelings of all beings are a common world, enclosing and surrounding everything else, just as the physical atmosphere surrounds the earth. This region is, as it were, the atmosphere or air of spiritland. All that a person has carried out in his life on earth in the service of the community, in selfless devotion to his fellowmen, will bear fruit here because through this service, through this self-giving, he has lived in a reflection of the third region of spiritland. The great benefactors of the human race, the self-sacrificing natures, those who render great services to communities, have gained their ability to render them in this region after having acquired for themselves the readiness for a special relation to it during their previous earthly careers.

It is evident that the three regions of spiritland just described stand in a certain relation to the worlds below them, to the physical and soul worlds, because they contain the archetypes, the living thought beings, that take up corporeal or soul existence in those worlds. Only the fourth region is the pure spiritland, but even this region is not quite that in the fullest sense of the word. It differs from the three lower regions owing to the fact that in them we meet with the archetypes of those physical and soul relations that man finds existing in the physical and soul worlds before he himself begins to participate in them. The circumstances of everyday life link themselves with the things and beings that man finds already present in the world. The transitory things of this world direct his gaze to their eternal primal foundation, and his fellow creatures also, to whom he selflessly devotes himself, do not owe their presence to him. It is, however, through him that there are in the world all the creations of the arts, sciences, engineering, states and governments — in short, all that he has embodied in the world as original creations of his spirit. Without his activity these could not manifest themselves in the physical world. The archetypes of these purely human creations are in the fourth region of the spiritland. All that we develop during earthly life in the way of scientific discoveries, of artistic ideas and forms, of technical conceptions, bears fruit in this fourth region. It is out of this region therefore that artists, scientists and inventors draw their impulses and enhance their genius during their stay in spiritland in order during another incarnation to be able to assist in fuller measure the further evolution of human culture. But we must not imagine that this fourth region of spiritland possesses importance only for specially prominent human beings. It has great importance for all men. All that occupies us in our physical life outside the sphere of everyday living, wishing and willing has its source in this region. If we did not pass through it in the period between death and a new birth, we would in our subsequent life have no interests leading out beyond the narrow circle of our personal life-conduct to what is common to all humanity.

It has already been said above that even this region cannot be called pure spiritland in the full sense of the word. This is the case because the stage at which men have left civilization on earth continues to influence their spiritual existence. They can enjoy in spiritland only the fruits of what it was possible for them to carry out in accordance with their talents and the stage of development of the folk, state and nation into which they were born.

In the still higher regions of the spiritland the human spirit is now freed from every earthly fetter. It rises to the pure spiritland in which it experiences the intentions, the aims, that the spirit set itself to accomplish by means of the earthly life. All that has been already realized in the earthly world brings into existence only a more or less weak copy of the highest intentions and aims. Each crystal, each tree, each animal, and all that is being realized in the domain of human creation — all this gives only copies of what the spirit intends, and man during his incarnations can only link himself with these imperfect copies of the perfect intentions and aims. Thus during one of his incarnations he himself can only be an image of what, in the kingdom of the spirit, he is intended to be. What he really is as spirit in spiritland comes, therefore, into view only when he rises to the fifth region of spiritland in the interval between two incarnations. What he is here is really he himself — the being who receives an external existence in the numerous and varied incarnations. In this region the true self of man can freely live and expand in all directions, and this self is thus the being who appears ever anew in each incarnation as the one. This self brings with it the faculties that have developed in the lower regions of the spiritland. It consequently carries the fruits of former lives over into those following. It is the bearer of the results of former incarnations.

When the self lives in the fifth region of the spiritland, it is in the kingdom of intentions and purposes. Just as the architect learns from the imperfections that have come to light in his work, and just as he brings into his new designs only what he was able to change from imperfections to perfections, so does the self in the fifth region discard from the results of its former lives whatever is bound up with the imperfections of the lower worlds, and with these results it impregnates the purposes of the spiritland — purposes with which it now lives. It is clear that the force that can be drawn from this region will depend upon how much the self during its incarnation has acquired in the form of results fit to be taken up into the world of purposes. The self that has sought to realize the purposes of the spirit during earthly life through an active thought life, or through wise love expressed in deeds, will establish a strong claim upon this region. The self that has expended its efforts entirely on the events of everyday life, that has lived only in the transitory, has sown no seeds that can be fruitful in the purposes of the external world order. Only the small portion of its activities that extended beyond the interests of everyday life can unfold as fruit in these higher regions of the spiritland. It must not be supposed that what comes into consideration here is chiefly earthly fame or anything akin to it. No, the important thing to realize here is that in the narrowest walks of life even the least event has its significance in the eternal progressive course of existence.

We must make ourselves familiar with the thought that in this region our judgments must be different from those in the physical life. For instance, if a man has acquired little that is related to this fifth region, the craving arises in him to imprint an impulse upon himself for the following life that will cause that life to run its course in such a way that in its destiny (karma) the corresponding effect of that deficiency will come to light. Experiences, which in the following earth life appear as a painful destiny, seen from that life — and perhaps deeply bewailed as such — are, nevertheless, the very experiences that a man in this region of spiritland finds absolutely necessary for himself.

Since a man in the fifth region lives in his own true self, he is lifted out of everything from the lower worlds that envelops him during his incarnations. He is what he ever was and ever will be during the course of his incarnations. He lives in the governing power of the intentions that prevail during these incarnations, and that he grafts into his own self. He looks back on his own past and feels that all he has experienced in it will be brought into service in the intentions he has to realize in the future. There flash forth a kind of remembrance of his earlier, and a prophetic vision of his future lives. We see, therefore, that what we call in this book spirit self lives in this region, as far as it is developed, in the reality that is appropriate to it. It develops itself still further and prepares itself to make possible in a new incarnation the fulfillment of the spiritual intentions in the realities of earthly life.

If, during a succession of sojourns in spiritland, the spirit self has evolved so far that it can move about quite freely there, it will evermore seek there its true home. Life in the world of spirit will be as familiar to it as life in physical reality is to the earthly man. The view-points of the spirit world operate from now on as the dominating ones, which it makes its own more or less consciously or unconsciously for its succeeding earth lives. The self can feel itself to be a member of the divine world order. The limitations and laws of the earthly life do not affect it in its innermost being. Power for all that it carries out comes to it from this spiritual world. The spiritual world, however, is a unity. He who lives in it knows how the Eternal has worked creatively upon the past. Out of the Eternal he can determine the direction for the future. His view over the past widens into a perfect one. The man who has reached this stage sets before himself aims that he intends to carry out in a coming incarnation. From out the spiritland he influences his future so that it runs its course in harmony with the true and spiritual. Such a person during the stages between two incarnations finds himself in the presence of all those exalted beings before whose gaze divine wisdom lies spread out unveiled, because he has climbed up to the stage at which he can understand it.

In the sixth region of the spiritland a man will fulfill in all his actions what is most in accord with the true being of the world. He cannot seek after what profits himself, but only after what ought to happen according to the right course of the world order.

In the seventh region of the spiritland the limit of the three worlds is reached. Man stands in the presence of the life-kernels, which are transplanted from higher worlds into the three already described in order that in them they may fulfill their tasks. When a man has reached the boundary of the three worlds, he recognizes himself in his own life-kernel. This implies that for him the problems of these three worlds have been solved. He has a complete view of the entire life of these worlds. In physical life the powers of the soul, through which it obtains the experiences in the spiritual world here described, remain unconscious under ordinary circumstances. They work in their unconscious depths upon the bodily organs, which bring about the consciousness of the physical world. That is precisely the reason why these powers remain imperceptible for this world. The eye, too, does not see itself because forces are at work in it that make other things visible. If one would judge to what extent a human life running its course between birth and death can be the result of preceding earth lives, one must take into consideration the fact that a point of view that lies within this same life, and at the outset is the natural one, can yield no possibility of correct judgment. For such a point of view, for instance, an earth life could appear full of suffering, imperfect. Yet, seen from an extra-earthly view-point, this very configuration of the earth life with its suffering, its imperfections, would prove to be the result of previous earth lives. By treading the path of knowledge as this is described in the next chapter, the soul sets itself free from the conditions of bodily life. Thus it can perceive in a picture the experiences that it undergoes between death and a new birth. Perception of this kind makes it possible to describe what happens in spiritland as has been done here in but little more than outline. Only when we do not neglect to hold before our minds the fact that the whole disposition of the soul is different in the physical body from its disposition during purely spiritual experiences, only then shall we see the description given here in the right light.

The Physical World and Its Connection with the Soul and Spiritland

The formations in the soul world and in spiritland cannot be the objects of external sense perception. The objects of this sense perception are to be added as a third world to the two already described. Man lives during his bodily existence simultaneously in the three worlds. He perceives the things of the sensory world and acts upon them. The formations of the soul world act upon him through their forces of sympathy and antipathy, and his own soul excites waves in the soul world by its likes and dislikes, desires and wishes. The spiritual being of things, on the other hand, mirrors itself in his thought world and he himself, as thinking spirit-being, is a citizen of spiritland and a companion of all that lives in that region of the world. This makes it evident that the sensory world is only a part of what surrounds us. This part stands out from our general surrounding with a certain independence because it can be perceived by senses that disregard the soul and spiritual parts. These, however, belong just as much to this surrounding world as does the material part. Just as a piece of floating ice is substance of the surrounding water although it stands out prominently owing to particular qualities, so are the things perceptible to the senses substance of the surrounding soul and spirit worlds. They stand out from these worlds owing to particular qualities that make them perceptible to the senses. They are, speaking somewhat metaphorically, condensed spirit and soul formations, and the condensation makes it possible for the senses to acquire knowledge of them. In fact, just as ice is only a form in which water exists, so are the objects of the senses only a form in which soul and spirit beings exist. If this has been grasped, it can also be understood that as water can pass over into ice, so the spirit world can pass over into the soul world, and the soul world into that of the senses.

Looked at from this point of view it can be seen why we can form thoughts about the things of the senses. Thus, there is a question that everyone who thinks must ask himself, "In what relation does the thought that we have about a stone stand to the stone itself?" This question rises in full clearness in the minds of those persons who look with especial penetration into external nature. They feel the consonance of the human thought world with the structure and order of nature. The great astronomer, Kepler, for example, speaks in a beautiful way about this harmony. He says, "True it is that the divine call that bids man study astronomy stands written in the world, not indeed in words and syllables, but factually by virtue of the adaptability of the human senses and concepts to the concatenations of the heavenly bodies and conditions." Only because the things of the sensible world are nothing but condensed spirit beings is the man who lifts himself by means of his thoughts to these spirit beings able by thinking to understand the things. Sense objects originate in the spirit world. They are only another form of the spirit beings, and when a man forms thoughts about things, his inner nature is merely directed away from the sensible form and out towards the spiritual archetypes of these things.

To understand an object by means of thought is a process that may be likened to the liquefaction of a solid body by fire in order that the chemist may examine it in its liquid form.

The spiritual archetypes of the sense world are to be found in the various regions of the spiritland. In the fifth, sixth and seventh regions these archetypes are still found as living germ-points. In the four lower regions they shape themselves into spiritual structures. The human spirit perceives a shadowy reflection of these spiritual formations when by thinking it tries to gain understanding of the things of the senses. How these formations have condensed until they form the sense world is a problem for the seeker who strives towards a spiritual understanding of the world around him.

For human sense perception this surrounding world is divided primarily into four distinctly separate stages — the mineral, plant, animal and human. The mineral kingdom is perceived by the senses and comprehended by thought. Thus, when we form a thought about a mineral body, we have to do with two things — the sense object and the thought. Accordingly, we must imagine that this sense object is a condensed thought being. Now, one mineral being acts on another in an external way. It impinges on it and moves it. It warms it, lights it up, dissolves it, and so forth. This external kind of action can be expressed in thoughts. We form thoughts about the way mineral things act on each other externally in accordance with law. By this means our separate thoughts expand into a thought picture of the whole mineral world, and this thought picture is a reflection of the archetype of the whole mineral world of the senses. It is to be found as a complete whole in the spirit world.

In the plant kingdom the phenomena of growth and propagation are added to the phenomenon of external action of one thing or another. The plant grows and brings forth from itself beings like itself. Life is here added to what confronts us in the mineral kingdom. The simple recollection of this fact leads to a view that is enlightening in this connection. The plant has the power to create its living shape and to reproduce it in a being of its own kind. In between the shapeless character of mineral matter as we meet it in gases, liquids, etc. and the living shape of the plant world, stand the forms of the crystals. In the crystals we have to seek the transition from the shapeless mineral world to the plant kingdom that has the capacity for forming living shapes. In this externally sensory formative process in both kingdoms, mineral and plant, we must see the sensory condensation of the purely spiritual process that takes place when the spiritual germs of the three higher regions of the spiritland form themselves into the spirit shapes of the lower regions. The transition from the formless spiritual germ to the formed structure corresponds in the spiritual world to the process of crystallization. This transition is the spiritual archetype of the process of crystallization. If this transition condenses so that the senses can perceive it in its outcome, it then exhibits itself in the world of senses as the process of mineral crystallization.   There is, however, also in the plant being a fashioned spirit germ. Here the living, fashioning capacity is still retained in the shaped being. In the crystal the spirit germ has lost its constructive power during the process of fashioning. It has exhausted its life in the shape produced. The plant has shape and in addition it has the capacity to produce a shape. The characteristic belonging to the spirit germs in the higher regions of the spiritland has been preserved in the plant life. The plant has, therefore, form like the crystal, and to that is added the shaping or formative force. Besides the form that the primal beings have assumed in the plant shape, there is another form working on that shape that bears the impress of the spirit beings of the higher regions. Only what manifests itself in the completed shape of the plant, however, is sensibly perceptible. The formative beings who give life to this shape are present but imperceptible in the plant kingdom. The physical eye sees the lily small today and some time later sees it grown larger. The formative force that evolves the latter out of the former is not seen by this eye. This formative force being is the part of the plant world that acts imperceptibly to the senses. The spirit germs have descended a stage in order to work in the kingdom of shapes. In spiritual science elementary kingdoms are spoken of. If we designate the primal forms, which has as yet no shape, as the first elementary kingdom, then the force beings who work invisible to the senses as the craftsmen of plant growth may be designated as belonging to the second elementary kingdom.

In the animal world sensation and impulse are added to the capacities for growth and propagation. These are manifestations of the soul world. A being endowed with these belongs to the soul world, receives impressions from it and reacts on it. Now, every sensation and every impulse that arises in the animal is brought forth from the foundations of the animal soul. The shape is more enduring than the feeling or impulse. One may say that the life of sensation bears the same relation to the more enduring living shape that the self-changing plant shape bears to the rigid crystal. The plant exhausts itself to a certain extent in the shape-forming force; during its life it continues to add new shapes to itself. First it sends forth roots, then its leafy structure, later flowers, and finally its fruit and seeds. The animal is enclosed within a shape complete within itself and develops within this the changeful life of feeling and impulse. This life has its existence in the soul world. The plant grows and propagates itself; the animal feels and develops its impulses. They constitute for the animal the formless that is always developing into new forms. They have their archetypal processes ultimately in the highest regions of spiritland, but they carry out their activities in the soul world. There are thus in the animal world in addition to the force beings who, invisible to the senses, direct growth and propagation, others who have descended a stage deeper into the soul world. In the animal kingdom formless beings who clothe themselves in soul sheaths are present as the master builders bringing about sensations and impulses. They are the real architects of the animal forms. In spiritual science this region to which they belong may be called the third elementary kingdom.

Man, in addition to having the capacities named in plant and animal, is furnished also with the power of elaborating his sensations into ideas and thoughts and of controlling his impulses by thinking. The thought, which appears in the plant as shape and in the animal as soul force, makes its appearance in man in its own form as thought itself. The animal is soul; man is spirit. The spirit being, which in the animal is engaged in soul development, has now descended a stage deeper still. In the animal it is soul forming. In man it has entered into the world of sensory matter itself. The spirit is present within the human sensory body, and because it appears in a sensory garment, it can appear only as the shadowy reflection of the spirit being that thought represents. The spirit manifests in man conditioned by the physical brain organism, but at the same time it has become the inner being of man. Thought is the form that the formless spirit being assumes in man, just as it takes on shape in the plant and soul in the animal. Consequently, man, insofar as he is a thinking being, is subject to no elementary kingdom fashioning him from without. His elementary kingdom works in his physical body. Only to the extent that man is shape and sentient being is he worked upon by elementary beings of the same kind as those working upon plants and animals. The thought organism of man is elaborated entirely from within his physical body. In the spirit organism of man, in his nervous system that has developed into the perfect brain, we have sensibly visible before us what works on plants and animals as non-sensory force being. That is, the animal shows self-feeling, but man self-consciousness. In the animal, spirit feels itself as soul. It does not yet grasp itself as spirit. In man, the spirit recognizes itself as spirit although, owing to physical limitations, merely as a shadowy reflection of the spirit, as thought.

The threefold world, accordingly, falls into the following categories:

1. Realm of archetypal formless beings — first elementary kingdom

2. Realm of shape-creating beings — secondary elementary kingdom
3. Realm of soul beings — third elementary kingdom

4. Realm of created shapes (crystal forms) — mineral kingdom

5. Realm whose forms are sensibly perceptible and in which the shape-creating beings are active — plant kingdom

6. Realm whose forms are sensibly perceptible and in which the shape-creating and soul beings are active — animal kingdom

7. Realm whose forms are sensibly perceptible and in which the shape-creating and soul beings are active, and in which the spirit fashions itself in the form of thought within the sense world — human kingdom.

From this can be seen how the basic constituents of man living in the body are connected with the spiritual world. The physical body, the ether body, the sentient soul body and the intellectual soul are to be regarded as archetypes of the spiritland condensed in the sensory world. The physical body comes into existence through condensation of the human archetype to the point of sensory appearance. For this reason one can call this physical body also a being of the first elementary kingdom condensed to sensory perceptibility. The ether body comes into existence through the fact that the shape thus engendered maintains its mobility through a being that extends its activity into the kingdom of the senses but is not itself visible to the senses. If one wishes to characterize this being fully, it must be described as having its origin in the highest regions of spiritland and thence shaping itself in the second region into an archetype of life. As such an archetype of life it works in the sensory world. In a similar way, the being that builds up the sentient soul body has its origin in the highest regions of the spiritland, forms itself in the third spirit region into the archetype of the soul world, and as such works in the sensory world. The intellectual soul, however, comes into existence when in the fourth region of the spiritland the archetype of the thinking man gives itself a thought form in which it acts directly as thinking man in the world of the senses. Thus man stands within the world of the senses. Thus the spirit works on his physical body, ether body and sentient soul body. Thus the spirit comes into manifestation in the intellectual soul. Archetypes in the form of beings who in a certain sense are external to man work upon the three lower members of his being. In his intellectual soul he himself becomes a conscious worker upon himself. The beings who work on his physical body are the same as those who form mineral nature. Beings of the kind that live in the plant kingdom work on his ether body, and those beings such as live in the animal kingdom work on his sentient soul body. Both are imperceptible to the senses but extend their activity into these kingdoms.

Thus do the different worlds combine in action. The universe man lives in is the expression of this combined activity.

*　　*　　*

When we have grasped the sensory world in this way, the understanding opens up for beings of a kind different from those having their existence in the above mentioned four kingdoms of nature. One example of such beings is what may be called the Folk or National Spirit. This being does not manifest itself directly in a sensibly perceptible way, but lives its life entirely in the sensations, feelings, tendencies and impulses observable in the common characteristics of a whole nation. This is a being who does not incarnate in the sense world, but just as man forms his body out of substances sensibly visible, so does this Folk Spirit form its body out of the substance of the soul world. This soul body of the National Spirit is like a cloud in which the members of a nation live. Its influences become evident in the souls of the men concerned, but it does not originate in these souls themselves. The National Spirit remains merely a shadowy conception of the mind without being or life, an empty abstraction, to the man who does not picture it in this way.

Something similar may be said in reference to what one calls the Spirit of the Age (Zeitgeist). Indeed, the spiritual outlook is extended in this way over a variety of other beings, both lower and higher, that live in the human environment unseen by the bodily senses. Those who have powers of spiritual sight perceive such beings and can describe them. To the lower species of such beings belongs all that is described by observers of the spiritual world as salamanders, sylphs, undines and gnomes. It should not be necessary to say that such descriptions are not to be considered reproductions of the reality that underlies them. If they were, then the world in question would be not a spiritual, but a grossly sensory one. They are attempts at making clear a spiritual reality that can only be represented in this way, this is, by similes. It is quite comprehensible that anyone who admits the validity of physical vision only, regards such beings as the offspring of confused fantasy and superstition. They can, of course, never become visible to the sensory eye because they have no sensory bodies. The superstition does not consist in regarding such beings as real, but in believing that they appear in a way perceptible to the physical senses. Beings of such forms co-operate in the construction of the world, and we come into contact with them as soon as we enter the higher regions closed to the bodily senses. Those people are not superstitious who see in such descriptions pictures of spiritual realities, but rather those who believe in the sensory existence of the pictures, as well as those who deny the spirit, because they think they must deny the sensory picture.

Mention must also be made of those beings who do not descend to the soul world, but whose vestment is composed of the formations of spiritland alone. Man perceives them and becomes their companion when he opens his spiritual eye and ear to them. Through such an opening much becomes intelligible to him that previously he could only stare at uncomprehendingly. It becomes bright around him, and he sees the primal causes of what takes place as effects in the world of the senses. He comprehends what he either denied entirely when he had no spiritual eye, or in reference to which he had to content himself with saying, "There are more things in heaven and earth than are dreamed of in thy philosophy." People with fine, spiritual feelings become uneasy when they begin to have a glimmering, when they become vaguely aware of a world different from the sensory one surrounding them, one in which they have to grope about as the blind grope among visible objects. Nothing but the clear vision of these higher regions of existence and a thorough understanding and penetration of what takes place in them can really fortify a man and lead him to his proper goal. Through insight into what lies hidden from the senses, man expands his nature in such a way that he feels his life prior to this expansion as "a mere dreaming about the world."

Thought Forms and the Human Aura

It has been said that the formations of any one of the three worlds can have reality for man only when he has the capacities or the organs for perceiving them. He perceives certain occurrences in space as light phenomena only because he has a correctly constructed eye. How much of what really exists reveals itself to a being depends upon his receptivity. A man, therefore, should never say that what is real is only what he can perceive. Much can be real that he cannot perceive for lack of organs.

Now, the soul world and the spirit world are just as real as the sensory world. Indeed, they are real in a much higher sense. No physical eye can see feelings and thoughts, yet they are real. Just as man by means of his outer senses has the corporeal world before him as an object of perception, so do feelings, instincts, and thoughts become objects of perception for his spiritual organs. Exactly as occurrences in space can be seen with the sensory eye as color phenomena, so can the above named soul and spiritual occurrences become, by means of the inner senses, perceptions that are analogous to the sensory color phenomena. To understand fully in what sense this is meant is only possible for one who has followed the path of knowledge described in the following chapter and has as a result developed his inner senses. For such a person the psychic phenomena in the soul region surrounding him, and the spiritual phenomena in the spiritual region, become supersensibly visible. The feelings of other beings that he experiences ray out to him from them like light phenomena, and thoughts to which he directs his attention surge through spiritual space. For him, the thought of one man about another is not something imperceptible but, on the contrary, is a perceptible occurrence. The content of a thought lives as such only in the soul of the thinker, but this content excites effects in the spirit world. They are the perceptible occurrence to the spiritual eye. The thought streams out as an actual reality from one man and flows to the other, and the way this thought acts on the other person is experienced as a perceptible occurrence in the spiritual world. Thus the physically perceptible man is only part of the whole man for the one whose spiritual senses are unfolded. This physical man becomes the center of soul and spiritual outpourings. It is impossible to do more than faintly indicate the richly varied world that discloses itself here to the seer. A human thought, which otherwise lives only in the understanding of the listener, appears, for example, as a spiritually perceptible color phenomenon. Its color corresponds with the character of the thought. A thought that springs forth from a sensual impulse in a person has a different color from a thought conceived in the service of pure knowledge, noble beauty or the eternally good. Thoughts that spring from the sensual life course through the soul world in shades of red. A thought by which the thinker rises to higher knowledge appears in beautiful light yellow. A thought that springs from devoted and unselfish love rays out in glorious rose red. Just as the content of a thought comes to expression in its supersensibly visible form, so also does the greater or lesser degree of its definiteness. The precise thought of the thinker shows itself as a formation with definite outlines; the confused idea appears as a wavering, cloudy formation.

In this way the soul and spirit nature of man appear as the supersensible part of the whole human being.

The color effects perceptible to the spirit eye that ray out around the physical man observed in his activity, and that envelop him like a somewhat egg-shaped cloud, are the human aura. The size of this aura varies in different people, but we may say that the entire man appears on the average twice as long and four times as wide as the physical man.

The most varied shades of color flood the aura. This color flooding is a true picture of the inner human life. As this changes, so do the shades of color change. Certain permanent qualities such as talents, habits and traits of character, however, express themselves also in permanent fundamental color shades.

Misunderstandings can arise in men who at present stand remote from the experiences of the path of knowledge described in a later chapter of this book — in regard to the nature of what is here described as the aura. We might imagine that what are here described as colors would stand before the soul just as the physical colors stand before the physical eye, but such a soul color would be nothing but hallucination. Spiritual science is not in the least concerned with hallucinatory impressions, and they are, in any case, not what is meant in the description now before us. We reach a correct conception if we keep the following in mind. With a physical color, the soul experiences not only the sense impression, but through it, it has a soul-experience. When through the eye the soul perceives a yellow surface, this soul-experience is different from what it is when it perceives a blue surface. One may call this experience "living in yellow" or "living in blue." Now the soul that has followed the path of knowledge has a similar "experience in yellow" when observing the active soul-experience of other beings; an "experience in blue" when observing devotional soul-moods. The essential thing is not that the seer in visualization of another soul sees blue just as he sees this blue in the physical world, but that he has an experience that justifies his calling the visualization blue; just as the physical man calls a curtain blue, for instance. Further, it is essential that the seer should be conscious of standing in an experience free of the body so that he gains the possibility of speaking about the value and the meaning of the soul-life in a world whose perception is not mediated through the human body. Although this meaning of the description must be taken into account, yet it is altogether a matter of course for the seer to speak of blue, yellow, green, and so forth, in the aura. The aura varies greatly according to the different temperaments and dispositions of people. It likewise varies in accordance with the stages of spiritual development. A man who yields completely to his animal impulses has an entirely different aura from one who lives much in the world of thought. The aura of a religiously disposed nature differs essentially from one that loses itself in the trivial experiences of the day. In addition to this, all varying moods, all inclinations, joys and pains, find their expression in the aura.

We have to compare the auras of various soul-experiences with each other in order to learn to understand the meaning of the color shades. To begin with, take soul-experiences shot through with strongly marked emotions. They may be divided into two kinds — those in which the soul is impelled to these emotions chiefly by the animal nature, and those in which these passions take a more subtle form, in which they are, so to speak, strongly influenced by reflection. In the first kind of experiences brown and reddish-yellow streams of color surge through the aura in definite locations. In persons with more subtle passions there appear in the same locations brighter reddish-yellow and green shades. One can notice that as intelligence increases the green shades become more frequent. Persons who are very intelligent, but who give themselves over entirely to satisfying their animal impulses, show much green in their aura, but this green will always have an admixture more or less of brown or brownish-red. Unintelligent people show a great part of their aura permeated by brownish-red or even by dark blood-red currents.

The auras of quiet, meditative, thoughtful soul-moods are essentially different from those of such passionate conditions. The brownish and reddish tones become less prominent and various shades of green emerge. In strenuous thinking the aura shows a pleasing green undertone. This is to a special degree the appearance of those natures who know how to adapt themselves to every condition of life.

Shades of blue appear in soul-moods full of devotion. The more a man places his self in the service of a cause, the more pronounced become the blue shades. In this class also one finds two quite different kinds of people. There are natures who are not in the habit of exerting their power of thought — passive souls who, as it were, have nothing to throw into the streams of events in the world but their good nature. Their aura glimmers with beautiful blue. This is also the appearance of many religious and devotional natures. Compassionate souls and those who find pleasure in giving themselves up to a life of benevolence have a similar aura. If such people are intelligent in addition, green and blue currents alternate, or the blue itself perhaps takes on a greenish shade. It is the peculiarity of the active souls in contrast to the passive, that their blue saturates itself from within with bright shades of color. Inventive natures, having fruitful thoughts, radiate bright shades of color as if from an inner center. This is true to the highest degree in those persons whom we call wise, and especially in those full of fruitful ideas. Generally speaking, all that implies spiritual activity takes more the form of rays spreading out from within, while everything that arises from the animal nature has the form of irregular clouds surging through the aura.

The variations in color nuances showing themselves in the corresponding aura formations depend on whether thoughts, sprinting from the soul's activity, are at the service of the soul's animal nature or that of an ideal, objective interest. The inventive person who applies all his thoughts to the satisfaction of his sensual passions shows dark blue-red shades. He, on the contrary, who places his thoughts selflessly at the service of an interest outside himself shows light reddish-blue color tones. A spiritual life combined with noble devotion and capacity for sacrifice shows rose-pink or light violet colors.

Not only does the fundamental disposition of the soul show its color surgings in the aura, but also transient passions, moods and other inner experiences. A violent anger that breaks out suddenly creates red streams; feelings of injured dignity that expend themselves in a sudden welling up can be seen appearing in dark green clouds. Color phenomena, however, do not appear only in irregular cloud forms but also in distinctly defined, regularly shaped figures. If we observe a man under the influence of an attack of fear, we see this, for instance, in his aura from top to bottom as undulating stripes of blue color suffused with a bluish-red shimmer. When we observe a person who expects some particular event with anxiety, we can see red-blue stripes like rays constantly streaming through his aura from within outwards.

Every sensation received from without can be observed by the one who has developed the faculty of exact spiritual perception. Persons who are greatly excited by every external impression show a continuous flickering of small bluish-red spots and flecks in the aura. In people who do not feel intensely, these flecks have an orange-yellow or even a beautiful yellow coloring. So-called absent-mindedness shows bluish flecks playing over into green and more or less changing in form.

By means of a more highly developed spiritual vision three aspects of color phenomena can be distinguished within the aura radiating and surging round a person. Firstly, there are colors that bear more or less the character of opaqueness and dullness. Certainly, if we compare them with colors seen with our physical eyes, they appear fugitive and transparent in comparison. Within the supersensible world itself, however, they make the space that they fill, comparatively speaking, opaque. They fill it in the manner of mist formations. A second species of colors consists of those that are light itself, as it were. They light up the space they fill so that it becomes through them itself a space of light. Color phenomena of the third kind are quite different from the first two. They have a raying, sparkling, glittering character. They fill space not merely with light but with glistening, glittering rays. There is something active and inherently mobile in these colors. The others are somewhat quiet and lack brilliance. These, on the contrary, continuously produce themselves out of themselves, as it were. Space is filled by the first two species of colors with a subtle fluidity that remains quietly in it. By the third, space is filled with an ever self-enkindling life, with never resting activity.

These three species of colors, however, are not ranged alongside each other in the human aura. They are not each enclosed in a separate section of space, but they interpenetrate and suffuse each other in the most varied ways. All three species can be seen playing through each other in one region of the aura, just a physical body, such as a bell, can simultaneously be heard and seen. The aura thus becomes an exceedingly complicated phenomenon because we have to do with three auras within each other, interpenetrating each other. We can, however, overcome the difficulty by directing our attention to the three species alternately. In the supersensible world we then do something similar to what we do in the sensible, for example, when we close our eyes in order to give ourselves up fully to the impressions of a piece of music. The seer has three different organs for the three species of color, and in order to observe undisturbed, he can open or close any one of the organs to impressions. As a rule only one kind of organ can at first be developed by a seer, namely, the organ for the first species of color. A person at this stage can see only the one aura; the other two remain invisible to him. In the same way a person may be accessible to impressions from the first two but not from the third. The higher stage of the gift of seeing consists in a person's being able to see all three auras, and for the purpose of study to direct his attention to the one or the other.

The threefold aura is thus the supersensibly visible expression of the being of man. The three members, body, soul and spirit, come to expression in it.

The first aura is a mirror of the influence the body exercises on the human soul; the second characterizes the life of the soul itself, the soul that has raised itself above the direct influence of the senses, but is not yet devoted to the service of the eternal; the third mirrors the mastery the eternal spirit has won over the transitory man. When descriptions of the aura are given, as here, it must be emphasized that these things are not only difficult to observe but above all difficult to describe. No one, therefore, should see in a description like this anything more than a stimulus to thought.

Thus, for the seer, the peculiarity of the soul's life expresses itself in the constitution of the aura. When he encounters a soul life that is given up entirely to passing impulses, passions and momentary external incitements, he sees the first aura in loudest colors; the second, on the contrary is only slightly developed. He sees in it only scanty color formations, while the third is barely indicated. Only here and there a small glittering spark of color shows itself, indicating that even in such a soul-mood the eternal already lives in man as a germ, but that it is driven into the background by the action of the sensory nature as has been indicated. The more a man gets rid of his lower impulses, the less obtrusive becomes the first part of the aura. The second part then grows larger and larger, filling the color body within which the physical man lives ever more completely with its illuminating force. The more a man proves himself to be a servant of the eternal, the more does the wonderful third aura show itself to be the part that bears witness to the extent to which he has become a citizen of the spiritual world because the divine self radiates into the earthly life through this part of the human aura. Insofar as men show this aura, they are flames through whom the Godhead illumines this world. They show through this part of the aura how far they know how to live not for themselves, but for the eternally True, the nobly Beautiful and the Good. They show how far they have wrung from their narrower self the power to offer themselves up on the altar of cosmic world activity.

Thus there comes to expression in the aura what a man has made of himself in the course of his incarnation.

All three parts of the aura contain colors of the most varied shades, but the character of these shades changes with the stage of man's development. In the first part of the aura there can be seen the undeveloped life of impulse in all shades from red to blue. These shades have a dull, muddy character. The obtrusive red shades point to the sensual desires, to the fleshly lusts, to the passion for the enjoyments of the palate and the stomach. Green shades appear to be found especially in those lower natures that incline to obtuseness and indifference, greedily giving themselves over to each enjoyment, but nevertheless shunning the exertions necessary to bring them to satisfaction. Where the desires are passionately bent on some goal beyond the reach of the capacities already acquired, brownish-green and yellowish-green auric colors appear. Certain modern modes of life actually breed this kind of aura.

A personal conceit that is entirely rooted in low inclinations, thus representing the lowest stage of egotism, shows itself in tones of muddy yellow to brown. Now it is clear that the animal life of impulse can take on a pleasing character. There is a purely natural capacity for self-sacrifice, a high form of which is to be found even in the animal kingdom. This development of an animal impulse finds its most beautiful consummation in natural mother love. These selfless natural impulses come to expression in the first aura in light reddish to rose-red shades of color. Cowardly fear and timidity in the face of external causes show themselves in the aura in brown-blue and grey-blue colors.

The second aura again shows the most varied grades of colors. Brown and orange colored formations point to strongly developed conceit, pride and ambition. Inquisitiveness also announces its presence through red-yellow flecks. A bright yellow mirrors clear thinking and intelligence; green expresses understanding of life and the world. Children who learn easily have much green in this part of the aura. A green yellow in the second aura seems to betoken a good memory. Rose-red indicates a benevolent, affectionate nature; blue is the sign of piety. The more piety approaches religious fervor, the more does the blue pass over into violet. Idealism and an earnest view of life in a higher sense is to be seen as indigo blue.

The fundamental colors of the third aura are yellow, green and blue. Bright yellow appears here if the thinking is filled with lofty, comprehensive ideas that grasp the details as part of the whole of the divine world order. If the thinking is intuitive and also completely purified of all sensuous visualizations, the yellow has a golden brilliance. Green expresses love towards all beings; blue is the sign of a capacity for selfless sacrifice for all beings. If this capacity for sacrifice rises to the height of strong willing, devoting itself to the active service of the world, the blue brightens to light violet. If pride and desire for honor, as last remnants of personal egoism, are still present despite a more highly developed soul nature, others verging on orange appear beside the yellow shades. It must be remarked, however, that in this part of the aura the colors are quite different from the shades we are accustomed to see in the world of the senses. The seer beholds a beauty and an exaltedness with which nothing in the ordinary world can be compared.

This presentation of the aura cannot be rightly judged by anyone who does not attach the chief weight to the fact that the seeing of the aura implies an extension and enrichment of what is perceived in the physical world — an extension, indeed, that aims at knowing the form of the soul life that possesses spiritual reality apart from the world of the senses. This whole presentation has nothing whatever to do with reading character or a man's thoughts from an aura perceived in the manner of a hallucination. It seeks to expand knowledge in the direction of the spiritual world and has nothing in common with the questionable art of reading human souls from their auras.

The Path of Knowledge

Knowledge of the spiritual science that is aimed at in this book can be acquired by every man for himself. Descriptions of the kind given here present a thought picture of the higher worlds, and they are in a certain respect the first step towards personal vision. Man is a thought being and he can find his path to knowledge only when he makes thinking his starting-point. A picture of the higher worlds given to his intellect is not without value for him even if for the time being it is only like a story about higher facts into which he has not yet gained insight through his own perception. The thoughts that are given him represent in themselves a force that continues working in this thought world. This force will be active in him; it will awaken slumbering capacities. Whoever is of the opinion that it is superfluous to give himself up to such a thought picture is mistaken because he regards thought as something unreal and abstract. Thought is a living force, and just as for one who has knowledge, thought is present as a direct expression of what is seen in the spirit, so the imparting of this expression acts in the one to whom it is communicated as a germ that brings forth from itself the fruit of knowledge.

Anyone disdaining the application of strenuous mental exertion in the effort to attain the higher knowledge, and preferring to make use of other forces in man to that end, fails to take into account the fact that thinking is the highest of the faculties possessed by man in the world of his senses.

To him who asks, "How can I gain personal knowledge of the higher truths of spiritual science?" the answer must be given, "Begin by making yourself acquainted with what is communicated by others concerning such knowledge." Should he reply, "I wish to see for myself; I do not wish to know anything about what others have seen," one must answer, "It is in the very assimilating of the communications of others that the first step towards personal knowledge consists." If he then should answer, "Then I am forced to have blind faith to begin with," one can only reply, "In regard to something communicated it is not a case of belief or unbelief, but merely of an unprejudiced assimilation of what one hears." The true spiritual researcher never speaks with the expectation of meeting blind faith in what he says. He merely says, "I have experienced this in the spiritual regions of existence and I narrate my experiences." He knows also that the reception of these experiences by another and the permeation of his thoughts with such an account are living forces making for spiritual development.

What is here to be considered will only be rightly viewed by one who takes into account the fact that all knowledge of the worlds of soul and spirit slumbers in the profoundest depths of the human soul. It can be brought to light through the path of knowledge. We can grasp, however, not only what we have ourselves brought to light, but also what someone else has brought up from those depths of the soul. This is so even when we have ourselves not yet made any preparations for the treading of that path of knowledge. Correct spiritual insight awakens the power of comprehension in anyone whose inner nature is not beclouded by preconceptions and prejudices. Unconscious knowledge flashes up to meet the spiritual fact discovered by another, and this "flashing up" is not blind faith but the right working of healthy human understanding. In this same healthy comprehension we should see a far better starting-point even for first hand cognition of the spiritual world than in dubious mystical contemplations or anything of a similar nature, in which we often fancy that we have something better than what is recognized by the healthy human understanding, when the results of genuine spiritual research are brought before it.

One cannot, in fact, emphasize strongly enough how necessary it is that anyone who wishes to develop his capacity for higher knowledge should undertake the earnest cultivation of his powers of thought. This emphasis must be all the more pressing because many persons who wish to become seers actually estimate lightly this earnest, self-denying labor of thinking. They say, "Thinking cannot help me reach anything; the chief thing is sensation or feeling." In reply it must be said that no one can in the higher sense, and means in truth, become a seer who has not previously worked himself into the life of thought. In this connection a certain inner laziness plays an injurious role with many persons. They do not become conscious of this laziness because it clothes itself in a contempt of abstract thought and idle speculation. We completely misunderstand what thinking is, however, if we confuse it with a spinning of idle, abstract trains of thought. Just as this abstract thinking can easily kill supersensible knowledge, so vigorous thinking, full of life, must be the groundwork on which it is based.

It would, indeed, be more comfortable if one could reach the higher power of seeing while shunning the labor of thinking. Many would like this, but in order to reach it an inner firmness is necessary, an assurance of soul to which thinking alone can lead. Otherwise there results merely a meaningless flickering of pictures here and there, a distracting display of soul phenomena that indeed gives pleasure to many, but that has nothing to do with a true penetration into the higher worlds. Further, if we consider what purely spiritual experiences take place in a man who really enters the higher world, we shall then understand that the matter has still another aspect. Absolute healthiness of the soul life is essential to the condition of being a seer. There is no better means of developing this healthiness than genuine thinking. In fact, it is possible for this healthiness to suffer seriously if the exercises for higher development are not based on thinking. Although it is true that the power of spiritual sight makes a healthy and correctly thinking man still healthier and more capable in life than he is without it, it is equally true that all attempts to develop oneself while shirking the effort of thought, all vague dreamings in this domain, lend strength to fantasy and illusion and tend to place the seeker in a false attitude towards life. No one who wishes to develop himself to higher knowledge has anything to fear if he pays heed to what is said here, but the attempt should only be made under the above pre-supposition. This pre-supposition has to do only with man's soul and spirit. To speak of any conceivable kind of injurious influence upon the bodily health is absurd under this assumption.

Unfounded disbelief is indeed injurious. It works in the recipient as a repelling force. It hinders him from receiving fructifying thoughts. Not blind faith, but just this reception of the thought world of spiritual science is the prerequisite to the development of the higher senses. The spiritual researcher approaches his student with the injunction, "You are not required to believe what I tell you but to think it, to make it the content of your own thought world, then my thoughts will of themselves bring about your recognition of their truth." This is the attitude of the spiritual researcher. He gives the stimulus. The power to accept what is said as true springs forth from the inner being of the learner himself. It is in this manner that the views of spiritual science should be studied. Anyone who has the self-control to steep his thoughts in them may be sure that after a shorter or longer period of time they will lead him to personal perception.

In what has been said here, there is already indicated one of the first qualities that everyone wishing to acquire a vision of higher facts has to develop. It is the unreserved, unprejudiced laying of oneself open to what is revealed by human life or by the world external to man. If a man approaches a fact in the world around him with a judgment arising from his life up to the present, he shuts himself off by this judgment from the quiet, complete effect that the fact can have on him. The learner must be able each moment to make of himself a perfectly empty vessel into which the new world flows. Knowledge is received only in those moments in which every judgment, every criticism coming from ourselves, is silent. For example, when we meet a person, the question is not at all whether we are wiser than he. Even the most unreasoning child has something to reveal to the greatest sage. If he approaches the child with prejudgment, be it ever so wise, he pushes his wisdom like a dulled glass in front of what the child ought to reveal to him.

Complete inner selflessness is necessary for this yielding of oneself up to the revelations of the new world. If a man tests himself to find out in what degree he possesses this accessibility to its revelations, he will make astonishing discoveries regarding himself. Anyone who wishes to tread the path of higher knowledge must train himself to be able at any moment to obliterate himself with all his prejudices. As long as he obliterates himself the revelations of the new world flow into him. Only a high grade of such selfless surrender enables a man to receive the higher spiritual facts that surround him on all sides. We can consciously develop this capacity in ourselves. We can try, for example, to refrain from any judgment on people around us. We should obliterate within ourselves the gauge of "attractive" and "repellent," of "stupid" or "clever," that we are accustomed to apply and try without this gauge to understand persons purely from and through themselves. The best exercises can be made with people for whom one has an aversion. We should suppress this aversion with all our power and allow everything that they do to affect us without bias. Or, if we are in an environment that calls forth this or that judgment, we should suppress the judgment and free from criticism, lay ourselves open to impressions.

We should allow things and events to speak to us rather than speak about them ourselves, and we also should extend this to our thought world. We should suppress in ourselves what prompts this or that thought and allow only what is outside to produce the thoughts. Only when such exercises are carried out with holiest earnestness and perseverance do they lead to the goal of higher knowledge. He who undervalues such exercises knows nothing of their worth, and he who has experience in such things knows that selfless surrender and freedom from prejudice are true producers of power. Just as heat applied to the steam boiler is transformed into the motive power of the locomotive, so do these exercises in selfless, spiritual self-surrender transforms themselves in man into the power of seeing in the spiritual worlds.

By this exercise a man makes himself receptive to all that surrounds him, but to this receptivity he must allow correct valuation also to be added. As long as he is inclined to value himself too highly at the expense of the world around him, he bars himself from the approach to higher knowledge. The seeker who yields himself up to the pleasure or pain that any thing or event in the world causes him is enmeshed by such an overvaluation of himself. Through his pleasure and his pain he learns nothing about the things, but merely something about himself. If I feel sympathy with a man, I feel to begin with nothing by my relation to him. If I make myself mainly dependent on this feeling of pleasure, of sympathy, for my judgment and my conduct, I place my personality in the foreground — I obtrude it upon the world. I want to thrust myself into the world just as I am, instead of accepting the world in an unbiased way, allowing it to assert itself in accordance with the forces acting on it. In other words I am tolerant only of what harmonizes with my peculiarities. In regard to everything else I exert a repelling force. As long as a man is enmeshed by the sensible world, he acts in an especially repelling way on all influences that are non-sensory. The learner must develop in himself the capacity to conduct himself toward things and people in accordance with their own peculiar natures, and to allow each of them to count at its due worth and significance. Sympathy and antipathy, pleasure and displeasure, must be made to play quite new roles. It is not a question here of man's eradicating them, of his blunting himself to sympathy and antipathy. On the contrary, the more a man develops the capacity to refrain from allowing immediately by a judgment, an action, the finer will his sensitivity become. He will find that sympathies and antipathies take on a higher character if he curbs those he already has. Even something that is at first most unattractive has hidden qualities. It reveals them if a man does not in his conduct obey his selfish feelings. A person who has developed himself in this respect has in every way a greater delicacy of feeling than one who is undeveloped because he does not allow his own personality to make him unimpressionable. Every inclination that a man follows blindly blunts the power to see things in his environment in their true light. By obeying inclination we thrust ourselves through the environment instead of laying ourselves open to it and feeling its true worth.

Man becomes independent of the changing impressions of the outer world when each pleasure and pain, each sympathy and antipathy, no longer call forth in him an egotistical response and conduct. The pleasure we feel in a thing makes us at once dependent on it. We lose ourselves in it. A man who loses himself in the pleasure or pain caused by every varying impression cannot tread the path of spiritual knowledge. He must accept pleasure and pain with equanimity. Then he ceases to lose himself in them and begins instead to understand them. A pleasure to which I surrender myself devours my being in the moment of surrender. I should use the pleasure only in order to arrive through it at an understanding of the thing that arouses pleasure in me. The important point should not be that the thing has aroused pleasure in me. I should experience the pleasure and through it the nature of the thing. The pleasure should only be an intimation to me that there is in the thing a quality capable of giving pleasure. This quality I must learn to understand. If I go no farther than the pleasure, if I allow myself to be entirely absorbed in it, then it is only myself who lives in it. If the pleasure is only the opportunity for me to experience a quality or property of the thing itself, I enrich my inner being through this experience. To the seeker, pleasure and displeasure, joy and pain, must be opportunities for learning about things. The seeker does not become blunted to pleasure or pain through this. He raises himself above them in order that they may reveal to him the nature of the things. By developing himself in this respect, he will learn to understand what instructors pleasure and pain are. He will feel with every being and thereby receive the revelation of its inner nature. The seeker never says to himself merely, "Oh, how I suffer!" or "Oh, how glad I am!" but always, "How does suffering speak? How does joy speak?" He eliminates the element of self in order that pleasure and joy from the outer world may work on him. By this means there develops in a man a completely new manner of relating himself to things. Formerly he responded to this or that impression by this or that action, only because the impressions caused him joy or unhappiness. Now he causes pleasure and displeasure to become also the organs by which things tell him what they themselves really are in their own nature. Pleasure and pain change from mere feelings within him to organs of sense by which the external world is perceived. Just as the eye does not act itself when it sees something, but causes the hand to act, so pleasure and pain do not bring about anything in the spiritual seeker insofar as he employs them as means of knowledge, but they receive impressions, and what is experienced through pleasure and displeasure causes the action When a man uses pleasure and displeasure in such a way that they become organs of transmission, they build up for him within his soul the actual organs through which the soul world opens up to view. The eye can serve the body only by being an organ for the transmission of sense impressions. Pleasure and pain become the eyes of the soul when they cease to be of value merely to themselves and begin to reveal to one's soul the other soul outside it.

By means of the qualities mentioned, the seeker for knowledge places himself in a condition that allows what is really present in the world around him to act upon him without disturbing influences from his own peculiarities. He has also to fit himself into the spiritual world around him in the right way because he is as a thinking being a citizen of the spiritual world. He can be this in the right way only if during mental activity he makes his thoughts run in accordance with the eternal laws of truth, the laws of the spiritland. Only thus can that land act on him and reveal its facts to him. A man never reaches the truth as long as he gives himself up to the thoughts continually coursing through his ego. If he permits this, his thoughts take a course imposed on them by the fact of their coming into existence within the bodily nature. The thought world of a man who gives himself up to a mental activity determined primarily by his physical brain looks irregular and confused. In it a thought enters, breaks off, is driven out of the field by another. Anyone who tests this by listening to a conversation between two people, or who observes himself in an unprejudiced way, will gain an idea of this mass of confused thoughts. As long as a man devotes himself only to the calls of the life of the senses, his confused succession of thoughts will always be set right again by the facts of reality. I may think ever so confusedly but in my actions everyday facts force upon me the laws corresponding to the reality. My mental picture of a city may be most confused, but if I wish to walk along a certain road in the city, I must accommodate myself to the conditions it imposes on me. The mechanic can enter his workshop with ever so varied a whirl of ideas, but the laws of his machines compel him to adopt the correct procedure in his work. Within the world of the senses facts exercise their continuous corrective on thought. If I come to a false opinion by thinking about a physical phenomenon or the shape of a plant, the reality confronts me and sets my thinking right.

It is quite different when I consider my relations to the higher regions of existence. They reveal themselves to me only if I enter their worlds with already strictly controlled thinking. There my thinking must give me the right, the sure impulse, otherwise I cannot find proper paths. The spiritual laws prevailing within these worlds are not condensed so as to become sensibly perceptible, and therefore they are unable to exert on me the compulsion described above. I am able to obey these laws only when they are allied to my own as those of a thinking being. Here I must be my own sure guide. The seeker for knowledge must therefore make his thinking something that is strictly regulated in itself. His thoughts must by degrees disaccustom themselves entirely from taking the ordinary daily course. They must in their whole sequence take on the inner character of the spiritual world. He must be able constantly to keep watch over himself in this respect and have himself in hand. With him, one thought must not link itself arbitrarily with another, but only in the way that corresponds with the severely exact contents of the thought world. The transition from one idea to another must correspond with the strict laws of thought. The man as thinker must be, as it were, constantly a copy of these thought laws. He must shut out from his train of thought all that does not flow out of these laws. Should a favorite thought present itself to him, he must put it aside if it disturbs the proper sequence. If a personal feeling tries to force upon his thoughts a direction not inherent in them, he must suppress it.

Plato required those who wished to attend his school first to go through a course of mathematical training. Mathematics with its strict laws, which do not accommodate themselves to the course of ordinary sensory phenomena, form a good preparation for the seeker of knowledge. If he wishes to make progress in the study of mathematics, he has to renounce all personal, arbitrary choice, all disturbances. The seeker prepares himself for his task by overcoming through his own choice all the arbitrary thinking that naturally rules in him. He learns thereby to follow purely the demands of thought. So, too, he must learn to do this in all thinking intended to serve spiritual knowledge. This thought life must itself be a copy of undisturbed mathematical judgments and conclusions. The seeker must strive wherever he goes and in whatever he does to be able to think after this manner. Then there will flow into him the intrinsic characteristic laws of the spirit world that pass over and through him without a trace as long as his thinking bears its ordinary confused character. Regulated thinking brings him from sure starting points to the most hidden truths. What has been said, however, must not be looked at in a one-sided way. Although mathematics act as a good discipline for the mind, one can arrive at pure healthy, vital thinking without mathematics.

What the seeker of knowledge strives for in his thinking, he must also strive for in his actions. He must be able to act in accordance with the laws of the nobly beautiful and the eternally true without any disturbing influences from his personality. These laws must be able constantly to direct him. Should he begin to do something he has recognized as right and find his personal feelings not satisfied by that action, he must not for that reason forsake the road he has entered on. On the other hand, he must not pursue it just because it gives him joy, if he finds that it is not in accordance with the laws of the eternally beautiful and true. In everyday life people allow their actions to be decided by what satisfies them personally, by what bears fruit for themselves. In so doing they force upon the world's events the direction of their personality. They do not bring to realization the true that is traced out in the laws of the spirit world, rather do they realize the demands of their self-will. We only act in harmony with the spiritual world when we follow its laws alone. From what is done only out of the personality, there result no forces that can form a basis for spiritual knowledge. The seeker of knowledge may not ask only, "What brings me advantages; what will bring me success?" He must also be able to ask, "What have I recognized as the good?" Renunciation of the fruits of action for his personality, renunciation of all self-will; these are the stern laws that he must prescribe for himself. Then he treads the path of the spiritual world, his whole being penetrated by these laws. He becomes free from all compulsion from the sense world; his spirit man raises itself out of the sensory sheath. He thus makes actual progress on the path towards the spiritual and thus he spiritualizes himself. One may not say, "Of what use to me are the resolutions to follow purely the laws of the true when I am perhaps mistaken concerning what is true?" The important thing is the striving, and the spirit in which one strives. Even when the seeker is mistaken, he possesses, in his very striving for the true, a force that turns him away from the wrong road. Should he be mistaken, this force seizes him and guides him to the right road. The very objection, "But I may be mistaken," is itself harmful unbelief. It shows that the man has no confidence in the power of the true. The important point is that he should not presume to decide on his aims in accordance with his own egotistical views, but that he should selflessly yield himself up to the guidance of the spirit itself. It is not the self-seeking will of man that can prescribe for the true. On the contrary, what is true must itself become lord in man, must permeate his whole being, make him a copy of the eternal laws of the spiritland. He must fill himself with these eternal laws in order to let them stream out into life.

Just as the seeker of knowledge must be able to have strict control of thinking, so he must also have control of his will. Through this he becomes in all modesty — without presumption — a messenger of the world of the true and the beautiful. Through this he ascends to be a participant in the spirit world. Through this he is lifted from stage to stage of development because one cannot reach the spiritual life by merely seeing it. On the contrary, one has to reach it by experiencing it, by living it.

If the seeker of knowledge observes the laws here described, his soul experiences relating to the spiritual world will take on an entirely new form. He will no longer live merely within them. They will no longer have a significance merely for his personal life. They will develop into soul perceptions of the higher world. In this soul the feelings of pleasure and displeasure, of joy and pain, do not live for themselves only, but grow into soul organs, just as in his body eyes and ears do not lead a life for themselves alone but selflessly allow external impressions to pass through them. Thereby the seeker of knowledge wins that calmness and assurance in his soul constitution necessary for research in the spiritual world. A great pleasure will no longer make him merely jubilant, but may be the messenger to him of qualities in the world that have hitherto escaped him. It will leave him calm, and through the calm the characteristics of the pleasure-giving beings will reveal themselves to him. Pain will no longer merely fill him with grief, but be able to tell him also what the qualities are of the being that causes the pain. Just as the eye does not desire anything for itself but shows man the direction of the road he has to take, so will pleasure and pain guide the soul safely along its path. This is the state of balance of soul that the seeker of knowledge must reach. The less pleasure and pain exhaust themselves in the waves that they throw up in the inner life of the seeker of knowledge, the more will they form eyes for the supersensible world. As long as a man lives in pleasure and pain he cannot gain knowledge by means of them. When he learns how to live by means of them, when he withdraws his feeling of self from them, then they become his organs of perception and he sees by means of them, attaining through them to knowledge. It is incorrect to think that the seeker of knowledge becomes a dry, colorless being, incapable of experiencing joy and sorrow. Joy and sorrow are present in him, but when he seeks knowledge in the spiritual world, they are present in a transformed shape; they have become eyes and ears.

As long as we live in a personal relationship with the world, things reveal only what links them with our personality. This, however, is their transitory path. If we withdraw ourselves from our transitory part and live with our feeling of self, with our "I," in our permanent part, then our transitory part becomes an intermediary for us. What reveals itself through it is an imperishable, an eternal in the things. The seeker of knowledge must be able to establish this relationship between his own eternal part and the eternal in the things. Even before he begins other exercises of the kind described, and also during them, he should direct his thought to this imperishable part. When I observe a stone, a plant, an animal or a man, I should be able to remember that in each of them an eternal expresses itself. I should be able to ask myself, "What is the permanent that lives in the transitory stone, in the transitory man? What will outlast the transitory sensory appearance?" We ought not to think that to direct the spirit to the eternal in this way destroys our careful consideration of, and sense for, the qualities of everyday affairs and estranges us from the immediate realities. On the contrary, every leaf, every little insect will unveil to us innumerable mysteries when not only our eyes but through the eyes of spirit is directed upon them. Every sparkle, every shade of color, every cadence will remain vividly perceptible to the senses. Nothing will be lost, but in addition, unlimited new life will be gained. Indeed, the person who does not understand how to observe even the tiniest thing with the eye, will only attain to pale, bloodless thoughts, not to spiritual sight.

It depends upon the attitude of mind we acquire in this direction. What stage we shall succeed in reaching will depend on our capacities. We have only to do what is right and leave everything else to evolution. It must be enough for us at first to direct our minds to the permanent. If we do this, the knowledge of the permanent will awaken in us through this. We must wait until it is given, and it is given at the right time to each one who with patience waits and works. A man soon notices during such exercises what a mighty transformation takes place within him. He learns to consider each thing as important or unimportant only insofar as he recognizes it to be related to a permanent, to an eternal. He comes to a valuation and estimate of the world different from the one he has hitherto had. His whole feeling takes on a new relationship toward the entire surrounding world. The transitory no longer attracts him merely for its own sake as formerly. It becomes for him a member, an image of the eternal, and this eternal, living in all things, he learns to love. It becomes familiar, just as the transitory was formerly familiar to him. This again does not cause his estrangement from life. He only learns to value each thing according to its true significance. Even the vain trifles of life will not pass him by quite without trace, but the man seeking after the spiritual no longer loses himself in them, but recognizes them at their limited worth. He sees them in their true light. He is a poor discerner of the spiritual who would go wandering in the clouds losing sight of life. From his high summit a true discerner with his power of clear survey and his just and healthy feeling for everything will know how to assign to each thing its proper place.

Thus there opens out to the seeker of knowledge the possibility of ceasing to obey only the unreliable influences of the external world of the senses that turn his will now here, now there. Through higher knowledge he has seen the eternal being of things. By means of the transformations of his inner world he has gained the capacity for perceiving this eternal being. For the seeker of knowledge the following thoughts have a special weight. When he acts out of himself, he is then conscious of acting also out of the eternal being of things because the things give utterance to him in their being. He, therefore, acts in harmony with the eternal world order when he directs his action out of the eternal living within him. He thus knows himself no longer merely as a being impelled by things. He knows that he impels them according to the law implanted within them that have become the laws of his own being. This ability to act out of his inner being can only be an ideal towards which he strives. The attainment of the goal lies in the far distance, but the seeker of knowledge must have the will to recognize clearly this road. This is his will to freedom, for freedom is action out of one's inner being. Only he may act out of his inner being who draws his motives from the eternal. A being who does not do this, acts according to other motives than those implanted in things. Such a person opposes the world order, and the world order must then prevail against him. That is to say, what he plans to carry through by his will cannot in the last resort take place. He cannot become free. The arbitrary will of the individual being annihilates itself through the effects of its deeds.

*   *   *

Whoever is able to work upon his inner life in such a way climbs upwards from stage to stage in spiritual knowledge. The reward of his exercises will be the unfolding of certain vistas of the supersensible world to his spiritual perception. He learns the real meaning of the truths communicated about this world, and he will receive confirmation of them through his own experience. If this stage is reached, he encounters an experience that can only come through treading this path. Something occurs whose significance can only now become clear to him. Through the great spiritual guiding powers of the human race there is bestowed on him what is called initiation. He becomes a disciple of wisdom. The less one sees in such initiation something that consists in an outer human relationship, the more correct will be his conception of it. What the seeker of knowledge now experiences can only be indicated here. He receives a new home. He becomes thereby a conscious dweller in the supersensible world. The source of spiritual insight now flows to him from a higher region. The light of knowledge from this time forth does not shine upon him from without, but he is himself placed at its fountainhead where the problems that the world offers receive a new illumination. Henceforth he holds converse no longer with the things that are shaped by the spirit, but with the shaping spirit itself. At the moments of attaining spiritual knowledge, the personality's own life exists now only in order to be a conscious image of the eternal. Doubts about the spirit that could formerly arise in him vanish because only he can doubt who is deluded by things regarding the spirit ruling in them. Since the disciple of wisdom is able to hold intercourse with the spirit itself, each false form vanishes in which he had previously imagined the spirit. The false form under which one conceives the spirit is superstition. The initiate has passed beyond all superstition because he has knowledge of the spirit's true form. Freedom from the prejudices of the personality, of doubt, and of superstition — these are the characteristics of the seeker who has attained to discipleship on the path of higher knowledge. We must not confuse this state in which the personality becomes one with the all-embracing spirit of life, with an absorption into the universal spirit that annihilates the personality. Such a disappearance does not take place in a true development of the personality. Personality continues to be preserved as such in the relationship into which it enters with the spirit world. It is not the subjection of the personality, but its highest development that occurs. If we wish to have a simile for this coincidence or union of the individual spirit with the all-encompassing spirit, we cannot choose that of many different coinciding circles that are lost in one circle, but we must choose the picture of many circles, each of which has a quite distinct shade of color. These variously colored circles coincide, but each separate shade preserves its color existence within the whole. Not one loses the fullness of its individual power.

The further description of the path will not be given here. It is given as far as possible in my Occult Science, an Outline, which forms a continuation of this book.

What is said here about the path of spiritual knowledge can all too easily, through failure to understand it, tempt us to consider it as a recommendation to cultivate certain moods of soul that would lead us to turn away from the immediate, joyous and strenuously active, experience of life. As against this, it must be emphasized that the particular attitude of the soul that renders it fit to experience directly the reality of the spirit, cannot be extended as a general demand over the entire life. It is possible for the seeker after spiritual existence to bring his soul for the purpose of research into the necessary condition of being withdrawn from the realities of the senses, without that withdrawal estranging him from the world. On the other hand, however, it must be recognized that a knowledge of the spiritual world, not merely a knowledge gained by treading the path, but also a knowledge acquired through grasping the truths of spiritual science with the unprejudiced, healthy human intellect, leads also to a higher moral status in life, to a knowledge of sensory existence that is in accord with the truth, to certainty in life, and to inward health of the soul.

An Esoteric Cosmology

The Birth of the Intellect and the Mission of Christianity

It is only of recent times that the truths of occultism have been the subject of public lectures. Formerly, these truths were only revealed in secret societies, to those who had passed through certain degrees of initiation and had sworn to obey the laws of the Order through the whole of their life. Today, man is entering upon a very critical period. Occult truths are beginning to be disclosed to the public. In a matter of twenty years or so, a certain number of them will already be common knowledge. Why is this? The reason is that humanity is entering upon a new phase which it is the object of this lecture to explain.

In the Middle Ages, occult truths were known in the Rosicrucian Movement. But whenever they leaked out, they were either misunderstood or distorted. In the eighteenth century they entered upon a phase of much dilletantism and charlatanry and at the beginning of the nineteenth century they were put entirely in the background by the physical sciences. It is only in our day that they are beginning to re-emerge and in the coming centuries they will play an important part in the development of mankind. In order to understand this, we must glance at the centuries preceding the advent of Christianity and follow the progress that has been made.

It does not require any very profound knowledge to realise the difference between a man of pre-Christian times and a man of today. Although his scientific knowledge was far less, man of olden times had deeper feelings and intuitions. He lived more in the world beyond — which he also perceived — than in the world of sense. There were some who entered into direct and actual communication with the astral and spiritual world. In the Middle Ages, when earthly existence was by no means comfortable, man still lived with his head in the heavens. True, the mediaeval cities were somewhat primitive, but they were a far truer representation of man's inner world than the cities of today. Not only the cathedrals but the houses and porches with their symbols reminded men of their faith, their inner feelings, their aspirations, and the home of their soul. Today, we have knowledge of many, many things and the relations among human beings have multiplied ad infinitum. But we live in cities that are like deafening factories in awful Babels, with nothing to remind us of our inner world. Our communion with this inner world is not through contemplation but through books. We have passed from intuition into intellectualism.

To find the origin of the stream of intellectualism we must go back further than the Middle Ages. The epoch of the birth of human intellect, the period when this transformation took place, lies about a thousand years before the Christian era. It is the epoch of Thales, Pythagoras, Buddha. Then for the first time arose philosophy and science, that is to say truth presented to the reason in the form of logic. Before this age, truth presented itself in the form of religion, of revelation received by the teachers and accepted by the masses. In our times, truth passes into the individual intelligence and would fain be proved by argument, would like to have its own wings clipped.

What has happened in the inner nature of man to justify this transition of his consciousness from one plane to another, from the plane of intuition to that of logic? Here we touch upon one of the fundamental laws of history — a law no longer recognised by contemporary thought. It is this: Humanity evolves in a way which enables the different elements and principles of man's being to unfold and develop in successive stages. What are these principles?

To begin with, man has a physical body in common with the mineral kingdom. The whole mineral world is found again in the chemistry of the body. He has an etheric body, which is, properly speaking, the vital principle within him. He has this etheric body in common with the plants. This principle engenders the process of nutrition and the forces of growth and re-production. Man has also an astral body in which feelings and sentiments, the power of enjoyment and of suffering are enkindled. He has the astral body in common with the animals.

Finally, there is a principle in man which cannot be spoken of as a body. It is his innermost essence, distinguishing him from all other entities, mineral, plant and animal. It is the self, the soul, the divine spark. The Hindus spoke of it as Manas; The Rosicrucians as the 'Inexpressible.' A body, in effect, is only part and parcel of another body, but the self, the 'I' of man exists in and by itself alone — "I am I." This principle is addressed by others as 'thou,' or 'you;' it cannot be confused with anything else in the universe. By virtue of this inexpressible, incommunicable self, man rises above all created things of the Earth, above the animals, indeed above all creation. And only through this principle can he commune with the Infinite Self, with God. That is why, at certain definite times, the officiating hierophant in the ancient Hebrew sanctuaries said to the High Priest: Shem-Ham-Phores, which means: What is his name (the name of God)? He-Vo-He, or — in one word — Jev or Joph, meaning God, Nature, Man; or again, the inexpressible 'I' of man which is both human and divine.

These principles of man's being were laid down in remote ages of his vast evolutionary cycle — but they only unfold slowly, one by one.

The special mission of the period which began about a thousand years before the Christian era has been to develop the human Ego in the intellectual sense. But above the intellectual plane there is the plane of Spirit. It is the world of Spirit to which man will attain in the centuries to come, and to which he will be wending his way from now onwards. The germs of this future development have been cast into the world by the Christ and by true Christianity.

Before speaking of this world of Spirit, we must understand one of the forces by means of which humanity en masse passed from the astral to the intellectual plane. It was by virtue of a new kind of marriage. In olden times, marriages were made in the bosom of the same tribe or of the same clan — which was only an extension of the family. Sometimes, indeed, brothers and sisters married. Later on, men sought their wives outside the clan, the tribe, the civic community. The beloved became the stranger, the unknown. Love — which in days of yore had been merely a natural and social function — became personal desire, and marriage a matter of free choice. This is indicated in certain Greek myths like that of the rape of Helen and again in the Scandinavian and Germanic myths of Sigurd and Gudrun. Love becomes an adventure, woman a conquest from afar.

This change from patriarchial marriage to free marriage corresponds to the new development of man's intellectual faculties, of the Ego. There is a temporary eclipse of the astral faculties of vision and the power of reading directly in the astral and spiritual world — faculties which are included in ordinary speech under the name of inspiration.

Let us now turn to Christianity. The brotherhood of man and the cult of the One God are certainly features of it but they only represent the external, social aspect, not the inner, spiritual reality. The new, mysterious and transcendental element in Christianity is that it creates divine Love, the power which transforms man from within, the leaven by which the whole world is raised. Christ came to say: "If you leave not mother, wife and your own body, you cannot be my disciple"

That does not imply the cessation of natural links. Love extends beyond the bounds of family to all human beings and is changed into vivifying, creative, transmuting power.

This Love was the fundamental principle of Rosicrucian thought but it was never understood by the outer world. It is destined to change the very essence of all religion, of all cults, of all science.

The progress of humanity is from unconscious spirituality (pre-Christian), through intellectualism (the present age), to conscious spirituality, where the astral and intellectual faculties unite once more and become dynamic through the power of the Spirit of Love, divine and human. In this sense, Theology will tend to become Theosophy.

What, in effect, is Theology? A knowledge of God imposed from without under the form of dogma, as a kind of supernatural logic. And what is Theosophy? A knowledge of God which blossoms like a flower in the depths of the individual soul. God, having vanished from the world, is reborn in the depths of the human heart.

In the Rosicrucian sense, Christianity is at once the highest development of individual freedom and universal religion. There is a community of free souls. The tyranny of dogma is replaced by the radiance of divine Wisdom, embracing intelligence, love and action.

The science which arises from this cannot be measured by its power of abstract reasoning but by its power to bring souls to flower and fruition. That is the difference between 'Logia' and 'Sophia,' between science and divine Wisdom, between Theology and Theosophy.

In this sense, Christ is the centre of the esoteric evolution of the West. Certain modern Theologians — above all in Germany — have tried to represent Christ as a simple, naive human being. This is a terrible error. The most sublime consciousness, the most profound Wisdom live in Him, as well as the most divine Love. Without such consciousness, how could He be a supreme manifestation in the life of our whole planetary evolution? What gave Him this power to rise so high above His own time? Whence came transcendental qualities?

The Mission of Manicheism

The purpose of this lecture is to expand and deepen what was said in the preceding lecture.

The difference between Occult Brotherhoods before and after Christianity is that before the advent of Christianity their chief mission was to guard the sacred tradition; afterwards, it was to form and mould the future. Occult science is not abstract and dead but active and living.

Christian occultism is derived from the Manicheans whose founder, Manes, lived on the Earth three hundred years after Jesus the Christ. The essence of Manichean teaching relates to the doctrine of Good and Evil. In ordinary thought, the Good and the Evil are two irreducible qualities, one of which — the Good — must destroy the other — the Evil. To the Manicheans, however, Evil is an integral part of the cosmos, collaborating in its evolution, finally to be absorbed and transfigured by the Good. The great feature of Manicheism is that it studies the function of Evil and of suffering in the world.

To understand the development of humanity, it must be viewed in its whole range. Only so can we see its high ideal. To believe that an ideal is not necessary for action is a great error. A man without ideals is a man without power. The function of an ideal in life is like that of steam in an engine. Steam comprises in a small area a vast expanse of 'condensed space' — hence its tremendous power of expansion. The magic power of thought is of the same nature. Let us then rise to the thought of the ideal of humanity as a whole, guided by the thread of its evolution through the epochs of time.

Systems like that of Darwin are also seeking for this guiding thread. The grandeur of Darwinian thought is not disputed, but it does not explain the integral evolution of man. It only sees the lower, inferior elements. So it is with all purely physical explanations which do not recognise the spiritual essence of man's being. Theories of evolution based entirely on physical facts, attribute to man an animal origin because science has established that in fossilised man the brow is lacking. Occultism, knowing that physical man is but an expression of etheric man, sees something very different. At the present point of time, the etheric body of man has practically the same form as his physical body, although extending a little beyond it. But the farther back we go in history, the greater is the difference in size between the etheric head and the physical head. The etheric head is found to be much larger. Especially was this so in the period of earthly development which precedes our own. The men living at that time were Atlanteans.

Geologians, indeed, are beginning to discover traces of ancient Atlantis, of the minerals and flora of this ancient continent now submerged under the ocean that bears its name. Traces of man himself have not yet been discovered but that is only a matter of time. Occult prophecies have always preceded authentic history.

The frontal part of the human head began to develop in the European races which followed those of Atlantis. The focus-point of consciousness in the Atlanteans lay outside the brow, in the etheric head. Today it lies within the physical head, a little higher than the nose.

Nifelheim or Nebelheim (the land of mists) in Germanic mythology is the country of the Atlanteans. In that age the Earth was hotter and still enveloped by vaporous clouds. The continent of Atlantis was destroyed by a series of deluges, as a consequence of which the terrestrial atmosphere cleared, — Then and only then came the blue sky, the storm, rain, the rainbow. That is why the Bible says that when Noah's Ark had come to rest, the rainbow, the "bow in the cloud" was a new token of alliance between God and man.

The 'I' of the Ayran race could only be consciously realised when the etheric body was centralised in the physical brain. Not until then could man begin to say: 'I.' The Atlanteans spoke of themselves in the third person.

Darwinism has made many errors in regard to the differentiation expressed by the races actually existing on the Earth. The higher races have not descended from the lower races; on the contrary, the latter represent the degeneration of the higher races which have preceded them. Suppose there are two brothers — one of whom is handsome and intelligent, the other ugly and dull-witted. Both proceed from the same father. What should we think of a man who believed that the intelligent brother descends from the idiot? That is the kind of error made by Darwinism in regard to the races. Man and animal have a common origin; the animals represent a degeneration of the one common ancestor, whose higher development comes to expression in man.

This should not give rise to pride, for it is only thanks to the lower kingdoms that the higher races have been able to develop.

Christ washes the feet of the Apostles. That is a symbol of the humility of the Initiate in face of his inferiors. The Initiate owes his existence to those who are not initiated. Hence the deep humility of those who truly know in face of those who do not. The tragic aspect of cosmic evolution is that one class of beings must abase themselves in order that the other may rise. In this sense we can appreciate the beauty of Paracelsus' words: "I have observed all beings — stones, plants, animals — and they seem to me nothing but scattered letters, man being the word, living and whole."

The animals are crystallised passions.

In the course of human and animal evolution the inferior descends from the superior.

The contradictions in man, the way in which the elements mingle in him, constitute his karma, his destiny.

Just as man has wrested himself from the animal so will he wrest himself from evil. But never yet has he passed through a crisis as severe as that of the present age.

The evil and the good are still within man just as in days of yore the animals were within him.

The aim of Manicheism is to sublimate men to be redeemers.

The Master must be the servant of all.

True morality flows from an understanding of the mighty laws of the universe.

God, Man, Nature

One of the fundamental tenets of occultism, founded on the law of analogies, is that Nature can reveal to us what is taking place within our own being.

A striking and typical example of this law, but one which is wholly ignored by orthodox science, is given in the Philosopher's Stone, known to the Rosicrucians. In a German magazine published at the end of the eighteenth century, we find mention of this Philosopher's Stone. It is spoken of as something quite real and the writer says: "Everyone contacts it frequently although he knows it not." This is literally true. In order to understand this mystery we must penetrate into the laboratory of Nature even more deeply than is the habit of modern science.

All the world knows that man inhales oxygen and exhales carbonic acid. In Yoga this has both a physical and spiritual significance. Man cannot inhale carbonic acid for the purposes of nourishing his being. He would die, whereas the carbonic acid keeps the plants alive. The plants provide man with the oxygen which gives him life; they renew the air and make it fit to breathe. On the other side, man and the animals provide the plants with the carbonic acid by which they, in their turn, are nourished. What does the plant do with the carbonic acid it absorbs? It builds up its own body. We know that the corpse of the plant is coal. Coal is thus crystallised carbonic acid.

The red blood in man must be refreshed and renewed with oxygen, for the carbonic acid cannot be used for the purpose of building up the body. The exercises of Yoga are a training which enables man to make the red blood into a body-builder. In this sense the Yogi works at his body by means of his blood, just as the plant works with the carbonic acid.

Thus we see that the power of transmutation in Nature is represented in coal which is a crystallised plant. The Philosopher's Stone, in its most general sense, signifies this power of transmutation.

The law of regression, as well as the law of ascension, is true for all beings. The minerals are plants which have degenerated; the plants are the remnants of animal life; animals and man (his physical body) have a common ancestor. Man has ascended, the animal has descended. The spiritual part of man proceeds from the Gods. In this sense, man is a God who has degenerated, and Lamartine's words are literally true: "Man is a fallen god who remembers the heavens."

There was an epoch when all life on the Earth was semi-plant and semi-animal. The Earth herself was, as it were, a great animal-being. Her whole surface was one mass of peat-like 'turf' with gigantic forest growing from it. This is the epoch when the Earth and the Moon were united in one body. The Moon represents the feminine element of the Earth.

There are beings whose progress is checked, who remain at a lower stage of evolution. The mistletoe, for instance, is a token of this ancient epoch. It is a survival of the parasitic plant-beings which once lived on the Earth as upon a plant. Hence its peculiar, occult properties, known to the Druids who spoke of it as the most sacred of all plants. Mistletoe is a survival from the lunar epoch of the Earth. It is parasitic because it has not learned, like other plants, to live directly upon mineral substance.

Disease is something of an analogy. It is a regression, caused by the parasitic elements in the organism. The Druids and the Skalds knew of the relation between the mistletoe and man. There is an echo of this in the legend of Baldur. The God Baldur is put to death by the mistletoe because the mistletoe is a hostile element from the preceding epoch — an element no longer united — with man. The other plants, having adapted themselves to the subsequent epoch, swore friendship to him.

When this plant-earth became mineral, it acquired, through the metals, a new property — that of reflecting the light.

A star is visible in the heavens only when it has become mineral. Thus there are many heavenly bodies imperceptible to the physical eye of man and visible only to clairvoyant vision.

The Earth has been "mineralised," so also has the physical body of man. But the characteristic feature of man is that a twofold movement takes places in him. As a physical being, man has descended; as a spiritual being he has ascended. St. Paul spoke of this truth when he declared that there is one law for the body and another for the Spirit. Thus man represents both an end and a beginning.

The vital point, the point of intersection and of change in the ascending life of man, lies at the time of the separation of the sexes. There was an age when the two sexes were united in the being of man. Even Darwin recognised this as a probability. As the result of the separation of the sexes, a new, all-embracing element came to birth: the element of love. The attraction of love is so powerful, so mysterious, that tropical butterflies of different sexes, brought to Europe and then released to the air, will fly back again and meet each other half-way.

There is some analogy between the relations established by the world of man with the divine world and by the human kingdom with the animal kingdom. Oxygen and carbonic acid are in-breathed and out-breathed by man. The plant-kingdom breathes out oxygen; man breathes out love — since the separation of the sexes. The Gods are nourished by this effluence of love.

How comes it that the animals and man out-breathe love?

The occultist sees in the man of today a being in the full swing of evolution. Man is at the same time a fallen God and a God in the becoming.

The kingdom of the heavens is nourished by the effluence of human love. Ancient Greek mythology expresses this reality when it speaks of nectar and ambrosia. The Gods are so far above man that their natural tendency would be to subjugate him. But there is a half-way state of being between man and the Gods, just as the mistletoe is half-way between the plant and the animal. It is represented by Lucifer and the Luciferian element.

The interest of the Gods is the element of human love by means of which their life is sustained.

When Lucifer, in the form of the serpent, induces man to seek for knowledge, Jehovah is wrath. Lucifer is here understood as the fallen God who instills into man the desire for personal knowledge. This sets him in opposition to the Divine Will which has created him in its image.

Rosicrucian science explains the rôle of Lucifer in the world. We shall return to this later on. Here we will merely recall the following saying of the Rosicrucian Order: "Know, O man, that through thy being flows a current which ascends and a current which descends."

Involution and Evolution

There is a phenomenon of physical life which has never been explained by exoteric thought — the chaotic life bound up with sleep and called the life of dream.

What is the dream? It is an activity which has survived from prehistoric times. To understand it by analogy, let us consider certain phenomena which do not any longer belong, properly speaking, to physical life — organs which have now become useless, rudimentary organisms of which the naturalist can make nothing. Such are the motor organs of the ear and eye which function no longer, the appendix and, — notably, the pineal gland in the brain which has the form of a tiny pine cone. Naturalists explain it as a product of degeneration, as a parasitic growth in the brain. This is not correct. In the lasting creations of Nature, nothing is without its use. The pineal gland is the surviving remnant of an organ of great significance in primitive man, an organ of perception which served simultaneously as antenna, eye and ear. This organ existed in man during his rudimentary period of development, in days when the semi-fluid, semi-vaporous Earth was still united with the Moon. Man moved through the semi-fluid, semi-gaseous element like a fish, guiding his way by means of this organ. His perceptions were of a visionary, allegoric nature. Currents of warmth evoked in him the impression of dazzling red and of powerful sound. Currents of cold evoked the impression of shades of green and blue, silvery, rippling sounds.

The rôle played by the pineal gland was thus of great significance. But with the mineralisation of the Earth, other organs of sense made their appearance, and with us the pineal gland has no apparent purpose.

Let us now turn to the phenomenon of the dream.

The dream is a rudimentary function of our life — seemingly without use or purpose. In reality it represents an atrophied function — a function which in days of yore gave rise to a very different mode of perception.

Before the Earth became metallic, it was only perceptible in the astral sense. All perceptions are relative; they are merely symbolic. The central core of truth is ineffable and divine. This is wonderfully expressed in the words of Goethe: "All things transitory are but symbols."

Astral vision (which is still present in the dream) is allegoric and symbolic.

Examples of dreams provoked by physical and bodily causes:

A student dreams that a companion gives him a blow, whereupon a duel is fought and he himself is wounded. He wakes up to find that the cause of the dream is a chair that has fallen over. Again someone may dream of a trotting horse but the sound is really caused by the ticking of a watch.

The bodily nature of man lies at the root of certain dreams but others are directly related to the astral and spiritual worlds. This latter class of dreams are the origin of myths.

In the opinion of modern scholars, the myths are poetic interpretations of the phenomena of Nature. If, however, we study certain folk-legends, we shall find that they are more than this. Myths and legends are based upon astral visions which have been travestied, changed and added to by tradition.

Think of the Slavonic legend of the 'Woman of Noonday.' If peasants who are labouring at the harvest in the oppressive heat of summer lie down to rest on the ground at midday instead of going to their homes, the figure of a woman appears and places a number of enigmas before them. If the sleeper can solve these enigmas, he is saved; if not, the woman slays and cuts him in two with a scythe. The legend goes on to say that this phantom can be exorcised by reciting the verses of the Lord's Prayer in backward order. Occultism teaches us that the Woman of Noonday is an astral figure, an incubus who appears and oppresses man during his sleep. The reversed Lord's Prayer indicates that in the astral world everything is reflected as in a mirror (inversion). In The Riddle of the Sphinx, Ludwig Laistner says that the origin of the legend of the sphinx is to be found among all races. He also proves that all legends have been conceived in a condition of higher sleep where realities are perceived, and that the sphinx is in truth a daemonic figure.

A state of dream-consciousness, or perception of a real world in astral symbols-this, then, is the origin of all the myths. Myths describe the astral world seen in symbolic visions.

In the course of history we find that the creation of myths ceases when the life of logic and intellectuality begins to develop.

A law known to occultism is that with every new stage of evolution, an element from the past makes its appearance. Ancient faculties, survivals from past epochs which have atrophied in the being of man, act as ferments for subsequent development; they are like the yeast which makes the dough rise. Man's present faculty of dreaming will beget a new kind of vision, a perception of the astral and spiritual world.

The man of today lives only in his senses and intellect which elaborates what the senses tell him. The intellect of man of the future will awaken to the full light of consciousness and he will live consciously in the astral world.

The trance of the hypnotised subject and of the medium is an atavistic phenomenon, bound up with lowered consciousness. The initiated clairvoyant is not an unbalanced visionary; he possesses, in advance, the consciousness which will be possessed by all men in future ages; he has his feet on solid ground just as firmly as the most matter-of-fact human being; his reason is just as clear and certain but he sees in two worlds.

It is a law of evolution that certain organs atrophy, subsequently to take on new functions.

The pineal gland has a certain physiological relation with the lymphatic system. In olden times this gland was the organ of perception of the outer world and it is still to be seen near the top of the head of newly-born babes where the soft matter recalls the nature of man's body in olden times.

In our life of intellect, the dream plays a rôle similar to that of the pineal gland in the physiology of the human body.

Why is there a descending and an ascending process in evolution? What is the purpose of evil? These are weighty questions which have never been solved by science or religion. Yet the whole problem of education depends upon their solution.

We cannot speak of evil in the absolute sense. Evil, indeed, plays a part in the development of beings and the unfolding of freedom.

The materialist will not admit that the thoughts stimulated in us by Nature are, in fact, already contained in her being. He imagines that we infuse our thoughts into Nature.

The Rosicrucians in the Middle Ages were wont to place a glass of water before the neophyte and say to him: 'This water would not be in the glass if some being had not put it there.' Thus it is in regard to the ideas we find expressed in Nature. They must have been implanted there by divine Intelligences, by servants of the Logos.

The thoughts we derive from the universe are actually there. All that we create is contained somewhere in the universe.

It is a false idea on the part of certain mystics to disparage the value of the physical body. It has just as much value as the astral body; its mission is to become the temple of the soul.

Think of the marvelous structure of the femur, of the bone which bears the whole body. Its construction is such that the maximum amount of strength is produced with the minimum amount of substance. No engineer could create such a wonder-structure. In comparison with the physical body, the astral body — the seat of passions and desires — is rudimentary and crude. The physical world is the expression of wisdom incarnate, divine wisdom. The Rosicrucians taught that the Earth, in primeval times, was an Earth of wisdom. Today we may call it an Earth of love. The mission of man is to accomplish for the imperfect part of his being what divine wisdom once accomplished for his physical body. He must ennoble his astral body and therewith the world around him.

All that has entered into us without our conscious will under the influence of divine wisdom — that is Involution. All that we must bring out of ourselves by dint of conscious will — that is Evolution.

The pyramids will perish in the course of the centuries but the ideas which gave them birth will develop onwards. The cathedral of today will take another form. Raphael's pictures will fall into dust but the soul of Raphael and the ideas which his creations represent will be living powers forever. The Art of today will be the Nature of tomorrow and will blossom again in her. Thus does Involution become Evolution.

Here we have the point of intersection between the divine and the human, the twofold power which brings God to man and raises man to God.

Yoga in East and West

Before embarking on this subject, we must realise that since occultism has been popularised, a certain class of theosophical literature has given rise to mistaken ideas as to the real goal of occult science. It has been contended that the goal is the annihilation of the body through asceticism and that reality is an illusion which must be conquered, reference being made to the 'maya' spoken of by Hindu philosophy. This is more than exaggeration; it is an actual error, contradicted by the science and practice of occultism.

Greek imagery compares the soul to a bee and this is much truer to the facts. Just as the bee emerges from the hive and gathers the juice of flowers to distil and make it into honey, so does the soul come forth from the Spirit, penetrates into reality and gathers its essence which is then borne back again to the Spirit.

Occultism does not disdain reality but seeks rather to understand and make use of it. The body is not merely the vesture, it is the instrument of the Spirit. Occultism is not a science which subordinates the body but teaches us how to use it for higher ends. Could we be said to understand the nature of a magnet if we described it merely as a piece of iron shaped like a horse-shoe? No, indeed. But we have understood if we say: 'The magnet is a piece of iron having the power to attract other pieces of iron.' Visible reality is wholly pervaded with a deeper reality and it is this deeper reality which the soul tries to penetrate and master.

For thousands of years the higher wisdom was guarded in profound secrecy by Occult Brotherhoods. A man had to belong to one of these Brotherhoods before he could learn even the elements of occult science. To enter a Brotherhood he had to pass certain tests and swear not to make wrong use of the truths revealed to him. But the conditions of civilisation, and particularly of the human intellect, have entirely changed since the sixteenth century and above all in the last hundred years under the influence of scientific discoveries. As the result of science, a certain number of truths pertaining to Nature and the world of sense — which in olden times were known only to Initiates — have become public property. Knowledge possessed by science today was once in the keeping of the Mysteries. The Initiates have always known that which all men were destined, in time, to know. That is why the Initiates have been called prophets.

The advent of Christianity wrought a great change in the manner of Initiation. Initiation since the time of Christ Jesus has not been the same as before His coming. We can only understand this by studying the nature of man and the seven fundamental principles of his being.

(1) The physical body, visible to the natural eye and familiar to science. As a purely physical being, man corresponds to the mineral world; he is a combination of all the physical forces of the universe.

(2) The etheric body. How does it become perceptible?

We know that hypnosis induces a different state of consciousness, not only in the hypnotised subject but also in the hypnotist, who suggests anything he pleases to his subject. He can make him think that a chair is a horse, or that the chair is not there, or again that there is nobody in a room which is really full of people. The Initiate consciously exercises a power whereby he can blot out from his vision the physical body of the person in front of him. Then, in place of the physical body he beholds, not an empty space, but the etheric body. This body somewhat resembles the physical body and yet it is different. It takes on the form of the physical body, extending slightly beyond it. The etheric body is more or less luminous and fluidic. Instead of organs there are currents of diverse colours, the heart being a veritable vortex of forces and streaming currents. The etheric body is the 'etheric double' of the material body. Man possesses it in common with the plants. It is not produced by the physical body as naturalists might be led to believe; on the contrary, the etheric body is the builder of every living organism. In the plant, as well as in man, it is the force of growth, rhythm and reproduction.

(3) The astral body has neither the form of the etheric nor of the physical body. It is an ovoid and extends beyond the body like a cloud, an aura. The astral body can take on all the colours of the rainbow, according to the passion by which it is animated. Each passion has its astral colour. Besides this, the astral body is, in a certain sense, the synthesis of the physical and etheric bodies, for the reason that the etheric body always has a contrary character to the sex of the physical body. The etheric body of a man is female; the etheric body of a woman is male. In both man and woman, the astral body is bisexual. In this sense, therefore, it is a synthesis of the two other bodies.

(4) The self — Manas in Sanscrit, Joph in Hebrew — is the intelligent, rational soul. It is the indestructible individuality which can learn to build the other bodies — the 'inexpressible,' the human self and the divine self.

The union of these four elements was venerated by Pythagoras in the sign of the tetragram.

The evolution of man consists in transforming the lower bodies with the aid of the self into spiritualised bodies. The physical body is the most ancient principle — hence the most perfect — of man's being. The task of the present epoch of human evolution is to transform the astral body.

In civilised man, the astral body is divided into two parts — a lower and a higher. The lower part is still chaotic and dark, the higher is luminous, penetrated even now by the forces of Manas — that is to say, it has a certain order and regularity.

When the Initiate has purified his astral body of all animal passions, when it has become wholly luminous (the first phase of Initiation), he has arrived at the stage of catharsis. Only then can he work at his etheric body and by this means 'affix his seal' to the physical body. Of itself, the astral body has no direct influence upon the physical body. Its forces must pass by way of the etheric body. The task of the disciple, therefore, is concerned with the transformation of the astral and etheric bodies in order, finally, to acquire full and complete control of the physical body. This is how he becomes a master. We are touching here upon a marvelous law of human nature, proving that the self and Manas are the central points of man's development. When Manas dominates the astral and etheric bodies, man acquires new faculties and these in turn influence the spiritual and divine form of man. When Manas works upon the etheric body, light and power for the purpose of man's spiritual being (Budhi) are generated. When Manas works upon the physical body, light and power for man's divine Spirit (Atma) are generated. The evolution of man, therefore, amounts to a transformation of the lower bodies by the higher Self.

We have a paramount example of the working of the lower self in an anecdote told by Darwin. On one of his journeys he conversed with a cannibal and asked, through an interpreter, if he felt no repugnance against eating human flesh. Whereupon the savage burst into laughter, saying: "One must have tasted human flesh before one can know whether it is good to eat. And you know nothing about it whatever!"

The transformation of the astral body goes hand in hand with the control of feelings and their purification.

The lower part of the astral body of man in our age is dark; the higher part is limpid and full of colour. The higher part has been transmuted and permeated by the self but not the lower part as yet. When man has transformed the whole of his astral body we say that he has changed it into Manas. Not until then can he begin to work on the etheric body. There is a reason why this is so. Everything in the astral body is ephemeral.) Everything that happens in the etheric body leaves an indelible trace which is, furthermore, impressed like a seal into the physical body.

The higher stages of Initiation consist in controlling all the phenomena connected with the physical body, in mastering and controlling them at will. The Initiate possesses Atma to the extent to which he achieves this; he becomes a sage and has power over Nature.

The difference between Eastern and Western Initiation lies in the method by which the master brings the pupil to the point of being able to work on his etheric body. Here we must consider the different conditions in which man finds himself during sleep and waking life.

During sleep the astral body is partly freed from the physical body and is in a condition of inactivity, but the vegetative activity of the etheric body continues.

At death, the etheric and astral bodies are wholly severed from the physical body. In the etheric body — which is the bearer of memory — inheres a remembrance of the past life and at the moment the etheric body frees itself, the dying have before them a tableau of their whole life. Freed from the physical body, the etheric body becomes much more sensitive and impressionable because it is no longer impeded by physical substance.

Oriental Initiation consisted in a process whereby the etheric and astral bodies of the neophyte were forced out of his physical body. He lay in a trance lasting three days and during this time the hierophant controlled his freed etheric body, poured impulses into him and taught him wisdom which remained as a powerful, lasting impression. When he awoke from the trance, the new Initiate found himself in possession of this wisdom, for the reason that memory inheres in the etheric body. The wisdom was occult doctrine but it bore the permanent and personal stamp of the hierophant who had imparted it. A man who had passed through this Initiation was said to be 'twice-born.'

The process of Western Initiation is quite different. Eastern Initiation takes place while man is in a state of sleep; Western Initiation must be achieved in a state of wakefulness. In other words, there is no separation of the etheric and physical bodies. In Western Initiation the neophyte is free; the master simply plays the rôle of an awakener. He does not try to dominate or convert; he simply recounts what he himself has seen, — And how ought we to listen? There are three ways of listening: to accept the words as infallible authority; to be sceptical and fight against what is heard; to pay heed to what is said without servile, blind credulity and without systematic opposition, allowing the ideas to work upon us and observing their effects. This latter is the attitude which the pupil should adopt towards his master in Western Initiation.

The Initiator knows that he who is master must also be servant. It is not his task to mould the soul of his pupil to his own image but to discover and solve the enigma of this soul. The teaching given by the Initiator is not dogma; it is simply an impulse for development. Every truth that is not at the same time a vital impulse, is a sterile truth. That is why all thought must be filled with the element of soul. Thought must be permeated with feeling; otherwise it will not pass into the realm of soul and it will be stillborn thought.

Yoga In East and West, Conclusion

The first thing to realise is that Yoga is not a sudden, convulsive event, but a process of gradual training, inner transformation. It does not consist, as is often supposed, in a series of external adjustments and ascetic practices. Everything must run its course in the depths of the soul.

It is often said that the first steps of Initiation are fraught with perils and grave dangers. There is a measure of truth in this. Initiation, or Yoga, is a coming-to-birth of the higher soul which lies latent in every human being. The astral body is faced with dangers analogous to those attending physical birth; there is travail before the divine soul comes forth from the desire-nature of man. The difference is that the birth of Spirit is a much longer process than that of physical birth.

Let us take another comparison. The higher soul is closely linked with the animal soul. By their fusion the passions are tempered, spiritualised and dominated according to the strength of man's intelligence and will. This fusion is of benefit to man but he pays for it by the loss of clairvoyance. Imagine to yourself a green liquid, produced by a combination of blue and yellow elements. If you succeed in separating them, the yellow will descend and the blue will rise to the surface. Something analogous happens when, through Yoga, the animal-soul is separated from the higher soul. The latter acquires clairvoyant vision; the former is left to its own devices if it has not been purified by the self and it is then given over to its passions and desires. This often happens in the case of mediums. The 'Guardian of the Threshold' protects man from this danger.

The first condition requisite for the Initiate is that his character shall be strong and that he shall be master of his passions. Yoga must be preceded by a rigorous discipline and the attainment of certain qualities, the first of which is inner calm. Ordinary 'morality' is not enough, for this relates merely to man's conduct in the outer world. Yoga is related to the inner man.

If it is said that compassion suffices, our answer will be: compassion is good and necessary but has nothing directly to do with occult training. Compassion without wisdom is weak and powerless.

The task of the occultist, of the true Initiate, is to change the direction of his life's current. The actions of man today are impelled and determined by his feelings — that is to say, by impulses from the outer world. Actions determined by space and time have no significance. Space and time must be transcended. How can we achieve this?

(1) Control of thought. We must be able to concentrate our thought upon a single object and hold it there.

(2) Control of actions. Our attitude to all actions, be they trivial or significant, must be to dominate, regulate and hold them under the control of the will. They must be the outcome of inner initiative.

(3) Equilibrium of soul. There must be moderation in sorrow and in joy. Goethe has said that the soul who loves is, till death, equally happy, equally sad. The occultist must bear the deepest joy and the deepest sorrow with the same equanimity of soul.

(4) Optimism — the attitude which looks for the good in everything. Even in crime and in seeming absurdity there is some element of good. A Persian legend says that Christ once passed by the corpse of a dog and that His disciples turned from it in disgust. But the Christ said: 'Lo! the teeth are beautiful.'

(5) Confidence. The mind must be open to every new phenomenon. We must never allow our judgments to be determined by the past.

(6) Inner balance, which is the result of these preparatory measures. Man is then ripe for the inner training of the soul. He is ready to set his feet upon the path.

(7) Meditation. We must be able to make ourselves blind and deaf to the outer world and our memories of it, to the point where even the shot of a gun does not disturb. This is the prelude to meditation. When this inner void has been created, man is able to receive the prompting of his inner being. The soul must then be awakened in its very depths by certain ideas able to impel it towards its source.

In the book Light on the Path, there are four sentences which may be employed in meditation and inner concentration. They are very ancient and have been used for centuries by Initiates. Their meaning is profound and many-sided.

"Before the eyes can see, they must be incapable of tears."

"Before the ear can hear, it must have lost it's sensitiveness."

"Before the voice can speak in the presence of the masters, it must have lost the power to wound."

"Before the soul can stand in the presence of the masters, its feet must be washed in the blood of the heart."

These four sentences have magical power. But we must bring them to life within us, we must love them as a mother loves her child.

This, the first stage of training, has power to develop the etheric body and particularly its upper part which corresponds to the head. Having trained the upper part of the etheric body, the disciple must begin to control the systems of breathing and blood, the lungs and the heart. In remote ages of earthly evolution, man lived in the waters and breathed through gills like fish. Sacred literature indicates the time when he began to breathe the airs of heaven. Genesis says "God breathed into his nostrils the breath of life."

The disciple must purify and bring about changes in his breathing system. All development proceeds from chaos to harmony, from lack of rhythm to rhythm (eurhythmy). Rhythm must be brought into the instincts.

In ancient times, the various degrees of Initiation were called by particular names:

First degree: The Raven (he who remains at the threshold). The raven appears in all mythologies. In the Edda, he whispers into the ear of Wotan what he sees afar off.

Second degree: the hidden Scholar, or the Occultist.

Third degree: the Warrior (struggle and strife).

Fourth degree: the Initiate bears the name of his people — he is a "Persian" or a "Greek" because his soul has grown to a point where it includes the soul of his people.

Sixth degree: the Initiate is a Sun-Hero, or Sun-Messenger, because his progress is as harmonious and, rhythmic as that of the Sun.

Seventh degree: the Initiate is a 'Father,' because he has power to make disciples of men and to be the protector of all; he is the Father of the new being, the 'twice-born' in the risen soul.

The Sun represents the vivifying movement and rhythm of the planetary system. The legend of Icarus is a legend of Initiation. Icarus has attempted to reach the Sun-sphere prematurely, without adequate preparation, and is cast down.

The new rhythm of breathing produces a change in the blood. Man is purified to the point of himself being able to generate blood without the aid of plant-nourishment. Prolonged meditation changes the nature of the blood. Man begins to exhale less carbon; he retains a certain amount and uses it for building up his body. The air he exhales is pure. He gradually becomes able to live on the forces contained in his own breath. He accomplishes an alchemical transmutation.

What are the higher stages of Yoga?

(1) The Initiate finds calm within his soul. Astral vision — where everything is a symbolic image of reality is acquired. This astral vision which arises during the sleeping state, is still incomplete.

(2) Dreams cease to be chaotic. Man understands the relation between dream-symbolism and reality; he gains control of the astral world. And then the inner astral light awakens in the soul who perceives other souls in their real being.

(3) Continuity of consciousness is set up between the waking state and the sleeping state. Astral life is reflected in dreams but in deep sleep, pure sounds

arise. The soul experiences the inner words issuing from all beings as a mighty harmony. This harmony is a manifestation of reality; it was called by Plato and Pythagoras, the harmony of the spheres. This is not a poetic metaphor but a reality experienced by the soul as a vibration emanating from the soul of the world.

Goethe, who was initiated between the periods of his life at Leipzig and Strasburg, knew of the harmony of the spheres. He expressed it at the beginning of Faust in words spoken by the Archangel Raphael:

"The Sun makes music as of old   Amid the sister-spheres of heaven. On its predestined circle rolls   With roar of thunder."

In deep sleep, the Initiate hears these sounds as if they were the notes of trumpets and the rolling of thunder.

The Gospel of St. John

The role of Christianity in human history is unique. The coming of Christianity represents, in a sense, the central moment, the turning point between involution and evolution. That is why it radiates so brilliant a light — a light that is nowhere so pregnant with life as in the Gospel of St. John. Truth to tell it is only in this Gospel that the full power of the light is made manifest.

It cannot be said that modern theology has this conception of the Gospel. From the historical point of view it is considered inferior to the three synoptic Gospels, as being, in a sense, apocryphal. The very fact that its authorship is said by some to have taken place in the second century after Christ has made certain theologians of the school of Bible criticism regard it as a work of mystical poetry and Alexandrian philosophy.

Occultism has quite another conception of the Gospel of St. John.

During the Middle Ages a number of Brotherhoods saw in this Gospel the essential source of Christian truth. Such Brotherhoods were the Brothers of St. John, the Albigenses, the Catharists, the Templars and the Rosicrucians. All were engaged in practical occultism and looked to this Gospel as to their Bible. It may be said in a sense that the legend of the Grail, Parsifal and Lohengrin emanated from these Brotherhoods and that it was the popular expression of the secret doctrines.

All the members of these different parent Orders were considered to possess the secret. They were the precursors of a Christianity which should spread over the world in later times. In the Gospel of St. John they found the secret, for its words contained eternal truth — truth applicable to all times. Such truth as this regenerates the souls of all who become aware of it in the depths of their being. The Gospel was never regarded or read merely as a gem of literature. It was used as an instrument for developing the mystic life of the soul. Let us, to begin with, leave its purely historical value out of account.

The first fourteen verses of this Gospel were the subject of daily meditation among the Rosicrucians. These verses were held to possess a magical power — a fact well known to occultists. By repeating these verses at the same hour, day by day without intermission, the Rosicrucians began to see in dream-visions all the events recorded in the Gospel and lived through them in inner experience.

Thus in spiritual vision the Rosicrucians saw the life of Christ — nay indeed the Christ Himself being born in the depths of the soul. They believed, of course, in the actual and historic existence of the Christ, for to know the inner Christ is also to recognise the outer Christ.

A materialist of today might ask whether the fact that the Rosicrucians had these visions is any proof of the actual existence of Christ. To this the occultist will reply: 'If there were no eye to perceive the sun, there would be no sun; but if there were no sun in the heavens, there would be no eye to perceive it. For it is the sun which in the course of ages has formed and built the eye in order that it may behold the light.' In this sense the Rosicrucians said: — 'The Gospel of St. John awakens thine inner senses but if there were no living Christ, He could not live within thee.'

The mission accomplished by Christ Jesus cannot be understood in all its depths unless we realise the difference between the Ancient Mysteries and the Christian Mystery.

The Ancient Mysteries were held in the temple-sanctuaries. The Initiates were the awakened ones. They had learnt to work upon the etheric body and were the 'twice-born' because they could perceive truth in a two-fold sense: directly, through dream and astral vision, indirectly, through sense-perception and logic. The initiation through which they passed was accomplished, in three stages: life, death and resurrection. The disciple spent three days in a sarcophagus in a tomb of the temple. His Spirit was released from his body; but on the third day, at the call of the hierophant, the Spirit came down again into the body from the cosmic spaces of universal life. The man was a transformed, new-born being. The greatest Greek writers have spoken of these mysteries with great awe and inspiration. Plato goes so far as to say that the Initiate alone is worthy of the name of man. This ancient initiation has its crowning-point 'in Christ.' Christ represents the crystallised initiation of the life of sense. All that was supersensibly seen in the Ancient Mysteries becomes, in Christ, historic fact on the physical plane. The death undergone by the ancient Initiates was only a partial death in the etheric world. The death of Christ was a full and complete death in the physical world.

The Raising of Lazarus may be regarded as a moment of transition from the ancient initiation to the Christian initiation. In the fourth Gospel no mention is made of John himself until after the story of the death of Lazarus. "The disciple whom Jesus loved" is he who passed through the stages of death and resurrection in initiation and who was called to new life by the voice of Christ Himself. John is Lazarus who came forth from the tomb after his initiation; he lived through the death undergone by Christ. Such is the mystic path concealed in the depths of Christianity.

The marriage at Cana expresses one of the most profound mysteries of the spiritual history of mankind. It is related to the saying of Hermes: "The above is as the below." In the marriage at Cana, water is changed into wine. The symbolic meaning of this miracle is that the sacrifice of water was to be replaced for a time by the sacrifice of wine.

There were ages in the history of man when wine was not known. In the days of the Vedas it was practically unknown. In the ages when there was no drinking of alcohol, the idea of previous existences and of many lives was universally held; nobody doubted its truth. As soon as man began to drink wine, however, the knowledge of re-incarnation rapidly faded away, ultimately to disappear entirely from the consciousness of man. It existed only among the Initiates who took no alcohol. Alcohol has a peculiarly potent effect on the human organism, especially on the etheric body which is the seat of memory. Alcohol obscures the intimate depths of memory. 'Wine induces forgetfulness' — so the saying goes. The forgetfulness is not only superficial or momentary, but deep and permanent and there is a deadening of the power of memory in the etheric body. That is why, little by little, men lost their instinctive knowledge of reincarnation when they began to drink wine.

Belief in reincarnation and the law of Karma had a great influence not only upon the individual but upon his social sentiment. It helped him to bear with the inequalities of human life. When the unhappy Egyptian labourer was working at the Pyramids, or the lowest caste of Hindu building the gigantic Indian temples in the heart of the mountains, he said to himself that another existence would compensate him for labours patiently accomplished, that his master if he were good had already undergone similar tests or that he would have to undergo them in the future if he were unjust and cruel.

As the era of Christianity drew near, man was destined to enter upon an epoch of concentration upon earthly efforts; he was to work towards the amelioration of earthly existence, the development of intellect, of logical and scientific understanding of Nature. The knowledge of re-incarnation, therefore, was to be lost for two thousand years and wine was the means to this end.

Such is the profound background of the cult of Bacchus, the God of wine and intoxication. (Bacchus is the popular expression of the God Dionysos of the Ancient Mysteries to whom quite a different significance must be attached.) Such, too, is the symbolic meaning of the Marriage at Cana. Water served the purpose of the ancient sacrifice; wine was to serve the purpose of the new. The words of Christ, "Happy are they who have not seen and yet have believed," refer to the new epoch when man — wholly given up to his earthly tasks — was to live without remembrance of his incarnations and without immediate vision of the divine world.

Christ has left us a testament in the scene on Mount Tabor, in the Transfiguration before Peter, James and John. The disciples see Him between Elias and Moses. Elias represents the Way of Truth; Moses, the Truth itself; Christ, the Life that epitomises them. That is why Christ can say of Himself: "I am the Way, the Truth and the Life."

All life is thus concentrated, illumined, deepened and transfigured in Christ. He epitomises the past of the human soul back to its primal source and prefigures its future to the point of union with God. Christianity is not only a power of the past but of the future. In common with the Rosicrucians, the occultist of our day teaches of the Christ in the inner being of each individual and of the Christ, in the future, in all mankind.

The Christian Mystery

Christian initiation has existed since the founding of Christianity. Through the Middle Ages and in our own time it has remained the same among a number of religious Orders as well as among the Rosicrucians. It consists of a spiritual training which culminates in certain identical and invariable symptoms. The Brotherhoods where, in profound secrecy, this training used to be given, are the home of all spiritual life and religious progress.

In certain respects the Christian initiation is more difficult of attainment than the initiation of ancient times. It is bound up with the essence and mission of Christianity which came into the world at a time when man had descended most deeply into matter. This descent was to imbue him with a new consciousness, but the struggle involved in rising from the depths of materialism demands greater effort and renders initiation more difficult. That is why the Christian masters demand intense humility and devotion of their pupils.

The Christian initiation has always consisted of seven stages, four of which correspond to four of the Stations of Calvary. The stages are: —

1. The Washing of the Feet.
2. The Scourging.
3. The Crowning with Thorns.
4. The Bearing of the Cross.
5. The Mystic Death.
6. The Entombment.
7. The Resurrection.

The Washing of the Feet is a preparatory exercise of a moral character, relating to the scene where Christ washes the feet of the disciples before the Easter Festival (St. John 13): "Verily, verily I say unto you, the servant is not greater than his Lord; neither he that is sent greater than he that sent him." Theology gives a purely moral interpretation to this act and looks upon it merely as an example of the profound humility and devotion of the Master to His disciples and His work. The Rosicrucians also held this view but in a deeper sense, relating the story to the evolution of all beings in Nature. The scene is really an allusion to the law that the higher is a product of the lower. The plant might say to the mineral: I am above you since I have a life which you have not; yet without you I could not exist, for the substances which nourish me are drawn from you. The animal again might say to the plant: I am above you, for I have feeling, desires, the capacity for voluntary movement which you have not; but without the food which you provide, without your leaves and fruits I could not live. And man should say to the plants: I am above you, but to you I owe the oxygen which I breathe. To the animals he should say: I have a soul and you have not; yet we are brothers and companions, involved in the great process of evolution. The esoteric meaning of the Washing of the Feet is that Jesus the Christ, the Messiah, the Son of God, could not exist without the Apostles.

The neophyte who meditates on this theme for months and years has a vision of the Washing of the Feet in the astral world during sleep. Then he is ready to pass to the second stage of the Christian initiation.

The Scourging, — At this stage man learns to resist the scourgings of life. Life brings sufferings of all kinds — physical, moral, intellectual, spiritual. Life is felt to be a dreadful and incessant torture. The disciple must endure it with perfect equanimity of soul and heroic courage. He must cease to know physical or moral fear. When he has become fearless, he sees, in dream, the scene of the Scourging. In another vision he sees himself in the Christ Who is scourged. Certain symptoms in physical life accompany this event. There is an intensification of the life of feeling, a wider sense of life and of love. We have an example of heightened sensibility transferred to the world of intelligence, in the life of Goethe. After lengthy osteological studies of the skeleton of man and of the animals, as well as comparative embryological research, Goethe came to the conclusion that the intermaxillary bone must exist in man. Before his time, science denied the existence of this bone in the upper jaw of man. Goethe himself says that he was overcome with joy and a kind of ecstasy when he actually discovered the intermaxillary bone in the human jaw, adding that it was one of the most wonderful experiences of his life. During his Italian journey he again had the same experience. He was looking at a fragment of a sheep's skull, and another idea came to him — an idea still more significant in regard to human evolution — that the human brain, the seat of intelligence, the centre of voluntary movements, is a development and a metamorphosis of the spinal marrow, just as the flower is a culmination and synthesis of root and stem. What faculty was it that enabled Goethe to make these marvelous discoveries which by themselves deserve to make his name immortal? It was his sublime intelligence on the one hand, but also his intense sympathy with all living beings and the whole of Nature. Such sensitiveness is a refinement and an extension of the forces of life and love. It corresponds to the second stage of Christian initiation and is the recompense for the trial of the Scourging. Man acquires a feeling of love for all beings and this gives him a sense of living in the heart of Nature herself.

The Crowning with Thorns, — At this stage man must learn to brave the world morally and intellectually, to desist from anger when all that is most dear to him is being attacked. The capacity to remain aloof when everything is tumbling about our ears, to say "Yea" when the rest of the world says "Nay" — that is what must be acquired before the next step can be taken. This gives rise to a new symptom, namely a dissociation, or rather the power of a momentary dissociation of three faculties which, in man, are united: the faculties of willing, feeling and thinking. We must learn to separate and to re-unite them at will. So long, for example, as some outer event carries us away with uncontrolled enthusiasm, we are immature, for such enthusiasm comes from the event, not from ourselves, and we may even exercise a shattering influence of which we are not master.

The enthusiasm of the disciple must have its well-spring in the depths of his inner life. He must therefore be able to remain impassive in the face of any event, no matter how catastrophic. That is the only way to reach freedom. The dissociation of feeling, thinking and willing produces in the brain a change that is symbolised by the Crown of Thorns. If this test is to be passed without danger, the powers inherent in the personality must be sufficiently intense and in perfect equilibrium. If the disciple has not reached this stage, or if he receives wrong guidance, the change in the brain may lead to insanity. Insanity is nothing but an involuntary separation of these faculties without the possibility of their re-union by dint of the inner will. The disciple brings about the separation by an act of conscious volition. A flash of his will re-establishes the link between the organs and the activities of soul. In the lunatic, the cleft may be incurable and produce a physical lesion in the nerve-centres.

In the course of the stage in the Christian initiation known as the Crowning with Thorns, there arises the phenomenon known as the Guardian of the Threshold — the appearance of the lower double of man. The spiritual being of man, composed of his impulses of will, his desires and his thoughts, appears to the Initiate in visible form. It is a form that is sometimes repugnant and terrible, for it is the offspring of his good and bad desires and of his karma — it is their personification in the astral world, the Evil Pilot of the Egyptian Book of the Dead. This form must be conquered by man before he can find the higher Self. The Guardian of the Threshold which has been a phenomenon of astral vision from times immemorial, is the origin of all the myths concerning the struggles of Heroes with monsters, of Perseus and Hercules with the Hydra, of St. George and Siegfried with the dragon.

The premature appearance of the astral world and the sudden apparition of the Double or Guardian of the Threshold may lead a man who is not fully prepared or who has not taken all the precautions necessary for the disciple, to madness and insanity.

The Bearing of the Cross refers, symbolically, to a virtue of the soul. This virtue which consists in a sense of having 'the world on one's conscience' as Atlas bore the world on his shoulders, may be called a feeling of indentification with the whole Earth, or in the words of oriental occultism the cessation of the feeling of separateness.

In general, and above all in modern times, men identify themselves with the body. (In his Ethics, Spinoza says that the basic and fundamental idea of man is the idea of the body in action.) The disciple must cultivate the idea that in the sum-total of things, his body in itself is of no more importance than any other body, whether it, be the body of an animal, a table or a piece of marble. The self is not bounded by the skin; it is united with the great organism of the universe as the hand is united with the rest of the body. The hand alone would be as dust and ashes. What would the body of man be without the soil on which he rests, without the air he breathes? It would die, for it is but a tiny organ of the Earth and the air. That is why the disciple must sink himself in every other being and identify himself with the Spirit of the Earth.

Goethe has given a marvelous description of this stage at the beginning of Faust. The Spirit of the Earth to whom Faust aspires, appears before him and speaks these words:

"In the tides of life, in Action's storm, A fluctuant wave, A shuttle free, Birth and the Grave, An eternal sea, A weaving, flowing Life, all-glowing; Thus at Time's humming loom 'tis my hand prepares The garments of Life which the Divinity weaves."

To identify oneself with all beings does not mean that the body is to be despised. It must be borne as some exterior object, even as Christ bore His Cross. The Spirit must wield the body as the hand wields the hammer. At this stage the disciple is conscious of the occult powers lying latent in his body. In the course of his meditations. the stigmata may even appear on his skin. This is the sign that he is ripe for the fifth stage, where, in sudden illumination, the Mystic Death is revealed to him.

The Mystic Death, — In the grip of the greatest of all suffering the disciple recognises that the world of the senses is illusion. He is actually aware of death and of descending into the world of shades, but then the darkness breaks and a new light-the astral light-shines out. The veil of the temple is 'rent in twain.' This light has nothing in common with the physical light of the sun. It rays forth from the inner being of man. The impression it makes is wholly unlike that made by outer light. The following comparison will give us some idea of what is meant. We imagine that we are leaving a turbulent city behind us and entering a dense forest. The noises gradually cease and the silence becomes complete. We finally begin to be aware of what lies beyond the silence, to pass the zero point at which all external sound has ceased. And now sound arises again for the inner ear from the other side of existence. Such is the experience of the soul of one who enters the astral world. He is then in contact with the inverse quality of the things with which he was familiar, just as in arithmetic, beneath the zero point, we enter into the growing series of negative numbers.

Thus do we need to lose all in order to regain all, and this applies to our own existence. In the moment of losing all we appear to die to ourselves and it is in the world around us that we begin to live again.

Such is the Mystic Death. When a man has passed this stage, the time has come for the next:

The Entombment, — Man feels that he is freed from his own body and is one with the planet. He is one with the Earth and finds himself again within the planetary life.

The Resurrection, — This is a sublime experience, impossible of description unless it be within the walls of the sanctuary. The last stage of Christian initiation transcends all words and all analogy fails. At this stage man acquires the power of healing. Yet it must be realised that he who possesses it, possesses at the same time the inverse power to bring about disease. The negative invariably goes in hand with the positive. Hence the tremendous responsibility attaching to this power which may be characterised by the saying: The creative word issues from the soul aflame.

The Astral World

How are we to conceive of the astral world? The three different worlds of which occultism speaks are as follows: —

(1) The physical world. (2) The astral world (Purgatory). (3) The spiritual world, or Devachan in Sanscrit terminology (The Christian Heaven).

There are yet other worlds above and beyond these three but they will not concern us in these lectures. They are, moreover, beyond all human conception. Even the highest Initiates can have but a faint presentiment of them. We will concern ourselves here with planetary evolution within the confines of our solar system.

The physical world encloses us in the narrow span of material existence between birth and death. Between two incarnations we live and move in the astral and devachanic worlds. The kernel of man's being is immutable, reincarnating perpetually but not eternally. The rhythm of incarnation and reincarnation had a beginning and will have an end. Man comes from other-where and passes other-where.

The astral world is not a place but a state, a condition of existence. It surrounds us and we are immersed in it while we live on Earth. We live in it as beings born blind who guide themselves by touch. If sight is opened up for them by operation they see for the first time the forms and colours with which they have always been surrounded.

Thus does the astral world open up to clairvoyant sight. It is another state of consciousness. In Goethe's scientific works there is a wonderful passage on the essence of the light as the language of Nature:

"It is useless to attempt to express the nature of a thing abstractedly. Effects we can perceive, and a complete history of those effects would, in fact, sufficiently define the nature of the thing itself. We should try in vain to describe a man's character, but let his acts be collected and an idea of the character will be presented to us.

"The colours are acts of light — its active and passive modifications: thus considered, we may expect from them some explanation respecting light itself. Colours and light, it is true, stand in the most intimate relation to each other, but we should think of both as belonging to Nature as a whole, for it is Nature as a whole which manifests itself by their means in an especial manner to the sense of sight.

"The completeness of Nature displays itself to another sense in a similar way. Let the eye be closed, let the sense of hearing be excited, and from the lightest breath to the wildest din, from the simplest sound to the highest harmony, from the most vehement and impassioned cry to the gentlest word of reason, still it is Nature that speaks and manifests her presence, her power, her pervading life and the vastness of her relations; so that a blind man to whom the infinite visible is denied, can still comprehend an infinite vitality by means of another organ.

"And thus as we descend the scale of being, Nature speaks to the senses — to known, misunderstood, and unknown senses: so speaks she with herself and to us in a thousand modes. To the attentive observer who is nowhere dead nor silent, she has even a secret agent in inflexible matter, in a metal, the smallest portions of which tell us what is passing in the entire mass." [Theory of Colours. Preface.]

Let us endeavour to form some conception of the astral world. We must accustom ourselves to quite a different mode of vision. To begin with, everything is confused and chaotic.

The first thing to realise is that in the astral world, everything that exists is revealed as it were in a mirror, inversed. In the astral light the cipher 365 must be read backwards: 563. If an event unfolds before us, it is perceived in inverse sequence. In the astral world the cause comes after the effect, whereas on Earth, the effect follows the cause. In the astral world, the aim appears as the cause — proving that the aim and the cause are identical, acting in an inverse sense according to the sphere of life in which we are functioning. The teleological problem which no metaphysician has been able to solve by dint of abstract thought is thus solved by clairvoyance.

Another result of this inverse unraveling of things in the astral world is that it teaches man to know himself. Feelings and passions are expressed by plant and animal forms. When man begins to behold his passions in the astral world he sees them as animal forms. These forms proceed from himself, but he sees them as if they were assailing him. This is because his own being is objectivised — otherwise he could not behold himself. Thus it is only in the astral world that man learns true self knowledge in contemplating the images of his passions in the animal forms which hurl, themselves upon him. A feeling of hatred entertained against another being appears as an attacking demon.

This astral self-knowledge occurs in an abnormal way in those who are troubled with Psychical illnesses which consist in constant visions of being pursued by animals and menacing entities. The sufferers are seeing the mirror images of their emotions and desires.

No psychical trouble arises in true initiation, but the premature and sudden flashing-up of the astral world may give rise to insanity. In clairvoyance, man is liberated from his physical body. Hence the dangers that may threaten the mind and brain of one who attempts this kind of training without being absolutely balanced.

The Rosicrucian initiation involved a discipline which was directed to making man objective to himself, to producing, as it were, an objective self. We must begin by seeing ourselves objectively. This outer personification of the self makes it possible for the astral body to go forth from the physical body.

What happens at the moment of death? After death, the etheric body, the astral body and the Ego of man have left the physical body. The corpse alone remains in the physical world. A short time after death the etheric and astral bodies unite. The etheric body imprints in the astral body the memory of the life just passed; then the etheric body slowly dissolves and the astral body passes alone into the astral world.

The astral body then contains all the desires generated by life and, being bereft of the physical body, has no means of satisfying them. This gives rise to a sensation of devouring thirst — the basis of the imagination of the punishment of Tantalus in Greek Mythology. There is also the impression of being immersed in fire — Gehenna or Purgatory. The idea of the fire of Purgatory which is laughed at by materialists is a true expression of the subjective state of man after death. By contrast, unsatisfied thirst for action produces the sensation of cold in the soul. It is this cold — born of action unrealised on Earth — that is said to be sensed by the spirits in mediumistic séances. The soul living in the astral body must learn to break free from the forces of the physical organs and acquire a new organism for existence in the astral world.

The soul now begins to live through the past life in backward order, beginning at death and going back to birth. Not until the life has been lived through in this purifying fire to the point of birth is the soul ready to pass into the spiritual world — into Devachan. Such is the import of Christ's words to His disciples: "Verity, verily I say unto you, unless ye become as little children, ye cannot enter into the kingdom of heaven."

Man is impelled by desire when he is descending to earthly incarnation. Not for nothing is desire for the Earth born in man. The end and aim is that he shall learn.

We learn through all our experiences and they enrich our store of knowledge. But in order that man may learn on the Earth, he must be allured by, [or] involved in enjoyment.

When the soul is experiencing the past life in the astral world after death, in backward order, there must be abnegation of enjoyment, while the essence of the experience itself is retained. The passage through the astral world is thus a purification whereby the soul learns to forego all taste for physical pleasures.

Such is the purification of the Hindu Kamaloca, of the 'consuming fire.' Man must grow accustomed to existence without a physical body. Death gives rise, at first, to the impression of an immeasurable void.

In cases of violent death and of suicide, the impressions of emptiness, thirst and burning are much more terrible. An astral body that is not prepared for existence outside the physical body, separates with great travail, whereas in natural death the detachment of the matured astral body takes place easily and smoothly. In the case of violent death that is not caused by the will of man, the process of separation is less distressing than in the case of suicide. During life itself a kind of spiritual death may occur, caused by a premature separation of the Spirit from the body. The astral world is confused with the physical world. Nietzsche is an example of this. In his book Beyond Good and Evil, Nietzsche has all-unconsciously transferred the astral into the physical world. The result is a confusion and chaos of ideas, culminating in error, insanity and death.

The dim, dreamy life of many mediums is an analogous phenomenon. The medium invariably loses his orientation between these different worlds and is unable to distinguish the true from the false.

A lie in the physical world becomes an agent of destruction in the astral world. A lie is a murder in the astral world. This phenomenon is the origin of black magic. The earthly commandment, Thou shalt not kill, may therefore be translated into Thou shalt not lie, in reference to the astral world. The lie is nothing but a word, an illusion. It may do untold harm, but nothing is actually destroyed. In the astral world, every feeling, every idea is a visible form, a living force. The astral lie brings about an impact between the false and true forms, resulting in death.

The white magician would impart to other souls the spiritual life he bears within him. The black magician has the urge to kill, to create a void around him in the astral world because this void affords him a field in which his egoistic desires may disport themselves. He needs the power which he acquires by taking the vital force of everything that lives, that is to say, by killing it.

That is why the first sentence on the tables of black magic is: Life must be conquered. For the same reason, in certain schools of black magic the followers are taught the horrible and diabolical practice of gashing living animals with a knife at the precise part of the body which will generate this or that force in the wielder of the knife. From the purely external aspect, there are certain points in common between black magic and vivisection. On account of its materialism, modern science has need of vivisection. The anti-vivisection movements are inspired by deeply moral motives. But it will not be possible to abolish vivisection in science until clairvoyance has been restored to medicine. It is only because clairvoyance has been lost that medicine has had to resort to vivisection. When man has regained conscious access to the astral world, clairvoyance will enable doctors to enter spiritually into the inner conditions of diseased organs and vivisection will be abandoned as worthless.

Knowledge of life in the astral world leads us to a conclusion of fundamental importance, namely that the physical world is the product of the astral world.

The epidemics which raged notably in the Middle Ages are one example among thousands of the relation of human sins to astral events, as well as of the repercussion in the astral world of sins committed in earthly life. Leprosy was the result of the terror caused by the invasions of the Huns and hordes of Asiatic peoples. The Mongolians, the descendants of the Atlanteans, bore within them the germs of degeneracy. This contact with the European populace produced, in the first instance, the moral malady of fear in the astral world; the substance of the astral body decomposed and this field of astral decomposition became a field for the development of bacteria, giving rise, on Earth, to diseases such as leprosy.

All that we throw out of ourselves into the astral world at one time will reappear in times to come, on the physical plane. What we sow in the astral world we reap on Earth in future times. We are reaping today the fruits of the narrow, materialistic thoughts strewn by our ancestors in the astral world.

This will make us realise how essential it is to nourish ourselves with occult truths. If science would accept the truths of occultism — merely as hypotheses to begin with — the very world would change. Materialism has cast man into such depths that a mighty concentration of forces is necessary to raise him again. He is subject to illnesses of the nervous system which are veritable epidemics of the life of the soul.

What on the Earth we call feeling comes back again to Earth in the form of actuality, event, fact. The nerve-storms that exhaust man have their origin in the astral world.

It is for this reason that the Occult Brotherhoods decided to demonstrate and reveal the hidden truths. For humanity is passing through a crisis and must be helped to regain health and equilibrium. Only by virtue of spirituality can this health and equilibrium be restored.

The occultist will never dream of imposing dogmas. He is one who tells what he has seen and tested in the astral and spiritual worlds or what has been revealed to him by trustworthy and reliable teachers. He does not desire to convert but to quicken in others the sense that has awakened in him and to enable them to see likewise.

Here we shall consider man as an astral being as he is revealed by clairvoyant vision. The astral being of man includes the whole world of feelings, passions, emotions and impulses of the soul. To inner sight these are changed into forms and colours. The astral body itself is a cloud-like, ovoid form, permeating and enveloping man. We can perceive it from within.

In man as a physical being, we have to consider the substance and form of the body. The astral substance entirely changes in the course of seven years, but the form remains. Behind substance is the constructive, upbuilding principle — the etheric body. We do not, in the ordinary way, perceive it; we only see its accomplished work, in the physical body. The eye of sense only sees what is finished, not what is in the state of becoming.

The contrary is the case when we are able to see the astral body — that is to say, our own astral body. We become aware of it from within through our desires and the various movements of the soul.

Seership consists in learning to see from without that which in ordinary life we feel from within. Feelings, desires and thoughts then become living and visible forms, constituting the aura around the physical sheath.

The etheric body builds and moulds the physical body; the astral body is made up of desires. Every human aura has its own individual shades and predominating colours. There is one fundamental colour in which the others play. The aura of a man with a melancholic temperament, for example, is of a bluish hue. But so many impressions coming from without flow through it that the observer may easily be deceived, above all if he is looking at his own aura. The clairvoyant sees his own aura reversed, as it were, the outer as the inner, the inner as the outer, because he is observing it from outside.

All the great Founders of religions have been possessed of clairvoyant sight. They are the spiritual Guides of mankind, and their precepts are precepts of the moral life based on astral and spiritual truths. This explains the similarities in all the religions. There is a certain similarity, for instance, between the Eight-fold Path of the Buddha and the Eight Beatitudes of Christ. The same underlying truth is that whenever man develops one of the virtues, he unfolds a new faculty of perception. Why are eight stages mentioned? Because the seer knows that the faculties which may be transmuted into organs of perception are eight in number.

The astral organs of perception are called in occultism, the 'lotus-flowers' (sacred wheels, chakra). The lotus-flower with sixteen petals lies in the region of the larynx. In very ancient times this lotus-flower turned from right to left — that is to say in the opposite direction to the hands of a clock. In the man of today, this lotus-flower has ceased to turn. In the clairvoyant seer it begins to move in the opposite direction — from left to right. In earlier times, eight of the sixteen petals were visible, the others undeveloped. In future ages they will all be visible, for the first eight are the result of the action of unconscious initiation, the other eight of the conscious initiation attained by dint of personal effort. The eight new petals correspond to the Beatitudes of Christ. Another lotus-flower (with twelve petals) is situated in the region of the heart. In earlier times, six petals only were visible. The acquisition of six virtues will, in times to come, develop the other six. These six virtues are: control of thought, power of initiative, balance of the faculties, optimism which enables a man always to see the positive side of things, freedom from prejudice, and finally, harmony in the life of soul. When these virtues have been acquired, the twelve petals begin to move. They express the sacred quality of the number twelve which we have in the twelve Apostles, the twelve knights of King Arthur, and again in all creation, in all action. Everything in the world develops according to twelve different aspects. We have another example in Goethe's poem, Die Geheimnisse, which expresses the ideal of the Rosicrucians. According to the explanation given by Goethe to certain students, each of the twelve Companions of the Rose Cross represents a religious creed.

We find these virtues expressed again in signs and symbols, for symbols are not arbitrary inventions — they are realities. The symbol of the Cross, for instance, as well as that of the Swastika, represents the four-petalled chakram in man. The twelve-petalled flower is expressed in the symbol of the Rose Cross and the twelve Companions. The thirteenth among them, the invisible Companion who unites them all, represents the truth that unites all religions.   This truth underlies the rites and ceremonies of the various religions. Divine wisdom speaks through the rites and cults which have been founded by seers. The astral world expresses itself through them in the physical world. As in a reflection, the rite represents what is happening in higher worlds. This fact appears again in masonic ritual and in certain Asiatic religions. At the birth of a new religion, an Initiate gives the foundations upon which the ritual of the outer cult is built. As evolution proceeds, the rite — a living picture of the spiritual world — tends towards the domain of Art. Art, too, comes from the astral world; the rite becomes beauty. This came to pass notably at the time of Greek civilisation. Art is an astral event of which the cause has been forgotten.

We have an example in the Mysteries and Gods of Greece. In the Mysteries, the hierophant retraced the development of man in its three stages: man the animal, man the human, man the God (the true Superman, not the false Superman of Nietzsche). The hierophant projected these three supersensible types as living images into the astral light, where they were visible to those who had been initiated into the Mysteries. At the same time they were expressed in poetry and sculpture by three symbols: (1) the Satyr, or bestial type; (2) the human type: Hermes, or Mercury; (3) the divine type: Zeus, or Jupiter. Each of these figures, together with everything around them, represents a cycle of human evolution. That is the way in which the disciples of the Mysteries carried over into Art what they had seen in the astral light. The zenith of the earthly life of man is reached at about the age of thirty-five. Why is this so? Why does Dante begin his journey at the age of thirty-five, the middle point of human life? Before this moment, man's activity has been concentrated on the development of the physical body but he can now begin his ascent to the spiritual worlds and apply his forces for the unfolding of seership. Dante became a seer at the age of thirty-five. It is the age when the physical forces cease to forestall the influx of Spirit; liberated from the body, these same forces can be transformed into clairvoyant faculties. Here we are touching upon a deep mystery: the law of the transformation of organs. Transformation of the organs constitutes man's evolution. The highest in him is the product of what once was the lowest and which has been transfigured. At the time of the separation of the sexes, the astral body of man divided: the lower part producing the sexual (physical) organism and the higher part giving rise to thought, imagination, speech.

In days of yore, the sexual organs (the procreative forces) and the organ of the voice (the word creative) were united. Two poles have appeared in man's being, where formerly there was but one single organ. The negative pole (animal) and the positive pole (divine) were once united and have separated. The third aspect of the Logos is the creative power of the word (as expressed at the beginning of the Gospel of St. John), of which the words of human speech are the reflection. In the old myths and legends this truth was represented in the figure of Vulcan, the cripple. His mission was to guard the sacred fire. He is crippled because, in initiation, man must lose something of his lower, physical forces; the lower part of the body is a product of the past. Raised to the heights of initiation, the lower nature must fall away, to rise thereafter to a yet higher stage. Thus in the course of his evolution man has divided into a lower and higher nature.

In certain mediaeval pictures, the human body is divided into two parts by a straight line; the head and left upper part of the body are above, the right upper part and the lower part of the body are below the line. This division is an indication of the past and the future of the human body.

The two-petalled lotus-flower lies beneath the forehead, at the root of the nose. As yet it is an undeveloped astral organ which will one day unfold into two antennae or wings. The symbol of them can already be seen in the horns traditionally represented on the head of Moses.

Viewed from above downwards, head and sexual organ, man is synthetic and one. All this is the product of the past. Left and right he is symmetrical, representing the present and the future. These two symmetrical parts, however, have not the same value. Why is man usually right-handed? The right hand which is the more active of the two today, is destined subsequently to atrophy. The left hand will survive when the two 'wings' on the forehead have developed. The heart will be the brain of the chest — an organ of knowledge.

Before man assumed the upright posture there was a time when he moved on all fours. Such is the origin of the riddle of the Sphinx: 'Who is the being who in infancy walks on four legs, in middle age on two, in old age on three?' Oedipus answers that this being is man, who when, a baby crawls on all fours, and in old age leans on a stick. In reality, riddle and answer refer to the whole evolution of humanity, past, present and future, as it was known in, the ancient Mysteries. Quadruped in a previous epoch of development, man walks today on two feet; in the future he will 'fly' and will indeed make use of three auxiliary organs, namely the two wings developed from the two-petall ed lotus which will be the motive organ of his will, and for the rest, the organ arising by a metamorphosis of the left half of the chest, and the left hand. Such will be the organs of movement in the future.

The present organs of reproduction will atrophy as well as the right side and the right hand. Man will give birth to his like by the force of the word; his word will mould ethereal bodies like his own.

The Devachanic World (Heaven)

Devachan is the Sanscrit term for the long period of time lying between the death and rebirth of man. After death, in the astral world, the soul first learns to cast off the instincts that are connected with the body. After this, the soul passes into Devachan for the long period that lies between two incarnations. The devachanic world is a state or condition of existence. It surrounds us even in earthly life, but we do not perceive it. In order, by way of analogy, to understand devachanic existence and its functions in earthly and cosmic life, it will be best to take our start from a consideration of the state of sleep.

For the vast majority of human beings, sleep is a condition full of enigmas. During sleep, man's etheric body remains with his physical body and continues its vegetative, restorative functions, but the astral body and individual Ego leave the sleeping body and live an independent existence.

The physical body is used up, consumed, as it were, by our conscious life. From morning till night man spends his forces; the astral body transmits sensations to the physical body which gradually exhaust it. At night, the astral body functions in quite a different way. It no longer transmits sensations which come from outside; it works upon them and brings order and harmony into what the waking life, with its chaotic perceptions, has thrown into disorder. By day, the function of the astral body is to receive and transmit; by night, during sleep, its function is to bring order, to build up and refresh the spent forces.

In man's present stage of evolution, it is not possible for the astral body to do this work of restoration by night and at the same time to observe what is happening in the surrounding astral world. How, then, can man arrive at the point of being able to relieve his astral body of its work, in order to set it free for conscious existence in the astral world?

The procedure adopted by the adept in order to release his astral body is, on the one hand, to train and develop such feelings and thoughts as possess, in themselves, a certain rhythm which can then be communicated to the physical body and, on the other, to avoid those which give rise to physical disorder. Joy or suffering that runs to extremes is avoided. The adept teaches the necessity for equanimity of soul.

Nature is governed by one sovereign law which is that rhythm must enter into all manifestation. When the twelve-petalled lotus-flower which constitutes man's organ of astral-spiritual perception has developed, he can begin to work upon his body and imbue it with a new rhythm whereby its fatigue is healed. Thanks to this rhythm and the restoration of harmony it is no longer necessary for the astral body to perform the restorative work on the sleeping physical body which alone prevents it from falling into ruin.

The whole of waking life is a process destructive of the physical body. Illnesses are caused by excessive activity of the astral body. Eating to excess affords a stimulus to the astral body which re-acts in a disturbing way on the physical body. That is why fasting is laid down in certain religions. The effect of fasting is that the astral body, having greater quiet and less to do, partially detaches itself from the physical body. Its vibrations are modulated and communicate a regular rhythm to the etheric body. Rhythm is thus set going in the etheric body by means of fasting. Harmony is brought into life (etheric body) and form (physical body). In other words, harmony reigns between the universe and man.

This gives us some idea of the function performed by the astral body during sleep. Where is the Self, the Ego of man? In the world of Devachan, but he has no consciousness of it. We must distinguish between sleep that is filled with dreams and the state of deep sleep. Sleep that is filled with dreams is an expression of astral consciousness. Deep, dreamless sleep — the sleep that follows the first dreams — corresponds to the devachanic state. Nothing of it is remembered because it is a condition of unconsciousness for the physical being of ordinary man. Only after the attainment of higher initiation is man aware of his experiences in deep sleep. In the Initiate there is continuity of consciousness through waking life, dream life and dreamless sleep.

Let us now consider the condition of man in Devachan, after death. At the end of a certain time, the etheric body disperses into the forces of the living ether.

What is the next task of the astral body and Ego? A new etheric body has to be built for the incarnation that is to follow. Devachanic existence is devoted, in part, to this work. The substance of the etheric body, like that of the physical body, is not conserved. The substance of which the physical body is composed, is constantly changing — to the point of being wholly renewed in the course of seven years. Similarly, etheric substance is renewed, although its principles of form and inner structure remain the same under the influence of the higher Self. At death, this substance is given completely over to the ether-world and nothing remains from one incarnation to another, any more than the substance of the physical body remains. In each successive incarnation, therefore, the etheric body of man is entirely renewed. That is why there is such a change in the physiognomy and bodily form of man from one incarnation to another. The physiognomy and bodily form do not depend upon the will of the individual but upon his karma, his desires, passions and his involuntary actions.

It is quite different in the case of an initiated disciple. He develops his etheric body in earthly existence in such a way that it is conserved and is fit to pass into

Devachan after death. Here on Earth he is able to awaken, within his etheric forces, a 'Life-Spirit' which constitutes one of the imperishable principles of his being. The Sanscrit term for the etheric body which has developed into Life-Spirit is Budhi. When this principle of Life-Spirit has developed in the disciple. it is no longer necessary for him entirely to re-mould his etheric body between two incarnations. His period of devachanic existence is then much shorter and for this reason the same character, temperament and outstanding traits are carried forward from one incarnation to another. When the master in occultism has reached the point of conscious control not only of his etheric but of his physical body, another, higher spiritual principle comes into being — Spirit-Man (in Sanscrit, Atma). At this stage the Initiate preserves the characteristics of his physical body every time he incarnates on Earth. With unbroken consciousness, he passes from earthly to heavenly life, from one incarnation to another. Here we have the origin of the legend referring to Initiates who lived for a thousand or two thousand years. For them there is neither Kamaloca or Devachan but unbroken consciousness through deaths and births.

The following objection to the idea of re-incarnation is sometimes made: When a man has accomplished his task in the physical world, he knows the Earth. Why, then, should he return? This objection would be justifiable if man were to return under similar conditions. But as a general rule, he returns to find a new Earth, a new humanity, even a new Nature. For all have evolved and he can enter a new apprenticeship, fulfil a new mission.

These changing conditions of the Earth which determine the times of rebirth, are themselves determined by the passage of the Sun through the Zodiac. Eight centuries before Jesus the Christ, the vernal equinox fell with the Sun in the sign of the Ram. Reference is made to this in the legend of the Golden Fleece and in the name of the Lamb of God — the Christ. 2,160 years before that, the vernal equinox fell with the Sun in the sign of the Bull, a fact expressed in the cults of the Egyptian Apis or the Mithras Bull in Persia. 2,160 years before that again, the vernal equinox fell with the Sun in the sign of the Twins and we find this expressed in the cosmogony of the very ancient Persians, in the two opposing figures of Ormuzd and Ahriman. When the civilisation of Atlantis was destroyed and the age of the Vedas was beginning, the Sun at the vernal equinox was in the sign of Cancer, (inscribed as the sign of cancer) indicating the end of one period and the beginning of another.

There has always been some consciousness among the peoples of the Earth of their relation to the heavenly constellations. The great periods of human civilisation are subject to the heavenly cycles and the movement of the Earth in its relation to Sun and stars. This fact explains the different characteristics of the various epochs and gives new meaning to the incarnations occurring in them. 2,160 years is approximately the time needed for the accomplishment of a male and a female incarnation — that is to say, for the two aspects under which the human being gathers all the experiences of one epoch.

A new flora and a new fauna on Earth are brought forth on Earth by the Devas; they are an expression of the forms of Devachan.

Darwin tries to explain the process of earthly evolution by the struggle for existence — but that is no explanation. The occultist knows that the flora and fauna of Earth are shaped by forces issuing from Devachan. The more man has advanced in his evolution, the more he can participate in this process. His influence upon the moulding of Nature is measured by the extent to which his consciousness has developed.

The Initiate can work in the sphere where the germs of new plants come into being, for Devachan is the region where vegetation receives its form. In Kamaloca, man works at building up the animal kingdom. Kamaloca belongs to the Moon-sphere; Devachan to the Sun-sphere.

Thus man is bound up with all the kingdoms of Nature. Plato speaks of the symbol of the Cross, saying that the soul of the world is bound to the body of the world as it were upon a Cross. What is the meaning of this symbol? It is an image of the soul passing through the kingdoms of Nature. In contrast to the human being, the plant has its root beneath and its organs of generation above, turned towards the Sun. The animal is at the intermediary stage, its organism lying, generally speaking, in the horizontal direction. Man and the plants stand vertically upright and with the animal form a Cross — the Cross of the world.

In future ages there will be conscious participation on the part of man in the higher worlds after death in the work of building up the lower kingdoms of Nature. The consciousness of man will govern the circumstances whereby a new civilisation comes into being, concurrently with the appearance of a new flora. The divine mission of the Spirit is to forge the future. A time will come when there will be no question of 'miracle' or chance. Flora and fauna will be a conscious expression of the transfigured soul of man. Creative works on Earth are wrought by the Devas and by man. If we build a cathedral, we are working on the mineral kingdom. The mountains, the banks of the holy Nile are the work of the Devas the temples on the banks of the Nile are the work of man. And the aim is one and the same — the transfiguration of the Earth.

In future ages man will learn to mould all the kingdoms of Nature with the same consciousness with which today he can give shape to mineral substances. He will give form to living beings and take upon himself the labours of the Gods. Thus will he transform the Earth into Devachan.

Devachan (abode of the Gods) corresponds to the heaven of the Christians, the spiritual world of the occultists.

These regions of existence are beyond the range of our physical senses, although they are intimately connected with this world. In attempting to describe them, we must have recourse to allegories and symbols. The words of human language are only adapted to express the world of sense.

There are seven distinct stages or degrees of Devachan. The seven stages are not definite 'localities' but conditions or states of the life of soul and Spirit. Devachan is everywhere present; it envelops us as does the astral world, only it is invisible. By dint of training, the Initiate acquires, one by one, the faculties necessary for beholding it.

At the first stage of clairvoyance, greater order enters into dreams; man sees marvelous forms and hears words that are pregnant with meaning. It becomes more and more possible to decipher the meaning of dreams and to relate them to actuality. We may dream, for example, that a friend's house is on fire and then hear that he is ill. The first faint glimpses of Devachan give the impression of a sky streaked with clouds which gradually turn into living forms.

At the second stage of clairvoyance, dreams become precise and clear. The geometrical and symbolic figures employed as the sacred signs of the great religions are, properly speaking, the language of the creative Word, the living hieroglyphs of cosmic speech. Among such symbols are: the cross, the sign of life; the pentagram or five-pointed star, the sign of sound or word; the hexagram or six-pointed star (two interlaced triangles) the sign of the macrocosm reflected in the microcosm, and so forth. At the second stage of clairvoyance, these signs — which we today delineate in abstract lines — appear full of colour, life and radiance on a background of light. They are not, as yet, the garment of living beings, but they indicate, so to say, the norms and laws of creation. These signs were the basis of the animal forms chosen by the earliest Initiates to express the passage of the Sun through the Zodiacal constellations. The Initiates translated their visions into such signs and symbols. The most ancient characters employed in Sanscrit, Egyptian, Greek and Runic scripts — every letter of which has ideographic meaning — were the expressions of heavenly ciphers.

At this stage of his seership, the disciple is still at the threshold of Devachan. His task is to penetrate into Devachan, to find the path leading from the astral world to the first stage of the devachanic world proper. This path was known to all the occult schools and even during the first centuries, Christianity contained esoteric teaching of which traces can be found. The ancient methods of Initiation, however, were abandoned from the beginning. In the Acts of the Apostles, mention is made of Dionysius the Areopagite. He was an initiated disciple of St. Paul and taught an esoteric Christianity. Later on, at the Court of Charles the Bald in the ninth century, John Scotus Erigena again taught the esoteric doctrines. Esoteric Christianity was then gradually obscured by dogma. When the Initiate has penetrated into Devachan, however, he finds that the descriptions given by Dionysius of this world are correct.

The rhythmic breathing practised in Yoga was one of the methods by means of which man was enabled to penetrate the world of Devachan. A certain sign that this entrance has been made is a conscious experience indicated in Vedic philosophy by the words: tat twam asi (Thou art That).

In dream, man beholds his own bodily form from without. He sees his body stretched on the couch but merely as an empty sheath. Around this empty form shines a radiant, ovoid form — the astral body. It has the appearance of an aura from which the body has been eliminated. The body itself seems like a hollow, empty mould. It is a vision where everything is reversed as in a photographic negative. The soul of crystal, plant and animal is seen as a kind of radiation, whereas the physical substance appears as an empty sheath. But it is only the phenomena of Nature that so appear-nothing that has been made by the hands of men. At the first stage of Devachan, we are contemplating the astral counterparts of the phenomena of the physical world. This region has been spoken of as the 'continents' of Devachan — the 'negative' forms of the valleys, mountains and physical continents.

If he enters into deep meditation while the breath is held, man reaches the second stage of Devachan. The moulds which represent physical substance are seen to be filled with spiritual currents — the currents of life universal. This is the ocean of Devachan. At this stage the Initiate enters the well-spring of all life. This life has the appearance of a network of vast streams with their tributaries. At the same time there is a strange and new experience of living within the metals. Reichenbach, the author of L'Od, speaks of this phenomenon in connection with sensitive subjects who were able to detect different metals wrapped in paper.

The Beings living in the region which becomes perceptible at the second stage of clairvoyant vision are called by Dionysius the Areopagite, the Archangels. [In German, Erzengel, — Erz = ore, mineral.] They represent the living soul of the minerals.

To attain the third stage of Devachan, thought must be freed from bondage to the things of the physical world. Man can then live consciously in the world of thought, quite independently of the actual content of thought. The pupil must experience the function of pure intellect, apart from its content. A new world will then be revealed. To the perception of the 'continents' and 'waters' of Devachan (the astral soul of things and the streaming currents of life) will be added the perception of its 'air' or 'atmosphere.' This atmosphere is altogether different from our own; its substance is living, sonorous, sensitive. Waves, gleams of light and sounds arise in response to our gestures, acts and thoughts. Everything that happens on Earth reverberates in colours, light and sound. Whether it be in sleep or after death, the echoes of Earth can be experienced in these 'airs' of Devachan. It is possible, for example, to experience the effects of a battle. We do not actually see the battle, nor hear the cries of the soldiers and the booming of the cannons.

Strife and passions appear in the form of lightning and thunder. Thus Devachan does not separate us from the Earth, but reveals it to us from outside, as it were. We do not experience sorrow and joy as if they were arising in ourselves; we behold them objectively, as a spectacle. Devachan is a school of apprenticeship where we learn to regard sorrows and joys from a higher point of view, where we strive to transmute suffering into joy, failures into renewed efforts, death into resurrection.

This has nothing in common with the passive contemplation and more or less egotistic bliss of heaven conceived of by certain writers on religion who think that the sufferings of the damned are part of the bliss of the elect. Devachan is a living heaven, where the overwhelming urge to sympathy and action contained in the human soul is faced with a boundless field of activity and a vista of infinity.

At the fourth stage of Devachan, the archetypes of things arise — not the 'negatives' but the original types. This is the laboratory of the Cosmos wherein all forms are contained, whence creation has proceeded; it is the home of the Ideas of Plato, the 'Realm of the Mothers' of which Goethe speaks in Faust in connection with Helena. In this realm of Devachan, the Akashic Record of Indian philosophy is revealed. In our modern terminology we speak of this Record as the astral impression of all the events of the world. Everything that passes through the astral bodies of men is 'fixed' in the infinitely subtle substance of this Record as in a sensitive plate. To understand the images which hover in the astral nimbus of the Earth, we must have recourse to analogies. The human voice pronounces words which set up waves of sound, penetrating by the ears into the brains of others, where images and thoughts are evoked. Each of these words is a wave of sound with an absolutely definite form which — if we could see it — is distinct from all others. Let us imagine these words congealing somewhat as water congeals to ice by sudden, intense cold. In such a case the words would descend to Earth as congealed air and we could recognise each word by its form.

And now, instead of a process of densification, let us imagine the reverse. We know that matter can pass through the most solid to the most rarified states: solid, liquid, gaseous. Matter can be subtilised to a point at which we are led over to 'negative' matter — Akasha. Events on Earth impress themselves into this akashic substance and can be rediscovered there even those which occurred in far remote ages of the past.

Akashic pictures are not static and immobile. They unroll before the eye of the seer as living tableaux where objects and persons move and even speak. The astral form of Dante would speak as he spoke in his own milieu. It is almost invariably this kind of image that is seen in spiritualistic séances, where it is thought to be the spirit of the dead.

Our task is to learn how to decipher the pages of this book of living images and to unroll the innumerable scrolls of the 'Chronicle' of the universe. This can only be done if we are able to distinguish between appearance and reality, between the human sheath and the living soul. Daily discipline and long training are necessary if false interpretations are to be prevented. Definite answers to questions, for example, might be received from the form of Dante thus perceived. But they do not emanate from the individuality of Dante, for the individuality continues to evolve; they emanate from the ancient figure of Dante, 'fixed' in the etheric milieu of his time.

The fifth realm of Devachan is the sphere of heavenly harmony. The higher regions of Devachan are characterised by the fact that all sounds have a greater clarity, brilliance and richness. In a mighty harmony we hear the voice of all beings. This harmony was called by Pythagoras, the 'Music of the Spheres.' It is the living, Cosmic Word. To the clairvoyant who has now become clairaudient, each being communicates his true name in a definite sound or tone. In Genesis, Jehovah takes the hand of Adam and Adam gives all beings their names. On Earth, the individual is lost among the crowd of other beings. In the highest sphere of Devachan, each being has his own particular sound; yet at the same time the Initiate is united with all beings, becomes one with his environment.

The Initiate who has attained to this degree is called the 'Swan.' He hears the sounds through which his master speaks to him and then communicates them to the world. The singing swan of Apollo brings to the ears of men the tones of the Beyond. The swan is said to come from the land of the Hyperboreans — that is to say from the world where the Sun sinks to rest, from heaven.

At this point, the Initiate passes to a sphere beyond the world of stars. He no longer reads the Akashic Records from the side of the Earth but from the side of the heavens. The Akashic Record becomes the occult script of the stars and the Initiate experiences the primal source of the universe, of the Logos.

In the myths, we find indications of this degree of the Swan, notably in the Middle Ages in the Grail stories which give expression to experiences in the devachanic world. All the exploits there described are by knights of the Grail, who represent the great spiritual impulses given to mankind by command of the masters.

The time when the legend of the Grail was composed, under the inspiration of high Initiates, is the age when the reign of the Bourgeoisie began and when the movement connected with the freedom of great cities had its rise, coming from Scotland into England and thence to France and Germany. When he is a free citizen, man aspires unconsciously to truth and divine life. In the legend of Lohengrin, Elsa represents the soul of man in the Middle Ages, striving to develop what is always expressed in occultism by a female figure. Lohengrin, the knight who comes from an unknown country, from the Castle of the Holy Grail, to deliver Elsa, represents the master who is the bearer of truth. He is the messenger of the Initiate and is borne by the symbolic swan. The messenger of the great

Initiates is a "Swan." None may ask his true name nor whence he comes. His authority may not be doubted. By his words he must be believed; by the truth shining in his countenance he must be recognised. He who has not this faith is incapable of understanding, unworthy to listen. That is why Lohengrin forbids Elsa to ask his name and whence he comes. The Swan is the chela who bears the master.

The disciple who has reached the fifth degree of initiation is sent by the master into the world. The legend of Lohengrin is a description of events occurring in the higher worlds. The light of the Logos — the solar and planetary Word — shines through the myths and legends of the ages.

The Logos and the World

We will endeavour in contemplation to retrace the stages of man's evolution to the Logos by Whom this world was created.

Modern exoteric science goes back to the Stone Age — an epoch when man lived in caves, using shaped stones as his only instruments. His existence was primitive in the extreme, his horizon narrow, his thought limited to the search for food and means for defending his life.

Occult science leads us back beyond this Stone Age to the epoch of Atlantis. In those times, man's physical appearance was not at all the same as it is today. It is known that the brow of prehistoric man was not developed, for, in effect, the development of the brow and forehead runs parallel with the development of the brain and of thinking. In days of yore, the physical brain was much smaller than the corresponding ether-form which extended beyond it on all sides. In the course of evolution, the etheric and physical brains have become more or less equal in size. A certain centre in the etheric brain which is now inside the skull, was in the evolution of Atlantean man, this centre moved to the interior of the skull. It was a moment of cardinal importance, for as soon as man began to think, to be conscious of his own being and to say 'I,' he began to associate ideas and to calculate — which he could not do before. On the other hand, the earliest Atlanteans possessed a far stronger and truer memory. Their knowledge was based, not upon the relations between facts but on their memory of these facts. They knew, by their memory, that a certain event would invariably give rise to a series of others; but they did not grasp the causes of these facts, nor could they think about them. In addition to this powerful memory, they possessed another faculty — a mighty power of will. Today, man can no longer work directly with his will upon the life forces. He cannot, for example, hasten the growth of plants by an act of will. The Atlantean had this power and was, moreover, able to draw from the plants ether forces which he knew how to use. He did this instinctively, without the help of intellect and the faculties of logical reasoning which are associated today with what we call the 'scientific mind.' To the measure in which intellectuality, the faculty of reflective thought and calculation unfolded in the men of Atlantis, to that measure their powers of instinctive clairvoyance declined.

If we go still further back in the history of Atlantis, we come to a very remote period when expression through speech, that is to say, expression in articulate sounds, first became possible. This was the age when man began to walk upright, for speech and the expression of articulate sounds can only be a faculty of beings who stand upright.

Before the great Atlantean race, of which all European and Asiatic races were the offshoots, there existed another continent and other peoples, still nearer to the animal nature — the Lemurian race. Science only admits its existence as a hypothesis. Certain islands to the South of Asia and the North of Australia are, nevertheless, evidences of this continent; they are the metamorphosed remains of old Lemuria. The temperature of the Earth in those times was much higher than it is today. The atmosphere was vaporous, full of currents. In Lemuria, we find rudimentary human forms, breathing not through the nasal organs but through organs more like gills.

In the course of human evolution, organs are perpetually being transformed both as to character and appearance. Thus primitive man walked on four feet; he could not utter articulate sounds; he had no ears with which to hear. Movement in the semi-liquid, semi-gaseous element surrounding him was made possible by an organ which enabled him to float and swim. When the elements differentiated and man found himself on solid earth, this organ changed into the lungs, the gills into ears and the frontal parts of his structure into arms and hands-free instruments for action. Besides this, he began to utter articulate sounds — the words of speech.

This great transformation was of cardinal importance to man. In Genesis (II.7), we read: "And the Lord God ... breathed into his nostrils the breath of life; and man became a living soul." This passage describes the period when the gills once possessed by man changed into lungs and he began to breathe the outer air. Simultaneously with the power to breathe, he acquired an inner soul and with this soul, the possibility of inner consciousness, of becoming aware of the self living within the soul.

When man began to breathe air through the lungs, his blood was invigorated and it was then that a soul higher than the group-soul of the animals, a soul individualised by the Ego-principle, could incarnate in him to carry evolution forward to its fully human and then divine phases. Before the body breathed air, the soul of man could not descend to incarnation, for air is an element enfilled with soul. At that time, therefore, man actually inbreathed the divine soul which came from the heavens. The words of Genesis, in their evolutionary sense, are to be taken quite literally. To breathe is to be permeated with Spirit. This truth was the basis of the exercises given in ancient systems of yoga. These exercises were founded upon the rhythm of breathing, their purpose being to render the body fit to receive the impouring Spirit. When we breathe, we commune with the world-soul. The inbreathed air is the bodily vesture of this higher soul, just as the flesh is the vesture of man's lower being.

These changes in the breathing-process mark the transition from ancient consciousness which was merely a play of pictures, to consciousness as it is in our time. Sense perceptions are received from the body; consciousness has a purely objective character. Consciousness in pictures (imaginative) created its own inner content by means of an inherent, plastic force. The further we go into the past, the more we find the soul of man living, not within him, but around him. We reach a point when the sense-organs existed only in germ and when man merely received from external objects impressions which gave rise to attraction or repulsion, sympathy or antipathy. The movements of this being — whom we cannot really call 'man' in our sense of the word — were governed by these feelings of attraction or repulsion. He had no reasoning faculty and the pineal gland — an organ of cardinal importance in those times — was his only 'brain'.

The existence of this imaginative consciousness is the answer to endless philosophical discussions on the objective nature and reality of the world and it is the refutation of all purely subjectivist philosophies, such, for instance, as that of Berkeley. Two poles of being and of life are essential to evolution. The 'subjective universal' becomes the objective universe; man proceeds, first, from the subjective to the objective and he will finally be led from the objective to the subjective by the development of Spirit-Self (Manas), Life-Spirit (Budhi), Spirit-Man (Atma).

Dream-consciousness is an atavistic survival of the picture consciousness of olden times. One quality of this picture consciousness is that it is creative. It creates forms and colours which do not exist in physical reality.

Objective consciousness is by nature analytic subjective consciousness is by nature plastic and has magical power. (This is indicated by the etymology of the word 'image'). The subjective, plastic consciousness of man was thus superseded by objective, analytic consciousness. The procedure by which the soul (which, to begin with, enveloped man like a cloud) subsequently penetrated into the physical body, may be compared with that of a snail secreting its own shell and then shrinking back inside it. The soul first gave form to the body and then penetrated within this body, having prepared the organs of perception from outside. The power of sight with which the human eye is endowed today is the same power which once was exercised upon the eye from without, in order that it might take shape.

The change from outer to inner activity of soul is expressed by a hieroglyph. This is the sign of Cancer in the Zodiac, expressing a dual action or movement — one from without inwards, the other from within outwards.

The middle of the third (Lemurian) epoch was the time when the soul passed into its self-created dwelling place and began to 'animate' the body from within. Before this point of time we find an astral humanity indwelling a purely astral

Earth. Before that again, man and Earth existed merely in a devachanic condition. There was as yet no picture consciousness. Cosmic thoughts poured into and through the being of man. His higher soul was still part and parcel of the whole Cosmos, participating in cosmic thought.

The further we retrace the parallel development of man and Earth, the more do we find them existing in a fluid, embryonic condition and the nearer to Spirit. Today, we have reached the lowest point on the curve of descent; man and Earth have reached the greatest degree of solidification and are about to re-ascend, through the action of individual will, towards the Spiritual.

What underlies this great process of evolution? Where was the home of human beings when, at the beginning, they existed merely in germ? Whence has man proceeded? Who created him? It is here that we must try to envisage a life and power of manifestation infinitely more sublime than all human, nay, than all planetary life. This power is the Logos.

In what does human and planetary life differ from the life of the Logos? — This question would seem to demand a flight into the unknown, into a universe of another order. And yet there are analogies which help us to understand or at least to divine something of the creative power of the Logos. Let us try to envisage an all-embracing mind, a mind to which all earthly and planetary experiences are known. Such a mind could live through all and every form of evolution. But with this power alone, it could not rise beyond the point of the creation of man and of the planetary system. It would remain in the sphere of what can be and has been proved by man. Human intelligence cannot pass beyond this limit.

But we can rise to a consciousness other than that wherein our experiences are merely realised in the mind. There are certain states of creative activity in which the spirit of man can give birth to something new, something never seen before. Such, for instance, is the consciousness of a sculptor at the moment he conceives or sees in a flash the form of a statue before his inner eye. He has never seen a model, he creates his statue. Such too, is the consciousness of a poet who conceives a poem in one flash of inspiration, in creative, spiritual vision.

This creative power is not generated by any intellectual idea but rather by a spiritual sense, — Think of a hen sitting on its eggs. It is wholly given up to this brooding activity and is filled with a kind of warm, almost voluptuous pleasure in which there arises a dreamy pre-vision of the hatching of the little winged chicken. This bliss in the work of creation exists at every stage of cosmic life, and warmth pours from it. In the sphere of Cosmic Intelligence — which may be conceived as the world of thoughts accessible to the higher Self (Manas) — this warmth seems to pervade the whole universe, emanating from the creative life of soul (Budhi). We can divine the presence of a creative sphere in existence before our Earth and 'brooding' over it. This is to ascend from Spirit-Self to Life-Spirit, and from Life-Spirit to Spirit-Man. The Ego or 'I' Principle of man is created by the third Logos.

We should try to conceive the power of the higher Ego as being suffused through the whole universe as a life-begetting warmth and then we reach the conception of the second Logos by Whom macrocosmic life is quickened and Who is reflected in the creative activities of the human soul.

The one primal source and centre of manifestation is the first Logos — the unfathomable Godhead.

The Logos and the Man

In the last lecture we retraced the past of man more particularly from the point of view of his form and his body. We will now consider the past as regards his states of consciousness.

The following questions often arise before the mind: Is man the only being upon Earth who possesses self consciousness? Or again: What is the relation between the consciousness of man and that of the animals, plants and metals? Have these lower kingdoms of life any consciousness at all?

Imagine that a tiny insect crawling on the body of a man could see only his finger. It could have no conception whatever of the organism as a whole, nor of the soul. We ourselves are in exactly the same position as regards the Earth and other beings indwelling it. A materialist has no conception of the soul of the Earth and, as a natural result, he is not aware of the existence of his own soul. Similarly, if a tiny insect is unaware of the soul of man, this is because it has no soul with which to perceive.

The Earth-soul is much more sublime than the soul of man and man knows nothing of it. In reality, all beings have consciousness but man's consciousness is quite different, inasmuch as in our age it is perfectly attuned to the physical world.

As well as the waking state (corresponding to the physical world), man passes through other conditions of consciousness. During dreamless sleep, his consciousness lives in the devachanic world. The consciousness of the plant is always devachanic. If a plant 'suffers,' the suffering brings about a change in devachanic consciousness. The animal has astral consciousness, corresponding to the dream-life of man.

These three states of consciousness are very different. In the physical world we evolve ideas simply by means of the sense organs and the outer realities with which these organs put us into touch. In the astral world, we perceive the surrounding milieu only in the form of pictures, feeling at the same time as if we were part of them.

Why does man, who is conscious in the physical world, feel himself separate from all that is not himself? It is because he receives all his impressions from a milieu which he perceives very distinctly outside his body. In the astral world, on the contrary, we do not perceive by means of the senses but by the sympathy which makes us penetrate to the heart of everything we encounter. Astral consciousness is not confined within a relatively limited field; in a certain sense it is liquid, fluidic. In the devachanic world, consciousness is as diffused as a gas might be. There is no resemblance whatever with physical consciousness, into which nothing penetrates except by way of the senses.

What was the object of this shutting-off of consciousness which followed the stage of imaginative consciousness? If such a shutting-off had not taken place, man could never have said 'I' of himself. The divine germ could not have penetrated into his being in the course of evolution if it had not been for the crystallisation of his physical body. Where, then, was this divine Spirit before the solidification of the Earth and of consciousness? Genesis tells us: "The Spirit of God moved upon the face of the waters." The divine Spirit, the spark of the Ego, was still in the astral world.

In higher Devachan, beyond the fourth degree, referred to in occultism as Arupa (without body), where Akasha (negative substance) has its rise — there is the home of the consciousness of the minerals. We must try to reach a deep and true understanding of the mineral kingdom and discover our moral link with it. The Rosicrucians in the Middle Ages taught their disciples to revere the chastity of the mineral, — "Imagine," they said, "that while retaining his faculties of thinking and feeling, a man becomes as pure and free from desire as the mineral, — He then possesses an infallible power — a spiritual power." — If we can say that the spirits of the several minerals are living in Devachan, we can say equally correctly that the spirit of the minerals is like a man who might live only with devachanic consciousness.

In other beings, then, the existence of consciousness must not be denied. Man has traversed all these degrees of consciousness on the descending curve of evolution. Originally he resembled the minerals, in this sense, that his Ego lived in a higher world and guided him from above. But the aim of evolution is to free man from being subject to beings endowed with a consciousness higher than his own and to bear him to a point where he himself is fully conscious in higher worlds.

All these levels of consciousness are contained within man today:

1. The consciousness of the mineral-corresponding to deep sleep.
2. The consciousness of the plant-ordinary sleep.
3. Animal consciousness-dream-life.
4. Physical, objective consciousness-the normal waking state. The two former states are atavistic survivals.
5. A consciousness which repeats the third stage but retains the acquired quality of objectivity. Images have definite colours and are realised as being quite distinct from the perceiver. The subjective sense of attraction or repulsion vanishes. In this new imaginative consciousness, the faculty of reason that has

been acquired in the physical world retains its own powers.   6. Sleep itself —
not the dream — here becomes a conscious state. We   do not only behold
images but we enter into the living essence of beings and hear their inner tones.
In the physical world we give names to things but the names are merely outer
appellations. Only man can express his own being from within by saying 'I' — the
ineffable name of conscious individuality. By this word we distinguish our own
personality from the rest of the universe. But when we become conscious of the
world of sound, each being, each thing communicates its own true name; in
clairaudience we hear the sound which expresses its innermost being and rings
forth as a tone in the universe that is distinct from all others.

7. One stage further and deep sleep becomes a conscious state. Description is
impossible, for this condition passes beyond the limits of comparison. All that can
be said is that it exists.

Such are the seven states of consciousness through which man passes, and he
will pass through others too. There is always one central state, with three beneath
and three above. The three higher states reproduce, in a higher sense, the three
lower. A traveler is always at the centre of the horizon. Each state of
consciousness develops through seven states of life, and each state of life through
seven states of form. Thus seven states of form always constitute one state of life;
seven states of life compose one whole period of planetary evolution, for example
that of our Earth.

The seven states of life culminate in the formation of seven kingdoms, of which
four are actually visible: the mineral, plant, animal and human kingdoms. In each
state of consciousness, therefore, man passes through 7 x 7 states of form this
brings us to 7 x 7 x 7 metamorphoses (343).

If we could envisage in one single tableau the 343 states of form, we should
have a picture of the third Logos.

If we could envisage the 49 states of life, we should have a picture of the
second Logos.

If we could envisage the 7 states of consciousness, we should have a conception
of the first Logos.

Evolution consists in the mutual interaction of all these seven forms. In order
to pass from one form to the other, a new spirit is necessary (the action of the
Holy Spirit). In order to pass from one state of life to another, a new power is
necessary (the action of the Son). In order to pass from one state of consciousness
to another, a new consciousness is necessary (the action of the Father).

Christ Jesus brought a new state of life and was in very truth the Word made
Flesh. With the coming of the Christ, a new force entered into the world,
preparing a new Earth in a new relationship with the heavens.

The Evolution of Planets and Earth

To gain an idea of this evolution we must have recourse not to abstractions but to pictures, for pictures have a living, creative quality that is not contained in the pure idea. The picture is a symbol in one world but corresponds to a reality in a higher world.

We know that before developing to its present stage, our Earth passed through a phase called the Old Moon period. But this Old Moon phase of evolution is not to be confused with the satellite we now see in the sky, nor to any other planet that astronomy might ever discover. The heavenly bodies visible today are bodies which have been mineralised. The human eye can only see objects which contain mineral elements and reflect the light, in other words, objects which have a physical body. When the occultist speaks of the mineral kingdom, he is not merely referring to the stones but to the milieu at the central core of which the consciousness of man unfolds. Many scholars regard living beings as mere machines and reject the idea of a vital force. This mentality is a result of the fact that our organism is unable really to behold life. The occultist, on the other hand, says that in our age man lives in the mineral world.

Think of the human eye. It is a highly complicated mechanism, a kind of 'dark chamber,' with the pupil as a window and the crystalline as a lens. The whole body of man is composed of a number of physical organs, equally delicate and complicated. The ear is like a harpsichord with a key-board and fibres for strings. And the same may be said of every sense-organ.

The consciousness of modern man is only awakened if connection is established with his physical or mineral body. True, it awakens first in the physical world, but it must none the less gradually light up in the other members of man's being — in the member that is constituted by the life-forces (the plant-nature of man), in the member that is chiefly dominated by the forces of feeling (the animal-nature), and finally in the Ego.

Truth to tell, man only knows what is mineral in the universe. He does not know the essential laws underlying the animal's life of instinct and feeling, and the growth of plants. He simply sees their physical expressions. Try to conceive a plant in super physical existence, having lost its mineral substance — it would be invisible to our physical eyes.

But even though man knows only the mineral, at least he has it in his power. He works it, moulds it, smelts and combines it. He fashions the face of the Earth anew. He is able to do this in our age with the help of machines. If we go back to remote historic ages when as yet no human hand had been laid on the Earth, we find it as it issued from the hands of the Gods. But ever since man began to exercise control over the mineral kingdom, the Earth has been changing, and we may foresee an age when the whole face of the Earth — which at the beginning was the work of the Gods — will have received the stamp imparted by the hand of man.

In the beginning, form was given to all created things by the Gods. This power of giving form has passed from the Gods to men, in so far as the mineral kingdom is concerned. In ancient traditions it was taught that man must accomplish the task of transforming the Earth in fulfillment of a threefold goal, namely the realisation of truth, beauty, goodness. It is for man to make the Earth into a temple of truth, beauty and goodness. And then, those who come after him will look upon his work as we now look upon the mineral world which came forth from the hands of the Gods. Neither cathedrals nor machines have been built in vain. The Gods have given form to the crystal which we extract from the Earth, just as we build our monuments and our machines. Just as in the past the Gods created the mineral world from a chaotic mass, so our cathedrals, inventions and even our institutions are the germs from which a future world will come to birth.

Having transformed the mineral world, man will learn to transform the plants. This denotes a higher power. Today, man erects buildings; in future times he will be able to create and give shape to plant-life by working upon plant-substance. At a still higher stage, he will give form not only to living beings but to conscious beings. He will have power over animal life. When he has reached the stage of being able to reproduce his like by an act of conscious will, he will accomplish, at a higher level, what he accomplishes today in the mineral world.

The germ of this sublime power of generation, cleansed of all element of sensuality, is the word. Man became a conscious being when he drew his first breath; consciousness will reach its stage of perfection when he is able to pour into the words he utters, the same creative power with which his thought is endowed today. In this age, it is only words that he communicates to the air. When he has reached the stage of higher creative consciousness, he will be able to communicate images to the air. The word will then be an Imagination — wholly permeated with life. In giving body to these images, he will be giving body to the word which bears and sustains the image. When we no longer simply embody our thoughts in objects, as for instance when we make a watch, but give body to these images, they will live.

And when man knows how to impart life to what is highest in him, these 'images' will lead a real and actual existence, comparable to animal existence. At the highest stage of evolution, man will thus be able, finally, to reproduce his own being. At the end of the process of the Earth's transformation, the whole atmosphere will resound with the power of the Word. Thus man must evolve to a stage where he will have the power to mould his environment in the image of his inner being. The initiate only precedes him along this path. It is evident that the Earth today cannot produce human bodies such as will be produced at the final stage of evolution. When that final stage has come, these bodies will be a fit expression of the Logos. The one great Messenger, He alone Who manifested in a human body like our own, this power of the Logos, is Christ. He came at the central turning-point of evolution, to reveal its goal.

And now let us enquire into the form in which the Spirit of man lived before this Spirit entered into him by way of the breath. The Earth is a reincarnation of an earlier planet — of the Old Moon. In this lunar period of evolution, the pure mineral did not yet exist. The planetary body was composed of a substance somewhat akin to the nature of wood a substance midway between the mineral and the plant. Its surface was not hard like the mineral — indeed it was liken to turf. It brought forth beings by nature half-plant, half-mollusc, and was inhabited by a third kingdom of beings at a stage of existence midway between the human being and animal. These beings were endowed with a dreamlike, imaginative consciousness. We can envisage the kind of matter of which their 'bodies' were composed, by thinking of the nerve-substance of the crayfish. This matter densified to become the substance of which the brain is now composed. On the Old Moon, this matter remained in a more fluid state but on Earth it required a protective sheath of bone — the skull. In this sense, all the substances of which we are composed are 'extracts' of the macrocosm. All this preparatory activity in the universe was necessary in order that the Ego might descend into man.

We have heard that man was only ready to receive the germ of his Ego, when, on Earth, he began to breathe the air around him. Did he then breathe on the Moon?

The further we go back in the periods of evolution, the higher the temperature. Atlantis was bathed in hot vapours. In earlier times still, the air was pure warmth; before that again, fire. Fire was there in the place of air. The Lemurians breathed fire. That is why it is said in occult writings that the first Teachers of men were the Spirits of Fire. When physical man appeared on the Earth, air became his element of life. But man changes this air, in that he transforms it into carbonic acid and the breathing-process has thus caused the materialisation of our globe to descend still one degree lower. The equilibrium is restored by the plant-world.

In times to come, the physical body will disappear; man and the Earth will live as astral forms. Physical substance destroys itself by its own forces. But before this metamorphosis comes about, a cosmic night will fall, just as a previous cosmic night marked the transition of the Old Moon evolution to that of our present Earth.

The atmosphere of the Moon contained nitrogen, just as today the atmosphere of the Earth contains oxygen, and it was the predominance of nitrogen which brought about the end of the Old Moon period and the onset of a cosmic night. The cyanides on Earth are survivals from the conditions existing at the final stages of the Old Moon evolution. That is why they have a destructive effect on Earth, for the Earth is not their proper sphere. They are the poisonous remains of life in another age.

Animal-man, as he lived on the old Moon, is thus the ancestor of earthly, physical man; the Spirit within man is the offspring of the Spirits of Fire in the lunar period. The Beings who on the Old Moon were incarnate in the fire, incarnated, on Earth, in the air. But now, has anything of the action of these Spirits of Fire remained in man? On the Old Moon, living beings had no warm blood. What was it that gave rise to the warmth of the blood and, as a consequence, to the life of passions? — The fire which was inbreathed by the beings of the Old Moon and which lives again on Earth in their blood. And the Spirit of the air surrounds the body which contains the heritage of the Old Moon evolution, namely, the warmth of the blood, the brain, the spinal fluid, the nerves.

These examples serve to show that a close study of the transformation of substances is required before we can begin to understand the great processes of metamorphosis which took place during the earlier periods of the Earth's evolution. At a stage still earlier than that of the Old Moon, the planetary sphere which has now become our Earth had a body composed merely of gaseous substance; before that again, we can only speak of a body of sound. It is in this sound — the Cosmic Word — that man's evolution has its origin, proceeding thence towards light, fire, air. Only in the fourth condition does consciousness flash up in the Spirit of man. From this point onwards, the directing force bestowed by the Logos has its rise from within man's own being and his conscience becomes his rightful guide. His primordial being comes to expression in the 'I,' the Ego. The conscious Ego is the realisation in man of the Christ Principle.

Earthquakes, Volcanoes, and Human Will

In a preceding lecture we went back in human evolution to the time when the division of the sexes occurred. This moment is in itself the climax of a long cosmic preparation. After the night which separated the phase of the ancient moon from the terrestrial phase, the earth to begin with appeared combined with the forces of the present sun and moon. They formed but one body which, little by little, became differentiated thus giving birth to the three bodies as we now know them. The present division of the sexes is the result of the separation between the moon forces and the earthly forces. The feminine forces of reproduction have remained under the influence of the moon. The moon still rules over the forces of propagation both in man and animal. Thus occult knowledge reveals the forces that are at play in the planetary system.

At the time when the sun was still united both with the earth and the moon, neither plants nor animals nor human beings existed as we know them today. In fact, only a plant kingdom existed then but under totally different conditions from our own. This kingdom preserved a particular connection with the forces of the sun similar to that of the animal with the moon and of man with the earth. As long as the sun was united with the earth-moon, the plants directed their blossoms toward the center of the globe; when the sun separated off they oriented themselves in accordance with it and directed their flowers heavenward. We have seen in an earlier lecture (XI) that the plants have thus adopted an inverted position in relation to man; both manifest themselves in the vertical whereas the animal is found to be half way between the human orientation and that of the plant world. The spinal column of the animal is in the horizontal. It is by means of the gradual separation of the three heavenly bodies that the different kingdoms on earth have become as we now know them: the plant kingdom at the time of the separation of the sun, the animal when the separation of the moon occurred. The pristine composition of these forces contained in germ what was later to take on physical manifestation. Let us imagine a substance which is heated to a high temperature and then cooled; one would then see the various elements which it contains taking on form.

At the time of the ancient moon we also find the solar forces which during a certain period are concentrated in a celestial body outside the moon. The moon was revolving around the ancient sun but in such a manner that it always turned the same side to the sun; the orbit of the moon around the earth is a continuation of the motion formerly described around the ancient sun. These bodies, both at the beginnings and at the end of this cosmic period, became one — just as the earth, the moon and the sun were united at the beginning of earth evolution and will again be united at the end. These two ancient cosmic bodies would never have been able to be active in evolution had they not recast their forces after their separation. The moon, during the time it was separated from the sun, developed in such a way that forces were engendered which later made it possible for a third body to appear. In fact, it was during this separation that man was able to develop within himself what later took on physical embodiment and gave him the possibility of developing objective, waking consciousness on earth.

The period which preceded the lunar one is referred to as the solar. At this time of evolution everything was pure solar life. Occultism sees the sun as a fixed star which had previously been a planet and similarly it recognizes the earth as a planet destined to become the sun of a future cosmic system. During the solar period, man was only endowed with a consciousness akin to that of dreamless sleep.

Yet another state preceded the solar period; at that time the sun was not even a planet. The human being was only endowed with a deep trance consciousness or deep sleep. He was not yet the being of light which he would become on the ancient sun; he simply vibrated like a tone in the pure harmony of this Saturn period, but it should be noted that our present Saturn has nothing to do with this condition.

After our earthly period of clear physical consciousness, a fifth condition will dawn of conscious astral imagination during a period known as Jupiter. This will be followed by a period of Venus where we shall become conscious of what today is the unconsciousness of sleep. Finally, a period of Vulcan will come into being which corresponds to the highest state of consciousness which can be attained by an initiate.

But this does not exhaust the relationships of the earth and the planets. We in fact can divide our present terrestrial stage into two parts. During the first it came about that our blood is red. What has given us our red blood? During the separation of the earth and the sun, this globe composed of fluid substance was shot through by other fluid forces emanating from the planet Mars. Before this passage of Mars not the slightest trace of iron existed on this earth. In fact, that is a result of this passage; all substances containing iron such as our blood have been subjected to the influence of Mars. Mars has colored the substance of the earth. And the appearance of red blood is the result of its influence. That is why the first half of earth evolution is referred to as the period of Mars.

At that time, iron was a fluid substance and the metals only hardened later on. Mercury is the only metal which has not solidified. When this will have happened the soul of man will have become totally independent of the physical body and astral imaginative vision will have become conscious. This fact is connected with the forces of Mercury which influence the second part of Earth evolution during which they will densify and finally become solid. The Earth is both Mars and Mercury. And it is this which Initiates have woven into our language by indicating that the days of the week belong to the planets of our evolution: Mars and Mercury are placed between the Moon and Jupiter.

The Interior of the Earth

Physical science as yet only knows of the terrestrial crust, a mineral layer which in fact is only like a thin skin at the surface of the earth. In reality the earth consists of a succession of concentric layers which we shall now describe:

1) The mineral layer contains all the metals which are found in the physical bodies of everything that lives at the surface. This crust is formed like a skin around the living being of the earth. It is only a few miles in depth.   2) The second layer can only be understood if we envisage a substance which is the very opposite of what we know. It is negative life, the opposite of life. All life is extinguished there. Were a plant or an animal plunged into it, it would be destroyed immediately. It would be totally dissolved. This second shell — half liquid — which envelopes the earth is truly a sphere of death.

3) The third layer is a circle of inverted consciousness. All sorrow appears there as joy. And all joy is experienced as sorrow. Its substance, composed of vapors, is related to our feelings in the same negative manner as the second layer is in regard to life. If we now abstract these three layers by means of our thinking, we would then find the earth in the condition in which it was before the separation of the moon. If one is able by means of concentration to attain a conscious astral vision, one would then see the activities in these two layers: the destruction of life in the second and the transformation of feelings in the third.

4) The fourth layer is known as water-earth, soul-earth, or form-earth, It is endowed with a remarkable property. Let us imagine a cube and now picture it reversed inasmuch as its substance is concerned. Where there was substance there is now nothing: the space occupied by the cube would now be empty while its substance, its substantial form, would now be spread around it; hence the term 'earth of form.' Here this whirlwind of forms, instead of being a negative emptiness, becomes a positive substance.

5) This layer is known as the earth of growth. It contains the archetypal source of all terrestrial life. Its substance consists of burgeoning, teeming energies.

6) This fire-earth is composed of pure will, of elemental vital forces — of constant movement — shot through by impulses and passions, truly a reservoir of will forces. If one were to exert pressure on this substance it would resist.

If now again in thought one were to abstract these last three layers just described, one would arrive at the condition in which our globe was when Sun, Moon and Earth were still interwoven.

The following layers are only accessible to a conscious observation which is not only that of dreamless sleep but a conscious condition in deep sleep.

7) This layer is the mirror of the earth. It is similar to a prism which decomposes everything that is reflected in it and brings to expression its complementary aspect; seen through an emerald it would appear red.

8) In this layer everything appears fragmented and reproduced to infinity. If one takes a plant or a crystal and one concentrates on this layer the plant or the crystal would appear multiplied indefinitely.

9) This last layer is composed of a substance endowed with moral action. But this morality is the opposite of the one that is to be elaborated on the earth. Its essence, its inherent force, is one of separation, of discord, and of hate. It is here in the hell of Dante that we find Cain the fratricide. This substance is the opposite of everything which among human beings is good and worthy. The activity of humanity in order to establish brotherhood on the earth diminishes the power of this sphere. It is the power of Love which will transform it inasmuch as it will spiritualize the very body of the Earth. This ninth layer represents the substantial origin of what appears on earth as black magic, that is, a magic founded on egoism.

These various layers are connected by means of rays which unite the center of the earth with its surface. Underneath the solid earth there are a large number of subterranean spaces which communicate to the sixth layer, that of fire. This element of the fire-earth is intimately connected with the human will. It is this element which has produced the tremendous eruptions that brought the Lemurian epoch to an end. At that time the forces which nourish the human will went through a trial which unleashed the fire catastrophe that destroyed the Lemurian continent. In the course of evolution this sixth layer receded more and more toward the center and as a result volcanic eruptions became less frequent. And yet they are still produced as a result of the human will which, when it is evil and chaotic, magnetically acts on this layer and disrupts it. Nevertheless, when the human will is devoid of egoism, it is able to appease this fire. Materialistic periods are mostly accompanied and followed by natural cataclysms, earthquakes, etc. Growing powers of evolution are the only alchemy capable of transforming, little by little, the organism and the soul of the earth.

The following is an example of the relationship that exists between the human will and telluric cataclysms: in human beings who perish as a result of earthquakes or volcanic eruptions one notices, during their next incarnation, inner qualities which are quite different. They bring from birth great spiritual pre-dispositions because, through their death, they were brought in touch with forces which showed them the true nature of reality and the illusion of material life.

One has also noticed a relationship between certain births and seismic and volcanic catastrophes.

During such catastrophes materialistic souls incarnate, drawn sympathetically by volcanic phenomena — by the convulsions of the evil soul of the earth. And these births can in their turn bring about new cataclysms because reciprocally the evil souls exert an exciting influence on the terrestrial fire. The evolution of our planet is intimately connected with the evolution of the forces of humanity and civilizations.

Redemption and Liberation

There are seven mysteries of life which up till now have never been spoken of outside the ranks of Occult Brotherhoods. Only in our age is it possible to speak of them openly. They have been called the seven 'inexpressible' or 'unutterable' mysteries. We shall attempt to deal with the fourth mystery, that of Death. These mysteries are as follows:

1. The mystery of the Abyss.
2. The mystery of Number (which can be studied in Pythagorean philosophy).

3. The mystery of Alchemy. (We can learn something of this mystery in the works of Paracelsus and Jacob Boehme).
4. The mystery of Death.
5. The mystery of Evil (to which reference is made in the Apocalypse).
6. The mystery of the Word, of the Logos.
7. The mystery of Divine Bliss. (This mystery is the most occult).

In speaking of the planetary body which preceded our Earth — the Old Moon phase of evolution — we distinguished three kingdoms of Nature, very different from those we know. Our mineral kingdom did not then exist. It came into being as the result of condensation and crystallisation of what on the Old Moon was half-mineral, half-plant. Our plant-world has sprung from the lunar plant-animal. Similarly, the animal world has arisen from the lunar animal-man. So we see that on the Earth, each of these lunar kingdoms makes a descent into materiality. The same thing happens to the Beings who on the Old Moon were higher than animal-man: the Spirits of Fire. In that period man breathed fire, just as today we breathe air. This is why the legends and myths speak of fire as the primary manifestation of the Gods. Goethe alludes to this in Faust, in the words: "Let us kindle fire in order that the Spirits may clothe themselves as in a garment." These Fire-Spirits of the ancient Moon descended to the air in the Earth period proper. They too have descended into denser materiality, into the air we inbreathe and outbreathe.

Now it is just because these Spirits have descended into the air that man can, by their help, rise to the Divine. A twofold movement occurred in the innermost nature of the beings dwelling in the Old Moon. Animal-man divided into two groups. In the one group, a brain developed under the influence of the inspiration and action of the Spirits of Fire who became Spirits of Air. The other group descended towards the animal kingdom. This division is now apparent in the very constitution of man, for the lower part of his being is more akin to the animal, while the higher rises towards the Spirit. According to whether the one or the other characteristic was more or less pronounced, two groups of human beings came into existence: the one bound by a lower nature to the Earth — the other more developed and free of the Earth. The first group grew more like the animals. The beings of the other group received the Divine Spark, the consciousness of 'I.' Such is the relation between man of today and the animals, more particularly the ape.

The physical correlate of this spiritual evolution was the growth and development of the human brain into a veritable temple of God. But if this had been the only evolution, something would have been lacking. There would have been minerals, plants, animals and human beings possessing a brain and a human form and figure, but something would have remained at the lunar stage of evolution. On the Old Moon there was neither birth nor death.

Try to conceive of man without a physical body. He would not pass through death; the renewal of his being would not be brought about by birth as we know it, but by some other means. Certain parts of the astral body and the etheric body would be subject to change, that is all. Around an imperishable centre, the surrounding sheaths alone would be the media of communication with the environment, — such was the condition of man during the Old Moon period of evolution; his being was subject to metamorphoses, not to birth or death. But in this state he had no consciousness in our sense of the word. The Gods who had given him form were around him, behind him, not within him. They were to him what the tree is to the branch or what the brain is to the hand. The hand moves, but the consciousness of the movement is in the brain. Man was a branch of the divine tree and if earthly evolution had not changed this condition of things, his brain would have been but a flower of the same divine tree, his thoughts would have been reflected in his countenance as in a mirror but he would have had no consciousness of his own thoughts. Our Earth would have been a world of beings endowed with thoughts, but not with consciousness, a world of statues ensouled by the Gods, above all by Jahve or Jehovah. What was it that changed this order of things and how has man arrived at independence?

The Gods of the nature of Jahve were able to descend into the human brain. But other Spirits who, on the Moon, had been of the order of the Spirits of Fire, had not completed their evolution, and instead of penetrating into the brain of man on the Earth they mingled with his astral body. The astral body is composed of instincts, desires, passions, and it was there that those Spirits of Fire who had not attained the goal of evolution on the Moon, took refuge. They found a home in the animal nature of man where the passions unfold, and at the same time they imbued these passions with higher qualities. They poured the capacity for higher enthusiasm into the blood and the astral body of man. The gift of the Jehovistic Gods was the pure, cold form of the idea; but under the influence of these Spirits — we may speak of them as Luciferian Spirits — man became capable of enthusiasm for ideas, of being passionately for them or against them. The Jehovistic Gods gave form and shape to the human brain; the Luciferian Spirits set up the connection between the brain and the physical senses; they live in the nerve branches which end in the sense-organs. Lucifer has lived in us for as long as Jehovah.   The fact that his senses give man an objective consciousness of the world around him is due to the Luciferian Spirits. Human thought is the gift of the Gods; human consciousness is the gift of Lucifer. Lucifer lives in the astral body of man, and Lucifer's activity comes to expression at the point where the nerves give rise to feeling and perception. That is why the Serpent in Genesis says: 'Your eyes shall be opened.' These words must be taken literally, for it was by the Luciferian Spirits that the senses of man were opened.

The individualisation of consciousness is due to the senses. If man's thoughts were not related to the sense-world they would simply be reflections of the Divine — not knowledge but belief. The contradiction between faith and science is due to this dual origin of human thought. Faith turns to the eternal Ideas, the 'Mother-Ideas' lying in the bosom of the Gods. All science, all knowledge of the outer world by means of the senses owes its existence to the Luciferian Spirits. In man, the Luciferian principle and Divine Intelligence are combined. It is this fusion of opposing principles which makes evil possible for man but it also gives him the power of self-consciousness, choice and freedom. Only a being capable of individualisation could be thus helped by opposing elements within his being. If when he descended into matter, man had only received the form given by Jehovah, he would have remained an impersonal being. And so it was due to Lucifer that man was able to become truly man, a being independent of the Gods. Christ, or the Logos made manifest in man, is the Principle which enables him to ascend once again to God.

Before the Coming of Christ, man embodied the principle of Jehovah (form) and that of Lucifer (individualisation). He was divided between obedience to the Law and the revolt of the principle of individuality. But the principle of Christ came to establish equilibrium between the two. Christ taught man how to find the Law which was originally laid down from outside, within the centre of individual being. This is what St. Paul meant when he said that freedom and love are the highest principles of Christianity. The ancient world was ruled by Law; Love is the governing principle of the new order of things. Thus three principles are inseparable from and essential to man's evolution — Jehovah, Lucifer, Christ. Christ Jesus is not only a Universal Principle; Christ is a Being who appeared once, and once only, at a definite moment in history. In human form, He revealed by His words and His life, a state of perfection which it is possible for all men ultimately to acquire by their own free-will. Christ came to the Earth at a critical moment, when the descending arc of human evolution was about to reach its lowest point of materialisation. In order that the Christ-Principle might awaken in man, the life of Christ Himself on Earth was necessary in a human body.

Karma is the law of cause and effect in the spiritual world; it represents the spiral process of evolution. The Christ Impulse intervenes in this karmic process and becomes its central pivot. Since He came to Earth the Christ has lived in the depths of every human soul.

When karma is conceived as a necessity imposed on man in order that his wrong doings may be redressed and his errors redeemed by an implacable justice working over from one incarnation to another, the objection is sometimes raised that karma must do away with the rôle of Christ as the Redeemer. In reality, karma is a redemption of man by himself, by dint of his own efforts as he gradually ascends to freedom through the series of incarnations. It is through karma that man is able to draw near to Christ.

The Christ-Impulse transforms implacable Law into Freedom, and the source of this Impulse is the person and example of Christ Jesus. Karma is not to be conceived as fatalism but as an instrument essential to the attainment of that supreme freedom which is life in Christ — a freedom attained not by defying the world-order but by fulfilling it.

Another objection is one that may be made from the point of view of oriental philosophy. It is said that the idea of a Redeemer of men does away with the logical concatenations of karma and substitutes for it an act of a miraculous Providence which intervenes in the universal laws of evolution. It is surely right and just that those who have committed sins should bear the weight of them. This is an error of thought. Karma is the law of cause and effect in the spiritual world, just as mechanical action is the law of cause and effect in the material world. At every moment of life karma represents something like a balance sheet, an exact statement of debit and credit. By every action, bad or good, man augments his debit or credit. Those who will not admit the possibility of an act of freedom are like a business man who will not venture to embark upon a new transaction because he does not wish to run any risk; he prefers always to keep the same balance sheet.

A purely logical conception of karma would prohibit one from helping a man in adversity. But there, too, such fatalism would be false. The help we give freely to another opens up a new era in his destiny. Our destinies are woven of these impulses, of these acts of grace. If we accept the idea of individual help, may we not conceive that a far mightier Being could help, not one man alone, but all men, could give a new impulse to all humanity? Such, indeed, was the act of a God Who was made man, not in order to defy the laws of karma but to fulfil them. Karma and Christ — the means of salvation and the Saviour. Through karma, the

Act of Christ becomes cosmic law, and through the Christ-Principle karma achieves its aim — the liberation of conscious souls and their identification with God. Karma is gradual redemption, Christ is the Redeemer.

If men would steep themselves in these ideas, they would realise that they belong to one another; they would understand the law recognised in all true occult brotherhoods — namely that each individual suffers and lives for others. There will come a time in the future when outer redemption will coincide in each man with the interior act of the Redeemer. It is not revelation but truth which makes men free: "You shall know the Truth and the Truth shall make you free."

The path of evolution leads to freedom. When man has awakened in himself all those qualities which were prophetically manifest in the Christ, he will be a free being. For if necessity is the law of the material world, freedom is the law of the spiritual world. Freedom is only acquired step by step and it will not be fully manifest in man until the end of his evolution, when his nature will be truly spiritualised.

The Apocalypse

It has been said many times in the course of these lectures that Christianity marks the turning point of human evolution. All the religions have their raison d'etre and have been partial manifestations of the Logos, but none have changed the world so deeply as Christianity. — Those who 'have not seen' are those who have not known the Mysteries. Through Christianity, certain fundamental teachings of the ancient Mysteries — for instance those which dealt with morality, the immortality of the soul by Resurrection or the 'second birth' — were given to the whole world.

Before Christianity, supersensible truth was revealed in the rites and dramatic ritual of the Mysteries. Since then, we have believed in it as it was revealed in the Divine Personality of Christ. But in every epoch there has been a difference between esoteric truth as known to the Initiates and its exoteric form which has been adapted to the multitude and expressed in the religions. The same applies to Christianity. What is written in the Gospels is the message, the good tidings announced to all the world. But there was a more profound teaching; it is contained in the Apocalypse in the form of symbols

There is a way of reading the Apocalypse which only now can be made public. But it was practised in the Middle Ages, in the occult schools of the Rosicrucians. They paid less attention to the historic aspect of the writing, the question of its author and all the problems which occupy the minds of modern theologians who only seek to discover the outer, historical circumstances. Theology today only knows the shell of the Apocalypse and has neglected its essence and core. The Rosicrucians were concerned with the prophetic utterances, with the eternal truths.

Occultism in general is not concerned with the history of a single evolutionary cycle or period but with the inner history of human evolution as a whole. True, occultism is at pains to discover the first manifestations of the life of our planetary system and the earlier stages of man's existence, but it looks forward through the millennia to a divine humanity, to a time when the Earth herself will have changed in substance and in form. Is it possible to predict the far distant future? It is indeed possible, because all that has finally to become physical in the future, already exists in germ, in archetypal form. The plan of evolution is contained in archetypal thought. Nothing comes into being in the physical world which in its broad lines has not been foreseen and prefigured in the devachanic world.

Individual freedom and power of initiative depends upon the manner of the realisation of this truth.

Esoteric Christianity is not based upon vague and sentimental idealism, but upon a realisation born of a knowledge of the higher worlds. Such was the knowledge possessed by the author of the Apocalypse, the Seer of Patmos, who gave a picture of the future of humanity.

Let us try to envisage this future in the light of the cosmological principles which we have been studying in these lectures. Certain visions of the past and also of the future were revealed to the pupils in the Rosicrucian Schools and then, in order that they might interpret these visions, they were told to study the Apocalypse. We will proceed in the same way and consider how man has gradually become what he is today and what lies before him in the future. We have spoken of the ancient continent of Atlantis, and of the Atlanteans who had only a primitive consciousness of the 'I' towards the end of their period. The Post-Atlantean civilisations were as follows:

1. Pre-Vedic civilisation in the south of Asia and in India-the beginning of Aryan culture.

2. The epoch of Zoroaster, comprising the civilisation of ancient Persia. 3 . Egyptian civilisation (including the Chaldean and Semitic). The first germs of Christianity were laid down in this epoch among the Hebrew peoples.

4. Graeco-Roman civilisation, the era of the birth of Christianity.

5. A new epoch commenced at the time of the migrations of the peoples and of the invasions.

The heritage of the Graeco-Roman civilisation was taken over by the races of the North: the Celts, the Germanic peoples and the Slavs. We ourselves are living in this epoch. It is a later transformation of the Graeco-Roman culture, brought about by the invigorating impulses of new races under the influence of Christianity mingled with the leaven of the East which was brought into Europe by the Arabs. The essential mission of this epoch of civilisation is to adapt man to the physical plane to develop reason and practical logic, to immerse intelligence in physical matter so that matter may be understood and finally mastered. In this hard and difficult task which is reaching its culminating point in our own day, man has temporarily forgotten the higher worlds whence he came. If we compare our intellectuality with that of the Chaldeans, for example, it is easy to see how much we have acquired and yet how much we have lost. When a Chaldean Magus looked at the sky — which for us simply presents problems of heavenly mechanics — his feelings were quite different from ours. Whereas modern astronomy is concerned with calculations and abstractions, the Magus of old Chaldea sensed the deep harmony of the heavens as that of a living and divine

Being. When he looked at Mercury, Venus, Moon or Sun, he not only perceived the physical light of these celestial bodies; he perceived their souls and he knew that his own soul was in communion with these mighty souls of the heavens. Their forces of attraction or repulsion seemed to be a marvelous symphony of divine will; the music of the macrocosm sounded in his being. Thus the 'Music of the Spheres' was a reality uniting man to the heavens. The superiority of the scholar in our modern age lies in a knowledge of the physical world, of mineral matter. What was once spiritual knowledge has descended to the physical world, to the world we know so well. But from now onwards we must strive to reach a knowledge of the astral world and of the world of pure Spirit by true clairvoyance.

This descent into materialism was necessary in order that the fifth epoch might fulfil its mission. It was essential that astral and spiritual clairvoyance should grow dim in order that the intellect might develop by dint of precise, minute and mathematical observation of the physical world. Physical Science must be supplemented by Spiritual Science. Here is an example: Comparisons are often made between Ptolemy's chart of the heavens and that of Copernicus. It is said that Ptolemy's chart is erroneous. Now this in itself is not correct. Both are true from different points of view. Ptolemy's chart is concerned with the astral world where the Earth is seen in the centre of the planets, including the Sun. The map of the heavens given by Copernicus was prepared from the point of view of the physical world — the Sun is at the centre of the solar system. The significance of Ptolemy's system will be recognised again in ages to come.

Our fifth epoch will be followed by another, the sixth. This sixth epoch will see the development of brotherhood among men, clairvoyance and creative power. What will Christianity be in the sixth epoch? To the priest in the Mysteries before Christ, there was harmony between science and faith. Science and faith were one and the same. When he looked up to the heavens, the priest knew that the soul was a drop of water from the celestial ocean, led down to Earth by the great streams of life flowing through space. Now that the attention of men is wholly directed to the physical world, faith has need of a refuge, of religion. Hence the separation between science and faith. Faith in the Person of Christ, of the God-Man on Earth has temporarily replaced Occult Science and the Mysteries of antiquity. But in the sixth epoch, the two streams will again unite. Mechanical science will become spiritually creative. This will be Gnosis-spiritual consciousness. This sixth epoch which will be radically different from our own, will be preceded by mighty cataclysms. It will be as spiritual as ours has been material. But the transformation can only be brought about by physical catastrophes. The sixth epoch will prepare for a seventh epoch. This seventh epoch will be the end of the Post-Atlantean civilisations and conditions of earthly life will be entirely different from those we know. At the end of the seventh epoch there will be a revolution of the elements analogous to that which put an end to Atlantis, and the subsequent eras will know a spirituality prepared by the two preceding Post-Atlantean periods.

Thus there are seven great epochs of Aryan civilisation in which the laws of evolution slowly come to expression. At first, man has within him what he later sees around him. All that is actually around us now, passed out from us in a preceding epoch when our being was still mingled with the Earth, Moon and Sun. This cosmic being from whom the man of today and all the kingdoms of nature have issued, is referred to in the Cabala as Adam-Cadmon. Adam-Cadmon embraced all the manifold aspects of man as we know him today in the various races and peoples.

All that lives today in the inner being of man, his thoughts, his feelings, will find expression in the outer world and become his surroundings. The future lies within man. He is free to make it good or evil. Just as he has already left the animal kingdom behind him, so the evil in him today will form a race of degenerate beings. In our age man can to a certain extent hide the good or evil within him. But a time will come when he will no longer be able to do so, when the good and the evil will be written in indelible characters upon his countenance, upon his body, nay even upon the very face of the Earth.

Humanity will then divide into two races. Just as today we see rocks or animals, in that future age we shall encounter beings who are wholly evil, wholly ugly. In our time it is only the clairvoyant who is able to see moral goodness or moral ugliness in human beings. But when man's very features express his karma, human beings will divide into groups of themselves, according to the stream to which they manifestly belong, according to whether the lower nature has been conquered or whether it has conquered the Spirit. This differentiation is beginning to operate little by little. When we derive understanding of the future from the past, and strive to realise the ideal of this future, its plan begins to unfold before us. A new race will come into being to be the link between the man of the present and the spiritual man of the future.

It was taught in Manicheism that from our age onwards the souls of men would begin to transmute into good the evil which will manifest in full force in the sixth epoch. In other words: human souls must be strong enough to bring good out of evil by a process of spiritual alchemy.

When the Earth begins to recapitulate the previous phases of its evolution, there will first be a re-union with the Moon, and then of this Earth-Moon with the Sun. The re-union with the Moon will mark the culminating point of evil on the Earth; the re-union with the Sun will signify, on the other hand, the advent of happiness, the reign of the 'elect.' Man will bear the signs of the seven great phases of the Earth. The Book with the Seven Seals, spoken of in the Apocalypse, will be opened. The Woman clothed with the Sun who has the Moon under her feet, refers to the age when the Earth will once again be united with Sun and Moon. The Trumpets of Judgment will sound for the Earth will have passed into the Devachanic condition where the ruling principle is not light but sound. The hallmark of the end of earthly existence will be that the Christ-Principle permeates all humanity. Having become like unto Christ, men will gather around Him as the hosts around the Lamb, and the great harvest of evolution will constitute the new Jerusalem.

Intuitive Thinking as a Spiritual Path

Conscious Human Action

IS man in his thinking and acting a spiritually free being, or is he compelled by the iron necessity of purely natural law? There are few questions upon which so much sagacity has been brought to bear. The idea of the freedom of the human will has found enthusiastic supporters and stubborn opponents in plenty. There are those who, in their moral fervor, label anyone a man of limited intelligence who can deny so patent a fact as freedom. Opposed to them are others who regard it as the acme of unscientific thinking for anyone to believe that the uniformity of natural law is broken in the sphere of human action and thinking. One and the same thing is thus proclaimed, now as the most precious possession of humanity, now as its most fatal illusion. Infinite subtlety has been employed to explain how human freedom can be consistent with the laws working in nature, of which man, after all, is a part. No less is the trouble to which others have gone to explain how such a delusion as this could have arisen. That we are dealing here with one of the most important questions for life, religion, conduct, science, must be felt by anyone who includes any degree of thoroughness at all in his make-up. It is one of the sad signs of the superficiality of present-day thought that a book which attempts to develop a new faith out of the results of recent scientific research, has nothing more to say on this question than these words: With the question of the freedom of the human will we are not concerned. The alleged freedom of indifferent choice has been recognized as an empty illusion by every philosophy worthy of the name. The moral valuation of human action and character remains untouched by this problem. It is not because I consider that the book in which it occurs has any special importance that I quote this passage, but because it seems to me to express the view to which the thinking of most of our contemporaries manages to rise in this matter. Everyone who claims to have grown beyond the kindergarten stage of science appears to know nowadays that freedom cannot consist in choosing, at one's pleasure, one or other of two possible courses of action. There is always, so we are told, a perfectly definite reason why, out of several possible actions, we carry out just one and no other. This seems obvious. Nevertheless, down to the present day, the main attacks of the opponents of freedom are directed only against freedom of choice. Even Herbert Spencer, whose doctrines are gaining ground daily, says, That everyone is at liberty to desire or not to desire, which is the real proposition involved in the dogma of free will, is negated as much by the analysis of consciousness, as by the contents of the preceding chapter. Others, too, start from the same point of view in combating the concept of free will. The germs of all the relevant arguments are to be found as early as Spinoza. All that he brought forward in clear and simple language against the idea of freedom has since been repeated times without number, but as a rule enveloped in the most hair-splitting theoretical doctrines, so that it is difficult to recognize the straightforward train of thought which is all that matters. Spinoza writes in a letter of October or November, 1674, I call a thing free which exists and acts from the pure necessity of its nature, and I call that unfree, of which the being and action are precisely and fixedly determined by something else. Thus, for example, God, though necessary, is free because he exists only through the necessity of his own nature. Similarly, God cognizes himself and all else freely, because it follows solely from the necessity of his nature that he cognizes all. You see, therefore, that for me freedom consists not in free decision, but in free necessity. But let us come down to created things which are all determined by external causes to exist and to act in a fixed and definite manner. To perceive this more clearly, let us imagine a perfectly simple case. A stone, for example, receives from an external cause acting upon it a certain quantity of motion, by reason of which it necessarily continues to move, after the impact of the external cause has ceased. The continued motion of the stone is due to compulsion, not to the necessity of its own nature, because it requires to be defined by the thrust of an external cause. What is true here for the stone is true also for every other particular thing, however complicated and many-sided it may be, namely, that everything is necessarily determined by external causes to exist and to act in a fixed and definite manner. Now, please, suppose that this stone during its motion thinks and knows that it is striving to the best of its ability to continue in motion. This stone, which is conscious only of its striving and is by no means indifferent, will believe that it is absolutely free, and that it continues in motion for no other reason than its own will to continue. But this is just the human freedom that everybody claims to possess and which consists in nothing but this, that men are conscious of their desires, but ignorant of the causes by which they are determined. Thus the child believes that he desires milk of his own free will, the angry boy regards his desire for vengeance as free, and the coward his desire for flight. Again, the drunken man believes that he says of his own free will what, sober again, he would fain have left unsaid, and as this prejudice is innate in all men, it is difficult to free oneself from it. For, although experience teaches us often enough that man least of all can temper his desires, and that, moved by conflicting passions, he sees the better and pursues the worse, yet he considers himself free because there are some things which he desires less strongly, and some desires which he can easily inhibit through the recollection of something else which it is often possible to recall. Because this view is so clearly and definitely expressed it is easy to detect the fundamental error that it contains. The same necessity by which a stone makes a definite movement as the result of an impact, is said to compel a man to carry out an action when impelled thereto by any reason. It is only because man is conscious of his action that he thinks himself to be its originator. But in doing so he overlooks the fact that he is driven by a cause which he cannot help obeying. The error in this train of thought is soon discovered. Spinoza, and all who think like him, overlook the fact that man not only is conscious of his action, but also may become conscious of the causes which guide him. Nobody will deny that the child is unfree when he desires milk, or the drunken man when he says things which he later regrets. Neither knows anything of the causes, working in the depths of their organisms, which exercise irresistible control over them. But is it justifiable to lump together actions of this kind with those in which a man is conscious not only of his actions but also of the reasons which cause him to act? Are the actions of men really all of one kind? Should the act of a soldier on the field of battle, of the scientific researcher in his laboratory, of the statesman in the most complicated diplomatic negotiations, be placed scientifically on the same level with that of the child when it desires milk: It is no doubt true that it is best to seek the solution of a problem where the conditions are simplest. But inability to discriminate has before now caused endless confusion. There is, after all, a profound difference between knowing why I am acting and not knowing it. At first sight this seems a self-evident truth. And yet the opponents of freedom never ask themselves whether a motive of action which I recognize and see through, is to be regarded as compulsory for me in the same sense as the organic process which causes the child to cry for milk. Eduard von Hartmann asserts that the human will depends on two chief factors, the motives and the character. If one regards men as all alike, or at any rate the differences between them as negligible, then their will appears as determined from without, that is to say, by the circumstances which come to meet them. But if one bears in mind that a man adopts an idea, or mental picture, as the motive of his action only if his character is such that this mental picture arouses a desire in him, then he appears as determined from within and not from without. Now because, in accordance with his character, he must first adopt as a motive a mental picture given to him from without, a man believes he is free, that is, independent of external impulses. The truth, however, according to Eduard von Hartmann, is that even though we ourselves first adopt a mental picture as a motive, we do so not arbitrarily, but according to the necessity of our characterological disposition, that is, we are anything but free. Here again the difference between motives which I allow to influence me only after I have permeated them with my consciousness, and those which I follow without any clear knowledge of them, is absolutely ignored. This leads us straight to the standpoint from which the subject will be considered here. Have we any right to consider the question of the freedom of the will by itself at all? And if not, with what other question must it necessarily be connected? If there is a difference between a conscious motive of action and an unconscious urge, then the conscious motive will result in an action which must be judged differently from one that springs from blind impulse. Hence our first question will concern this difference, and on the result of this enquiry will depend what attitude we shall have to take towards the question of freedom proper. What does it mean to have knowledge of the reasons for one's action? Too little attention has been paid to this question because, unfortunately, we have torn into two what is really an inseparable whole: Man. We have distinguished between the knower and the doer and have left out of account precisely the one who matters most of all — the knowing doer. It is said that man is free when he is controlled only by his reason and not by his animal passions. Or again, that to be free means to be able to determine one's life and action by purposes and deliberate decisions. Nothing is gained by assertions of this sort. For the question is just whether reason, purposes, and decisions exercise the same kind of compulsion over a man as his animal passions. If without my co-operation, a rational decision emerges in me with the same necessity with which hunger and thirst arise, then I must needs obey it, and my freedom is an illusion. Another form of expression runs: to be free does not mean to be able to want as one wills, but to be able to do as one wills. This thought has been expressed with great clearness by the poet-philosopher Robert Hamerling. Man can certainly do as he wills, but he cannot want as he wills, because his wanting is determined by motives. He cannot want as he wills? Let us consider these phrases more closely. Have they any intelligible meaning: Freedom of will would then mean being able to want without ground, without motive. But what does wanting mean if not to have grounds for doing, or trying to do, this rather than that: To want something without ground or motive would be to want something without wanting it. The concept of wanting cannot be divorced from the concept of motive. Without a determining motive the will is an empty faculty; only through the motive does it become active and real. It is, therefore, quite true that the human will is not "free" inasmuch as its direction is always determined by the strongest motive. But on the other hand it must be admitted that it is absurd, in contrast with this "unfreedom", to speak of a conceivable freedom of the will which would consist in being able to want what one does not want. Here again, only motives in general are mentioned, without taking into account the difference between unconscious and conscious motives. If a motive affects me, and I am compelled to act on it because it proves to be the "strongest" of its kind, then the thought of freedom ceases to have any meaning. How should it matter to me whether I can do a thing or not, if I am forced by the motive to do it? The primary question is not whether I can do a thing or not when a motive has worked upon me, but whether there are any motives except such as impel me with absolute necessity. If I am compelled to want something, then I may well be absolutely indifferent as to whether I can also do it. And if, through my character, or through circumstances prevailing in my environment, a motive is forced on me which to my thinking is unreasonable, then I should even have to be glad if I could not do what I want. The question is not whether I can carry out a decision once made, but how the decision comes about within me. What distinguishes man from all other organic beings arises from his rational thinking. Activity he has in common with other organisms. Nothing is gained by seeking analogies in the animal world to clarify the concept of freedom as applied to the actions of human beings. Modern science loves such analogies. When scientists have succeeded in finding among animals something similar to human behavior, they believe they have touched on the most important question of the science of man. To what misunderstandings this view leads is seen, for example, in the book The Illusion of Freewill, by P. Rée, where the following remark on freedom appears: It is easy to explain why the movement of a stone seems to us necessary, while the volition of a donkey does not. The causes which set the stone in motion are external and visible, while the causes which determine the donkey's volition are internal and invisible. Between us and the place of their activity there is the skull of the ass. ... The determining causes are not visible and therefore thought to be non-existent. The volition, it is explained, is, indeed, the cause of the donkey's turning round, but is itself unconditioned; it is an absolute beginning. Here again human actions in which there is a consciousness of the motives are simply ignored, for Rée declares that "between us and the place of their activity there is the skull of the ass." To judge from these words, it has not dawned on Rée that there are actions, not indeed of the ass, but of human beings, in which between us and the action lies the motive that has become conscious. Rée demonstrates his blindness once again, a few pages further on, when he says,

We do not perceive the causes by which our will is determined, hence we think it is not causally determined at all.

But enough of examples which prove that many argue against freedom without knowing in the least what freedom is.

That an action, of which the agent does not know why he performs it, cannot be free, goes without saying. But what about an action for which the reasons are known? This leads us to the question of the origin and meaning of thinking. For without the recognition of the thinking activity of the soul, it is impossible to form a concept of knowledge about anything, and therefore of knowledge about an action. When we know what thinking in general means, it will be easy to get clear about the role that thinking plays in human action. As Hegel rightly says,

It is thinking that turns the soul, which the animals also possess, into spirit.

Hence it will also be thinking that gives to human action its characteristic stamp.

On no account should it be said that all our action springs only from the sober deliberations of our reason. I am very far from calling human in the highest sense only those actions that proceed from abstract judgment. But as soon as our conduct rises above the sphere of the satisfaction of purely animal desires, our motives are always permeated by thoughts. Love, pity, and patriotism are driving forces for actions which cannot be analysed away into cold concepts of the intellect. It is said that here the heart, the mood of the soul, hold sway. No doubt. But the heart and the mood of the soul do not create the motives. They presuppose them and let them enter. Pity enters my heart when the mental picture of a person who arouses pity appears in my consciousness. The way to the heart is through the head, Love is no exception. Whenever it is not merely the expression of bare sexual instinct, it depends on the mental picture we form of the loved one. And the more idealistic these mental pictures are, just so much the more blessed is our love. Here too, thought is the father of feeling. It is said that love makes us blind to the failings of the loved one. But this can be expressed the other way round, namely, that it is just for the good qualities that love opens the eyes. Many pass by these good qualities without noticing them. One, however, perceives them, and just because he does, love awakens in his soul. What else has he done but made a mental picture of what hundreds have failed to see? Love is not theirs, because they lack the mental picture.

However we approach the matter, it becomes more and more clear that the question of the nature of human action presupposes that of the origin of thinking. I shall, therefore, turn next to this question

The Fundamental Desire for Knowledge

Two souls reside, alas, within my breast,
And each one from the other would be parted.
The one holds fast, in sturdy lust for love,
With clutching organs clinging to the world;
The other strongly rises from the gloom
To lofty fields of ancient heritage.
Faust I, Scene 2, lines 1112-1117.

    In these words Goethe expresses a characteristic feature which is deeply rooted in human nature. Man is not organized as a self-consistent unity. He always demands more than the world, of its own accord, gives him. Nature has endowed us with needs; among them are some that she leaves to our own activity to satisfy. Abundant as are the gifts she has bestowed upon us, still more abundant are our desires. We seem born to be dissatisfied. And our thirst for knowledge is but a special instance of this dissatisfaction. We look twice at a tree. The first time we see its branches at rest, the second time in motion. We are not satisfied with this observation. Why, we ask, does the tree appear to us now at rest, now in motion? Every glance at Nature evokes in us a multitude of questions. Every phenomenon we meet sets us a new problem. Every experience is a riddle. We see that from the egg there emerges a creature like the mother animal, and we ask the reason for the likeness. We observe a living being grow and develop to a certain degree of perfection, and we seek the underlying conditions for this experience. Nowhere are we satisfied with what Nature spreads out before our senses. Everywhere we seek what we call the explanation of the facts.

    The something more which we seek in things, over and above what is immediately given to us in them, splits our whole being into two parts. We become conscious of our antithesis to the world. We confront the world as independent beings. The universe appears to us in two opposite parts: I and World.

    We erect this barrier between ourselves and the world as soon as consciousness first dawns in us. But we never cease to feel that, in spite of all, we belong to the world, that there is a connecting link between it and us, and that we are beings within, and not without, the universe.

    This feeling makes us strive to bridge over this antithesis, and in this bridging lies ultimately the whole spiritual striving of mankind. The history of our spiritual life is a continuing search for the unity between ourselves and the world. Religion, art and science follow, one and all, this aim. The religious believer seeks in the revelation which God grants him the solution to the universal riddle which his I, dissatisfied with the world of mere appearance, sets before him. The artist seeks to embody in his material the ideas that are in his I, in order to reconcile what lives in him with the world outside. He too feels dissatisfied with the world of mere appearance and seeks to mould into it that something more which his I, transcending it, contains. The thinker seeks the laws of phenomena, and strives to penetrate by thinking what he experiences by observing. Only when we have made the world-content into our thought-content do we again find the unity out of which we had separated ourselves. We shall see later that this goal can be reached only if the task of the research scientist is conceived at a much deeper level than is often the case. The whole situation I have described here presents itself to us on the stage of history in the conflict between the one-world theory, or monism, and the two-world theory, or dualism.

Dualism pays attention only to the separation between I and World which the consciousness of man has brought about. All its efforts consist in a vain struggle to reconcile these opposites, which it calls now spirit and matter, now subject and object, now thinking and appearance. It feels that there must be a bridge between the two worlds but is not in a position to find it. In that man is aware of himself as "I", he cannot but think of this "I" as being on the side of the spirit; and in contrasting this "I" with the world, he is bound to put on the world's side the realm of percepts given to the senses, that is, the world of matter. In doing so, man puts himself right into the middle of this antithesis of spirit and matter. He is the more compelled to do so because his own body belongs to the material world. Thus the "I", or Ego, belongs to the realm of spirit as a part of it; the material objects and events which are perceived by the senses belong to the "World". All the riddles which relate to spirit and matter, man must inevitably rediscover in the fundamental riddle of his own nature.

Monism pays attention only to the unity and tries either to deny or to slur over the opposites, present though they are. Neither of these two points of view can satisfy us, for they do not do justice to the facts. Dualism sees in spirit (I) and matter (World) two fundamentally different entities, and cannot, therefore, understand how they can interact with one another. How should spirit be aware of what goes on in matter, seeing that the essential nature of matter is quite alien to spirit? Or how in these circumstances should spirit act upon matter, so as to translate its intentions into actions? The most ingenious and the most absurd hypotheses have been propounded to answer these questions. Up to the present, however, monism is not in a much better position. It has tried three different ways of meeting the difficulty. Either it denies spirit and becomes materialism; or it denies matter in order to seek its salvation in spiritualism; or it asserts that even in the simplest entities in the world, spirit and matter are indissolubly bound together so that there is no need to marvel at the appearance in man of these two modes of existence, seeing that they are never found apart.

Materialism can never offer a satisfactory explanation of the world. For every attempt at an explanation must begin with the formation of thoughts about the phenomena of the world. Materialism thus begins with the thought of matter or material processes. But, in doing so, it is already confronted by two different sets of facts: the material world, and the thoughts about it. The materialist seeks to make these latter intelligible by regarding them as purely material processes. He believes that thinking takes place in the brain, much in the same way that digestion takes place in the animal organs. Just as he attributes mechanical and organic effects to matter, so he credits matter in certain circumstances with the capacity to think. He overlooks that, in doing so, he is merely shifting the problem from one place to another. He ascribes the power of thinking to matter instead of to himself. And thus he is back again at his starting point. How does matter come to think about its own nature? Why is it not simply satisfied with itself and content just to exist? The materialist has turned his attention away from the definite subject, his own I, and has arrived at an image of something quite vague and indefinite. Here the old riddle meets him again. The materialistic conception cannot solve the problem; it can only shift it from one place to another.

What of the spiritualistic theory? The genuine spiritualist denies to matter all independent existence and regards it merely as a product of spirit. But when he tries to use this theory to solve the riddle of his own human nature, he finds himself driven into a corner. Over against the "I" or Ego, which can be ranged on the side of spirit, there stands directly the world of the senses. No spiritual approach to it seems open. Only with the help of material processes can it be perceived and experienced by the "I". Such material processes the "I" does not discover in itself so long as it regards its own nature as exclusively spiritual. In what it achieves spiritually by its own effort, the sense-perceptible world is never to be found. It seems as if the "I" had to concede that the world would be a closed book to it unless it could establish a non-spiritual relation to the world. Similarly, when it comes to action, we have to translate our purposes into realities with the help of material things and forces. We are, therefore, referred back to the outer world. The most extreme spiritualist — or rather, the thinker who through his absolute idealism appears as extreme spiritualist — is Johann Gottlieb Fichte. He attempts to derive the whole edifice of the world from the "I". What he has actually accomplished is a magnificent thought-picture of the world, without any content of experience. As little as it is possible for the materialist to argue the spirit away, just as little is it possible for the spiritualist to argue away the outer world of matter.

When man reflects upon the "I", he perceives in the first instance the work of this "I" in the conceptual elaboration of the world of ideas. Hence a world-conception that inclines towards spiritualism may feel tempted, in looking at man's own essential nature, to acknowledge nothing of spirit except this world of ideas. In this way spiritualism becomes one-sided idealism. Instead of going on to penetrate through the world of ideas to the spiritual world, idealism identifies the spiritual world with the world of ideas itself. As a result, it is compelled to remain fixed with its world-outlook in the circle of activity of the Ego, as if bewitched.

A curious variant of idealism is to be found in the view which Friedrich Albert Lange has put forward in his widely read History of Materialism. He holds that the materialists are quite right in declaring all phenomena, including our thinking, to be the product of purely material processes, but, conversely, matter and its processes are for him themselves the product of our thinking.

The senses give us only the effects of things, not true copies, much less the things themselves. But among these mere effects we must include the senses themselves together with the brain and the molecular vibrations which we assume to go on there.

That is, our thinking is produced by the material processes, and these by the thinking of our I. Lange's philosophy is thus nothing more than the story, in philosophical terms, of the intrepid Baron Münchhausen, who holds himself up in the air by his own pigtail.

The third form of monism is the one which finds even in the simplest entity (the atom) both matter and spirit already united. But nothing is gained by this either, except that the question, which really originates in our consciousness, is shifted to another place. How comes it that the simple entity manifests itself in a two-fold manner, if it is an indivisible unity?

Against all these theories we must urge the fact that we meet with the basic and primary opposition first in our own consciousness. It is we ourselves who break away from the bosom of Nature and contrast ourselves as "I" with the "World". Goethe has given classic expression to this in his essay Nature, although his manner may at first sight be considered quite unscientific: "Living in the midst of her (Nature) we are strangers to her. Ceaselessly she speaks to us, yet betrays none of her secrets." But Goethe knows the reverse side too: "Men are all in her and she in all."

However true it may be that we have estranged ourselves from Nature, it is none the less true that we feel we are in her and belong to her. It can be only her own working which pulsates also in us.

We must find the way back to her again. A simple reflection can point this way out to us. We have, it is true, torn ourselves away from Nature, but we must none the less have taken something of her with us into our own being. This element of Nature in us we must seek out, and then we shall find the connection with her once more. Dualism fails to do this. It considers human inwardness as a spiritual entity utterly alien to Nature, and then attempts somehow to hitch it on to Nature. No wonder that it cannot find the connecting link. We can find Nature outside us only if we have first learned to know her within us. What is akin to her within us must be our guide. This marks out our path of enquiry. We shall attempt no speculations concerning the interaction of Nature and spirit. Rather shall we probe into the depths of our own being, to find there those elements which we saved in our flight from Nature.

Investigation of our own being must give us the answer to the riddle. We must reach a point where we can say to ourselves, "Here we are no longer merely 'I', here is something which is more than 'I'."

I am well aware that many who have read thus far will not find my discussion "scientific", as this term is used today. To this I can only reply that I have so far been concerned not with scientific results of any kind, but with the simple description of what every one of us experiences in his own consciousness. The inclusion of a few phrases about attempts to reconcile man's consciousness and the world serves solely to elucidate the actual facts. I have therefore made no attempt to use the various expressions "I", "Spirit", "World", "Nature", in the precise way that is usual in psychology and philosophy. The ordinary consciousness is unaware of the sharp distinctions made by the sciences, and my purpose so far has been solely to record the facts of everyday experience. I am concerned, not with the way in which science, so far, has interpreted consciousness, but with the way in which we experience it in every moment of our lives.

Thinking in the service of Knowledge

WHEN I observe how a billiard ball, when struck, communicates its motion to another, I remain entirely without influence on the course of this observed process. The direction of motion and the velocity of the second ball are determined by the direction and velocity of the first. As long as I remain a mere spectator, I can only say anything about the movement of the second ball when it has taken place. It is quite different when I begin to reflect on the content of my observation. The purpose of my reflection is to form concepts of the occurrence. I connect the concept of an elastic ball with certain other concepts of mechanics, and take into consideration the special circumstances which obtain in the instance in question. I try, in other words, to add to the occurrence which takes place without my assistance a second process which takes place in the conceptual sphere. This latter one is dependent on me. This is shown by the fact that I can rest content with the observation, and renounce all search for concepts if I have no need of them. If however, this need is present, then I am not satisfied until I have brought the concepts Ball, Elasticity, Motion, Impact, Velocity, etc., into a certain connection, to which the observed process is related in a definite way. As surely as the occurrence goes on independently of me, so surely is the conceptual process unable to take place without my assistance.

We shall have to consider later whether this activity of mine really proceeds from my own independent being, or whether those modern physiologists are right who say that we cannot think as we will, but that we must think just as those thoughts and thought-connections determine that happen to be present in our consciousness. For the present we wish merely to establish the fact that we constantly feel obliged to seek for concepts and connections of concepts, which stand in a certain relation to the objects and events which are given independently of us. Whether this activity is really ours or whether we perform it according to an unalterable necessity, is a question we need not decide at present. That it appears in the first instance to be ours is beyond question. We know for certain that we are not given the concepts together with the objects. That I am myself the agent in the conceptual process may be an illusion, but to immediate observation it certainly appears to be so. The question is, therefore: What do we gain by supplementing an event with a conceptual counterpart?

There is a profound difference between the ways in which, for me, the parts of an event are related to one another before, and after, the discovery of the corresponding concepts. Mere observation can trace the parts of a given event as they occur, but their connection remains obscure without the help of concepts. I see the first billiard ball move towards the second in a certain direction and with a certain velocity. What will happen after the impact I must await, and again I can only follow it with my eyes. Suppose someone, at the moment of impact, obstructs my view of the field where the event is taking place, then, as mere spectator, I remain ignorant of what happens afterwards. The situation is different if prior to the obstruction of my view I have discovered the concepts corresponding to the pattern of events. In that case I can say what will happen even when I am no longer able to observe. An event or an object which is merely observed, does not of itself reveal anything about its connection with other events or objects. This connection becomes evident only when observation is combined with thinking.

Observation and thinking are the two points of departure for all the spiritual striving of man, in so far as he is conscious of such striving. The workings of common sense, as well as the most complicated scientific researches, rest on these two fundamental pillars of our spirit. Philosophers have started from various primary antitheses: idea and reality, subject and object, appearance and thing-in-itself, "I" and "Not-I", idea and will, concept and matter, force and substance, the conscious and the unconscious. It is easy to show, however, that all these antitheses must be preceded by that of observation and thinking, this being for man the most important one.

Whatever principle we choose to lay down, we must either prove that somewhere we have observed it, or we must enunciate it in the form of a clear thought which can be re-thought by any other thinker. Every philosopher who sets out to discuss his fundamental principles must express them in conceptual form and thus use thinking. He therefore indirectly admits that his activity presupposes thinking. Whether thinking or something else is the chief factor in the evolution of the world will not be decided at this point. But that without thinking, the philosopher can gain no knowledge of such evolution, is clear from the start. In the occurrence of the world phenomena, thinking may play a minor part; but in the forming of a view about them, there can be no doubt that, its part is a leading one.

As regards observation, our need of it is due to the way we are constituted. Our thinking about a horse and the object "horse" are two things which for us emerge apart from each other. This object is accessible to us only by means of observation. As little as we can form a concept of a horse by merely staring at the animal, just as little are we able by mere thinking to produce a corresponding object.

In sequence of time, observation does in fact come before thinking. For even thinking we must get to know first through observation. It was essentially a description of an observation when, at the beginning of this chapter, we gave an account of how thinking lights up in the presence of an event and goes beyond what is merely presented. Everything that enters the circle of our experience, we first become aware of through observation. The content of sensation, perception and contemplation, all feelings, acts of will, dreams and fancies, mental pictures, concepts and ideas, all illusions and hallucinations, are given to us through observation.

But thinking as an object of observation differs essentially from all other objects. The observation of a table, or a tree, occurs in me as soon as these objects appear upon the horizon of my experience. Yet I do not, at the same time, observe my thinking about these things. I observe the table, and I carry out the thinking about the table, but I do not at the same moment observe this. I must first take up a standpoint outside my own activity if, in addition to observing the table, I want also to observe my thinking about the table. Whereas observation of things and events, and thinking about them, are everyday occurrences filling up the continuous current of my life, observation of the thinking itself is a kind of exceptional state. This fact must be properly taken into account when we come to determine the relationship of thinking to all other contents of observation. We must be quite clear about the fact that, in observing thinking, we are applying to it a procedure which constitutes the normal course of events for the study of the whole of the rest of the world-content, but which in this normal course of events is not applied to thinking itself.

Someone might object that what I have said about thinking applies equally to feeling and to all other spiritual activities. Thus for instance, when I have a feeling of pleasure, the feeling is also kindled by the object, and it is this object that I observe, but not the feeling of pleasure. This objection, however, is based on an error. Pleasure does not stand at all in the same relation to its object as the concept formed by thinking. I am conscious, in the most positive way, that the concept of a thing is formed through my activity; whereas pleasure is produced in me by an object in the same way as, for instance, a change is caused in an object by a stone which falls on it. For observation, a pleasure is given in exactly the same way as the event which causes it. The same is not true of the concept. I can ask why a particular event arouses in me a feeling of pleasure, but I certainly cannot ask why an event produces in me a particular set of concepts. The question would be simply meaningless. In reflecting upon an event, I am in no way concerned with an effect upon myself. I can learn nothing about myself through knowing the concepts which correspond to the observed change in a pane of glass by a stone thrown against it. But I do very definitely learn something about my personality when I know the feeling which a certain event arouses in me. When I say of an observed object, "This is a rose," I say absolutely nothing about myself; but when I say of the same thing that "it gives me a feeling of pleasure," I characterize not only the rose, but also myself in my relation to the rose.

There can, therefore, be no question of putting thinking and feeling on a level as objects of observation. And the same could easily be shown of other activities of the human spirit. Unlike thinking, they must be classed with other observed objects or events. The peculiar nature of thinking lies just in this, that it is an activity which is directed solely upon the observed object and not on the thinking personality. This is apparent even from the way in which we express our thoughts about an object, as distinct from our feelings or acts of will. When I see an object and recognize it as a table, I do not as a rule say, "I am thinking of a table," but, "this is a table." On the other hand, I do say, "I am pleased with the table." In the former case, I am not at all interested in stating that I have entered into a relation with the table; whereas in the latter case, it is just this relation that matters. In saying, "I am thinking of a table," I already enter the exceptional state characterized above, in which something that is always contained — though not as an observed object — within our spiritual activity, is itself made into an object of observation.

This is just the peculiar nature of thinking, that the thinker forgets his thinking while actually engaged in it. What occupies his attention is not his thinking, but the object of his thinking, which he is observing.

The first observation which we make about thinking is therefore this: that it is the unobserved element in our ordinary mental and spiritual life.

The reason why we do not observe the thinking that goes on in our ordinary life is none other than this, that it is due to our own activity. Whatever I do not myself produce, appears in my field of observation as an object; I find myself confronted by it as something that has come about independently of me. It comes to meet me. I must accept it as something that precedes my thinking process, as a premise. While I am reflecting upon the object, I am occupied with it, my attention is focussed upon it. To be thus occupied is precisely to contemplate by thinking. I attend, not to my activity, but to the object of this activity. In other words, while I am thinking I pay no heed to my thinking, which is of my own making, but only to the object of my thinking, which is not of my making.

I am, moreover, in the same position when I enter into the exceptional state and reflect on my own thinking. I can never observe my present thinking; I can only subsequently take my experiences of my thinking process as the object of fresh thinking. If I wanted to watch my present thinking, I should have to split myself into two persons, one to think, the other to observe this thinking. But this I cannot do. I can only accomplish it in two separate acts. The thinking to be observed is never that in which I am actually engaged, but another one. Whether, for this purpose, I make observations of my own former thinking, or follow the thinking process of another person, or finally, as in the example of the motions of the billiard balls, assume an imaginary thinking process, is immaterial.

There are two things which are incompatible with one another: productive activity and the simultaneous contemplation of it. This is recognized even in Genesis (1, 31). Here God creates the world in the first six days, and only when it is there is any contemplation of it possible: "And God saw everything that he had made and, behold, it was very good." The same applies to our thinking. It must be there first, if we would observe it.

The reason why it is impossible to observe thinking in the actual moment of its occurrence, is the very one which makes it possible for us to know it more immediately and more intimately than any other process in the world. Just because it is our own creation do we know the characteristic features of its course, the manner in which the process takes place. What in all other spheres of observation can be found only indirectly, namely, the relevant context and the relationship between the individual objects, is, in the case of thinking, known to us in an absolutely direct way. I do not on the face of it know why, for my observation, thunder follows lightning; but I know directly, from the very content of the two concepts, why my thinking connects the concept of thunder with the concept of lightning. It does not matter in the least whether I have the right concepts of lightning and thunder. The connection between those concepts that I do have is clear to me, and this through the very concepts themselves.

This transparent clearness concerning our thinking process is quite independent of our knowledge of the physiological basis of thinking. Here I am speaking of thinking in so far as we know it from the observation of our own spiritual activity. How one material process in my brain causes or influences another while I am carrying out a thinking operation, is quite irrelevant. What I observe about thinking is not what process in my brain connects the concept lightning with the concept thunder but what causes me to bring the two concepts into a particular relationship. My observation shows me that in linking one thought with another there is nothing to guide me but the content of my thoughts; I am not guided by any material processes in my brain. In a less materialistic age than our own, this remark would of course be entirely superfluous. Today, however, when there are people who believe that once we know what matter is we shall also know how it thinks, we do have to insist that one may talk about thinking without trespassing on the domain of brain physiology.

Many people today find it difficult to grasp the concept of thinking in its purity. Anyone who challenges the description of thinking which I have given here by quoting Cabanis' statement that "the brain secretes thoughts as the liver does gall or the spittle-glands spittle ...", simply does not know what I am talking about. He tries to find thinking by a process of mere observation in the same way that we proceed in the case of other objects that make up the world. But he cannot find it in this way because, as I have shown, it eludes just this ordinary observation. Whoever cannot transcend materialism lacks the ability to bring about the exceptional condition I have described, in which he becomes conscious of what in all other spiritual activity remains unconscious. If someone is not willing to take this standpoint, then one can no more discuss thinking with him than one can discuss color with a blind man. But in any case he must not imagine that we regard physiological processes as thinking. He fails to explain thinking because he simply does not see it.

For everyone, however, who has the ability to observe thinking — and with good will every normal man has this ability — this observation is the most important one he can possibly make. For he observes something of which he himself is the creator; he finds himself confronted, not by an apparently foreign object, but by his own activity. He knows how the thing he is observing comes into being. He sees into its connections and relationships. A firm point has now been reached from which one can, with some hope of success, seek an explanation of all other phenomena of the world.

The feeling that he had found such a firm point led the father of modern philosophy, Descartes, to base the whole of human knowledge on the principle: I think, therefore I am. All other things, all other events, are there independently of me. Whether they be truth, or illusion, or dream, I know not. There is only one thing of which I am absolutely certain, for I myself give it its certain existence; and that is my thinking. Whatever other origin it may ultimately have, may it come from God or from elsewhere, of one thing I am certain: that it exists in the sense that I myself bring it forth. Descartes had, to begin with, no justification for giving his statement more meaning than this. All that he had any right to assert was that within the whole world content I apprehend myself in my thinking as in that activity which is most uniquely my own. What the attached "therefore I am" is supposed to mean has been much debated. It can have a meaning on one condition only. The simplest assertion I can make of a thing is that it is, that it exists. How this existence can be further defined in the case of any particular thing that appears on the horizon of my experience, is at first sight impossible to say. Each object must first be studied in its relation to others before we can determine in what sense it can be said to exist. An experienced event may be a set of percepts or it may be a dream, an hallucination, or something else. In short, I am unable to say in what sense it exists. I cannot gather this from the event in itself, but I shall find it out when I consider the event in its relation to other things. But here again I cannot know more than just how it stands in relation to these other things. My investigation touches firm ground only when I find an object which exists in a sense which I can derive from the object itself. But I am myself such an object in that I think, for I give to my existence the definite, self-determined content of the thinking activity. From here I can go on to ask whether other things exist in the same or in some other sense.

When we make thinking an object of observation, we add to the other observed contents of the world something which usually escapes our attention. But the way we stand in relation to the other things is in no way altered. We add to the number of objects of observation, but not to the number of methods. While we are observing the other things, there enters among the processes of the world — among which I now include observation — one process which is overlooked. Something is present which is different from all other processes, something which is not taken into account. But when I observe my own thinking, no such neglected element is present. For what now hovers in the background is once more just thinking itself. The object of observation is qualitatively identical with the activity directed upon it. This is another characteristic feature of thinking. When we make it an object of observation, we are not compelled to do so with the help of something qualitatively different, but can remain within the same element.

When I weave an independently given object into my thinking, I transcend my observation, and the question arises: What right have I to do this? Why do I not simply let the object impress itself upon me? How is it possible for my thinking to be related to the object? These are questions which everyone must put to himself who reflects on his own thought processes. But all these questions cease to exist when we think about thinking itself. We then add nothing to our thinking that is foreign to it, and therefore have no need to justify any such addition.

Schelling says, "To know Nature means to create Nature." If we take these words of this bold Nature-philosopher literally, we shall have to renounce for ever all hope of gaining knowledge of Nature. For Nature is there already, and in order to create it a second time, we must first know the principles according to which it has originated. From the Nature that already exists we should have to borrow or crib the fundamental principles for the Nature we want to begin by creating. This borrowing, which would have to precede the creating, would however mean knowing Nature, and this would still be so even if after the borrowing no creation were to take place. The only kind of Nature we could create without first having knowledge of it would be a Nature that does not yet exist.

What is impossible for us with regard to Nature, namely, creating before knowing, we achieve in the case of thinking. Were we to refrain from thinking until we had first gained knowledge of it, we would never come to it at all. We must resolutely plunge right into the activity of thinking, so that afterwards, by observing what we have done, we may gain knowledge of it. For the observation of thinking, we ourselves first create an object; the presence of all other objects is taken care of without any activity on our part.

My contention that we must think before we can examine thinking might easily be countered by the apparently equally valid contention that we cannot wait with digesting until we have first observed the process of digestion. This objection would be similar to that brought by Pascal against Descartes, when he asserted that we might also say, "I walk, therefore I am." Certainly I must go straight ahead with digesting and not wait until I have studied the physiological process of digestion. But I could only compare this with the study of thinking if, after digestion, I set myself not to study it by thinking, but to eat and digest it. It is after all not without reason that, whereas digestion cannot become the object of digestion, thinking can very well become the object of thinking.

This then is indisputable, that in thinking we have got hold of one corner of the whole world process which requires our presence if anything is to happen. And this is just the point upon which everything turns. The very reason why things confront me in such a puzzling way is just that I play no part in their production. They are simply given to me, whereas in the case of thinking I know how it is done. Hence for the study of all that happens in the world there can be no more fundamental starting point than thinking itself.

I should now like to mention a widely current error which prevails with regard to thinking. It is often said that thinking, as it is in itself, is nowhere given to us: the thinking that connects our observations and weaves a network of concepts about them is not at all the same as that which we subsequently extract from the objects of observation in order to make it the object of our study. What we first weave unconsciously into the things is said to be quite different from what we consciously extract from them again.

Those who hold this view do not see that it is impossible in this way to escape from thinking. I cannot get outside thinking when I want to study it. If we want to distinguish between thinking before we have become conscious of it, and thinking of which we have subsequently become aware, we should not forget that this distinction is a purely external one which has nothing to do with the thing itself. I do not in any way alter a thing by thinking about it. I can well imagine that a being with quite differently constructed sense organs and with a differently functioning intelligence, would have a very different mental picture of a horse from mine, but I cannot imagine that my own thinking becomes something different through the fact that I observe it. I myself observe what I myself produce. Here we are not talking of how my thinking looks to an intelligence other than mine, but of how it looks to me. In any case the picture of my thinking which another intelligence might have cannot be a truer one than my own. Only if I were not myself the being doing the thinking, but if the thinking were to confront me as the activity of a being quite foreign to me, might I then say that although my own picture of the thinking may arise in a particular way, what the thinking of that being may be like in itself, I am quite unable to know.

So far, there is not the slightest reason why I should regard my own thinking from any point of view other than my own. After all, I contemplate the rest of the world by means of thinking. Why should I make my thinking an exception?

I believe I have give sufficient reasons for making thinking the starting point for my study of the world. When Archimedes had discovered the lever, he thought he could lift the whole cosmos from its hinges, if only he could find a point of support for his instrument. He needed something that was supported by itself and by nothing else. In thinking we have a principle which subsists through itself. Let us try, therefore, to understand the world starting from this basis. We can grasp thinking by means of itself. The question is, whether we can also grasp anything else through it.

I have so far spoken of thinking without taking account of its vehicle, human consciousness. Most present-day philosophers would object that before there can be thinking, there must be consciousness. Hence we ought to start, not from thinking, but from consciousness. There is no thinking, they say, without consciousness. To this I must reply that in order to clear up the relation between thinking and consciousness, I must think about it. Hence I presuppose thinking. Nevertheless one could still argue that although, when the philosopher tries to understand consciousness he makes use of thinking and to that extent presupposes it, yet in the ordinary course of life thinking does arise within consciousness and therefore presupposes consciousness.

Now if this answer were given to the world creator when he was about to create thinking, it would doubtless be to the point. Naturally it is not possible to create thinking before consciousness. The philosopher, however, is not concerned with creating the world but with understanding it. Accordingly he has to seek the starting points not for the creation of the world but for the understanding of it. It seems to me very strange that the philosopher should be reproached for troubling himself first and foremost about the correctness of his principles instead of turning straight to the objects which he seeks to understand. The world creator had above all to know how to find a vehicle for thinking, but the philosopher has to seek a secure foundation for his attempts to understand what already exists. How does it help us to start with consciousness and subject it to the scrutiny of thinking, if we do not first know whether thinking is in fact able to give us insight into things at all?

We must first consider thinking quite impartially, without reference to a thinking subject or a thought object. For both subject and object are concepts formed by thinking. There is no denying that before anything else can be understood, thinking must be understood. Whoever denies this fails to realize that man is not the first link in the chain of creation but the last. Hence, in order to explain the world by means of concepts, we cannot start from the elements of existence which came first in time, but we must begin with that element which is given to us as the nearest and most intimate. We cannot at one bound transport ourselves back to the beginning of the world in order to begin our studies from there, but we must start from the present moment and see whether we can ascend from the later to the earlier. As long as Geology invented fabulous catastrophes to account for the present state of the earth, it groped in darkness. It was only when it began to study the processes at present at work on the earth, and from these to argue back to the past, that it gained a firm foundation. As long as

Philosophy goes on assuming all sorts of basic principles, such as atom, motion, matter, will, or the unconscious, it will hang in the air. Only if the philosopher recognizes that which is last in time as his first point of attack, can he reach his goal. This absolutely last thing at which world evolution has arrived is in fact thinking.

There are people who say it is impossible to ascertain with certainty whether our thinking is right or wrong, and thus our starting point is in any case a doubtful one. It would be just as sensible to doubt whether a tree is in itself right or wrong. Thinking is a fact, and it is meaningless to speak of the truth or falsity of a fact. I can, at most, be in doubt as to whether thinking is correctly applied, just as I can doubt whether a certain tree supplies wood adapted to the making of this or that useful object. To show how far the application of thinking to the world is right or wrong, is precisely the task of this book. I can understand anyone doubting whether, by means of thinking, we can gain knowledge of the world, but it is incomprehensible to me how anyone can doubt the rightness of thinking in itself.

The World as Percept

THROUGH thinking, concepts and ideas arise. What a concept is cannot be expressed in words. Words can do no more than draw our attention to the fact that we have concepts. When someone sees a tree, his thinking reacts to his observation, an ideal element is added to the object, and he considers the object and the ideal counterpart as belonging together. When the object disappears from his field of observation, only the ideal counterpart of it remains. This latter is the concept of the object. The more our range of experience is widened, the greater becomes the sum of our concepts. But concepts certainly do not stand isolated from one another. They combine to form a systematically ordered whole. The concept "organism", for instance, links up with those of "orderly development" and "growth". Other concepts which are based on single objects merge together into a unity. All concepts I may form of lions merge into the collective concept "lion". In this way all the separate concepts combine to form a closed conceptual system in which each has its special place. Ideas do not differ qualitatively from concepts. They are but fuller, more saturated, more comprehensive concepts. I must attach special importance to the necessity of bearing in mind, here, that I make thinking my starting point, and not concepts and ideas which are first gained by means of thinking. For these latter already presuppose thinking. My remarks regarding the self-supporting and self-determined nature of thinking cannot, therefore, be simply transferred to concepts. (I make special mention of this, because it is here that I differ from Hegel, who regards the concept as something primary and original.)

Concepts cannot be gained through observation. This follows from the simple fact that the growing human being only slowly and gradually forms the concepts corresponding to the objects which surround him. Concepts are added to observation.

A philosopher widely read at the present day — Herbert Spencer — describes the mental process which we carry out with respect to observation as follows:

If, when walking through the fields some day in September, you hear a rustle a few yards in advance, and on observing the ditch-side where it occurs, see the herbage agitated, you will probably turn towards the spot to learn by what this sound and motion are produced. As you approach there flutters into the ditch a partridge; on seeing which your curiosity is satisfied — you have what you call an explanation of the appearances. The explanation, mark, amounts to this; that whereas throughout life you have had countless experiences of disturbance among small stationary bodies, accompanying the movement of other bodies among them, and have generalized the relation between such disturbances and such movements, you consider this particular disturbance explained on finding it to present an instance of the like relation.

A closer analysis shows matters to stand very differently from the way described above. When I hear a noise, I first look for the concept which fits this observation. It is this concept which first leads me beyond the mere noise. If one thinks no further, one simply hears the noise and is content to leave it at that. But my reflecting makes it clear to me that I have to regard the noise as an effect. Therefore not until I have connected the concept of effect with the perception of the noise, do I feel the need to go beyond the solitary observation and look for the cause. The concept of effect calls up that of cause, and my next step is to look for the object which is being the cause, which I find in the shape of the partridge. But these concepts, cause and effect, I can never gain through mere observation, however many instances the observation may cover. Observation evokes thinking, and it is thinking that first shows me how to link one separate experience to another.

If one demands of a "strictly objective science" that it should take its content from observation alone, then one must at the same time demand that it should forego all thinking. For thinking, by its very nature, goes beyond what is observed.

We must now pass from thinking to the being that thinks; for it is through the thinker that thinking is combined with observation. Human consciousness is the stage upon which concept and observation meet and become linked to one another. In saying this we have in fact characterized this (human) consciousness. It is the mediator between thinking and observation. In as far as we observe a thing it appears to us as given; in as far as we think, we appear to ourselves as being active. We regard the thing as object and ourselves as thinking subject. Because we direct our thinking upon our observation, we have consciousness of objects; because we direct it upon ourselves, we have consciousness of ourselves, or self-consciousness. Human consciousness must of necessity be at the same time self-consciousness because it is a consciousness which thinks. For when thinking contemplates its own activity, it makes its own essential being, as subject, into a thing, as object.

It must, however, not be overlooked that only with the help of thinking am I able to determine myself as subject and contrast myself with objects. Therefore thinking must never be regarded as a merely subjective activity. Thinking lies beyond subject and object. It produces these two concepts just as it produces all others. When, therefore, I, as thinking subject, refer a concept to an object, we must not regard this reference as something purely subjective. It is not the subject that makes the reference, but thinking. The subject does not think because it is a subject; rather it appears to itself as subject because it can think. The activity exercised by man as a thinking being is thus not merely subjective. Rather is it something neither subjective nor objective, that transcends both these concepts.

I ought never to say that my individual subject thinks, but much more that my individual subject lives by the grace of thinking. Thinking is thus an element which leads me out beyond myself and connects me with the objects. But at the same time it separates me from them, inasmuch as it sets me, as subject, over against them.

It is just this which constitutes the double nature of man. He thinks, and thereby embraces both himself and the rest of the world. But at the same time it is by means of thinking that he determines himself as an individual confronting the things.

We must next ask ourselves how that other element, which we have so far simply called the object of observation and which meets the thinking in our consciousness, comes into our consciousness at all.

In order to answer this question we must eliminate from our field of observation everything that has been imported by thinking. For at any moment the content of our consciousness will already be interwoven with concepts in the most varied ways.

We must imagine that a being with fully developed human intelligence originates out of nothing and confronts the world. What it would be aware of, before it sets its thinking in motion, would be the pure content of observation. The world would then appear to this being as nothing but a mere disconnected aggregate of objects of sensation: colors, sounds, sensations of pressure, of warmth, of taste and smell; also feelings of pleasure and pain. This aggregate is the content of pure, unthinking observation. Over against it stands thinking, ready to begin its activity as soon as a point of attack presents itself. Experience shows at once that this does happen. Thinking is able to draw threads from one element of observation to another. It links definite concepts with these elements and thereby establishes a relationship between them. We have already seen how a noise which we hear becomes connected with another observation by our identifying the former as the effect of the latter.

If now we recollect that the activity of thinking is on no account to be considered as merely subjective, then we shall also not be tempted to believe that the relationships thus established by thinking have merely subjective validity.

Our next task is to discover by means of thoughtful reflection what relation the immediately given content of observation mentioned above has to the conscious subject.

The ambiguity of current speech makes it necessary for me to come to an agreement with my readers concerning the use of a word which I shall have to employ in what follows. I shall apply the word "percept" to the immediate objects of sensation enumerated above, in so far as the conscious subject apprehends them through observation. It is, then, not the process of observation but the object of observation which I call the "percept".

I do not choose the term "sensation", since this has a definite meaning in physiology which is narrower than that of my concept of "percept". I can speak of a feeling in myself (emotion) as percept, but not as sensation in the physiological sense of the term. Even my feeling becomes known to me by becoming a percept for me. And the way in which we gain knowledge of our thinking through observation is such that thinking too, in its first appearance for our consciousness, may be called a percept.

The naïve man regards his percepts, such as they appear to his immediate apprehension, as things having an existence wholly independent of him. When he sees a tree he believes in the first instance that it stands in the form which he sees, with the colors of its various parts, and so on, there on the spot towards which his gaze is directed. When the same man sees the sun in the morning appear as a disc on the horizon, and follows the course of this disc, he believes that all this actually exists and happens just as he observes it. To this belief he clings until he meets with further percepts which contradict his former ones. The child who as yet has no experience of distance grasps at the moon, and only corrects its picture of the reality, based on first impressions, when a second percept contradicts the first. Every extension of the circle of my percepts compels me to correct my picture of the world. We see this in everyday life, as well as in the spiritual development of mankind. The picture which the ancients made for themselves of the relation of the earth to the sun and other heavenly bodies had to be replaced by another when Copernicus found that it was not in accordance with some percepts, which in those early days were unknown. A man who had been born blind said, when operated on by Dr. Franz, that the picture of the size of objects which he had formed by his sense of touch before his operation, was a very different one. He had to correct his tactual percepts by his visual percepts.

How is it that we are compelled to make these continual corrections to our observations?

A simple reflection gives the answer to this question. When I stand at one end of an avenue, the trees at the other end, away from me, seem smaller and nearer together than those where I stand. My percept-picture changes when I change the place from which I am looking. Therefore the form in which it presents itself to me is dependent on a condition which is due not to the object but to me, the perceiver. It is all the same to the avenue wherever I stand. But the picture I have of it depends essentially on just this viewpoint. In the same way, it makes no difference to the sun and the planetary system that human beings happen to look at them from the earth; but the percept-picture of the heavens presented to them is determined by the fact that they inhabit the earth. This dependence of our percept-picture on our place of observation is the easiest one to understand. The matter becomes more difficult when we realize how our world of percepts is dependent on our bodily and spiritual organization. The physicist shows us that within the space in which we hear a sound there are vibrations of the air, and also that the body in which we seek the origin of the sound exhibits a vibrating movement of its parts. We perceive this movement as sound only if we have a normally constructed ear. Without this the world would be for ever silent for us. Physiology tells us that there are people who perceive nothing of the magnificent splendor of color which surrounds us. Their percept-picture has only degrees of light and dark. Others are blind only to one color, for example, red. Their world picture lacks this hue, and hence it is actually a different one from that of the average man. I should like to call the dependence of my percept-picture on my place of observation, "mathematical", and its dependence on my organization, "qualitative". The former determines the proportions of size and mutual distances of my percepts, the latter their quality. The fact that I see a red surface as red — this qualitative determination — depends on the organization of my eye.

My percept-pictures, then, are in the first instance subjective. The recognition of the subjective character of our percepts may easily lead us to doubt whether there is any objective basis for them at all. When we realize that a percept, for example that of a red color or of a certain tone, is not possible without a specific structure of our organism, we may easily be led to believe that it has no permanency apart from our subjective organization and that, were it not for our act of perceiving it as an object, it would not exist in any sense. The classical representative of this view is George Berkeley, who held that from the moment we realize the importance of the subject for perception, we are no longer able to believe in the existence of a world without a conscious Spirit.

Some truths there are so near and obvious to the mind that man need only open his eyes to see them. Such I take this important one to be, to wit, that all the choir of heaven and furniture of the earth, in a word, all those bodies which compose the mighty frame of the world, have not any subsistence without a mind, that their being is to be perceived or known; that, consequently, so long as they are not actually perceived by me, or do not exist in my mind or that of any other created spirit, they must either have no existence at all, or else subsist in the mind of some Eternal Spirit.

On this view, when we take away the fact of its being perceived, nothing remains of the percept. There is no color when none is seen, no sound when none is heard. Extension, form, and motion exist as little as color and sound apart from the act of perception. Nowhere do we see bare extension or shape, but these are always bound up with color or some other quality unquestionably dependent upon our subjectivity. If these latter disappear when we cease to perceive them, then the former, being bound up with them, must disappear likewise.

To the objection that there must be things that exist apart from consciousness and to which the conscious percept-pictures are similar, even though figure, color, sound, and so on, have no existence except within the act of perceiving, the above view would answer that a color can be similar only to a color, a figure only to a figure. Our percepts can be similar only to our percepts and to nothing else. Even what we call an object is nothing but a collection of percepts which are connected in a particular way. If I strip a table of its shape, extension, color, etc. — in short, of all that is merely my percept — then nothing remains over. This view, followed up logically, leads to the assertion that the objects of my perceptions exist only through me, and indeed only in as far as, and as long as, I perceive them; they disappear with my perceiving and have no meaning apart from it. Apart from my percepts, I know of no objects and cannot know of any.

No objection can be made to this assertion as long as I am merely referring to the general fact that the percept is partly determined by the organization of myself as subject. The matter would appear very different if we were in a position to say just what part is played by our perceiving in the bringing forth of a percept. We should then know what happens to a percept while it is being perceived, and we should also be able to determine what character it must already possess before it comes to be perceived.

This leads us to turn our attention from the object of perception to the subject of perception. I perceive not only other things, but also myself. The percept of myself contains, to begin with, the fact that I am the stable element in contrast to the continual coming and going of the percept-pictures. The percept of my "I" can always come up in my consciousness while I am having other percepts. When I am absorbed in the perception of a given object I am for the time being aware only of this object. To this the percept of my self can be added. I am then conscious not only of the object but also of my own personality which confronts the object and observes it. I do not merely see a tree, but I also know that it is I who am seeing it. I know, moreover, that something happens in me while I am observing the tree. When the tree disappears from my field of vision, an after-effect of this process remains in my consciousness — a picture of the tree. This picture has become associated with my self during my observation. My self has become enriched; its content has absorbed a new element. This element I call my mental picture of the tree. I should never have occasion to speak of mental pictures did I not experience them in the percept of my own self. Percepts would come and go; I should let them slip by. Only because I perceive my self, and observe that with each percept the content of my self, too, is changed, am I compelled to connect the observation of the object with the changes in my own condition, and to speak of my mental picture.

I perceive the mental picture in my self in the same sense as I perceive color, sound, etc., in other objects. I am now also able to distinguish these other objects that confront me, by calling them the outer world, whereas the content of my percept of my self I call my inner world. The failure to recognize the true relationship between mental picture and object has led to the greatest misunderstandings in modern philosophy. The perception of a change in me, the modification my self undergoes, has been thrust into the foreground, while the object which causes this modification is lost sight of altogether. It has been said that we perceive not objects but only our mental pictures. I know, so it is said, nothing of the table in itself, which is the object of my observation, but only of the change which occurs within me while I am perceiving the table. This view should not be confused with the Berkeleyan theory mentioned above. Berkeley maintains the subjective nature of the content of my percepts, but he does not say that my knowledge is limited to my mental pictures. He limits my knowledge to my mental pictures because, in his opinion, there are no objects apart from mental picturing. What I take to be a table no longer exists, according to Berkeley, when I cease to look at it. This is why Berkeley holds that my percepts arise directly through the omnipotence of God. I see a table because God calls up this percept in me. For Berkeley, therefore, there are no real beings other than God and human spirits. What we call the "world" exists only in these spirits. What the naïve man calls the outer world, or corporeal nature, is for Berkeley non-existent. This theory is confronted by the now predominant Kantian view which limits our knowledge of the world to our mental pictures, not because it is convinced that things cannot exist beyond these mental pictures, but because it believes us to be so organized that we can experience only the changes of our own selves, but not the things-in-themselves that cause these changes. This view concludes from the fact that I know only my mental pictures, not that there is no reality independent of them, but only that the subject cannot directly assimilate such reality. The subject can merely, "through the medium of its subjective thoughts, imagine it, invent it, think it, cognize it, or perhaps even fail to cognize it." This (Kantian) conception believes it gives expression to something absolutely certain, something which is immediately evident, requiring no proof.

The first fundamental proposition which the philosopher must bring to clear consciousness is the recognition that our knowledge, to begin with, is limited to our mental pictures. Our mental pictures are the only things that we know directly, experience directly; and just because we have direct experience of them, even the most radical doubt cannot rob us of our knowledge of them. On the other hand, the knowledge which goes beyond my mental pictures — taking mental pictures here in the widest possible sense, so as to include all psychical processes — is not proof against doubt. Hence, at the very beginning of all philosophizing we must explicitly set down all knowledge which goes beyond mental pictures as being open to doubt.

These are the opening sentences of Volkelt's book on Immanuel Kant's Theory of Knowledge. What is here put forward as an immediate and self-evident truth is in reality the result of a thought operation which runs as follows: The naïve man believes that things, just as we perceive them, exist also outside our consciousness.

Physics, physiology, and psychology, however, seem to teach us that for our percepts our organization is necessary, and that therefore we cannot know anything about external objects except what our organization transmits to us. Our percepts are thus modifications of our organization, not things-in-themselves. This train of thought has in fact been characterized by Eduard von Hartmann as the one which must lead to the conviction that we can have direct knowledge only of our mental pictures. Because, outside our organism, we find vibrations of physical bodies and of the air which are perceived by us as sound, it is concluded that what we call sound is nothing more than a subjective reaction of our organism to these motions in the external world. Similarly, it is concluded that color and warmth are merely modifications of our organism. And, further, these two kinds of percepts are held to be produced in us through processes in the external world which are utterly different from what we experience as warmth or as color. When these processes stimulate the nerves in my skin, I have the subjective percept of warmth; when they stimulate the optic nerve, I perceive light and color. Light, color, and warmth, then, are the responses of my sensory nerves to external stimuli. Even the sense of touch reveals to me, not the objects of the outer world, but only states of my own body. In the sense of modern physics one could somehow think that bodies consist of infinitely small particles called molecules, and that these molecules are not in direct contact, but are at certain distances from one another. Between them, therefore, is empty space. Across this space they act on one another by forces of attraction and repulsion. If I put my hand on a body, the molecules of my hand by no means touch those of the body directly, but there remains a certain distance between body and hand, and what I experience as the body's resistance is nothing but the effect of the force of repulsion which its molecules exert on my hand. I am absolutely external to the body and perceive only its effects on my organism.

In amplification of this discussion, there is the theory of the so-called Specific Nerve Energies, advanced by J. Müller (1801–1858). It asserts that each sense has the peculiarity that it responds to all external stimuli in one particular way only. If the optic nerve is stimulated, perception of light results, irrespective of whether the stimulation is due to what we call light, or whether mechanical pressure or an electric current works upon the nerve. On the other hand, the same external stimulus applied to different senses gives rise to different percepts. The conclusion from these facts seems to be that our senses can transmit only what occurs in themselves, but nothing of the external world. They determine our percepts, each according to its own nature.

Physiology shows that there can be no direct knowledge even of the effects which objects produce on our sense organs. Through following up the processes which occur in our own bodies, the physiologist finds that, even in the sense organs, the effects of the external movement are transformed in the most manifold ways. We can see this most clearly in the case of eye and ear. Both are very complicated organs which modify the external stimulus considerably before they conduct it to the corresponding nerve. From the peripheral end of the nerve the already modified stimulus is then conducted to the brain. Only now can the central organs be stimulated. Therefore it is concluded that the external process undergoes a series of transformations before it reaches consciousness. What goes on in the brain is connected by so many intermediate links with the external process, that any similarity to the latter is out of the question. What the brain ultimately transmits to the soul is neither external processes, nor processes in the sense organs, but only such as occur in the brain. But even these are not perceived directly by the soul. What we finally have in consciousness are not brain processes at all, but sensations. My sensation of red has absolutely no similarity to the process which occurs in the brain when I sense red. The redness, again, only appears as an effect in the soul, and the brain process is merely its cause. This is why Hartmann says, "What the subject perceives, therefore, are always only modifications of his own psychical states and nothing else." When I have the sensations, however, they are as yet very far from being grouped into what I perceive as "things". Only single sensations can be transmitted to me by the brain. The sensations of hardness and softness are transmitted to me by the sense of touch, those of color and light by the sense of sight. Yet all these are to be found united in one and the same object. This unification, therefore, can only be brought about by the soul itself; that is, the soul combines the separate sensations, mediated through the brain, into bodies. My brain conveys to me singly, and by widely different paths, the visual, tactile, and auditory sensations which the soul then combines into the mental picture of a trumpet. It is just this very last link in a process (the mental picture of the trumpet) which for my consciousness is the very first thing that is given. In it nothing can any longer be found of what exists outside me and originally made an impression on my senses. The external object has been entirely lost on the way to the brain and through the brain to the soul.

It would be hard to find in the history of human culture another edifice of thought which has been built up with greater ingenuity, and which yet, on closer analysis, collapses into nothing. Let us look a little closer at the way it has been constructed. One starts with what is given in naïve consciousness, with the thing as perceived. Then one shows that none of the qualities which we find in this thing would exist for us had we no sense organs. No eye — no color. Therefore the color is not yet present in that which affects the eye. It arises first through the interaction of the eye and the object. The latter is, therefore, colorless. But neither is the color in the eye, for in the eye there is only a chemical or physical process which is first conducted by the optic nerve to the brain, and there initiates another process. Even this is not yet the color. That is only produced in the soul by means of the brain process. Even then it does not yet enter my consciousness, but is first transferred by the soul to a body in the external world. There, upon this body, I finally believe myself to perceive it. We have traveled in a complete circle. We became conscious of a colored body. That is the first thing. Here the thought operation starts. If I had no eye, the body would be, for me, colorless. I cannot therefore attribute the color to the body. I start on the search for it. I look for it in the eye — in vain; in the nerve — in vain; in the brain — in vain once more; in the soul — here I find it indeed, but not attached to the body. I find the colored body again only on returning to my starting point. The circle is completed. I believe that I am cognizing as a product of my soul that which the naïve man regards as existing outside him, in space.

As long as one stops here everything seems to fit beautifully. But we must go over the whole thing again from the beginning. Hitherto I have been dealing with something — the external percept — of which, from my naïve standpoint, I have had until now a totally wrong conception. I thought that the percept, just as I perceive it, had objective existence. But now I observe that it disappears together with my mental picture, that it is only a modification of my inner state of soul. Have I, then, any right at all to start from it in my arguments? Can I say of it that it acts on my soul? I must henceforth treat the table, of which formerly I believed that it acted on me and produced a mental picture of itself in me, as itself a mental picture. But from this it follows logically that my sense organs and the processes in them are also merely subjective. I have no right to speak of a real eye but only of my mental picture of the eye. Exactly the same is true of the nerve paths, and the brain process, and no less of the process in the soul itself, through which things are supposed to be built up out of the chaos of manifold sensations. If, assuming the truth of the first circle of argumentation, I run through the steps of my act of cognition once more, the latter reveals itself as a tissue of mental pictures which, as such, cannot act on one another. I cannot say that my mental picture of the object acts on my mental picture of the eye, and that from this interaction my mental picture of color results. Nor is it necessary that I should say this. For as soon as I see clearly that my sense organs and their activity, my nerve and soul processes, can also be known to me only through perception, the train of thought which I have outlined reveals itself in its full absurdity. It is quite true that I can have no percept without the corresponding sense organ. But just as little can I be aware of a sense organ without perception. From the percept of a table I can pass to the eye which sees it, or the nerves in the skin which touch it, but what takes place in these I can, in turn, learn only from perception. And then I soon notice that there is no trace of similarity between the process which takes place in the eye and the color which I perceive. I cannot eliminate my color percept by pointing to the process which takes place in the eye during this perception. No more can I rediscover the color in the nerve or brain processes. I only add new percepts, localized within the organism, to the first percept, which the naïve man localizes outside his organism. I merely pass from one percept to another.

Moreover there is a gap in the whole argument. I can follow the processes in my organism up to those in my brain, even though my assumptions become more and more hypothetical as I approach the central processes of the brain. The path of external observation ceases with the process in my brain, more particularly with the process which I should observe if I could deal with the brain using the instruments and methods of physics and chemistry. The path of inner observation begins with the sensation, and continues up to the building of things out of the material of sensation. At the point of transition from brain process to sensation, the path of observation is interrupted.

The way of thinking here described, known as critical idealism, in contrast to the standpoint of naïve consciousness known as naïve realism, makes the mistake of characterizing the one percept as mental picture while taking the other in the very same sense as does the naïve realism which it apparently refutes. It wants to prove that percepts have the character of mental pictures by naïvely accepting the percepts connected with one's own organism as objectively valid facts; and over and above this, it fails to see that it confuses two spheres of observation, between which it can find no connection.

Critical idealism can refute naïve realism only by itself assuming, in naïve-realistic fashion, that one's own organism has objective existence. As soon as the idealist realizes that the percepts connected with his own organism are exactly of the same nature as those which naïve realism assumes to have objective existence, he can no longer use those percepts as a safe foundation for his theory. He would have to regard even his own subjective organization as a mere complex of mental pictures. But this removes the possibility of regarding the content of the perceived world as a product of our spiritual organization. One would have to assume that the mental picture "color" was only a modification of the mental picture "eye". So-called critical idealism cannot be proved without borrowing from naïve realism. Naive realism can be refuted only if, in another sphere, its own assumptions are accepted without proof as being valid.

This much, then, is certain: Investigation within the world of percepts cannot establish critical idealism, and consequently, cannot strip percepts of their objective character.

Still less can the principle "the perceived world is my mental picture" be claimed as obvious and needing no proof. Schopenhauer begins his chief work with the words:

The world is my mental picture — this is a truth which holds good for everything that lives and cognizes, though man alone can bring it into reflective and abstract consciousness. If he really does this, he has attained to philosophical discretion. It then becomes clear and certain to him that he knows no sun and no earth, but only an eye that sees a sun, a hand that feels an earth; that the world which surrounds him is there only as mental picture, that is, only in relation to something else, to the one who pictures it, which is he himself. If any truth can be asserted a priori, it is this one, for it is the expression of that form of all possible and thinkable experience which is more universal than all others, than time, space, or causality, for all these presuppose it ...

This whole theory is wrecked by the fact, already mentioned, that the eye and the hand are percepts no less than the sun and the earth. Using Schopenhauer's expressions in his own sense, we could reply: My eye that sees the sun, my hand that feels the earth, are my mental pictures just as much as the sun and the earth themselves. That with this the whole theory cancels itself, is clear without further argument. For only my real eye and my real hand could have the mental pictures "sun" and "earth" as modifications of themselves; the mental pictures "eye" and "hand" cannot have them. Yet it is only of these mental pictures that critical idealism is allowed to speak.

Critical idealism is totally unfitted to form an opinion about the relationship between percept and mental picture. It cannot begin to make the distinction, mentioned above, between what happens to the percept in the process of perception and what must be inherent in it prior to perception. We must, therefore, tackle this problem in another way.

The Act of Knowing the World

FROM the foregoing considerations it follows that it is impossible to prove by investigating the content of our observation that our percepts are mental pictures. Such proof is supposed to be established by showing that, if the process of perceiving takes place in the way in which — on the basis of naïve-realistic assumptions about our psychological and physiological constitution — we imagine that it does, then we have to do, not with things in themselves, but only with our mental pictures of things. Now if naïve realism, when consistently thought out, leads to results which directly contradict its presuppositions, then these presuppositions must be discarded as unsuitable for the foundation of a universal philosophy. In any case, it is not permissible to reject the presuppositions and yet accept the consequences, as the critical idealist does when he bases his assertion that the world is my mental picture on the line of argument already described. (Eduard von Hartmann gives a full account of this line of argument in his work, Das Grundproblem der Erkenntnistheorie.)

The truth of critical idealism is one thing, the force of its proof another. How it stands with the former will appear later on in the course of this book, but the force of its proof is exactly nil. If one builds a house, and the ground floor collapses while the first floor is being built, then the first floor collapses also. Naïve realism and critical idealism is related as ground floor to the first floor in this simile.

For someone who believes that the whole perceived world is only an imagined one, a mental picture, and is in fact the effect upon my soul of things unknown to me, the real problem of knowledge is naturally concerned not with the mental pictures present only in the soul but with the things which are independent of us and which lie outside our consciousness. He asks: How much can we learn about these things indirectly, seeing that we cannot observe them directly? From this point of view, he is concerned not with the inner connection of his conscious percepts with one another but with their causes which transcend his consciousness and exist independently of him, since the percepts, in his opinion, disappear as soon as he turns his senses away from things. Our consciousness, on this view, works like a mirror from which the pictures of definite things disappear the moment its reflecting surface is not turned toward them. If, now, we do not see the things themselves but only their reflections, then we must learn indirectly about the nature of things by drawing conclusions from the behavior of the reflections. Modern science takes this attitude in that it uses percepts only as a last resort in obtaining information about the processes of matter which lie behind them, and which alone really "are." If the philosopher, as critical idealist, admits real existence at all, then his search for knowledge through the medium of mental pictures is directed solely toward this existence. His interest skips over the subjective world of mental pictures and goes straight for what produces these pictures.

The critical idealist can, however, go even further and say: I am confined to the world of my mental pictures and escape from it. If I think of a thing as being behind my mental picture, then thought is again nothing but a mental picture. An idealist of this type will either deny the thing-in-itself entirely or at any rate assert that it has no significance for human beings, in other words, that it is as good as non-existent since we can know nothing of it.

To this kind of critical idealist the whole world seems a dream, in the face of which all striving for knowledge is simply meaningless. For him there can be only two sorts of men: victims of the illusion that their own dream structures are real things, and the wise ones who see through the nothingness of this dream world and who must therefore gradually lose all desire to trouble themselves further about it. From this point of view, even one's own personality may become a mere dream phantom. Just as during sleep there appears among my dream images an image of myself, so in waking consciousness the mental picture of my own I is added to the mental picture of the outer world. We have then given to us in consciousness, not our real I, but only our mental picture of our I. Whoever denies that things exist, or at least that we can know anything of them, must also deny the existence, or at least the knowledge, of one's own personality. The critical idealist then comes to the conclusion that "All reality resolves itself into a wonderful dream, without a life which is dreamed about, and without a spirit which is having the dream; into a dream which hangs together in a dream of itself."

For the person who believes that he recognizes our immediate life to be a dream, it is immaterial whether he postulates nothing more behind this dream or whether he relates his mental pictures to actual things. In both cases life must lose all academic interest for him. But whereas all learning must be meaningless for those who believe that the whole of the accessible universe is exhausted in dreams, yet for others who feel entitled to argue from mental pictures to things, learning will consist in the investigation of these "things-in-themselves." The first of these theories may be called absolute illusionism, the second is called transcendental realism by its most rigorously logical exponent, Eduard von Hartmann.

Both these points of views have this in common with naïve realism, that they seek to gain a footing in the world by means of an investigation of perceptions. Within this sphere, however, they are unable to find a firm foundation.

One of the most important questions for an adherent of transcendental realism would have to be: How does the Ego produce the world of mental pictures out of itself? A world of mental pictures which was given to us, and which disappeared as soon as we shut our senses to the external world, might kindle as earnest desire for knowledge, in so far as it was a means of investigating indirectly the world of the I-in-itself. If the things of our experience were "mental pictures", then our everyday life would be like a dream, and the discovery of the true state of affairs would be like waking. Now our dream images interest us as long as we dream and consequently do not detect their dream character. But as soon as we wake, we no longer look for the inner connections of our dream images among themselves, but rather for the physical, physiological and psychological processes which underlie them. In the same way, a philosopher who holds the world to be his mental picture cannot be interested in the mutual relations of the details within the picture. If he allows for the existence of a real Ego at all, then his question will be, not how one of his mental pictures is linked with another, but what takes place in the independently existing soul while a certain train of mental pictures passes through his consciousness. If I dream that I am drinking wine which makes my throat dry, and then wake up with a cough (see fn 3), I cease, the moment I wake, to be interested in progress of the dream for its own sake. My attention is now concerned only with the physiological and psychological processes by means of which the irritation which causes me to cough comes to be symbolically expressed in the dream picture. Similarly, once the philosopher is convinced that the given world consists of nothing but mental pictures, his interest is bound to switch at once from this world to the real soul which lies behind. The matter is more serious, however, for the adherent of illusionism who denies altogether the existence of an Ego-in-itself behind the mental pictures, or at least holds this Ego to be unknowable. We might very easily be led to such a view by the observation that, in contrast to dreaming, there is indeed the waking state in which we have the opportunity of seeing through our dreams and referring them to the real relations of things, but that there is no state of the self which is related similarly to our waking conscious life. Whoever takes this view fails to see that there is, in fact, something which is related to mere perceiving in the way that our waking experience is related to our dreaming. This something is thinking.

The naïve man cannot be charged with the lack of insight referred to here. He accepts life as it is, and regards things as real just as they present themselves to him in experience. The first step, however, which we take beyond this standpoint can be only this, that we ask how thinking is related to percept. It makes no difference whether or no the percept, in the shape given to me, exists continuously before and after my forming a mental picture; if I want to assert anything whatever about it, I can do so only with the help of thinking. If I assert that the world is my mental picture, I have enunciated the result of an act of thinking. and if my thinking is not applicable to the world, then this result is false. Between a percept and every kind of assertion about it there intervenes thinking.

The reason why we generally overlook thinking in our consideration of things has already been given. It lies in the fact that our attention is concentrated only on the object we are thinking about, but not at the same time on the thinking itself. The naïve consciousness, therefore, treats thinking as something which has nothing to do with things, but stands altogether aloof from them and contemplates them. The picture which the thinker makes of the phenomena of the world is regarded not as something belonging to the things but as existing only in the human head. The world is complete in itself without this picture. It is finished and complete with all its substances and forces, and of this ready-made world man makes a picture. Whoever thinks thus need only be asked one question. What right have you to declare the world to be complete without thinking? Does not the world produce thinking in the heads of men with the same necessity as it produces the blossom on a plant? Plant a seed in the earth. It puts forth root and stem, it unfolds into leaves and blossoms. Set the plant before yourself. It connects itself, in your mind, with a definite concept. Why should this concept belong any less to the whole plant than leaf and blossom? You say the leaves and blossoms exist quite apart from a perceiving subject, but the concept appears only when a human being confronts the plant. Quite so. But leaves and blossoms also appear on the plant only if there is soil in which the seed can be planted, and light and air in which the leaves and blossoms can unfold. Just so the concept of a plant arises when a thinking consciousness approaches the plant.

It is quite arbitrary to regard the sum of what we experience of a thing through bare perception as a totality, as the whole thing, while that which reveals itself through thoughtful contemplation is regarded as a mere accretion which has nothing to do with the thing itself. If I am given a rosebud today, the picture that offers itself to my perception is complete only for the moment. If I put the bud into water, I shall tomorrow get a very different picture of my object. If I watch the rosebud without interruption, I shall see today's state change continuously into tomorrow's through an infinite number of intermediate stages. The picture which presents itself to me at any one moment is only a chance cross-section of an object which is in a continual process of development. If I do not put the bud into water, a whole series of states which lay as possibilities within the bud will not develop. Similarly I may be prevented tomorrow from observing the blossom further, and will thereby have an incomplete picture of it.

It would be a quite unobjective and fortuitous kind of opinion that declared of the purely momentary appearance of a thing: this is the thing.

Just as little is it legitimate to regard the sum of perceptual characteristics as the thing. It might be quite possible for a spirit to receive the concept at the same time as, and united with, the percept. It would never occur to such a spirit that the concept did not belong to the thing. It would have to ascribe to the concept an existence indivisibly bound up with the thing.

I will make myself clearer by an example. If I throw a stone horizontally through the air, I perceive it in different places one after the other. I connect these places so as to form a line. Mathematics teaches me to know various kinds of lines, one of which is the parabola. I know the parabola to be a line which is produced when a point moves according to a particular law. If I examine the conditions under which the stone thrown by me moves, I find the path traversed is identical with the line I know as a parabola. That the stone moves just in a parabola is a result of the given conditions and follows necessarily from them. The form of the parabola belongs to the whole phenomenon as much as any other feature of it does. The spirit described above who has no need of the detour of thinking would find itself presented not only a sequence of visual percepts at different points but, as part and parcel of these phenomena, also with the parabolic form of the path which we add to the phenomenon only by thinking.

It is not due to the objects that they are given us at first without the corresponding concepts, but to our mental organization. Our whole being functions in such a way that from every real thing the relevant elements come to us from two sides, from perceiving and from thinking.

The way I am organized for apprehending the things has nothing to do with the nature of the things themselves. The gap between perceiving and thinking exists only from the moment that I as spectator confront the things. Which elements do, and which do not, belong to the things cannot depend at all on the manner in which I obtain my knowledge of these elements.

Man is a limited being. First of all, he is a being among other beings. His existence belongs to space and time. Thus, only a limited part of the total universe that can be given him at any one time. This limited part, however, is linked up with other parts in all directions both in time and in space. If our existence were so linked up with the things that every occurrence in the world were at the same time also an occurrence in us, the distinction between ourselves and the things would not exist. But then there would be no separate things at all for us. All occurrences would pass continuously one into the other. The cosmos would be a unity and a whole, complete in itself. The stream of events would nowhere be interrupted. It is owing to our limitations that a thing appears to us as single and separate when in truth it is not a separate thing at all. Nowhere, for example, is the single quality "red" to be found by itself in isolation. It is surrounded on all sides by other qualities to which it belongs, and without which it could not subsist. For us, however, it is necessary to isolate certain sections of the world and to consider them by themselves. Our eye can grasp only single colors one after another out of a manifold totality of color, and our understanding, can grasp only single concepts out of a connected conceptual system. This separating off is a subjective act, which is due to the fact that we are not identical with the world process, but are a single being among other beings.

The all important thing now is to determine how the being that we ourselves are is related to the other entities. This determination must be distinguished from merely becoming conscious of ourselves. For this latter self-awareness we depend on perceiving just as we do for our awareness of any other thing. The perception of myself reveals to me a number of qualities which I combine into my personality as a whole, just as I combine the qualities yellow, metallic, hard, etc., in the unity "gold." The perception of myself does not take me beyond the sphere of what belongs to me. This perceiving of myself must be distinguished from determining myself by means of thinking. Just as, by means of thinking, I fit any single external percept into the whole world context, so by means of thinking I integrate into the world process the percepts I have made of myself. My self-perception confines me within certain limits, but my thinking is not concerned with these limits. In this sense I am a two-sided being. I am enclosed within the sphere which I perceive as that of my personality, but I am also the bearer of an activity which, from a higher sphere, defines my limited existence. Our thinking is not individual like our sensing and feeling; it is universal. It receives an individual stamp in each separate human being only because it comes to be related to his individual feelings and sensations. By means of these particular colorings of the universal thinking, individual men differentiate themselves from one another. There is only one single concept of "triangle". It is quite immaterial for the content of this concept whether it is grasped in A's consciousness or in B's. It will, however, be grasped by each of the two in his own individual way.

This thought is opposed by a common prejudice very hard to overcome. This prejudice prevents one from seeing that the concept of a triangle that my head grasps is the same as the concept that my neighbor's head grasps. The naïve man believes himself to be the creator of his concepts. Hence he believes that each person has his own concepts. It is a fundamental requirement of philosophic thinking that it should overcome this prejudice. The one uniform concept of "triangle" does not become a multiplicity because it is thought by many persons. For the thinking of the many is itself a unity.

In thinking, we have that element given us which welds our separate individuality into one whole with the cosmos. In so far as we sense and feel (and also perceive), we are single beings; in so far as we think, we are the all-one being that pervades everything. This is the deeper meaning of our two-sided nature: We see coming into being in us a force complete and absolute in itself, a force which is universal but which we learn to know, not as it issues from the center of the world, but rather at a point in the periphery. Were we to know it at its source, we should understand the whole riddle of the universe the moment we became conscious. But since we stand at a point in the periphery, and find that our own existence is bounded by definite limits, we must explore the region which lies outside our own being with the help of thinking, which projects into us from the universal world existence.

The fact that the thinking, in us, reaches out beyond our separate existence and relates itself to the universal world existence, gives rise to the fundamental desire for knowledge in us. Beings without thinking do not have this desire. When they are faced with other things, no questions arise for them. These other things remain external to such beings. But in thinking beings the concept rises up when they confront the external thing. It is that part of the thing which we receive not from outside but from within. To match up, to unite the two elements, inner and outer, is the task of knowledge.

The percept is thus not something finished and self-contained, but one side of the total reality. The other side is the concept. The act of knowing is the synthesis of percept and concept. Only percept and concept together constitute the whole thing.

The foregoing arguments show that it is senseless to look for any common element in the separate entities of the world other than the ideal content that thinking offers us. All attempts to find a unity in the world other than this internally coherent ideal content, which we gain by a thoughtful contemplation of our percepts, are bound to fail. Neither a humanly personal God, nor force, nor matter, nor the blind will (Schopenhauer), can be valid for us as a universal world unity. All these entities belong only to limited spheres of our observation. Humanly limited personality we perceive only in ourselves; force and matter in external things. As far as the will is concerned, it can be regarded only as the expression of the activity of our finite personality. Schopenhauer wants to avoid making "abstract" thinking the bearer of unity in the world, and seeks instead something which presents itself to him immediately as real. This philosopher believes that we can never approach the world so long as we regard it as "external" world.

In point of fact, the sought for meaning of the world which confronts me is nothing more than mental picture, or the passage from the world as mere mental picture of the knowing subject to whatever it may be besides this, could never be found at all if the investigator himself were nothing more than the purely knowing subject (a winged cherub without a body). But he himself is rooted in that world: he finds himself in it as an individual, that is to say, his knowledge, which is the determining factor supporting the whole world as mental picture, is thus always given through the medium of a body, whose affections are, for the intellect, the starting point for the contemplation of that world, as we have shown. For the purely knowing subject as such, this body is a mental picture like any other, an object among objects; its movements and actions are so far known to him in precisely the same way as the changes of all other perceived objects, and would be just as strange and incomprehensible to him if their sense were not made clear for him in an entirely different way. ... To the subject of knowledge, who appears as an individual through his identity with the body, this body is given in two entirely different ways: once as a mental picture for intelligent consideration, as an object among objects and obeying their laws; but at the same time, in quite a different way, namely as the thing immediately known to everyone by the word will. Every true act of his will is at once and without exception also a movement of his body: he cannot will the act without at the same time perceiving that it appears as a movement of the body. The act of will and the action of the body are not two things objectively known to be different, which the bond of causality unites; they do not stand in the relation of cause and effect; they are one and the same, but they are given in two entirely different ways: once quite directly and once in contemplation for the intellect.

Schopenhauer considers himself entitled by these arguments to find in the human body the "objectivity" of the will. He believes that in the activities of the body he feels an immediate reality — the thing-in-itself in the concrete. Against these arguments it must be said that the activities of our body come to our consciousness only through percepts of the self, and that, as such, they are in no way superior to other percepts. If we want to know their real nature, we can do so only by a thinking investigation, that is, by fitting them into the ideal system of our concepts and ideas.

Rooted most deeply in the naïve consciousness of mankind is the opinion that thinking is abstract, without any concrete content; it can at most give us an "ideal" counterpart of the unity of the world, but never the unity itself. Whoever judges in this way has never made it clear to himself what a percept without the concept really is. Let us see what this world of percepts is like: a mere juxtaposition in space, a mere succession in time, a mass of unconnected details — that is how it appears. None of the things which come and go on the stage of perception has any direct connection, that can be perceived, with any other. The world is thus a multiplicity of objects of equal value. None plays any greater part in the whole machinery of the world than any other. If it is to become clear to us that this or that fact has greater significance than another, we must consult our thinking. Were thinking not to function, the rudimentary organ of an animal which has no significance in its life would appear equal in value to the most important limb of its body. The separate facts appear in their true significance, both in themselves and for the rest of the world only when thinking spins its threads from one entity to another. This activity of thinking is one full of content. For it is only through a quite definite concrete content that I can know why the snail belongs to a lower level of organization than the lion. The mere appearance, the percept, gives me no content which could inform me as to the degree of perfection of the organization.

Thinking offers this content to the percept, from man's world of concepts and ideas. In contrast to the content of percept which is given to us from without, the content of thinking appears inwardly. The form in which this first makes its appearance we will call intuition. Intuition is for thinking what observation is for percept. Intuition and observation are the sources of our knowledge. An observed object of the world remains unintelligible to us until we have within ourselves the corresponding intuition which adds that part of reality which is lacking in the percept. To anyone who is incapable of finding intuitions corresponding to the things, the full reality remains inaccessible. Just as the color-blind person sees only differences of brightness without any color qualities, so can the person without intuition observe only unconnected perceptual fragments.

To explain a thing, to make it intelligible, means nothing else than to place it into the context from which it has been torn by the peculiar character of our organization as already described. A thing cut off from the world-whole does not exist. All isolating has only subjective validity for our organization. For us the universe divides itself up into above and below, before and after, cause and effect, thing and mental picture, matter and force, object and subject, etc. What appears to us in observation as separate parts becomes combined, bit by bit, through the coherent, unified world of our intuitions. By thinking we fit together again into one piece all that we have taken apart through perceiving.

The enigmatic character of an object consists in its separateness. But this separation is our own making and can, within the world of concepts, be overcome again.

Except through thinking and perceiving nothing is given to us directly. The question now arises: What is the significance of the percept, according to our line of argument? We have learnt that the proof which critical idealism offers of the subjective nature of perceptions collapses. But insight into the falsity of the proof is not alone sufficient to show that the doctrine itself is erroneous. Critical idealism does not base its proof on the absolute nature of thinking, but relies on the argument of naïve realism, when followed to its logical conclusion, cancels itself out. How does the matter appear when we have recognized the absoluteness of thinking?

Let us assume that a certain perception, for example, red, appears in my consciousness. To continued observation, this percept shows itself to be connected with other percepts, for example, a definite figure and with certain temperature- and touch-percepts. This combination I call an object belonging to the sense-perceptible world. I can now ask myself: Over and above the percepts just mentioned, what else is there in the section of space in which they appear? I shall then find mechanical, chemical and other processes in that section of space. I next go further and study the processes I find on the way from the object to my sense organs. I can find movements in an elastic medium, which by their very nature have not the slightest in common with the percepts from which I started. I get the same result when I go on and examine the transmission from sense organs to brain. In each of these fields I gather new percepts, but the connecting medium which weaves through all these spatially and temporally separated percepts is thinking. The air vibrations which transmit sound are given to me as percepts just like the sound itself. Thinking alone links all these percepts to one another and shows them to us in their mutual relationship. We cannot speak of anything existing beyond what is directly perceived except what can be recognized through the ideal connections of percepts, that is, connections accessible to thinking). The way objects as percepts are related to the subject as percept — a relationship that goes beyond what is merely perceived — is therefore purely ideal, that is, it can be expressed only by means of concepts. Only if I could perceive how the percept object affects the percept subject, or, conversely, could watch the building up of the perceptual pattern by the subject, would it be possible to speak as modern physiology and the critical idealism based on it do. Their view confuses an ideal relation (that of the object to the subject) with a process which we could speak of only if it were possible to perceive it. The proposition, "No color without a color-sensing eye," cannot be taken to mean that the eye produces the color, but only that an ideal relation, recognizable by thinking, subsists between the percept "color" and the percept "eye". Empirical science will have to ascertain how the properties of the eye and those of the colors are related to one another, by what means the organ of sight transmits the perception of colors, and so forth. I can trace how one percept succeeds another in time and is related to others in space, and I can formulate these relations in conceptual terms, but I can never perceive how a percept originates out of the non-perceptible. All attempts to seek any relations between percepts other than thought relations must of necessity fail.

What, then is a percept? The question, asked in this general way, is absurd. A percept emerges always as something perfectly definite, as a concrete content. This content is directly given and is completely contained in what is given. The only question one can ask concerning the given content is what it is apart from perception, that is, what it is for thinking? The question concerning the "what" of a percept can, therefore, only refer to the conceptual intuition that corresponds to this percept. From this point of view, the question of the subjectivity of percepts, in the sense of critical idealism, cannot be raised at all. Only what is perceived as belonging to the subject can be termed "subjective." To form a link between something subjective and something objective is impossible for any process that is "real" in the naïve sense, that is, one that can be perceived; it is possible only for thinking. Therefore what appears for our perception to be external to the percept of myself as subject is for us "objective". The percept of myself as subject remains perceptible to me after the table which now stands before me has disappeared from my field of observation. The observation of the table has produced in me a modification which likewise persists. I retain the faculty to produce later on an image of the table. This faculty of producing an image remains connected with me. Psychology calls this image as a memory-picture. It is in fact the only thing which can justifiably be called the mental picture of the table. For it corresponds to the perceptible modification of my own state through the presence of the table in my visual field. Moreover, it does not mean a modification of some "Ego-in-itself" standing behind the percept of the subject, but the modification of the perceptible subject itself. The mental picture is, therefore, a subjective percept, in contrast with the objective percept which occurs when the object is present in the field of vision. Confusing the subjective percept with the objective percept leads to the misconception of contained in idealism — that the world is my mental picture.

Our next task must be to define the concept of "mental picture" more closely. What we have said about it so far does not give us the concept of it but only shows us whereabouts in the perceptual field the mental picture is to be found. The exact concept of mental picture will make it possible for us also to obtain a satisfactory explanation of the way that mental picture and object are related. This will then lead us over the border line where the relationship between the human subject and the object belonging to the world is brought down from the purely conceptual field of cognition into concrete individual life. Once we know what to make of the world, it will be a simple matter to direct ourselves accordingly. We can only act with full energy when we know what it is in the world to which we devote our activity.

Human Individuality

IN explaining mental pictures, philosophers have found the chief difficulty in the fact that we ourselves are not the outer things, and yet our mental pictures must have a form corresponding to the things. But on closer inspection it turns out that this difficulty does not really exist. We certainly are not the external things, but we belong together with them to one and the same world. That section of the world which I perceive to be myself as subject is permeated by the stream of the universal cosmic process. To my perception I am, in the first instance, confined within the limits bounded by my skin. But all that is contained within this skin belongs to the cosmos as a whole. Hence, for a relation to subsist between my organism and an object external to me, it is by no means necessary that something of the object should slip into me, or make an impression on my mind, like a signet ring on wax. The question: "How do I get information about that tree ten feet away from me?" is utterly misleading. It springs from the view that the boundaries of my body are absolute barriers, through which information about things filters into me. The forces which are at work inside my body are the same as those which exist outside. Therefore I really am the things; not, however, "I" in so far as I am a percept of myself as subject, but "I" in so far as I am a part of the universal world process. The percept of the tree belongs to the same whole as my I. This universal world process produces equally the percept of the tree out there and the percept of my I in here. Were I not a world knower, but world creator, object and subject (percept and I) would originate in one act. For each implies the other. In so far as these are entities that belong together, I can as world knower discover the common element in both only through thinking, which relates one to the other by means of concepts.

The most difficult to drive from the field are the so-called physiological proofs of the subjectivity of our percepts. When I exert pressure on my skin I perceive it as a pressure sensation. This same pressure can be sensed as light by the eye, as sound by the ear. An electric shock is perceived by the eye as light, by the ear as noise, by the nerves of the skin as impact, and by the nose as a phosphoric smell. What follows from these facts? Only this: I perceive an electric shock (or a pressure, as the case may be) followed by an impression of light, or sound, or perhaps a certain smell, and so on. If there were no eye present, then no perception of light would accompany the perception of the mechanical disturbance in my environment; without the presence of the ear, no perception of sound, and so on. But what right have we to say that in the absence of sense organs the whole process would not exist at all? Those who, from the fact that an electrical process calls forth light in the eye, conclude that what we sense as light is only a mechanical process of motion when outside our organism, forget that they are only passing from one percept to another, and not at all to something lying beyond percepts. Just as we can say that the eye perceives a mechanical process of motion in its surroundings as light, so we could equally well say that a regular and systematic change in an object is perceived by us as a process of motion. If I draw twelve pictures of a horse on the circumference of a rotating disc, reproducing exactly the attitudes which the horse's body successively assumes when galloping, I can produce the illusion of movement by rotating the disc. I need only look through an opening in such a way that, in the proper intervals, I see the successive positions of the horse. I do not see twelve separate pictures of a horse but the picture of a single galloping horse.

The physiological fact mentioned above cannot therefore throw any light on the relation of percept to mental picture. We must go about it rather differently.

The moment a percept appears in my field of observation, thinking also becomes active through me. An element of my thought system, a definite intuition, a concept, connects itself with the percept. Then, when the percept disappears from my field of vision, what remains? My intuition, with the reference to the particular percept which it acquired in the moment of perceiving. The degree of vividness with which I can subsequently recall this reference depends on the manner in which my mental and bodily organism is working. A mental picture is nothing but an intuition related to a particular percept; it is a concept that was once connected with a certain percept, and which retains the reference to this percept. My concept of a lion is not formed out of my percepts of lions; but my mental picture of a lion is very definitely formed according to a percept. I can convey the concept of a lion to someone who has never seen a lion. I cannot convey to him a vivid mental picture without the help of his own perception.

Thus the mental picture is an individualized concept. And now we can see how real objects can be represented to us by mental pictures. The full reality of a thing is given to us in the moment of observation through the fitting together of concept and percept. By means of a percept, the concept acquires an individualized form, a relation to this particular percept. In this individualized form, which carries the reference to the percept as a characteristic feature, the concept lives on in us and constitutes the mental picture of the thing in question. If we come across a second thing with which the same concept connects itself, we recognize the second as belonging to the same kind as the first; if we come across the same thing a second time, we find in our conceptual system, not merely a corresponding concept, but the individualized concept with its characteristic relation to the same object, and thus we recognize the object again.

Thus the mental picture stands between percept and concept. It is the particularized concept which points to the percept.

The sum of those things about which I can form mental pictures may be called my total experience. The man who has the greater number of individualized concepts will be the man of richer experience. A man who lacks all power of intuition is not capable of acquiring experience. He loses the objects again when they disappear from his field of vision, because he lacks the concepts which he should bring into relation with them. A man whose faculty of thinking is well developed, but whose perception functions badly owing to his clumsy sense organs, will just as little be able to gather experience. He can, it is true, acquire concepts by one means or another; but his intuitions lack the vivid reference to definite things. The unthinking traveler and the scholar living in abstract conceptual systems are alike incapable of acquiring a rich sum of experience.

Reality shows itself to us as percept and concept; the subjective representative of this reality shows itself to us as mental picture.

If our personality expressed itself only in cognition, the totality of all that is objective would be given in percept, concept and mental picture.

However, we are not satisfied merely to refer the percept, by means of thinking, to the concept, but we relate them also to our particular subjectivity, our individual Ego. The expression of this individual relationship is feeling, which manifests itself as pleasure or displeasure.

Thinking and feeling correspond to the two-fold nature of our being to which reference has already been made. Thinking is the element through which we take part in the universal cosmic process; feeling is that through which we can withdraw ourselves into the narrow confines of our own being.

Our thinking links us to the world; our feeling leads us back into ourselves and thus makes us individuals. Were we merely thinking and perceiving beings, our whole life would flow along in monotonous indifference. Were we able merely to know ourselves as selves, we should be totally indifferent to ourselves. It is only because we experience self-feeling with self-knowledge, and pleasure and pain with the perception of objects, that we live as individual beings whose existence is not limited to the conceptual relations between us and the rest of the world, but who have besides this a special value for ourselves.

One might be tempted to see in the life of feeling an element that is more richly saturated with reality than is the contemplation of the world through thinking. But the reply to this is that the life of feeling, after all, has this richer meaning only for my individual self. For the universe as a whole my life of feeling can have value only if, as a percept of my self, the feeling enters into connection with a concept and in this roundabout way links itself to the cosmos.

Our life is a continual oscillation between living with the universal world process and being our own individual selves. The farther we ascend into the universal nature of thinking where in the end what is individual interests us only as an example or specimen of the concept, the more the character of the separate being, of the quite definite single personality, becomes lost in us. The farther we descend into the depths of our own life and allow our feelings to resound with our experiences of the outer world, the more we cut ourselves off from universal being. A true individuality will be the one who reaches up with his feelings to the farthest possible extent into the region of the ideal. There are men in whom even the most general ideas that enter their heads still bear that peculiar personal tinge which shows unmistakably the connection with their author. There are others whose concepts come before us without the least trace of individual character as if they had not been produced by a man of flesh and blood at all.

Making mental pictures gives our conceptual life at once an individual stamp. Each one of us has his own particular place from which he surveys the world. His concepts link themselves to his percepts. He thinks the general concepts in his own special way. This special determination results for each of us from the place where we stand in the world, from the range of percepts peculiar to our place in life.

Distinct from this determination is another which depends on our particular organization. Our organization is indeed a special, fully determined entity. Each of us combines special feelings, and these in the most varying degrees of intensity, with his percepts. This is just the individual element in the personality of each one of us. It is what remains over when we have allowed fully for all the determining factors in our surroundings.

A life of feeling, wholly devoid of thinking, would gradually lose all connection with the world. But man is meant to be a whole, and for him knowledge of things will go hand in hand with the development and education of the life of feeling.

Feeling is the means whereby, in the first instance, concepts gain concrete life.

Are There Limits to Knowledge?

WE have established that the elements for the explanation of reality are to be found in the two spheres: perceiving and thinking. It is due, as we have seen, to our organization that the full, complete reality, including our own selves as subjects, appears at first as a duality. The act of knowing overcomes this duality by fusing the two elements of reality, the percept and the concept gained by thinking, into the complete thing. Let us call the manner in which the world presents itself to us, before it has taken on its true nature through our knowing it, "the world of appearance," in contrast to the unified whole composed of percept and concept. We can then say: The world is given to us as a duality, and knowledge transforms it into a unity. A philosophy which starts from this basic principle may be called a monistic philosophy, or monism. Opposed to this is the two-world theory, or dualism. The latter does not assume just that there are two sides of a single reality which are kept apart merely by our organization, but that there are two worlds absolutely distinct from one another. It then tries to find in one of these two worlds the principles for the explanation of the other.

Dualism rests on a false conception of what we call knowledge. It divides the whole of existence into two spheres, each of which has its own laws, and it leaves these two worlds standing apart and opposed.

It is from a dualism such as this that there arises the distinction between the perceptual object and the thing-in-itself, which Kant introduced into philosophy, and which, to the present day, we have not succeeded in eradicating. According to our line of argument, it is due to the nature of our mental organization that a particular thing can be given to us only as a percept. Thinking then overcomes this particularity by assigning to each percept its rightful place in the world as a whole. As long as we designate the separated parts of the world as percepts, we are simply following, in this separating out, a law of our subjectivity. If, however, we regard the sum of all percepts as the one part, and contrast with this a second part, namely, the things-in-themselves, then we are philosophizing into the blue. We are merely playing with concepts. We construct an artificial pair of opposites, but we can gain no content for the second of these opposites, since such content for a particular thing can be drawn only from perception.

Every kind of existence that is assumed outside the realm of percept and concept must be relegated to the sphere of unjustified hypotheses. To this category belongs the "thing-in-itself". It is quite natural that a dualistic thinker should be unable to find the connection between the world principle which he hypothetically assumes and the things given in experience. A content for the hypothetical world principle can be arrived at only by borrowing it from the world of experience and then shutting one's eyes to the fact of the borrowing. Otherwise it remains an empty concept, a non-concept which has nothing but the form of a concept. Here the dualistic thinker usually asserts that the content of this concept is inaccessible to our knowledge; we can know only that such a content exists, but not what it is that exists. In both cases it is impossible to overcome dualism. Even though one were to import a few abstract elements from the world of experience into the concept of the thing-in-itself, it would still remain impossible to derive the rich concrete life of experience from these few qualities which are, after all, themselves taken from perception. DuBois-Reymond considers that the imperceptible atoms of matter produce sensation and feeling by means of their position and motion, and then comes to the conclusion that we can never find a satisfactory explanation of how matter and motion produce sensation and feeling, for "it is absolutely and for ever incomprehensible that it should be other than indifferent to a number of atoms of carbon, hydrogen, nitrogen, and so on, how they lie and move, how they lay and moved, or how they will lie and will move. It is impossible to see how consciousness could come into existence through their interaction." This conclusion is characteristic of this whole trend of thought. Position and motion are abstracted from the rich world of percepts. They are then transferred to the notional world of atoms. And then astonishment arises that real life cannot be evolved out of this self-made principle borrowed from the world of percepts.

That the dualist can reach no explanation of the world, working as he does with a completely empty concept of the "in-itself" of a thing, follows at once from the very definition of his principle given above.

In every case the dualist finds himself compelled to set impassable barriers to our faculty of knowledge. The follower of a monistic world conception knows that everything he needs for the explanation of any given phenomenon in the world must lie within this world itself. What prevents him from reaching it can be only accidental limitations in space and time, or defects of his organization, that is, not of human organization in general, but only of his own particular one.

It follows from the concept of the act of knowing as we have defined it, that one cannot speak of limits to knowledge. Knowing is not a concern of the world in general, but an affair which man must settle for himself. Things demand no explanation. They exist and act on one another according to laws which can be discovered through thinking. They exist in indivisible unity with these laws. Our Egohood confronts them, grasping at first only that part of them we have called percepts. Within our Egohood, however, lies the power to discover the other part of the reality as well. Only when the Egohood has taken the two elements of reality which are indivisibly united in the world and has combined them also for itself, is our thirst for knowledge satisfied — the I has then arrived at the reality once more.

Thus the conditions necessary for an act of knowledge to take place are there through the I and for the I. The I sets itself the problems of knowledge; and moreover it takes them from an element that is absolutely clear and transparent in itself: the element of thinking. If we set ourselves questions which we cannot answer, it must be because the content of the questions is not in all respects clear and distinct. It is not the world which sets us the questions, but we ourselves.

I can imagine that it would be quite impossible for me to answer a question which I happened to find written down somewhere, without knowing the sphere from which the content of the question was taken.

In our knowledge we are concerned with questions which arise for us through the fact that a sphere of percepts, conditioned by place, time, and our subjective organization, is confronted by a sphere of concepts pointing to the totality of the universe. My task consists in reconciling these two spheres, with both of which I am well acquainted. Here one cannot speak of a limit to knowledge. It may be that, at any particular moment, this or that remains unexplained because, through our place in life, we are prevented from perceiving the things involved. What is not found today, however, may be found tomorrow. The limits due to these causes are only transitory, and can be overcome by the progress of perception and thinking.

Dualism makes the mistake of transferring the antithesis of object and subject, which has meaning only within the perceptual realm, to purely notional entities outside this realm. But since the separate things within the perceptual field remain separated only so long as the perceiver refrains from thinking (which cancels all separation and shows it to be due to purely subjective factors), the dualist is therefore transferring to entities behind the perceptible realm determining factors which even for this realm have no absolute validity, but only relative. He thus splits up the two factors concerned in the process of knowledge, namely percept and concept, into four: (1) the object in itself; (2) the precept which the subject has of the object; (3) the subject; (4) the concept which relates the precept to the object in itself. The relation between subject and object is a real one; the subject is really (dynamically) influenced by the object. This real process is said not to appear in consciousness. But it is supposed to evoke in the subject a response to the stimulation from the object. The result of this response is said to be the percept. Only at this stage does it enter our consciousness. The object is said to have an objective (independent of the subject) reality, the percept a subjective reality. This subjective reality is referred by the subject to the object. This reference is called an ideal one. With this the dualist therefore splits up the process of knowledge into two parts. The one part, namely, the production of the perceptual object out of the thing-in-itself, he conceives of as taking place outside consciousness, whereas the other, the combination of percept with concept and the reference of the concept to the object, takes place, according to him, within consciousness.

With these presuppositions, it is clear why the dualist believes his concepts to be merely subjective representatives of what is there prior to his consciousness. The objectively real process in the subject by means of which the percept comes about, and still more the objective relations between things-in-themselves, remain for such a dualist inaccessible to direct knowledge; according to him, man can obtain only conceptual representatives of the objectively real. The bond of unity which connects things with one another and also objectively with the individual mind of each of us (as thing-in-itself) lies beyond our consciousness in a being-in-itself of whom, once more, we can have in our consciousness merely a conceptual representative.

The dualist believes that he would dissolve away the whole world into a mere abstract. scheme of concepts, did he not insist on real connections between the objects besides the conceptual ones. In other words, the ideal principles which thinking discovers seem too airy for the dualist, and he seeks, in addition, real principles with which to support them.

Let us examine these real principles a little more closely. The naïve man (naïve realist) regards the objects of external experience as realities. The fact that his hands can grasp these objects, and his eyes see them, is for him sufficient proof of their reality. "Nothing exists that cannot be perceived" is, in fact, the first axiom of the naïve man; and it is held to be equally valid in its converse: "Everything which can be perceived exists." The best evidence for this assertion is the naïve man's belief in immortality and ghosts. He thinks of the soul as refined material substance which may, in special circumstances, become visible even to the ordinary man (naïve belief in ghosts).

In contrast with this real world of his, the naïve realist regards everything else, especially the world of ideas, as unreal or "merely ideal". What we add to objects by thinking is nothing more than thoughts about the things. Thought adds nothing real to the percept.

But it is not only with reference to the existence of things that the naïve man regards sense perception as the sole proof of reality, but also with reference to events. A thing, according to him, can act on another only when a force actually present to sense perception issues from the one and seizes upon the other. In the older physics it was thought that very fine substances emanate from the objects and penetrate through the sense organs into the soul. The actual seeing of these substances is impossible only because of the coarseness of our sense organs relative to the fineness of these substances. In principle, the reason for attributing reality to these substances was the same as for attributing it to the objects of the sense-perceptible world, namely because of their mode of existence, which was thought to be analogous to that of sense-perceptible reality.

The self-contained nature of what can be experienced through ideas is not regarded by the naïve mind as being real in the same way that sense experience is. An object grasped in "mere idea" is regarded as a chimera until conviction of its reality can be given through sense perception. In short, the naïve man demands the real evidence of his senses in addition to the ideal evidence of his thinking. In this need of the naïve man lies the original ground for primitive forms of the belief in revelation. The God who is given through thinking remains to the naïve mind always a merely "notional" God. The naïve mind demands a manifestation that is accessible to sense perception. God must appear in the flesh, and little value is attached to the testimony of thinking, but only to proof of divinity such as changing water into wine in a way that can be testified by the senses.

Even the act of knowing itself is pictured by the naïve man as a process analogous to sense perception. Things, it is thought, make an impression on the soul, or send out images which enter through our senses, and so on.

What the naïve man can perceive with his senses he regards as real, and what he cannot thus perceive (God, soul, knowledge, etc.) he regards as analogous to what he does perceive.

A science based on naïve realism would have to be nothing but an exact description of the content of perception. For naïve realism, concepts are only the means to an end. They exist to provide ideal counterparts of percepts, and have no significance for the things themselves. For the naïve realist, only the individual tulips which he sees (or could see) are real; the single idea of the tulip is to him an abstraction, the unreal thought-picture which the soul has put together out of the characteristics common to all tulips.

Naive realism, with its fundamental principle of the reality of all perceived things, is contradicted by experience, which teaches us that the content of percepts is of a transitory nature. The tulip I see is real today; in a year it will have vanished into nothingness. What persists is the species tulip. For the naïve realist, however, this species is "only" an idea, not a reality. Thus this theory of the world find itself in the position of seeing its realities arise and perish, while what it regards as unreal, in contrast with the real, persists. Hence naïve realism is compelled to acknowledge, in addition to percepts, the existence of something ideal. It must admit entities which cannot be perceived by the senses. In doing so, it justifies itself by conceiving their existence as being analogous to that of sense-perceptible objects. Just such hypothetical realities are the invisible forces by means of which the sense-perceptible objects act on one another. Another such thing is heredity, which works on beyond the individual and is the reason why a new being which develops from the individual is similar to it, thereby serving to maintain the species. Such a thing again is the life-principle permeating the organic body, the soul for which the naïve mind always finds a concept formed in analogy with sense realities, and finally the naïve man's Divine Being. This Divine Being is thought of as acting in a manner exactly corresponding to the way in which man himself is seen to act; that is, anthropomorphically.

Modern physics traces sensations back to processes of the smallest particles of bodies and of an infinitely fine substance, called ether, or to other such things. For example, what we experience as warmth is, within the space occupied by the warmth-giving body, the movement of its parts. Here again something imperceptible is conceived in analogy with what is perceptible. In this sense, the perceptual analogue to the concept "body" would be, shall we say, the interior of a totally enclosed space, in which elastic spheres are moving in all directions, impinging one on another, bouncing on and off the walls, and so on.

Without such assumptions the world would fall apart for the naïve realist into an incoherent aggregate of percepts without mutual relationships and with no tendency to unite. It is clear, however, that naïve realism can make these assumptions only by an inconsistency. If it would remain true to its fundamental principle that only what is perceived is real, then it ought not to assume a reality where it perceives nothing. The imperceptible forces which proceed from the perceptible things are in fact unjustified hypotheses from the standpoint of naïve realism. And because naïve realism knows no other realities, it invests its hypothetical forces with perceptual content. It thus ascribes a form of existence (perceptible existence) to a sphere where the only means of making any assertion about such existence, namely, sense perception, is lacking.

This self-contradictory theory leads to metaphysical realism. This constructs, in addition to the perceptible reality, an imperceptible reality which it conceives on the analogy of the perceptible one. Therefore metaphysical realism is of necessity dualistic.

Wherever the metaphysical realist observes a relationship between perceptible things (such as when two things move towards each other, or when something objective enters consciousness), there he sees a reality. However, the relationship which he notices can only be expressed by means of thinking; it cannot be perceived. The purely ideal relationship is then arbitrarily made into something similar to a perceptible one. Thus, according to this theory, the real world is composed of the objects of perception which are in ceaseless flux, arising and disappearing, and of imperceptible forces which produce the objects of perception, and are the things that endure.

Metaphysical realism is a contradictory mixture of naïve realism and idealism. Its hypothetical forces are imperceptible entities endowed with the qualities of percepts. The metaphysical realist has made up his mind to acknowledge, in addition to the sphere which he is able to know through perception, another sphere for which this means of knowledge fails him and which can be known only by means of thinking. But he cannot make up his mind at the same time to acknowledge that the mode of existence which thinking reveals, namely, the concept (idea), is just as important a factor as the percept. If we are to avoid the contradiction of imperceptible percepts, we must admit that the relationships which thinking establishes between the percepts can have no other mode of existence for us than that of concepts. If we reject the untenable part of metaphysical realism, the world presents itself to us as the sum of percepts and their conceptual (ideal) relationships. Metaphysical realism would then merge into a view of the world which requires the principle of perceivability for percepts and that of conceivability for the relationships between the percepts. This view of the world can admit no third sphere — in addition to the world of percepts and the world of concepts — in which both the so-called "real" and "ideal" principles are simultaneously valid.

When the metaphysical realist asserts that, besides the ideal relationship between the percept of the object and the percept of the subject, there must also exist a real relationship between the "thing-in-itself" of the percept and the "thing-in-itself" of the perceptible subject (that is, of the so-called individual spirit), he is basing his assertion on the false assumption of a real process, analogous to the processes in the sense world but imperceptible. Further, when the metaphysical realist asserts that we enter into a conscious ideal relationship to our world of percepts, but that to the real world we can have only a dynamic (force) relationship, he repeats the mistake we have already criticized. One can talk of a dynamic relationship only within the world of percepts (in the sphere of the sense of touch), but not outside that world.

Let us call the view which we have characterized above, into which metaphysical realism merges when it discards its contradictory elements, monism, because it combines one-sided realism with idealism into a higher unity.

For naïve realism, the real world is an aggregate of perceived objects (percepts); for metaphysical realism, not only percepts but also imperceptible forces are real; monism replaces forces by ideal connections which are gained through thinking. The laws of nature are just such connections. A law of nature is in fact nothing but the conceptual expression of the connection between certain percepts.

Monism never finds it necessary to ask for any principles of explanation for reality other than percepts and concepts. It knows that in the whole field of reality there is no occasion for this question. In the perceptual world, as it presents itself directly to perception, it sees one half of the reality; in the union of this world with the world of concepts it finds the full reality.

The metaphysical realist may object to the adherent of monism: It may be that for your organization, your knowledge is complete in itself, with no part lacking; but you do not know how the world is mirrored in an intelligence organized differently from your own. To this the monist will reply: If there are intelligences other than human, and if their percepts are different from ours, all that concerns me is what reaches me from them through perception and concept. Through my perceiving, that is, through this specifically human mode of perceiving, I, as subject, am confronted with the object. The connection of things is thereby interrupted. The subject restores this connection by means of thinking. In doing so it puts itself back into the context of the world as a whole. Since it is only through the subject that the whole appears cut in two at the place between our percept and our concept, the uniting of those two gives us true knowledge. For beings with a different perceptual world (for example, if they had twice our number of sense organs), the continuum would appear broken in another place, and the reconstruction would accordingly have to take a form specific for such beings. The question concerning the limits of knowledge exists only for naïve and metaphysical realism, both of which see in the contents of the soul only an ideal representation of the real world. For these theories, what exists outside the subject is something absolute, founded in itself, and what is contained within the subject is a picture of this absolute, but quite external to it. The completeness of knowledge depends on the greater or lesser degree of resemblance between the picture and the absolute object. A being with fewer senses than man will perceive less of the world, one with more senses will perceive more. The former will accordingly have a less complete knowledge than the latter.

For monism, the situation is different. The manner in which the world continuum appears to be rent asunder into subject and object depends on the organization of the perceiving being. The object is not absolute, but merely relative, with reference to this particular subject. Bridging over the antithesis, therefore, can again take place only in the quite specific way that is characteristic of the particular human subject. As soon as the I, which is separated from the world in the act of perceiving, fits itself back into the world continuum through thoughtful contemplation, all further questioning ceases, having been but a consequence of the separation.

A differently constituted being would have a differently constituted knowledge. Our own knowledge suffices to answer the questions put by our own nature.

Metaphysical realism has to ask: By what means are our percepts given? What is it that affects the subject?

Monism holds that percepts are determined through the subject. But at the same time, the subject has in thinking the means for canceling this self-produced determination.

The metaphysical realist is faced by a further difficulty when he seeks to explain the similarity between the world pictures of different human individuals. He has to ask himself: How is it that the picture of the world which I build up out of my subjectively determined percepts and my concepts turns out to be the same as the one which another individual is also building up out of the same two subjective factors? How can I, in any case, draw conclusions from my own subjective picture of the world about that of another human being? The fact that people can understand and get on with one another in practical life leads the metaphysical realist to conclude that their subjective world pictures must be similar. From the similarity of these world pictures he then further concludes that the "individual spirits" behind the single human subjects as percepts, or the "I-in-itself" behind the subjects, must also be like one another.

This is an inference from a sum of effects to the character of the underlying causes. We believe that we can understand the situation well enough from a sufficiently large number of instances to know how the inferred causes will behave in other instances. Such an inference is called an inductive inference. We shall be obliged to modify its results if further observation yields some unexpected element, because the character of our conclusion is, after all, determined only by the particular form of our actual observations. The metaphysical realist asserts that this knowledge of causes, though conditional, is nevertheless quite sufficient for practical life.

Inductive inference is the method underlying modern metaphysical realism. At one time it was thought that we could evolve something out of concepts that is no longer a concept. It was thought that the metaphysical realities, which metaphysical realism after all requires, could be known by means of concepts. This kind of philosophizing is now out of date. Instead it is thought that one can infer from a sufficiently large number of perceptual facts the character of the thing-in-itself which underlies these facts. Whereas formerly it was from concepts, now it is from percepts that people seek to evolve the metaphysical. Since one has concepts before oneself in transparent clearness, it was thought that one might be able to deduce the metaphysical from them with absolute certainty. Percepts are not given with the same transparent clearness. Each subsequent one is a little different from others of the same kind which preceded it. Basically, therefore, anything inferred from past percepts will be somewhat modified by each subsequent percept. The character of the metaphysical thus obtained can, therefore, be only relatively true, since it is subject to correction by further instances. Eduard von Hartmann's metaphysics has a character determined by this basic method, as expressed in the motto on the title page of his first important book: "Speculative results following the inductive method of Natural Science."

The form which the metaphysical realist nowadays gives to his things-in-themselves is obtained by inductive inferences. Through considerations of the process of knowledge he is convinced of the existence of an objectively real world continuum, over and above the "subjective" world continuum which we know through percepts and concepts. The nature of this reality he thinks he can determine by inductive inferences from his percepts.

The Factors of Life

LET us recapitulate what we have achieved in the previous chapters. The world faces man as a multiplicity, as a mass of separate details. One of these separate things, one entity among others, is man himself. This aspect of the world we simply call the given, and inasmuch as we do not evolve it by conscious activity, but just find it, we call it percept. Within this world of percepts we perceive ourselves. This percept of self would remain merely one among many other percepts, if something did not arise from the midst of this percept of self which proves capable of connecting all percepts with one another and, therefore, the sum of all other percepts with the percept of our own self. This something which emerges is no longer merely percept; neither is it, like percepts, simply given. It is produced by our activity. To begin with, it appears to be bound up with what we perceive as our own self. In its inner significance, however, it transcends the self. To the separate percepts it adds ideally determined elements, which, however, are related to one another, and are rooted in a totality. What is obtained by perception of self is ideally determined by this something in the same way as are all other percepts, and is placed as subject, or "I", over against the objects. This something is thinking, and the ideally determined elements are the concepts and ideas. Thinking, therefore, first reveals itself in the percept of the self. But it is not merely subjective, for the self characterizes itself as subject only with the help of thinking. This relationship in thought of the self to itself is what, in life, determines our personality. Through it we lead a purely ideal existence. Through it we feel ourselves to be thinking beings. This determination of our life would remain a purely conceptual (logical) one, if no other determinations of our self were added to it. We should then be creatures whose life was expended in establishing purely ideal relationships between percepts among themselves and between them and ourselves. If we call the establishment of such a thought connection an "act of cognition", and the resulting condition of ourself "knowledge", then, assuming the above supposition to be true, we should have to consider ourselves as beings who merely cognize or know.

The supposition, however, does not meet the case. We relate percepts to ourselves not merely ideally, through concepts, but also, as we have already seen, through feeling. Therefore we are not beings with a merely conceptual content to our life. In fact the naïve realist holds that the personality lives more genuinely in the life of feeling than in the purely ideal element of knowledge. From his point of view he is quite right when he describes the matter in this way. To begin with, feeling is exactly the same, on the subjective side, as the percept is on the objective side. From the basic principle of naïve realism — that everything that can be perceived is real — it follows that feeling must be the guarantee of the reality of one's own personality. Monism, however, as here understood, must grant the same addition to feeling that it considers necessary for percepts, if these are to stand before us as full reality. Thus, for monism, feeling is an incomplete reality, which, in the form in which it first appears to us, does not yet contain its second factor, the concept or idea. This is why, in actual life, feelings, like percepts, appear prior to knowledge. At first, we have merely a feeling of existence; and it is only in the course of our gradual development that we attain to the point at which the concept of self emerges from within the dim feeling of our own existence. However, what for us appears only later, is from the first indissolubly bound up with our feeling. This is why the naïve man comes to believe that in feeling he is presented with existence directly, in knowledge only indirectly. The cultivation of the life of feeling, therefore, appears to him more important than anything else. He will only believe that he has grasped the pattern of the universe when he has received it into his feeling. He attempts to make feeling, rather than knowing, the instrument of knowledge. Since a feeling is something entirely individual, something equivalent to a percept, the philosopher of feeling is making a universal principle out of something that has significance only within his own personality. He attempts to permeate the whole world with his own self. What the monist, in the sense we have described, strives to grasp through concepts, the philosopher of feeling tries to attain through feelings, and he regards this kind of connection with the objects as the more direct.

The tendency just described, the philosophy of feeling, is often called mysticism. The error in a mystical outlook based upon mere feeling is that it wants to experience directly what it ought to gain through knowledge; that it wants to raise feeling, which is individual, into a universal principle.

Feeling is a purely individual affair; it is the relation of the external world to ourself as subject, in so far as this relation finds expression in a merely subjective experience.

There is yet another expression of human personality. The I, through its thinking, shares the life of the world in general. In this manner, in a purely ideal way (that is, conceptually), it relates the percepts to itself, and itself to the percepts. In feeling, it has direct experience of a relation of the objects to itself as subject. In the will, the case is reversed. In willing, we are concerned once more with a percept, namely, that of the individual relation of our self to what is objective. Whatever there is in willing that is not a purely ideal factor, is just as much mere object of perception as is any object in the external world.

Nevertheless, the naïve realist believes here again that he has before him something far more real than can be attained by thinking. He sees in the will an element in which he is directly aware of an occurrence, a causation, in contrast with thinking which only grasps the event afterwards in conceptual form. According to such a view, what the I achieves through its will is a process which is experienced directly. The adherent of this philosophy believes that in the will he has really got hold of the machinery of the world by one corner. Whereas he can follow other occurrences only from the outside by means of perception, he is confident that in his will he experiences a real process quite directly. The mode of existence in which the will appears within the self becomes for him a concrete principle of reality. His own will appears to him as a special case of the general world process; hence the latter appears as universal will. The will becomes the principle of the universe just as, in mysticism, feeling becomes the principle of knowledge. This kind of theory is called the philosophy of will (thelism). It makes something that can be experienced only individually into a constituent factor of the world.

The philosophy of will can as little be called scientific as can the mysticism based on feeling. For both assert that the conceptual understanding of the world is inadequate. Both demand a principle of existence which is real, in addition to a principle which is ideal. To a certain extent this is justified. But since perceiving is our only means of apprehending these so-called real principles, the assertion of both the mysticism of feeling and the philosophy of will comes to the same thing as saying that we have two sources of knowledge, thinking and perceiving, the latter presenting itself as an individual experience in feeling and will. Since the results that flow from the one source, the experiences, cannot on this view be taken up directly into those that flow from the other source, thinking, the two modes of knowledge, perceiving and thinking, remain side by side without any higher form of mediation between them. Besides the ideal principle which is accessible to knowledge, there is said to be a real principle which cannot be apprehended by thinking but can yet be experienced. In other words, the mysticism of feeling and the philosophy of will are both forms of naïve realism, because they subscribe to the doctrine that what is directly perceived is real. Compared with naïve realism in its primitive form, they are guilty of the yet further inconsistency of accepting one particular form of perceiving (feeling or will, respectively) as the one and only means of knowing reality, whereas they can only do this at all if they hold in general to the fundamental principle that what is perceived is real. But in that case they ought to attach equal value, for the purposes of knowledge, also to external perception.

The philosophy of will turns into metaphysical realism when it places the element of will even into those spheres of existence where it cannot be experienced directly, as it can in the individual subject. It assumes, outside the subject, a hypothetical principle for whose real existence the sole criterion is subjective experience. As a form of metaphysical realism, the philosophy of will is subject to the criticism made in the preceding chapter, in that it has to get over the contradictory stage inherent in every form of metaphysical realism, and must acknowledge that the will is a universal world process only in so far as it is ideally related to the rest of the world.

The Idea of Freedom

FOR our cognition, the concept of the tree is conditioned by the percept of the tree. When faced with a particular percept, I can select only one particular concept from the general system of concepts. The connection of concept and percept is determined by thinking, indirectly and objectively, at the level of the percept. This connection of the percept with its concept is recognized after the act of perceiving; but that they do belong together lies in the very nature of things.

The process looks different when we examine knowledge, or rather the relation of man to the world which arises within knowledge. In the preceding chapters the attempt has been made to show that an unprejudiced observation of this relationship is able to throw light on its nature. A proper understanding of this observation leads to the insight that thinking can be directly discerned as a self-contained entity. Those who find it necessary for the explanation of thinking as such to invoke something else, such as physical brain processes or unconscious spiritual processes lying behind the conscious thinking which they observe, fail to recognize what an unprejudiced observation of thinking yields. When we observe our thinking, we live during this observation directly within a self-supporting, spiritual web of being. Indeed, we can even say that if we would grasp the essential nature of spirit in the form in which it presents itself most immediately to man, we need only look at the self-sustaining activity of thinking.

When we are contemplating thinking itself, two things coincide which otherwise must always appear apart, namely, concept and percept. If we fail to see this, we shall be unable to regard the concepts which we have elaborated with respect to percepts as anything but shadowy copies of these percepts, and we shall take the percepts as presenting to us the true reality. We shall, further, build up for ourselves a metaphysical world after the pattern of the perceived world; we shall call this a world of atoms, a world of will, a world of unconscious spirit, or whatever, each according to his own kind of mental imagery. And we shall fail to notice that all the time we have been doing nothing but building up a metaphysical world hypothetically, after the pattern of our own world of percepts. But if we recognize what is present in thinking, we shall realize that in the percept we have only one part of the reality and that the other part which belongs to it, and which first allows the full reality to appear, is experienced by us in the permeation of the percept by thinking. We shall see in this element that appears in our consciousness as thinking, not a shadowy copy of some reality, but a self-sustaining spiritual essence. And of this we shall be able to say that it is brought into consciousness for us through intuition. Intuition is the conscious experience — in pure spirit — of a purely spiritual content. Only through an intuition can the essence of thinking be grasped.

Only if, by means of unprejudiced observation, one has wrestled through to the recognition of this truth of the intuitive essence of thinking will one succeed in clearing the way for an insight into the psyche-physical organization of man. One will see that this organization can have no effect on the essential nature of thinking. At first sight this seems to be contradicted by patently obvious facts. For ordinary experience, human thinking makes its appearance only in connection with, and by means of, this organization. This form of its appearance comes so much to the fore that its real significance cannot be grasped unless we recognize that in the essence of thinking this organization plays no part whatever. Once we appreciate this, we can no longer fail to notice what a peculiar kind of relationship there is between the human organization and the thinking itself. For this organization contributes nothing to the essential nature of thinking, but recedes whenever the activity of thinking makes its appearance; it suspends its own activity, it yields ground; and on the ground thus left empty, the thinking appears. The essence which is active in thinking has a twofold function: first, it represses the activity of the human organization; secondly, it steps into its place. For even the former, the repression of the physical organization, is a consequence of the activity of thinking, and more particularly of that part of this activity which prepares the manifestation of thinking. From this one can see in what sense thinking finds its counterpart in the physical organization. When we see this, we can no longer misjudge the significance of this counterpart of the activity of thinking. When we walk over soft ground, our feet leave impressions in the soil. We shall not be tempted to say that these footprints have been formed from below by the forces of the ground. We shall not attribute to these forces any share in the production of the footprints. Just as little, if we observe the essential nature of thinking without prejudice, shall we attribute any share in that nature to the traces in the physical organism which arise through the fact that the thinking prepares its manifestation by means of the body.

An important question, however, emerges here. If the human organization has no part in the essential nature of thinking, what is the significance of this organization within the whole nature of man? Now, what happens in this organization through the thinking has indeed nothing to do with the essence of thinking, but it has a great deal to do with the arising of the ego-consciousness out of this thinking. Thinking, in its own essential nature, certainly contains the real I or ego, but it does not contain the ego-consciousness. To see this we have but to observe thinking with an open mind. The "I" is to be found within the thinking; the "ego-consciousness" arises through the traces which the activity of thinking engraves upon our general consciousness, in the sense explained above. (The ego-consciousness thus arises through the bodily organization. However, this must not be taken to imply that the ego-consciousness, once it has arisen, remains dependent on the bodily organization. Once arisen, it is taken up into thinking and shares henceforth in thinking's spiritual being.)

The "ego-consciousness" is built upon the human organization. Out of the latter flow our acts of will. Following the lines of the preceding argument, we can gain insight into the connections between thinking, conscious I, and act of will, only by observing first how an act of will issues from the human organization.

In any particular act of will we must take into account the motive and the driving force. The motive is a factor with the character of a concept or a mental picture; the driving force is the will-factor belonging to the human organization and directly conditioned by it. The conceptual factor, or motive, is the momentary determining factor of the will; the driving force is the permanent determining factor of the individual. A motive for the will may be a pure concept, or else a concept with a particular reference to a percept, that is, a mental picture. Both general concepts and individual ones (mental pictures) become motives of will by affecting the human individual and determining him to action in a particular direction. But one and the same concept, or one and the same mental picture, affects different individuals differently. They stimulate different men to different actions. An act of will is therefore not merely the outcome of the concept or the mental picture but also of the individual make-up of the person. Here we may well follow the example of Eduard von Hartmann and call this individual make-up the characterological disposition. The manner in which concept and mental picture affects the characterological disposition of a man gives to his life a definite moral or ethical stamp.

The characterological disposition is formed by the more or less permanent content of our subjective life, that is, by the content of our mental pictures and feelings. Whether a mental picture which enters my mind at this moment stimulates me to an act of will or not, depends on how it relates itself to the content of all my other mental pictures and also to my idiosyncrasies of feeling. But after all, the general content of my mental pictures is itself conditioned by the sum total of those concepts which have, in the course of my individual life, come into contact with percepts, that is, have become mental pictures. This sum, again, depends on my greater or lesser capacity for intuition and on the range of my observations, that is, on the subjective and objective factors of experience, on my inner nature and situation in life. My characterological disposition is determined especially by my life of feeling. Whether I shall make a particular mental picture or concept into a motive of action or not, will depend on whether it gives me joy or pain.

These are the elements which we have to consider in an act of will. The immediately present mental picture or concept, which becomes the motive, determines the aim or the purpose of my will; my characterological disposition determines me to direct my activity towards this aim. The mental picture of taking a walk in the next half-hour determines the aim of my action. But this mental picture is raised to the level of a motive for my will only if it meets with a suitable characterological disposition, that is, if during my past life I have formed the mental pictures of the sense and purpose of taking a walk, of the value of health, and further, if the mental picture of taking a walk is accompanied in me by a feeling of pleasure.

We must therefore distinguish (1) the possible subjective dispositions which are capable of turning certain mental pictures and concepts into motives, and (2) the possible mental pictures and concepts which are in a position to influence my characterological disposition so that an act of will results. For our moral life the former represent the driving force, and the latter, its aims.

The driving force in the moral life can be discovered by finding out the elements of which individual life is composed.

The first level of individual life is that of perceiving, more particularly perceiving through the senses. This is the region of our individual life in which perceiving translates itself directly into willing, without the intervention of either a feeling or a concept. The driving force here involved is simply called instinct. The satisfaction of our lower, purely animal needs (hunger, sexual intercourse, etc.) comes about in this way. The main characteristic of instinctive life is the immediacy with which the single percept releases the act of will. This kind of determination of the will, which belongs originally only to the life of the lower senses, may however become extended also to the percepts of the higher senses. We may react to the percept of a certain event in the external world without reflecting on what we do, without any special feeling connecting itself with the percept, as in fact happens in our conventional social behaviour. The driving force of such action is called tact or moral good taste. The more often such immediate reactions to a percept occur, the more the person concerned will prove himself able to act purely under the guidance of tact; that is, tact becomes his characterological disposition.

The second level of human life is feeling. Definite feelings accompany the percepts of the external world. These feelings may become the driving force of an action. When I see a starving man, my pity for him may become the driving force of my action. Such feelings, for example, are shame, pride, sense of honour, humility, remorse, pity, revenge, gratitude, piety, loyalty, love, and duty.

The third level of life amounts to thinking and forming mental pictures. A mental picture or a concept may become the motive of an action through mere reflection. Mental pictures become motives because, in the course of life, we regularly connect certain aims of our will with percepts which recur again and again in more or less modified form. Hence with people not wholly devoid of experience it happens that the occurrence of certain percepts is always accompanied by the appearance in consciousness of mental pictures of actions that they themselves have carried out in a similar case or have seen others carry out. These mental pictures float before their minds as patterns which determine all subsequent decisions; they become parts of their characterological disposition. The driving force in the will, in this case, we can call practical experience. Practical experience merges gradually into purely tactful behaviour. This happens when definite typical pictures of actions have become so firmly connected in our minds with mental pictures of certain situations in life that, in any given instance, we skip over all deliberation based on experience and go straight from the percept to the act of will.

The highest level of individual life is that of conceptual thinking without regard to any definite perceptual content. We determine the content of a concept through pure intuition from out of the ideal sphere. Such a concept contains, at first, no reference to any definite percepts. If we enter upon an act of will under the influence of a concept which refers to a percept, that is, under the influence of a mental picture, then it is this percept which determines our action indirectly by way of the conceptual thinking. But if we act under the influence of intuitions, the driving force of our action is pure thinking. As it is the custom in philosophy to call the faculty of pure thinking "reason", we may well be justified in giving the name of practical reason to the moral driving force characteristic of this level of life. The clearest account of this driving force in the will has been given by Kreyenbuehl. In my opinion his article on this subject is one of the most important contributions to present-day philosophy, more especially to Ethics. Kreyenbuehl calls the driving force we are here discussing, the practical a priori, that is, an impulse to action issuing directly from my intuition.

It is clear that such an impulse can no longer be counted in the strictest sense as belonging to the characterological disposition. For what is here effective as the driving force is no longer something merely individual in me, but the ideal and hence universal content of my intuition. As soon as I see the justification for taking this content as the basis and starting point of an action, I enter upon the act of will irrespective of whether I have had the concept beforehand or whether it only enters my consciousness immediately before the action, that is, irrespective of whether it was already present as a disposition in me or not.

Since a real act of will results only when a momentary impulse to action, in the form of a concept or mental picture, acts on the characterological disposition, such an impulse then becomes the motive of the will.

The motives of moral conduct are mental pictures and concepts. There are Moral Philosophers who see a motive for moral behaviour also in the feelings; they assert, for instance, that the aim of moral action is to promote the greatest possible quantity of pleasure for the acting individual. Pleasure itself, however, cannot become a motive; only an imagined pleasure can. The mental picture of a future feeling, but not the feeling itself, can act on my characterological disposition. For the feeling itself does not yet exist in the moment of action; it has first to be produced by the action.

The mental picture of one's own or another's welfare is, however, rightly regarded as a motive of the will. The principle of producing the greatest quantity of pleasure for oneself through one's action, that is, of attaining individual happiness, is called egoism. The attainment of this individual happiness is sought either by thinking ruthlessly only of one's own good and striving to attain it even at the cost of the happiness of other individuals (pure egoism), or by promoting the good of others, either because one anticipates a favourable influence on one's own person indirectly through the happiness of others, or because one fears to endanger one's own interest by injuring others (morality of prudence). The special content of the egoistical principles of morality will depend on the mental pictures which we form of what constitutes our own, or others', happiness. A man will determine the content of his egoistical striving in accordance with what he regards as the good things of life (luxury, hope of happiness, deliverance from various evils, and so on).

The purely conceptual content of an action is to be regarded as yet another kind of motive. This content refers not to the particular action only, as with the mental picture of one's own pleasures, but to the derivation of an action from a system of moral principles. These moral principles, in the form of abstract concepts, may regulate the individual's moral life without his worrying himself about the origin of the concepts. In that case, we simply feel that submitting to a moral concept in the form of a commandment overshadowing our actions, is a moral necessity. The establishment of this necessity we leave to those who demand moral subjection from us, that is, to the moral authority that we acknowledge (the head of the family, the state, social custom, the authority of the church, divine revelation). It is a special kind of these moral principles when the commandment is made known to us not through an external authority but through our own inner life (moral autonomy). In this case we hear the voice to which we have to submit ourselves, in our own souls. This voice expresses itself as conscience.

It is a moral advance when a man no longer simply accepts the commands of an outer or inner authority as the motive of his action, but tries to understand the reason why a particular maxim of behaviour should act as a motive in him. This is the advance from morality based on authority to action out of moral insight. At this level of morality a man will try to find out the requirements of the moral life and will let his actions be determined by the knowledge of them. Such requirements are

1. the greatest possible good of mankind purely for its own sake;   2. the progress of civilization, or the moral evolution of mankind towards ever greater perfection;   3. the realization of individual moral aims grasped by pure intuition.

The greatest possible good of mankind will naturally be understood in different ways by different people. This maxim refers not to any particular mental picture of this "good" but to the fact that everyone who acknowledges this principle strives to do whatever, in his opinion, most promotes the good of mankind.

The progress of civilization, for those to whom the blessings of civilization bring a feeling of pleasure, turns out to be a special case of the foregoing moral principle. Of course, they will have to take into the bargain the decline and destruction of a number of things that also contribute to the general good. It is also possible, however, that some people regard the progress of civilization as a moral necessity quite apart from the feeling of pleasure that it brings. For them, this becomes a special moral principle in addition to the previous one.

The principle of the progress of civilization, like that of the general good, is based on a mental picture, that is, on the way we relate the content of our moral ideas to particular experiences (percepts). The highest conceivable moral principle, however, is one that from the start contains no such reference to particular experiences, but springs from the source of pure intuition and only later seeks any reference to percepts, that is, to life. Here the decision as to what is to be willed proceeds from an authority very different from that of the foregoing cases. If a man holds to the principle of the general good, he will, in all his actions, first ask what his ideals will contribute to this general good. If a man upholds the principle of the progress of civilization, he will act similarly. But there is a still higher way which does not start from one and the same particular moral aim in each case, but sees a certain value in all moral principles and always asks whether in the given case this or that principle is the more important. It may happen that in some circumstances a man considers the right aim to be the progress of civilization, in others the promotion of the general good, and in yet another the promotion of his own welfare, and in each case makes that the motive of his action. But if no other ground for decision claims more than second place, then conceptual intuition itself comes first and foremost into consideration. All other motives now give way, and the idea behind an action alone becomes its motive.

Among the levels of characterological disposition, we have singled out as the highest the one that works as pure thinking or practical reason. Among the motives, we have just singled out conceptual intuition as the highest. On closer inspection it will at once be seen that at this level of morality driving force and motive coincide; that is, neither a predetermined characterological disposition nor the external authority of an accepted moral principle influences our conduct. The action is therefore neither a stereotyped one which merely follows certain rules, nor is it one which we automatically perform in response to an external impulse, but it is an action determined purely and simply by its own ideal content.

Such an action presupposes the capacity for moral intuitions. Whoever lacks the capacity to experience for himself the particular moral principle for each single situation, will never achieve truly individual willing.

Kant's principle of morality — Act so that the basis of your action may be valid for all men — is the exact opposite of ours. His principle means death to all individual impulses of action. For me, the standard can never be the way all men would act, but rather what, for me, is to be done in each individual case.

A superficial judgment might raise the following objection to these arguments: How can an action be individually made to fit the special case and the special situation, and yet at the same time be determined by intuition in a purely ideal way? This objection rests upon a confusion of the moral motive with the perceptible content of an action. The latter may be a motive, and actually is one in the case of the progress of civilization, or when we act from egoism, and so forth, but in an action based on pure moral intuition it is not the motive. Of course, my "I" takes notice of these perceptual contents, but it does not allow itself to be determined by them. The content is used only to construct a cognitive concept, but the corresponding moral concept is not derived by the "I" from the object. The cognitive concept of a given situation facing me is at the same time a moral concept only if I take the standpoint of a particular moral principle. If I were to base my conduct only on the general principle of the development of civilization, then my way through life would be tied down to a fixed route. From every occurrence which I perceive and which concerns me, there springs at the same time a moral duty: namely, to do my little bit towards seeing that this occurrence is made to serve the development of civilization. In addition to the concept which reveals to me the connections of events or objects according to the laws of nature, there is also a moral label attached to them which for me, as a moral person, gives ethical directions as to how I have to conduct myself. Such a moral label is justified on its own ground; at a higher level it coincides with the idea which reveals itself to me when I am faced with the concrete instance.

Men vary greatly in their capacity for intuition. In one, ideas just bubble up; another acquires them with much labour. The situations in which men live and which provide the scenes of their actions are no less varied. The conduct of a man will therefore depend on the manner in which his faculty of intuition works in a given situation. The sum of ideas which are effective in us, the concrete content of our intuitions, constitutes what is individual in each of us, notwithstanding the universality of the world of ideas. In so far as this intuitive content applies to action, it constitutes the moral content of the individual. To let this content express itself in life is both the highest moral driving force and the highest motive a man can have, who sees that in this content all other moral principles are in the end united. We may call this point of view ethical individualism.

The decisive factor of an intuitively determined action in any concrete instance is the discovery of the corresponding purely individual intuition. At this level of morality one can only speak of general concepts of morality (standards, laws) in so far as these result from the generalization of the individual impulses. General standards always presuppose concrete facts from which they can be derived. But the facts have first to be created by human action.

If we seek out the rules (conceptual principles) underlying the actions of individuals, peoples, and epochs, we obtain a system of ethics which is not so much a science of moral laws as a natural history of morality. It is only the laws obtained in this way that are related to human action as the laws of nature are related to a particular phenomenon. These laws, however, are by no means identical with the impulses on which we base our actions. If we want to understand how a man's action arises from his moral will, we must first study the relation of this will to the action. Above all, we must keep our eye on those actions in which this relation is the determining factor. If I, or someone else, reflect upon such an action afterwards, we can discover what moral principles come into question with regard to it. While I am performing the action I am influenced by a moral maxim in so far as it can live in me intuitively; it is bound up with my love for the objective that I want to realize through my action. I ask no man and no rule, "Shall I perform this action?" — but carry it out as soon as I have grasped the idea of it. This alone makes it my action. If a man acts only because he accepts certain moral standards, his action is the outcome of the principles which compose his moral code. He merely carries out orders. He is a superior automaton. Inject some stimulus to action into his mind, and at once the clockwork of his moral principles will set itself in motion and run its prescribed course, so as to result in an action which is Christian, or humane, or seemingly unselfish, or calculated to promote the progress of civilization. Only when I follow my love for my objective is it I myself who act. I act, at this level of morality, not because I acknowledge a lord over me, or an external authority, or a so-called inner voice; I acknowledge no external principle for my action, because I have found in myself the ground for my action, namely, my love of the action. I do not work out mentally whether my action is good or bad; I carry it out because I love it. My action will be "good" if my intuition, steeped in love, finds its right place within the intuitively experienceable world continuum; it will be "bad" if this is not the case. Again, I do not ask myself, "How would another man act in my position?" — but I act as I, this particular individuality, find I have occasion to do. No general usage, no common custom, no maxim applying to all men, no moral standard is my immediate guide, but my love for the deed. I feel no compulsion, neither the compulsion of nature which guides me by my instincts, nor the compulsion of the moral commandments, but I want simply to carry out what lies within me.

Those who defend general moral standards might reply to these arguments that if everyone strives to live his own life and do what he pleases, there can be no distinction between a good deed and a crime; every corrupt impulse that lies within me has as good a claim to express itself as has the intention of serving the general good. What determines me as a moral being cannot be the mere fact of my having conceived the idea of an action, but whether I judge it to be good or evil. Only in the former case should I carry it out.

My reply to this very obvious objection, which is nevertheless based on a misapprehension of my argument, is this: If we want to understand the nature of the human will, we must distinguish between the path which leads this will to a certain degree of development and the unique character which the will assumes as it approaches this goal. On the path towards this goal the standards play their rightful part. The goal consists of the realization of moral aims grasped by pure intuition. Man attains such aims to the extent that he is able to raise himself at all to the intuitive world of ideas. In any particular act of will such moral aims will generally have other elements mixed in with them, either as driving force or as motive. Nevertheless intuition may still be wholly or partly the determining factor in the human will. What one should do, that one does; one provides the stage upon which obligation becomes deed; one's own action is what one brings forth from oneself. Here the impulse can only be wholly individual. And, in truth, only an act of will that springs from intuition can be an individual one. To regard evil, the deed of a criminal, as an expression of the human individuality in the same sense as one regards the embodiment of pure intuition is only possible if blind instincts are reckoned as part of the human individuality. But the blind instinct that drives a man to crime does not spring from intuition, and does not belong to what is individual in him, but rather to what is most general in him, to what is equally present in all individuals and out of which a man works his way by means of what is individual in him. What is individual in me is not my organism with its instincts and its feelings but rather the unified world of ideas which lights up within this organism. My instincts, urges and passions establish no more than that I belong to the general species man; it is the fact that something of the idea world comes to expression in a particular way within these urges, passions and feelings that establishes my individuality. Through my instincts and cravings, I am the sort of man of whom there are twelve to the dozen; through the particular form of the idea by means of which I designate myself within the dozen as "I", I am an individual. Only a being other than myself could distinguish me from others by the difference in my animal nature; through my thinking, that is, by actively grasping what expresses itself in my organism as idea, I distinguish myself from others. Therefore one cannot say of the action of a criminal that it proceeds from the idea within him. Indeed, the characteristic feature of criminal actions is precisely that they spring from the non-ideal elements in man.

An action is felt to be free in so far as the reasons for it spring from the ideal part of my individual being; every other part of an action, irrespective of whether it is carried out under the compulsion of nature or under the obligation of a moral standard, is felt to be unfree.

Man is free in so far as he is able to obey himself in every moment of his life. A moral deed is my deed only if it can be called a free one in this sense. We have here considered what conditions are required for an intentional action to be felt as a free one; how this purely ethically understood idea of freedom comes to realization in the being of man will be shown in what follows.

Acting out of freedom does not exclude the moral laws; it includes them, but shows itself to be on a higher level than those actions which are merely dictated by such laws. Why should my action be of less service to the public good when I have done it out of love than when I have done it only because I consider serving the public good to be my duty? The mere concept of duty excludes freedom because it does not acknowledge the individual element but demands that this be subject to a general standard. Freedom of action is conceivable only from the standpoint of ethical individualism.

But how is a social life possible for man if each one is only striving to assert his own individuality? This objection is characteristic of a false understanding of moralism. Such a moralist believes that a social community is possible only if all men are united by a communally fixed moral order. What this kind of moralist does not understand is just the unity of the world of ideas. He does not see that the world of ideas working in me is no other than the one working in my fellow man. Admittedly, this unity is but an outcome of practical experience. But in fact it cannot be anything else. For if it could be known in any other way than by observation, then in its own sphere universal standards rather than individual experience would be the rule. Individuality is possible only if every individual being knows of others through individual observation alone. I differ from my fellow man, not at all because we are living in two entirely different spiritual worlds, but because from the world of ideas common to us both we receive different intuitions. He wants to live out his intuitions, I mine. If we both really conceive out of the idea, and do not obey any external impulses (physical or spiritual), then we cannot but meet one another in like striving, in common intent. A moral misunderstanding, a clash, is impossible between men who are morally free. Only the morally unfree who follow their natural instincts or the accepted commands of duty come into conflict with their neighbours if these do not obey the same instincts and the same commands as themselves. To live in love towards our actions, and to let live in the understanding of the other person's will, is the fundamental maxim of free men. They know no other obligation than what their will puts itself in unison with intuitively; how they will direct their will in a particular case, their faculty for ideas will decide.

Were the ability to get on with one another not a basic part of human nature, no external laws would be able to implant it in us. It is only because human individuals are one in spirit that they can live out their lives side by side. The free man lives in confidence that he and any other free man belong to one spiritual world, and that their intentions will harmonize. The free man does not demand agreement from his fellow man, but expects to find it because it is inherent in human nature. I am not here referring to the necessity for this or that external institution, but to the disposition, the attitude of soul, through which a man, aware of himself among his fellows, most clearly expresses the ideal of human dignity.

There are many who will say that the concept of the free man which I have here developed is a chimera nowhere to be found in practice; we have to do with actual human beings, from whom we can only hope for morality if they obey some moral law, that is, if they regard their moral task as a duty and do not freely follow their inclinations and loves. I do not doubt this at all. Only a blind man could do so. But if this is to be the final conclusion, then away with all this hypocrisy about morality! Let us then simply say that human nature must be driven to its actions as long as it is not free. Whether his unfreedom is forced on him by physical means or by moral laws, whether man is unfree because he follows his unlimited sexual desire or because he is bound by the fetters of conventional morality, is quite immaterial from a certain point of view. Only let us not assert that such a man can rightly call his actions his own, seeing that he is driven to them by a force other than himself. But in the midst of all this framework of compulsion there arise men who establish themselves as free spirits in all the welter of customs, legal codes, religious observances, and so forth. They are free in so far as they obey only themselves, unfree in so far as they submit to control. Which of us can say that he is really free in all his actions? Yet in each of us there dwells a deeper being in which the free man finds expression.

Our life is made up of free and unfree actions. We cannot, however, think out the concept of man completely without coming upon the free spirit as the purest expression of human nature. Indeed, we are men in the true sense only in so far as we are free.

This is an ideal, many will say. Doubtless; but it is an ideal which is a real element in us working its way to the surface of our nature. It is no ideal just thought up or dreamed, but one which has life, and which announces itself clearly even in the least perfect form of its existence. If man were merely a natural creature, there would be no such thing as the search for ideals, that is, for ideas which for the moment are not effective but whose realization is required. With the things of the outer world, the idea is determined by the percept; we have done our share when we have recognized the connection between idea and percept. But with the human being it is not so. The sum total of his existence is not fully determined without his own self; his true concept as a moral being (free spirit) is not objectively united from the start with the percept-picture "man" needing only to be confirmed by knowledge afterwards. Man must unite his concept with the percept of man by his own activity. Concept and percept coincide in this case only if man himself makes them coincide. This he can do only if he has found the concept of the free spirit, that is, if he has found the concept of his own self. In the objective world a dividing line is drawn by our organization between percept and concept; knowledge overcomes this division. In our subjective nature this division is no less present; man overcomes it in the course of his development by bringing the concept of himself to expression in his outward existence. Hence not only man's intellectual but also his moral life leads to his twofold nature, perceiving (direct experience) and thinking. The intellectual life overcomes this two-fold nature by means of knowledge, the moral life overcomes it through the actual realization of the free spirit. Every existing thing has its inborn concept (the law of its being and doing), but in external objects this concept is indivisibly bound up with the percept, and separated from it only within our spiritual organization. In man concept and percept are, at first, actually separated, to be just as actually united by him.

One might object: At every moment of a man's life there is a definite concept corresponding to our percept of him just as with everything else. I can form for myself the concept of a particular type of man, and I may even find such a man given to me as a percept; if I now add to this the concept of a free spirit, then I have two concepts for the same object.

Such an objection is one-sided. As object of perception I am subjected to continual change. As a child I was one thing, another as a youth, yet another as a man. Indeed, at every moment the percept-picture of myself is different from what it was the moment before. These changes may take place in such a way that it is always the same man (the type) who reveals himself in them, or that they represent the expression of a free spirit. To such changes my action, as object of perception, is subjected.

The perceptual object "man" has in it the possibility of transforming itself, just as the plant seed contains the possibility of becoming a complete plant. The plant transforms itself because of the objective law inherent in it; the human being remains in his incomplete state unless he takes hold of the material for transformation within him and transforms himself through his own power. Nature makes of man merely a natural being; society makes of him a law-abiding being; only he himself can make of himself a free man. Nature releases man from her fetters at a definite stage in his development; society carries this development a stage further; he alone can give himself the final polish.

The standpoint of free morality, then, does not declare the free spirit to be the only form in which a man can exist. It sees in the free spirit only the last stage of man's evolution. This is not to deny that conduct according to standards has its justification as one stage in evolution. Only we cannot acknowledge it as the absolute standpoint in morality. For the free spirit overcomes the standards in the sense that he does not just accept commandments as his motives but orders his action according to his own impulses (intuitions).

When Kant says of duty: "Duty! Thou exalted and mighty name, thou that dost comprise nothing lovable, nothing ingratiating, but demandest submission," thou that "settest up a law ... before which all inclinations are silent, even though they secretly work against it," then out of the consciousness of the free spirit, man replies: "Freedom! Thou kindly and human name, thou that dost comprise all that is morally most lovable, all that my manhood most prizes, and that makest me the servant of nobody, thou that settest up no mere law, but awaitest what my moral love itself will recognize as law because in the face of every merely imposed law it feels itself unfree."

This is the contrast between a morality based on mere law and a morality based on inner freedom.

The philistine, who sees the embodiment of morality in an external code, may see in the free spirit even a dangerous person. But that is only because his view is narrowed down to a limited period of time. If he were able to look beyond this, he would at once find that the free spirit just as seldom needs to go beyond the laws of his state as does the philistine himself, and certainly never needs to place himself in real opposition to them. For the laws of the state, one and all, just like all other objective laws of morality, have had their origin in the intuitions of free spirits. There is no rule enforced by family authority that was not at one time intuitively grasped and laid down as such by an ancestor; similarly the conventional laws of morality are first of all established by definite men, and the laws of the state always originate in the head of a statesman. These leading spirits have set up laws over other men, and the only person who feels unfree is the one who forgets this origin and either turns these laws into extra-human commandments, objective moral concepts of duty independent of man, or else turns them into the commanding voice within himself which he supposes, in a falsely mystical way, to be compelling him. On the other hand, the person who does not overlook this origin, but seeks man within it, will count such laws as belonging to the same world of ideas from which he, too, draws his moral intuitions. If he believes he has better intuitions, he will try to put them into the place of the existing ones; if he finds the existing ones justified, he will act in accordance with them as if they were his own.

We must not coin the formula: Man exists only in order to realize a moral world order which is quite distinct from himself. Anyone who maintains that this is so, remains, in his knowledge of man, at the point where natural science stood when it believed that a bull has horns in order to butt. Scientists, happily, have thrown out the concept of purpose as a dead theory. Ethics finds it more difficult to get free of this concept. But just as horns do not exist for the sake of butting, but butting through the presence of horns, so man does not exist for the sake of morality, but morality through the presence of man. The free man acts morally because he has a moral idea; he does not act in order that morality may come into being. Human individuals, with the moral ideas belonging to their nature, are the prerequisites of a moral world order.

The human individual is the source of all morality and the centre of earthly life. State and society exist only because they have arisen as a necessary consequence of the life of individuals. That state and society should in turn react upon individual life is no more difficult to comprehend than that the butting which is the result of the presence of horns reacts in turn upon the further development of the horns of the bull, which would become stunted through prolonged disuse. Similarly, the individual would become stunted if he led an isolated existence outside human society. Indeed, this is just why the social order arises, so that it may in turn react favourably upon the individual.

Freedom — Philosophy and Monism

THE naïve man, who acknowledges as real only what he can see with his eyes and grasp with his hands, requires for his moral life, also, a basis for action that shall be perceptible to the senses. He requires someone or something to impart the basis for his action to him in a way that his senses can understand. He is ready to allow this basis for action to be dictated to him as commandments by any man whom he considers wiser or more powerful than himself, or whom he acknowledges for some other reason to be a power over him. In this way there arise, as moral principles, the authority of family, state, society, church and God, as previously described. A man who is very narrow minded still puts his faith in some one person; the more advanced man allows his moral conduct to be dictated by a majority (state, society). It is always on perceptible powers that he builds. The man who awakens at last to the conviction that basically these powers are human beings as weak as himself, seeks guidance from a higher power, from a Divine Being, whom he endows, however, with sense perceptible features. He conceives this Being as communicating to him the conceptual content of his moral life, again in a perceptible way — whether it be, for example, that God appears in the burning bush, or that He moves about among men in manifest human shape, and that their ears can hear Him telling them what to do and what not to do.

The highest stage of development of naïve realism in the sphere of morality is that where the moral commandment (moral idea) is separated from every being other than oneself and is thought of, hypothetically, as being an absolute power in one's own inner life. What man first took to be the external voice of God, he now takes as an independent power within him, and speaks of this inner voice in such a way as to identify it with conscience.

But in doing this he has already gone beyond the stage of naïve consciousness into the sphere where the moral laws have become independently existing standards. There they are no longer carried by real bearers, but have become metaphysical entities existing in their own right. They are analogous to the invisible "visible forces" of metaphysical realism, which does not seek reality through the part of it that man has in his thinking, but hypothetically adds it on to actual experience. These extra-human moral standards always occur as accompanying features of metaphysical realism. For metaphysical realism is bound to seek the origin of morality in the sphere of extra-human reality. Here there are several possibilities. If the hypothetically assumed entity is conceived as in itself unthinking, acting according to purely mechanical laws, as materialism would have it, then it must also produce out of itself, by purely mechanical necessity, the human individual with all his characteristic features. The consciousness of freedom can then be nothing more than an illusion. For though I consider myself the author of my action, it is the matter of which I am composed and the movements going on in it that are working in me. I believe myself free; but in fact all my actions are nothing but the result of the material processes which underlie my physical and mental organization. It is said that we have the feeling of freedom only because we do not know the motives compelling us.

We must emphasize that the feeling of freedom is due to the absence of external compelling motives ... Our action is necessitated as is our thinking.

Another possibility is that a man may picture the extra-human Absolute that lies behind the world of appearances as a spiritual being. In this case he will also seek the impulse for his actions in a corresponding spiritual force. He will see the moral principles to be found in his own reason as the expression of this being itself, which has its own special intentions with regard to man. To this kind of dualist the moral laws appear to be dictated by the Absolute, and all that man has to do is to use his intelligence to find out the decisions of the absolute being and then carry them out. The moral world order appears to the dualist as the perceptible reflection of a higher order standing behind it. Earthly morality is the manifestation of the extra-human world order. It is not man that matters in this moral order, but the being itself, that is, the extra-human entity. Man shall do as this being wills. Eduard von Hartmann, who imagines this being itself as a Godhead whose very existence is a life of suffering, believes that this Divine Being has created the world in order thereby to gain release from His infinite suffering. Hence this philosopher regards the moral evolution of humanity as a process which is there for the redemption of God.

Only through the building up of a moral world order by intelligent self-conscious individuals can the world process be led towards its goal. ... True existence is the incarnation of the Godhead; the world process is the Passion of the incarnated Godhead and at the same time the way of redemption for Him who was crucified in the flesh; morality, however, is the collaboration in the shortening of this path of suffering and redemption.

Here man does not act because he wants to, but he shall act, because it is God's will to be redeemed. Whereas the materialistic dualist makes man an automaton whose actions are only the result of a purely mechanical system, the spiritualistic dualist (that is, one who sees the Absolute, the Being-in-itself, as something spiritual in which man has no share in his conscious experience) makes him a slave to the will of the Absolute. As in materialism, so also in one-sided spiritualism, in fact in any kind of metaphysical realism inferring but not experiencing something extra-human as the true reality, freedom is out of the question.

Metaphysical as well as naïve realism, consistently followed out, must deny freedom for one and the same reason: they both see man as doing no more than putting into effect, or carrying out, principles forced upon him by necessity. Naive realism destroys freedom by subjecting man to the authority of a perceptible being or of one conceived on the analogy of a perceptible being, or eventually to the authority of the abstract inner voice which it interprets as "conscience"; the metaphysician, who merely infers the extra-human reality, cannot acknowledge freedom because he sees man as being determined, mechanically or morally, by a "Being-in-itself".

Monism will have to recognize that naïve realism is partially justified because it recognizes the justification of the world of percepts. Whoever is incapable of producing moral ideas through intuition must accept them from others. In so far as a man receives his moral principles from without, he is in fact unfree. But monism attaches as much significance to the idea as to the percept. The idea, however, can come to manifestation in the human individual. In so far as man follows the impulses coming from this side, he feels himself to be free. But monism denies all justification to metaphysics, which merely draws inferences, and consequently also to the impulses of action which are derived from so-called "Beings-in-themselves". According to the monistic view, man may act unfreely-when he obeys some perceptible external compulsion; he can act freely, when he obeys none but himself. Monism cannot recognize any unconscious compulsion hidden behind percept and concept. If anyone asserts that the action of a fellow man is done unfreely, then he must identify the thing or the person or the institution within the perceptible world, that has caused the person to act; and if he bases his assertion upon causes of action lying outside the world that is real to the senses and the spirit, then monism can take no notice of it.

According to the monistic view, then, man's action is partly unfree, partly free. He finds himself to be unfree in the world of percepts, and he realizes within himself the free spirit.

The moral laws which the metaphysician who works by mere inference must regard as issuing from a higher power, are, for the adherent of monism, thoughts of men; for him the moral world order is neither the imprint of a purely mechanical natural order, nor that of an extra-human world order, but through and through the free creation of men. It is not the will of some being outside him in the world that man has to carry out, but his own; he puts into effect his own resolves and intentions, not those of another being. Monism does not see, behind man's actions, the purposes of a supreme directorate, foreign to him and determining him according to its will, but rather sees that men, in so far as they realize their intuitive ideas, pursue only their own human ends. Moreover, each individual pursues his own particular ends. For the world of ideas comes to expression, not in a community of men, but only in human individuals. What appears as the common goal of a whole group of people is only the result of the separate acts of will of its individual members, and in fact, usually of a few outstanding ones who, as their authorities, are followed by the others. Each one of us has it in him to be a free spirit, just as every rose bud has in it a rose.

Monism, then, in the sphere of true moral action, is a freedom philosophy. Since it is a philosophy of reality, it rejects the metaphysical, unreal restrictions of the free spirit as completely as it accepts the physical and historical (naïvely real) restrictions of the naïve man. Since it does not consider man as a finished product, disclosing his full nature in every moment of his life, it regards the dispute as to whether man as such is free or not, to be of no consequence. It sees in man a developing being, and asks whether, in the course of this development, the stage of the free spirit can be reached.

Monism knows that Nature does not send man forth from her arms ready made as a free spirit, but that she leads him up to a certain stage from which he continues to develop still as an unfree being until he comes to the point where he finds his own self.

Monism is quite clear that a being acting under physical or moral compulsion cannot be a truly moral being. It regards the phases of automatic behavior (following natural urges and instincts) and of obedient behavior (following moral standards) as necessary preparatory stages of morality, but it also sees that both these transitory stages can be overcome by the free spirit. Monism frees the truly moral world conception both from the mundane fetters of naïve moral maxims and from the transcendental moral maxims of the speculative metaphysician. Monism can no more eliminate the former from the world than it can eliminate percepts; it rejects the latter because it seeks all the principles for the elucidation of the world phenomena within that world, and none outside it.

Just as monism refuses even to think of principles of knowledge other than those that apply to men (see Chapter 7), so it emphatically rejects even the thought of moral maxims other than those that apply to men. Human morality, like human knowledge, is conditioned by human nature. And just as beings of a different order will understand knowledge to mean something very different from what it means to us, so will other beings have a different morality from ours. Morality is for the monist a specifically human quality, and spiritual freedom the human way of being moral.

World Purpose and Life Purpose (The Ordering of Man's Destiny)

AMONG the manifold currents in the spiritual life of mankind, there is one to be followed up which can be described as the overcoming of the concept of purpose in spheres where it does not belong. Purposefulness is a special kind of sequence of phenomena. True purposefulness really exists only if, in contrast to the relationship of cause and effect where the earlier event determines the later, the reverse is the case and the later event influences the earlier one. To begin with, this happens only in the case of human actions. One performs an action of which one has previously made a mental picture, and one allows this mental picture to determine one's action. Thus the later (the deed) influences the earlier (the doer) with the help of the mental picture. For there to be a purposeful connection, this detour through the mental picture is absolutely necessary.

In a process which breaks down into cause and effect, we must distinguish percept from concept. The percept of the cause precedes the percept of the effect; cause and effect would simply remain side by side in our consciousness, if we were not able to connect them with one another through their corresponding concepts. The percept of the effect must always follow upon the percept of the cause. If the effect is to have a real influence upon the cause, it can do so only by means of the conceptual factor. For the perceptual factor of the effect simply does not exist prior to the perceptual factor of the cause. Anyone who declares that the blossom is the purpose of the root, that is, that the former influences the latter, can do so only with regard to that factor in the blossom which is established in it by his thinking. The perceptual factor of the blossom is not yet in existence at the time when the root originates.

For a purposeful connection to exist, it is not only necessary to have an ideal, law-determined connection between the later and the earlier, but the concept (law) of the effect must really influence the cause, that is, by means of a perceptible process. A perceptible influence of a concept upon something else, however, is to be observed only in human actions. Hence this is the only sphere in which the concept of purpose is applicable.

The naïve consciousness, which regards as real only what is perceptible, attempts — as we have repeatedly pointed out — to introduce perceptible elements where only ideal elements are to be found. In the perceptible course of events it looks for perceptible connections, or, failing to find them, it simply invents them. The concept of purpose, valid for subjective actions, is an element well suited for such invented connections. The naïve man knows how he brings an event about and from this he concludes that nature will do it in the same way. In the connections of nature which are purely ideal he finds not only invisible forces but also invisible real purposes. Man makes his tools according to his purposes; the naïve realist would have the Creator build organisms on the same formula. Only very gradually is this mistaken concept of purpose disappearing from the sciences. In philosophy, even today, it still does a good deal of mischief. Here people still ask after the extra-mundane purpose of the world, the extra-human ordering of man's destiny (and consequently also his purpose), and so on.

Monism rejects the concept of purpose in every sphere, with the sole exception of human action. It looks for laws of nature, but not for purposes of nature. Purposes of nature are arbitrary assumptions no less than are imperceptible forces (see Chapter 7). But even purposes of life not set by man himself are unjustified assumptions from the standpoint of monism. Nothing is purposeful except what man has first made so, for purposefulness arises only through the realization of an idea. In a realistic sense, an idea can become effective only in man. Therefore human life can only have the purpose and the ordering of destiny that man gives it. To the question: What is man's task in life? there can be for monism but one answer: The task he sets himself. My mission in the world is not predetermined, but is at every moment the one I choose for myself. I do not set out upon my journey through life with fixed marching orders.

Ideas are realized purposefully only by human beings. Consequently it is not permissible to speak of the embodiment of ideas by history. All such phrases as "history is the evolution of mankind towards freedom," or "... the realization of the moral world order," and so on, are, from a monistic point of view, untenable.

The supporters of the concept of purpose believe that, by surrendering it, they would also have to surrender all order and uniformity in the world. Listen, for example, to Robert Hamerling:

As long as there are instincts in nature, it is folly to deny purposes therein.

Just as the formation of a limb of the human body is not determined and conditioned by an idea of this limb, floating in the air, but by its connection with the greater whole, the body to which the limb belongs, so the formation of every natural object, be it plant, animal or man, is not determined and conditioned by an idea of it floating in the air, but by the formative principle of the totality of nature which unfolds and organizes itself in a purposeful manner.

And on page 191 of the same volume we read:

The theory of purpose maintains only that, in spite of the thousand discomforts and distresses of this mortal life, there is a high degree of purpose and plan unmistakably present in the formations and developments of nature — a degree of plan and purposefulness, however, which is realized only within the limits of natural law, and which does not aim at a fool's paradise where life faces no death, growth no decay, with all their more or less unpleasant but quite unavoidable intermediary stages.

When the opponents of the concept of purpose set a laboriously collected rubbish-heap of partial or complete, imaginary or real maladaptations against a whole world of miracles of purposefulness, such as nature exhibits in all her domains, then I consider this just as quaint ...

What is here meant by purposefulness? The coherence of percepts to form a whole. But since underlying all percepts there are laws (ideas) which we discover through our thinking, it follows that the systematic coherence of the parts of a perceptual whole is simply the ideal coherence of the parts of an ideal whole contained in this perceptual whole. To say that an animal or a man is not determined by an idea floating in the air is a misleading way of putting it, and the point of view he is disparaging automatically loses its absurdity as soon as the expression is put right. An animal certainly is not determined by an idea floating in the air, but it definitely is determined by an idea inborn in it and constituting the law of its being. It is just because the idea is not external to the object, but works within it as its very essence, that we cannot speak of purposefulness. It is just the person who denies that natural beings are determined from without (and it does not matter, in this context, whether it be by an idea floating in the air or existing outside the creature in the mind of a world creator) who must admit that such beings are not determined by purpose and plan from without, but by cause and law from within. I construct a machine purposefully if I connect its parts together in a way that is not given in nature. The purposefulness of the arrangement consists in just this, that I embody the working principle of the machine, as its idea, into the machine itself. The machine becomes thereby an object of perception with the idea corresponding to it. Natural objects are also entities of this kind. Whoever calls a thing purposeful simply because it is formed according to a law, may, if he wish, apply the same term to the objects of nature. But he must not confuse this kind of lawfulness with that of subjective human action. For purpose to exist, it is absolutely necessary that the effective cause shall be a concept, in fact the concept of the effect. But in nature we can nowhere point to concepts acting as causes; the concept invariably turns out to be nothing but the ideal link connecting cause and effect. Causes are present in nature only in the form of percepts.

Dualism may talk of world purposes and natural purposes. Wherever there is a systematic linking of cause and effect for our perception, the dualist may assume that we see only the carbon copy of a connection in which the absolute cosmic Being has realized its purposes. For monism, with the rejection of an absolute cosmic Being — never experienced but only hypothetically inferred — all ground for assuming purposes in the world and in nature also falls away.

Moral Imagination (Darwinism and Morality)

A free spirit acts according to his impulses, that is, according to intuitions selected from the totality of his world of ideas by thinking. For an unfree spirit, the reason why he singles out a particular intuition from his world of ideas in order to make it the basis of an action, lies in the world of percepts given to him, that is, in his past experiences. He recalls, before coming to a decision, what someone else has done or recommended as suitable in a comparable case, or what God has commanded to be done in such a case, and so on, and he acts accordingly. For a free spirit, these prior conditions are not the only impulses to action. He makes a completely first-hand decision. What others have done in such a case worries him as little as what they have decreed. He has purely ideal reasons which lead him to select from the sum of his concepts just one in particular, and then to translate it into action. But his action will belong to perceptible reality. What he achieves will thus be identical with a quite definite content of perception. The concept will have to realize itself in a single concrete occurrence. As a concept it will not be able to contain this particular event. It will refer to the event only in the same way as a concept is in general related to a percept, for example, the concept of the lion to a particular lion. The link between concept and percept is the mental picture (see Chapter 6). For the unfree spirit, this link is given from the outset. Motives are present in his consciousness from the outset in the form of mental pictures. Whenever there is something he wants to carry out, he does it as he has seen it done, or as he has been told to do it in the particular case. Hence authority works best through examples, that is, through providing quite definite particular actions for the consciousness of the unfree spirit. A Christian acts not so much according to the teaching as according to the example of the Saviour. Rules have less value for acting positively than for refraining from certain actions. Laws take on the form of general concepts only when they forbid actions, but not when they prescribe them. Laws concerning what he ought to do must be given to the unfree spirit in quite concrete form: Clean the street in front of your door! Pay your taxes, amounting to the sum here given, to the Tax Office at X! and so on. Conceptual form belongs to laws for inhibiting actions: Thou shalt not steal! Thou shalt not commit adultery! These laws, too, influence the unfree spirit only by means of a concrete mental picture, for example, that of the appropriate secular punishment, or the pangs of conscience, or eternal damnation, and so on.

Whenever the impulse for an action is present in a general conceptual form (for example, Thou shalt do good to thy fellow men! Thou shalt live so that thou best promotest thy welfare!) then for each particular case the concrete mental picture of the action (the relation of the concept to a content of perception) must first be found. For the free spirit who is impelled by no example, nor fear of punishment or the like, this translation of the concept into a mental picture is always necessary.

Man produces concrete mental pictures from the sum of his ideas chiefly by means of the imagination. Therefore what the free spirit needs in order to realize his ideas, in order to be effective, is moral imagination. This is the source of the free spirit's action. Therefore it is only men with moral imagination who are, strictly speaking, morally productive. Those who merely preach morality, that is, people who merely spin out moral rules without being able to condense them into concrete mental pictures, are morally unproductive. They are like those critics who can explain very intelligibly what a work of art ought to be like, but who are themselves incapable of even the slightest productive effort.

Moral imagination, in order to realize its mental picture, must set to work in a definite sphere of percepts. Human action does not create percepts, but transforms already existing percepts and gives them a new form. In order to be able to transform a definite object of perception, or a sum of such objects, in accordance with a moral mental picture, one must have grasped the principle at work within the percept picture, that is, the way it has hitherto worked, to which one wants to give a new form or a new direction. Further, it is necessary to discover the procedure by which it is possible to change the given principle into a new one. This part of effective moral activity depends on knowledge of the particular world of phenomena with which one is concerned. We shall, therefore, look for it in some branch of learning in general. Moral action, then, presupposes, in addition to the faculty of having moral ideas (moral intuition) and moral imagination, the ability to transform the world of percepts without violating the natural laws by which these are connected. This ability is moral technique. It can be learnt in the same sense in which any kind of knowledge can be learnt. Generally speaking, men are better able to find concepts for the existing world than to evolve productively, out of their imagination, the not-yet-existing actions of the future. Hence it is perfectly possible for men without moral imagination to receive such mental pictures from others, and to embody them skillfully into the actual world. Conversely, it may happen that men with moral imagination lack technical skill, and must make use of other men for the realization of their mental pictures.

In so far as knowledge of the objects within our sphere of action is necessary for acting morally, our action depends upon such knowledge. What we are concerned with here are laws of nature. We are dealing with natural science, not ethics.

Moral imagination and the faculty of having moral ideas can become objects of knowledge only after they have been produced by the individual. By then, however, they no longer regulate life, for they have already regulated it. They must now be regarded as effective causes, like all others (they are purposes only for the subject). We therefore deal with them as with a natural history of moral ideas.

Ethics as a science that sets standards, in addition to this, cannot exist.

Some people have wanted to maintain the standard-setting character of moral laws, at least in so far as they have understood ethics in the sense of dietetics, which deduces general rules from the organism's requirements in life as a basis for influencing the body in a particular way (e.g., Paulsen, in his System der Ethik). This comparison is false, because our moral life is not comparable with the life of the organism. The functioning of the organism occurs without any action on our part; we come upon its laws in the world ready-made and can therefore seek them and apply them when found. Moral laws, on the other hand, are first created by us. We cannot apply them until we have created them. The error arises through the fact that, as regards their content, moral laws are not newly created at every moment, but are inherited. Those that we have taken over from our ancestors appear to be given, like the natural laws of the organism. But a later generation will certainly not be justified in applying them as if they were dietetic rules. For they apply to individuals and not, as natural laws do, to specimens of a general type. Considered as an organism, I am such a generic specimen and I shall live in accordance with nature if I apply the natural laws of my general type to my particular case; as a moral being, I am an individual and have laws of my very own.

This view appears to contradict the fundamental doctrine of modern natural science known as the theory of evolution. But it only appears to do so. Evolution is understood to mean the real development of the later out of the earlier in accordance with natural law. In the organic world, evolution is understood to mean that the later (more perfect) organic forms are real descendants of the earlier (imperfect) forms, and have developed from them in accordance with natural laws. The adherents of the theory of organic evolution ought really to picture to themselves that there was once a time on our earth when a being could have followed with his own eyes the gradual development of reptiles out of proto-amniotes, had he been able to be there at the time as an observer, endowed with a sufficiently long span of life. Similarly, evolutionists ought to picture to themselves that a being could have watched the development of the solar system out of the Kant-Laplace primordial nebula, had he been able to remain in a suitable spot out in the cosmic world ether during that infinitely long time. That with such mental pictures, the nature of both the proto-amniotes and the Kant-Laplace cosmic nebula would have to be thought of differently from the way the materialist thinkers do, is here irrelevant. But no evolutionist should ever dream of maintaining that he could get the concept of the reptile, with all its characteristics, out of his concept of the proto-amniotic animal, if he had never seen a reptile. Just as little would it be possible to derive the solar system from the concept of the Kant-Laplace nebula, if this concept of a primordial nebula is thought of as being directly determined only by the percept of the primordial nebula. In other words, if the evolutionist is to think consistently, he is bound to maintain that later phases of evolution do actually result from earlier ones, and that once we have been given the concept of the imperfect and that of the perfect, we can see the connection; but on no account should he agree that the concept attained from the earlier is, in itself, sufficient for evolving the later out of it. From this it follows for ethics that, though we can certainly see the connection between later moral concepts and earlier, we cannot get even a single new moral idea out of the earlier ones. As a moral being, the individual produces his own content. For the student of ethics, the content thus produced is just as much a given thing as reptiles are a given thing for the scientist. Reptiles have developed out of proto-amniotes, but the scientist cannot get the concept of reptiles out of the concept of the proto-amniotes. Later moral ideas evolve out of earlier, but the student of ethics cannot get the moral concepts of a later civilization out of those of an earlier one. The confusion arises because, as scientists, we start with the facts before us, and then get to know them, whereas in moral action we ourselves first create the facts which we then get to know. In the process of evolution of the moral world order we accomplish something that, at a lower level, is accomplished by nature: we alter something perceptible. The ethical standard thus cannot start, like a law of nature, by being known, but only by being created. Only when it is there, can it become an object of knowledge.

But can we not then make the old a measure for the new? Is not every man compelled to measure the products of his moral imagination by the standard of traditional moral doctrines? For something that should reveal itself as morally productive, this would be just as absurd as to want to measure a new form in nature by an old one and say that, because reptiles do not conform to the proto-amniotes, they are an unjustifiable (pathological) form.

Ethical individualism, then, is not in opposition to a rightly understood theory of evolution, but follows directly from it. Haeckel's genealogical tree, from protozoa up to man as an organic being, ought to be capable of being continued without an interruption of natural law and without a break in the uniformity of evolution, up to the individual as a being that is moral in a definite sense. But on no account could the nature of a descendant species be deduced from the nature of an ancestral one. However true it is that the moral ideas of the individual have perceptibly developed out of those of his ancestors, it is equally true that the individual is morally barren unless he has moral ideas of his own.

The same ethical individualism that I have developed on the basis of views already given could also be derived from the theory of evolution. The final conviction would be the same; only the path by which it was reached would be different.

The appearance of completely new moral ideas through moral imagination is, for the theory of evolution, no more miraculous than the development of a new animal species out of an old one ; only, as a monistic view of the world, this theory must reject, in morality as in science, every transcendental (metaphysical) influence, every influence that is merely inferred and cannot be experienced ideally. In doing so, the theory follows the same principle that guides it when it seeks the causes of new organic forms without invoking the interference of an extra-mundane Being who produces every new species, in accordance with a new creative thought, by supernatural influence. Just as monism has no use for supernatural creative thoughts in explaining living organisms, so it is equally impossible for it to derive the moral world order from causes which do not lie within the experienceable world. It cannot admit that the moral nature of will is completely accounted for by being traced back to a continuous supernatural influence upon moral life (divine government of the world from the outside), or to an act of revelation at a particular moment in history (giving of the ten commandments), or to God's appearance on the earth (as Christ). What happens to man, and in man, through all this, becomes a moral element only when, in human experience, it becomes an individual's own. For monism, moral processes are products of the world like everything else that exists, and their causes must be sought in the world, that is, in man, since man is the bearer of morality.

Ethical individualism, then, is the crowning feature of the edifice that Darwin and Haeckel have striven to build for natural science. It is spiritualized theory of evolution carried over into moral life.

Anyone who, in a narrow-minded way, restricts the concept of the natural from the outset to an arbitrarily limited sphere may easily conclude that there is no room in it for free individual action. The consistent evolutionist cannot fall a prey to such narrow-mindedness. He cannot let the natural course of evolution terminate with the ape, and allow man to have a "supernatural" origin; in his very search for the natural progenitors of man, he is bound to seek spirit in nature; again, he cannot stop short at the organic functions of man, and take only these as natural, but must go on to regard the free moral life as the spiritual continuation of organic life.

If he is to keep to his fundamental principles, the evolutionist can state only that the present form of moral action evolves from other forms of activity in the world; the characterizing of an action, that is, whether it is a free one, he must leave to the immediate observation of the action. In fact, he maintains only that men have developed out of ancestors that were not yet human. What men are actually like must be determined by observation of men themselves. The results of this observation cannot contradict the properly understood history of evolution.

Only the assertion that the results are such as to exclude a natural ordering of the world would contradict recent trends in the natural sciences.

Ethical individualism has nothing to fear from a natural science that understands itself: for observation shows that the perfect form of human action has freedom as its characteristic quality. This freedom must be allowed to the human will, in so far as the will realizes purely ideal intuitions. For these intuitions are not the results of a necessity acting upon them from without, but are due only to themselves. If a man finds that an action is the image of such an ideal intuition, then he feels it to be free. In this characteristic of an action lies its freedom.

What are we to say, from this standpoint, about the distinction mentioned earlier (see Chapter 1) between the two propositions, "To be free means to be able to do as one wills" and, "To be at liberty to desire or not to desire is the real proposition involved in the dogma of freewill"? Hamerling bases his view of free will precisely on this distinction, by declaring the first statement to be correct but the second to be an absurd tautology. He says, "I can do as I will. But to say I can want as I will is an empty tautology." Whether I am able to do, that is, to translate into reality, what I will, that is, what I have set before myself as my idea of action, depends on external circumstances and on my technical skill (see above). To be free means to be able of one's own accord to determine by moral imagination those mental pictures (motives) which underlie the action. Freedom is impossible if anything other then myself (mechanical process or merely inferred extra-mundane God) determines my moral ideas. In other words, I am free only when I myself produce these mental pictures, not when I am merely able to carry out the motives which another being has implanted in me. A free being is one who can want what he himself considers right. Whoever does anything other than what he wants must be impelled to it by motives which do not lie within him. Such a man is unfree in his action. To be at liberty to want what one considers right or what one considers wrong, would therefore mean to be at liberty to be free or unfree. This is, of course, just as absurd as to see freedom in the ability to do what one is compelled to will. But this last is just what Hamerling maintains when he says, "It is perfectly true that the will is always determined by motives, but it is absurd to say that on this account it is unfree; for a greater freedom can neither be desired nor conceived than the freedom to realize oneself in proportion to one's own strength and determination." In deed it can! It is certainly possible to desire a greater freedom, and this for the first time the true one: namely, to decide for oneself the motives for one's will.

Under certain conditions a man may be induced to abandon the execution of his will. To allow others to prescribe to him what he ought to do — in other words, to want what another, and not he himself, considers right — to this a man will submit only to the extent that he does not feel free.

External powers may prevent me from doing as I will. Then they simply condemn me to do nothing or to be unfree. Not until they would enslave my spirit, drive my motives out of my head, and put their own motives in the place of mine, do they really aim at making me unfree. For this reason the Church sets itself not only against the mere doing, but especially against the impure thoughts, that is, the motives of my action. The Church makes me unfree if, for her, all those motives she has not herself enunciated seem impure. A Church or other community produces unfreedom when its priests or teachers make themselves into keepers of consciences, that is, when the faithful are obliged to go to them (to the confessional) for the motives of their actions.

The Value of Life (Optimism and Pessimism)

A COUNTERPART to the question concerning the purpose of life, or the ordering of its destiny (see Chapter 11), is the question concerning its value. We meet here with two mutually opposed views, and between them all conceivable attempts at compromise. One view says that this world is the best that could conceivably exist, and that to live and to act in it is a blessing of untold value. Everything that exists displays harmonious and purposeful co-operation and is worthy of admiration. Even what is apparently bad and evil may, from a higher point of view, be seen to be good, for it represents an agreeable contrast with the good; we are the more able to appreciate the good when it is clearly contrasted with evil. Moreover, evil is not genuinely real; what we feel as evil is only a lesser degree of good. Evil is the absence of good; it has no significance in itself.

The other view maintains that life is full of misery and want; everywhere pain outweighs pleasure, sorrow outweighs joy. Existence is a burden, and non-existence would in all circumstances be preferable to existence.

The chief representatives of the former view, optimism, are Shaftesbury and Leibnitz; those of the latter, pessimism, are Schopenhauer and Eduard von Hartmann.

Leibnitz believes the world is the best of all possible worlds. A better one is impossible. For God is good and wise. A good God wants to create the best possible world; a wise God knows which is the best possible — He is able to distinguish the best from all other possible worse ones. Only an evil or an unwise God would be able to create a world worse than the best possible.

Whoever starts from this point of view will find it easy to lay down the direction that human action must follow in order to make its contribution to the greatest good of the world. All that man need do is to find out the counsels of God and to behave in accordance with them. If he knows what God's intentions are concerning the world and mankind, he will be able to do what is right. And he will be happy in the feeling that he is adding his share to the other good in the world. From this optimistic standpoint, then, life is worth living. It must stimulate us to co-operative participation.

Schopenhauer pictures things quite differently. He thinks of the foundation of the world not as an all-wise and all-beneficent being, but as blind urge or will. Eternal striving, ceaseless craving for satisfaction which is ever beyond reach, this is the fundamental characteristic of all active will. For no sooner is one goal attained, than a fresh need springs up, and so on. Satisfaction, when it occurs, lasts only for an infinitesimal time. The entire remaining content of our life is unsatisfied craving, that is, dissatisfaction and suffering. If at last blind craving is dulled, then all content is gone from our lives; an infinite boredom pervades our existence. Hence the best we can do is to stifle all wishes and needs within us and exterminate the will. Schopenhauer's pessimism leads to complete inactivity; his moral aim is universal idleness.

By a very different argument von Hartmann attempts to establish pessimism and to make use of it for ethics. He attempts, in keeping with a favourite tendency of our times, to base his world view on experience. From the observation of life he hopes to discover whether pleasure or pain outweighs the other in the world. He parades whatever appears to men as blessing and fortune before the tribunal of reason, in order to show that all alleged satisfaction turns out on closer inspection to be illusion. It is illusion when we believe that in health, youth, freedom, sufficient income, love (sexual satisfaction), pity, friendship and family life, self-respect, honour, fame, power, religious edification, pursuit of science and of art, hope of a life hereafter, participation in the progress of civilization — that in all these we have sources of happiness and satisfaction. Soberly considered, every enjoyment brings much more evil and misery into the world than pleasure. The disagreeableness of the hangover is always greater than the agreeableness of getting drunk. Pain far outweighs pleasure in the world. No man, even though relatively the happiest, would, if asked, wish to live through this miserable life a second time. Now, since Hartmann does not deny the presence of an ideal factor (wisdom) in the world, but rather gives it equal standing with blind urge (will), he can credit his primal Being with the creation of the world only if he allows the pain in the world to serve a wise world-purpose. The pain of created beings is, however, nothing but God's pain itself, for the life of the world as a whole is identical with the life of God. An all-wise Being can, however, see his goal only in release from suffering, and, since all existence is suffering, in release from existence. To transform existence into the far better state of non-existence is the purpose of all creation. The course of the world is a continuous battle against God's pain, which ends at last with the annihilation of all existence. The moral life of men, therefore, will consist in taking part in the annihilation of existence. God has created the world so that through it He may free Himself from His infinite pain. The world is "to be regarded, more or less, as an itching eruption upon the Absolute," by means of which the unconscious healing power of the Absolute rids itself of an inward disease, "or even as a painful poultice which the All-One applies to himself in order first to divert the inner pain outwards, and then to get rid of it altogether." Human beings are integral parts of the world. In them God suffers. He has created them in order to disperse His infinite pain. The pain which each one of us suffers is but a drop in the infinite ocean of God's pain.

Man has to permeate his whole being with the recognition that the pursuit of individual satisfaction (egoism) is a folly, and that he ought to be guided solely by the task of dedicating himself to the redemption of God by unselfish devotion to the progress of the world. Thus, in contrast to Schopenhauer's, von Hartmann's pessimism leads us to activity devoted to a sublime task.

But is it really based on experience?

To strive for satisfaction means that our activity reaches out beyond the actual content of our lives. A creature is hungry, that is, it strives for repletion, when its organic functions, if they are to continue, demand the supply of fresh means of life in the form of nourishment. The striving for honour means that a man only regards what he personally does or leaves undone as valuable when his activity is approved by others. The striving for knowledge arises when a man finds that something is missing from the world that he sees, hears, and so on, as long as he has not understood it. The fulfillment of the striving creates pleasure in the striving individual, failure creates pain. It is important here to observe that pleasure and pain are dependent only upon the fulfillment or non-fulfillment of my striving. The striving itself can by no means be counted as pain. Hence, if it happens that in the very moment in which a striving is fulfilled a new striving at once arises, this is no ground for saying that, because in every ease enjoyment gives rise to a desire for its repetition or for a fresh pleasure, my pleasure has given birth to pain. I can speak of pain only when desire runs up against the impossibility of fulfillment. Even when an enjoyment that I have had creates in me the desire for the experience of greater or more refined pleasure, I cannot speak of this desire as a pain created by the previous pleasure until the means of experiencing the greater or more refined pleasure fail me. Only when pain appears as a natural consequence of pleasure, as for instance when a woman's sexual pleasure is followed by the suffering of childbirth and the cares of a family, can I find in the enjoyment the originator of the pain. If striving by itself called forth pain, then each reduction of striving would have to be accompanied by pleasure. But the opposite is the case. To have no striving in one's life creates boredom, and this is connected with displeasure. Now, since it may be a long time before striving meets with fulfillment, and since, in the interval, it is content with the hope of fulfillment, we must acknowledge that the pain has nothing whatever to do with the striving as such, but depends solely on the non-fulfillment of the striving. Schopenhauer, then, is in any case wrong to take desiring or striving (will) as being in itself the source of pain.

In fact, just the opposite is correct. Striving (desiring) in itself gives pleasure. Who does not know the enjoyment given by the hope of a remote but intensely desired goal? This joy is the companion of all labour that gives us its fruits only in the future. It is a pleasure quite independent of the attainment of the goal. For when the goal has been reached, the pleasure of fulfillment is added as something new to the pleasure of striving. If anyone were to argue that the pain caused by an unsatisfied aim is increased by the pain of disappointed hope, and that thus, in the end, the pain of non-fulfillment will eventually outweigh the possible pleasure of fulfillment, we shall have to reply that the reverse may be the case, and that the recollection of past enjoyment at a time of unfulfilled desire will just as often mitigate the pain of non-fulfillment. Whoever exclaims in the face of shattered hopes, "I have done my part," is a proof of this assertion. The blissful feeling of having tried one's best is overlooked by those who say of every unsatisfied desire that not only is the joy of fulfillment absent but the enjoyment of the desiring itself has been destroyed.

The fulfillment of a desire brings pleasure and its nonfulfillment brings pain. But from this we must not conclude that pleasure is the satisfaction of a desire, and pain its non-satisfaction. Both pleasure and pain can be experienced without being the consequence of desire. Illness is pain not preceded by desire. If anyone were to maintain that illness is unsatisfied desire for health, he would be making the mistake of regarding the unconscious wish not to fall ill, which we all take for granted, as a positive desire. When someone receives a legacy from a rich relative of whose existence he had not the faintest idea, this fills him with pleasure without any preceding desire.

Hence, if we set out to enquire whether the balance is on the side of pleasure or of pain, we must take into account the pleasure of desiring, the pleasure at the fulfillment of a desire, and the pleasure which comes to us without any striving. On the other side of the account we shall have to enter the displeasure of boredom, the pain of unfulfilled striving, and lastly the pain which comes to us without any desiring on our part. Under this last heading we shall have to put also the displeasure caused by work, not chosen by ourselves, that has been forced upon us.

This leads to the question: What is the right method for striking the balance between these credit and debit columns? Eduard von Hartmann believes that it is reason that holds the scales. It is true that he says, "Pain and pleasure exist only in so far as they are actually felt." It follows that there can be no yardstick for pleasure other than the subjective one of feeling. I must feel whether the sum of my disagreeable feelings together with my agreeable feelings leaves me with a balance of pleasure or of pain. But for all that, von Hartmann maintains that, "though the value of the life of every person can be set down only according to his own subjective measure, yet it by no means follows that every person is able to arrive at the correct algebraic sum from all the collected emotions in his life — or, in other words, that his total estimate of his own life, with regard to his subjective experiences, would be correct." With this, the rational estimation of feeling is once more made the evaluator.

Anyone who follows fairly closely the line of thought of such thinkers as Eduard von Hartmann may believe it necessity, in order to arrive at a correct valuation of life, to clear out of the way those factors which falsify our judgement about the balance of pleasure and pain. He can try to do this in two ways. Firstly, by showing that our desire (instinct, will) interferes with our sober estimation of feeling values in a disturbing way. Whereas, for instance, we ought to say to ourselves that sexual enjoyment is a source of evil, we are misled by the fact that the sexual instinct is very strong in us into conjuring up the prospect of a pleasure which just is not there in that degree at all. We want to enjoy ourselves; hence we do not admit to ourselves that we suffer under the enjoyment. Secondly, he can do it by subjecting feelings to a critical examination and attempting to prove that the objects to which our feelings attach themselves are revealed as illusions by the light of reason, and that they are destroyed from the moment that our ever growing intelligence sees through the illusions.

He can think of the matter in the following way. If an ambitious man wants to determine clearly whether, up to the moment of his enquiry, there has been a surplus of pleasure or of pain in his life, then he has to free himself from two sources of error that may affect his judgment. Being ambitious, this fundamental feature of his character will make him see the joys due to the recognition of his achievements through a magnifying glass, and the humiliations due to his rebuffs through a diminishing glass. At the time when he suffered the rebuffs he felt the humiliations just because he was ambitious; in recollection they appear to him in a milder light, whereas the joys of recognition to which he is so susceptible leave a far deeper impression. Now, for an ambitious man it is an undeniable blessing that it should be so. The deception diminishes his pain in the moment of self-analysis. None the less, his judgment is wrong. The sufferings over which a veil is now drawn were actually experienced by him in all their intensity, and hence he enters them at a wrong valuation in his life's account book. In order to arrive at a correct estimate, an ambitious man would have to lay aside his ambition for the time of his enquiry. He would have to review his past life without any distorting glasses before his mind's eye. Otherwise he would resemble a merchant who, in making up his books, enters among the items on the credit side his own zeal in business.

But the holder of this view can go even further. He can say: The ambitious man will even make clear to himself that the recognition he pursues is a worthless thing. Either by himself, or through the influence of others, he will come to see that for an intelligent man recognition by others counts for very little, seeing that "in all such matters, other than those that are questions of sheer existence or that are already finally settled by science," one can be quite sure "that the majority is wrong and the minority right.... Whoever makes ambition the lode-star of his life puts his life's happiness at the mercy of such a judgment." If the ambitious man admits all this to himself, then he must regard as illusion what his ambition had pictured as reality, and thus also the feelings attached to these illusions of his ambition. On this basis it could then be said that such feelings of pleasure as are produced by illusion must also be struck out of the balance sheet of life's values; what then remains represents the sum total of life's pleasures stripped of all illusion, and this is so small compared with the sum total of pain that life is no joy and non-existence preferable to existence.

But while it is immediately evident that the deception produced by the instinct of ambition leads to a false result when striking the balance of pleasure, we must none the less challenge what has been said about the recognition of the illusory character of the objects of pleasure. The elimination from the credit side of life of all pleasurable feelings which accompany actual or supposed illusions would positively falsify the balance of pleasure and pain. For an ambitious man has genuinely enjoyed the acclamations of the multitude, irrespective of whether subsequently he himself, or some other person, recognizes that this acclamation is an illusion. The pleasant sensation he has had is not in the least diminished by this recognition. The elimination of all such "illusory" feelings from life's balance does not make our judgment about our feelings more correct, but rather obliterates from life feelings which were actually there.

And why should these feelings be eliminated? For whoever has them, they are certainly pleasure-giving; for whoever has conquered them, a purely mental but none the less significant pleasure arises through the experience of self-conquest (not through the vain emotion: What a noble fellow I am! but through the objective sources of pleasure which lie in the self-conquest). If we strike out feelings from the pleasure side of the balance on the ground that they are attached to objects which turn out to have been illusory, we make the value of life dependent not on the quantity but on the quality of pleasure, and this, in turn, on the value of the objects which cause the pleasure. But if I want to determine the value of life in the first place by the quantity of pleasure or pain which it brings, I may nor presuppose something else which already determines the positive or negative value of the pleasure. If I say I want to compare the quantity of pleasure with the quantity of pain in order to see which is greater, I am bound to bring into my account all pleasures and pains in their actual intensities, whether they are based on illusions or not. Whoever ascribes a lesser value for life to a pleasure which is based on an illusion than to one which can justify itself before the tribunal of reason, makes the value of life dependent on factors other than pleasure.

Whoever puts down pleasure as less valuable when it is attached to a worthless object, resembles a merchant who enters the considerable profits of a toy factory in his account at a quarter of their actual amount on the ground that the factory produces nothing but playthings for children.

If the point is simply to weigh quantity of pleasure against quantity of pain, then the illusory character of the objects causing certain feelings of pleasure must be left right out of the question.

The method recommended by von Hartmann, that is, rational consideration of the quantities of pleasure and pain produced by life, has thus led us to the point where we know how we are to set out our accounts, what we are to put down on the one side of our book and what on the other. But how is the calculation now to be made? Is reason actually capable of striking the balance?

A merchant has made a mistake in his reckoning if his calculated profit does not agree with the demonstrable results or expectations of his business. Similarly, the philosopher will undoubtedly have made a mistake in his estimate if he cannot demonstrate in actual feeling the surplus of pleasure, or pain, that he has somehow extracted from his accounts.

For the present I shall not look into the calculations of those pessimists whose opinion of the world is measured by reason; but if one is to decide whether to carry on the business of life or not, one will first demand to be shown where the alleged surplus of pain is to be found.

Here we touch the point where reason is not in a position to determine by itself the surplus of pleasure or of pain, but where it must demonstrate this surplus as a percept in life. For man reaches reality not through concepts alone but through the interpenetration of concepts and percepts (and feelings are percepts) which thinking brings about. A merchant, after all, will give up his business only when the losses calculated by his accountant are confirmed by the facts. If this does not happen, he gets his accountant to make the calculation over again. That is exactly what a man will do in the business of life. If a philosopher wants to prove to him that the pain is far greater than the pleasure, but he himself does not feel it to be so, then he will reply, "You have gone astray in your reckoning; think it all out again." But should there come a time in a business when the losses are really so great that the firm's credit no longer suffices to satisfy the creditors, then bankruptcy will result if the merchant fails to keep himself informed about the state of his affairs by careful accounting. Similarly, if the quantity of pain in a man's life became at any time so great that no hope of future pleasure (credit) could help him to get over the pain, then the bankruptcy of life's business would inevitably follow.

Now the number of those who kill themselves is relatively unimportant when compared with the multitude of those who live bravely on. Only very few men give up the business of life because of the pain involved. What follows from this? Either that it is untrue to say that the quantity of pain is greater than the quantity of pleasure, or that we do not at all make the continuation of life dependent on the quantity of pleasure or pain that is felt.

In a very curious way, Eduard von Hartmann's pessimism comes to the conclusion that life is valueless because it contains a surplus of pain and yet affirms the necessity of going on with it. This necessity lies in the fact that the world purpose mentioned above can be achieved only by the ceaseless, devoted labour of human beings. But as long as men still pursue their egotistical cravings they are unfit for such selfless labour. Not until they have convinced themselves through experience and reason that the pleasures of life pursued by egoism cannot be attained, do they devote themselves to their proper tasks. In this way the pessimistic conviction is supposed to be the source of unselfishness. An education based on pessimism should exterminate egoism by making it see the hopelessness of its case.

According to this view, then, the striving for pleasure is inherent in human nature from the outset. Only when fulfillment is seen to be impossible does this striving retire in favour of higher tasks for mankind.

It cannot be said that egoism is overcome in the true sense of the word by an ethical world conception that expects a devotion to unselfish aims in life through the acceptance of pessimism. The moral ideals are said not to be strong enough to dominate the will until man has learnt that selfish striving after pleasure cannot lead to any satisfaction. Man, whose selfishness desires the grapes of pleasure, finds them sour because he cannot reach them, and so he turns his back on them and devotes himself to an unselfish way of life. Moral ideals, then, according to the opinion of pessimists, are not strong enough to overcome egoism; but they establish their dominion on the ground previously cleared for them by the recognition of the hopelessness of egoism.

If men by nature were to strive after pleasure but were unable to reach it, then annihilation of existence, and salvation through non-existence, would be the only rational goal. And if one holds the view that the real bearer of the pain of the world is God, then man's task would consist in bringing about the salvation of God. Through the suicide of the individual, the realization of this aim is not advanced, but hindered. Rationally, God can only have created men in order to bring about his salvation through their actions. Otherwise creation would be purposeless. And it is extra-human purposes that such a world conception has in mind. Each one of us has to perform his own particular task in the general work of salvation. If he withdraws from the task by suicide, then the work which was intended for him must be done by another. Somebody else must bear the torment of existence in his stead. And since within every being it is God who actually bears all pain, the suicide does not in the least diminish the quantity of God's pain, but rather imposes upon God the additional difficulty of providing a substitute.

All this presupposes that pleasure is the yardstick for the value of life. Now life manifests itself through a number of instinctive desires (needs). If the value of life depended on its producing more pleasure than pain, an instinct which brought to its owner a balance of pain would have to be called valueless. Let us, therefore, examine instinct and pleasure to see whether the former can be measured by the latter. In order not to arouse the suspicion that we consider life to begin only at the level of "aristocracy of the intellect", we shall begin with the "purely animal" need, hunger.

Hunger arises when our organs are unable to continue their proper function without a fresh supply of food. What a hungry man wants first of all is to satisfy his hunger. As soon as the supply of nourishment has reached the point where hunger ceases, everything that the instinct for food craves has been attained. The enjoyment that comes with being satisfied consists primarily in putting an end to the pain caused by hunger. But to the mere instinct for food a further need is added. For man does not merely desire to repair the disturbance in the functioning of his organs by the consumption of food, or to overcome the pain of hunger; he seeks to effect this to the accompaniment of pleasurable sensations of taste. If he feels hungry and is within half an hour of an appetizing meal, he may even refuse inferior food, which could satisfy him sooner, so as not to spoil his appetite for the better fare to come. He needs hunger in order to get the full enjoyment from his meal. Thus for him hunger becomes at the same time a cause of pleasure. Now if all the existing hunger in the world could be satisfied, we should then have the total quantity of enjoyment attributable to the presence of the need for nourishment. To this would still have to be added the special pleasure which the gourmet achieves by cultivating his palate beyond the common measure.

This quantity of pleasure would reach the highest conceivable value if no need aiming at the kind of enjoyment under consideration remained unsatisfied, and if with the enjoyment we had not to accept a certain amount of pain into the bargain.

Modern science holds the view that nature produces more life than it can sustain, that is to say, more hunger than it is able to satisfy. The surplus of life thus produced must perish in pain in the struggle for existence. Admittedly the needs of life at every moment in the course of the world are greater than the available means of satisfaction, and that the enjoyment of life is affected as a result. Such enjoyment as actually does occur, however, is not in the least reduced. Wherever a desire is satisfied, the corresponding quantity of pleasure exists, even though in the desiring creature itself or in its fellows there are plenty of unsatisfied instincts. What is, however, diminished by all this is the value of the enjoyment of life. If only a part of the needs of a living creature finds satisfaction, it experiences a corresponding degree of enjoyment. This pleasure has a lower value, the smaller it is in proportion to the total demands of life in the field of the desires in question. One can represent this value by a fraction, of which the numerator is the pleasure actually experienced while the denominator is the sum total of needs. This fraction has the value 1 when the numerator and the denominator are equal, that is, when all needs are fully satisfied. The fraction becomes greater than 1 when a creature experiences more pleasure than its desires demand; and it becomes smaller than 1 when the quantity of pleasure falls short of the sum total of desires. But the fraction can never become zero as long as the numerator has any value at all, however small. If a man were to make up a final account before his death, and were to think of the quantity of enjoyment connected with a particular instinct (for example, hunger) as being distributed over the whole of his life together with all the demands made by this instinct, then the pleasure experienced might perhaps have a very small value, but it could never become valueless. If the quantity of pleasure remains constant, then, with an increase in the needs of the creature, the value of the pleasure diminishes. The same is true for the sum of life in nature. The greater the number of creatures in proportion to those which are able to satisfy their instincts fully, the smaller is the average value of pleasure in life. The cheques on life's pleasure which are drawn in our favour in the form of our instincts, become less valuable if we cannot expect to cash them for the full amount. If I get enough to eat for three days and as a result must then go hungry for another three days, the actual pleasure on the three days of eating is not thereby diminished. But I have now to think of it as distributed over six days, and thus its value for my food-instinct is reduced by half. In just the same way the magnitude of pleasure is related to the degree of my need. If I am hungry enough for two pieces of bread and can only get one, the pleasure I derive from it had only half the value it would have had if the eating of it has satisfied my hunger. This is the way that the value of a pleasure is determined in life. It is measured by the needs of life. Our desires are the yardstick; pleasure is the thing that is measured. The enjoyment of satisfying hunger has a value only because hunger exists; and it has a value of a definite magnitude through the proportion it bears to the magnitude of the existing hunger.

Unfulfilled demands of our life throw their shadow even upon satisfied desires, and thus detract from the value of pleasurable hours. But we can also speak of the present value of a feeling of pleasure. This value is the lower, the smaller the pleasure is in proportion to the duration and intensity of our desire.

A quantity of pleasure has its full value for us when in duration and degree it exactly coincides with our desire. A quantity of pleasure which is smaller than our desire diminishes the value of the pleasure; a quantity which is greater produces a surplus which has not been demanded and which is felt as pleasure only so long as, whilst enjoying the pleasure, we can increase the intensity of our desire. If the increase in our desire is unable to keep pace with the increase in pleasure, then pleasure turns into displeasure. The thing that would otherwise satisfy us now assails us without our wanting it and makes us suffer. This proves that pleasure has value for us only to the extent that we can measure it against our desires. An excess of pleasurable feeling turns into pain. This may be observed especially in people whose desire for a particular kind of pleasure is very small. In people whose instinct for food is stunted, eating readily becomes nauseating. This again shows that desire is the standard by which we measure the value of pleasure.

Now the pessimist might say that an unsatisfied instinct for food brings into the world not only displeasure at the lost enjoyment, but also positive pain, misery and want. He can base this statement upon the untold misery of starving people and upon the vast amount of suffering which arises indirectly for such people from their lack of food. And if he wants to extend his assertion to nature outside man as well, he can point to the suffering of animals that die of starvation at certain times of the year. The pessimist maintains that these evils far outweigh the amount of pleasure that the instinct for food brings into the world.

There is indeed no doubt that one can compare pleasure and pain and can estimate the surplus of one or the other much as we do in the case of profit and loss. But if the pessimist believes that because there is a surplus of pain he can conclude that life is valueless, he falls into the error of making a calculation that in real life is never made.

Our desire, in any given case, is directed to a particular object. As we have seen, the value of the pleasure of satisfaction will be the greater, the greater is the amount of pleasure in relation to the intensity of our desire . On this intensity of desire also will depend how much pain we are willing to bear as part of the price of achieving the pleasure. We compare the quantity of pain not with the quantity of pleasure but with the intensity of our desire. If someone takes great delight in eating, he will, by reason of his enjoyment in better times, find it easier to bear a period of hunger than will someone for whom eating is no pleasure. A woman who wants to have a child compares the pleasure that would come from possessing it not with the amount of pain due to pregnancy, childbirth, nursing and so on, but with her desire to possess the child.

We never aim at a certain quantity of pleasure in the abstract, but at concrete satisfaction in a perfectly definite way. If we are aiming at a pleasure which must be satisfied by a particular object or a particular sensation, we shall not be satisfied with some other object or some other sensation that gives us an equal amount of pleasure. If we are aiming at satisfying our hunger, we cannot replace the pleasure this would give us by a pleasure equally great, but produced by going for a walk. Only if our desire were, quite generally, for a certain fixed quantity of pleasure as such, would it disappear as soon as the price of achieving it were seen to be a still greater quantity of pain. But since satisfaction of a particular kind is being aimed at, fulfillment brings the pleasure even when, along with it, a still greater pain has to be taken into the bargain. But because the instincts of living creatures move in definite directions and go after concrete goals, the quantity of pain endured on the way to the goal cannot be set down as an equivalent factor in our calculations. Provided the desire is sufficiently intense to be present in some degree after having overcome the pain — however great that pain in itself may be — then the pleasure of satisfaction can still be tasted to the full. The desire, therefore, does not compare the pain directly to the pleasure achieved, but compares it indirectly by relating its own intensity to that of the pain. The question is not whether the pleasure to be gained is greater than the pain, but whether the desire for the goal is greater than the hindering effect of the pain involved. If the hindrance is greater than the desire, then the desire gives way to the inevitable, weakens and strives no further. Since our demand is for satisfaction in a particular way, the pleasure connected with it acquires a significance such that, once we have achieved satisfaction, we need take the quantity of pain into account only to the extent that it has reduced the intensity of our desire. If I am a passionate admirer of beautiful views, I never calculate the amount of pleasure which the view from the mountain top gives me as compared directly with the pain of the toilsome ascent and descent; but I reflect whether, after having overcome all difficulties, my desire for the view will still be sufficiently intense. Only indirectly, through the intensity of the desire, can pleasure and pain together lead to a result. Therefore the question is not at all whether there is a surplus of pleasure or of pain, but whether the will for pleasure is strong enough to overcome the pain.

A proof for the correctness of this statement is the fact that we put a higher value on pleasure when it has to be purchased at the price of great pain than when it falls into our lap like a gift from heaven. When suffering and misery have toned down our desire and yet after all our goal is reached, then the pleasure, in proportion to the amount of desire still left, is all the greater. Now, as I have shown, this proportion represents the value of the pleasure. A further proof is given through the fact that living creatures (including man) give expression to their instincts as long as they are able to bear the pain and misery involved. The struggle for existence is but a consequence of this fact. All existing life strives to express itself, and only that part of it whose desires are smothered by the overwhelming weight of difficulties abandons the struggle. Every living creature seeks food until lack of food destroys its life. Man, too, does not turn his hand against himself until he believes, rightly or wrongly, that those aims in life that are worth his striving are beyond his reach. So long as he still believes in the possibility of reaching what, in his view, is worth striving for, he will battle against all misery and pain. Philosophy would first have to convince him that an act of will makes sense only when the pleasure is greater than the pain; for by nature he will strive for the objects of his desire if he can bear the necessary pain, however great it may be. But such a philosophy would be mistaken because it would make the human will dependent on a circumstance (the surplus of pleasure over pain) which is originally foreign to man. The original measure of his will is desire, and desire asserts itself as long as it can. When it is a question of pleasure and pain in the satisfaction of a desire, the calculation that is made, not in philosophical theory, but in life, can be compared with the following. If in buying a certain quantity of apples I am obliged to take twice as many rotten ones as sound ones — because the seller wants to clear his stock — I shall not hesitate for one moment to accept the bad apples as well, if the smaller quantity of good ones are worth so much to me that in addition to their purchase price I am also prepared to bear the expense of disposing of the bad ones. This example illustrates the relation between the quantities of pleasure and pain resulting from an instinct. I determine the value of the good apples not by subtracting the total number of the good ones from that of the bad ones but by assessing whether the good ones still have value for me in spite of the presence of the bad ones.

Just as I leave the bad apples out of account in the enjoyment of the good ones, so I give myself up to the satisfaction of a desire after having shaken off the unavoidable pain.

Even if pessimism were right in its assertion that there is more pain then pleasure in the world, this would have no influence on the will, since living creatures would still strive after the pleasure that remains. The empirical proof that pain outweighs joy (if such proof could be given) would certainly be effective for showing up the futility of the school of philosophy that sees the value of life in a surplus of pleasure (eudaemonism) but not for showing that the will, as such, is irrational; for the will is not set upon a surplus of pleasure, but upon the amount of pleasure that remains after getting over the pain. This still appears as a goal worth striving for.

Some have tried to refute pessimism by stating that it is impossible to calculate the surplus of pleasure or of pain in the world. That any calculation can be done at all depends on whether the things to be calculated can be compared in respect of their magnitudes. Every pain and every pleasure has a definite magnitude (intensity and duration). Further, we can compare pleasurable feelings of different kinds one with another, at least approximately, with regard to their magnitudes. We know whether we derive more entertainment from a good cigar or from a good joke. Therefore there can be no objection to comparing different sorts of pleasure and pain in respect of their magnitudes. And the investigator who sets himself the task of determining the surplus of pleasure or pain in the world starts from fully justified assumptions. One may declare the conclusions of pessimism to be false, but one cannot doubt that quantities of pleasure and pain can be scientifically estimated, and the balance of pleasure thereby determined. It is, however, quite wrong to claim that the result of this calculation has any consequences for the human will. The cases where we really make the value of our activity dependent on whether pleasure or pain shows a surplus are those where the objects towards which our activity is directed are all the same to us. If it is only a question whether, after the day's work, I am to amuse myself by a game or by light conversation, and if I am totally indifferent to what I do as long as it serves the purpose, then I simply ask myself: What gives me the greatest surplus of pleasure? And I shall most certainly abandon the activity if the scales incline towards the side of displeasure. If we are buying a toy for a child we consider, in selecting, what will give him the greatest happiness. In all other cases we do not base our decision exclusively on the balance of pleasure.

Therefore, if the pessimists believe that by showing pain to be present in greater quantity than pleasure they are preparing the ground for unselfish devotion to the work of civilization, they forget that the human will, by its very nature, does not allow itself to be influenced by this knowledge. Human striving is directed towards the measure of satisfaction that is possible after all difficulties are overcome. Hope of such satisfaction is the foundation of all human activity. The work of every individual and of the whole of civilization springs from this hope. Pessimistic ethics believes that it must present the pursuit of happiness as an impossibility for man in order that he may devote himself to his proper moral tasks. But these moral tasks are nothing but the concrete natural and spiritual instincts; and man strives to satisfy them in spite of the incidental pain. The pursuit of happiness which the pessimist would eradicate is therefore nowhere to be found. But the tasks which man has to fulfill, he does fulfill, because from the very nature of his being he wants to fulfill them, once he has properly recognized their nature. Pessimistic ethics declares that only when a man has given up the quest for pleasure can he devote himself to what he recognizes as his task in life. But no system of ethics can ever invent any life tasks other than the realization of the satisfactions that human desires demand and the fulfillment of man's moral ideals. No ethics can deprive man of the pleasure he experiences in the fulfillment of his desires. When the pessimist says, "Do not strive for pleasure, for you can never attain it; strive rather for what you recognize to be your task," we must reply, "But this is just what man does, and the notion that he strives merely for happiness is no more than the invention of an errant philosophy." He aims at the satisfaction of what he himself desires, and he has in view the concrete objects of his striving, not "happiness" in the abstract; and fulfillment is for him a pleasure. When pessimistic ethics demands, "Strive not for pleasure, but for the attainment of what you see as your life's task," it hits on the very thing that man, in his own being, wants. Man does not need to be turned inside out by philosophy, he does not need to discard his human nature, before he can be moral. Morality lies in striving for a goal that one recognizes as justified; it is human nature to pursue it as long as the pain incurred does not inhibit the desire for it altogether. This is the essence of all genuine will. Ethical behaviour is not based upon the eradication of all striving for pleasure to the end that bloodless abstract ideas may establish their dominion unopposed by any strong yearnings for the enjoyment of life, but rather upon a strong will sustained by ideal intuitions, a will that reaches its goal even though the path be thorny.

Moral ideals spring from the moral imagination of man. Their realization depends on his desire for them being intense enough to overcome pain and misery. They are his intuitions, the driving forces which his spirit harnesses; he wants them, because their realization is his highest pleasure. He needs no ethics to forbid him to strive for pleasure and then to tell him what he shall strive for. He will strive for moral ideals if his moral imagination is sufficiently active to provide him with intuitions that give his will the strength to make its way against all the obstacles inherent in his constitution, including the pain that is necessarily involved.

If a man strives for sublimely great ideals, it is because they are the content of his own being, and their realization will bring him a joy compared to which the pleasure that a limited outlook gets from the gratification of commonplace desires is a mere triviality. Idealists revel, spiritually, in the translation of their ideals into reality.

Anyone who would eradicate the pleasure brought by the fulfillment of human desires will first have to make man a slave who acts not because he wants to but only because he must. For the achievement of what one wanted to do gives pleasure. What we call good is not what a man must do but what he will want to do if he develops the true nature of man to the full. Anyone who does not acknowledge this must first drive out of man all that man himself wants to do, and then, from outside, prescribe the content he is to give to his will.

Man values the fulfillment of a desire because the desire springs from his own being. What is achieved has its value because it has been wanted. If we deny any value to what man himself wants, then aims that do have value will have to be found in something that man does not want.

An ethics built on pessimism arises from the disregard of moral imagination. Only if one considers that the individual human spirit is itself incapable of giving content to its striving can one expect the craving for pleasure to account fully for all acts of will. A man without imagination creates no moral ideas. They must be given to him. Physical nature sees to it that he strives to satisfy his lower desires. But the development of the whole man also includes those desires that originate in the spirit. Only if one believes that man has no such spiritual desires can one declare that he must receive them from without. Then one would also be entitled to say that it is man's duty to do what he does not want. Every ethical system that demands of man that he should suppress his own will in order to fulfill tasks that he does not want, reckons not with the whole man but with one in which the faculty of spiritual desire is lacking. For a man who is harmoniously developed, the so-called ideals of virtue lie, not without, but within the sphere of his own being. Moral action consists not in the eradication of a one-sided personal will but in the full development of human nature. Those who hold that moral ideals are attainable only if man destroys his own personal will, are not aware that these ideals are wanted by man just as he wants the satisfaction of the so-called animal instincts.

It cannot be denied that the views here outlined may easily be misunderstood. Immature people without moral imagination like to look upon the instincts of their half-developed natures as the fullest expression of the human race, and reject all moral ideas which they have not themselves produced, in order that they may "live themselves out" undisturbed. But it goes without saying that what is right for a fully developed human being does not hold good for half-developed human natures. Anyone who still needs to be educated to the point where his moral nature breaks through the husk of his lower passions, will not have the same things expected of him as of a mature person. However, it was not my intention to show what needs to be impressed upon an undeveloped person, but what lies within the essential nature of a mature human being. My intention was to demonstrate the possibility of freedom, and freedom is manifested not in actions performed under constraint of sense or soul but in actions sustained by spiritual intuitions.

The mature man gives himself his own value. He does not aim at pleasure, which comes to him as a gift of grace on the part of Nature or of the Creator; nor does he fulfill an abstract duty which he recognizes as such after he has renounced the striving for pleasure. He acts as he wants to act, that is, in accordance with the standard of his ethical intuitions; and he finds in the achievement of what he wants the true enjoyment of life. He determines the value of life by measuring achievements against aims. An ethics which replaces "would" with mere "should", inclination with mere duty, will consequently determine the value of man by measuring his fulfillment of duty against the demands that it makes. It measures man with a yardstick external to his own being.

The view which I have here developed refers man back to himself. It recognizes as the true value of life only what each individual regards as such, according to the standard of his own will. It no more acknowledges a value of life that is not recognized by the individual than it does a purpose of life that has not originated in him. It sees in the individual who knows himself through and through, his own master and his own assessor.

Individuality and Genus

THE view that man is destined to become a complete, self-contained, free individuality seems to be contested by the fact that he makes his appearance as a member of a naturally given totality (race, people, nation, family, male or female sex) and also works within a totality (state, church, and so on). He bears the general characteristics of the group to which he belongs, and he gives to his actions a content that is determined by the position he occupies among many others.

This being so, is individuality possible at all? Can we regard man as a totality in himself, seeing that he grows out of one totality and integrates himself into another?

Each member of a totality is determined, as regards its characteristics and functions, by the whole totality. A racial group is a totality and all the people belonging to it bear the characteristic features that are inherent in the nature of the group. How the single member is constituted, and how he will behave, are determined by the character of the racial group. Therefore the physiognomy and conduct of the individual have something generic about them. If we ask why some particular thing about a man is like this or like that, we are referred back from the individual to the genus. The genus explains why something in the individual appears in the form we observe.

Man, however, makes himself free from what is generic. For the generic features of the human race, when rightly understood, do not restrict man's freedom, and should not artificially be made to do so. A man develops qualities and activities of his own, and the basis for these we can seek only in the man himself. What is generic in him serves only as a medium in which to express his own individual being. He uses as a foundation the characteristics that nature has given him, and to these he gives a form appropriate to his own being. If we seek in the generic laws the reasons for an expression of this being, we seek in vain. We are concerned with something purely individual which can be explained only in terms of itself. If a man has achieved this emancipation from all that is generic, and we are nevertheless determined to explain everything about him in generic terms, then we have no sense for what is individual.

It is impossible to understand a human being completely if one takes the concept of genus as the basis of one's judgment. The tendency to judge according to the genus is at its most stubborn where we are concerned with differences of sex. Almost invariably man sees in woman, and woman in man, too much of the general character of the other sex and too little of what is individual. In practical life this does less harm to men than to women. The social position of women is for the most part such an unworthy one because in so many respects it is determined not as it should be by the particular characteristics of the individual woman, but by the general picture one has of woman's natural tasks and needs. A man's activity in life is governed by his individual capacities and inclinations, whereas a woman's is supposed to be determined solely by the mere fact that she is a woman. She is supposed to be a slave to what is generic, to womanhood in general. As long as men continue to debate whether a woman is suited to this or that profession "according to her natural disposition", the so-called woman's question cannot advance beyond its most elementary stage. What a woman, within her natural limitations, wants to become had better be left to the woman herself to decide. If it is true that women are suited only to that profession which is theirs at present, then they will hardly have it in them to attain any other. But they must be allowed to decide for themselves what is in accordance with their nature. To all who fear an upheaval of our social structure through accepting women as individuals and not as females, we must reply that a social structure in which the status of one half of humanity is unworthy of a human being is itself in great need of improvement.

Anyone who judges people according to generic characters gets only as far as the frontier where people begin to be beings whose activity is based on free self-determination. Whatever lies short of this frontier may naturally become matter for academic study. The characteristics of race, people, nation and sex are the subject matter of special branches of study. Only men who wish to live as nothing more than examples of the genus could possibly conform to a general picture such as arises from academic study of this kind. But none of these branches of study are able to advance as far as the unique content of the single individual. Determining the individual according to the laws of his genus ceases where the sphere of freedom (in thinking and acting) begins. The conceptual content which man has to connect with the percept by an act of thinking in order to have the full reality (see Chapter 5 ff.) cannot be fixed once and for all and bequeathed ready-made to mankind. The individual must get his concepts through his own intuition. How the individual has to think cannot possibly be deduced from any kind of generic concept. It depends simply and solely on the individual. Just as little is it possible to determine from the general characteristics of man what concrete aims the individual may choose to set himself. If we would understand the single individual we must find our way into his own particular being and not stop short at those characteristics that are typical. In this sense every single human being is a separate problem. And every kind of study that deals with abstract thoughts and generic concepts is but a preparation for the knowledge we get when a human individuality tells us his way of viewing the world, and on the other hand for the knowledge we get from the content of his acts of will. Whenever we feel that we are dealing with that element in a man which is free from stereotyped thinking and instinctive willing, then, if we would understand him in his essence, we must cease to call to our aid any concepts at all of our own making. The act of knowing consists in combining the concept with the percept by means of thinking. With all other objects the observer must get his concepts through his intuition; but if we are to understand a free individuality we must take over into our own spirit those concepts by which he determines himself, in their pure form (without mixing our own conceptual content with them). Those who immediately mix their own concepts into every judgment about another person, can never arrive at the understanding of an individuality. Just as the free individuality emancipates himself from the characteristics of the genus, so must the act of knowing emancipate itself from the way in which we understand what is generic.

Only to the extent that a man has emancipated himself in this way from all that is generic, does he count as a free spirit within a human community. No man is all genus, none is all individuality. But every man gradually emancipates a greater or lesser sphere of his being, both from the generic characteristics of animal life and from domination by the decrees of human authorities.

As regards that part of his nature where a man is not able to achieve this freedom for himself, he constitutes a part of the whole organism of nature and spirit. In this respect he lives by copying others or by obeying their commands. But only that part of his conduct that springs from his intuitions can have ethical value in the true sense. And those moral instincts that he possesses through the inheritance of social instincts acquire ethical value through being taken up into his intuitions. It is from individual ethical intuitions and their acceptance by human communities that all moral activity of mankind originates. In other words, the moral life of mankind is the sum total of the products of the moral imagination of free human individuals. This is the conclusion reached by monism.

The Consequences of Monism

THE uniform explanation of the world, that is, the monism we have described, derives the principles that it needs for the explanation of the world from human experience. In the same way, it looks for the sources of action within the world of observation, that is, in that part of human nature which is accessible to our self-knowledge, more particularly in moral imagination. Monism refuses to infer in an abstract way that the ultimate causes of the world that is presented to our perceiving and thinking are to be found in a region outside this world. For monism, the unity that thoughtful observation — which we can experience — brings to the manifold multiplicity of percepts is the same unity that man's need for knowledge demands, and through which it seeks entry into the physical and spiritual regions of the world. Whoever seeks another unity behind this one only proves that he does not recognize the identity of what is discovered by thinking and what is demanded by the urge for knowledge. The single human individual is not actually cut off from the universe. He is a part of it, and between this part and the totality of the cosmos there exists a real connection which is broken only for our perception. At first we take this part of the universe as something existing on its own, because we do not see the belts and ropes by which the fundamental forces of the cosmos keep the wheel of our life revolving.

Whoever remains at this standpoint sees a part of the whole as if it were actually an independently existing thing, a monad which receives information about the rest of the world in some way from without. Monism, as here described, shows that we can believe in this independence only so long as the things we perceive are not woven by our thinking into the network of the conceptual world. As soon as this happens, all separate existence turns out to be mere illusion due to perceiving. Man can find his full and complete existence in the totality of the universe only through the experience of intuitive thinking. Thinking destroys the illusion due to perceiving and integrates our individual existence into the life of the cosmos. The unity of the conceptual world, which contains all objective percepts, also embraces the content of our subjective personality. Thinking gives us reality in its true form as a self-contained unity, whereas the multiplicity of percepts is but a semblance due to the way we are organized. To recognize true reality, as against the illusion due to perceiving, has at all times been the goal of human thinking. Scientific thought has made great efforts to recognize reality in percepts by discovering the systematic connections between them. Where, however, it was believed that the connections ascertained by human thinking had only subjective validity, the true basis of unity was sought in some entity lying beyond our world of experience (an inferred God, will, absolute spirit, etc.). On the strength of this belief, the attempt was made to obtain, in addition to the knowledge accessible to experience, a second kind of knowledge which transcends experience and shows how the world that can be experienced is connected with the entities that cannot (a metaphysics arrived at by inference, and not by experience). It was thought that the reason why we can grasp the connections of things in the world through disciplined thinking was that a primordial being had built the world upon logical laws, and, similarly, that the grounds for our actions lay in the will of such a being. What was not realized was that thinking embraces both the subjective and the objective in one grasp, and that through the union of percept with concept the full reality is conveyed. Only as long as we think of the law and order that permeates and determines the percept as having the abstract form of a concept, are we in fact dealing with something purely subjective. But the content of a concept, which is added to the percept by means of thinking, is not subjective. This content is not taken from the subject, but from reality. It is that part of the reality that cannot be reached by the act of perceiving. It is experience, but not experience gained through perceiving. If someone cannot see that the concept is something real, he is thinking of it only in the abstract form in which he holds it in his mind. But only through our organization is it present in such isolation, just as in the case of the percept. After all, the tree that one perceives has no existence by itself, in isolation. It exists only as a part of the immense machinery of nature, and can only exist in real connection with nature. An abstract concept taken by itself has as little reality as a percept taken by itself. The percept is the part of reality that is given objectively, the concept the part that is given subjectively (through intuition). Our mental organization tears the reality apart into these two factors. One factor presents itself to perception, the other to intuition. Only the union of the two, that is, the percept fitting systematically into the universe, constitutes the full reality. If we take mere percepts by themselves, we have no reality but rather a disconnected chaos; if we take by itself the law and order connecting the percepts, then we have nothing but abstract concepts. Reality is not contained in the abstract concept; it is, however, contained in thoughtful observation, which does not one-sidedly consider either concept or percept alone, but rather the union of the two.

That we live in reality (that we are rooted in it with our real existence) will not be denied by even the most orthodox of subjective idealists. He will only deny that we reach the same reality with our knowing, with our ideas, as the one we actually live in. Monism, on the other hand, shows that thinking is neither subjective nor objective, but is a principle that embraces both sides of reality. When we observe with our thinking, we carry out a process which itself belongs to the order of real events. By means of thinking, within the experience itself, we overcome the one-sidedness of mere perceiving. We cannot argue out the essence of reality by means of abstract conceptual hypotheses (through pure conceptual reflection), but in so far as we find the ideas that belong to the percepts, we are living in the reality. Monism does not seek to add to experience something non-experienceable (transcendental), but finds the full reality in concept and percept. It does not spin a system of metaphysics out of mere abstract concepts, because it sees in the concept by itself only one side of the reality, namely, the side that remains hidden from perception, and only makes sense in connection with the percept. Monism does, however, give man the conviction that he lives in the world of reality and has no need to look beyond this world for a higher reality that can never be experienced. It refrains from seeking absolute reality anywhere else but in experience, because it is just in the content of experience that it recognizes reality. Monism is satisfied by this reality, because it knows that thinking has the power to guarantee it. What dualism seeks only beyond the observed world, monism finds in this world itself. Monism shows that with our act of knowing we grasp reality in its true form, and not as a subjective image that inserts itself between man and reality. For monism, the conceptual content of the world is the same for all human individuals. According to monistic principles, one human individual regards another as akin to himself because the same world content expresses itself in him. In the unitary world of concepts there are not as many concepts of the lion as there are individuals who think of a lion, but only one. And the concept that A fits to his percept of the lion is the same that B fits to his, only apprehended by a different perceiving subject. Thinking leads all perceiving subjects to the same ideal unity in all multiplicity. The unitary world of ideas expresses itself in them as in a multiplicity of individuals. As long as a man apprehends himself merely by means of self-perception, he sees himself as this particular man; as soon as he looks at the world of ideas that lights up within him, embracing all that is separate, he sees within himself the absolute reality living and shining forth. Dualism defines the divine primordial Being as that which pervades and lives in all men. Monism finds this divine life, common to all, in reality itself. The ideas of another human being are in substance mine also, and I regard them as different only as long as I perceive, but no longer when I think. Every man embraces in his thinking only a part of the total world of ideas, and to that extent individuals differ even in the actual content of their thinking. But all these contents are within a self-contained whole, which embraces the thought contents of all men. Hence every man, in his thinking, lays hold of the universal primordial Being which pervades all men. To live in reality, filled with the content of thought, is at the same time to live in God. A world beyond, that is merely inferred and cannot be experienced, arises from a misconception on the part of those who believe that this world cannot have the foundation of its existence within itself. They do not realize that through thinking they find just what they require for the explanation of the percept. This is the reason why no speculation has ever brought to light any content that was not borrowed from the reality given to us. The God that is assumed through abstract inference is nothing but a human being transplanted into the Beyond; Schopenhauer's Will is human will-power made absolute; Hartmann's Unconscious, a primordial Being made up of idea and will, is but a compound of two abstractions drawn from experience. Exactly the same is true of all other transcendental principles based on thought that has not been experienced.

The truth is that the human spirit never transcends the reality in which we live, nor has it any need to do so, seeing that this world contains everything the human spirit requires in order to explain it. If philosophers eventually declare themselves satisfied with the deduction of the world from principles they borrow from experience and transplant into an hypothetical Beyond, then it should be just as possible to be satisfied when the same content is allowed to remain in this world, where for our thinking as experienced it does belong. All attempts to transcend the world are purely illusory, and the principles transplanted from this world into the Beyond do not explain the world any better than those which remain within it. If thinking understands itself it will not ask for any such transcendence at all, since every content of thought must look within the world and not outside it for a perceptual content, together with which it forms something real. The objects of imagination, too, are no more than contents which become justified only when transformed into mental pictures that refer to a perceptual content. Through this perceptual content they become an integral part of reality. A concept that is supposed to be filled with a content lying beyond our given world is an abstraction to which no reality corresponds. We can think out only the concepts of reality; in order to find reality itself, we must also have perception. A primordial world being for which we invent a content is an impossible assumption for any thinking that understands itself. Monism does not deny ideal elements, in fact, it considers a perceptual content without an ideal counterpart as not fully real; but in the whole realm of thinking it finds nothing that could require us to step outside the realm of our thinking's experience by denying the objective spiritual reality of thinking itself. Monism regards a science that limits itself to a description of percepts without penetrating to their ideal complements as incomplete. But it regards as equally incomplete all abstract concepts that do not find their complements in percepts, and that fit nowhere into the conceptual network that embraces the whole observable world. Hence it knows no ideas that refer to objective factors lying beyond our experience and which are supposed to form the content of a purely hypothetical system of metaphysics. All that mankind has produced in the way of such ideas monism regards as abstractions borrowed from experience, the fact of borrowing having been overlooked by the originators.

Just as little, according to monistic principles, can the aims of our action be derived from an extra-human Beyond. In so far as we think them, they must stem from human intuition. Man does not take the purposes of an objective (transcendental) primordial Being and make them his own, but he pursues his own individual purposes given him by his moral imagination. The idea that realizes itself in an action is detached by man from the unitary world of ideas and made the basis of his will. Therefore it is not the commandments injected into this world from the Beyond that live in his action, but human intuitions belonging to this world itself. Monism knows no such world-dictator who sets our aims and directs our actions from outside. Man finds no such primal ground of existence whose counsels he might investigate in order to learn from it the aims to which he has to direct his actions. He is thrown back upon himself. It is he himself who must give content to his action. If he looks outside the world in which he lives for the grounds determining his will, he will look in vain. If he is to go beyond merely satisfying his natural instincts, for which Mother Nature has provided, then he must seek these grounds in his own moral imagination, unless he finds it more convenient to let himself be determined by the moral imaginations of others; in other words, either he must give up action altogether, or else he must act for reasons that he gives himself out of his world of ideas or that others select for him out of theirs. If he advances beyond merely following his life of sensuous instincts or carrying out the commands of others, then he will be determined by nothing but himself. He must act out of an impulse given by himself and determined by nothing else. It is true that this impulse is determined ideally in the unitary world of ideas; but in practice it is only by man that it can be taken from that world and translated into reality. The grounds for the actual translation of an idea into reality by man, monism can find only in man himself. If an idea is to become action, man must first want it, before it can happen. Such an act of will therefore has its grounds only in man himself. Man is then the ultimate determinant of his action. He is free.

An Introduction to Waldorf Education and Other Essays

An Introduction to Waldorf Education

The aims Emil Molt is trying to realize through the Waldorf School are connected with quite definite views on the social tasks of the present day and the near future. The spirit in which the school should be conducted must proceed from these views. It is a school attached to an industrial undertaking. The peculiar place modern industry has taken in the evolution of social life in actual practice sets its stamp upon the modern social movement. Parents who entrust their children to this school are bound to expect that the children shall be educated and prepared for the practical work of life in a way that takes due account of this movement. This makes it necessary, in founding the school, to begin from educational principles that have their roots in the requirements of modern life. Children must be educated and instructed in such a way that their lives fulfill demands everyone can support, no matter from which of the inherited social classes one might come. What is demanded of people by the actualities of modern life must find its reflection in the organization of this school. What is to be the ruling spirit in this life must be aroused in the children by education and instruction.

It would be fatal if the educational views upon which the Waldorf School is founded were dominated by a spirit out of touch with life. Today, such a spirit may all too easily arise because people have come to feel the full part played in the recent destruction of civilization by our absorption in a materialistic mode of life and thought during the last few decades. This feeling makes them desire to introduce an idealistic way of thinking into the management of public affairs. Anyone who turns his attention to developing educational life and the system of instruction will desire to see such a way of thinking realized there especially. It is an attitude of mind that reveals much good will. It goes without saying that this good will should be fully appreciated. If used properly, it can provide valuable service when gathering manpower for a social undertaking requiring new foundations. Yet it is necessary in this case to point our how the best intentions must fail if they set to work without fully regarding those first conditions that are based on practical insight.

This, then, is one of the requirements to be considered when the founding of any institution such as the Waldorf School is intended. Idealism must work in the spirit of its curriculum and methodology; but it must be an idealism that has the power to awaken in young, growing human beings the forces and faculties they will need in later life to be equipped for work in modern society and to obtain for themselves an adequate living.

The pedagogy and instructional methodology will be able to fulfill this requirement only through a genuine knowledge of the developing human being. Insightful people are today calling for some form of education and instruction directed not merely to the cultivation of one-sided knowledge, but also to abilities; education directed not merely to the cultivation of intellectual faculties, but also to the strengthening of the will. The soundness of this idea is unquestionable; but it is impossible to develop the will (and that healthiness of feeling on which it rests) unless one develops the insights that awaken the energetic impulses of will and feeling. A mistake often made presently in this respect is not that people instill too many concepts into young minds, but that the kind of concepts they cultivate are devoid of all driving life force. Anyone who believes one can cultivate the will without cultivating the concepts that give it life is suffering from a delusion. It is the business of contemporary educators to see this point clearly; but this clear vision can only proceed from a living understanding of the whole human being.

It is now planned that the Waldorf School will be a primary school in which the educational goals and curriculum are founded upon each teacher's living insight into the nature of the whole human being, so far as this is possible under present conditions. Children will, of course, have to be advanced far enough in the different school grades to satisfy the standards imposed by the current views. Within this framework, however, the pedagogical ideals and curriculum will assume a form that arises out of this knowledge of the human being and of actual life.

The primary school is entrusted with the child at a period of its life when the soul is undergoing a very important transformation. From birth to about the sixth or seventh year, the human being naturally gives himself up to everything immediately surrounding him in the human environment, and thus, through the imitative instinct, gives form to his own nascent powers. From this period on, the child's soul becomes open to take in consciously what the educator and teacher gives, which affects the child as a result of the teacher's natural authority. The authority is taken for granted by the child from a dim feeling that in the teacher there is something that should exist in himself, too. One cannot be an educator or teacher unless one adopts out of full insight a stance toward the child that takes account in the most comprehensive sense of this metamorphosis of the urge to imitate into an ability to assimilate upon the basis of a natural relationship of authority. The modern world view, based as it is upon natural law, does not approach these fact of human development in full consciousness. To observe them with the necessary attention, one must have a sense of life's subtlest manifestations in the human being. This kind of sense must ran through the whole an of education; it must shape the curriculum; it must live in the spirit uniting teacher and pupil. In educating, what the teacher does can depend only slightly on anything he gets from a general, abstract pedagogy: it must rather be newly born every moment from a live understanding of the young human being he or she is teaching. One may, of course, object that this Lively kind of education and instruction breaks down in large classes. This objection is no doubt justified in a limited sense. Taken beyond those limits, however, the objection merely shows that the person who makes it proceeds from abstract educational norms, for a really living an of education based on a genuine knowledge of the human being carries with it a power that rouses the interest of every single pupil so that there is no need for direct "individual" work in order to keep his attention on the subject. One can put forth the essence of one's teaching in such a form that each pupil assimilates it in his own individual way. This requires simply that whatever the teacher does should be sufficiently alive. If anyone has a genuine sense for human nature, the developing human being becomes for him such an intense, Living riddle that the very attempt to solve it awakens the pupil's living interest empathetically. Such empathy is more valuable than individual work, which may all too easily cripple the child's own initiative. It might indeed be asserted — again, within limitations — that large classes led by teachers who are imbued with the life that comes from genuine knowledge of the human being, will achieve better results than small classes led by teachers who proceed from standard educational theories and have no chance to put this life into their work.

Not so outwardly marked as the transformation the soul undergoes in the sixth or seventh year, but no less important for the art of educating, is a change that a penetrating study of the human being shows to take place around the end of the ninth year. At this time, the sense of self assumes a form that awakens in the child a relationship to nature and to the world about him such that one can now talk to him more about the connections between things and processes themselves, whereas previously he was interested almost exclusively in things and processes only in relationship to man. Facts of this kind in a human being's development ought to be most carefully observed by the educator. For if one introduces into the child's world of concepts and feelings what coincides just at that period of life with the direction taken by his own developing powers, one then gives such added vigor to the growth of the whole person that it remains a source of strength throughout life. If in any period of life one works against the grain of these developing powers, one weakens the individual.

Knowledge of the special needs of each life period provides a basis for drawing up a suitable curriculum. This knowledge also can be a basis for dealing with instructional subjects in successive periods. By the end of the ninth year, one must have brought the child to a certain level in all that has come into human life through the growth of civilization. Thus while the first school years are properly spent on teaching the child to write and read, the teaching must be done in a manner that permits the essential character of this phase of development to be served. If one teaches things in a way that makes a one-sided claim on the child's intellect and the merely abstract acquisition of skills, then the development of the native will and sensibilities is checked; while if the child learns in a manner that calls upon its whole being, he or she develops all around. Drawing in a childish fashion, or even a primitive kind of painting, brings out the whole human being's interest in what he is doing. Therefore one should let writing grow out of drawing. One can begin with figures in which the pupil's own childish artistic sense comes into play; from these evolve the letters of the alphabet. Beginning with an activity that, being artistic, draws out the whole human being, one should develop writing, which tends toward the intellectual. And one must let reading, which concentrates the attention strongly within the realm of the intellect, arise out of writing.

When people recognize how much is to be gained for the intellect from this early artistic education of the child, they will be willing to allow art its proper place in the primary school education. The arts of music, painting and sculpting will be given a proper place in the scheme of instruction. This artistic element and physical exercise will be brought into a suitable combination. Gymnastics and action games will be developed as expressions of sentiments called forth by something in the nature of music or recitation. Eurythmic movement — movement with a meaning — will replace those motions based merely on the anatomy and physiology of the physical body. People will discover how great a power resides in an artistic manner of instruction for the development of will and feeling. However, to teach or instruct in this way and obtain valuable results can be done only by teachers who have an insight into the human being sufficiently keen to perceive clearly the connection between the methods they are employing and the developmental forces that manifest themselves in any particular period of life. The real teacher, the real educator, is not one who has studied educational theory as a science of the management of children, but one in whom the pedagogue has been awakened by awareness of human nature.

Of prime importance for the cultivation of the child's feeling-life is that the child develops its relationship to the world in a way such as that which develops when we incline toward fantasy. If the educator is not himself a fantast, then the child is not in danger of becoming one when the teacher conjures forth the realms of plants and animals, of the sky and the stars in the soul of the child in fairy-tale fashion.

Visual aids are undoubtedly justified within certain limits; but when a materialistic conviction leads people to try to extend this form of teaching to every conceivable thing, they forget there are other powers in the human being which must be developed, and which cannot be addressed through the medium of visual observation. For instance, there is the acquisition of certain things purely through memory that is connected to the developmental forces at work between the sixth or seventh and the fourteenth year of life. It is this property of human nature upon which the teaching of arithmetic should be based. Indeed, arithmetic can be used to cultivate the faculty of memory. If one disregards this fact, one may perhaps be tempted (especially when teaching arithmetic) to commit the educational blunder of teaching with visual aids what should be taught as a memory exercise.

One may fall into the same mistake by trying all too anxiously to make the child understand everything one tells him. The will that prompts one to do so is undoubtedly good, but does not duly estimate what it means when, Later in life, we revive within our soul something that we acquired simply through memory when younger and now find, in our mature years, that we have come to understand it on our own. Here, no doubt, any fear of the pupil's not taking an active interest in a lesson learned by memory alone will have to be relieved by the teacher's lively way of giving it. If the teacher engages his or her whole being in teaching, then he may safely bring the child things for which the full understanding will come when joyfully remembered in later life. There is something that constantly refreshes and strengthens the inner substance of life in this recollection. If the teacher assists such a strengthening, he will give the child a priceless treasure to take along on life's road. In this way, too, the teacher will avoid the visual aid's degenerating into the banality that occurs when a lesson is overly adapted to the child's understanding. Banalities may be calculated to arouse the child's own activity, but such fruits lose their flavor with the end of childhood. The flame enkindled in the child from the living fire of the teacher in matters that still lie, in a way, beyond his "understanding," remains an active, awakening force throughout the child's life.

If, at the end of the ninth year, one begins to choose descriptions of natural history from the plant and animal world, treating them in a way that the natural forms and processes lead to an understanding of the human form and the phenomena of human life, then one can help release the forces that at this age are struggling to be born out of the depths of human nature. It is consistent with the character of the child's sense of self at this age to see the qualities that nature divides among manifold species of the plant and animal kingdoms as united into one harmonious whole at the summit of the natural world in the human being.

Around the twelfth year, another turning point in the child's development occurs. He becomes ripe for the development of the faculties that lead him in a wholesome way to the comprehension of things that must be considered without any reference to the human being: the mineral kingdom, the physical world, meteorological phenomena, and so on.

The best way to lead then from such exercises, which are based entirely on the natural human instinct of activity without reference to practical ends, to others that shall be a sort of education for actual work, will follow from knowledge of the character of the successive periods of life. What has been said here with reference to particular parts of the curriculum may be extended to everything that should be taught to the pupil up to his fifteenth year.

There need be no fear of the elementary schools releasing pupils in a state of soul and body unfit for practical life if their principles of education and instructions are allowed to proceed, as described, from the inner development of the human being. For human life itself is shaped by this inner development; and one can enter upon life in no better way than when, through the development of our own inner capacities, we can join with what others before us, from similar inner human capacities, have embodied in the evolution of the civilized world. It is true that to bring the two into harmony — the development of the pupil and the development of the civilized world — will require a body of teachers who do not shut themselves up in an educational routine with strictly professional interests, but rather take an active interest in the whole range of life. Such a body of teachers will discover how to awaken in the upcoming generation a sense of the inner, spiritual substance of life and also an understanding of life's practicalities. If instruction is carried on this way, the young human being at the age of fourteen or fifteen will not lack comprehension of important things in agriculture and industry, commerce and travel, which help to make up the collective life of mankind. He will have acquired a knowledge of things and a practical skill that will enable him to feel at home in the life which receives him into its stream.

If the Waldorf School is to achieve the aims its founder has in view, it must be built on educational principles and methods of the kind here described. It will then be able to give the kind of education that allows the pupil's body to develop healthily and according to its needs, because the soul (of which this body is the expression) is allowed to grow in a way consistent with the forces of its development. Before its opening, some preparatory work was attempted with the teachers so that the school might be able to work toward the proposed aim. Those concerned with the management of the school believe that in pursuing this aim they bring something into educational life in accordance with modern social thinking. They feel the responsibility inevitably connected with any such attempt; but they think that, in contemporary social demands, it is a duty to undertake this when the opportunity is afforded.

Individualism in Philosophy

If the human being were a mere creature of nature and not a creator at the same time, he would not stand questioningly before the phenomena of the world and would also not seek to fathom their essential being and laws. He would satisfy his drive to eat and to propagate in accordance with the inborn laws of his organism and otherwise allow the events of the world to take the course they happen to take. It would not occur to him at all to address a question to nature. Content and happy he would go through life like the rose of which Angelus Silesius says:

The rose has no "wherefore?"; it blooms because it blooms. It pays itself no mind, asks not if it is seen.

The rose can just be like this. What it is it is because nature has made it this way. But the human being cannot just be like this. There is a drive within him to add to the world lying before him yet another world that springs forth from him. He does not want to live with his fellowmen in the chance proximity into which nature has placed him; he seeks to regulate the way he lives with others in accordance with his reason. The form in which nature has shaped man and woman does not suffice for him; he creates the ideal figures of Greek sculpture. To the natural course of events in daily life he adds the course of events springing from his imagination as tragedy and comedy. In architecture and music, creations spring from his spirit that are hardly reminiscent at all of anything created by nature. In his sciences he draws up conceptual pictures through which the chaos of world phenomena passing daily before our senses appears to us as a harmoniously governed whole, as a structured organism. In the world of his own deeds, he creates a particular realm — that of historical happenings — which is essentially different from nature's course of events.

The human being feels that everything he creates is only a continuation of the workings of nature. He also knows that he is called upon to add something higher to what nature can do out of itself. He is conscious of the fact that he gives birth out of himself to another, higher nature in addition to outer nature.

Thus the human being stands between two worlds; between the world that presses in upon him from outside and the world that he brings forth out of himself. His effort is to bring these two worlds into harmony. For, his whole being aims at harmony. He would like to live like the rose that does not ask about the whys and wherefores but rather blooms because it blooms. Schiller demands this of the human being in the words:

Are you seeking the highest, the greatest? The plant can teach it to you. What it is will-lessly, you must be will-fully — that's it!

The plant can just be what it is. For no new realm springs forth from it, and therefore the fearful longing can also not arise in it: How am I to bring the two realms into harmony with each other?

The goal for which man has striven throughout all the ages of history is to bring what lies within him into harmony with what nature creates out of itself. The fact that he himself is fruitful becomes the starting point for his coming to terms with nature; this coming to terms forms the content of his spiritual striving.

There are two ways of coming to terms with nature. The human being either allows outer nature to become master over his inner nature, or he subjects this outer nature to himself. In the first case, he seeks to submit his own willing and existence to the outer course of events. In the second case, he draws the goal and direction of his willing and existence from himself and seeks to deal in some way or other with the events of nature that still go their own way.

Let us speak about the first case first. It is in accordance with his essential being for man, above and beyond the realm of nature, to create yet another realm that in his sense is a higher one. He can do no other. How he relates to the outer world will depend upon the feelings and emotions he has with respect to this his own realm. Now he can have the same feelings with respect to his own realm as he has with respect to the facts of nature. He then allows the creations of his spirit to approach him in the same way he allows an event of the outer world, wind and weather, for example, to approach him. He perceives no difference in kind between what occurs in the outer world and what occurs within his soul. He therefore believes that they are only one realm, i.e., governed by one kind of law. But he does feel that the creations of his spirit are of a higher sort. He therefore places them above the creations of mere nature. Thus he transfers his own creations into the outer world and lets nature be governed by them. Consequently he knows only an outer world. For he transfers his own inner world outside himself. No wonder then that for him even his own self becomes a subordinate part of this outer world.

One way man comes to terms with the outer world consists, therefore, in his regarding his inner being as something outer; he sets this inner being, which he has transferred into the outer world, both over nature and over himself as ruler and lawgiver.

This characterizes the standpoint of the religious person. A divine world order is a creation of the human spirit. But the human being is not clear about the fact that the content of this world order has sprung from his own spirit. He therefore transfers it outside himself and subordinates himself to his own creation.

The acting human being is not content simply to act. The flower blooms because it blooms. It does not ask about whys and wherefores. The human being relates to what he does. He connects feelings to what he does. He is either satisfied or dissatisfied with what he does. He makes value judgments about his actions. He regards one action as pleasing to him, and another as displeasing. The moment he feels this, the harmony of the world is disturbed for him. He believes that the pleasing action must bring about different consequences than one which evokes his displeasure. Now if he is not clear about the fact that, out of himself, he has attached the value judgments to his actions, he will believe that these values are attached to his actions by some outer power. He believes that an outer power differentiates the happenings of this world into ones that are pleasing and therefore good, and ones that are displeasing and therefore bad, evil. A person who feels this way makes no distinction between the facts of nature and the actions of the human being. He judges both from the same point of view. For him the whole cosmos is one realm, and the laws governing this realm correspond entirely to those which the human spirit brings forth out of itself.

This way of coming to terms with the world reveals a basic characteristic of human nature. No matter how unclear the human being might be about his relationship to the world, he nevertheless seeks within himself the yardstick by which to measure all things. Out of a kind of unconscious feeling of sovereignty he decides on the absolute value of all happenings. No matter how one studies this, one finds that there are countless people who believe themselves governed by gods; there are none who do not independently, over the heads of the gods, judge what pleases or displeases these gods. The religious person cannot set himself up as the lord of the world; but he does indeed determine, out of his own absolute power, the likes and dislikes of the ruler of the world.

One need only look at religious natures and one will find my assertions confirmed. What proclaimer of gods has not at the same time determined quite exactly what pleases these gods and what is repugnant to them? Every religion has its wise teachings about the cosmos, and each also asserts that its wisdom stems from one or more gods.

If one wants to characterize the standpoint of the religious person one must say: He seeks to judge the world out of himself, but he does not have the courage also to ascribe to himself the responsibility for this judgment; therefore he invents beings for himself in the outer world that he can saddle with this responsibility.

Such considerations seem to me to answer the question:

What is religion? The content of religion springs from the human spirit. But the human spirit does not want to acknowledge this origin to itself. The human being submits himself to his own laws, but he regards these laws as foreign. He establishes himself as ruler over himself. Every religion establishes the human "I" as regent of the world. Religion's being consists precisely in this, that it is not conscious of this fact. It regards as revelation from outside what it actually reveals to itself.

The human being wishes to stand at the topmost place in the world. But he does not dare to pronounce himself the pinnacle of creation. Therefore he invents gods in his own image and lets the world be ruled by them. When he thinks this way, he is thinking religiously.

Philosophical thinking replaces religious thinking. Wherever and whenever this occurs, human nature reveals itself to us in a very particular way.

For the development of Western thinking, the transition from the mythological thinking of the Greeks into philosophical thinking is particularly interesting. I would now like to present three thinkers from that time of transition: Anaximander, Thales, and Parmenides. They represent three stages leading from religion to philosophy.

It is characteristic of the first stage of this path that divine beings, from whom the content taken from the human "I" supposedly stems, are no longer acknowledged. But from habit one still holds fast to the view that this content stems from the outer world. Anaximander stands at this stage. He no longer speaks of gods as his Greek ancestors did. For him the highest principle, which rules the world, is not a being pictured in man's image. It is an impersonal being, the apeiron, the indefinite. It develops out of itself everything occurring in nature, not in the way a person creates, but rather out of natural necessity. But Anaximander always conceives this natural necessity to be analogous to actions that proceed according to human principles of reason. He pictures to himself, so to speak, a moral, natural lawfulness, a highest being, that treats the world like a human, moral judge without actually being one. For Anaximander, everything in the world occurs just as necessarily as a magnet attracts iron, but does so according to moral, i.e., human laws. Only from this point of view could he say: "Whence things arise, hence must they also pass away, in accordance with justice, for they must do penance and recompense because of unrighteousness in a way corresponding to the order of time."

This is the stage at which a thinker begins to judge philosophically. He lets go of the gods. He therefore no longer ascribes to the gods what comes from man. But he actually does nothing more than transfer onto something impersonal the characteristics formerly attributed to divine, i.e., personal beings.

Thales approaches the world in an entirely free way. Even though he is a few years older than Anaximander, he is philosophically much more mature. His way of thinking is no longer religious at all.

Within Western thinking Thales is the first to come to terms with the world in the second of the two ways mentioned above. Hegel has so often emphasized that thinking is the trait which distinguishes man from the animal. Thales is the first Western personality who dared to assign to thinking its sovereign position. He no longer bothered about whether gods have arranged the world in accordance with the order of thought or whether an apeiron directs the world in accordance with thinking. He only knew that he thought, and assumed that, because he thought, he also had a right to explain the world to himself in accordance with his thinking. Do not underestimate this standpoint of Thales! It represents an immense disregard for all religious preconceptions. For it was the declaration of the absoluteness of human thinking. Religious people say: The world is arranged the way we think it to be because God exists. And since they conceive of God in the image of man, it is obvious that the order of the world corresponds to the order of the human head. All that is a matter of complete indifference to Thales. He thinks about the world. And by virtue of his thinking he ascribes to himself the power to judge the world. He already has a feeling that thinking is only a human action; and accordingly he undertakes to explain the world with the help of this purely human thinking. With Thales the activity of knowing (das Erkennen) now enters into a completely new stage of its development. It ceases to draw its justification from the fact that it only copies what the gods have already sketched out. It takes from out of itself the right to decide upon the lawfulness of the world. What matters, to begin with, is not at all whether Thales believed water or anything else to be the principle of the world; what matters is that he said to himself: What the principle is, this I will decide by my thinking. He assumed it to be obvious that thinking has the power in such things. And therein lies his greatness.

Just consider what was accomplished. No less an event than that spiritual power over world phenomena was given to man. Whoever trusts in his thinking says to himself: No matter how violently the waves of life may rage, no matter that the world seems a chaos: I am at peace, for all this mad commotion does not disquiet me, because I comprehend it.

Heraclitus did not comprehend this divine peacefulness of the thinker who understands himself. He was of the view that all things are in eternal flux. That becoming is the essential beings of things. When I step into a river, it is no longer the same one as in the moment of my deciding to enter it. But Heraclitus overlooks just one thing. Thinking preserves what the river bears along with itself and finds that in the next moment something passes before my senses that is essentially the same as what was already there before.

Like Thales, with his firm belief in the power of human thinking, Heraclitus is a typical phenomenon in the realm of those personalities who come to terms with the most significant questions of existence. He does not feel within himself the power to master by thinking the eternal flux of sense-perceptible becoming. Heraclitus looks into the world and it dissolves for him into momentary phenomena upon which one has no hold. If Heraclitus were right, then everything in the world would flutter away, and in the general chaos the human personality would also have to disintegrate. I would not be the same today as I was yesterday, and tomorrow I would be different than today. At every moment, the human being would face something totally new and would be powerless. For, it is doubtful that the experiences he has acquired up to a certain day can guide him in dealing with the totally new experiences that the next day will bring.

Parmenides therefore sets himself in absolute opposition to Heraclitus. With all the one-sidedness possible only to a keen philosophical nature, he rejected all testimony brought by sense perception. For, it is precisely this ever-changing sense world that leads one astray into the view of Heraclitus. Parmenides therefore regarded those revelations as the only source of all truth which well forth from the innermost core of the human personality: the revelations of thinking. In his view the real being of things is not what flows past the senses; it is the thoughts, the ideas, that thinking discovers within this stream and to which it holds fast!

Like so many things that arise in opposition to a particular one-sidedness, Parmenides's way of thinking also became disastrous. It ruined European thinking for centuries. It undermined man's confidence in his sense perception. Whereas an unprejudiced, naive look at the sense world draws from this world itself the thought-content that satisfies the human drive for knowledge, the philosophical movement developing in the sense of Parmenides believed it had to draw real truth only out of pure, abstract thinking.

The thoughts we gain in living intercourse with the sense world have an individual character; they have within themselves the warmth of something experienced. We unfold our own personality by extracting ideas from the world. We feel ourselves as conquerors of the sense world when we capture it in the world of thoughts. Abstract, pure thinking has something impersonal and cold about it. We always feel a compulsion when we spin forth ideas out of pure thinking. Our feeling of self cannot be heightened through such thinking. For we must simply submit to the necessities of thought.

Parmenides did not take into account that thinking is an activity of the human personality. He took it to be impersonal, as the eternal content of existence. What is thought is what exists, he once said.

In the place of the old gods he thus set a new one. Whereas the older religious way of picturing things had set the whole feeling, willing, and thinking man as God at the pinnacle of the world, Parmenides took one single human activity, one part, out of the human personality and made a divine being out of it.

In the realm of views about the moral life of man Parmenides is complemented by Socrates. His statement that virtue is teachable is the ethical consequence of Parmenides's view that thinking is equitable with being. If this is true, then human action can claim to have raised itself to something worthily existing only when human action flows from thinking, from that abstract, logical thinking to which man must simply yield himself, i.e., which he has to acquire for himself as learner.

It is clear that a common thread can be traced through the development of Greek thought. The human being seeks to transfer into the outer world what belongs to him, what springs from his own being, and in this way to subordinate himself to his own being. At first he takes the whole fullness of his nature and sets likenesses of it as gods over himself; then he takes one single human activity, thinking, and sets it over himself as a necessity to which he must yield. That is what is so remarkable in the development of man, that he unfolds his powers, that he fights for the existence and unfolding of these powers in the world, but that he is far from being able to acknowledge these powers as his own.

One of the greatest philosophers of all time has made this great, human self-deception into a bold and wonderful system. This philosopher is Plato. The ideal world, the inner representations that arise around man within his spirit while his gaze is directed at the multiplicity of outer things, this becomes for Plato a higher world of existence of which that multiplicity is only a copy. "The things of this world which our senses perceive have no true being at all: they are always becoming but never are. They have only a relative existence; they are, in their totality, only in and through their relationship to each other; one can therefore just as well call their whole existence a non-existence. They are consequently also not objects of any actual knowledge. For, only about what is, in and for itself and always in the same way, can there be such knowledge; they, on the other hand, are only the object of what we, through sensation, take them to be. As long as we are limited only to our perception of them, we are like people who sit in a dark cave so firmly bound that they cannot even turn their heads and who see nothing, except, on the wall facing them, by the light of a fire burning behind them, the shadow images of real things which are led across between them and the fire, and who in fact also see of each other, yes each of himself, only the shadows on that wall. Their wisdom, however, would be to predict the sequence of those shadows which they have learned to know from experience." The tree that I see and touch, whose flowers I smell, is therefore the shadow of the idea of the tree. And this idea is what is truly real. The idea, however, is what lights up within my spirit when I look at the tree. What I perceive with my senses is thus made into a copy of what my spirit shapes through the perception.

Everything that Plato believes to be present as the world of ideas in the beyond, outside things, is man's inner world. The content of the human spirit, torn out of man and pictured as a world unto itself, as a higher, true world lying in the beyond: that is Platonic philosophy.

I consider Ralph Waldo Emerson to be right when he says: "Among books, Plato only is entitled to Omar's fanatical compliment to the Koran, when he said, 'Burn the libraries; for their value is in this book.' These sentences contain the culture of nations; these are the cornerstone of schools; these are the fountain-head of literatures. A discipline it is in logic, arithmetic, taste, symmetry, poetry, language, rhetoric, ontology, morals, or practical wisdom. There was never such range of speculation. Out of Plato come all things that are still written and debated among men of thought." Let me express the last sentence somewhat more exactly in the following form. The way Plato felt about the relationship of the human spirit to the world, this is how the overwhelming majority of people still feel about it today. They feel that the content of the human spirit — human feeling, willing, and thinking — does stand at the top of the ladder of phenomena; but they know what to do with this spiritual content only when they conceive of it as existing outside of man as a divinity or as some other kind of higher being such as a necessary natural order, or as a moral world order — or as any of the other names that man has given to what he himself brings forth.

One can understand why the human being does this. Sense impressions press in upon him from outside. He sees colors and hears sounds. His feelings and thoughts arise in him as he sees the colors and hears the sounds. These stem from his own nature. He asks himself: How can I, out of myself, add anything to what the world gives me? It seems to him completely arbitrary to draw something out of himself to complement the outer world.

But the moment he says to himself: What I am feeling and thinking, this I do not bring to the world out of myself; another, higher being has laid this into the world, and I only draw it forth from the world — at this moment he feels relieved. One only has to tell the human being: Your opinions and thoughts do not come from yourself; a god has revealed them to you — then he is reconciled with himself. And if he has divested himself of his belief in God, he then sets in His place the natural order of things, eternal laws. The fact that he cannot find this God, these eternal laws, anywhere outside in the world, that he must rather first create them for the world if they are to be there — this he does not want to admit to himself at first. It is difficult for him to say to himself: The world outside me is not divine; by virtue of my essential being, however, I assume the right to project the divine into the outer world.

What do the laws of the pendulum that arose in Galileo's spirit as he watched the swinging church lamp matter to the lamp? But man himself cannot exist without establishing a relationship between the outer world and the world of his inner being. His spiritual life is a continuous projecting of his spirit into the sense world. Through his own work, in the course of historical life, there occurs the interpenetration of nature and spirit. The Greek thinkers wanted nothing more than to believe that man was already born into a relationship which actually can come about only through himself. They did not want it to be man who first consummates the marriage of spirit and nature; they wanted to confront this as a marriage already consummated, to regard it as an accomplished fact.

Aristotle saw what is so contradictory in transferring the ideas — arising in man's spirit from the things of the world — into some supersensible world in the beyond. But even he did not recognize that things first receive their ideal aspect when man confronts them and creatively adds this aspect to them. Rather, he assumed that this ideal element, as entelechy, is itself at work in things as their actual principle. The natural consequence of this basic view of his was that he traced the moral activity of man back to his original, moral, natural potential. The physical drives ennoble themselves in the course of human evolution and then appear as willing guided by reason. Virtue consists in this reasonable willing.

Taken at face value, this seems to indicate that Aristotle believed that moral activity, at least, has its source in man's own personality, that man himself gives himself the direction and goal of his actions out of his own being and does not allow these to be prescribed for him from outside. But even Aristotle does not dare to stay with this picture of a human being who determines his own destiny for himself. What appears in man as individual, reasonable activity is, after all, only the imprint of a general world reason existing outside of him. This world reason does realize itself within the individual person, but has its own independent, higher existence over and above him. .

Even Aristotle pushes outside of man what he finds present only within man. The tendency of Greek thinking from Thales to Aristotle is to think that what is encountered within the inner life of man is an independent being existing for itself and to trace the things of the world back to this being.

Man's knowledge must pay the consequences when he thinks that the mediating of spirit with nature, which he himself is meant to accomplish, is accomplished by outer powers. He should immerse himself in his own inner being and seek there the point of connection between the sense world and the ideal world. If, instead of this, he looks into the outer world to find this point, then, because he cannot find it there, he must necessarily arrive eventually at the doubt in any reconciliation between the two powers. The period of Greek thought that follows Aristotle presents us with this stage of doubt. It announces itself with the Stoics and Epicureans and reaches its high-point with the Skeptics.

The Stoics and Epicureans feel instinctively that one cannot find the essential being of things along the path taken by their predecessors. They leave this path without bothering very much about finding a new one. For the older philosophers, the main thing was the world as a whole. They wanted to discover the laws of the world and believed that knowledge of man must result all by itself from knowledge of the world, because for them man was a part of the world-whole like all other things. The Stoics and Epicureans made man the main object of their reflections. They wanted to give his life its appropriate content. They thought about how man should live his life. Everything else was only a means to this end. The Stoics considered all philosophy to be worthwhile only to the extent that through it man could know how he is to live his life. They considered the right life for man to be one that is in harmony with nature. In order to realize this harmony with nature in one's own actions, one must first know what is in harmony with nature.

In the Stoics' teachings there lies an important admission about the human personality. Namely, that the human personality can be its own purpose and goal and that everything else, even knowledge, is there only for the sake of this personality.

The Epicureans went even further in this direction. Their striving consisted in shaping life in such a way that man would feel as content as possible in it or that it would afford him the greatest possible pleasure. One's own life stood so much in the foreground for them that they practiced knowledge only for the purpose of freeing man from superstitious fear and from the discomfort that befalls him when he does not understand nature.

A heightened human feeling of oneself runs through the views of the Stoics and Epicureans compared to those of older Greek thinkers.

This view appears in a finer, more spiritual way in the Skeptics. They said to themselves: When a person is forming ideas about things, he can form them only out of himself. And only out of himself can he draw the conviction that an idea corresponds to some thing. They saw nothing in the outer world that would provide a basis for connecting thing and idea. And they regarded as delusion and combated what anyone before them had said about any such bases.

The basic characteristic of the Skeptical view is modesty. Its adherents did not dare to deny that there is a connection in the outer world between idea and thing; they merely denied that man could know of any such connection. Therefore they did indeed make man the source of his knowing, but they did not regard this knowing as the expression of true wisdom.

Basically, Skepticism represents human knowing's declaration of bankruptcy. The human being succumbs to the preconception he has created for himself — that the truth is present outside him in a finished form — through the conviction he has gained that his truth is only an inner one, and therefore cannot be the right one at all.

Thales begins to reflect upon the world with utter confidence in the power of the human spirit. The doubt — that what human pondering must regard as the ground of the world could not actually be this ground — lay very far from his naive belief in man's cognitive ability. With the Skeptics a complete renunciation of real truth has taken the place of this belief.

The course of development taken by Greek thinking lies between the two extremes of naive, blissful confidence in man's cognitive ability and absolute lack of confidence in it. One can understand this course of development if one considers how man's mental pictures of the causes of the world have changed. What the oldest Greek philosophers thought these causes to be had sense-perceptible characteristics. Through this, one had a right to transfer these causes into the outer world. Like every other object in the sense world, the primal water of Thales belongs to outer reality. The matter became quite different when Parmenides stated that true existence lies in thinking. For, this thinking, in accordance with its true existence, is to be perceived only within man's inner being. Through Parmenides there first arose the great question: How does thought-existence, spiritual existence, relate to the outer existence that our senses perceive? One was accustomed then to picturing the relationship of the highest existence to that existence which surrounds us in daily life in the same way that Thales had thought the relationship to be between his sense-perceptible primal thing and the things that surround us. It is altogether possible to picture to oneself the emergence of all things out of the water that Thales presents as the primal source of all existence, to picture it as analogous to certain sense-perceptible processes that occur daily before our very eyes. And the urge to picture relations in the world surrounding us in the sense of such an analogy still remained even when, through Parmenides and his followers, pure thinking and its content, the world of ideas, were made into the primal source of all existence. Men were indeed ready to see that the spiritual world is a higher one than the sense world, that the deepest world-content reveals itself within the inner being of man, but they were not ready at the same time to picture the relationship between the sense world and the ideal world as an ideal one. They pictured it as a sense-perceptible relationship, as a factual emergence. If they had thought of it as spiritual, then they could peacefully have acknowledged that the content of the world of ideas is present only in the inner being of man. For then what is higher would not need to precede in time what is derivative. A sense-perceptible thing can reveal a spiritual content, but this content can first be born out of the sense-perceptible thing at the moment of revelation. This content is a later product of evolution than the sense world. But if one pictures the relationship to be one of emergence, then that from which the other emerges must also precede it in time. In this way the child — the spiritual world born of the sense world — was made into the mother of the sense world. This is the psychological reason why the human being transfers his world out into outer reality and declares — with reference to this his possession and product — that it has an objective existence in and for itself, and that he has to subordinate himself to it, or, as the case may be, that he can take possession of it only through revelation or in some other way by which the already finished truth can make its entry into his inner being.

This interpretation which man gives to his striving for truth, to his activity of knowing, corresponds with a profound inclination of his nature. Goethe characterized this inclination in his Aphorisms in Prose in the following words: "The human being never realizes just how anthropomorphic he is." And: "Fall and propulsion. To want to declare the movement of the heavenly bodies by these is actually a hidden anthropomorphism; it is the way a walker goes across a field. The lifted foot sinks down, the foot left behind strives forward and falls; and so on continuously from departing until arriving." All explanation of nature, indeed, consists in the fact that experiences man has of himself are interpreted into the object. Even the simplest phenomena are explained in this way. When we explain the propulsion of one body by another, we do so by picturing to ourselves that the one body exerts upon the other the same effect as we do when we propel a body.

In the same way as we do this with something trivial, the religious person does it with his picture of God. He takes human ways of thinking and acting and interprets them into nature; and the philosophers we have presented, from Parmenides to Aristotle, also interpreted human thought-processes into nature. Max Stirner has this human need in mind when he says: "What haunts the universe and carries on its mysterious, 'incomprehensible' doings is, in fact, the arcane ghost that we call the highest being. And fathoming this ghost, understanding it, discovering reality in it (proving the 'existence of God') — this is the task men have set themselves for thousands of years; they tormented themselves with the horrible impossibility, with the endless work of the Danaides, of transforming the ghost into a nonghost, the unreal into a real, the spirit into a whole and embodied person. Behind the existing world they sought the 'thing-in-itself,' the essential being; they sought the non-thing behind the thing."

The last phase of Greek philosophy, Neo-Platonism, offers a splendid proof of how inclined the human spirit is to misconstrue its own being and therefore its relationship to the world. This teaching, whose most significant proponent is Plotin, broke with the tendency to transfer the content of the human spirit into a realm outside the living reality within which man himself stands. The Neo-Platonist seeks within his own soul the place at which the highest object of knowledge is to be found. Through that intensification of cognitive forces which one calls ecstasy, he seeks within himself to behold the essential being of world phenomena. The heightening of the inner powers of perception is meant to lift the human spirit onto a level of life at which he feels directly the revelation of this essential being. This teaching is a kind of mysticism. It is based on a truth that is to be found in every kind of mysticism. Immersion into one's own inner being yields the deepest human wisdom. But man must first prepare himself for this immersion. He must accustom himself to behold a reality that is free of everything the senses communicate to us. People who have brought their powers of knowledge to this height speak of an inner light that has dawned for them. Jakob Böhme, the Christian mystic of the seventeenth century, regarded himself as inwardly illumined in this way. He sees within himself the realm he must designate as the highest one knowable to man. He says: "Within the human heart (Gemüt) there lie the indications (Signatur), quite artfully set forth, of the being of all being."

Neo-Platonism sets the contemplation of the human inner world in the place of speculation about an outer world in the beyond. As a result, the highly characteristic phenomenon appears that the Neo-Platonist regards his own inner being as something foreign. One has taken things all the way to knowledge of the place at which the ultimate part of the world is to be sought; but one has wrongly interpreted what is to be found in this place. The Neo-Platonist therefore describes the inner experiences of his ecstasy like Plato describes the being of his supersensible world.

It is characteristic that Neo-Platonism excludes from the essential being of the inner world precisely that which constitutes its actual core. The state of ecstasy is supposed to occur only when self-consciousness is silent. It was therefore only natural that in Neo-Platonism the human spirit could not behold itself, its own being, in its true light.

The courses taken by the ideas that form the content of Greek philosophy found their conclusion in this view. They represent the longing of man to recognize, to behold, and to worship his own essential being as something foreign.

In the normal course of development within the spiritual evolution of the West, the discovery of egoism would have to have followed upon Neo-Platonism. That means, man would have to have recognized as his own being what he had considered to be a foreign being. He would have to have said to himself: The highest thing there is in the world given to man is his individual "I" whose being comes to manifestation within the inner life of the personality.

This natural course of Western spiritual development was held up by the spread of Christian teachings. Christianity presents, in popular pictures that are almost tangible, what Greek philosophy expressed in the language of sages. When one considers how deeply rooted in human nature the urge is to renounce one's own being, it seems understandable that this teaching has gained such incomparable power over human hearts. A high level of spiritual development is needed to satisfy this urge in a philosophical way. The most naive heart suffices to satisfy this urge in the form of Christian faith. Christianity does not present — as the highest being of the world — a finely spiritual content like Plato's world of ideas, nor an experience streaming forth from an inner light which must first be kindled; instead, it presents processes with attributes of reality that can be grasped by the senses. It goes so far, in fact, as to revere the highest being in a single historical person. The philosophical spirit of Greece could not present us with such palpable mental pictures. Such mental pictures lay in its past, in its folk mythology. Hamann, Herder's predecessor in the realm of theology, commented one time that Plato had never been a philosopher for children. But that it was for childish spirits that "the holy spirit had had the ambition to become a writer."

And for centuries this childish form of human self-estrangement has had the greatest conceivable influence upon the philosophical development of thought. Like fog the Christian teachings have hung before the light from which knowledge of man's own being should have gone forth. Through all kinds of philosophical concepts, the church fathers of the first Christian centuries seek to give a form to their popular mental pictures that would make them acceptable also to an educated consciousness. And the later teachers in the church, of whom Saint Augustine is the most significant, continue these efforts in the same spirit. The content of Christian faith had such a fascinating effect that there could be no question of doubt as to its truth, but only of lifting up of this truth into a more spiritual, more ideal sphere. The philosophy of the teachers within the church is a transforming of the content of Christian faith into an edifice of ideas. The general character of this thought-edifice could therefore be no other than that of Christianity: the transferring of man's being out into the world, self-renunciation. Thus it came about that Augustine again arrives at the right place, where the essential being of the world is to be found, and that he again finds something foreign in this place. Within man's own being he seeks the source of all truth; he declares the inner experiences of the soul to be the foundations of knowledge. But the teachings of Christian faith have set an extra-human content at the place where he was seeking. Therefore, at the right place, he found the wrong beings.

There now follows a centuries-long exertion of human thinking whose sole purpose, by expending all the power of the human spirit, was to bring proof that the content of this spirit is not to be sought within this spirit but rather at that place to which Christian faith has transferred this content. The movement in thought that grew up out of these efforts is called Scholasticism. All the hair-splittings of the Schoolmen can be of no interest in the context of the present essay. For that movement in ideas does not represent in the least a development in the direction of knowledge of the personal "I."

The thickness of the fog in which Christianity enshrouded human self-knowledge becomes most evident through the fact that the Western spirit, out of itself, could not take even one step on the path to this self-knowledge. The Western spirit needed a decisive push from outside. It could not find upon the ground of the soul what it had sought so long in the outer world. But it was presented with proof that this outer world could not be constituted in such a way that the human spirit could find there the essential being it sought. This push was given by the blossoming of the natural sciences in the sixteenth century. As long as man had only an imperfect picture of how natural processes are constituted, there was room in the outer world for divine beings and for the working of a personal divine will. But there was no longer a place, in the natural picture of the world sketched out by Copernicus and Kepler, for the Christian picture. And as Galileo laid the foundations for an explanation of natural processes through natural laws, the belief in divine laws had to be shaken.

Now one had to seek in a new way the being that man recognizes as the highest and that had been pushed out of the external world for him.

Francis Bacon drew the philosophical conclusions from the presuppositions given by Copernicus, Kepler, and Galileo. His service to the Western world view is basically a negative one. He called upon man in a powerful way to direct his gaze freely and without bias upon reality, upon life. As obvious as this call seems, there is no denying that the development of Western thought has sinned heavily against it for centuries. Man's own "I" also belongs within the category of real things. And does it not almost seem as though man's natural predisposition makes him unable to look at this "I" without bias? Only the development of a completely unbiased sense, directed immediately upon what is real, can lead to self-knowledge. The path of knowledge of nature is also the path of knowledge of the "I."

Two streams now entered into the development of Western thought that tended, by different paths, in the direction of the new goals of knowledge necessitated by the natural sciences. One goes back to Jakob Böhme, the other to René Descartes.

Jakob Böhme and Descartes no longer stood under the influence of Scholasticism. Böhme saw that nowhere in cosmic space was there a place for heaven; he therefore became a mystic. He sought heaven within the inner being of man. Descartes recognized that the adherence of the Schoolmen to Christian teachings was only a matter of centuries-long habituation to these pictures. Therefore he considered it necessary first of all to doubt these habitual pictures and to seek a way of knowledge by which man can arrive at a kind of knowing whose certainty he does not assert out of habit, but which can be guaranteed at every, moment through his own spiritual powers.

Those are therefore strong initial steps which — both with Böhme and with Descartes — the human "I" takes to know itself. Both were nevertheless overpowered by the old preconceptions in what they brought forth later. It has already been indicated that Jakob Böhme has a certain spiritual kinship with the Neo-Platonists. His knowledge is an entering into his own inner being. But what confronts him within this inner being is not the "I" of man but rather only the Christian God again. He becomes aware that within his own heart (Gemüt) there lies what the person who needs knowledge is craving. Fulfillment of the greatest human longings streams toward him from there. But this does not lead him to the view that the "I," by intensifying its cognitive powers, is also able out of itself to satisfy its demands. This brings him, rather, to the belief that, on the path of knowledge into the human heart, he had truly found the God whom Christianity had sought upon a false path. Instead of self-knowledge, Jakob Böhme seeks union with God; instead of life with the treasures of his own inner being, he seeks a life in God.

It is obvious that the way man thinks about his actions, about his moral life, will also depend upon human self-knowledge or self-misapprehension. The realm of morality does in fact establish itself as a kind of upper story above the purely natural processes. Christian belief, which already regards these natural processes as flowing from the divine will, seeks this will all the more within morality. Christian moral teachings show more clearly than almost anything else the distortedness of this world view. No matter how enormous the sophistry is that theology has applied to this realm: questions remain which, from the standpoint of Christianity, show definite features of considerable contradiction. If a primal being like the Christian God is assumed, it is incomprehensible how the sphere of human action can fall into two realms: into that of the good and into that of the evil. For, all human actions would have to flow from the primal being and consequently bear traits homogeneous with their origin. Human actions would in fact have to be divine. Just as little can human responsibility be explained on this basis. Man is after all directed by the divine will. He can therefore give himself up only to this will; he can let happen through him only what God brings about.

In the views one held about morality, precisely the same thing occurred as in one's views about knowledge. Man followed his inclination to tear his own self out of himself and to set it up as something foreign. And just as in the realm of knowledge no other content could be given to the primal being — regarded as lying outside man — than the content drawn from his own inner being, so no moral aims and impulses for action could be found in this primal being except those belonging to the human soul. What man, in his deepest inner being, was convinced should happen, this he regarded as something willed by the primal being of the world. In this way a duality in the ethical realm was created. Over against the self that one had within oneself and out of which one had to act, one set one's own content as something morally determinative. And through this, moral demands could arise. Man's self was not allowed to follow itself; it had to follow something foreign. Selflessness in one's actions in the moral field corresponds to self-estrangement in the realm of knowledge. Those actions are good in which the "I" follows something foreign; those actions are bad, on the other hand, in which it follows itself. In self-will Christianity sees the source of all evil. That could never have happened if one had seen that everything moral can draw its content only out of one's own self. One can sum up all the Christian moral teachings in one sentence:

If man admits to himself that he can follow only the commandments of his own being and if he acts according to them, then he is evil; if this truth is hidden from him and if he sets — or allows to be set — his own commandments as foreign ones over himself in order to act according to them, then he is good.

The moral teaching of selflessness is elaborated perhaps more completely than anywhere else in a book from the fourteenth century, German Theology. The author of this book is unknown to us. He carried self-renunciation far enough to be sure that his name did not come down to posterity. In this book it is stated: "That is no true being and has no being which does not exist within the perfect; rather it is by chance or it is a radiance and a shining that is no being or has no being except in the fire from which the radiance flows, or in the sun, or in the light. The Bible speaks of faith and the truth: sin is nothing other than the fact that the creature turns himself away from the unchangeable good and toward the changeable good, which means that he turns from the perfect to the divided and to the imperfect and most of all to himself. Now mark. If the creature assumes something good — such as being, living, knowing, recognizing, capability, and everything in short that one should call good — and believes that he is this good, or that it is his or belongs to him, or that it is of him, no matter how often nor how much results from this, then he is going astray. What else did the devil do or what else was his fall and estrangement than that he assumed that he was also something and something would be his and something would also belong to him? That assumption and his "I" and his "me," his "for me" and his "mine," that was his estrangement and his fall. That is how it still is. For, everything that one considers good or should call good belongs to no one, but only to the eternal true good which God is alone, and whoever assumes it of himself acts wrongly and against God."

A change in moral views from the old Christian ones is also connected with the turn that Jakob Böhme gave to man's relationship to God. God still works as something higher in the human soul to effect the good, but He does at least work within this self and not from outside upon the self. An internalizing of moral action occurs thereby. The rest of Christianity demanded only an outer obedience to the divine will. With Jakob Böhme the previously separated entities — the really personal and the personal that was made into God — enter into a living relationship. Through this, the source of the moral is indeed now transferred into man's inner being, but the moral principle of selflessness seems to be even more strongly emphasized. If God is regarded as an outer power, then the human self is the one actually acting. It acts either in God's sense or against it. But if God is transferred into man's inner being, then man himself no longer acts, but rather God in him. God expresses himself directly in human life. Man foregoes any life of his own; he makes himself a part of the divine life. He feels himself in God, God in himself; he grows into the primal being; he becomes an organ of it.

In this German mysticism man has therefore paid for his participation in the divine life with the most complete extinguishing of his personality, of his "I." Jakob Böhme and the mystics who were of his view did not feel the loss of the personal element. On the contrary: they experienced something particularly uplifting in the thought that they were directly participating in the divine life, that they were members in a divine organism. An organism cannot exist, after all, without its members. The mystic therefore felt himself to be something necessary within the world-whole, as a being that is indispensable to God. Angelus Silesius, the mystic who felt things in the same spirit as Jakob Böhme, expresses this in a beautiful statement:

I know that without me God cannot live an instant, Came I to naught, he needs must yield the spirit.

And even more characteristically in another one:

Without me God cannot a single worm create; Do I not co-maintain it, it must at once crack open.

The human "I" asserts its rights here in the most powerful way vis-à-vis its own image which it has transferred into the outer world. To be sure, the supposed primal being is not yet told that it is man's own being set over against himself, but at least man's own being is considered to be the maintainer of the divine primal ground.

Descartes had a strong feeling for the fact that man, through his thought-development, had brought himself into a warped relationship with the world. Therefore, to begin with, he met everything that had come forth from this thought-development with doubt. Only when one doubts everything that the centuries have developed as truths can one — in his opinion — gain the necessary objectivity for a new point of departure. It lay in the nature of things that this doubt would lead Descartes to the human "I." For, the more a person regards everything else as something that he still must seek, the more he will have an intense feeling of his own seeking personality. He can say to himself: Perhaps I am erring on the paths of existence; then the erring one is thrown all the more clearly back upon himself. Descartes' Cogito, ergo sum (I think, therefore I am) indicates this. Descartes presses even further. He is aware that the way man arrives at knowledge of himself should be a model for any other knowledge he means to acquire. Clarity and definiteness seem to Descartes to be the most prominent characteristics of self-knowledge. Therefore he also demands these two characteristics of all other knowledge. Whatever man can distinguish just as clearly and definitely as his own existence: only that can stand as certain.

With this, the absolutely central place of the "I" in the world-whole is at least recognized in the area of cognitive methodology. Man determines the how of his knowledge of the world according to the how of his knowledge of himself, and no longer asks for any outer being to justify this how. Man does not want to think in the way a god prescribes knowing activity to be, but rather in the way he determines this for himself. From now on, with respect to the world, man draws the power of his wisdom from himself.

In connection with the what, Descartes did not take the same step. He set to work to gain mental pictures about the world, and — in accordance with the cognitive principle just presented — searched through his own inner being for such mental pictures. There he found the mental picture of God. It was of course nothing more than the mental picture of the human "I." But Descartes did not recognize this. The idea of God as the altogether most perfect being » brought his thinking onto a completely wrong path. This one characteristic, that of the altogether greatest perfection, outshone for him all the other characteristics of the central being. He said to himself: Man, who is himself imperfect, cannot out of himself create the mental picture of an altogether most perfect being. Consequently this altogether most perfect being exists. If Descartes had investigated the true content of his mental picture of God, he would have found that it is exactly the same as the mental picture of the "I," and that perfection is only a conceptual enhancement of this content. The essential content of an ivory ball is not changed by my thinking of it as infinitely large. Just as little does the mental picture of the "I" become something else through such an enhancement.

The proof that Descartes brings for the existence of God is therefore again nothing other than a paraphrasing of the human need to make one's own "I," in the form of a being outside man, into the ground of the world. But here indeed the fact presents itself with full clarity that man can find no content of its own for this primal being existing outside man, but rather can only lend this being the content of his mental picture of the "I" in a form that has not been significantly changed.

Spinoza took no step forward on the path that must lead to the conquest of the mental picture of the "I"; he took a step backward. For Spinoza has no feeling of the unique position of the human "I." For him the stream of world processes consists only in a system of natural necessity, just as for the Christian philosophers it consisted only in a system of divine acts of will. Here as there the human "I" is only a part within this system. For the Christian, man is in the hands of God; for Spinoza he is in those of natural world happenings. With Spinoza the Christian God received a different character. A philosopher who has grown up in a time when natural-scientific insights are blooming cannot acknowledge a God who directs the world arbitrarily; he can acknowledge only a primal being who exists because his existence, through itself, is a necessity, and who guides the course of the world according to the unchangeable laws that flow from his own absolutely necessary being. Spinoza has no consciousness of the fact that man takes the image in which he pictures this necessity from his own content. For this reason Spinoza's moral ideal also becomes something impersonal, unindividual. In accordance with his presuppositions he cannot indeed see his ideal to be in the perfecting of the "I," in the enhancement of man's own powers, but rather in the permeating of the "I" with the divine world content, with the highest knowledge of the objective God. To lose oneself in this God should be the goal of human striving.

The path Descartes took — to start with the "I" and press forward to world knowledge — is extended from now on by the philosophers of modern times. The Christian theological method, which had no confidence in the power of the human "I" as an organ of knowledge, at least was overcome. One thing was recognized: that the "I" itself must find the highest being. The path from there to the other point — to the insight that the content lying within the "I" is also the highest being — is, to be sure, a long one.

Less thoughtfully than Descartes did the two English philosophers Locke and Hume approach their investigation of the paths that the human "I" takes to arrive at enlightenment about itself and the world. One thing above all was lacking in both of them: a healthy, free gaze into man's inner being. Therefore they could also gain no mental picture of the great difference that exists between knowledge of outer things and knowledge of the human "I." Everything they say relates only to the acquisition of outer knowledge. Locke entirely overlooks the fact that man, by enlightening himself about outer things, sheds a light upon them that streams from his own inner being. He believes therefore that all knowledge stems from experience. But what is experience? Galileo sees a swinging church lamp. It leads him to find the laws by which a body swings. He has experienced two things: firstly, through his senses, outer processes; secondly, from out of himself, the mental picture of a law that enlightens him about these processes, that makes them comprehensible. One can now of course call both of these experience. But then one fails to recognize the difference, in fact, that exists between the two parts of this cognitive process. A being that could not draw upon the content of his being could stand eternally before the swinging church lamp: the sense perception would never complement itself with a conceptual law. Locke and all who think like him allow themselves to be deceived by something — namely by the way the content of what is to be known approaches us. It simply rises up, in fact, upon the horizon of our consciousness. Experience consists in what thus arises. But the fact must be recognized that the content of the laws of experience is developed by the "I" in its encounter with experience. Two things reveal themselves in Hume. One is that, as already mentioned, he does not recognize the nature of the "I," and therefore, exactly like Locke, derives the content of the laws from experience. The other thing is that this content, by being separated from the "I," loses itself completely in indefiniteness, hangs freely in the air without support or foundation. Hume recognizes that outer experience communicates only unconnected processes, that it does not at the same time, along with these processes, provide the laws by which they are connected. Since Hume knows nothing about the being of the "I," he also cannot derive from it any justification for connecting the processes. He therefore derives these laws from the vaguest source one could possibly imagine: from habit. A person sees that a certain process always follows upon another; the fall of a stone is followed by the indentation of the ground on which it falls. As a result man habituates himself to thinking of such processes as connected. All knowledge loses its significance if one takes one's start from such presuppositions. The connection between the processes and their laws acquires something of a purely chance nature.

We see in George Berkeley a person for whom the creative being of the "I" has come fully to consciousness. He had a clear picture of the "I's" own activity in the coming about of all knowledge. When I see an object, he said to himself, I am active. I create my perception for myself. The object of my perception would remain forever beyond my consciousness, it would not be there for me, if I did not continuously enliven its dead existence by my activity. I perceive only my enlivening activity, and not what precedes it objectively as the dead thing. No matter where I look within the sphere of my consciousness: everywhere I see myself as the active one, as the creative one. In Berkeley's thinking, the "I" acquires a universal life. What do I know of any existence of things, if I do not picture this existence?

For Berkeley the world consists of creative spirits who out of themselves form a world. But at this level of knowledge there again appeared, even with him, the old preconception. He indeed lets the "I" create its world for itself, but he does not give it at the same time the power to create itself out of itself. It must again proffer a mental picture of God. The creative principle in the "I" is God, even for Berkeley.

But this philosopher does show us one thing. Whoever really immerses himself into the essential being of the creative "I" does not come back out of it again to an outer being except by forcible means. And Berkeley does proceed forcibly. Under no compelling necessity he traces the creativity of the "I" back to God. Earlier philosophers emptied the "I" of its content and through this gained a content for their God. Berkeley does not do this. Therefore he can do nothing other than set, beside the creative spirits, yet one more particular spirit that basically is of exactly the same kind as they and therefore completely unnecessary, after all.

This is even more striking in the German philosopher Leibniz. He also recognized the creative activity of the "I." He had a very clear overview of the scope of this activity; he saw that it was inwardly consistent, that it was founded upon itself. The "I" therefore became for him a world in itself, a monad. And everything that has existence can have it only through the fact that it gives itself a self-enclosed content. Only monads, i.e., beings creating out of and within themselves, exist: separate worlds in themselves that do not have to rely on anything outside themselves. Worlds exist, no world. Each person is a world, a monad, in himself. If now these worlds are after all in accord with one another, if they know of each other and think the contents of their knowledge, then this can only stem from the fact that a predestined accord (pre-established harmony) exists. The world, in fact, is arranged in such a way that the one monad creates out of itself something which corresponds to the activity in the others. To bring about this accord Leibniz of course again needs the old God. He has recognized that the "I" is active, creative, within his inner being, that it gives its content to itself; the fact that the "I" itself also brings this content into relationship with the other content of the world remained hidden to him. Therefore he did not free himself from the mental picture of God. Of the two demands that lie in the Goethean statement — "If I know my relationship to myself and to the outer world, then I call it truth" — Leibniz understood only the one.

This development of European thought manifests a very definite character. Man must draw out of himself the best that he can know. He in fact practices self-knowledge. But he always shrinks back again from the thought of also recognizing that what he has created is in fact self-created. He feels himself to be too weak to carry the world. Therefore he saddles someone else with this burden. And the goals he sets for himself would lose their weight for him if he acknowledged their origin to himself; therefore he burdens his goals with powers that he believes he takes from outside. Man glorifies his child but without wanting to acknowledge his own fatherhood.

In spite of the currents opposing it, human self-knowledge made steady progress. At the point where this self-knowledge began to threaten man's belief in the beyond, it met Kant. Insight into the nature of human knowing had shaken the power of those proofs which people had thought up to support belief in the beyond. One had gradually gained a picture of real knowledge and therefore saw through the artificiality and tortured nature of the seeming ideas that were supposed to give enlightenment about other-worldly powers. A devout, believing man like Kant could fear that a further development along this path would lead to the disintegration of all faith. This must have seemed to his deeply religious sense like a great, impending misfortune for mankind. Out of his fear of the destruction of religious mental pictures there arose for him the need to investigate thoroughly the relationship of human knowing to matters of faith. How is knowing possible and over what can it extend itself? That is the question Kant posed himself, with the hope, right from the beginning, of being able to gain from his answer the firmest possible support for faith.

Kant took up two things from his predecessors. Firstly, that there is a knowledge in some areas that is indubitable. The truths of pure mathematics and the general teachings of logic and physics seem to him to be in this category. Secondly, he based himself upon Hume in his assertion that no absolutely sure truths can come from experience. Experience teaches only that we have so and so often observed certain connections; nothing can be determined by experience as to whether these connections are also necessary ones. If there are indubitable, necessary truths and if they cannot stem from experience: then from what do they stem? They must be present in the human soul before experience. Now it becomes a matter of distinguishing between the part of knowledge that stems from experience and the part that cannot be drawn from this source of knowledge. Experience occurs through the fact that I receive impressions. These impressions are given through sensations. The content of these sensations cannot be given us in any other way than through experience. But these sensations, such as light, color, tone, warmth, hardness, etc., would present only a chaotic tangle if they were not brought into certain interconnections. In these interconnections the contents of sensation first constitute the objects of experience. An object is composed of a definitely ordered group of the contents of sensation. In Kant's opinion, the human soul accomplishes the ordering of these contents of sensation into groups. Within the human soul there are certain principles present by which the manifoldness of sensations is brought into objective unities. Such principles are space, time, and certain connections such as cause and effect. The contents of sensation are given me, but not their spatial interrelationships nor temporal sequence. Man first brings these to the contents of sensation. One content of sensation is given and another one also, but not the fact that one is the cause of the other. The intellect first makes this connection. Thus there lie within the human soul, ready once and for all, the ways in which the contents of sensation can be connected. Thus, even though we can take possession of the contents of sensation only through experience, we can, nevertheless, before all experience, set up laws as to how these contents of sensation are to be connected. For, these laws are the ones given us within our own souls.

We have, therefore, necessary kinds of knowledge. But these do not relate to a content, but only to ways of connecting contents. In Kant's opinion, we will therefore never draw knowledge with any content out of the human soul's own laws. The content must come through experience. But the otherworldly objects of faith can never become the object of any experience. Therefore they also cannot be attained through our necessary knowledge. We have a knowledge from experience and another, necessary, experience-free knowledge as to how the contents of experience can be connected. But we have no knowledge that goes beyond experience. The world of objects surrounding us is as it must be in accordance with the laws of connection lying ready in our soul. Aside from these laws we do not know how this world is "in-itself." The world to which our knowledge relates itself is no such "in-itselfness" but rather is an appearance for us.

Obvious objections to these Kantian views force themselves upon the unbiased person. The difference in principle between the particulars (the contents of sensation) and the way of connecting these particulars does not consist, with respect to knowledge, in the way we connect things as Kant assumes it to. Even though one element presents itself to us from outside and the other comes forth from our inner being, both elements of knowledge nevertheless form an undivided unity. Only the abstracting intellect can separate light, warmth, hardness, etc., from spatial order, causal relationship, etc. In reality, they document, with respect to every single object, their necessary belonging together. Even the designation of the one element as "content" in contrast to the other element as a merely "connecting" principle is all warped. In truth, the knowledge that something is the cause of something else is a knowledge with just as much content as the knowledge that it is yellow. If the object is composed of two elements, one of which is given from outside and the other from within, it follows that, for our knowing activity, elements which actually belong together are communicated along two different paths. It does not follow, however, that we are dealing with two things that are different from each other and that are artificially coupled together.

Only by forcibly separating what belongs together can Kant therefore support his view. The belonging together of the two elements is most striking in knowledge of the human "I." Here one element does not come from outside and the other from within; both arise from within. And here both are not only one content but also one completely homogeneous content.

What mattered to Kant — his heart's wish that guided his thoughts far more than any unbiased observation of the real factors — was to rescue the teachings relative to the beyond. What knowledge had brought about as support for these teachings in the course of long ages had decayed. Kant believed he had now shown that it is anyway not for knowledge to support such teachings, because knowledge has to rely on experience, and the things of faith in the beyond cannot become the object of any experience. Kant believed he had thereby created a free space where knowledge could not get in his way and disrupt him as he built up there a faith in the beyond. And he demands, as a support for moral life, that one believe in the things in the beyond. Out of that realm from which no knowledge comes to us, there sounds the despotic voice of the categorical imperative which demands of us that we do the good. And in order to establish a moral realm we would in fact need all that about which knowledge can tell us nothing. Kant believed he had achieved what he wanted: "I therefore had to set knowledge aside in order to make room for faith."

The great philosopher in the development of Western thought who set out in direct pursuit of a knowledge of human self-awareness is Johann Gottlieb Fichte. It is characteristic of him that he approaches this knowledge without any presuppositions, with complete lack of bias. He has the clear, sharp awareness of the fact that nowhere in the world is a being to be found from which the "I" could be derived. It can therefore be derived only from itself. Nowhere is a power to be found from which the existence of the "I" flows. Everything the "I" needs, it can acquire only out of itself. Not only does it gain enlightenment about its own being through self-observation; it first posits this being into itself through an absolute, unconditional act. "The 'I' posits itself, and it is by virtue of this mere positing of itself; and conversely: The 'I' is, and posits its existence, by virtue of its mere existence. It is at the same time the one acting and the product of its action; the active one and what is brought forth by the activity; action and deed are one and the same; and therefore the 'I am' is the expression of an active deed." Completely undisturbed by the fact that earlier philosophers have transferred the entity he is describing outside man, Fichte looks at the "I" naively. Therefore the "I" naturally becomes for him the highest being. "That whose existence (being) merely consists in the fact that it posits itself as existing is the 'I' as absolute subject. In the way that it posits itself, it is, and in the way that it is, it posits itself: and the 'I' exists accordingly for the 'I,' simply and necessarily. What does not exist for itself is no 'I' ... One certainly hears the question raised: What was I anyway, before I came to self-awareness? The obvious answer to that is: I was not at all; for I was not I... To posit oneself and to be are, for the 'I,' completely the same." The complete, bright clarity about one's own "I," the unreserved illumination of one's personal, human entity, becomes thereby the starting point of human thinking. The result of this must be that man, starting here, sets out to conquer the world. The second of the Goethean demands mentioned above, knowledge of my relationship to the world, follows upon the first — knowledge of the relationship that the "I" has to itself. This philosophy, built upon self-knowledge, will speak about both these relationships, and not about the derivation of the world from some primal being. One could now ask: Is man then supposed to set his own being in place of the primal being into which he transferred the world origins? Can man then actually make himself the starting point of the world? With respect to this it must be emphasized that this question as to the world origins stems from a lower sphere. In the sequence of the processes given us by reality, we seek the causes for the events, and then seek still other causes for the causes, and soon. We are now stretching the concept of causation. We are seeking a final cause for the whole world. And in this way the concept of the first, absolute primal being, necessary in itself, fuses for us with the idea of the world cause. But that is a mere conceptual construction. When man sets up such conceptual constructions, they do not necessarily have any justification. The concept of a flying dragon also has none. Fichte takes his start from the "I" as the primal being, and arrives at ideas that present the relationship of this primal being to the rest of the world in an unbiased way, but not under the guise of cause and effect. Starting from the "I," Fichte now seeks to gain ideas for grasping the rest of the world. Whoever does not want to deceive himself about the nature of what one can call cognition or knowledge can proceed in no other way. Everything that man can say about the being of things is derived from the experiences of his inner being. "The human being never realizes just how anthropomorphic he is." (Goethe) In the » explanation of the simplest phenomena, in the propulsion of one body by another, for example, there lies an anthropomorphism. The conclusion that the one body propels the other is already anthropomorphic. For, if one wants to go beyond what the senses tell us about the occurrence, one must transfer onto it the experience our body has when it sets a body in the outer world into motion. We transfer our experience of propelling something onto the occurrence in the outer world, and also speak there of propulsion when we roll one ball and as a result see a second ball go rolling. For we can observe only the movements of the two balls, and then in addition think the propulsion in the sense of our own experiences. All physical explanations are anthropomorphisms, attributing human characteristics to nature. But of course it does not follow from this what has so often been concluded from this: that these explanations have no objective significance for the things. A part of the objective content lying within the things, in fact, first appears when we shed that light upon it which we perceive in our own inner being.

Whoever, in Fichte's sense, bases the being of the "I" entirely upon itself can also find the sources of moral action only within the "I" alone. The "I" cannot seek harmony with some other being, but only with itself. It does not allow its destiny to be prescribed, but rather gives any such destiny to itself. Act according to the basic principle that you can regard your actions as the most worthwhile possible. That is about how one would have to express the highest principle of Fichte's moral teachings. "The essential character of the 'I,' in which it distinguishes itself from everything that is outside it, consists in a tendency toward self-activity for the sake of self-activity; and it is this tendency that is thought when the 'I,' in and for itself, without any relationship to something outside it, is thought." An action therefore stands on an ever higher level of moral value, the more purely it flows from the self-activity and self-determination of the "I."

In his later life Fichte changed his self-reliant, absolute "I" back into an external God again; he therefore sacrificed true self-knowledge, toward which he had taken so many important steps, to that self-renunciation which stems from human weakness. The last books of Fichte are therefore of no significance for the progress of this self-knowledge.

The philosophical writings of Schiller, however, are important for this progress. Whereas Fichte expressed the self-reliant independence of the "I" as a general philosophical truth, Schiller was more concerned with answering the question as to how the particular "I" of the simple human individuality could live out this self-activity in the best way within itself.

Kant had expressly demanded the suppression of pleasure as a pre-condition for moral activity. Man should not carry out what brings him satisfaction; but rather what the categorical imperative demands of him. According to his view an action is all the more moral the more it is accomplished with the quelling of all feeling of pleasure, out of mere heed to strict moral law. For Schiller this diminishes human worth. Is man in his desire for pleasure really such a low being that he must first extinguish this base nature of his in order to be virtuous? Schiller criticizes any such degradation of man in the satirical epigram (Xenie):

Gladly I serve all my friends, but do so alas out of liking; Therefore it rankles me often that I'm not a virtuous man.

No, says Schiller, human instincts are capable of such ennobling that it is a pleasure to do the good. The strict "ought to" transforms itself in the ennobled man into a free "wanting to." And someone who with pleasure accomplishes what is moral stands higher on the moral world scale than someone who must first do violence to his own being in order to obey the categorical imperative.

Schiller elaborated this view of his in his Letters on the Aesthetic Education of the Human Race. There hovers before him the picture of a free individuality who can calmly give himself over to his egoistical drives because these drives, out of themselves, want what can be accomplished by the unfree, ignoble personality only when it suppresses its own needs. The human being, as Schiller expressed it, can be unfree in two respects: firstly, if he is able to follow only his blind, lower instincts. Then he acts out of necessity. His drives compel him; he is not free. Secondly, however, that person also acts unfreely who follows only his reason. For, reason sets up principles of behavior according to logical rules. A person who merely follows reason acts unfreely because he subjugates himself to logical necessity. Only that person acts freely out of himself for whom what is reasonable has united so deeply with his individuality , has gone over so fully into his flesh and blood, that he carries out with the greatest pleasure what someone standing morally less high can accomplish only through the most extreme self-renunciation and the strongest compulsion.

Friedrich Joseph Schelling wanted to extend the path Fichte had taken. Schelling took his start from the unbiased knowledge of the "I" that his predecessor had achieved. The "I" was recognized as a being that draws its existence out of itself. The next task was to bring nature into a relationship with this self-reliant "I." It is clear: If the "I" is not to transfer the actual higher being of things into the outer world again, then it must be shown that the "I," out of itself, also creates what we call the laws of nature. The structure of nature must therefore be the material system, outside in space, of what the "I," within its inner being, creates in a spiritual way. "Nature must be visible spirit, and spirit must be invisible nature. Here, therefore, in the absolute identity of the spirit in us and of nature outside of us, must the problem be solved as to how a nature outside of us is possible." "The outer world lies open before us, in order for us to find in it again the history of our spirit."

Schelling, therefore, sharply illuminates the process that the philosophers have interpreted wrongly for so long. He shows that out of one being the clarifying light must fall upon all the processes of the world; that the "I" can recognize one being in all happenings; but he no longer sets forth this being as something lying outside the "I"; he sees it within the "I." The "I" finally feels itself to be strong enough to enliven the content of world phenomena from out of itself. The way in which Schelling presented nature in detail as a material development out of the "I" does not need to be discussed here. The important thing in this essay is to show in what way the "I" has reconquered for itself the sphere of influence which, in the course of the development of Western thought, it had ceded to an entity that it had itself created. For this reason Schelling's other writings also do not need to be considered in this context. At best they add only details to the question we are examining. Exactly like Fichte, Schelling abandons clear self-knowledge again, and seeks then to trace the things flowing from the self back to other beings. The later teachings of both thinkers are reversions to views which they had completely overcome in an earlier period of life.

The philosophy of Georg Wilhelm Friedrich Hegel is a further bold attempt to explain the world on the basis of a content lying within the "I." Hegel sought, comprehensively and thoroughly, to investigate and present the whole content of what Fichte, in incomparable words to be sure, had characterized: the being of the human "I." For Hegel also regards this being as the actual primal thing, as the "in-itselfness of things." But Hegel does something peculiar. He divests the "I" of everything individual, personal. In spite of the fact that it is a genuine true "I" which Hegel takes as a basis for world phenomena, this "I" seems impersonal, unindividual, far from an intimate, familiar "I," almost like a god. In just such an unapproachable, strictly abstract form does Hegel, in his logic, expound upon the content of the in-itselfness of the world. The most personal thinking is presented here in the most impersonal way. According to Hegel, nature is nothing other than the content of the "I" that has been spread out in space and time. Nature is this ideal content in a different state. "Nature is spirit estranged from itself." Within the individual human spirit Hegel's stance toward the impersonal "I" is personal. Within self-consciousness, the being of the "I" is not an in-itself, it is also for-itself; the human spirit discovers that the highest world content is his own content.

Because Hegel seeks to grasp the being of the "I" at first impersonally, he also does not designate it as "I," but rather as idea. But Hegel's idea is nothing other than the content of the human "I" freed of all personal character. This abstracting of everything personal manifests most strongly in Hegel's views about the spiritual life, the moral life. It is not the single, personal, individual "I" of man that can decide its own destiny, but rather it is the great, objective, impersonal world "I," which is abstracted from man's individual "I"; it is the general world reason, the world idea. The individual "I" must submit to this abstraction drawn from its own being. The world idea has instilled the objective spirit into man's legal, state, and moral institutions, into the historical process. Relative to this objective spirit, the individual is inferior, coincidental. Hegel never tires of emphasizing again and again that the chance, individual "I" must incorporate itself into the general order, into the historical course of spiritual evolution. It is the despotism of the spirit over the bearer of this spirit that Hegel demands.

It is a strange last remnant of the old belief in God and in the beyond that still appears here in Hegel. All the attributes with which the human "I," turned into an outer ruler of the world, was once endowed have been dropped, and only the attribute of logical generality remains. The Hegelian world idea is the human "I," and Hegel's teachings recognize this expressly, for at the pinnacle of culture man arrives at the point, according to this teaching, of feeling his full identity with this world "I." In art, religion, and philosophy man seeks to incorporate into his particular existence what is most general; the individual spirit permeates itself with the general world reason. Hegel portrays the course of world history in the following way: "If we look at the destiny of world-historical individuals, they have had the good fortune to be the managing directors of a purpose that was one stage in the progress of the general spirit. One can call it a trick of world reason for it to use these human tools; for it allows them to carry out their own purposes with all the fury of their passion, and yet remains not only unharmed itself but even brings forth itself. The particular is usually too insignificant compared to the general: individuals are sacrificed and abandoned. World history thus presents itself as the battle of individuals, and in the field of this particularization, things take their completely natural course. Just as in animal nature the preservation of life is the purpose and instinct of the individual creature, and just as here, after all, reason, the general, predominates and the individuals fall, thus so do things in the spiritual world also take their course. The passions mutually destroy each other; only reason is awake, pursues its purpose, and prevails." But for Hegel, the highest level of development of human culture is also not presented in this sacrificing of the particular individuals to the good of general world reason, but rather in the complete interpenetration of the two. In art, religion, and philosophy, the individual works in such a way that his work is at the same time a content of the general world reason. With Hegel, through the factor of generality that he laid into the world "I," the subordination of the separate human "I" to this world "I" still remained.

Ludwig Feuerbach sought to put an end to this subordination by stating in powerful terms how man transfers the being of his "I" into the outer world in order then to place himself over against it, acknowledging, obeying, revering it as though it were a God. "God is the revealed inner being, the expressed self, of man; religion is the festive disclosing of the hidden treasures of man, the confessing of his innermost thoughts, the public declaration of his declarations of love." But even Feuerbach has not yet cleansed the idea of this "I" of the factor of generality. For him the general human "I" is something higher than the individual, single "I." And even though as a thinker he does not, like Hegel, objectify this general "I" into a cosmic being existing in itself, still, in the moral context, over against the single human being, he does set up the general concept of a generic man, and demands that the individual should raise himself above the limitations of his individuality.

Max Stirner, in his book The Individual and What Is His (Der Einzige und sein Eigentum), published in 1844, demanded of the "I" in a radical way that it finally recognize that all the beings it has set above itself in the course of time were cut by it from its own body and set up in the outer world as idols. Every god, every general world reason, is an image of the "I" and has no characteristics different from the human "I." And even the concept of the general "I" was extracted from the completely individual "I" of every single person.

Stirner calls upon man to throw off everything general about himself and to acknowledge to himself that he is an individual. "You are indeed more than a Jew, more than a Christian, etc., but you are also more than a man. Those are all ideas; you, however, are in the flesh. Do you really believe, therefore, that you can ever become 'man as such'?" "*I* am man! I do not first have to produce man in myself, because he already belongs to me as all my characteristics do." "Only I am not an abstraction alone; I am the all in all;... I am no mere thought, but I am at the same time full of thoughts, a thought-world. Hegel condemns what is one's own, what is mine ... 'Absolute thinking' is that thinking which forgets that it is my thinking, that I think, and that thinking exists only through me. As 'I,' however, I again swallow what is mine, am master over it; it is only my opinion that I can change at every moment, i.e., that I can destroy, that I can take back into myself and can devour." "The thought is only my own when I can indeed subjugate it, but it can never subjugate me, never fanaticize me and make me the tool of its realization." All the beings placed over the "I" finally shatter upon the knowledge that they have only been brought into the world by the "I." "The beginning of my thinking, namely, is not a thought, but rather I, and therefore I am also its goal, just as its whole course is then only the course of my self-enjoyment."

In Stirner's sense, one should not want to define the individual "I" by a thought, by an idea. For, ideas are something general; and through any such definition, the individual — at least logically — would thus be subordinated at once to something general. One can define everything else in the world by ideas, but we must experience our own "I" as something individual within us. Everything that is expressed about the individual in thoughts cannot take up his content into itself; it can only point to it. One says: Look into yourself; there is something for which any concept, any idea, is too poor to encompass in all its incarnate wealth, something that brings forth the ideas out of itself, but that itself has an inexhaustible spring within itself whose content is infinitely more extensive than everything this something brings forth. Stirner's response is: "The individual is a word and with a word one would after all have to be able to think something; a word would after all have to have a thought-content. But the individual is a word without thought; it has no thought-content. But what is its content then if not thought? Its content is one that cannot be there a second time and that consequently can also not be expressed, for if it could be expressed, really and entirely expressed, then it would be there a second time, would be there in the 'expression'... only when nothing of you is spoken out and you are only named, are you recognized as you. As long as something of you is spoken out, you will be recognized only as this something (man, spirit, Christian, etc.)." The individual "I" is therefore that which is everything it is only through itself, which draws the content of its existence out of itself and continuously expands this content from out of itself.

This individual "I" can acknowledge no ethical obligation that it does not lay upon itself. "Whether what I think and do is Christian, what do I care? Whether it is human, liberal, humane, or inhuman, unliberal, inhumane, I don't ask about that. If it only aims at what I want, if I satisfy only myself in it, then call it whatever you like: it's all the same to me ..." "Perhaps, in the very next moment I will turn against my previous thought; I also might very well change my behavior suddenly; but not because it does not correspond to what is Christian, not because it goes against eternal human rights, not because it hits the idea of mankind, humanity, humaneness in the face, but rather — because I am no longer involved, because I no longer enjoy it fully, because I doubt my earlier thought, or I am no longer happy with my recent behavior." The way Stirner speaks about love from this point of view is characteristic. "I also love people, not merely some of them but everyone. But I love them with the consciousness of egoism; I love them because love makes me happy; I love because loving is natural for me, because I like it. I know no 'commandment of love' ..." To this sovereign individual, all state, social, and church organizations are fetters. For, all organizations presuppose that the individual must be like this or like that so that it can fit into the community. But the individual will not let it be determined for him by the community how he should be. He wants to make himself into this or that. J. H. Mackay, in his book Max Stirner, His Life and Work, has expressed what matters to Stirner: "The annihilation, in the first place, of those foreign powers which seek in the most varied ways to suppress and destroy the "I"; and in the second place, the presentation of the relationships of our intercourse with each other, how they result from the conflict and harmony of our interests." The individual cannot fulfill himself in an organized community, but only in free intercourse or association. He acknowledges no societal structure set over the individual as a power. In him everything occurs through the individual. There is nothing fixed within him. What occurs is always to be traced back to the will of the individual. No one and nothing represents a universal will. Stirner does not want society to care for the individual, to protect his rights, to foster his well-being, and so on. When the organization is taken away from people, then their intercourse regulates itself on its own. "I would rather have to rely on people's self-interest than on their 'service of love,' their compassion, their pity, etc. Self-interest demands reciprocity (as you are to me, thus I am to you), does nothing 'for nothing,' and lets itself be won and — bought." Let human intercourse have its full freedom and it will unrestrictedly create that reciprocity which you could set up through a community after all, only in a restricted way.

"Neither a natural nor a spiritual tie holds a society (Verein) together, and it is no natural nor spiritual association (Bund). It is not blood nor a belief (i.e., spirit) that brings it about. In a natural association — such as a family, a tribe, a nation; yes, even mankind — individuals have value only as specimens of a species or genus; in a spiritual association — such as a community or church — the individual is significant only as a part of the common spirit; in both cases, what you are as an individual must be suppressed. Only in a society can you assert yourself as an individual, because the society does not possess you, but rather you possess it or use it."

The path by which Stirner arrived at his view of the individual can be designated as a universal critique of all general powers that suppress the "I." The churches, the political systems (political liberalism, social liberalism, humanistic liberalism), the philosophies — they have all set such general powers over the individual. Political liberalism establishes the "good citizen"; social liberalism establishes the worker who is like all the others in what they own in common; humanistic liberalism establishes the "human being as human being." As he destroys all these powers, Stirner sets up in their ruins the sovereignty of the individual. "What all is not supposed to be my cause! Above all the good cause, then God's cause, the cause of mankind, of truth, of freedom, of humaneness, of justice; furthermore the cause of my folk, of my prince, of my fatherland; finally, of course, the cause of the spirit and a thousand other causes. Only my cause is never supposed to be my cause. — Let us look then at how those people handle their cause for whose cause we are supposed to work, to devote ourselves, and to wax enthusiastic. You know how to proclaim many basic things about God, and for thousands of years have investigated 'the depths of the Divinity' and looked into His heart, so that you are very well able to tell us how God Himself conducts 'the cause of God' that we are called to serve. And you also do not keep the Lord's conduct secret. What is His cause then? Has He, as is expected of us, made a foreign cause, the cause of truth and love, into His own? Such lack of understanding enrages you and you teach us that God's cause is, to be sure, the cause of truth and love, but that this cause cannot be called foreign to Him because God is Himself, in fact, truth and love; you are enraged by the assumption that God could be like us poor worms in promoting a foreign cause as His own. 'God is supposed to take on the cause of truth when He is not Himself the truth?' He takes care only of His cause, but because He is the all in all, everything is also His cause; we, however, we are not the all in all, and our cause is small and contemptible indeed; therefore we must 'serve a higher cause.' — Now, it is clear that God concerns Himself only with what is His, occupies Himself only with Himself, thinks only about Himself, and has His eye on Himself; woe to anything that is not well pleasing to Him. He serves nothing higher and satisfies only Himself. His cause is a purely egoistical cause. How do matters stand with mankind, whose cause we are supposed to make into our own? Is its cause perhaps that of another, and does mankind serve a higher cause? No, mankind looks only at itself, mankind wants to help only mankind, mankind is itself its cause. In order to develop itself, mankind lets peoples and individuals torment themselves in its service, and when they have accomplished what mankind needs, then, out of gratitude, they are thrown by it onto the manure pile of history. Is the cause of mankind not a purely egoistical cause?" Out of this kind of a critique of everything that man is supposed to make into his cause, there results for Stirner that "God and mankind have founded their cause on nothing but themselves. I will then likewise found my cause upon myself, I, who like God am nothing from anything else, I, who am my all, I who am the single one."

That is Stirner's path. One can also take another path to arrive at the nature of the "I." One can observe the "I" in its cognitive activity. Direct your gaze upon a process of knowledge. Through a thinking contemplation of processes, the "I" seeks to become conscious of what actually underlies these processes. What does one want to achieve by this thinking contemplation? To answer this question we must observe: What would we possess of these processes without this contemplation, and what do we obtain through this contemplation? I must limit myself here to a meager sketch of these fundamental questions about world views, and can point only to the broader expositions in my books Truth and Science (Wahrheit und Wissenschaft) and The Philosophy of Spiritual Activity (Die Philosophic der Freiheit).

Look at any process you please. I throw a stone in a horizontal direction. It moves in a curved line and falls to earth after a time. I see the stone at successive moments in different places, after it has first cost me a certain amount of effort to throw it. Through my thinking contemplation I gain the following. During its motion the stone is under the influence of several factors. If it were only under the influence of the propulsion I gave it in throwing it, it would go on forever, in a straight line, in fact, without changing its velocity. But now the earth exerts an influence upon it which one calls gravity. If, without propelling it away from me, I had simply let go of it, it would have fallen straight to the ground, and in doing so its velocity would have increased continuously. Out of the reciprocal workings of these two influences there arises what actually happens. Those are all thought-considerations that I bring to what would offer itself to me without any thinking contemplation.

In this way we have in every cognitive process an element that would present itself to us even without any thinking contemplation, and another element that we can gain only through such thinking contemplation.

When we have then gained both elements, it is clear to us that they belong together. A process runs its course in accordance with the laws that I gain about it through my thinking. The fact that for me the two elements are separated and are joined together by my cognition is my affair. The process does not bother about this separation and joining. From this it follows, however, that the activity of knowing is altogether my affair. Something that I bring about solely for my own sake.

Yet another factor enters in here now. The things and processes would never, out of themselves, give me what I gain about them through my thinking contemplation. Out of themselves they give me, in fact, what I possess without that contemplation. It has already been stated in this essay that I take out of myself what I see in the things as their deepest being. The thoughts I make for myself about the things, these I produce out of my own inner being. They nevertheless belong to the things, as has been shown. The essential being of the things does not therefore come to me from them, but rather from me. My content is their essential being. I would never come to ask about the essential being of the things at all if I did not find present within me something I designate as this essential being of the things, designate as what belongs to them, but designate as what they do not give me out of themselves, but rather what I can take only out of myself.

Within the cognitive process I receive the essential being of the things from out of myself. I therefore have the essential being of the world within myself. Consequently I also have my own essential being within myself. With other things two factors appear to me: a process without its essential being and the essential being through me. With myself, process and essential being are identical. I draw forth the essential being of all the rest of the world out of myself, and I also draw forth my own essential being from myself.

Now my action is a part of the general world happening. It therefore has its essential being as much within me as all other happenings. To seek the laws of human action means, therefore, to draw them forth out of the content of the "I." Just as the believer in God traces the laws of his actions back to the will of his God, so the person who has attained the insight that the essential being of all things lies within the "I" can also find the laws of his action only within the "I." If the "I" has really penetrated into the essential nature of its action, it then feels itself to be the ruler of this action. As long as we believe in a world-being foreign to us, the laws of our action also stand over against us as foreign. They rule us; what we accomplish stands under the compulsion they exercise over us. If they are transformed from such foreign beings into our "I's" primally own doing, then this compulsion ceases. That which compels has become our own being. The lawfulness no longer rules over us, but rather rules within us over the happenings that issue from our "I." To bring about a process by virtue of a lawfulness standing outside the doer is an act of inner unfreedom; to do so out of the doer himself is an act of inner freedom. To give oneself the laws of one's actions out of oneself means to act as a free individual. The consideration of the cognitive process shows the human being that he can find the laws of his action only within himself.

To comprehend the "I" in thinking means to create the basis for founding everything that comes from the "I" also upon the "I" alone. The "I" that understands itself can make itself dependent upon nothing other than itself. And it can be answerable to no one but itself. After these expositions it seems almost superfluous to say that with this "I" only the incarnate real "I" of the individual person is meant and not any general "I" abstracted from it. For any such general "I" can indeed be gained from the real "I" only by abstraction. It is thus dependent upon the real individual. (Benj. R. Tucker and J. H. Mackay also advocate the same direction in thought and view of life out of which my two above-mentioned books have arisen. See Tucker's Instead of a Book and Mackay's The Anarchists.

In the eighteenth century and in the greater part of the nineteenth, man's thinking made every effort to win for the "I" its place in the universe. Two thinkers who are already keeping aloof from this direction are Arthur Schopenhauer and Eduard von Hartmann, who is still vigorously working among us. Neither any longer transfers the full being of our "I," which we find present in our consciousness, as primal being into the outer world. Schopenhauer regarded one part of this "I," the will, as the essential being of the world, and Hartmann sees the unconscious to be this being. Common to both of them is this striving to subordinate the "I" to their assumed general world-being. On the other hand, as the last of the strict individualists, Friedrich Nietzsche, taking his start from Schopenhauer, did arrive at views that definitely lead to the path of absolute appreciation of the individual "I." In his opinion, genuine culture consists in fostering the individual in such a way that he has the strength out of himself to develop everything lying within him. Up until now it was only an accident if an individual was able to develop himself fully out of himself. "This more valuable type has already been there often enough: but as a happy chance, as an exception, never as willed. Rather he was precisely the one feared the most; formerly he was almost the fearful thing; — and out of fear, the opposite type was willed, bred, attained: the domestic animal, the herd animal, the sick animal man, the Christian ..." Nietzsche transfigured poetically, as his ideal, his type of man in his Zarathustra. He calls him the Superman (Übermensch). He is man freed from all norms, who no longer wants to be the mere image of God, a being in whom God is well pleased, a good citizen, and so on, but rather who wants to be himself and nothing more — the pure and absolute egoist.

Reordering of Society
Capital and Credit

From various points of view the opinion has been expressed that all questions of money are so complicated as to be well-nigh impossible to grasp in clear and transparent thoughts. A similar view can be maintained regarding many questions of modern social life. But we should consider the consequences that must follow if men allow their social dealings to be guided by indefinite thoughts; for such thoughts do not merely signify a confusion in theoretic knowledge, they are potent forces in life; their vague character lives on in the institutions that arise under their influence, which in turn result in social conditions making life impossible ...

If we try to go the root of the social question, we are bound to see that even the most material demands can be grappled with only by proceeding to the thoughts that underlie the co-operation of men and women in a community. For example, people closely connected with the land have indicated how, under the influence of modern economic forces, the buying and selling of land has made land into a commodity, and they are of the opinion that this is harmful to society. Yet opinions such as these do not lead to practical results, for men in other spheres of life do not admit that they are justified ... We must take into account how the purely capitalistic tendency affects the valuation of land. Capital creates the laws of its own increase, which in certain spheres no longer accord with an increase on sound lines. This is specially evident in the case of land. Certain conditions may well make it necessary for a district to be fruitful in a particular way-they may be founded on spiritual and cultural peculiarities. But their fulfilment might result in a smaller interest on capital than investment elsewhere. As a consequence of the purely capitalistic tendency the land will then be exploited, not according to these spiritual or cultural points of view, but in such a way that the resulting interest on capital may equal that in other undertakings. And in this way values that may be very necessary to a real civilization are left undeveloped.

It is easy to jump to the conclusion: The capitalistic orientation of economic life has these results, and must therefore be abandoned ... But one who recognizes how modern life works through division of labour and of social function will rather have to consider how to exclude from social life the disadvantages which arise as a by-product of this capitalistic tendency ... The ideal is to work for a structure of society whereby the criterion of increase in capital will no longer be the only power to which production is subject-it should rather be the symptom, which shows that the economic life, by taking into account all the requirements of man's bodily and spiritual nature, is rightly formed and ordered ...

Now it is just in so far as they can be bought and sold for sums of capital in which their specific nature finds no expression, that economic values become commodities. But the commodity nature is only suited to those goods or values which are directly consumed by man. For the valuation of these, man has an immediate standard in his bodily and spiritual needs. There is no such standard in the case of land, nor in the case of means of production. The valuation of these depends on many factors, which only become apparent when one takes into account the social structure as a whole ...

Where 'supply and demand' are the determining factors, there the egoistic type of value is the only one that can come into reckon ing. The 'market' relationship must be superseded by associations regulating the exchange and production of goods by an intelligent observation of human needs. Such associations can replace mere supply and demand by contracts and negotiations between groups of producers and consumers, and between different groups of producers ...

Work done in confidence of the return achievements of others constitutes the giving of *credit* in social life. As there was once a transition from barter to the money system, so there has recently been a progressive transformation to a basis of credit. Life makes it necessary today for one man to work with means entrusted to him by another, or by a community, having confidence in his power to achieve a result. But under the capitalistic method the credit system involves a complete loss of the real and satisfying human relationship of a man to the conditions of his life and work. Credit is given when there is prospect of an increase of capital that seems to justify it; and work is always done subject to the view that the confidence or credit received will have to appear justified in the capitalistic sense. And what is the result? Human beings are subjected to the power of dealings in capital which take place in a sphere of finance remote from life. And the moment they become fully conscious of this fact, they feel it to be unworthy of their humanity ...

A healthy system of giving credit presupposes a social structure which enables economic values to be estimated by their relation to the satisfaction of men's bodily and spiritual needs. Men's economic dealings will take their form from this. Production will be considered from the point of view of needs, no longer by an abstract scale of capital and wages.

Economic life in a threefold society is built up by the cooperation of *associations* arising out of the needs of producers and the interests of consumers. In their mutual dealings, impulses from the spiritual sphere and sphere of rights will play a decisive part. These associations will not be bound to a purely capitalistic standpoint, for one association will be in direct mutual dealings with another, and thus the one-sided interests of one branch of production will be regulated and balanced by those of the other. The responsibility for the giving and taking of credit will thus devolve to the associations. This will not impair the scope and activity of individuals with special faculties; on the contrary, only this method will give individual faculties full scope: the individual is responsible to his association for achieving the best possible results. The association is responsible to other associations for using these individual achievements to good purpose. The individual's desire for gain will no longer be imposing production on the life of the community; production will be regulated by the needs of the community ...

All kinds of dealings are possible between the new associations and old forms of business — there is no question of the old having to be destroyed and replaced by the new. The new simply takes its place and will have to justify itself and prove its inherent power, while the old will dwindle away ... The essential thing is that the threefold idea will stimulate a real social intelligence in the men and women of the community. The individual will in a very definite sense be contributing to the achievements of the whole community ... The individual faculties of men, working in harmony with the human relationships founded in the sphere of rights, and with the production, circulation and consumption that are regulated by the economic associations, will result in the greatest possible efficiency. Increase of capital, and a proper adjustment of work and return for work, will appear as a final consequence

...Whether a man rejects this idea or makes it his own will depend on his summoning the will and energy to work his way through into the sphere of causes. If he does so, he will cease considering external institutions alone; his attention will be guided to the human beings who make the institutions. Division of labour separates men; the forces that come from the three spheres of social life, once these are made independent, will draw them together again ... This inevitable demand of the time is shown in a vivid light by such concrete facts as the continued intensification of the credit system ... In the long run, credit cannot work healthily unless the giver of credit feels himself responsible for all that is brought about through his giving credit. The receiver of credit, through the associations, must give him grounds to justify his taking this responsibility. For a healthy national economy, it is not merely important that credit should further the spirit of enterprise as such, but that the right methods and institutions should exist to enable the spirit of enterprise to work in a socially useful way.

The social thoughts that start from the threefold idea do not aim to replace free business dealings governed by supply and demand by a system of rations and regulations. Their aim is to realize the true relative values of commodities, with the underlying idea that the product of one man's labour should be equivalent in value to all the other commodities that he needs for his consumption during the time he spends in producing it.

Under the capitalistic system, demand may determine whether someone will undertake the production of a certain commodity. But demand alone can never determine whether it will be possible to produce it at a price corresponding to its value in the sense defined above. This can only be determined through methods and institutions by which society in all its aspects will bring about a sensible valuation of the different commodities. Anyone who doubts that this is worth striving for is lacking in vision. For he does not see that, under the mere rule of supply and demand, human needs whose satisfaction would uplift the civilized life of the community are being starved. And he has no feeling for the necessity of trying to include the satisfaction of such needs among the practical incentives of an organised community. The essential aim of the threefold society is to create a just balance between human needs and the value of the products of human work.

Reordering of Society Requirements of Spiritual, Social and Economic Life

In the social movement of the present day there is a great deal of talk about social organization but very little about social and unsocial human beings. Little regard is paid to that 'social question' which arises when one considers that the arrangements of society take their social or antisocial stamp from the people who work in them. Socialist thinkers expect to see in the control of the means of production by the community what will satisfy the needs of the wider population. They take for granted that under such control the co-operation between people must take a social form. They have seen that the industrial system of private capitalism has led to unsocial conditions. They think that if this industrial system were to disappear, the antisocial effects must also end.

Undoubtedly along with the modern capitalistic form of economy there have arisen social ills to the widest extent; but is this any proof that they are a necessary consequence of this economic system? An industrial system can of its own nature do nothing but put men into situations in life that enable them to produce goods for themselves or for others in a useful or a useless manner. The modern industrial system has brought the means of production into the power of individuals or groups of persons. The technical achievements could best be exploited by a concentration of economic power. So long as this power is employed only in the production of goods, its social effect is essentially different from when it trespasses on the fields of civil rights or spiritual culture. And it is this trespassing which in the course of the last few centuries has led to those social ills for whose abolition the modern social movement is pressing. He who is in possession of the means of production acquires economic domination over others. This has resulted in his allying himself with the forces helpful to him in administration and parliaments, through which he was able to procure positions of social advantage over those who were economically dependent on him; and which even in a democratic state bear in practice the character of rights. Similarly this economic domination has led to a monopolizing of the life of spiritual culture by those who held economic power.

Now the simplest thing seems to be to get rid of this economic predominance of individuals, and thereby to do away with their predominance in rights and spiritual culture as well. One arrives at this 'simplicity' of social conception when one fails to remember that the combination of technical and economic activity which modern life demands necessitates allowing the most fruitful expansion possible to individual initiative and personal worth within the business of economic life. The form which production must take under modern conditions makes this a necessity. The individual cannot make his abilities effective in business, if he is tied down in his work and decisions to the will of the community. However dazzling the thought of the individual producing not for himself but for society collectively, yet its justice within certain bounds should not hinder one from also recognizing the other truth, that society collectively is incapable of originating economic decisions that permit of being realized through individuals in the desirable way. Really practical thought, therefore, will not look to find the cure for social ills in a reshaping of economic life that would substitute communal for private management of the means of production. The endeavour should rather be to forestall the ills that can arise through management by individual initiative and personal worth, without impairing this management itself. This is only possible if the relations of civil rights amongst those engaged in industry are not influenced by the interests of economic life, and if that which should be done for people through the spiritual life is also independent of these interests.

Genuine interests of right can only spring up on a ground where the life of rights is separately cultivated, and where the only consideration will be what the rights of a matter are. When people proceed from such considerations to frame rules of right, the rules thus made will take effect in economic life. Then it will not be necessary to place a restriction on the individual acquiring economic power; for such power will only result in his rendering economic achievements proportionate to his abilities, but not in using this to obtain privileged rights ... Only when rights are ordered in a field where a business consideration cannot in any way come into question, where business can procure no power over this system of rights, will the two be able to work together in such a way that men's sense of right will not be injured, nor economic ability be turned from a blessing to a curse for the community as a whole.

When those who are economically powerful are in a position to use their power to wrest privileged rights for themselves, then among the economically weak there will grow up a corresponding opposition to these privileges; and this opposition must as soon as it has grown strong enough lead to revolutionary disturbances. If the existence of a special province of rights makes it impossible for such privileged rights to arise, then disturbances of this sort cannot occur. . . One will never really touch what is working up through the social movement to the surface of modern life, until one brings about social conditions in which, alongside the claims and interests of the economic life, those of rights can find realization and satisfaction on their own independent basis.

In a similar manner must one approach the question of the cultural life, and its connections with the life of civil rights and of industrial economy. The course of the last few centuries has been such that the cultural life itself has been cultivated under conditions which only allowed of its exercising to a limited extent an independent influence upon political life — that of civil rights — or upon economics. One of the most important branches of spiritual culture, the whole manner of education, was shaped by the interests of the civil power. The human being was taught and trained according as state interests required; and state power was reinforced by economic power. If anyone was to develop his capacities within the existing provisions for education, he had to do so on the basis of such finances as his place in life provided. Those spiritual forces that could find scope within the life of political rights or of industry accordingly acquired the stamp of the latter. Any free spiritual life had to forego all idea of carrying its results into the sphere of the state, and could only do so in the economic sphere in so far as this remained outside the sphere of activities of the state. In industry, after all, the necessity is obvious for allowing the competent person to find scope, since all fruitful activity dies out if left solely under the control of the incompetent whom circumstances may have endowed with economic power. If the tendency common amongst socialist thinkers were carried out and economic life were administered after the fashion of the political and legal, then the culture of the free spiritual life would be forced to withdraw altogether from the public field.

But a spiritual life that has to develop apart from civil and industrial realities loses touch with life. It is forced to draw its content from sources that are not in live connection with these realities; and in course of time it works this substance up into a shape which runs on like a sort of animated abstraction along side the actual realities, without having any practical effect on them. And so two different currents arise in spiritual life ... Consider what conceptions of the mind, what religious ideals, what artistic interests form the inner life of the shopkeeper, the manufacturer, or the government official, apart from his daily practical life; and then consider what ideas are contained in those activities expressed in his bookkeeping, or for which he is trained by the education and instruction that prepares him for his profession. A gulf lies between the two currents of spiritual life. The gulf has grown all the wider in recent years because the mode of conception which in natural science is quite justified has become the standard of man's relation to reality. This mode of conception proceeds from the knowledge of laws in things and processes lying outside the field of human activity and influence, so that man is as it were a mere spectator of that which he grasps in the laws of nature ...

A spiritual conception that penetrates to the being of man finds there motives for action which ethically are directly good; for the impulse to evil arises in man only because in his thoughts and sensations he silences the depths of his own nature. Hence social ideas arrived at through the spiritual conception here meant must by their very nature be ethical ideas as well. And not being drawn from thought alone but experienced in life, they have the strength to lay hold on the will and live on in action. For true spiritual conception, social thought and ethical thought flow into one ...

This kind of spirit can, however, thrive only when its growth is completely independent of all authority except such as is derived directly from the spiritual life itself. Legal regulations by the civil state for the nurture of the spirit sap the strength of the forces of spiritual life, whereas a spiritual life left to its own inherent interests and impulses will reach out into everything that man performs in social life ...

If the life of the spirit be a free one, evolved only from impulses within itself, then civil life will thrive in proportion as people are educated intelligently from living spiritual experience in the adjustment of their relationships of rights; and economic life will be fruitful in the measure in which men's spiritual nature has developed their capacities for it ...

Because the spirit at work in civil life and the round of industry is no longer one through which the spiritual life of the individual finds a channel, he sees himself in a social order which gives him, as individual, no scope civically nor economically. People who do not see this clearly will always object to a view of the social organism divided into three independently functioning systems of the cultural life, the rights state and the industrial economy, that such a differentiation would destroy the necessary unity of communal life. One must reply to them that this unity is destroying itself, in the effort to maintain itself intact ... It is just in separation that they will turn to unity, whereas in an artificial unity they become estranged.

Many socialist thinkers will dismiss such an idea with the phrase that conditions of life worth striving for cannot be brought about by this organic membering of society, but only through a suitable economic organization. They overlook the fact that the men at work in their organization are endowed with wills. If one tells them so they will smile, for they regard it as self-evident. Yet they envisage a social structure in which this 'self-evident' fact is left out of account. Their economic organization is to be controlled by a communal will, which must be the resultant wills of the people in the organization. These individual wills can never find scope, if the communal will is derived entirely from the idea of economic organization ...

Most people today still lack faith in the possibility of establishing a socially satisfying order of society based on individual wills, because such a faith cannot come from a spiritual life dependent on the life of the state and of the economy. The kind of spirit that develops not in freedom out of the life of the spirit itself but out of an external organization simply does not know what the potentialities of the spirit are. It looks round for something to direct it, not knowing how the spirit directs itself if only it can draw its strength from its own resources. For the new shaping of the social order, goodwill is not the only thing needed. It needs also that courage which can be a match for the lack of faith in the spirit's power. A true spiritual conception can inspire this courage; for it feels able to bring forth ideas that not only serve to give the soul its inward orientation, but which in their very birth bring with them seeds of life's practical configuration. The will to go down into the deep places of the spirit can become a will so strong as to bear a part in every thing that man performs ...

The experiments now being made to solve the social question afford such unsatisfactory results because many people have not yet become able to see what the true gist of the problem is. They see it arise in economic regions, and look to economic institutions to provide the answer. They think they will find the solution in economic transformations. They fail to recognize that these transformations can only come about through forces released from within human nature itself in the uprising of a new spiritual life and life of rights in their own independent realms.

Reordering of Society
The Fundamental Social Law

Briefly as the subject must be dealt with, there will always be some people whose feeling will lead them to recognize the truth of what it is impossible to discuss in all its fullness here. There is a fundamental social law which spiritual science teaches, and which is as follows:

'The well-being of a community of people working together will be the greater, the less the individual claims for himself the proceeds of his work, i.e. the more of these proceeds he makes over to his fellow-workers, the more his own needs are satisfied, not out of his own work but out of the work done by others'.

Every arrangement in a community that is contrary to this law will inevitably engender somewhere after a while distress and want. It is a fundamental law, which holds good for all social life with the same absoluteness and necessity as any law of nature within a particular field of natural causation. It must not be supposed, however, that it is sufficient to acknowledge this law as one for general moral conduct, or to try to interpret it into the sentiment that everyone should work in the service of his fellow men. No, this law only lives in reality as it should when a community of people succeeds in creating arrangements such that no one can ever claim the fruits of his own labour for himself, but that these go wholly to the benefit of the community. And he must himself be supported in return by the labours of his fellow men. The important point is, therefore, that working for one's fellow men and obtaining so much income must be kept apart, as two separate things.

Self-styled 'practical people' will of course have nothing but a smile for such 'outrageous idealism'. And yet this law is more practical than any that was ever devised or enacted by the 'practicians'. Anyone who really examines practical life will find that every community that exists or has ever existed anywhere has two sorts of arrangements, of which the one is in accordance with this law and the other contrary to it. It is bound to be so everywhere, whether men will it or not. Every community would indeed fall to pieces at once, if the work of the individual did not pass over into the totality. But human egoism has from of old run counter to this law, and sought to extract as much as possible for the individual out of his own work. And what has come about from of old in this way due to egoism has alone brought want, poverty and distress in its wake. This simply means that the part of human arrangements brought about by 'practicians' who calculated on the basis of either their own egotism or that of others must always prove impractical.

Now naturally it is not simply a matter of recognizing a law of this kind, but the real practical part begins with the question: How is one to translate this law into actual fact? Obviously this law says nothing less than this: man's welfare is the greater, in proportion as egoism is less. So for its translation into reality one must have people who can find their way out of egoism. In practice, however, this is quite impossible if the individual's share of weal and woe is measured according to his labour. He who labours for himself must gradually fall a victim to egoism. Only one who labours solely for the rest can gradually grow to be a worker without egoism.

But there is one thing needed to begin with. If any man works for another, he must find in this other man the reason for his work; and if anyone is to work for the community, he must perceive and feel the value, the nature and importance, of this community. He can only do this when the community is something quite different from a more or less indefinite summation of individual men. It must be informed by an actual spirit, in which each single one has his part. It must be such that each one says: 'It is as it should be, and I will that it be so'. The community must have a spiritual mission, and each individual must have the will to contribute towards the fulfilling of this mission. All the vague abstract ideals of which people usually talk cannot present such a mission. If there be nothing but these, then one individual here or one group there will be working without any clear overview of what use there is in their work, except it being to the advantage of their families, or of those particular interests to which they happen to be attached. In every single member, down to the most solitary, this spirit of the community must be alive ...

No one need try to discover a solution of the social question that shall hold good for all time, but simply to find the right form for his social thoughts and actions in the light of the immediate need of the time in which he lives. Indeed there is today no theoretical scheme which could be devised or carried into effect by any one person which in itself could solve the social question. For this he would need to possess the power to force a number of people into the conditions which he had created. But in the present day any such compulsion is out of the question. The possibility must be found of each person doing of his own free will that which he is called upon to do according to his strength and abilities. For this reason there can be no possible question of ever trying to work on people theoretically, by merely indoctrinating them with a view as to how economic conditions might best be arranged. A bald economic theory can never act as a force to counteract the powers of egoism. For a while such an economic theory may sweep the masses along with a kind of impetus that appears to resemble idealism; but in the long run it helps nobody. Anyone who implants such a theory into a mass of people without giving them some real spiritual substance along with it is sinning against the real meaning of human evolution. The only thing which can help is a spiritual world-conception which of itself, through what it has to offer, can live in the thoughts, in the feelings, in the will — in short, in a man's whole soul ...

The recognition of these principles means, it is true, the loss of many an illusion for various people whose ambition it is to be popular benefactors. It makes working for the welfare of society a really difficult matter — one of which the results, too, may in certain circumstances comprise only quite tiny part-results. Most of what is given out today by whole parties as panaceas for social life loses its value, and is seen to be a mere bubble and hollow phrase, lacking in due knowledge of human life. No parliament, no democracy, no popular agitation can have any meaning for a person who looks at all deeper, if they violate the law stated above; whereas everything of this kind may work for good if it works on the lines of this law. It is a mischievous delusion to believe that particular persons sent up to some parliament as delegates from the people can do anything for the good of mankind, unless their activity is in conformity with the fundamental social law.

Wherever this law finds outer expression, wherever anyone is at work on its lines — so far as is possible in that position in which he is placed within the community — good results will be attained, though it be but in the single case and in never so small a measure. And it is only a number of individual results attained in this way that will together combine to the healthy collective progress of society.

The healthy social life is found   When in the mirror of each human soul   The whole community is shaped,   And when in the community   Lives the strength of each human soul.

The Human Soul
in the Twilight of Dreams

If, within the limits of ordinary consciousness, the human being wishes to study his soul, it will not suffice for him simply to direct his mind's eye backward, so to speak, in order to discern by introspection his nature as someone who looks out upon the world. He will see nothing new by this means. He will perceive himself in his capacity as a spectator of the world — merely from a different direction. In his waking life man is almost entirely occupied with the external world. He lives by his senses. In their impressions the external world continues to live in his inner life. Thoughts weave into these impressions. The outer world lives in the thoughts as well. Only the force with which the world is grasped in thoughts can be experienced as man's autonomous being. The sensation of this force, however, is of an entirely general and vague character. By means of ordinary consciousness one can differentiate nothing within this sensation. If one had to discern the human soul in it, one would obtain no more about the soul than a vague sensation of self; one would be unable to identify what it was.

What is unsatisfying about self-observation along these lines is that the nature of the soul promptly eludes the attempt to grasp it. Because of this drawback, people who seriously strive after knowledge may be driven to despair of it entirely.

Thoughtful people, therefore, have almost always sought knowledge of the human soul in ways other than such selfobservation. In the realm of sense perception and ordinary thinking they have felt that the vague sensation of self is surrendered to the body. They have realized that the soul, so long as it remains in this surrender, can learn nothing of its own nature through self-observation.

A realm to which this feeling points is that of the dream. People have become aware that the world of images the dream conjures up has some connection with the vague sensation of self. This appears, as it were, as an empty canvas on which the dream paints its own pictures. And then it is realized that the canvas is really itself the painter painting on and within itself.

Dreaming thus becomes for them the fleeting activity of man's inner life, which fills the soul's vague feeling of self with content. A questionable content — but the only one to be had at the outset. It is a view, lifted out of the brightness of ordinary consciousness and thrust into the twilight of semi-consciousness. Yet this is the only form attainable in everyday life.

Despite this dimness, however, there occurs — not in thinking self-observation to be sure, but in an inward touching of the self — something very significant. A kinship between dreaming and creative fantasy can inwardly be touched [seelisch ertasten]. One has the feeling that the airy pictures of a dream are the same as those of creative fantasy, though the latter are controlled by the body from within. And this inner body [Korper-Innere] compels the dream-picturing power to desist from its arbitrariness and to transform itself into an activity that emulates, albeit in a free manner, what exists in the world of the senses.

Once one has struggled through to such a touching of the inner world, one soon advances a step further. One becomes aware how the dream-picturing power can form a still closer connection with the body. One sees this foreshadowed in the activity of recollection, of memory. In memory the body compels the dream-picturing power to an even stronger fidelity to the outer world than it does in fantasy.

If this is understood, then there remains but one step to the recognition that the dream-picturing force of the soul also lies at the basis of ordinary thinking and sense perception. It is then entirely surrendered to the body, while in fantasy and memory it still reserves something of its own weaving.

This, then, justifies the assumption that in dreaming the soul frees itself from the state of bondage to the body and lives according to its own nature.

Thus the dream has become the field of inquiry for many searchers after the soul.

It relegates man, however, to a quite uncertain province. In surrendering to the body, the human soul becomes harnessed to the laws which govern nature. The body is a part of nature. Insofar as the soul surrenders to the body, it binds itself at the same time to the regularity of nature. The means whereby the soul adapts to the existence of nature is experienced as logic. In logical thinking about nature the soul feels secure. But in the power of dream-making it tears itself away from this logical thinking about nature. It returns to its own sphere. Thereby it abandons, as it were, the welltended and well-trodden pathways of the inner life and sets forth on the flowing, pathless sea of spiritual existence.

The threshold of the spiritual world seems to have been crossed; after the crossing, however, only the bottomless, directionless spiritual element presents itself. Those who seek to cross the threshold in this way find the exciting but also doubt-riddled domain of the soul life.

It is full of riddles. At one time it weaves the external events of life into airy connections that scorn the regularity of nature; at another it shapes symbols of inner bodily processes and organs. A too violently beating heart appears in the dream as an oven; aching teeth as a fence with pickets in disrepair. What is more, man comes to know himself in a peculiar way. His instinctive life takes shape in the dream in images of reprehensible actions which, in the waking state, he would strongly resist. Those dreams that have a prophetic character arouse special interest among students of the soul, as do those in which the soul dreams up capacities that are entirely absent in the waking state.

The soul appears released from its bondage to bodily and natural activity. It wants to be independent, and it prepares itself for this independence. As soon as it tries to become active, however, the activity of the body and of nature follow it. The soul will have nothing to do with nature's regularity; but the facts of nature appear in dreams as travesties of nature. The soul is interested in the internal bodily organs or bodily activities. It cannot, however, make clear pictures of these organs or bodily activities, but only symbols which bear the character of arbitrariness. Experience of external nature is torn away from the certainty in which sense perception and thinking place it. The inner life of what is human begins; it begins, however, in dim form. Observation of nature is abandoned; observation of the self is not truly achieved. The investigation of the dream does not place man in a position to view the soul in its true form. It is true this is spiritually more nearly comprehensible through dreams than through thinking self-observation; it is, however, something he should actually see but can only grope after as if through a veil.

The following section will speak about the perception of the soul through spirit knowledge.

The Human Soul
in Courage and Fear

The habits of thinking that have come to be accepted in the modern study of nature [Naturerkenntnis] can yield no satisfying results for the study of the soul. What one would grasp with these habits of thinking must either be spread out in repose before the soul or, if the object of knowledge is in movement, the soul must feel itself extricated from this movement. For to participate in the movement of the object of knowledge means to lose oneself in it, to transform oneself, so to speak, into it.

How should the soul grasp itself, however, in an act of knowing in which it must lose itself? It can expect selfknowledge only in an activity in which, step by step, it comes into possession of itself.

This can only be an activity that is creative. Here, however, a cause for uncertainty arises at once for the knower. He believes he will lapse into personal arbitrariness.

It is precisely this arbitrariness that he gives up in the knowledge of nature. He excludes himself and lets nature hold sway. He seeks certainty in a realm which his individual soul being does not reach. In seeking self-knowledge he cannot conduct himself in this way. He must take himself along wherever he seeks to know. He therefore can find no nature on his path to self-knowledge. For where she would encounter him, there he is no longer to be found.

This, however, provides just the experience that is needed with regard to the spirit. One cannot expect other than to find the spirit when, through one's own activity, nature, as it were, melts away; that is, when one experiences oneself ever more strongly in proportion to one's feeling this melting away.

If one fills the soul with something that afterward proves to be like a dream in its illusory character, and one experiences the illusory in its true nature, then one becomes stronger in one's own experience of self. In confronting a dream, one's thinking corrects the belief one has in the dream's reality while dreaming. Concerning the activity of fantasy, this correction is not needed because one did not have this belief. Concerning the meditative soul activity, to which one devotes oneself for spirit-knowledge, one cannot be satisfied with mere thought correction. One must correct by experiencing. One must first create the illusory thinking with one's activity and then extinguish it by a different, equally strong, activity.

In this act of extinguishing, another activity awakens, the spirit-knowing activity. For if the extinguishing is real, then the force for it must come from an entirely different direction than from nature. With the experienced illusion one has dispersed what nature can give; what inwardly arises during the dispersion is no longer nature.

With this activity something is needed that does not come into consideration in the study of nature: inner courage. With it one must take hold of what inwardly arises. In the study of nature one needs to hold nothing inwardly. One lets oneself be held by what is external. Inner courage is not needed here. One forgets it. This forgetting then causes anxiety when the spiritual is to enter the sphere of knowledge. Fear is felt because one might grope in a void if one no longer could hold onto nature.

This fear meets one at the threshold to spirit knowledge. And fear causes one to recoil from this knowledge. One now becomes creative in recoiling instead of in pressing forward. One does not allow the spirit to shape creative knowledge in oneself; one invents for oneself a sham logic for disputing the justification of spirit knowledge. Every possible sham reason is brought forward to spare one from acknowledging the spiritual, because one retreats trembling in fear of it.

Instead of spirit knowledge, then, there arises out of the creative force that which now appears in the soul when it draws back from nature, the enemy of spirit knowledge: first, as doubt concerning all knowledge that extends beyond nature; and then, as the fear grows, as an anti-logic that would banish all spirit knowledge to the realm of the fantastic.

Whoever has learned to move cognitively in the spirit often sees in the refutations of this knowledge its strongest evidence; for it becomes clear to him how in the soul, step by step, the refuter chokes down his fear of the spirit, and how in choking it he creates this sham logic. With such a refuter there is no point in arguing, for the fear befalling him arises in the subconscious. The consciousness tries to rescue itself from this fear. It feels at first that should this anxiety arise, it would inundate the whole inner experience with weakness. It is true, the soul cannot escape from this weakness, for one feels it rising up from within. If one ran away it would follow one everywhere. He who proceeds further in the knowledge of nature and, in his dedication to it feels obliged to preserve his own self, never escapes from this fear if he cannot acknowledge the spirit. Fear will accompany him, unless he is willing to give up the knowledge of nature along with spirit knowledge. He must somehow rid himself of this fear in his pursuit of the science of nature. In reality he cannot do so. The fear is produced in the: subconscious during the study of nature. It continually attempts to rise up out of the subconscious into consciousness. Therefore one refutes in the thought world what one cannot remove from the reality of soul experience.

And this refutation is an illusory layer of thought covering the subconscious fear. The refuter has not found the courage to come to grips with the illusory, just as in the meditative life he has to obliterate illusion in order to attain spiritual reality. For this reason he interposes the false arguments of his refutation into that region of the life of the soul that now arises. They soothe his consciousness; he ceases to feel the fear that, all the same, remains in his subconscious.

The denial of the spiritual world is a desire to run away from one's own soul. This, however, represents an impossibility. One must remain with oneself. And because one may run away but not escape from oneself, one takes care that in running one loses sight of oneself. It is the same with the entire human being in the soul realm, however, as it is with the eye with a cataract. The eye can then no longer see. It is darkened within itself.

So, too, the denier of spirit knowledge darkens his soul. He causes its darkening through sham reasoning born of fear. He avoids healthy clarification of the soul; he creates for himself an unhealthy soul darkening. The denial of spirit knowledge has its origin in a cataract affliction of the soul.

Thus one is ultimately led to the inner spiritual strength of the soul when one is willing to see the justification of spirit knowledge. And the way to such a knowledge can be had only through the strengthening of the soul. The meditative activity, preparing the soul for spirit knowledge, is a gradual conquest of the soul's "fear of the void." This void, however, is only a "void of nature," in which the "fullness of the spirit" can manifest itself if one wishes to take hold of it. Nor does the soul enter this "fullness of the spirit" with the arbitrariness it has when acting through the body in natural life; the soul enters this fullness at the moment when the spirit reveals to the soul the creative will, before which the arbitrariness, existing only in natural life, dissolves in the same way as nature herself dissolves.

The Human Soul
in the Light of Spirit Vision

If one resorts to dream phenomena in order to acquire knowledge of the soul's nature, one ultimately is forced to admit that the object of one's search is wearing a mask. Behind the symbolizations of bodily conditions and processes, behind the fantastically connected memory experiences, one may surmise the soul's activity. It cannot be maintained, however, that one is face to face with the true form of the soul.

On awaking, one realizes how the active part of the dream is interwoven with the function of the body and thereby subject to the external world of nature. Through the backward-directed view of self-observation one sees in the soul life only the images of the external world, not the life of the soul itself. The soul eludes the ordinary consciousness at the very moment one would grasp it cognitively.

By studying dreams one cannot hope to arrive at the reality of the soul element. In order to preserve the soul activity in its innate form one would have to obliterate, through a strong inner activity, the symbolizations of the bodily conditions and processes, along with the memory of past experiences. Then one would have to be able to study that which had been retained. This is impossible. For the dreamer is in a passive state. He cannot undertake any autonomous activity. With the disappearance of the soul's mask, the sensation of one's own self disappears also.

It is different with the waking soul life. There the autonomous activity of the soul can not only be sustained when one erases all one perceives of the external world; it can also be strengthened in itself.

This happens if, while awake in the forming of mental pictures, one makes oneself as independent of the external world of the senses as one is in a dream. One becomes a fully conscious, wakeful imitator of the dream. Thereby, however, the illusory quality of the dream falls away. The dreamer takes his dream pictures for realities. If one is awake one can see through their unreality. No healthy person when awake and imitating the dream will take his dream images for realities. He will remain conscious of the fact that he is living in self-created illusions.

He will not be able to create these illusions, however, if he merely remains at the ordinary level of consciousness. He must see to it that he strengthens this consciousness. He can achieve this by a continually renewed self-kindling of thinking from within. The inner soul activity grows with these repeated kindlings.

(I have described in detail the appropriate inner activity in my books Knowledge of the Higher Worlds and its Attainment and An Outline of Occult Science).

In this way the work of the soul during the twilight of dreams can be brought into the clear light of consciousness. One accomplishes thereby the opposite of what happens in suggestion or auto-suggestion. With these, something out of the semi-darkness and within the semi-darkness is shifted into the soul-life, which is then taken to be reality. In the fully circumspect activity of the soul just described, something is placed before one's inner view in clear consciousness, something that one regards, in the fullest sense of the word, only as illusion.

One thus arrives at compelling the dream to manifest itself in the light of consciousness. Ordinarily this occurs only in the diminished half-awake consciousness. It shuns the clarity of consciousness. It disappears in its presence. The strengthened consciousness holds it fast.

In holding the dream fast it does not gain in strength. On the contrary it diminishes in strength. Consciousness, however, is thereby induced to supply its own strength. The same thing happens here in the soul. It is just as it is when, in physical life, one transforms a solid into steam. The solid has its own boundaries on all sides. One can touch these boundaries. They exist in themselves. If one transforms the solid into steam, then one must enclose it within solid boundaries so that it will not escape. Similarly the soul, if it would hold fast the dream while awake, must shape itself, as it were, into a strong container. It must strengthen itself from within.

The soul does not need to effect this strengthening when it perceives the images of the external world. Then the relationship of the body to the external world takes care that the soul is aroused to retain these images. If, however, the waking soul is to dream in sensory unreality, then it must hold fast this sensory unreality by its own strength.

In the fully conscious representation [Vorstellen] of sensory unreality one develops the strength to behold the spiritual reality.

In the dream state the autonomous activity of the soul is weak. The fleeting dream content overpowers this autonomous activity. This supremacy of the dream causes the soul to take the dream for reality. In ordinary waking consciousness the autonomous activity experiences itself as reality along with the reality of the sense world. This autonomous activity, however, cannot behold [anschauen] itself; its vision is occupied with the images of sense reality. If the autonomous activity learns to maintain itself by consciously filling itself with content unreal to the senses, then, little by little, it also brings to life self-contemplation [Anschauung] within itself. Then, it does not simply direct its gaze away from outer observation and back upon itself; it strides as soul activity backward and discovers itself as spiritual entity; this now becomes the content of its vision [Anschaung].

While the soul thus discovers itself within itself, the nature of dreaming is even more illumined for it. The soul discerns clearly what before it could only surmise: that dreaming does not cease in the waking state. It continues. The feeble activity of the dream, however, is drowned by the content of sense perception. Behind the brightness of consciousness, filled with the images of sense reality, there glimmers a dream world. And this world, while the soul is awake, is not illusory like the dream world of semi-consciousness. In the waking state man dreams — beneath the threshold of consciousness — about the inner processes of his body. While the external world is seen through the eye and is present in [vorgestallt] the soul, there lives in the background the dim dream of inner occurrences. Through the strengthening of the autonomous activity of the soul the vision of the external world is gradually dampened to the dimness of dream, and the vision of the inner world, in its reality, brightens.

In its vision of the external world the soul is receptive; it experiences the external world as the creative principle and the soul's own content as created in the image of the external world. In the inner vision, the soul recognizes itself to be the creative principle. And one's own body is revealed as created in the image of the soul. Thoughts of the external world are to be felt [empfunden] as images of the beings and processes of the external world. To the soul's true vision, achieved in the way described, the human body can be felt [empfunden] only as the image of the human soul which is spiritual.

In dreams, the soul activity is loosened from its firm union with the body, which it maintains in the ordinary waking state; it still retains, however, the loose relationship that fills it with the symbolic images of bodily senses and with the memory experiences that also are acquired through the body. In spiritual vision of itself the soul so grows in strength that its own higher reality becomes discernible, and the body becomes recognizable in its character of a reflected image of this reality.

The Human Soul
on the Path to Self-Observation

In a dream the soul comprehends itself in a fleeting form, which is really a mask. In dreamless sleep it apparently loses itself entirely. In spiritual self-contemplation [Anschaung], which is achieved through circumspect reconstruction [besonnen] of the dream-state, the soul comes into its own as a creative being, of which the physical body is the reflected image.

A dream, however, arises out of sleep. Whoever undertakes to raise the dream up into the clear light of consciousness must also feel the incentive to go still further. He does this when he tries consciously to experience dreamless sleep.

That seems to be impossible, precisely because in sleep consciousness ceases. The desire consciously to experience unconsciousness seems like folly.

The folly, however, takes on another light when one confronts the memories one can follow from a given point of time backward to one's last awakening. To do so one must proceed in such a way as to connect the memory pictures vividly with that which they recall. Then, if one tries — working backward — to proceed to the next conscious memory picture before that, this will be found before the last falling asleep. If one has really made the connection vivid with what is recalled, there arises an inner difficulty. One cannot join up the memory picture after awaking with the one before falling asleep.

Ordinary consciousness gets one over this difficulty by not vividly connecting what is recalled, but simply placing the waking image next to the image one has on falling asleep. The person who has raised his consciousness to a high degree of sensitiveness, however, through conscious imitation of the dream, finds that the two images fall apart from one another [fallen ausenander]. For him an abyss lies between them, but because he notices this abyss it already begins to fill itself up. For his self-awareness the dreamless sleep ceases to be an empty passage of time. Out of it there emerges like a memory a spiritual content of the "empty time," like a memory, it is true, of something that ordinary consciousness had not contained before. Even so this memory points to an experience of one's own soul like an ordinary memory. The soul, however, really looks thereby into that which in ordinary experience — in dreamless sleep — occurred unconsciously.

On this path the soul looks still more deeply within than it does in the condition that arises as a result of the conscious dream imitation. In this condition the soul beholds its own body-forming being. Through the conscious penetration of dreamless sleep, the soul perceives itself in its own being, completely detached from the body.

Now, however, the soul beholds not only the forming of the body but also, beyond that, the formation of its own willing [Wollen].

The inner nature of the will remains as unknown to ordinary consciousness as the events of dreamless sleep. One experiences a thought that contains the intention of the will. This thought sinks into the obscure world of the feelings and disappears into the darkness of the bodily processes. It emerges again as the external bodily process of an arm movement that is comprehended anew through a thought. Between the two thought contents there lies something like the sleep between the thoughts before falling asleep and those after waking.

Now as the inner working of the soul upon the body becomes comprehensible to the first level of vision, so does the will over and above the body to the second. The soul can follow the path to behold its inner working upon the body's organic development; and it can take the other path by which it learns to comprehend how the soul works on the body in such a way as to extract the will from it.

And just as dreaming lies between sleeping and waking, so feeling lies between willing and thinking. On the same path that leads to the illumination of the will process lies the illumination of the world of feeling also.

In the first kind of vision the soul's inner working on the organism is revealed. In the second the soul penetrates to the will. But an inner activity must precede the outward manifestation of the will. Before the arm can be raised, the creative current must flow into it so that in its metabolic processes, which run on quietly, processes are inserted that are clearly the result of feeling. Feeling is a willing that remains enclosed within the human being, a willing that is arrested at its inception.

The processes inserted into the body for feeling and willing reveal themselves for the second stage of vision as processes that are in opposition to those that support life. They are destructive processes. In the constructive processes life prospers; but the soul withers in them. The life of the body, which itself is built up by the soul, must be broken down so that the nature and activity of the soul can unfold out of the body.

To spiritual vision the working of the soul on the body is like a memory of something that the soul had first to accomplish before it could exist in its own activity.

Thereby, however, the soul experiences itself as a purely spiritual being that has let the forming of the body take precedence to the soul's own activity in order to have the body become the basis for the soul's inherent, purely spiritual development. The soul first devotes its creative effort to the body so that, after this has been done sufficiently, the soul can manifest itself in free spirituality.

And this development of the soul begins already with thinking that results from the perception of the senses. When one perceives an object, the soul commences its activity. It shapes the corresponding part of the body in such a way that it becomes adapted for developing, in the form of thought, a mirror image of the object. In experiencing this mirror image, the soul beholds the result of its own activity.

One will never find the spiritual nature of the soul by philosophizing about the thoughts that arise before ordinary consciousness. The spiritual activity of the soul does not lie in these thoughts but behind them. It is true that the thoughts which the soul experiences are the result of the brain's activity. The brain's activity, however, is first the result of the spiritual activity of the soul. In misunderstanding this fact lies what is unsound in the materialistic world view. This view is right when it demonstrates from every possible scientific presupposition that thoughts are the result of the brain's activity. Any other view that seeks to contradict this will always run up against the claims of materialism. The activity of the brain, however, is the product of the activity of the spirit. To realize this it is not sufficient to look back into the inner being of man. In doing so one encounters thoughts. And these contain only a pictorial reality. This pictorial reality is the product of the physical body. In observing retrospectively one must bring to life reinforced and strengthened soul capacities. One must wrest the dreaming soul from the twilight of the dream; then it will not evaporate into fantasies, but rather lay its mask aside so as to appear as a being active spiritually in the body. One must wrest the sleeping soul from the darkness of sleep; then the soul does not lose sight of itself but faces itself as an actual spiritual entity, which in the act of willing, by means of the bodily organism, creates above and beyond this body.

Answers to Some Questions
Concerning Karma

The following question has been asked: "According to the law of reincarnation, we are required to think that the human individuality possesses its talents, capacities, and so forth, as an effect of its previous lives. Is this not contradicted by the fact that such talents and capacities, for instance moral courage, musical gifts, and so forth, are directly inherited by the children from their parents?"

Answer: If we rightly conceive of the laws of reincarnation and karma, we cannot find a contradiction in what is stated above. Only those qualities of the human being which belong to his physical and ether body can be directly passed on by heredity. The ether body is the bearer of all life phenomena (the forces of growth and reproduction). Everything connected with this can be directly passed on by heredity. What is bound to the so-called soul-body can be passed on by heredity to a much lesser degree. This constitutes a certain disposition in the sensations. Whether we possess a vivid sense of sight, a well-developed sense of hearing, and so forth, may depend upon whether our ancestors have acquired such faculties and have passed them on to us by heredity. But nobody can pass on to his offsprings what is connected with the actual spiritual being of man, that is, for instance, the acuteness and accuracy of his life of thought, the reliability of his memory, the moral sense, the acquired capacities of knowledge and art.

These are qualities which remain enclosed within his individuality and which appear in his next incarnation as capacities, talents, character, and so forth. — The environment, however, into which the reincarnating human being enters is not accidental, but it is necessarily connected with his karma. Let us assume a human being has acquired in his previous life the capacity for a morally strong character. It is his karma that this capacity should unfold in his next incarnation. This would not be possible if he did not incarnate in a body which possesses a quite definite constitution. This bodily constitution, however, must be inherited from the forebears. The incarnating individuality strives, through a power of attraction inherent in it, toward those parents who are capable of giving it the suitable body. This is caused by the fact that, already before reincarnating, this individuality connects itself with the forces of the astral world which strive toward definite physical conditions. Thus the human being is born into that family which is able to transmit to him by heredity the bodily conditions which correspond to his karmic potentialities. It then looks, if we go back to the example of moral courage, as if the latter itself had been inherited from the parents. The truth is that man, through his individual being, has searched out that family which makes the unfoldment of moral courage possible for him. In addition to this it may be possible that the individualities of the children and the parents have already been connected in previous lives and for that very reason have found one another again. The karmic laws are so complicated that we may never base a judgment upon outer appearances. Only a person to whose spiritual sense-organs the higher worlds are at least partially manifest may attempt to form such a judgment. Whoever is able to observe the soul organism and the spirit, in addition to the physical body, is in a position to discriminate between what has been passed on to the human being by his forebears and what is his own possession, acquired in previous lives. For ordinary vision these things are not clearly distinguishable, and it may easily appear as if something were merely inherited which in reality is karmicly determined. — It is a thoroughly wise expression which states that children are "given" to their parents. In respect of the spirit this is absolutely the case. And children with certain spiritual qualities are given to them for the very reason that they, the parents, are capable of giving the children the opportunity to unfold these spiritual qualities.

Question: "Does Anthroposophy attribute no significance to 'chance'? I cannot imagine that it can be predestined by the karma of each individual person when five hundred persons are killed at the same time in a theater fire."

Answer: The laws of karma are so complicated that we should not be surprised when to the human intellect some fact appears at first as being contradictory to the general validity of this law. We must realize that this intellect is schooled by our physical world, and that, in general, it is accustomed to admit only what it has learned in this world. The laws of karma, however, belong to higher worlds. Therefore, if we try to understand an event which meets the human being as being brought about by karma in the same way in which justice is applied in the purely earthly-physical life, then we must of necessity run up against contradictions. We must realize that a common experience which several people undergo in the physical world may, in the higher world, mean something completely different for each individual person among them. Naturally, the opposite may also be true: common interrelations may become effective in common earthly experiences. Only one gifted with clear vision in the higher worlds can give information about particular cases. If the karmic interrelations of five hundred people become effective in the common death of these people in a theater fire, the following instances may be possible:

First: Not a single one of the five hundred people need be karmicly linked to the other victims. The common disaster is related in the same way to the karmas of each single person as the shadow-image of fifty people on a wall is related to the worlds of thought and feeling of these persons. These people had nothing in common an hour ago; nor will they have anything in common an hour hence.

What they experienced when they met at the same place will have a special effect for each one of them. Their association is expressed in the above-mentioned common shadow-image. Whoever were to attempt to conclude from this shadow-image that a common bond united these people would be decidedly in error.

Second: It is possible that the common experience of the five hundred people has nothing whatsoever to do with their karmic past, but that, just through this common experience, something is prepared which will unite them karmicly in the future. Perhaps these five hundred people will, in future ages, carry out a common undertaking, and through the disaster have been united for the sake of higher worlds. The experienced spiritual-scientist is thoroughly acquainted with the fact that many societies, formed today, owe their origin to the circumstance of a common disaster experienced in a more distant past by the people who join together today.

Third: The case in question may actually be the effect of former common guilt of the persons concerned. There are, however, still countless other possibilities. For instance, a combination of all three possibilities described might occur.

It is not unjustifiable to speak of "chance" in the physical world. And however true it is to say: there is no "chance" if we take into consideration all the worlds, yet it would be unjustifiable to eradicate the word "chance" if we are merely speaking of the interlinking of things in the physical world. Chance in the physical world is brought about through the fact that things take place in this world within sensible space. They must, in as far as they occur within this space, also obey the laws of this space. Within this space, things may outwardly meet which have inwardly nothing to do with each other. The causes which let a brick fall from a roof, injuring me as I pass by, do not necessarily have anything to do with my karma which stems from my past. Many people commit here the error of imagining karmic relations in too simple a fashion. They presume, for instance, that if a brick has injured a person, he must have deserved this injury karmicly. But this is not necessarily so. In the life of every human being events constantly take place which have nothing at all to do with his merits or his guilt in the past. Such events find their karmic adjustment in the future. If something happens to me today without being my fault, I shall be compensated for it in the future. One thing is certain: nothing remains without karmic adjustment. However, whether an experience of the human being is the effect of his karmic past or the cause of his karmic future will have to be determined in every individual instance. And this cannot be decided by the intellect accustomed to dealing with the physical world, but solely by occult experience and observation.

Question: "Is it possible to understand, according to the law of reincarnation and karma, how a highly developed human soul can be reborn in a helpless, undeveloped child? To many a person the thought that we have to begin over and over again at the childhood stage is unbearable and illogical."

Answer: How the human being can act in the physical world depends entirely upon the physical instrumentality of his body. Higher ideas, for instance, can come to expression in this world only if there is a fully developed brain. Just as the pianist must wait until the piano builder has made a piano on which he can express his musical ideas, so does the soul have to wait with its faculties acquired in the previous life until the forces of the physical world have built up the bodily organs to the point where they can express these faculties. The nature forces have to go their way, the soul, also, has to go its way. To be sure, from the very beginning of human life a cooperation exists between soul and body forces. The soul works in the flexible and supple body of the child until it is made ready to become a bearer of the forces acquired in former life periods. For it is absolutely necessary that the reborn human being adjust himself to the new life conditions.

Were he simply to appear in a new life with all he has acquired previously, he would not fit into the surrounding world. For he has acquired his faculties and forces under quite different circumstances in completely different surroundings. Were he simply to enter the world in his former state he would be a stranger in it. The period of childhood is gone through in order to bring about harmony between the old and the new conditions. How would one of the cleverest ancient Romans appear in our present world, were he simply born into our world with his acquired powers? A power can only be employed when it is in harmony with the surrounding world. For instance, if a genius is born, the power of genius lies in the innermost being of this man which may be called the causal-body. The lower spirit-body and the body of feeling and sensation are adaptable, and in a certain sense not completely determined. These two parts of the human being are now elaborated. In this work the causal-body acts from within and the surroundings from without. With the completion of this work, these two parts may become the instruments of the acquired forces. — The thought that we have to be born as a child is, therefore, neither illogical nor unbearable. On the contrary, it would be unbearable were we born as a fully developed man into a world in which we are a stranger.

Question: "Are two successive incarnations of a human being similar to one another? Will an architect, for instance, become again an architect, a musician again a musician?"

Answer: This might be the case, but not necessarily so. Such similarities occur, but are by no means the rule. It is easy in this field to arrive at false conceptions because we form thoughts concerning the laws of reincarnation which cling too much to externalities. Someone loves the south, for instance, and therefore believes he must have been a southerner in a former incarnation. Such inclinations, however, do not reach up to the causal-body. They have a direct significance only for the one life. Whatever sends its effects over from one incarnation into another must be deeply seated in the central being of man. Let us assume, for instance, that someone is a musician in his present life. The spiritual harmonies and rhythms which express themselves in tones reach into the causal-body. The tones themselves belong to the outer physical life. They sit in the parts of the human being which come into existence and pass away. The lower ego or spirit-body, which is, at one time, the proper vehicle for tones may, in a subsequent life, be the vehicle for the perception of number and space relations. And the musician may now become a mathematician. Just through this fact the human being develops, in the course of his incarnations, into an all-comprehensive being by passing through the most manifold life activities. As has been stated, there are exceptions to this rule. And these are explicable by the great laws of the spiritual world.

Question: "What are the karmic facts in the case of a human being who is condemned to idiocy because of a defective brain?"

Answer: A case like this ought not to be dealt with by speculation and hypotheses, but only by means of spiritual-scientific experience. Therefore, the question here will be answered by quoting an example which has really occurred.

In a previous life a certain person had been doomed to an existence of mental torpor because of an undeveloped brain. During the time between his death and a new birth he was able to work over in himself all the depressing experiences of such a life, such as his having been pushed around, subjected to the unkindness of people, and he was reborn as a veritable genius of benevolence. Such a case shows clearly how wrong we can be if we refer everything in life karmicly back to the past. We cannot say in every instance: this destiny is the result of this or that guilt in the past. It is very well possible that an event has no relation whatsoever to the past but is only the cause for a karmic compensation in the future. An idiot need not have deserved his destiny through his deeds in the past. But the karmic consequence of his destiny for the future will not fail to appear. Just as a businessman's balance account is determined by the figures of his ledger, while he is free to have new receipts and expenses, so new deeds and blows of destiny may enter the life of a human being in spite of his book of life showing a definite balance at every given moment. Therefore, karma must not be conceived of as an immutable fate: it is absolutely compatible with the freedom, the will of man. Karma does not demand surrender to an unalterable fate; on the contrary, it affords us the certainty that no deed, no experience of the human being remains without effect or runs its course outside of the laws of the world. It affords us the certainty that every deed or experience is joined to just and compensating law. Moreover, if there were no karma, arbitrariness would rule in the world. As it is, I may know that every one of my actions, every one of my experiences is inserted in a lawful interrelationship. My deed is free; its effect follows definite laws. It is the free deed of a businessman when he makes a good deal; its result, however, shows up in the balance sheet of his ledger in accordance with definite laws.

How Karma Works

Sleep has often been called the younger brother of death. This simile illustrates the paths of the human spirit more exactly than a superficial observation might feel inclined to assume. For it gives us an idea of the way in which the most manifold incarnations passed through by this human spirit are interrelated. In the first chapter of this book, Reincarnation and Karma, Concepts Compelled by the Modern Scientific Point of View, it has been shown that the present natural-scientific mode of thought, if it but understands itself properly, leads to the ancient teaching of the evolution of the eternal human spirit through many lives. This knowledge is necessarily followed by the question: how are these manifold lives interrelated? In what sense is the life of a human being the effect of his former incarnations, and how does it become the cause of the later incarnations? The picture of sleep presents an image of the relation of cause and effect in this field. I arise in the morning. My continuous activity was interrupted during the night. I cannot resume this activity arbitrarily if order and connection are to govern my life. What I have done yesterday constitutes the conditions for my actions of today. I must make a connection with the result of my activities of yesterday. It is true in the fullest sense of the word that my deeds of yesterday are my destiny of today. I myself have shaped the causes to which I must add the effects. And I encounter these causes after having withdrawn from them for a short time. They belong to me, although I was separated from them for some time.

The effects of my experiences of yesterday belong to me in still another sense. I myself have been changed by them. Let us suppose that I have undertaken something in which I succeeded only partially. I have pondered on the reason for this partial failure. If I have again to carry out a similar task, I avoid the mistakes I have recognized. That is, I have acquired a new faculty. Thereby my experiences of yesterday have become the causes of my faculties of today. My past remains united with me; it lives on in my present; and it will follow me into my future. Through my past, I have created for myself the position in which I find myself at present. And the meaning of life demands that I remain united with this position. Would it not be senseless if, under normal conditions, I should not move into a house I had caused to be built for myself?

If the effects of my deeds of yesterday were not to be my destiny of today, I should not have to wake up today, but I should have to be created anew, out of the nothing. And the human spirit would have to be newly created, out of the nothing, if the results of its former lives were not to remain linked to its later lives. Indeed, the human being cannot live in any other position but the one which has been created through his previous life. He can do this no more than can certain animals, which have lost their power of sight as a result of their migration to the caves of Kentucky, live anywhere else but in these caves. They have, through their deed, through migration, created for themselves the conditions for their later existence. A being which has once been active is henceforth no longer isolated in the world; it has inserted itself into its deeds. And its future development is connected with what arises from the deeds. This connection of a being with the results of its deeds is the law of karma which rules the whole world. Activity that has become destiny is karma.

And sleep is a good picture of death for the reason that the human being, during sleep, is actually withdrawn from the field of action upon which destiny awaits him. While we sleep, the events on this field of action run their course. For a time, we have no influence upon this course. Nevertheless, we find again the effects of our actions, and we must link up with them. In reality, our personality every morning incarnates anew in our world of deeds. What was separated from us during the night, envelops us, as it were, during the day.

It is the same with the deeds of our former incarnations. Their results are embodied in the world in which we were incarnated. Yet they belong to us just as the life in the caves belongs to the animals which, through this life, have lost the power of sight. Just as these animals can only live if they find again the surroundings to which they have adapted themselves, so the human spirit is only able to live in those surroundings which, through his deeds, he has created for himself and are suited to him.

Every new morning the human body is ensouled anew, as it were. Natural science admits that this involves a process which it cannot grasp if it employs merely the laws it has gained in the physical world. Consider what the natural scientist Du Bois-Reymond says about this in his address, Die Grenze des Naturerkennens (The Limits of the Cognition of Nature): "If a brain, for some reason unconscious, as for instance in dreamless sleep, were to be viewed scientifically" — (Du Bois-Reymond says "astronomically") — "it would hold no longer any secrets, and if we were to add to this the natural-scientific knowledge of the rest of the body, there would be a complete deciphering of the entire human machine with its breathing, its heartbeat, its metabolism, its warmth, and so forth, right up to the nature of matter and force. The dreamless sleeper is comprehensible to the same degree that the world is comprehensible before consciousness appeared. But just as the world became doubly incomprehensible with the first stirring of consciousness, so the sleeper becomes incomprehensible with the first dream picture that arises in him." This cannot be otherwise. For, what the scientist describes here as the dreamless sleeper is that part of the human being which alone is subject to physical laws. The moment, however, it appears again permeated by the soul, it obeys the laws of the soul-life. During sleep, the human body obeys the physical laws: the moment the human being wakes up, the light of intelligent action flashes forth, like a spark, into purely physical existence. We speak entirely in the sense of the scientist Du Bois-Reymond when we state: the sleeping body may be investigated in all its aspects, yet we shall not be able to find the soul in it. But this soul continues the course of its rational deeds at the point where this was interrupted by sleep. — Thus the human being, also in this regard, belongs to two worlds. In one world he lives his bodily life which may be observed by means of physical laws;in the other he lives as a spiritual-rational being, and about this life we are able to learn nothing by means of physical laws. If we wish to study the bodily life, we have to hold to the physical laws of natural science; but if we wish to grasp the spiritual life, we have to acquaint ourselves with the laws of rational action, such, for instance, as logic, jurisprudence, economics, aesthetics, and so forth.

The sleeping human body, subject only to physical laws, can never accomplish anything in the realm of the laws of reason. But the human spirit carries these laws of reason into the physical world. And just as much as he has carried into it will he find again when, after an interruption, he resumes the thread of his activity.

Let us hold on to the picture of sleep. If life is not to be meaningless, the personality has to link up today with its deeds of yesterday. It could not do so did it not feel itself joined to these deeds. I should be unable to pick up today the result of my activity of yesterday, had there not remained within myself something of this activity. If I had today forgotten everything that I have experienced yesterday, I should be a new human being, unable to link up with anything. It is my memory which enables me to link up with my deeds of yesterday. — This memory binds me to the effects of my action. That which, in the real sense, belongs to my life of reason, — logic, for instance, — is today the same it was yesterday. This is applicable also to that which did not enter my field of vision yesterday, indeed, which never entered it. My memory connects my logical action of today with my logical action of yesterday. If matters depended merely upon logic, we certainly might start a new life every morning. But memory retains what binds us to our destiny.

Thus I really find myself in the morning as a threefold being. I find my body again which during my sleep has obeyed its merely physical laws. I find again my own self, my human spirit, which is today the same it was yesterday, and which is today endowed with the gift of rational action with which it was endowed yesterday. And I find — preserved by memory — everything that my yesterday, that my entire past has made of me. —

And this affords us at the same time a picture of the threefold being of man. In every new incarnation the human being finds himself in a physical organism which is subject to the laws of external nature. And in every incarnation he is the same human spirit. As such he is the Eternal within the manifold incarnations.

Body and Spirit confront one another. Between these two there must lie something just as memory lies between my deeds of yesterday and those of today. And this something is the soul. It preserves the effects of my deeds from former lives and brings it about that the spirit, in a new incarnation, appears in the form which previous earth lives have given it. In this way, body, soul, and spirit are interrelated. The spirit is eternal; birth and death rule in the body according to the laws of the physical world; both are brought together again and again by the soul as it fashions our destiny out of our deeds. (Each of the above-mentioned principles: body, soul, and spirit, in turn consists of three members. Thus the human being appears to be formed of nine members. The body consists of: (1) the actual body, (2) the life-body, (3) the sentient-body. The soul consists of: (4) the sentient-soul, (5) the intellectual-soul, (6) the consciousness-soul. The spirit consists of: (7) spirit-self, (8) life-spirit, (9) spirit-man. In the incarnated human being, 3 and 4, and 6 and 7 unite, flowing into one another. Through this fact the nine members appear to have contracted into seven members.)

In regard to the comparison of the soul with memory we are also in a position to refer to modern natural science. The scientist Ewald Hering published a treatise in 1870 which bears the title: Ueber das Gedaechtnis als eine allgemeine Funktion der organisierten Materie (Memory as a General Function of Organized Matter). Ernst Haeckel agrees with Hering's point of view. He states the following in his treatise: Ueber die Wellenzeugung der Lebensteilchen (The Wave Generation of Living Particles): "Profound reflection must bring the conviction that without the assumption of an unconscious memory of living matter the most important life functions are utterly inexplicable. The faculty of forming ideas and concepts, of thinking and consciousness, of practice and habit, of nutrition and reproduction rests upon the function of the unconscious memory, the activity of which is much more significant than that of conscious memory. Hering is right in stating that it is memory to which we owe nearly everything that we are and have." And now Haeckel tries to trace back the processes of heredity within living creatures to this unconscious memory. The fact that the daughter-being resembles the mother-being, that the former inherits the qualities of the latter, is thus supposed to be due to the unconscious memory of the living, which in the course of reproduction retains the memory of the preceding forms. — It is not a question here of investigating how much of the presentations of Hering and Haeckel are scientifically tenable; for our purposes it suffices to draw attention to the fact that the natural scientist is compelled to assume an entity which he considers similar to memory; he is compelled to do so if he goes beyond birth and death, and presumes something that endures beyond death. He quite naturally seizes upon a supersensible force in the realm where the laws of physical nature do not suffice.

We must, however, realize that we are dealing here merely with a comparison, with a picture, when we speak of memory. We must not believe that by soul we understand something that is equivalent to conscious memory. Even in ordinary life it is not always conscious memory that is active when we make use of the experiences of the past. We bear within us the fruits of these experiences even if we do not always consciously remember what we have experienced. Who can remember all the details of his learning to read and write? Moreover, who was ever conscious of all those details? Habit, for instance, is a kind of unconscious memory. — By means of this comparison with memory we merely wish to point to the soul which inserts itself between body and spirit and constitutes the mediator between the Eternal and that which, as the Physical, is inwoven into the course of birth and death.

The spirit that reincarnates thus finds within the physical world the results of its deeds as its destiny; and the soul that is bound to it, mediates the spirit's linking up with this destiny. Now we may ask: how can the spirit find the results of its deeds, since, on reincarnating, it is certainly placed in a world completely different from the one in which it existed previously? This question is based upon a very externalized conception of the web of destiny. If I transfer my residence from Europe to America, I, too, find myself in completely new surroundings. Yet my life in America is completely dependent upon my previous life in Europe. If I have been a mechanic in Europe, my life in America will take on a form quite different from the one it would take on had I been a bank clerk. In the one case I shall probably be surrounded in America by machines, in the other by banking papers. In every case my previous life determines my surroundings, it attracts, as it were, out of the whole environment those things which are related to it. This is also the case with my spirit-soul. It surrounds itself quite necessarily with what it is related to out of its previous life. This cannot constitute a contradiction of the simile of sleep and death if we realize that we are dealing only with a simile, although a most striking one. That I find in the morning the situation which I myself have created on the previous day is brought about by the direct course of events. That I find on reincarnating an environment that corresponds to the result of my deeds of the previous life is brought about through the affinity of my reborn spirit-soul with the things of this environment.

What leads me into this environment? Directly the qualities of my spirit-soul on reincarnating. But I possess these qualities merely through the fact that the deeds of my previous lives have implanted them into the spirit-soul. These deeds, therefore, are the real cause of my being born into certain circumstances. And what I do today will be one of the causes of my finding myself in a later life within certain definite circumstances. — Thus man indeed creates his destiny for himself. This remains incomprehensible only as long as one considers the separate life as such and dos not regard it as a link in the chain of successive lives.

Thus we may say that nothing can happen to the human being in life for which he has not himself created the conditions. Only through insight into the law of destiny — karma — does it become comprehensible why "the good man has often to suffer, while the evil one may experience happiness." This seeming disharmony of the one life disappears when the view is extended upon many lives. — To be sure, the law of karma must not be conceived of as being so simple that we might compare it to an ordinary judge or to civil justice. This would be the same as if we were to imagine God as an old man with a white beard. Many people fall into this error. Especially the opponents of the idea of karma proceed from such erroneous premises. They fight against the conception which they impute to the believers in karma and not against the conception held by the true knowers.

What is the relation of the human being to his physical surroundings when he enters a new incarnation? This relation is composed of two factors: first, in the time between two consecutive incarnations he has had no part in the physical world; second, he passed through a certain development during that period. It is self-evident that no influence from the physical world can affect this development, for the spirit-soul then exists outside this physical world. Everything that takes place in the spirit-soul, it can, therefore, only draw out of itself, that is to say, out of the super-physical world. During its incarnation it was interwoven with the physical world of facts; after its discarnation through death, it is deprived of the direct influence of this factual world. It has merely retained from the latter that which we have compared to memory. — This "memory remnant" consists of two parts. These parts become evident if we consider what has contributed to its formation. — The spirit has lived in the body and through the body, therefore, it entered into relation with the bodily surroundings. This relation has found its expression through the fact that, by means of the body, impulses, desires, and passions have developed and that, through them, outer actions have been performed. Because he has a corporeal existence, the human being acts under the influence of impulses, desires, and passions. And these have a significance in two directions. On the one hand, they impress themselves upon the outer actions which the human being performs. And on the other, they form his personal character. The action I perform is the result of my desire; and I myself, as a personality, am what is expressed by this desire. The action passes over into the outer world;the desire remains within my soul just as the thought remains within my memory. And just as the thought image in my memory is strengthened through every new impression of like nature, so is the desire strengthened through every new action which I perform under its influence. Thus within my soul, because of corporeal existence, there lives a certain sum of impulses, desires, and passions. The sum total of these is designated by the expression "body of desire." — This body of desire is intimately connected with physical existence, for it comes into being under the influence of the physical corporeality. The moment the spirit is no longer incarnated it cannot continue the formation of this body of desire. The spirit must free itself from this desire-body in so far as it was connected, through it, with the single physical life. The physical life is followed by another in which this liberation occurs. We may ask: Does not death signify the destruction also of this body of desire? The answer is: No; for to the degree in which, at every moment of physical life, desire surpasses satisfaction, desire persists even when the possibility of satisfaction has ceased. Only a human being who does not desire anything of the physical world has no surplus of desire over satisfaction. Only a man of no desires dies without retaining in his spirit a certain amount of desire. And this amount must gradually diminish and fade away after death. The state of this fading away is called "the sojourn in the region of desire." It can easily be seen that the more the human being has felt bound to the sense life, the longer must this state persist.

The second part of the "memory remnant" is formed in a different way. Just as desire draws the spirit toward the past life, so this second part directs it toward the future. The spirit, through its activity in the body, has become acquainted with the world to which this body belongs. Each new exertion, each new experience enhances this acquaintance. As a rule the human being does a thing better the second time than he does it the first. Experience impresses itself upon the spirit, enhancing its capacities. Thus our experience acts upon our future, and if we have no longer the opportunity to have experiences, then the result of these experiences remains as memory remnant. — But no experience could affect us if we did not have the capacity to make use of it. The way in which we are able to absorb the experience, the use we are able to make of it, determines its significance for our future. For Goethe, an experience had a significance quite different from the significance it had for his valet; and it produced results for Goethe quite different from those it produced for his valet. What faculties we acquire through an experience depends, therefore, upon the spiritual work we perform in connection with the experience. — I always have within me, at any given moment of my life, a sum total of the results of my experience. And this sum total forms the potential of capacities which may appear in due course. — Such a sum total of experiences the human spirit possesses when it discarnates. This the human spirit takes with it into supersensible life. Now, when it is no longer bound to physical existence by bodily ties and when it has divested itself also of the desires which chain it to this physical existence, then the fruit of its experience has remained with the spirit. And this fruit is completely freed from the direct influence of the past life. The spirit can now devote itself entirely to what it is capable of fashioning out of this fruit for the future. Thus the spirit, after having left the region of desire, is in a state in which its experiences of former lives transform themselves into potentials — that is to say, talents, capacities — for the future. The life of the spirit in this state is designated as the sojourn in the "region of bliss." ("Bliss" may, indeed, designate a state in which all worry about the past is relegated to oblivion and which permits the heart to beat solely for the concerns of the future.) It is self-evident that the greater the potentiality exists at death for the acquirement of new capacities, the longer will this state in general last.

Naturally, it cannot be a question here of developing the complete scope of knowledge relating to the human spirit. We merely intend to show how the law of karma operates in physical life. For this purpose it is sufficient to know what the spirit takes out of this physical life into supersensible states and what it brings back again for a new incarnation. It brings with it the results of the experiences undergone in previous lives, transformed into the capacities of its being. — In order to realize the far-reaching character of this fact we need only elucidate the process by a single example. The philosopher, Kant, says: "Two things fill the soul with ever increasing wonder: the starry heavens above me and the moral law within me." Every thinking human being must admit that the starry heavens have not sprung out of nothingness but have come gradually into existence. And it is Kant himself who in 1755, in a basic treatise, tried to explain the gradual formation of a cosmos. Likewise, however, we must not accept the fact of moral law without an explanation. This moral law, too, has not sprung from nothingness. In the first incarnations through which man passed the moral law did not speak in him in the way it spoke in Kant. Primitive man acts in accordance with his desires. And he carries the experiences which he has undergone through such action into the supersensible states. Here they become higher faculties. And in a subsequent incarnation, mere desire no longer acts in him, but it is now guided by the effect of the previous experiences. And many incarnations are needed before the human being, originally completely given over to desires, confronts the surrounding world with the purified moral law which Kant designates as something demanding the same admiration as is demanded by the starry heavens.

The surrounding world into which the human being is born through a new incarnation confronts him with the results of his deeds, as his destiny. He himself enters this surrounding world with the capacities which he has fashioned for himself in the supersensible state out of his former experiences. Therefore his experiences in the physical world will, in general, be at a higher level the more often he has incarnated, or the greater his efforts were during his previous incarnations. Thus his pilgrimage through the incarnations will be an upward development. The treasure which his experiences accumulate in his spirit will become richer and richer. And he thereby confronts his surrounding world, his destiny, with greater and greater maturity. This makes him increasingly the master of his destiny. For what he gains through his experiences is the fact that he learns to grasp the laws of the world in which these experiences occur. At first the spirit does not find its way about in the surrounding world. It gropes in the dark. But with every new incarnation the world grows brighter. The spirit acquires a knowledge of the laws of its surrounding world; in other words, it accomplishes ever more consciously what it previously did in dullness of mind. The compulsion of the surrounding world decreases; the spirit becomes increasingly self-determinative. The spirit, however, which is self-determinative, is the free spirit. Action in the full clear light of consciousness is free action. (I have tried to present the nature of the free human spirit in my book, Philosophie der Freiheit, (Philosophy of Freedom — Spiritual Activity.) The full freedom of the human spirit is the ideal of its development. We cannot ask the question: is man free or unfree? The philosophers who put the question of freedom in this fashion can never acquire a clear thought about it. For the human being in his present state is neither free nor unfree; but he is on the way to freedom. He is partially free, partially unfree. He is free to the degree he has acquired knowledge and consciousness of world relations. — The fact that our destiny, our karma, meets us in the form of absolute necessity is no obstacle to our freedom. For when we act we approach this destiny with the measure of independence we have achieved. It is not destiny that acts, but it is we who act in accordance with the laws of this destiny.

If I light a match, fire arises according to necessary laws;but it was I who put these necessary laws into effect. Likewise, I can perform an action only in the sense of the necessary laws of my karma, but it is I who puts these necessary laws into effect. And new karma is created through the deed proceeding from me, just as the fire, according to necessary laws of nature, continues to be effective after I have kindled it.

This also throws light upon another doubt which may assail a person in regard to the effectiveness of the law of karma. Somebody might say: "If karma is an unalterable law, then it is wrong to help a person. For what befalls him is the consequence of his karma, and it is absolutely necessary that it should befall him." Certainly, I cannot eliminate the effects of the destiny which a human spirit has created for himself in former incarnations. But the matter of importance here is how he finds his way into this destiny, and what new destiny he may create for himself under the influence of the old one. If I help him, I may bring about the possibility of his giving his destiny a favorable turn through his deeds; if I refrain from helping him, the opposite may perhaps occur. Naturally, everything will depend upon whether my help is a wise or unwise one. [The fact that I am present to help may be a part of both his Karma and mine, or my presence and deed may be a free act.]

His advance through ever new incarnations signifies a higher development of the human spirit. This higher development comes to expression in the fact that the world in which the incarnations of the spirit take place is comprehended in increasing measure by this spirit. This world, however, comprises the incarnations themselves. In regard to the latter, too, the spirit gradually passes from a state of unconsciousness to one of consciousness. On the path of evolution there lies the point from which the human being is able to look back upon his successive incarnations with full consciousness. — This is a thought at which it is easy to mock; and it is easy to criticise it negatively. But whoever does this has no idea of the nature of such truths. And derision as well as criticism place themselves like a dragon in front of the portal of the sanctuary within which we may attain knowledge of these truths. For it is self-evident that truths, the realization of which lies for the human being in the future, cannot be found as facts in the present. There is only one way of convincing oneself of their reality: namely, to make every effort possible to attain this reality.

Reincarnation and Karma

Francesco Redi, the Italian natural scientist, was considered a dangerous heretic by the leading scholars of the seventeenth century because he maintained that even the lowest animals originate through reproduction. He narrowly escaped the martyr-destiny of Giordano Bruno or Galileo. For the orthodox scientist of that time believed that worms, insects, and even fish could originate out of lifeless mud. Redi maintained that which today is generally acknowledged: that all living creatures have descended from living creatures. He committed the sin of recognizing a truth two centuries before science found its "irrefutable" proof. Since Pasteur has carried out his investigations, there can be no longer any doubt about the fact that those cases were merely illusion in which people believed that living creatures could come into existence out of lifeless substances through "spontaneous generation". The life germs entering such lifeless substances escaped observation. With proper means, Pasteur prevented the entrance of such germs into substances in which, ordinarily, small living creatures come into existence, and not even a trace of the living was formed. Thus it was demonstrated that the living springs only from the life germ. Redi had been completely correct.

Today, the spiritual scientist, the anthroposophist, finds himself in a situation similar to that of the Italian scientist.

On the basis of his knowledge, he must maintain in regard to the soul what Redi maintained in regard to life. He must maintain that the soul nature can spring only from the soul. And if science advances in the direction it has taken since the seventeenth century, then the time will come when, out of its own nature, science will uphold this view. For — and this must be emphasized again and again — the attitude of thought which underlies the anthroposophical conception of today is no other than the one underlying the scientific dictum that insects, worms and fish originate from life germs and not from mud. The anthroposophical conception maintains the postulate: "Every soul originates out of the soul nature," in the same sense and with the same significance in which the scientist maintains: "Everything living originates out of the living."

Today's customs differ from those of the seventeenth century. The attitudes of mind underlying the customs have not changed particularly. To be sure, in the seventeenth century, heretical views were persecuted by means no longer considered human today. Today, spiritual scientists, anthroposophists, will not be threatened with burning at the stake: one is satisfied in rendering them harmless by branding them as visionaries and unclear thinkers. Current science designates them fools. The former execution through the inquisition has been replaced by modern, journalistic execution. The anthroposophists, however, remain steadfast; they console themselves in the consciousness that the time will come when some Virchow will say: "There was a time — fortunately it is now superceded — when people believed that the soul comes into existence by itself if certain complicated chemical and physical processes take place within the skull. Today, for every serious researcher this infantile conception must give way to the statement that everything pertaining to the soul springs from the soul."

One must by no means believe that spiritual science intends to prove its truths through natural science. It must be emphasized, however, that spiritual science has an attitude of mind similar to that of true natural science. The anthroposophist accomplishes in the sphere of the soul life what the nature researcher strives to attain in the domains perceptible to the eyes and audible to the ears. There can be no contradiction between genuine natural science and spiritual science. The anthroposophist demonstrates that the laws which he postulates for the soul life are correspondingly valid also for the external phenomena of nature. He does so because he knows that the human sense of knowledge can only feel satisfied if it perceives that harmony, and not discord, rules among the various phenomenal realms of existence. Today most human beings who strive at all for knowledge and truth are acquainted with certain natural-scientific conceptions. Such truths can be acquired, so to speak, with the greatest ease. The science sections of newspapers disclose to the educated and uneducated alike the laws according to which the perfect animals develop out of the imperfect, they disclose the profound relationship between man and the anthropoid ape, and smart magazine writers never tire of inculcating their readers with their conception of "spirit" in the age of the "great Darwin." They very seldom add that in Darwin's main treatise there is to be found the statement: "I hold that all organic beings that have ever lived on this earth have descended from one primordial form into which the creator breathed the breath of life." (Origin of Species, Vol. II, chapter XV.) — In our age it is most important to show again and again that Anthroposophy does not treat the conceptions of "the breathing in of life" and the soul as lightly as Darwin and many a Darwinian, but that its truths do not contradict the findings of true nature research. Anthroposophy does not wish to penetrate into the mysteries of spirit-life upon the crutches of natural science of the present age, but it merely wishes to say: "Recognize the laws of the spiritual life and you will find these sublime laws verified in corresponding form if you descend to the domain in which you can see with eyes and hear with ears." Natural science of the present age does not contradict spiritual science; on the contrary, it is itself elemental spiritual science. Only because Haeckel applied to the evolution of animal life the laws which the psychologists since ancient days have applied to the soul, did he achieve such beautiful results in the field of animal life. If he himself is not of this conviction, it does not matter; he simply does not know the laws of the soul, nor is he acquainted with the research which can be carried on in the field of the soul. The significance of his findings in his field is thereby not diminished. Great men have the faults of their virtues. Our task is to show that Haeckel in the field where he is competent is nothing but an anthroposophist. — By linking up with the natural-scientific knowledge of the present age, still another aid offers itself to the spiritual scientist. The objects of outer nature are, so to speak, to be grasped by our hands. It is, therefore, easy to expound their laws. It is not difficult to realize that plants change when they are transplanted from one region into another. Nor is it hard to visualize that a certain animal species loses its power of eyesight when it lives for a certain length of time in dark caves. By demonstrating the laws which are active in such processes, it is easy to lead over to the less manifest, less comprehensible laws which we encounter in the field of the soul life. — if the anthroposophist employs natural science as an aid, he merely does so in order to illustrate what he is saying. He has to show that anthroposophic truths, with respective modifications, are to be found in the domain of natural science, and that natural science cannot be anything but elemental spiritual science; and he has to employ natural-scientific concepts in order to lead over to his concepts of a higher nature.

The objection might be raised here that any inclination toward present-day natural-scientific conceptions might put spiritual science into an awkward position for the simple reason that these conceptions themselves rest upon a completely uncertain foundation. It is true: There are scientists who consider certain fundamental principles of Darwinism as irrefutable, and there are others who even today speak of a "crisis in Darwinism." The former consider the concepts of "the omnipotence of natural selection" and "the struggle for survival" to be a comprehensive explanation of the evolution of living creatures; the latter consider this "struggle for survival" to be one of the infantile complaints of modern science and speak of the "impotence of natural selection." — If matters depended upon these specific, problematic questions, it were certainly better for the anthroposophist to pay no attention to them and to wait for a more propitious moment when an agreement with natural science might be achieved. But matters do not depend upon these problems. What is important, however, is a certain attitude, a mode of thought within natural-scientific research in our age, certain definite great guiding lines, which are adhered to everywhere, even though the thoughts of various researchers and thinkers concerning specific questions diverge widely. It is true: Ernst Haeckel's and Virchow's conceptions of the "genesis of man" diverge greatly. But the anthroposophical thinker might consider himself fortunate if leading personalities were to think as clearly about certain comprehensive viewpoints concerning the soul life as these opponents think about that which they consider absolutely certain in spite of their disagreement.

Neither the adherents of Haeckel nor those of Virchow search today for the origin of worms in lifeless mud; neither the former nor the latter doubt that "all living creatures originate from the living," in the sense designated above. — In psychology we have not yet advanced so far. Clarity is completely lacking concerning a view point which might be compared with such scientific fundamental convictions. Whoever wishes to explain the shape and mode of life of a worm knows that he has to consider its ovum and ancestors; he knows the direction in which his research must proceed, although the viewpoints may differ concerning other aspects of the question, or even the statement may be made that the time is not yet ripe when definite thoughts may be formed concerning this or that point. — Where, in psychology, is there to be found a similar clarity? The fact that the soul has spiritual qualities, just as the worm has physical ones, does not cause the researcher to approach — as he should — the one fact with the same attitude of mind as he approaches the other. To be sure, our age is under the influence of thought habits which prevent innumerable people, occupied with these problems, from entering at all properly upon such demands. — True, it will be admitted that the soul qualities of a human being must originate somewhere just as do the physical ones. The reasons are being sought for the fact that the souls of a group of children are so different from one another, although the children all grew up and were educated under identical circumstances; that even twins differ from one another in essential characteristics, although they always lived at the same place and under the care of the same nurse. The case of the Siamese Twins is quoted, whose final years of life were, allegedly, spent in great discomfort in consequence of their opposite sympathies concerning the North-American Civil War. We do not deny that careful thought and observation have been directed upon such phenomena and that remarkable studies have been made and results achieved. But the fact remains that these efforts concerning the soul life are on a par with the efforts of a scientist who maintains that living creatures originate from lifeless mud. In order to explain the lower psychic qualities, we are undoubtedly justified in pointing to the physical forebears and in speaking of heredity, just as we do in the case of bodily traits. But we deliberately close our eyes to the most important aspect of the matter if we proceed in the same direction with respect to the higher soul qualities, the actually spiritual in man. We have become accustomed to regard these higher soul qualities as a mere enhancement, as a higher degree of the lower ones. And we therefore believe that an explanation might satisfy us which follows the same lines as the explanation offered for the soul qualities of the animal.

It is not to be denied that the observation of certain soul functions of higher animals may easily lead to this mistaken conception. We only need draw attention to the fact that dogs show remarkable proof of a faithful memory; that horses, noticing the loss of a horse shoe, walk of their own accord to the blacksmith who has shod them before; that animals which are shut up in a room, can by themselves open the door; we might quote many more of these astonishing facts. Certainly, the anthroposophist, too, will not refrain from admitting the possibility of continued enhancement of animal faculties. But must we, for that reason, obliterate the difference between the lower soul traits which man shares with the animal, and the higher spiritual qualities which man alone possesses? This can only be done by someone who is completely blinded by the dogmatic prejudice of a "science" which wishes to stick fast to the facts of the coarse, physical senses. Simply consider what is established by indisputable observation, namely, that animals, even the highest-developed ones, cannot count and therefore are unable to learn arithmetic. The fact that the human being is distinguished from the animal by his ability to count was considered a significant insight even in ancient schools of wisdom. — Counting is the simplest, the most insignificant of the higher soul faculties. For that very reason we cite it here, because it indicates the point where the animal-soul element passes over into the spirit-soul element, into the higher human element. Of course, it is very easy to raise objections here also. First, one might say that we have not yet reached the end of the world and that we might one day succeed in what we have not yet been able to do, namely, to teach counting to intelligent animals. And secondly, one might point to the fact that the brain has reached a higher stage of perfection in man than in the animal, and that herein lies the reason for the human brain's higher degrees of soul activity. We may fully concur with the persons who raise these objections. Yet we are in the same position concerning those people who, in regard to the fact that all living creatures spring from the living, maintain over and over again that the worm is governed by the same chemical and physical laws that govern the mud, only in a more complicated manner. Nothing can be done for a person who wishes to disclose the secrets of nature by means of trivialities and what is self-evident. There are people who consider the degree of insight they have attained to be the most penetrating imaginable and to whom, therefore, it never occurs that there might be someone else able to raise the same trivial objections, did he not see their worthlessness. — No objection can be raised against the conception that all higher processes in the world are merely higher degrees of the lower processes to be found in the mud. But just as it is impossible for a person of insight today to maintain that the worm originates from the mud, so is it impossible for a clear thinker to force the spirit-soul nature into the same concept-pattern as that of the animal-soul nature. Just as we remain within the sphere of the living in order to explain the descent of the living, so must we remain in the sphere of the soul-spirit nature in order to understand the soul-spirit nature's origin.

There are facts which may be observed everywhere and which are bypassed by countless people without their paying any attention to them. Then someone appears who, by becoming aware of one of these facts, discovers a fundamental and far-reaching truth. It is reported that Galileo discovered the important law of the pendulum by observing a swinging chandelier in the cathedral of Pisa. Up to that time, innumerable people had seen swinging church lamps without making this decisive observation. What matters in such cases is that we connect the right thoughts with the things we see. Now, there exists a fact which is quite generally accessible and which, when viewed in an appropriate manner, throws a clear light upon the character of the soul-spirit nature. This is the simple truth that every human being has a biography, but not the animal. To be sure, certain people will say: Is it not possible to write the life story of a cat or a dog? The answer must be: Undoubtedly it is; but there is also a kind of school exercise which requires the children to describe the fate of a pen. The important point here is that the biography has the same fundamental significance in regard to the individual human being as the description of the species has in regard to the animal. Just as I am interested in the description of the lion-species in regard to the lion, so am I interested in the biography in regard to the individual human being. By describing their human species, I have not exhaustively described Schiller, Goethe, and Heine, as would be the case regarding the single lion once I have recognized it as a member of its species. The individual human being is more than a member of his species. Like the animal, he shares the characteristics of his species with his physical forebears. But where these characteristics terminate, there begins for the human being his unique position, his task in the world. And where this begins, all possibility of an explanation according to the pattern of animal-physical heredity ceases. I may trace back Schiller's nose and hair, perhaps even certain characteristics of his temperament, to corresponding traits in his ancestors, but never his genius. And naturally, this does not only hold good for Schiller. This also holds good for Mrs. Miller of Gotham. In her case also, if we are but willing, we shall find soul-spiritual characteristics which cannot be traced back to her parents and grand-parents in the same way we can trace the shape of her nose or the blue color of her eyes. It is true, Goethe has said that he had received from his father his figure and his serious conduct of life, and from his little mother his joyous nature and power of fantasy, and that, as a consequence, nothing original was to be found in the whole man. But in spite of this, nobody will try to trace back Goethe's gifts to father and mother — and be satisfied with it — in the same sense in which we trace back the form and manner of life of the lion to his forebears. — This is the direction in which psychology must proceed if it wishes to parallel the natural-scientific postulate that "all living creatures originate from the living" with the corresponding postulate that "everything of the nature of the soul is to be explained by the soul-nature." We intend to follow up this direction and show how the laws of reincarnation and karma, seen from this point of view, are a natural-scientific necessity. It seems most peculiar that so many people pass by the question of the origin of the soul-nature simply because they fear that they might find themselves caught in an uncertain field of knowledge. They will be shown what the great scientist Carl Gegenbaur has said about Darwinism. Even if the direct assertions of Darwin may not be entirely correct, yet they have led to discoveries which without them would not have been made. In a convincing manner Darwin has pointed to the evolution of one form of life out of another one, and this has stimulated the research into the relationships of such forms. Even those who contest the errors of Darwinism ought to realize that this same Darwinism has brought clarity and certainty to the research into animal and plant evolution, thus throwing light into dark reaches of the working of nature. Its errors will be overcome by itself. If it did not exist, we should not have its beneficial consequences. In regard to the spiritual life, the person who fears uncertainty concerning the anthroposophical conception ought to concede to it the same possibility; even though anthroposophical teachings were not completely correct, yet they would, out of their very nature, lead to the light concerning the riddles of the soul. To them, too, we shall owe clarity and certainty. And since they are concerned with our spiritual destiny, our human destination, our highest tasks, the bringing about of this clarity and certainty ought to be the most significant concern of our life. In this sphere, striving for knowledge is at the same time a moral necessity, an absolute moral duty.

David Friedrich Strauss endeavored to furnish a kind of Bible for the "enlightened" human being in his book, Der alte und neue Glaube (Faith — Ancient and Modern). "Modern faith" is to be based on the revelations of natural science, and not on the revelations of "ancient faith" which, in the opinion of this apostle of enlightenment, have been superceded. This new Bible has been written under the impression of Darwinism by a personality who says to himself: Whoever, like myself, counts himself among the enlightened, has ceased, long before Darwin, to believe in "supernatural revelation" and its miracles. He has made it clear to himself that in nature there hold sway necessary, immutable laws, and whatever miracles are reported in the Bible would be disturbances, interruptions of these laws; and there cannot be such disturbances and interruptions. We know from the laws of nature that the dead cannot be reawakened to life: therefore, Jesus cannot have reawakened Lazarus. — However, — so this enlightened person continues — there was a gap in our explanation of nature. We were able to understand how the phenomena of the lifeless may be explained through immutable laws of nature; but we were unable to form a natural conception about the origin of the manifold species of plants and animals and of the human being himself. To be sure, we believed that in their case also we are concerned merely with necessary laws of nature; but we did not know their nature nor their mode of action. Try as we might, we were unable to raise reasonable objection to the statement of Carl von Linné, the great nature-researcher of the eighteenth century, that there exist as many "species in the animal and plant kingdom as were originally created in principle." Were we not confronted here with as many miracles of creation as with species of plants and animals? Of what use was our conviction that God was unable to raise Lazarus through a supernatural interference with the natural order, through a miracle, when we had to assume the existence of such supernatural deeds in countless numbers. Then Darwin appeared and showed us that, through immutable laws of nature (natural selection and struggle for life), the plant and animal species come into existence just as do the lifeless phenomena. Our gap in the explanation of nature was filled.

Out of the mood which this conviction engendered in him, David Friedrich Strauss wrote down the following statement of his "ancient and modern belief": "We philosophers and critical theologians spoke to no purpose in denying the existence of miracles; our authoritative decree faded away without effect because we were unable to prove their dispensability and give evidence of a nature force which could replace them in the fields where up to now they were deemed most indispensable. Darwin has given proof of this nature force, this nature process, he has opened the door through which a fortunate posterity will cast the miracle into oblivion. Everybody who knows what is connected with the concept 'miracle' will praise him as one of the greatest benefactors of the human race."

These words express the mood of the victor. And all those who feel like Strauss may disclose the following view of the "modern faith": Once upon a time, lifeless particles of matter have conglomerated through their inherent forces in such a way as to produce living matter. This living matter developed, according to necessary laws, into the simplest, most imperfect living creatures. These, according to similarly necessary laws, transformed themselves further into the worm, the fish, the snake, the marsupial, and finally into the ape. And since Huxley, the great English nature researcher, has demonstrated that human beings are more similar in their structure to the most highly developed apes than the latter are to the lower apes, what then stands in the way of the assumption that the human being himself has, according to the same natural laws, developed from the higher apes? And further, do we not find what we call higher human spiritual activity, what we call morals, in an imperfect condition already with the animal. May we doubt the fact that the animals — as their structure became more perfect, as it developed into the human form, merely on the basis of physical laws — likewise developed the indications of intellect and morals to be found in them to the human stage?

All this seems to be perfectly correct. Although everybody must admit that our knowledge of nature will not for a long time to come be in the position to conceive of how what has been described above takes place in detail, yet we shall discover more and more facts and laws; and thus the "modern faith" will gain more and firmer supports.

Now it is a fact that the research and study of recent years have not furnished such solid supports for this belief; on the contrary, they have contributed greatly to discredit it. Yet it holds sway in ever extending circles and is a great obstacle to every other conviction.

There is no doubt that if David Friedrich Strauss and those of like mind are right, then all talk of higher spiritual laws of existence is an absurdity; the "modern faith" would have to be based solely on the foundations which these personalities assert are the result of the knowledge of nature.

Yet, whoever with unprejudiced mind follows up the statements of these adherents of the "modern faith" is confronted by a peculiar fact. And this fact presses upon us most irresistibly if we look at the thoughts of those people who have preserved some degree of impartiality in the face of the self-assured assertions of these orthodox pioneers of progress.

For there are hidden corners in the creed of these modern believers. And if we uncover what exists in these corners, then the true findings of modern natural science shine forth in full brilliance, but the opinions of the modern believers concerning the human being begin to fade away.

Let us throw light into a few of these corners. At the outset, let us keep to that personality who is the most significant and the most venerable of these modern believers. On page 804 of the ninth edition of Haeckel's Natuerliche Schoepfungsgeschichte (Natural Genesis) we read: "The final result of a comparison of animals and man shows that between the most highly developed animal souls and the lowest human souls there exists only a small quantitative, but no qualitative difference; this difference is much smaller than the difference between the lowest and the highest human souls, or the difference between the highest and the lowest animal souls." Now, what is the modern believer's attitude toward such a fact? He announces: we must explain the difference between the lower and the higher animal souls as a consequence of necessary and immutable laws. And we study these laws. We ask ourselves: how did it come about that out of animals with a lower soul have developed those with a higher soul? We look in nature for conditions through which the lower may develop into the higher. We then find, for example, that animals which have migrated to the caves of Kentucky become blind there. It becomes clear to us that through the sojourn in the darkness the eyes have lost their function. In these eyes the physical and chemical processes no longer take place which were carried out during the act of seeing. The stream of nourishment which has formerly been used for this activity is now diverted to other organs. The animals change their shape. In this way, new animal species can arise out of existing ones if only the transformation which nature causes in these species is sufficiently great and manifold. — What actually takes place here? Nature brings about changes in certain beings; and these changes later also appear in their descendants. We say: they are transmitted by heredity. Thus the coming into existence of new animal and plant species is explained.

The modern believers now continue happily in the direction of their explanation. The difference between the lowest human souls and the highest animal souls is not particularly great. Therefore, certain life conditions in which the higher animal souls have been placed have brought about changes by means of which they became lower human souls. The miracle of the evolution of the human soul has been cast out of the temple of the "modern faith" into oblivion, to use an expression of Strauss', and man has been classified among the animals according to "eternal, necessary" laws. Satisfied, the modern believer retires into peaceful slumber; he does not wish to go further.

Honest thinking must disturb his slumber. For this honest thinking must keep alive around his couch the spirits which he himself has evoked. Let us consider more closely the above statement of Haeckel: "the difference (between higher animals and men) is much smaller than the difference between the lowest and the highest human souls." If the modern believer admits this, may he then indulge in peaceful slumber as soon as he — according to his opinion — has explained the evolution of the lower men out of the highest animals?

No, he must not do this, and if he does so nevertheless, then he denies the whole basis upon which he has founded his conviction. What would a modern believer reply to another who were to say: I have demonstrated how fish have originated from lower living creatures. This suffices. I have shown that everything evolves — therefore the species higher than the fish will doubtless have developed like the fish. There is no doubt that the modern believer would reply: Your general thought of evolution is useless; you must be able to show how the mammals originate; for there is a greater difference between mammals and fish than between fish and those animals on a stage directly below them. — And what would have to be the consequence of the modern believer's real faithfulness to his creed? He would have to say: the difference between the higher and lower human souls is greater than the difference between these lower souls and the animal souls on the stage directly below them; therefore I must admit that there are causes in the universe which effect changes in the lower human soul, transforming it in the same way as do the causes, demonstrated by me, which lead the lower animal form into the higher one. If I do not admit this, the species of human souls remain for me a miracle in regard to their origin, just as the various animal species remain a miracle to the one who does not believe in the transformation of living creatures through laws of nature.

And this is absolutely correct: the modern believers, who deem themselves so greatly enlightened because they believe they have "cast out" the miracle in the domain of the living, are believers in miracles, nay, even worshipers of the miracle in the domain of the soul life. And only the following fact differentiates them from the believers in miracles, so greatly despised by them: these latter honestly avow their belief; the modern believers, however, have not the slightest inkling of the fact that they themselves have fallen prey to the darkest superstition.

And now let us illumine another corner of the "modern belief." In his Anthropology, Dr. Paul Topinard has beautifully compiled the findings of the modern theory of the origin of man. At the end of his book he briefly recapitulates the evolution of the higher animal forms in the various epochs of the earth according to Haeckel: "At the beginning of the earth period designated by geologists the Laurentian period, the first nuclei of albumin were formed by a chance meeting of certain elements, i.e. carbon, oxygen, hydrogen, and nitrogen, under conditions probably only prevailing at that epoch. From them, through spontaneous generation, monads developed (the smallest, imperfect living creatures). These split and multiplied, rearranged themselves into organs, and finally, after a series of transformations which Haeckel estimates as nine, they bestowed life upon certain vertebrae such as the amphioxus lanceolatus." We may skip the description of the further animal species in the same direction and add here at once Topinard's concluding sentences: "In the twentieth earth epoch, we find the anthropoid ape approximately during the whole Miocene period; in the twenty-first, the man-ape which does not yet possess speech and a corresponding brain. In the twenty-second period, Man finally appears as we know him, at least in his less perfect forms." And now, after having cited what is to be understood as the "natural-scientific basis of the modern belief," Topinard, in a few words, makes a significant confession. He says: "Here the classification comes to an abrupt halt. Haeckel forgets the twenty-third degree in which the brilliant Lamarck and Newton appear."

A corner in the creed of the modern believer is thereby exposed in which he points with the utmost clarity to facts, concerning which he denies his creed. He is unwilling to rise into the human soul sphere with the concepts with which he tried to find his way in the other spheres of nature. — Were he to do this, were he, with his attitude of mind acquired through the observation of external nature, to enter upon the sphere which Topinard calls the twenty-third degree, then he would have to say to himself: just as I derive the higher animal species from the lower through evolution, so do I derive the higher soul nature from the lower through evolution. I cannot understand Newton's soul if I do not conceive of it as having sprung from a preceding soul being. And this soul being can never be looked for in the physical ancestors. Were I to look for it there, I would turn upside down the whole method of nature research. How could it ever occur to a scientist to show the evolution of one animal species out of another if the latter, in regard to its physical makeup, were as dissimilar to the former as Newton, in regard to his soul, is to his forebears: One conceives of one animal species having proceeded from a similar one which is merely one degree lower than itself.

Therefore, Newton's soul must have sprung from a soul similar to it, but only one degree lower, psychically. Newton's soul nature is comprised in his biography. I recognize Newton by his biography just as I recognize a lion by the description of its species. And I comprehend the species "lion" if I imagine that it has sprung from a species on a correspondingly lower stage. Thus I comprehend what is comprised in Newton's biography if I conceive of it as having developed from the biography of a soul which resembles it, is related to it as soul. From this follows that Newton's soul existed already in another form, just as the species "lion" existed previously in a different form.

For clear thought, there is no escape from this conception. Only because the modern believers do not have the courage to think their thoughts through to the end do they not arrive at this final conclusion. Through it, however, the reappearance of the being who is comprised in the biography is secured. — Either we must abandon the whole natural-scientific theory of evolution, or we must admit that it must be extended to include the evolution of the soul. There are only two alternatives: either, every soul is created by a miracle, just as the animal species would have to be created by miracles if they have not developed one out of the other, or, the soul has developed and has previously existed in another form, just as the animal species has existed in another form.

A few modern thinkers who have preserved some clarity and courage for logical thinking are a living proof of the above conclusion. They are just as unable to familiarize themselves with the thought of soul evolution, so strange to our age, as are the modern believers characterized above. But they at least possess the courage to confess the only other possible view, namely: the miracle of the creation of the soul. Thus, in the book on psychology by Professor Johannes Rehmke, one of the best thinkers of our time, we may read the following: "The idea of creation ... appears to us ... to be the only one suited to render comprehensible the mystery of the origin of the soul." Rehmke goes so far as to acknowledge the existence of a conscious Universal-Being who, "as the only condition for the origin of the soul, would have to be called the creator of the soul." Thus speaks a thinker who is unwilling to indulge in gentle spiritual slumber after having grasped the physical life processes, yet who is lacking the capacity of acknowledging the idea that each individual soul has evolved out of its previous form of existence. Rehmke has the courage to accept the miracle, since he is unable to have the courage to acknowledge the anthroposophical view of the reappearance of the soul, of reincarnation. Thinkers in whom the natural-scientific striving begins to be developed logically must of necessity arrive at this view. Thus, in the book, Neuchristentum und reale Religion (Neo-Christianity and Real Religion), by Julius Baumann, professor of philosophy at the University of Goettingen, we find the following (twenty-second) paragraph among the thirty-nine paragraphs of a Sketch of a Summary of Real-Scientific

Religion: "Just as in inorganic nature the physical-chemical elements and forces do not disappear but only change their combinations, so is this also to be assumed, according to the real scientific method, in respect of the organic and organic-spiritual forces. The Human soul as formal unity, as connecting Ego, returns in new human bodies and is thus enabled to pass through all the stages of human evolution."

Whoever possesses the full courage for the natural-scientific avowal of faith of the present age must arrive at this conception. This, however, must not be misunderstood;we do not maintain that the more prominent thinkers among the modern believers are cowardly persons, in the ordinary sense of the word. It needed courage, indescribable courage to carry to victory the natural-scientific view in face of the resisting forces of the nineteenth century. But this courage must be distinguished from the higher one in regard to logical thinking. Yet just those nature researchers of the present age who desire to erect a world conception out of the findings of their domain are lacking such logical thinking. For, is it not a disgrace if we have to hear a sentence like the following, which was pronounced by the Breslau chemist Albert Ladenburg, in a lecture at a recent (1903) Conference of scientists: "Do we know anything about a substratum of the soul? I have no such knowledge." After having made this confession, this same man continues: "What is your opinion concerning immortality? I believe that in regard to this question, more than in regard to any other, the wish is father to the thought, for I do not know a single scientifically proven fact which might serve as the basis for the belief in immortality." What would the learned gentleman say if we were confronted by a speaker who said: "I know nothing about chemical facts. I therefore deny the chemical laws, for I know not a single scientifically proven fact which might serve as the basis for these laws." Certainly, the professor would reply: "What do we care about your ignorance of chemistry? First study chemistry, then do your talking!" Professor Ladenburg does not know anything about a substratum of the soul; he, therefore, should not bother the world with the findings of his ignorance.

Just as the nature researcher, in order to understand certain animal forms, studies the animal forms out of which these former have evolved, so the psychologist, rooted in natural science, must, in order to understand a certain soul form, study the soul form out of which the former has evolved. The skull form of higher animals is explained by scientists as having arisen out of the transformation of the lower animal skull. Therefore, everything belonging to a soul's biography ought to be explained by them through the biography of the soul out of which this soul concerned has evolved. The later conditions are the effects of former ones. That is to say, the later physical conditions are the effects of former physical conditions; likewise, the later soul conditions are the effects of former soul conditions. This is the content of the Law of Karma which says: all my talents and deeds in my present life do not exist separately as a miracle, but they are connected as effect with the previous forms of existence of my soul and as cause with future ones.

Those who, with open spiritual eyes, observe human life and do not know this comprehensive law, or do not wish to acknowledge it, are constantly confronted by riddles of life. Let us quote one example for many. It is contained in Maurice Maeterlinck's book Le Temple Enseveli (The Buried Temple). This is a book which speaks of these riddles, which appear to present-day thinkers in a distorted shape because they are not conversant with the great laws in spiritual life of cause and effect, of Karma. Those who have fallen prey to the limited dogmas of the modern believers have no organ for the perception of such riddles. Maeterlinck puts [forth] one of these questions: "If I plunge into the water in zero weather in order to save my fellow man, or if I fall into the water while trying to push him into it, the consequences of the cold I catch will be exactly the same in both cases, and no power in heaven or earth beside myself or the man (if he is able to do so) will increase my suffering because I have committed a crime, or will relieve my pain because I performed a virtuous deed." Certainly; the consequences in question here appear to an observation which limits itself to physical facts to be the same in both cases. But may this observation, without further research, be considered complete? Whoever asserts this holds, as a thinker, the same view point as a person who observes two boys being taught by two different teachers, and who observes nothing else in this activity but the fact that in both cases the teachers are occupied with the two boys for the same number of hours and carry on the same studies. If he were to enter more deeply upon the facts, he would perhaps observe a great difference between the two cases, and he would consider it comprehensible that one boy grows up to be an inefficient man, while the other boy becomes an excellent and capable human being. — And if the person who is willing to enter upon soul-spiritual connections were to observe the above consequences for the souls of the human beings in question, he would have to say to himself: what happens there cannot be considered as isolated facts. The consequences of a cold are soul experiences, and I must, if they are not to be deemed a miracle, view them as causes and effects in the soul life. The consequences for the person who saves a life will spring from causes different from those for the criminal; or they will, in the one or the other case, have different effects. And if I cannot find these causes and effects in the present life of the people concerned, if all conditions are alike for this present life, then I must look for the compensation in the past and the future life. Then I proceed exactly like the natural scientist in the field of external facts; he, too, explains the lack of eyes in animals living in dark caves by previous experiences, and he presupposes that present-day experiences will have their effects in future formations of races and species.

Only he has an inner right to speak of evolution in the domain of outer nature who acknowledges this evolution also in the sphere of soul and spirit. Now, it is clear that this acknowledgment, this extension of knowledge of nature beyond nature is more than mere cognition. For it transforms cognition into life; it does not merely enrich man's knowledge, it provides him with the strength for his life's journey. It shows him whence he comes and whither he goes. And it will show him this whence and whither beyond birth and death if he steadfastly follows the direction which this knowledge indicates. He knows that everything he does is a link in the stream which flows from eternity to eternity. The point of view from which he regulates his life becomes higher and higher. The man who has not attained to this state of mind appears as though enveloped in a dense fog, for he has no idea of his true being, of his origin and goal. He follows the impulses of his nature, without any insight into these impulses. He must confess that he might follow quite different impulses, were he to illuminate his path with the light of knowledge. Under the influence of such an attitude of soul, the sense of responsibility in regard to life grows constantly. If the human being does not develop this sense of responsibility in himself, he denies, in a higher sense, his humanness. Knowledge lacking the aim to ennoble the human being is merely the satisfying of a higher curiosity. To raise knowledge to the comprehension of the spiritual, in order that it may become the strength of the whole life, is, in a higher sense, duty. Thus it is the duty of every human being to seek the understanding for the Whence and Whither of the Soul.

Knowledge of the State
Between Death and a New Birth

The following thoughts are intended as aphoristic sketches of a domain of knowledge that, in the form in which is it characterised here, is almost entirely rejected by the culture of our time. The aphoristic form has been chosen in order to give some idea of the fundamental character of this field of knowledge, and to show — at least in one direction — the prospects for life which it opens up. The narrow frame of an essay requires one to refer the reader to the literature of the subject for further information. The author is fully aware that precisely this form of presentation may easily be felt as presumptuous by many who, from the well-founded habits of thought of the culture of the day, must find what is here brought forward directly opposed to all that is scientific. It may be said in answer to this that the author, in spite of his 'spiritual-scientific' orientation, believes that he can agree with every scientist in his high estimation of the spirit and significance of scientific thinking. Only it seems clear to him that one can fully accept Natural Science without being thereby compelled to reject an independent Spiritual Science of the kind described here. A consequence of this relation to Natural Science will, at all events, be to guard true Spiritual Science from that amateurishness which is noticeable in many quarters to-day, and which usually indulges the more presumptuously in phrases about the 'crude materialism of Natural Science' the less the speakers are able to judge of the earnestness, rigour and scientific soundness of Natural Knowledge.

The writer wished to make these introductory remarks because the brevity of the discussions in this article may possibly obscure from the reader his attitude towards these matters.

He who speaks to-day of investigating the spiritual world encounters the sceptical objections of those whose habits of thought have been moulded by the outlook of Natural Science. His attention will be drawn to the blessings which this outlook has brought for a healthy development of human life, by destroying the illusions of a learning which professed to follow purely spiritual modes of cognition. Now these sceptical objections can be quite intelligible to the spiritual investigator. Indeed it ought to be perfectly clear to him that any kind of spiritual investigation which finds itself in conflict with established ideas of Natural Science cannot rest on a sure foundation. A spiritual investigator with a feeling for, and an understanding of the earnestness of scientific procedure, and insight into the achievements of Natural Knowledge for human life, will not wish to join the ranks of those who, from the standpoint of their 'spiritual sight,' criticise lightly the limitations of scientists, and imagine their own standpoint so much the higher the more every kind of Natural Knowledge is lost for them in unfathomable depths.

Natural Science and Spiritual Science could live in harmony if the former could rid itself of the erroneous belief that true spiritual investigation necessarily requires we [human beings] to reject attested knowledge of sensible reality and of the soul-life bound up with this. In this erroneous belief lies the source of innumerable misunderstandings which Spiritual Science has to encounter. Those who believe they stand, in their outlook on life, on the 'firm ground of Natural Science' hold that the spiritual investigator is compelled by his point of view to reject their knowledge. But this is not really the case. Genuine spiritual investigation is in full agreement with Natural Science. Thus spiritual investigation is not opposed on account of what it maintains, but for what people believe it could or must maintain.

With regard to human soul life the scientific thinker must maintain that the soul activities which reveal themselves as thinking, feeling and willing, ought, for the acquisition of scientific knowledge, to be observed without prejudice in the same way as the phenomena of light or heat in the outer world of Nature. He must reject all ideas about the entity of the soul which do not arise from such unprejudiced observation, and from which all kinds of conclusions are then drawn about the indestructibility of the soul, and its connection with the spiritual world. It is quite understandable that such a thinker begins his study of the facts of soul-life as Theodor Ziehen does in the first of his lectures on "Physiological Psychology." He says: "The psychology which I shall put before you, is not that old psychology which attempted to investigate soul phenomena in a more or less speculative way. This psychology has long been abandoned by those accustomed to think scientifically." True spiritual investigation need not conflict with the scientific attitude which may he in such an avowal. And yet, among those who take this attitude as a result of their scientific habits of thought, the opinion will be almost universally held to-day that the specific results of spiritual investigation are to be regarded as unscientific. Of course one will not encounter everywhere this rejection, on grounds of principle, of the investigation of spiritual facts; yet when specific results of such investigation are brought forward they will scarcely escape the objection that scientific thinking can do nothing with them. As a consequence of this,one can observe that there has recently grown up a science of the soul, forming its methods of investigation on the pattern of natural-scientific procedure, but unable to find the power to approach those highest questions which our inner need of knowledge must put when we turn our gaze to the fate of the soul. One investigates conscientiously the connection of soul phenomena with bodily processes, one tries to gain ideas on the way presentations associate and dissociate in the soul, how attention acts, how memory functions, what relation exists between thinking, feeling and willing; but for the higher questions of soul-life the words of Franz Brentano remain true. This acute psychologist, though rooted in the mode of thinking of Natural Science, wrote: "The laws of association of ideas, of the development of convictions and opinions and of the genesis of pleasure and love would be anything but a true compensation for the hopes of a Plato or an Aristotle of gaining certainty concerning the continued life of our better part after the dissolution of the body." And if the recent scientific mode of thinking really means "excluding the question of immortality," this exclusion would have great significance for psychology.

The fact is, that considerations which might tend in the direction of the 'hopes of a Plato and an Aristotle' are avoided in recent psychological writings which wish to satisfy the demands of scientific thought. Now the spiritual investigator will not come into conflict with the mode of procedure of recent scientific psychology if he has an understanding of its vital nerve. He will have to admit that this psychology proceeds, in the main, along right lines insofar as the study of the inner experiences of thinking, feeling and willing is concerned. Indeed his path of knowledge leads him to admit that thinking, feeling and willing reveal nothing that could fulfil the 'hopes of a Plato and an Aristotle' if these activities are only studied as they are experienced in ordinary human life. But his path of knowledge also shows that in thinking, feeling and willing something lies hidden which does not become conscious in the course of ordinary life, but which can be brought to consciousness through inner soul exercises. In this spiritual entity of the soul, hidden from ordinary consciousness, is revealed what in it is independent of the life of the body; and in this the relations of man to the spiritual world can be studied. To the spiritual investigator it appears just as impossible to fulfil the 'hopes of a Plato or an Aristotle' in regard to the existence of the soul independent of bodily life by observing ordinary thinking, feeling and willing, as it is impossible to investigate in water the properties of hydrogen. To learn these one must first extract the hydrogen from the water by an appropriate procedure. So it is also necessary to separate from the everyday life of the soul (which it leads in connection with the body) that entity which is rooted in the spiritual world, if this entity is to be studied.

The error which casts befogging misunderstandings in the way of Spiritual Science lies in the almost general belief that knowledge about the higher questions of soul-life must be gained from a study of such facts of the soul as are already to be found in ordinary life. But no other knowledge results from these facts than that to which research, conducted on what are at present called scientific lines, can lead. On this account Spiritual Science can be no mere heeding of what is immediately present in the life of the soul. It must first lay bare, by inner processes in the life of the soul, the world of facts to be studied. To this end spiritual investigation applies soul processes which are attained in inner experience. Its field of research lies entirely within the inner life of the soul. It cannot make its experiences outwardly visible. Nevertheless they are not on that account less independent of personal caprice than the true results of Natural Science. They have nothing in common with mathematical truths except that they, too, cannot be proved by outer facts, but are proved for anyone who grasps them in inner perception. Like mathematical truths they can at the most be outwardly symbolised but not represented in their full content, for it is this that proves them. The essential point, which can easily be misunderstood, is, that on the path pursued by spiritual investigation a certain direction is given, by inner initiative, to the experiences of the soul, thereby calling out forces which otherwise remain unconscious as in a kind of soul sleep. (The soul exercises which lead to this goal are described in detail in my books "Knowledge of the Higher Worlds and its Attainment" and "Occult Science." It is only intended to indicate here what transpires in the soul when it subjects itself to such exercises). If the soul proceeds in this way it inserts — as it were — its inner life into the domain of spiritual reality. It opens to the spiritual world its organs of perception so formed, as the senses open outwardly to physical reality.

One kind of such soul exercises consists in an intensive surrender to the process of thinking. One carries this surrender so far that one acquires the capacity of directing one's attention no longer to the thoughts present in thinking but solely to the activity of thinking itself. Every kind of thought content then disappears from consciousness and the soul experiences herself consciously in the activity of thinking. Thinking then becomes transformed into a subtle inner act of will which is completely illuminated by consciousness. In ordinary thinking, thoughts live; the process indicated extinguishes the thought in thinking. The experience thus induced is a weaving in an inner activity of will which bears its reality within itself. The point is that the soul, by continued inner experience in this direction, may make itself as familiar with the purely spiritual reality in which it weaves as sense observation is with physical reality. As in the outer world a reality can only be known as such by experiencing it, so, too, in this inner domain. He who objects that what is inwardly real cannot be proved only shows that he has not yet grasped that we become convinced of an outer reality in no other way than by experiencing its existence together with our own. A healthy life has direct experience of the difference between a genuine perception in the outer world and a vision or hallucination; in a similar way a healthily developed soul life can distinguish the spiritual reality it has approached from fantastic imagining; and dreamy reverie.

Thinking that has been developed in the manner stated perceives that it has freed itself from the soul force which ordinarily leads to memory. What is experienced in thinking which has become an inwardly experienced 'will-reality' cannot be remembered in the direct form in which it presents itself. Thus it differs from what is experienced in ordinary thinking. What one has thought about an event is incorporated into memory. It can be brought up again in the further course of life. But the 'will-reality' here described must be attained anew, if it is to be again experienced in consciousness. I do not mean that this reality cannot be indirectly incorporated into ordinary memory. This must indeed take place if the path of spiritual investigation is to be a healthy one. But what remains in memory is only an idea (Vorstellung) of this reality, just as what one remembers to-day of an experience of yesterday is only an idea (Vorstellung). Concepts, ideas, can be retained in memory: a spiritual reality must be experienced ever anew. By grasping vividly this difference between the cherishing of mere thoughts and a spiritual reality reached by developing the activity of thinking, one comes to experience oneself with this reality outside the physical body. What ordinary thinking must mostly regard as an impossibility commences; one experiences oneself outside the existence that is connected with the body. Ordinary thinking, regarding this experience 'outside the body' only from its own point of view, must at first hold this to be an illusion. Assurance of this experience can, indeed, only be won through the experience itself. And it is precisely through this experience that one understands only too well that those whose habits of thought have been formed by Natural Science cannot, at first, but regard such experiences as fantastic imaginings or dreamy reverie, perhaps as a weaving in illusions or hallucinations. Only he can fully understand what is here brought forward who has come to know that the path of true spiritual investigation releases forces in the soul which lie in a direction precisely opposite to those which induce pathological soul experiences. What the soul develops on the path of spiritual investigation are forces competent to oppose pathological states or to dissipate these where they tend to occur. No scientific investigation can see through what is visionary — of an hallucinatory nature — when this tries to get in man's way, as directly as true spiritual science, which can only unfold in a direction opposed to the unhealthy experiences mentioned.

In that moment when this 'experience outside the body' becomes a reality for him the spiritual investigator learns to know how ordinary thinking is bound to the physical processes of the body. He comes to see how thoughts acquired in outer experience necessarily arise in such a way that they can be remembered. This rests on the fact that these thoughts do not merely lead a spiritual life in the soul but share their life with the body. Thus the spiritual investigator comes not to reject but to accept what scientific thought must maintain about the dependence of the life of thought on bodily processes.

At first the inner experiences described above present themselves as anxious oppression of the soul. They appear to lead out of the domain of ordinary existence but not into a new reality. One knows, indeed, that one is living in a reality; one feels this reality as one's own spiritual being. One has found one's way out of sense reality, but one has only grasped oneself in a purely spiritual form of existence. A feeling of loneliness resembling fear can overtake the soul — a loneliness to experience oneself in a world, not merely to possess oneself. Yet another feeling arises. One feels one must lose again the acquired spiritual self-experience, if one cannot confront a spiritual environment. The spiritual state into which one thus enters may be roughly compared to what would be experienced if one had to clutch with one's hands in all directions without being able to lay hold of anything.

When, however, the path of spiritual investigation is pursued in the right way, the above experiences are, indeed, undergone, but they form only one side of the soul's development. The necessary completion is found in other experiences. As certain impulses given to the soul's experiences lead one to grasp the 'will-reality' within thinking, so other directions imparted to the processes of the soul lead to an experience of hidden forces within the activity of the will. (Here also we can only state what takes place in the inner being of man through such soul experiences. The books mentioned give a detailed description of what the soul must undertake in order to reach the indicated goal). In ordinary life the activity of the will is not perceived in the same way as an outer event. Even what is usually called introspection by no means puts one into the position of regarding one's own willing as one regards an outer event of Nature.

To achieve this — to be able to confront one's own willing as an observer stands before an outer fact of Nature — intensive soul processes, induced voluntarily, are again necessary. If these are induced in the appropriate way there arises something quite different from this view of one's own willing as of an outer fact. In ordinary perception a presentation (Vorstellung) emerges in the life of the soul and is, in a certain sense, an inner image of the outer fact. But in observing one's own willing this accustomed power of forming presentations fades out. One ceases to form presentations of outer things. In place of this a faculty of forming real images — a real perception — is released from the depths of willing, and breaks through the surface of the will's activity, bringing living spiritual reality with it. At first one's own hidden spiritual entity appears within this spiritual reality. One perceives that one carries a hidden spiritual man within one. This is no thought-picture but a real being — real in a higher sense than the outer bodily man. Now this spiritual man does not present himself like an outer being perceptible to the senses. He does not reveal his characteristic qualities outwardly. He reveals himself through his inner nature by developing an inner activity similar to the processes of consciousness in one's own soul. But, unlike the soul dwelling in man's body, this higher being is not turned towards sensible objects but towards spiritual events — in the first place towards the events of one's own soul-life as unfolded up till now. One really discovers in oneself a second human being who, as a spiritual being, is a conscious observer of one's ordinary soul-life. However fantastic this description of a spiritual man within the bodily may appear, it is nevertheless a sober description of reality for a soul-life appropriately trained. It is as different from anything visionary or of the nature of an illusion as is day from night.

Just as a reality partaking of the nature of will is discovered in the transformed thinking, so a consciousness partaking of the nature of being — and weaving in the spiritual — is discovered in the will. And these two prove, for fuller experience, to belong together. In a certain sense they are discovered on paths running in opposite directions, but turn out to be a unity. The feeling of anxiety experienced in the weaving of the 'will-reality' ceases when this 'will-reality,' born from developed thinking, unites itself with the higher being above described. Through this union man confronts, for the first time, the complete spiritual world. He encounters, not only himself, but beings and events of the spiritual world lying outside himself.

In the world into which man has thus entered, perception is an essentially different process from perception in the world of sense. Real beings and events of the spiritual world arise from out of the higher being revealed through developing the will. Through the interplay of these beings and events with the 'will-reality' resulting from developed thinking, these beings and events are spiritually perceived. What we know as memory in the physical world ceases to have significance for the spiritual world. We see that this soul force uses the physical body as a tool. But another force takes the place of memory in observing the spiritual world. Through this force a past event is not remembered in the form of mental presentations but perceived directly in a fresh experience. It is not like reading a sentence and remembering it later, but like reading and re-reading. The concept of the past acquires a new significance in this domain; the past appears to spiritual perception as present, and we recognise that something belongs to a past time by perceiving, not the passage of time, but the relation of one spiritual being or event to another.

The path into the spiritual world is thus traversed by laying bare what is contained in thinking and willing. Now feeling cannot be developed in a similar way by inner initiative of soul. Unlike the case of thinking and willing, nothing to take the place of what is experienced within the physical world as feeling can be developed in the spiritual world through transforming an inner force. What corresponds to feeling in the spiritual world arises quite of itself as soon as spiritual perception has been acquired in the described way. This experience of feeling, however, bears a different character from that borne by feeling in the physical world. One does not feel in oneself, but in the beings and events which one perceives. One enters into them with one's feeling; one feels their inner being, as in physical life one feels one's own being. We might put it in this way: as in the physical world one is conscious of experiencing objects and events as material, so in the spiritual world one is conscious of experiencing beings and facts through revelations of feeling which come from without like colours or sounds in the physical world.

A soul which has attained to the spiritual experience described knows it is in a world from out of which it can observe its own experiences in the physical word — just as physical perception can observe a sensible object. It is united with that spiritual entity which unites itself — at birth (or at conception) — with the physical body derived from one's ancestors; and this spiritual entity persists when this body is laid aside at death. The 'hopes of a Plato and an Aristotle' for the science of the soul can only be fulfilled through a perception of this entity. Moreover the perception of repeated earth-lives (between which are lives spent in the purely spiritual world) now becomes a fact inasmuch as man's psychic-spiritual kernel, thus discovered, perceives itself and its own weaving and becoming in the spiritual world. It learns to know its own being as the result of earlier earthlives and spiritual forms of existence lying between them. Within its present earth-life it finds a spiritual germ which must unfold in a future earth-life after passing through states between death and a new birth. As the plant germ contains the future plant potentially, so there develops, concealed in man, a psychic-spiritual germ. This reveals itself to spiritual perception through its own essence as the foundation of a future earth-life. It would be incorrect so to interpret the spiritual perception of life between death and a new birth as if such perception meant participating beforehand in the experience of the spiritual world entered at physical death. Such perception does not give a complete, disembodied experience of the spiritual world as experienced after death; it is only the knowledge of the actual experience that is experienced.

While still in one's body one can receive all of the disembodied experience between death and a new birth that is offered by the experiences of the soul described above, that is to say, when the 'will-reality' is released from thinking with the help of the consciousness set free from the will. In the spiritual world the feeling element revealing itself from without can first be experienced through entrance into this world. Strange as it may sound, experience in the spiritual world leads one to say: the physical world is present to man in the first place as a complex of outer facts, and man acquires knowledge of it after it has confronted him in this form; the spiritual world, on the other hand, sends knowledge of itself in advance, and the knowledge it kindles in the soul beforehand is the torch which must illumine the spiritual world if this world is to reveal itself as a fact. It is clear to one who knows this through spiritual perception that this light develops during bodily life on earth in the unconscious depths of the soul, and then, after death, illumines the regions of the spiritual world making them experiences of the human soul.

During bodily life on earth one can awaken this knowledge of the state between death and a new birth. This knowledge has an entirely opposite character to that developed for life in the physical world. One perceives through it what the soul will accomplish between death and a new birth, because one has present in spiritual perception the germ of what impels towards this accomplishment. The perception of this germ reveals that a creative connection with the spiritual world commences for the soul after death. It unfolds an activity which is directed towards the future earth life as its goal, whereas in physical perception its activity is directed — although imitatively and not creatively — towards the outer world of sense. Man's growth (Werden) as a spiritual being connected with the spiritual world lies in the field of vision of the soul between death and a new birth, as the existence (Sein) of the sense world lies in the field of view of the bodily man. Active perception of spiritual Becoming (Werden) characterises the conditions between death and a new birth. (It is not the task of this article to give details of these states. Those interested will find them in my books "Theosophy" and "Occult Science").

In contrast to experience in the body, spiritual experience is something to which we are completely unaccustomed, inasmuch as the idea of Being as acquired in the physical world loses all meaning. The spiritual world has nothing of the nature of Being. Everything is Becoming. To enter a spiritual environment is to enter an everlasting Becoming. But in contrast to this restless Becoming in our spiritual environment we have the soul's perception of itself as stationary consciousness within the never-ceasing movement into which it is placed. The awakened spiritual consciousness must accommodate itself to this reversal of inner experience with regard to the consciousness that lives in the body. It can thereby acquire a real knowledge of experience apart from the body. And only such knowledge can embrace the states between death and a new birth.

" . . . . In a certain sense all human beings are 'specialists' to-day so far as their souls are concerned. We are struck by this specialised mode of perception when we study the development of Art in humanity. And for this very reason a comprehensive understanding of spiritual life in its totality must again come into existence. True form in Art will arise from this comprehensive understanding of spiritual life . . . . "

Supersensible Knowledge

There are two experiences whence the soul may gain an understanding for the mode of knowledge to which the supersensible worlds will open out. The one originates in the science of Nature; the other, in the Mystical experience whereby the untrained ordinary consciousness contrives to penetrate into the supersensible domain. Both confront the soul of man with barriers of knowledge — barriers he cannot cross till he can open for himself the portals which by their very essence Natural Science, and ordinary Mysticism too, must hold fast closed.

Natural Science leads inevitably to certain conceptions about reality, which are like a stone wall to the deeper forces of the soul; and yet, this Science itself is powerless to remove them. He who fails to feel the impact, has not yet called to life the deeper needs of knowledge in his soul. He may then come to believe that it is impossible in any case for Man to attain any other than the natural-scientific form of knowledge. There is, however, a definite experience in Self-knowledge whereby one weans oneself of this belief. This experience consists in the insight that the whole of Natural Science would be dissolved into thin air if we attempted to fathom the above-named conceptions with the methods of Natural Science itself. If the conceptions of Natural Science are to remain spread out before the soul, these limiting conceptions must be left within the field of consciousness intact, without attempting to approach them with a deeper insight. There are many of them; here I will only mention two of the most familiar: Matter and Force. Recent developments in scientific theory may or may not be replacing these particular conceptions; the fact remains that Natural Science must invariably lead to some conception or another of this kind, impenetrable to its own methods of knowledge.

To the experience of soul, of which I am here speaking, these limiting conceptions appear like a reflecting surface which the human soul must place before it; while Natural Science itself is like the picture, made manifest with the mirror's help. Any attempt to treat the limiting conceptions themselves by ordinary scientific means is, as it were, to smash the mirror, and with the mirror broken, Natural Science itself dissolves away. Moreover, this experience reveals the emptiness of all talk about 'Things-in-themselves,' of whatsoever kind, behind the phenomena of Nature. He who seeks for such Things-in-themselves is like a man who longs to break the looking-glass, hoping to see what there is behind the reflecting surface to cause his image to appear.

It goes without saying that the validity of such an experience of soul cannot be 'proved,' in the ordinary sense of the word, with the habitual thoughts of presentday Natural Science. For the point will be, what kind of an inner experience does the process of the 'proof' call forth in us; and this must needs transcend the abstract proof. With inner experience in this sense, we must apprehend the question: How is it that the soul is forced to confront these barriers of knowledge in order to have before it the phenomena of Nature? Mature self-knowledge brings us an answer to this question. We then perceive which of the forces of man's soul partakes in the erection of these barriers to knowledge. It is none other than the force of soul which makes man capable, within the world of sense, of unfolding Love out of his inner being. The faculty of Love is somehow rooted in the human organisation; and the very thing which gives to man the power of love — of sympathy and antipathy with his environment of sense, — takes away from his cognition of the things and processes of Nature the possibility to make transparent such pillars of Reality as 'Matter' and 'Force.' To the man who can experience himself in true self-knowledge, on the one hand in the act of knowing Nature, and on the other hand in the unfolding of Love, this peculiar property of the human organisation becomes straightway apparent.

We must, however, beware of misinterpreting this perception by lapsing again into a way of thought which, within Natural Science itself, is no doubt inevitable. Thus it would be a misconstruction to assume, that an insight into the true essence of the things and processes of Nature is withheld from man because he lacks the organisation for such insight. The opposite is the case. Nature becomes sense-perceptible to man through the very fact that his being is capable of Love. For a being incapable of Love within the field of sense, the whole human picture of Nature would dissolve away. It is not Nature who on account of his organisation reveals only her external aspect. No; it is man, who, by that force of his organisation which makes him in another direction capable of Love, is placed in a position to erect before his soul images and forms of Reality whereby Nature reveals herself to him.

Through the experience above-described the fact emerges, that the scientific frontiers of knowledge depend on the whole way in which man, as a sense-endowed being, is placed within this world of physical reality. His vision of Nature is of a kind, appropriate to a being who is capable of Love. He would have to tear the faculty of Love out of his inner life if he wished no longer to be faced with limits in his perception of Nature. But in so doing he would destroy the very force whereby Nature is made manifest to him. The real object of his quest for knowledge is not, by the same methods which he applies in his outlook upon Nature, to remove the limitations of that outlook. No, it is something altogether different, and once this has been perceived, man will no longer try to penetrate into a supersensible world through the kind of knowledge which is effective in Natural Science. Rather will he tell himself, that to unveil the supersensible domain an altogether different activity of knowledge must be evolved than that which he applies to the science of Nature.

Many people, more or less consciously aware of the above experience of soul, turn away from Natural Science when it is a question of opening the supersensible domain, and seek to penetrate into the latter by methods which are commonly called Mystical. They think that what is veiled to outwardly directed vision may be revealed by plunging into the depths of one's own being. But a mature self-knowledge reveals in the inner life as well a frontier of knowledge. In the field of the senses the faculty of Love erects, as it were, an impenetrable background whereat Nature is reflected; in the inner life of man the power of Memory erects a like background. The same force of soul, which makes the human being capable of Memory, prevents his penetrating, in his inner being, down to that experience which would enable him to meet — along this inward path — the supersensible reality for which he seeks. Invariably, along this path, he reaches only to that force of soul which recalls to him in Memory the experiences he has undergone through his bodily nature in the past. He never penetrates into the region where with his own supersensible being he is rooted in a supersensible world. For those who fail to see this, mystical pursuits will give rise to the worst of illusions. For in the course of life, the human being receives into his inner life untold experiences, of which in the receiving he is not fully conscious. But the Memory retains what is thus half-consciously or subconsciously experienced. Long afterwards it frequently emerges into consciousness — in moods, in shades of feeling and the like, if not in clear conceptions. Nay more, it often undergoes a change, and comes to consciousness in quite a different form from that in which it was experienced originally. A man may then believe himself confronted by a supersensible reality arising from the inner being of the soul, whereas, in fact, it is but an outer experience transformed — an experience called forth originally by the world of sense — which comes before his mental vision. He alone is preserved from such illusions, who recognises that even on a mystic path man cannot penetrate into the supersensible domain so long as he applies methods of knowledge dependent on the bodily nature which is rooted in the world of sense. Even as our picture of Nature depends for its existence on the faculty of Love, so does the immediate consciousness of the human Self depend upon the power of Memory. The same force of the soul, endowing man in the physical world with the Self-consciousness that is bound to the bodily nature, stands in the way to obstruct his inner union with the supersensible world. Thus, even that which is often considered Mysticism provides no way into the supersensible realms of existence.

For him who would penetrate with full conscious clarity of understanding into the supersensible domain, the two experiences above described are, however, preparatory stages. Through them he recognises that man is shut off from the supersensible world by the very thing which places him, as a self-conscious being, in the midst of Nature. Now one might easily conclude from this, that man must altogether forego the effort to gain knowledge of the Supersensible. Nor can it be denied that many who are loath to face the painful issue, abstain from working their way through to a clear perception of the two experiences. Cherishing a certain dimness of perception on these matters, they either give themselves up to the belief that the limitations of Natural Science may be transcended by some intellectual and philosophic exercise; or else they devote themselves to Mysticism in the ordinary sense, avoiding the full enlightenment as to the nature of Self-consciousness and Memory which would reveal its insufficiency.

But to one who has undergone them and reached a certain clarity withal, these very experiences will open out the possibility and prospect of true supersensible knowledge. For in the course of them he finds that even in the ordinary action of human consciousness there are forces holding sway within the soul, which are not bound to the physical organisation; forces which are in no way subject to the conditions whereon the faculties of Love and Memory within this physical organisation depend. One of these forces reveals itself in Thought. True, it remains unnoticed in the ordinary conscious life; indeed there are even many philosophers who deny it. But the denial is due to an imperfect self-observation. There is something at work in Thought which does not come into it from the faculty of Memory. It is something that vouches to us for the correctness of a present thought, not when a former thought emerging from the memory sustains it, but when the correctness of the present thought is experienced directly. This experience escapes the every-day consciousness, because man completely spends the force in question for his life of thought-filled perception. In Perception permeated by Thought this force is at work. But man, perceiving, imagines that the perception alone is vouching for the correctness of what he apprehends by an activity of soul where Thought and Perception in reality always flow together. And when he lives in Thought alone, abstracted from perceptions, it is but an activity of Thought which finds its supports in Memory. In this abstracted Thought the physical organism is cooperative. For the every-day consciousness, an activity of Thought unsubjected to the bodily organism is only present while man is in the act of Sense-perception. Sense-perception itself depends upon the organism. But the thinking activity, contained in and co-operating with it, is a purely supersensible element in which the bodily organism has no share. In it the human soul rises out of the bodily organism. As soon as man becomes distinctly, separately conscious of this Thinking in the act of Perception, he knows by direct experience that he has himself as a living soul, quite independently of the bodily nature.

This is man's first experience of himself as a supersensible soul-being, arising out of an evolved self-knowledge. The same experience is there unconsciously in every act of perception. We need only sharpen our selfobservation so as to

Observe the fact: in the act of Perception a supersensible element reveals itself. Once it is thus revealed, this first, faint suggestion of an experience of the soul within the Supersensible can be evolved, as follows: In living, meditative practice, man unfolds a Thinking wherein two activities of the soul flow together, namely that which lives in the ordinary consciousness in Sense-perception, and that which is active in ordinary Thought. The meditative life thus becomes an intensified activity of Thought, receiving into itself the force that is otherwise spent in Perception. Our Thinking in itself must grow so strong, that it works with the same vivid quality which is otherwise only there in Sense-perception. Without perception by the senses we must call to life a Thinking which, unsupported by memories of the past, experiences in the immediate present a content of its own, such as we otherwise only can derive from Sense-perception. From the Thinking that co-operates in perception, this meditative action of the soul derives its free and conscious quality, its inherent certainty that it receives no visionary content raying into the soul from unconscious organic regions. A visionary life of whatsoever kind is the very antithesis of what is here intended. By self-observation we must become thoroughly and clearly familiar with the condition of soul in which we are in the act of perception through any one of the senses. In this state of soul, fully aware that the content of our ideation does not arise out of the activity of the bodily organism, we must learn to experience ideas which are called forth in consciousness without external perceptions, just as are those of which we are conscious in ordinary life when engaged in reflective thought, abstracted from the enter world. (As to the right ways of developing this meditative practice, detailed indications are given in the book 'Knowledge of the Higher Worlds and its Attainment' and in several of my other writings.)

In evolving the meditative life above-described, the human soul rises to the conscious feeling perception of itself, as of a supersensible Being independent of the bodily organisation. This is man's first experience of himself as a supersensible Being; and it leads on to a second stage in supersensible self-knowledge. At the former stage he can only be aware that he is a supersensible Being; at the second he feels this Being filled with real content, even as the 'I' of ordinary waking life is felt by means of the bodily organisation. It is of the utmost importance to realise that the transition from the one stage to the other takes place quite independently of any co-operation from outside the soul's domain — namely from the mere organic life. If we experienced the transition, in relation to our own bodily nature, any differently from the process of drawing a logical conclusion for example, it would be a visionary experience, not what is intended here. The process here intended differs from the act of drawing logical conclusions, not in respect of its relationship to the bodily nature, but in quite another regard; namely in the consciousness that a supersensible, purely spiritual content is entering the feeling and perception of the Self.

The kind of meditative life hitherto described gives rise to the supersensible self-consciousness. But this self-consciousness would be left without any supersensible environment if the above form of meditation were unaccompanied by another. We come to an understanding of this latter kind by turning our self-observation to the activity of the Will. In every-day life the activity of the Will is consciously directed to external actions. There is, however, another concomitant expression of the Will to which the human being pays little conscious attention. It is the activity of Will which carries him from one stage of development to another in the course of life. For not only is he filled with different contents of soul day after day; his soul-life itself, on each succeeding day, has evolved out of his soul-life of the day before. The driving force in this evolving process is the Will, which in this field of its activity remains for the most part unconscious. Mature self-knowledge can, however, raise this Will, with all its peculiar quality, into the conscious life. When this is done, man comes to the perception of a life of Will which has absolutely nothing to do with any processes of a sense-perceptible external world, but is directed solely to the inner evolution of the soul — independent of this world. Once it is known to him, he learns by degrees to enter into the living essence of this Will, just as in the former kind of meditative life he entered into the fusion of the soul's experiences of Thinking and Perception. And the conscious experience in this element of Will expands into the experience of a supersensible external world. Evolved in the way above described, and transplanted now into this element of Will, the supersensible self-consciousness finds itself in a supersensible environment, filled with spiritual Beings and events. While the supersensible Thinking leads to a self-consciousness independent of the power of Memory which is bound to the bodily nature, the supersensible Willing comes to life in such a way as to be permeated through and through by a spiritualised faculty of Love. It is this faculty of Love which enables the supersensible self-consciousness of man to perceive and grasp the supersensible external world. Thus the power of supersensible knowledge is established by a self-consciousness which eliminates the ordinary Memory and lives in the intuitive perception of the spiritual world through the power of Love made spiritual.

Only by realising this essence of the supersensible faculty of knowledge, does one become able to understand the real meaning of man's knowledge of Nature. In effect, the knowledge of Nature is inherently connected with what is being evolved in man within this physical world of sense. It is in this world that man incorporates, into his spiritual Being, Self-consciousness and the faculty of Love. Once he has instilled these two into his nature, he can carry them with him into the super sensible world. In supersensible perception, the ordinary power of Memory is eliminated. Its place is taken by an immediate vision of the past — a vision for which the past appears as we look backward in spiritual observation, just as for sense-perception the things we pass by as we walk along appear when we turn round to look behind us. Again the ordinary faculty of Love is bound to the physical organism. In conscious supersensible experience, its place is taken by a power of Love made spiritual, which is to say, a power of perception.

It may already be seen, from the above description, that supersensible experience takes place in a mood of soul which must be held apart, in consciousness, from that of ordinary Perception, Thinking, Feeling and Willing. The two ways of looking out upon the world must be kept apart by the deliberate control of man himself, just as in another sphere the waking consciousness is kept apart from the dream life. He who lets play the picture-complexes of his dreams into his waking life becomes a listless and fantastic fellow, abstracted from realities. He, on the other hand, who holds to the belief that the essence of causal relationships experienced in waking life can be extended into the life of dreams, endows the dream-pictures with an imagined reality which will make it impossible for him to experience their real nature. So with the mode of thought which governs our outlook upon Nature, or of inner experience which determines ordinary Mysticism: — he who lets them play into his supersensible experience, will not behold the supersensible, but weave himself in figments of the mind, which, far from bringing him nearer to it, will cut him off from the higher world he seeks. A man who will not hold his experience in the supersensible apart from his experience in the world of the physical senses, will mar the fresh and unembarrassed outlook upon Nature which is the true basis for a healthy sojourn in this earthly life. Moreover, he will permeate with the force of spiritual perception the faculty of Love that is connected with the bodily nature, thus tending to bring it into a deceptive relationship with the physical experience. All that the human being experiences and achieves within the field of sense, receives its true illumination — an illumination which the deepest needs of the soul require — through the science of things that are only to be experienced supersensibly. Yet must the latter be held separate in consciousness from the experience in the world of sense. It must illumine our knowledge of Nature, our ethical and social life; yet so, that the illumination always proceeds from a sphere of experience apart. Mediately, through the attunement of the human soul, the Supersensible must indeed shed its light upon the Sensible. For if it did not do so, the latter would be relegated to darkness of thought, chaotic wilfulness of instinct and desire.

Many human beings, well knowing this relationship which has to be maintained in the soul between the experience of the supersensible and that of the world of sense, hold that the supersensible knowledge must on no account be given full publicity. It should remain, so they consider, the secret knowledge of a few, who have attained by strict self-discipline the power to establish and maintain the true relationship. Such guardians of supersensible knowledge base their opinion on the very true assertion that a man who is in any way inadequately prepared for the higher knowledge will feel an irresistible impulse to mingle the Supersensible with the Sensible in life; and that he will inevitably thus call forth, both in himself and others, all the ill effects which we have here characterised as the result of such confusion. On the other hand — believing as they do, and with good reason, that man's outlook upon Nature must not be left to grope in utter darkness, nor his life to spend itself in blind forces of instinct and desire, — they have founded self-contained and closed Societies, or Occult Schools, within which human beings properly prepared are guided stage by stage to supersensible discovery. Of such it then becomes the task to pour the fruits of their knowledge into life, without, however, exposing the knowledge itself to publicity.

In past epochs of human evolution this idea was undoubtedly justified. For the propensity above described, leading to the misuse of supersensible knowledge, was then the only thing to be considered, and against it there stood no other circumstance to call for publication of the higher knowledge. It might at most be contended that the superiority of those initiated into the higher knowledge gave into their hands a mighty power to rule over those who had no such knowledge.

None the less, an enlightened reading of the course of History will convince us that such conflux of power into the hands of a few, fitted by self-discipline to wield it, was indeed necessary.

In present time, however — meaning 'present' in the wider sense — the evolution of mankind has reached a point whenceforward it becomes not only impossible but harmful to prolong the former custom. The irresistible impulse to misuse the higher knowledge is now opposed by other factors, making the — at any rate partial — publication of such knowledge a matter of necessity, and calculated also to remove the ill effects of the above tendency. Our knowledge of Nature has assumed a form wherein it beats perpetually, in a destructive way, against its own barriers and limitations. In many branches of Science, the laws and generalisations in which man finds himself obliged to clothe certain of the facts of Nature, are in themselves of such a kind as to call his attention to his own supersensible powers. The latter press forward into the conscious life of the soul. In former ages, the knowledge of Nature which was generally accessible had no such effect. Through Natural Science, however, in its present form — expanding as it is in ever widening circles — mankind would be led astray in either of two directions, if a publication of supersensible knowledge were not now to take place. Either the possibility of a supersensible world-outlook would be repudiated altogether and with growing vehemence; and this would presently result in an artificial repression of supersensible faculties which the time is actually calling forth. Such repression would make it more and more impossible for man to see his own Being in a true light. Emptiness, chaos and dissatisfaction of the inner life, instability of soul, perversity of will; and, in the sequel, even physical degeneration and illhealth would be the outcome. Or else the supersensible faculties-uncontrolled by conscious knowledge of these things-would break out in a wild tangle of obtuse, unconscious, undirected forces of cognition, and the life of knowledge would degenerate in a chaotic mass of nebulous conceptions. This would be to create a world of scientific phantoms, which, like a curtain, would obscure the true supersensible world from the spiritual eye of man. For either of these aberrations, a proper publication of supersensible knowledge is the only remedy.

As to the impulse to abuse such knowledge in the way above described, it can be counteracted in our time, as follows: the training of thought which modern Natural Science has involved can be fruitfully employed to clothe in words the truths that point towards the supersensible. Itself, this Science of Nature cannot penetrate into the supersensible world; but it lends the human mind an aptitude for combinations of thought whereby the higher knowledge can be so expressed that the irresistible impulsion to misuse it need not arise. The thought-combinations of the Nature-knowledge of former times were more pictorial, less inclined to the domain of pure Thought. Supersensible perceptions, clothed in them, stirred up — without his being conscious of it — those very instincts in the human being which tend towards misuse.

This being said, it cannot on the other hand be emphasised too strongly that he who gives out supersensible knowledge in our time will the better fulfil his responsibilities to mankind the more he contrives to express this knowledge in forms of thought borrowed from the modern Science of Nature. For the receiver of knowledge thus imparted will then have to apply, to the overcoming of certain difficulties of understanding, faculties of soul which would otherwise remain inactive and tend to the above misuse. The popularising of supersensible knowledge, so frequently desired by overzealous and misguided people, should be avoided. The truly earnest seeker does not call for it; it is but the banale, uncultured craving of persons indolent in thought.

In the ethical and social life as well, humanity has reached a stage of development which makes it impossible to exclude all knowledge of the supersensible from public life and thought. In former epochs the ethical and social instincts contained within them spiritual guiding forces, inherited from primaeval ages of mankind. Such forces tended instinctively to a community life which answered also to the needs of individual soul. But the inner life of man has grown more conscious than in former epochs. The spiritual instincts have thus been forced into the background. The Will, the impulses of men must now be guided consciously, lest they become vagrant and unstable. That is to say, the individual, by his own insight, must be in a position to illumine the life in the physical world of sense by the knowledge of the supersensible, spiritual Being of man.

Conceptions formed in the way of natural-scientific knowledge cannot enter effectively into the conscious guiding forces of the ethical and social life. Destined as it is — within its own domain — to bear the most precious fruits, Natural Science will be led into an absolutely fatal error if it be not perceived that the mode of thought which dominates it is quite unfitted to open out an understanding of, or to give impulses for, the moral and social life of humanity. In the domain of ethical and social life our conception of underlying principles, and the conscious guidance of our action, can only thrive when illumined from the aspect of the Supersensible. Between the rise of a highly evolved Natural Science, and present-day developments in the human life of Will — with all the underlying impulses and instincts — there is indeed a deep, significant connection. The force of knowledge that has gone into our science of Nature, is derived from the former spiritual content of man's impulses and instincts. From the fountain-head of supersensible Realities, the latter must now be supplied with fresh impulsive forces.

We are living in an age when supersensible knowledge can no longer remain the secret possession of a few. No, it must become the common property of all, in whom the meaning of life within this age is stirring as a very condition of their soul's existence. In the unconscious depths of the souls of men this need is already working, far more widespread than many people dream. And it will grow, more and more insistently, to the demand that the science of the Supersensible shall be treated on a like footing with the science of Nature.

How to Know Higher Worlds

How Is Knowledge of the Higher Worlds Attained?

There slumber in every human being faculties by means of which he can acquire for himself a knowledge of higher worlds. Mystics, Gnostics, Theosophists — all speak of a world of soul and spirit which for them is just as real as the world we see with our physical eyes and touch with our physical hands. At every moment the listener may say to himself: that, of which they speak, I too can learn, if I develop within myself certain powers which today still slumber within me. There remains only one question — how to set to work to develop such faculties. For this purpose, they only can give advice who already possess such powers. As long as the human race has existed there has always been a method of training, in the course of which individuals possessing these higher faculties gave instruction to others who were in search of them. Such a training is called occult (esoteric) training, and the instruction received therefrom is called occult (esoteric) teaching, or spiritual science. This designation naturally awakens misunderstanding. The one who hears it may very easily be misled into the belief that this training is the concern of a special, privileged class, withholding its knowledge arbitrarily from its fellow-creatures. He may even think that nothing of real importance lies behind such knowledge, for if it were a true knowledge — he is tempted to think — there would be no need of making a secret of it; it might be publicly imparted and its advantages made accessible to all. Those who have been initiated into the nature of this higher knowledge are not in the least surprised that the uninitiated should so think, for the secret of initiation can only be understood by those who have to a certain degree experienced this initiation into the higher knowledge of existence. The question may be raised: how, then, under these circumstances, are the uninitiated to develop any human interest in this so-called esoteric knowledge? How and why are they to seek for something of whose nature they can form no idea? Such a question is based upon an entirely erroneous conception of the real nature of esoteric knowledge. There is, in truth, no difference between esoteric knowledge and all the rest of man's knowledge and proficiency. This esoteric knowledge is no more of a secret for the average human being than writing is a secret for those who have never learned it. And just as all can learn to write who choose the correct method, so, too, can all who seek the right way become esoteric students and even teachers. In one respect only do the conditions here differ from those that apply to external knowledge and proficiency. The possibility of acquiring the art of writing may be withheld from someone through poverty, or through the conditions of civilization into which he is born; but for the attainment of knowledge and proficiency in the higher worlds, there is no obstacle for those who earnestly seek them.

Many believe that they must seek, at one place or another, the masters of higher knowledge in order to receive enlightenment. Now in the first place, whoever strives earnestly after higher knowledge will shun no exertion and fear no obstacle in his search for an initiate who can lead him to the higher knowledge of the world. On the other hand, everyone may be certain that initiation will find him under all circumstances if he gives proof of an earnest and worthy endeavor to attain this knowledge. It is a natural law among all initiates to withhold from no man the knowledge that is due him but there is an equally natural law which lays down that no word of esoteric knowledge shall be imparted to anyone not qualified to receive it. And the more strictly he observes these laws, the more perfect is an initiate. The bond of union embracing all initiates is spiritual and not external, but the two laws here mentioned form, as it were, strong clasps by which the component parts of this bond are held together. You may live in intimate friendship with an initiate, and yet a gap severs you from his essential self, so long as you have not become an initiate yourself. You may enjoy in the fullest sense the heart, the love of an initiate, yet he will only confide his knowledge to you when you are ripe for it. You may flatter him; you may torture him; nothing can induce him to betray anything to you as long as you, at the present stage of your evolution, are not competent to receive it into your soul in the right way.

The methods by which a student is prepared for the reception of higher knowledge are minutely prescribed. The direction he is to take is traced with unfading, everlasting letters in the worlds of the spirit where the initiates guard the higher secrets. In ancient times, anterior to our history, the temples of the spirit were also outwardly visible; today, because our life has become so unspiritual, they are not to be found in the world visible to external sight; yet they are present spiritually everywhere, and all who seek may find them.

Only within his own soul can a man find the means to unseal the lips of an initiate. He must develop within himself certain faculties to a definite degree, and then the highest treasures of the spirit can become his own.

He must begin with a certain fundamental attitude of soul. In spiritual science this fundamental attitude is called the path of veneration, of devotion to truth and knowledge. Without this attitude no one can become a student. The disposition shown in their childhood by subsequent students of higher knowledge is well known to the experienced in these matters. There are children who look up with religious awe to those whom they venerate. For such people they have a respect which forbids them, even in the deepest recess of their heart, to harbor any thought of criticism or opposition. Such children grow up into young men and women who feel happy when they are able to look up to anything that fills them with veneration. From the ranks of such children are recruited many students of higher knowledge. Have you ever paused outside the door of some venerated person, and have you, on this your first visit, felt a religious awe as you pressed on the handle to enter the room which for you is a holy place? If so, a feeling has been manifested within you which may be the germ of your future adherence to the path of knowledge. It is a blessing for every human being in process of development to have such feelings upon which to build. Only it must not be thought that this disposition leads to submissiveness and slavery. What was once a childlike veneration for persons becomes, later, a veneration for truth and knowledge. Experience teaches that they can best hold their heads erect who have learnt to venerate where veneration is due; and veneration is always fitting when it flows from the depths of the heart.

If we do not develop within ourselves this deeply rooted feeling that there is something higher than ourselves, we shall never find the strength to evolve to something higher. The initiate has only acquired the strength to lift his head to the heights of knowledge by guiding his heart to the depths of veneration and devotion. The heights of the spirit can only be climbed by passing through the portals of humility. You can only acquire right knowledge when you have learnt to esteem it. Man has certainly the right to turn his eyes to the light, but he must first acquire this right. There are laws in the spiritual life, as in the physical life. Rub a glass rod with an appropriate material and it will become electric, that is, it will receive the power of attracting small bodies. This is in keeping with a law of nature. It is known to all who have learnt a little physics. Similarly, acquaintance with the first principles of spiritual science shows that every feeling of true devotion harbored in the soul develops a power which may, sooner or later, lead further on the path of knowledge.

The student who is gifted with this feeling, or who is fortunate enough to have had it inculcated in a suitable education, brings a great deal along with him when, later in life, he seeks admittance to higher knowledge. Failing such preparation, he will encounter difficulties at the very first step, unless he undertakes, by rigorous self-education, to create within himself this inner life of devotion. In our time it is especially important that full attention be paid to this point. Our civilization tends more toward critical judgment and condemnation than toward devotion and selfless veneration. Our children already criticize far more than they worship. But every criticism, every adverse judgment passed, disperses the powers of the soul for the attainment of higher knowledge in the same measure that all veneration and reverence develops them. In this we do not wish to say anything against our civilization. There is no question here of leveling criticism against it. To this critical faculty, this self-conscious human judgment, this "test all things and hold fast what is best," we owe the greatness of our civilization. Man could never have attained to the science, the industry, the commerce, the rights relationships of our time, had he not applied to all things the standard of his critical judgment. But what we have thereby gained in external culture we have had to pay for with a corresponding loss of higher knowledge of spiritual life. It must be emphasized that higher knowledge is not concerned with the veneration of persons but the veneration of truth and knowledge.

Now, the one thing that everyone must acknowledge is the difficulty for those involved in the external civilization of our time to advance to the knowledge of the higher worlds. They can only do so if they work energetically at themselves. At a time when the conditions of material life were simpler, the attainment of spiritual knowledge was also easier. Objects of veneration and worship stood out in clearer relief from the ordinary things of the world. In an epoch of criticism ideals are lowered; other feelings take the place of veneration, respect, adoration, and wonder. Our own age thrusts these feelings further and further into the background, so that they can only be conveyed to man through his every-day life in a very small degree. Whoever seeks higher knowledge must create it for himself. He must instill it into his soul. It cannot be done by study; it can only be done through life. Whoever, therefore, wishes to become a student of higher knowledge must assiduously cultivate this inner life of devotion. Everywhere in his environment and his experiences he must seek motives of admiration and homage. If I meet a man and blame him for his shortcomings, I rob myself of power to attain higher knowledge; but if I try to enter lovingly into his merits, I gather such power. The student must continually be intent upon following this advice. The spiritually experienced know how much they owe to the circumstance that in face of all things they ever again turn to the good, and withhold adverse judgement. But this must not remain an external rule of life; rather it must take possession of our innermost soul. Man has it in his power to perfect himself and, in time, completely to transform himself. But this transformation must take place in his innermost self, in his thought-life. It is not enough that I show respect only in my outward bearing; I must have this respect in my thoughts. The student must begin by absorbing this devotion into this thought-life. He must be wary of thoughts of disrespect, of adverse criticism, existing in his consciousness, and he must endeavor straightaway to cultivate thoughts of devotion.

Every moment that we set ourselves to discover in our consciousness whatever there remains in it of adverse, disparaging and critical judgement of the world and of life; every such moment brings us nearer to higher knowledge. And we rise rapidly when we fill our consciousness in such moments with thoughts evoking in us admiration, respect and veneration for the world and for life. It is well known to those experienced in these matters that in every such moment powers are awakened which otherwise remain dormant. In this way the spiritual eyes of man are opened. He begins to see things around him which he could not have seen before. He begins to understand that hitherto he had only seen a part of the world around him. A human being standing before him now presents a new and different aspect. Of course, this rule of life alone will not yet enable him to see, for instance, what is described as the human aura, because for this still higher training is necessary. But he can rise to this higher training if he has previously undergone a rigorous training in devotion. (In the last chapter of his book Theosophy, the author describes fully the Path of Knowledge; here it is intended to give some practical details.)

Noiseless and unnoticed by the outer world is the treading of the Path of Knowledge. No change need be noticed in the student. He performs his duties as hitherto; he attends to his business as before. The transformation goes on only in the inner part of the soul hidden from outward sight. At first his entire inner life is flooded by this basic feeling of devotion for everything which is truly venerable. His entire soul-life finds in this fundamental feeling its pivot. Just as the sun's rays vivify everything living, so does reverence in the student vivify all feelings of the soul.

It is not easy, at first, to believe that feelings like reverence and respect have anything to do with cognition. This is due to the fact that we are inclined to set cognition aside as a faculty by itself — one that stands in no relation to what otherwise occurs in the soul. In so thinking we do not bear in mind that it is the soul which exercises the faculty of cognition; and feelings are for the soul what food is for the body. If we give the body stones in place of bread, its activity will cease. It is the same with the soul. Veneration, homage, devotion are like nutriment making it healthy and strong, especially strong for the activity of cognition. Disrespect, antipathy, underestimation of what deserves recognition, all exert a paralyzing and withering effect on this faculty of cognition. For the spiritually experienced this fact is visible in the aura. A soul which harbors feelings of reverence and devotion produces a change in its aura. Certain spiritual colorings, as they may be called, yellow-red and brown-red in tone, vanish and are replaced by blue-red tints. Thereby the cognitional faculty is ripened; it receives intelligence of facts in its environment of which it had hitherto no idea. Reverence awakens in the soul a sympathetic power through which we attract qualities in the beings around us, which would otherwise remain concealed.

The power obtained through devotion can be rendered still more effective when the life of feeling is enriched by yet another quality. This consists in giving oneself up less and less to impressions of the outer world, and to develop instead a vivid inner life. A person who darts from one impression of the outer world to another, who constantly seeks distraction, cannot find the way to higher knowledge. The student must not blunt himself to the outer world, but while lending himself to its impressions, he should be directed by his rich inner life.

When passing through a beautiful mountain district, the traveler with depth of soul and wealth of feeling has different experiences from one who is poor in feeling. Only what we experience within ourselves unlocks for us the beauties of the outer world. One person sails across the ocean, and only a few inward experiences pass through his soul; another will hear the eternal language of the cosmic spirit; for him are unveiled the mysterious riddles of existence. We must learn to remain in touch with our own feelings and ideas if we wish to develop any intimate relationship with the outer world. The outer world with all its phenomena is filled with splendor, but we must have experienced the divine within ourselves before we can hope to discover it in our environment.

The student is told to set apart moments in his daily life in which to withdraw into himself, quietly and alone. He is not to occupy himself at such moments with the affairs of his own ego. This would result in the contrary of what is intended. He should rather let his experiences and the messages from the outer world re-echo within his own completely silent self. At such silent moments every flower, every animal, every action will unveil to him secrets undreamt of. And thus he will prepare himself to receive quite new impressions of the outer world through quite different eyes. The desire to enjoy impression after impression merely blunts the faculty of cognition; the latter, however, is nurtured and cultivated if the enjoyment once experienced is allowed to reveal its message. Thus the student must accustom himself not merely to let the enjoyment reverberate, as it were, but rather to renounce any further enjoyment, and work upon the past experience. The peril here is very great. Instead of working inwardly, it is very easy to fall into the opposite habit of trying to exploit the enjoyment. Let no one underestimate the fact that immense sources of error here confront the student. He must pass through a host of tempters of his soul. They would all harden his ego and imprison it within itself. He should rather open it wide to all the world. It is necessary that he should seek enjoyment, for only through enjoyment can the outer world reach him. If he blunts himself to enjoyment he is like a plant which cannot any longer draw nourishment from its environment. Yet if he stops short at the enjoyment he shuts himself up within himself. He will only be something to himself and nothing to the world. However much he may live within himself, however intensely he may cultivate his ego — the world will reject him. To the world he is dead. The student of higher knowledge considers enjoyment only as a means of ennobling himself for the world. Enjoyment is to him like a scout informing him about the world; but once instructed by enjoyment, he passes on to work. He does not learn in order to accumulate learning as his own treasure, but in order that he may devote his learning to the service of the world.

In all spiritual science there is a fundamental principle which cannot be transgressed without sacrificing success, and it should be impressed on the student in every form of esoteric training. It runs as follows: All knowledge pursued merely for the enrichment of personal learning and the accumulation of personal treasure leads you away from the path; but all knowledge pursued for growth to ripeness within the process of human ennoblement and cosmic development brings you a step forward. This law must be strictly observed, and no student is genuine until he has adopted it as a guide for his whole life. This truth can be expressed in the following short sentence: Every idea which does not become your ideal slays a force in your soul; every idea which becomes your ideal creates within you life-forces.

Inner Tranquility

At the very beginning of his course, the student is directed to the path of veneration and the development of the inner life. Spiritual science now also gives him practical rules by observing which he may tread that path and develop that inner life. These practical rules have no arbitrary origin. They rest upon ancient experience and ancient wisdom, and are given out in the same manner, wheresoever the ways to higher knowledge are indicated. All true teachers of the spiritual life are in agreement as to the substance of these rules, even though they do not always clothe them in the same words. This difference, which is of a minor character and is more apparent than real, is due to circumstances which need not be dwelt upon here.

No teacher of the spiritual life wishes to establish a mastery over other persons by means of such rules. He would not tamper with anyone's independence. Indeed, none respect and cherish human independence more than the spiritually experienced. It was stated in the preceding pages that the bond of union embracing all initiates is spiritual, and that two laws form, as it were, clasps by which the component parts of this bond are held together. Whenever the initiate leaves his enclosed spiritual sphere and steps forth before the world, he must immediately take a third law into account. It is this: Adapt each one of your actions, and frame each one of your words in such a way that you infringe upon no one's free-will.

The recognition that all true teachers of the spiritual life are permeated through and through with this principle will convince all who follow the practical rules proffered to them that they need sacrifice none of their independence.

One of the first of these rules can be expressed somewhat in the following words of our language: Provide for yourself moments of inner tranquility, and in these moments learn to distinguish between the essential and the non-essential. It is said advisedly: "expressed in the words of our language." Originally all rules and teachings of spiritual science were expressed in a symbolical sign-language, some understanding of which must be acquired before its whole meaning and scope can be realized. This understanding is dependent on the first steps toward higher knowledge, and these steps result from the exact observation of such rules as are here given. For all who earnestly will, the path stands open to tread.

Simple, in truth, is the above rule concerning moments of inner tranquility; equally simple is its observation. But it only achieves its purpose when it is observed in as earnest and strict a manner as it is, in itself, simple. How this rule is to be observed will, therefore, be explained without digression.

The student must set aside a small part of his daily life in which to concern himself with something quite different from the objects of his daily occupation. The way, also, in which he occupies himself at such a time must differ entirely from the way in which he performs the rest of his daily duties. But this does not mean that what he does in the time thus set apart has no connection with his daily work. On the contrary, he will soon find that just these secluded moments, when sought in the right way, give him full power to perform his daily task[s]. Nor must it be supposed that the observance of this rule will really encroach upon the time needed for the performance of his duties. Should anyone really have no more time at his disposal, five minutes a day will suffice. It all depends on the manner in which these five minutes are spent.

During these periods the student should wrest himself entirely free from his work-a-day life. His thoughts and feelings should take on a different coloring. His joys and sorrows, his cares, experiences and actions must pass in review before his soul; and he must adopt such a position that he may regard all his sundry experiences from a higher point of view.

We need only bear in mind how, in ordinary life, we regard the experiences and actions of others quite differently from our own. This cannot be otherwise, for we are interwoven with our own actions and experiences, whereas those of others we only contemplate. Our aim in these moments of seclusion must be so to contemplate and judge our own actions and experiences as though they applied not to ourselves but to some other person. Suppose, for example, a heavy misfortune befalls us. How different would be our attitude toward a similar misfortune had it befallen our neighbor. This attitude cannot be blamed as unjustifiable; it is part of human nature, and applies equally to exceptional circumstances and to the daily affairs of life. The student must seek the power of confronting himself, at certain times, as a stranger. He must stand before himself with the inner tranquility of a judge. When this is attained, our own experiences present themselves in a new light. As long as we are interwoven with them and stand, as it were, within them, we cling to the non-essential just as much as to the essential. If we attain the calm inner survey, the essential is severed from the non-essential. Sorrow and joy, every thought, every resolve, appear different when we confront ourselves in this way. It is as though we had spent the whole day in a place where we beheld the smallest objects at the same close range as the largest, and in the evening climbed a neighboring hill and surveyed the whole scene at a glance. Then the various parts appear related to each other in different proportions from those they bore when seen from within. This exercise will not and need not succeed with present occurrences of destiny, but it should be attempted by the student in connection with the events of destiny already experienced in the past. The value of such inner tranquil self-contemplation depends far less on what is actually contemplated than on our finding within ourselves the power which such inner tranquility develops.

For every human being bears a higher man within himself besides what we may call the work-a-day man. This higher man remains hidden until he is awakened. And each human being can himself alone awaken this higher being within himself. As long as this higher being is not awakened, the higher faculties slumbering in every human being, and leading to supersensible knowledge, will remain concealed. The student must resolve to persevere in the strict and earnest observation of the rule here given, so long as he does not feel within himself the fruits of this inner tranquility. To all who thus persevere the day will come when spiritual light will envelop them, and a new world will be revealed to an organ of sight of whose presence within them they were never aware.

And no change need take place in the outward life of the student in consequence of this new rule. He performs his duties and, at first, feels the same joys, sorrows, and experiences as before. In no way can it estrange him from life; he can rather devote himself the more thoroughly to this life for the remainder of the day, having gained a higher life in the moments set apart. Little by little this higher life will make its influence felt on his ordinary life. The tranquility of the moments set apart will also affect everyday existence. In his whole being he will grow calmer; he will attain firm assurance in all his actions, and cease to be put out of countenance by all manner of incidents. By thus advancing he will gradually become more and more his own guide, and allow himself less and less to be led by circumstances and external influences. He will soon discover how great a source of strength is available to him in these moments thus set apart. He will begin no longer to get angry at things which formerly annoyed him; countless things he formerly feared cease to alarm him. He acquires a new outlook on life. Formerly he may have approached some occupation in a fainthearted way. He would say: "Oh, I lack the power to do this as well as I could wish." Now this thought does not occur to him, but rather a quite different thought. Henceforth he says to himself: "I will summon all my strength to do my work as well as I possibly can." And he suppresses the thought which makes him faint-hearted; for he knows that this very thought might be the cause of a worse performance on his part, and that in any case it cannot contribute to the improvement of his work. And thus thought after thought, each fraught with advantage to his whole life, flows into the student's outlook. They take the place of those that had a hampering, weakening effect. He begins to steer his own ship on a secure course through the waves of life, whereas it was formerly battered to and fro by these waves.

This calm and serenity react on the whole being. They assist the growth of the inner man, and, with the inner man, those faculties also grow which lead to higher knowledge. For it is by his progress in this direction that the student gradually reaches the point where he himself determines the manner in which the impressions of the outer world shall affect him. Thus he may hear a word spoken with the object of wounding or vexing him. Formerly it would indeed have wounded or vexed him, but now that he treads the path to higher knowledge, he is able — before the word has found its way to his inner self — to take from it the sting which gives it the power to wound or vex. Take another example. We easily become impatient when we are kept waiting, but — if we tread the path to higher knowledge — we so steep ourselves in our moments of calm with the feeling of the uselessness of impatience that henceforth, on every occasion of impatience, this feeling is immediately present within us. The impatience that was about to make itself felt vanishes, and an interval which would otherwise have been wasted in expressions of impatience will be filled by useful observations, which can be made while waiting.

Now, the scope and significance of these facts must be realized. We must bear in mind that the higher man within us is in constant development. But only the state of calm and serenity here described renders an orderly development possible. The waves of outward life constrain the inner man from all sides if, instead of mastering this outward life, it masters him. Such a man is like a plant which tries to expand in a cleft in the rock and is stunted in growth until new space is given it. No outward forces can supply space to the inner man. It can only be supplied by the inner calm which man himself gives to his soul. Outward circumstances can only alter the course of his outward life; they can never awaken the inner spiritual man. The student must himself give birth to a new and higher man within himself.

This higher man now becomes the inner ruler who directs the circumstances of the outer man with sure guidance. As long as the outer man has the upper hand and control, this inner man is his slave and therefore cannot unfold his powers. If it depends on something other than myself whether I should get angry or not, I am not master of myself, or, to put it better, I have not yet found the ruler within myself. I must develop the faculty of letting the impressions of the outer world approach me only in the way in which I myself determine; then only do I become in the real sense a student. And only in as far as the student earnestly seeks this power can he reach the goal. It is of no importance how far anyone can go in a given time; the point is that he should earnestly seek. Many have striven for years without noticing any appreciable progress; but many of those who did not despair, but remained unshaken, have then quite suddenly achieved the inner victory.

No doubt a great effort is required in many stations of life to provide these moments of inner calm; but the greater the effort needed, the more important is the achievement. In spiritual science everything depends upon energy, inward truthfulness, and uncompromising sincerity with which we confront our own selves, with all our deeds and actions, as a complete stranger.

But only one side of the student's inner activity is characterized by this birth of his own higher being. Something else is needed in addition. Even if he confronts himself as a stranger it is only himself that he contemplates; he looks on those experiences and actions with which he is connected through his particular station of life. He must now disengage himself from it and rise beyond to a purely human level, which no longer has anything to do with his own special situation. He must pass on to the contemplation of those things which would concern him as a human being, even if he lived under quite different circumstances and in quite a different situation. In this way something begins to live within him which ranges above the purely personal. His gaze is directed to worlds higher than those with which every-day life connects him. And thus he begins to feel and realize, as an inner experience, that he belongs to those higher worlds. These are worlds concerning which his senses and his daily occupation can tell him nothing. Thus he now shifts the central point of his being to the inner part of his nature. He listens to the voices within him which speak to him in his moments of tranquility; he cultivates an intercourse with the spiritual world. He is removed from the every-day world. Its noise is silenced. All around him there is silence. He puts away everything that reminds him of such impressions from without. Calm inward contemplation and converse with the purely spiritual world fill his soul. — Such tranquil contemplation must become a natural necessity in the life of the student. He is now plunged in a world of thought. He must develop a living feeling for this silent thought-activity. He must learn to love what the spirit pours into him. He will soon cease to feel that this thought-world is less real than the every-day things which surround him. He begins to deal with his thoughts as with things in space, and the moment approaches when he begins to feel that which reveals itself in the silent inward thought-work to be much higher, much more real, than the things in space. He discovers that something living expresses itself in this thought-world. He sees that his thoughts do not merely harbor shadow-pictures, but that through them hidden beings speak to him. Out of the silence, speech becomes audible to him. Formerly sound only reached him through his ear; now it resounds through his soul. An inner language, an inner word is revealed to him. This moment, when first experienced, is one of greatest rapture for the student. An inner light is shed over the whole external world, and a second life begins for him. Through his being there pours a divine stream from a world of divine rapture.

This life of the soul in thought, which gradually widens into a life in spiritual being, is called by Gnosis, and by Spiritual Science, Meditation (contemplative reflection). This meditation is the means to supersensible knowledge. But the student in such moments must not merely indulge in feelings; he must not have indefinite sensations in his soul. That would only hinder him from reaching true spiritual knowledge. His thoughts must be clear, sharp and definite, and he will be helped in this if he does not cling blindly to the thoughts that rise within him. Rather must he permeate himself with the lofty thoughts by which men already advanced and possessed of the spirit were inspired at such moments. He should start with the writings which themselves had their origin in just such revelation during meditation. In the mystic, gnostic and spiritual scientific literature of today the student will find such writings, and in them the material for his meditation. The seekers of the spirit have themselves set down in such writings the thoughts of the divine science which the Spirit has directed his messengers to proclaim to the world.

Through such meditation a complete transformation takes place in the student. He begins to form quite new conceptions of reality. All things acquire a fresh value for him. It cannot be repeated too often that this transformation does not alienate him from the world. He will in no way be estranged from his daily tasks and duties, for he comes to realize that the most insignificant action he has to accomplish, the most insignificant experience which offers itself to him, stands in connection with cosmic beings and cosmic events. When once this connection is revealed to him in his moments of contemplation, he comes to his daily activities with a new, fuller power. For now he knows that his labor and his suffering are given and endured for the sake of a great, spiritual, cosmic whole. Not weariness, but strength to live springs from meditation.

With firm step the student passes through life. No matter what it may bring him, he goes forward erect. In the past he knew not why he labored and suffered, but now he knows. It is obvious that such meditation leads more surely to the goal if conducted under the direction of experienced persons who know of themselves how everything may best be done; and their advice and guidance should be sought. Truly, no one loses his freedom thereby. What would otherwise be mere uncertain groping in the dark becomes under this direction purposeful work. All who apply to those possessing knowledge and experience in these matters will never apply in vain, only they must realize that what they seek is the advice of a friend, not the domination of a would-be ruler. It will always be found that they who really know are the most modest of men, and that nothing is further from their nature than what is called the lust for power.

When, by means of meditation, a man rises to union with the spirit, he brings to life the eternal in him, which is limited by neither birth nor death. The existence of this eternal being can only be doubted by those who have not themselves experienced it. Thus meditation is the way which also leads man to the knowledge, to the contemplation of his eternal, indestructible, essential being; and it is only through meditation that man can attain to such knowledge. Gnosis and Spiritual Science tell of the eternal nature of this being and of its reincarnation. The question is often asked: Why does a man know nothing of his experiences beyond the borders of life and death? Not thus should we ask, but rather: How can we attain such knowledge? In right meditation the path is opened. This alone can revive the memory of experiences beyond the border of life and death. Everyone can attain this knowledge; in each one of us lies the faculty of recognizing and contemplating for ourselves what genuine Mysticism, Spiritual Science, Anthroposophy, and Gnosis teach. Only the right means must be chosen. Only a being with ears and eyes can apprehend sounds and colors; nor can the eye perceive if the light which makes things visible is wanting. Spiritual Science gives the means of developing the spiritual ears and eyes, and of kindling the spiritual light; and this method of spiritual training: (1) Preparation; this develops the spiritual senses. (2) Enlightenment; this kindles the spiritual light. (3) Initiation; this establishes intercourse with the higher spiritual beings.

The Stages of Initiation

The information given in the following chapters constitutes steps in an esoteric training, the name and character of which will be understood by all who apply this information in the right way. It refers to the three stages through which the training of the spiritual life leads to a certain degree of initiation. But only so much will here be explained as can be publicly imparted. These are merely indications extracted from a still deeper and more intimate doctrine. In esoteric training itself a quite definite course of instruction is followed. Certain exercises enable the soul to attain to a conscious intercourse with the spiritual world. These exercises bear about the same relation to what will be imparted in the following pages, as the instruction given in a higher strictly disciplined school bears to the incidental training. But impatient dabbling, devoid of earnest perseverance, can lead to nothing at all. The study of Spiritual Science can only be successful if the student retain what has already been indicated in the preceding chapter, and on the basis of this proceed further.

The three stages which the above-mentioned tradition specifies, are as follows: (1) preparation; (2) enlightenment; (3) initiation. It is not altogether necessary that the first of these three stages should be completed before the second can be begun, nor that the second, in turn, be completed before the third be started. In certain respects it is possible to partake of enlightenment, and even of initiation, and in other respects still be in the preparatory stage. Yet it will be necessary to spend a certain time in the stage of preparation before any enlightenment can begin; and, at least in some respects, enlightenment must be completed before it is even possible to enter upon the stage of initiation. But in describing them it is necessary, for the sake of clarity, that the three stages be made to follow in order.

Preparation

Preparation consists in a strict and definite cultivation of the life of thought and feeling, through which the psycho-spiritual body becomes equipped with higher senses and organs of activity in the same way that natural forces have fitted the physical body with organs built out of indeterminate living matter.

To begin with, the attention of the soul is directed to certain events in the world that surrounds us. Such events are, on the one hand, life that is budding, growing, and flourishing, and on the other hand, all phenomena connected with fading, decaying, and withering. The student can observe these events simultaneously, wherever he turns his eyes and on every occasion they naturally evoke in him feelings and thoughts; but in ordinary circumstances he does not devote himself sufficiently to them. He hurries on too quickly from impression to impression. It is necessary, therefore, that he should fix his attention intently and consciously upon these phenomena. Wherever he observes a definite kind of blooming and flourishing, he must banish everything else from his soul, and entirely surrender himself, for a short time, to this one impression. He will soon convince himself that a feeling which heretofore in a similar case, would merely have flitted through his soul, now swells out and assumes a powerful and energetic form. He must now allow this feeling to reverberate quietly within himself while keeping inwardly quite still. He must cut himself off from the outer world, and simply and solely follow what his soul tells him of this blossoming and flourishing.

Yet it must not be thought that much progress can be made if the senses are blunted to the world. First look at the things as keenly and as intently as you possibly can; then only let the feeling which expands to life, and the thought which arises in the soul, take possession of you. The point is that the attention should be directed with perfect inner balance upon both phenomena. If the necessary tranquility be attained and you surrender yourself to the feeling which expands to life in the soul, then, in due time, the following experience will ensue. Thoughts and feelings of a new kind and unknown before will be noticed uprising in the soul. Indeed, the more often the attention be fixed alternately upon something growing, blossoming and flourishing, and upon something else that is fading and decaying, the more vivid will these feelings become. And just as the eyes and ears of the physical body are built by natural forces out of living matter, so will the organs of clairvoyance build themselves out of the feelings and thoughts thus evoked. A quite definite form of feeling is connected with growth and expansion, and another equally definite with all that is fading and decaying. But this is only the case if the effort be made to cultivate these feelings in the way indicated. It is possible to describe approximately what these feelings are like. A full conception of them is within the reach of all who undergo these inner experiences.

If the attention be frequently fixed on the phenomena of growing, blooming and flourishing, a feeling remotely allied to the sensation of a sunrise will ensue, while the phenomena of fading and decaying will produce an experience comparable, in the same way, to the slow rising of the moon on the horizon. Both these feelings are forces which, when duly cultivated and developed to ever increasing intensity, lead to the most significant spiritual results. A new world is opened to the student if he systematically and deliberately surrenders himself to such feelings. The soul-world, the so-called astral plane, begins to dawn upon him. Growth and decay are no longer facts which make indefinite impressions on him as of old, but rather they form themselves into spiritual lines and figures of which he had previously suspected nothing. And these lines and figures have, for the different phenomena, different forms. A blooming flower, an animal in the process of growth, a tree that is decaying, evoke in his soul different lines. The soul world (astral plane) broadens out slowly before him. These lines and figures are in no sense arbitrary. Two students who have reached the corresponding stage of development will always see the same lines and figures under the same conditions. Just as a round table will be seen as round by two normal persons, and not as round by one and square by the other, so too, at the sight of a flower, the same spiritual figure is presented to the soul. And just as the forms of animals and plants are described in ordinary natural history, so too, the spiritual scientist describes or draws the spiritual forms of the process of growth and decay, according to species and kind.

If the student has progressed so far that he can perceive the spiritual forms of those phenomena which are physically visible to his external sight, he is then not far from the stage where he will behold things which have no physical existence, and which therefore remain entirely hidden (occult) from those who have not received suitable instruction and training.

It should be emphasized that the student must never lose himself in speculations on the meaning of one thing or another. Such intellectualizing will only draw him away from the right road. He should look out on the world with keen, healthy senses and quickened power of observation, and then give himself up to the feeling that arises within him. He should not try to make out, through intellectual speculation, the meaning of things, but rather allow the things to disclose themselves. It should be remarked that artistic feeling, when coupled with a quiet introspective nature, forms the best preliminary condition for the development of spiritual faculties. This feeling pierces through the superficial aspect of things, and in so doing touches their secrets.

A further point of importance is what spiritual science calls orientation in the higher worlds. This is attained when the student is permeated, through and through, with the conscious realization that feelings and thoughts are just as much veritable realities as are tables and chairs in the world of the physical senses. In the soul and thought world, feelings and thoughts react upon each other just as do physical objects in the physical world. As long as the student is not vividly permeated with this consciousness, he will not believe that a wrong thought in his mind may have as devastating an effect upon other thoughts that spread life in the thought world as the effect wrought by a bullet fired at random upon the physical objects it hits. He will perhaps never allow himself to perform a physically visible action which he considers to be wrong, though he will not shrink from harboring wrong thoughts and feelings, for these appear harmless to the rest of the world. There can be no progress, however, on the path to higher knowledge unless we guard our thoughts and feelings in just the same way we guard out steps in the physical world. If we see a wall before us, we do not attempt to dash right through it, but turn aside. In other words, we guide ourselves by the laws of the physical world. There are such laws, too, for the soul and thought world, only they cannot impose themselves on us from without. They must flow out of the life of the soul itself. This can be attained if we forbid ourselves to harbor wrong thoughts and feelings. All arbitrary flitting to and fro in thought, all accidental ebbing and flowing of emotion must be forbidden in the same way. In so doing we do not become deficient in feeling. On the contrary, if we regulate our inner life in this way, we shall soon find ourselves becoming rich in feelings and creative with genuine imagination. In the place of petty emotionalism and capricious flights of thought, there appear significant emotions and thoughts that are fruitful. Feelings and thoughts of this kind lead the student to orientation in the spiritual world. He gains a right position in relation to the things of the spiritual world; a distinct and definite result comes into effect in his favor. Just as he, as a physical man, finds his way among physical things, so, too, his path now leads him between growth and decay, which he has already come to know in the way described above. On the one hand, he follows all processes of growing and flourishing and, on the other, of withering and decaying in a way that is necessary for his own and the world's advancement.

The student has also to bestow a further care on the world of sound. He must discriminate between sounds that are produced by the so-called inert (lifeless) bodies, for instance, a bell, or a musical instrument, or a falling mass, and those which proceed from a living creature (an animal or a human being.) When a bell is struck, we hear the sound and connect a pleasant feeling with it; but when we hear the cry of an animal, we can, besides our own feeling, detect through it the manifestation of an inward experience of the animal, whether of pleasure or pain. It is with the latter kind of sound that the student sets to work. He must concentrate his whole attention on the fact that the sound tells him of something that lies outside his own soul. He must immerse himself in this foreign thing. He must closely unite his own feeling with the pleasure or pain of which the sound tells him. He must get beyond the point of caring whether, for him, the sound is pleasant or unpleasant, agreeable or disagreeable, and his soul must be filled with whatever is occurring in the being from which the sound proceeds. Through such exercises, if systematically and deliberately performed, the student will develop within himself the faculty of intermingling, as it were, with the being from which the sound proceeds. A person sensitive to music will find it easier than one who is unmusical to cultivate his inner life in this way; but no one should suppose that a mere sense for music can take the place of this inner activity. The student must learn to feel in this way in the face of the whole of nature. This implants a new faculty in his world of thought and feeling. Through her resounding tones, the whole of nature begins to whisper her secrets to the student. What was hitherto merely incomprehensible noise to his soul becomes by this means a coherent language of nature. And whereas hitherto he only heard sound from the so-called inanimate objects, he now is aware of a new language of the soul. Should he advance further in this inner culture, he will soon learn that he can hear what hitherto he did not even surmise. He begins to hear with the soul.

To this, one thing more must be added before the highest point in this region can be attained. Of very great importance for the development of the student is the way in which he listens to others when they speak. He must accustom himself to do this in such a way that, while listening, his inner self is absolutely silent. If someone expresses an opinion and another listens, assent or dissent will, generally speaking, stir in the inner self of the listener. Many people in such cases feel themselves impelled to an expression of their assent, or more especially, of their dissent. In the student, all such assent or dissent must be silenced. It is not imperative that he should suddenly alter his way of living by trying to attain at all times to this complete inner silence. He will have to begin by doing so in special cases, deliberately selected by himself. Then quite slowly and by degrees, this new way of listening will creep into his habits, as of itself. In spiritual research this is systematically practiced. The student feels it his duty to listen, by way of practice, at certain times to the most contradictory views and, at the same time, bring entirely to silence all assent, and more especially, all adverse criticism. The point is that in so doing, not only all purely intellectual judgment be silenced, but also all feelings of displeasure, denial, or even assent. The student must at all times be particularly watchful lest such feelings, even when not on the surface, should still lurk in the innermost recess of the soul. He must listen, for example, to the statements of people who are, in some respects, far beneath him, and yet while doing so suppress every feeling of greater knowledge or superiority. It is useful for everyone to listen in this way to children, for even the wisest can learn incalculably much from children. The student can thus train himself to listen to the words of others quite selflessly, completely shutting down his own person and his opinions and way of feeling. When he practices listening without criticism, even when a completely contradictory opinion is advanced, when the most hopeless mistake is committed before him, he then learns, little by little, to blend himself with the being of another and become identified with it. Then he hears through the words into the soul of the other. Through continued exercise of this kind, sound becomes the right medium for the perception of soul and spirit. Of course it implies the very strictest self-discipline, but the latter leads to a high goal. When these exercises are practiced in connection with the other already given, dealing with the sounds of nature, the soul develops a new sense of hearing. She is now able to perceive manifestations from the spiritual world which do not find their expression in sounds perceptible to the physical ear. The perception of the "inner word" awakens. Gradually truths reveal themselves to the student from the spiritual world. He hears speech uttered to him in a spiritual way. Only to those who, by selfless listening, train themselves to be really receptive from within, in stillness, unmoved by personal opinion or feeling only to such can the higher beings speak of whom spiritual science tells. As long as one hurls any personal opinion or feeling against the speaker to whom one must listen, the beings of the spiritual world remain silent.

All higher truths are attained through such inwardly instilled speech, and what we hear from the lips of a true spiritual teacher has been experienced by him in this manner. But this does not mean that it is unimportant for us to acquaint ourselves with the writings of spiritual science before we can ourselves hear such inwardly instilled speech. On the contrary, the reading of such writings and the listening to the teachings of spiritual science are themselves means of attaining personal knowledge. Every sentence of spiritual science we hear is of a nature to direct the mind to the point which must be reached before the soul can experience real progress. To the practice of all that has here been indicated must be added the ardent study of what the spiritual researchers impart to the world. In all esoteric training such study belongs to the preparatory period, and all other methods will prove ineffective if due receptivity for the teachings of the spiritual researcher is lacking. For since these instructions are culled from the living inner word, from the living inwardly instilled speech, they are themselves gifted with spiritual life. They are not mere words; they are living powers. And while you follow the words of one who knows, while you read a book that springs from real inner experience, powers are at work in your soul which make you clairvoyant, just as natural forces have created out of living matter your eyes and your ears.

Enlightenment

Enlightenment proceeds from very simple processes. Here, too, it is a matter of developing certain feelings and thoughts which slumber in every human being and must be awakened. It is only when these simple processes are carried out with unfailing patience, continuously and conscientiously, that they can lead to the perception of the inner light-forms. The first step is taken by observing different natural objects in a particular way; for instance, a transparent and beautifully formed stone (a crystal), a plant, and an animal. The student should endeavor, at first, to direct his whole attention to a comparison of the stone with the animal in the following manner. The thoughts here mentioned should pass through his soul accompanied by vivid feelings, and no other thought, no other feeling, must mingle with them and disturb what should be an intensely attentive observation. The student says to himself: "The stone has a form; the animal also has a form. The stone remains motionless in its place. The animal changes its place. It is instinct (desire) which causes the animal to change its place. Instincts, too, are served by the form of the animal. Its organs and limbs are fashioned in accordance with these instincts. The form of the stone is not fashioned in accordance with desires, but in accordance with desireless force." (The fact here mentioned, in its bearing on the contemplation of crystals, is in many ways distorted by those who have only heard of it in an outward, exoteric manner, and in this way such practices as crystal-gazing have their origin Such manipulations are based on a misunderstanding. They have been described in many books, but they never form the subject of genuine esoteric teaching.)

By sinking deeply into such thoughts, and while doing so, observing the stone and the animal with rapt attention, there arise in the soul two quite separate kinds of feelings. From the stone there flows into the soul the one kind of feeling, and from the animal the other kind. The attempt will probably not succeed at first, but little by little, with genuine and patient practice, these feelings ensue. Only, this exercise must be practiced over and over again. At first the feelings are only present as long as the observation lasts. Later on they continue, and then they grow to something which remains living in the soul. The student has then but to reflect, and both feelings will always arise, even without the contemplation of an external object. Out of these feelings and the thoughts that are bound up with them, the organs of clairvoyance are formed. If the plant should then be included in this observation, it will be noticed that the feeling flowing from it lies between the feelings derived from the stone and the animal, in both quality and degree. The organs thus formed are spiritual eyes. The students gradually learns, by their means, to see something like soul and spirit colors. The spiritual world with its lines and figures remains dark as long as he has only attained what has been described as preparation; through enlightenment this world becomes light. Here it must also be noted that the words "dark" and "light," as well as the other expressions used, only approximately describe what is meant. This cannot be otherwise if ordinary language is used, for this language was created to suit physical conditions. Spiritual science describes that which, for clairvoyant organs, flows from the stone, as blue, or blue-red; and that which is felt as coming from the animal as red or red-yellow. In reality, colors of a spiritual kind are seen. The color proceeding the plant is green which little by little turns into a light ethereal pink. The plant is actually that product of nature which in higher worlds resembles, in certain respects, its constitution in the physical world. The same does not apply to the stone and the animal. It must now be clearly understood that the above-mentioned colors only represent the principal shades in the stone, plant and animal kingdom. In reality, all possible intermediate shades are present. Every stone, every plant, every animal has its own particular shade of color. In addition to these there are also the beings of the higher worlds who never incarnate physically, but who have their colors, often wonderful, often horrible.

Indeed, the wealth of color in these higher worlds is immeasurably greater than in the physical world.

Once the faculty of seeing with spiritual eyes has been acquired, one then encounters sooner or later the beings here mentioned, some of them higher, some lower than man himself--beings that never enter physical reality.

If this point has been reached, the way to a great deal lies open. But it is inadvisable to proceed further without paying careful heed to what is said or otherwise imparted by the spiritual researcher. And for that, too, which has been described, attention paid to such experienced guidance is the very best thing. Moreover, if a man has the strength and the endurance to travel so far that he fulfills the elementary conditions of enlightenment, he will assuredly seek and find the right guidance.

But in any circumstances, one precaution is necessary, failing which it were better to leave untrodden all steps on the path to higher knowledge. It is necessary that the student should lose none of his qualities as a good and noble man, or his receptivity for all physical reality. Indeed, throughout his training he must continually increase his moral strength, his inner purity, and his power of observation. To give an example: during the elementary exercises on enlightenment, the student must take care always to enlarge his sympathy for the animal and the human worlds, and his sense for the beauty of nature. Failing this care, such exercises would continually blunt that feeling and that sense; the heart would become hardened, and the senses blunted, and that could only lead to perilous results.

How enlightenment proceeds if the student rises, in the sense of the foregoing exercises, from the stone, the plant, and the animal, up to man, and how, after enlightenment, under all circumstances the union of the soul with the spiritual world is effected, leading to initiation--with these things the following chapters will deal, in as far as they can and may do so.

In our time the path to spiritual science is sought by many. It is sought in many ways, and many dangerous and even despicable practices are attempted. It is for this reason that they who claim to know something of the truth in these matters place before others the possibility of learning something of esoteric training. Only so much is here imparted as accords with this possibility. It is necessary that something of the truth should become known, in order to prevent error causing great harm. No harm can come to anyone following the way here described, so long as he does not force matters. Only, one thing should be noted: no student should spend more time and strength upon these exercises than he can spare with due regard to his station in life and to his duties; nor should he change anything, for the time being, in the external conditions of his life through taking this path. Without patience no genuine results can be attained. After doing an exercise for a few minutes, the student must be able to stop and continue quietly his daily work, and no thought of these exercises should mingle with the day's work. NO one is of use as an esoteric student or will ever attain results of real value who has not learned to wait in the highest and best sense of the word.

The Control of Thoughts and Feelings

When the student seeks the path leading to higher knowledge in the way described in the preceding chapter, he should not omit to fortify himself; throughout his work, with one ever present thought. He must never cease repeating to himself that he may have made quite considerable progress after a certain interval of time, though it may not be apparent to him in the way he perhaps expected; otherwise he can easily lose heart and abandon all attempts after a short time. The powers and faculties to be developed are of a most subtle kind, and differ entirely in their nature from the conceptions previously formed by the student. He had been accustomed to occupy himself exclusively with the physical world; the world of spirit and soul had been concealed from his vision and concepts. It is therefore not surprising if he does not immediately notice the powers of soul and spirit now developing in him. In this respect there is a possibility of discouragement for those setting out on the path to higher knowledge, if they ignore the experience gathered by responsible investigators. The teacher is aware of the progress made by his pupil long before the latter is conscious of it He knows how the delicate spiritual eyes begin to form themselves long before the pupil is aware of this, and a great part of what he has to say is couched in such terms as to prevent the pupil from losing patience and perseverance before he can himself gain knowledge of his own progress. The teacher, as we know, can confer upon the pupil no powers which are not already latent within him, and his sole function is to assist in the awakening of slumbering faculties. But what he imparts out of his own experience is a pillar of strength for the one wishing to penetrate through darkness to light. Many abandon the path to higher knowledge soon after having set foot upon it, because their progress is not immediately apparent to them. And even when the first experiences begin to dawn upon the pupil, he is apt to regard them as illusions, because he had formed quite different conceptions of what he was going to experience. He loses courage, either because he regards these first experiences as being of no value, or because they appear to him to be so insignificant that he cannot believe they will lead him to any appreciable results within a measurable time. Courage and self-confidence are two beacons which must never be extinguished on the path to higher knowledge. No one will ever travel far who cannot bring himself to repeat, over and over again, an exercise which has failed, apparently, for a countless number of times.

Long before any distinct perception of progress, there rises in the student, from the hidden depths of the soul, a feeling that he is on the right path. This feeling should be cherished and fostered, for it can develop into a trustworthy guide. Above all, it is imperative to extirpate the idea that any fantastic, mysterious practices are required for the attainment of higher knowledge. It must be clearly realized that a start has to be made with the thoughts and feelings with which we continually live, and that these feelings and thoughts must merely be given a new direction. Everyone must say to himself: "In my own world of thought and feeling the deepest mysteries lie hidden, only hitherto I have been unable to perceive them." In the end it all resolves itself into the fact that man ordinarily carries body, soul and spirit about with him, and yet is conscious in a true sense only of his body, and not of his soul and spirit. The student becomes conscious of soul and spirit, just as the ordinary person is conscious of his body. Hence it is highly important to give the proper direction to thoughts and feelings, for then only can the perception be developed of all that is invisible in ordinary life. One of the ways by which this development may be carried out will now be indicated. Again, like almost everything else so far explained, it is quite a simple matter. Yet its results are of the greatest consequence, if the necessary devotion and sympathy be applied.

Let the student place before himself the small seed of a plant, and while contemplating this insignificant object, form with intensity the right kind of thoughts, and through these thoughts develop certain feelings. In the first place let him clearly grasp what he really sees with his eyes. Let him describe to himself the shape, color and all other qualities of the seed. Then let his mind dwell upon the following train of thought: "Out of the seed, if planted in the soil, a plant of complex structure will grow." Let him build up this plant in his imagination, and reflect as follows: "What I am now picturing to myself in my imagination will later on be enticed from the seed by the forces of earth and light. If I had before me an artificial object which imitated the seed to such a deceptive degree that my eyes could not distinguish it from a real seed, no forces of earth or light could avail to produce from it a plant." If the student thoroughly grasps this thought so that it becomes an inward experience, he will also be able to form the following thought and couple it with the right feeling: "All that will ultimately grow out of the seed is now secretly enfolded within it as the force of the whole plant. In the artificial imitation of the seed there is no such force present. And yet both appear alike to my eyes. The real seed, therefore, contains something invisible which is not present in the imitation." It is on this invisible something that thought and feeling are to be concentrated. (Anyone objecting that a microscopical examination would reveal the difference between the real seed and the imitation would only show that he had failed to grasp the point. The intention is not to investigate the physical nature of the object, but to use it for the development of psycho-spiritual forces.)

Let the student fully realize that this invisible something will transmute itself later on into a visible plant, which he will have before him in its shape and color. Let him ponder on the thought: "The invisible will become visible. If I could not think, then that which will only become visible later on could not already make its presence felt to me." Particular stress must be laid on the following point: what the student thinks he must also feel with intensity. In inner tranquility, the thought mentioned above must become a conscious inner experience, to the exclusion of all other thoughts and disturbances. And sufficient time must be taken to allow the thought and the feeling which is coupled with it to bore themselves into the soul, as it were. If this be accomplished in the right way, then after a time — possibly not until after numerous attempts — an inner force will make itself felt. This force will create new powers of perception. The grain of seed will appear as if enveloped in a small luminous cloud. In a sensible-supersensible way, it will be felt as a kind of flame. The center of this flame evokes the same feeling that one has when under the impression of the color lilac, and the edges as when under the impression of a bluish tone. What was formerly invisible now becomes visible, for it is created by the power of the thoughts and feelings we have stirred to life within ourselves. The plant itself will not become visible until later, so that the physically invisible now reveals itself in a spiritually visible way.

It is not surprising that all this appears to many as illusion. "What is the use of such visions," they ask, "and such hallucinations?" And many will thus fall away and abandon the path. But this is precisely the important point: not to confuse spiritual reality with imagination at this difficult stage of human evolution, and further-more, to have the courage to press onward and not become timorous and faint-hearted. On the other hand, however, the necessity must be emphasized of maintaining unimpaired and of perpetually cultivating that healthy sound sense which distinguishes truth from illusion. Fully conscious self-control must never be lost during all these exercises, and they must be accompanied by the same sane, sound thinking which is applied to the details of every-day life. To lapse into reveries would be fatal. The intellectual clarity, not to say the sobriety of thought, must never for a moment be dulled. The greatest mistake would be made if the student's mental balance were disturbed through such exercises, if he were hampered in judging the matters of his daily life as sanely and as soundly as before. He should examine himself again and again to find out if he has remained unaltered in relation to the circumstances among which he lives, or whether he may perhaps have become unbalanced. Above all, strict care must be taken not to drift at random into vague reveries, or to experiment with all kinds of exercises. The trains of thought here indicated have been tested and practiced in esoteric training since the earliest times, and only such are given in these pages. Anyone attempting to use others devised by himself, or of which he may have heard or read at one place or another, will inevitably go astray and find himself on the path of boundless chimera.

As a further exercise to succeed the one just described, the following may be taken: Let the student place before him a plant which has attained the stage of full development. Now let him fill his mind with the thought that the time will come when this plant will wither and die. "Nothing will be left of what I now see before me. But this plant will have developed seeds which, in their turn, will develop to new plants. I again become aware that in what I see, something lies hidden which I cannot see. I fill my mind entirely with the thought: this plant with its form and colors, will in time be no more. But the reflection that it produces seeds teaches me that it will not disappear into nothing. I cannot at present see with my eyes that which guards it from disappearance, any more than I previously could discern the plant in the grain of seed. Thus there is something in the plant which my eyes cannot see. If I let this thought live within me, and if the corresponding feeling be coupled with it, then, in due time, there will again develop in my soul a force which will ripen into a new perception." Out of the plant there again grows a kind of spiritual flame-form, which is, of course, correspondingly larger than the one previously described. The flame can be felt as being greenish-blue in the center, and yellowish-red at the outer edge.

It must be explicitly emphasized that the colors here described are not seen as the physical eyes see colors, but that through spiritual perception the same feeling is experienced as in the case of a physical color-impression. To apprehend blue spiritually means to have a sensation similar to the one experienced when the physical eye rests on the color blue. This fact must be noted by all who intend to rise to spiritual perception. Otherwise they will expect a mere repetition of the physical in the spiritual. This could only lead to the bitterest deception.

Anyone having reached this point of spiritual vision is the richer by a great deal, for he can perceive things not only in their present state of being but also in their process of growth and decay. He begins to see in all things the spirit, of which physical eyes can know nothing. And therewith he has taken the first step toward the gradual solution, through personal vision, of the secret of birth and death. For the outer senses a being comes into existence through birth, and passes away through death. This, however, is only because these senses cannot perceive the concealed spirit of the being. For the spirit, birth and death are merely a transformation, just as the unfolding of the flower from the bud is a transformation enacted before our physical eyes. But if we desire to learn this through personal vision we must first awaken the requisite spiritual sense in the way here indicated.

In order to meet another objection, which may be raised by certain people who have some psychic experience, let it at once be admitted that there are shorter and simpler ways, and that there are persons who have acquired knowledge of the phenomena of birth and death through personal vision, without first going through all that has here been described. There are, in fact, people with considerable psychic gifts who need but a slight impulse in order to find themselves already developed. But they are the exceptions, and the methods described above are safer and apply equally to all. It is possible to acquire some knowledge of chemistry in an exceptional way, but if you wish to become a chemist you must follow the recognized and reliable course.

An error fraught with serious consequences would ensue if it were assumed that the desired result could be reached more easily if the grain of seed or the plant mentioned above were merely imagined, were merely pictured in the imagination. This might lead to results, but not so surely as the method here. The vision thus attained would, in most cases, be a mere fragment of the imagination, the transformation of which into genuine spiritual vision would still remain to be accomplished. It is not intended arbitrarily to create visions, but to allow reality to create them within oneself. The truth must well up from the depths of our own soul; it must not be conjured forth by our ordinary ego, but by the beings themselves whose spiritual truth we are to contemplate.

Once the student has found the beginnings of spiritual vision by means of such exercises, he may proceed to the contemplation of man himself. Simple phenomena of human life must first be chosen. But before making any attempt in this direction it is imperative for the student to strive for the absolute purity of his moral character. He must banish all through of ever using knowledge gained in this way for his own personal benefit. He must be convinced that he would never, under any circumstances, avail himself in an evil sense of any power he may gain over his fellow-creatures. For this reason, all who seek to discover through personal vision the secrets in human nature must follow the golden rule of true spiritual science. This golden rule is as follows: For every one step that you take in the pursuit of higher knowledge, take three steps in the perfection of your own character. If this rule is observed, such exercise as the following may be attempted:

Recall to mind some person whom you may have observed when he was filled with desire for some object. Direct your attention to this desire. It is best to recall to memory that moment when the desire was at its height, and it was still uncertain whether the object of the desire would be attained. And now fill your mind with this recollection, and reflect on what you can thus observe. Maintain the utmost inner tranquility. Make the greatest possible effort to be blind and deaf to everything that may be going on around you, and take special heed that through the conception thus evoked a feeling should awaken in your soul. Allow this feeling to rise in your soul like a cloud on the cloudless horizon. As a rule, of course, your reflection will be interrupted, because the person whom it concerns was not observed in this particular state of soul for a sufficient length of time. The attempt will most likely fail hundreds and hundreds of times. It is just a question of not losing patience. After many attempts you will succeed in experiencing a feeling In your soul corresponding to the state of soul of the person observed, and you will begin to notice that through this feeling a power grows in your soul that leads to spiritual insight into the state of soul of the other. A picture experienced as luminous appears in your field of vision. This spiritually luminous picture is the so-called astral embodiment of the desire observed in that soul. Again the impression of this picture may be described as flame-like, yellowish-red in the center, and reddish-blue or lilac at the edges. Much depends on treating such spiritual experiences with great delicacy. The best thing is not to speak to anyone about them except to your teacher, if you have one. Attempted descriptions of such experiences in inappropriate words usually only lead to gross self-deception. Ordinary terms are employed which are not intended for such things, and are therefore too gross and clumsy. The consequence is that in the attempt to clothe the experience in words we are misled into blending the actual experience with all kinds of fantastic delusions. Here again is another important rule for the student: know how to observe silence concerning your spiritual experiences. Yes, observe silence even toward yourself. Do not attempt to clothe in words what you contemplate in the spirit, or to pore over it with clumsy intellect. Lend yourself freely and without reservation to these spiritual impressions, and do not disturb them by reflecting and pondering over them too much. For you must remember that your reasoning faculties are, to begin with, by no means equal to your new experience. You have acquired these reasoning faculties in a life hitherto confined to the physical world of the senses; the faculties you are not acquiring transcend this world. Do not try, therefore, to apply to the new and higher perceptions the standard of the old. Only he who has gained some certainty and steadiness in the observation of inner experiences can speak about them, and thereby stimulate his fellow-men.

The exercise just described may be supplemented by the following: Direct your attention in the same way upon a person to whom the fulfillment of some wish, the gratification of some desire, has been granted. If the same rules and precautions be adopted as in the previous instance, spiritual insight will once more be attained. A spiritual insight will once more be attained. A spiritual flame-form will be distinguished, creating an impression of yellow in the center and green at the edges.

By such observation of his fellow-creatures, the student may easily lapse into a moral fault. He may become cold-hearted. Every conceivable effort must be made to prevent this. Such observation should only be practiced by one who has already risen to the level on which complete certainty is found that thoughts are real things. He will then no longer allow himself to think of his fellow-men in a way that is incompatible with the highest reverence for human dignity and human liberty. The thought that a human being could be merely an object of observation must never for a moment be entertained. Self-education must see to it that this insight into human nature should go hand in hand with an unlimited respect for the personal privilege of each individual, and with the recognition of the sacred and inviolable nature of that which dwells in each human being. A feeling of reverential awe must fill us, even in our recollections.

For the present, only these two examples can be given to show how enlightened insight into human nature may be achieved; they will at least serve to point out the way to be taken. By gaining the inner tranquility and repose indispensable for such observation, the student will have undergone a great inner transformation. He will then soon reach the point where this enrichment of his inner self will lend confidence and composure to his outward demeanor. And this transformation of his outward demeanor will again react favorably on his soul. Thus he will be able to help himself further along the road. He will find ways and means of penetrating more and more into the secrets of human nature which are hidden from our external senses, and he will then also become ripe for a deeper insight into the mysterious connections between human nature and all else that exists in the universe. By following this path the student approaches closer and closer to the moment when he can effectively take the first steps of initiation. But before these can be taken, one thing more is necessary, though at first its need will be least of all apparent; later on, however, the student will be convinced of it.

The would-be initiate must bring with him a certain measure of courage and fearlessness. He must positively go out of his way to find opportunities for developing these virtues. His training should provide for their systematic cultivation. In this respect, life itself is a good school — possibly the best school. The student must learn to look danger calmly in the face and try to overcome difficulties unswervingly. For instance, when in the presence of some peril, he must swiftly come to the conviction that fear is of no possible use; I must not feel afraid; I must only think of what is to be done. And he must improve to the extent of feeling, upon occasions which formerly inspired him with fear, that to be frightened, to be disheartened, are things that are out of the question as far as his own inmost self is concerned. By self-discipline in this direction, quite definite qualities are develop which are necessary for initiation into the higher mysteries. Just as man requires nervous force in his physical being in order to use his physical sense, so also he requires in his soul nature the force which is only developed in the courageous and the fearless. For in penetrating to the higher mysteries he will see things which are concealed from ordinary humanity by the illusion of the senses. If the physical senses do not allow us to perceive the higher truth, they are for this very reason our benefactors. Things are thereby hidden from us which, if realized without due preparation, would throw us into unutterable consternation, and the sight of which would be unendurable. The student must be fit to endure this sight. He loses certain supports in the outer world which he owes to the very illusion surrounding him. It is truly and literally as if the attention of someone were called to a danger which had threatened him for a long time, but of which he knew nothing. Hitherto he felt no fear, but now that he knows, he is overcome by fear, though the danger has not been rendered greater by his knowing it.

The forces at work in the world are both destructive and constructive; the destiny of manifested beings is birth and death. The seer is to behold the working of these forces and the march of destiny. The veil enshrouding the spiritual eyes in ordinary life is to be removed. But man is interwoven with these forces and with this destiny. His own nature harbors destructive and constructive forces. His own soul reveals itself to the seer as undisguised as the other objects. He must not lose strength in the face of this self-knowledge; but strength will fail him unless he brings a surplus on which to draw. For this purpose he must learn to maintain inner calm and steadiness in the face of difficult circumstances; he must cultivate a strong trust in the beneficent powers of existence. He must be prepared to find that many motives which had actuated him hitherto will do so no longer. He will have to recognize that previously he thought and acted in a certain way only because he was still in the throes of ignorance. Reasons that influenced him formerly will now disappear. He often acted out of vanity; he will now see how utterly futile all vanity is for the seer. He often acted out of greed; he will now become aware how destructive all greed is. He will have to develop quite new motives for his thoughts and actions, and it is just for this purpose that courage and fearlessness are required.

It is pre-eminently a question of cultivating this courage and this fearlessness in the inmost depths of thought-life. The student must learn never to despair over failure. He must be equal to the thought: I shall forget that I have failed in this matter, and I shall try once more as though this had not happened. Thus he will struggle through to the firm conviction that the fountain-head of strength from which he may draw is inexhaustible. He struggles ever onward to the spirit which will uplift him and support him, however weak and impotent his earthly self may have proved. He must be capable of pressing on to the future undismayed by any experiences of the past. If the student has acquired these faculties up to a certain point, he is then ripe to hear the real names of things, which are the key to higher knowledge. For initiation consists in this very act of learning to call the things of the world by those names which they bear in the spirit of their divine authors. In these, their names, lies the mystery of things. It is for this reason that the initiates speak a different language from the uninitiated, for the former know the names by which the beings themselves are called into existence.

In as far as initiation itself can be discussed, this will be done in the following chapter.

Initiation

Initiation is the highest stage in an esoteric training concerning which it is possible to give some indications in a book intended for the genuine public. Whatever lives beyond forms a subject difficult to understand, yet the way to it can be found by all who have passed through preparation, enlightenment, and initiation as far as the lesser mysteries.

The knowledge and proficiency conferred by initiation cannot be obtained in any other manner, except in some far distant future, after many incarnations, by quite different means and in quite a different form. The initiate of today undergoes experiences which would otherwise come to him much later, under quite different circumstances.

The secrets of existence are only accessible to an extent corresponding to man's own degree of maturity. For this reason alone the path to the higher stages of knowledge and power is beset with obstacles. A firearm should not be used until sufficient experience has been gained to avoid disaster, caused by its use. A person initiated today without further ado would lack the experience which he will gain during his future incarnations before he can attain to higher knowledge in the normal course of his development. At the portal of initiation, therefore, this experience must be supplied in some other way. Thus the first instructions given to the candidate for initiation serve as a substitute for these future experiences. These are the so-called trials, which he has to undergo, and which constitute a normal course of inner development resulting from due application to such exercises as are described in the preceding chapters.

These trials are often discussed in books, but it is only natural that such discussions should as a rule give quite false impressions of their nature; for without passing through preparation and enlightenment no one can know anything of these tests and appropriately describe them.

The would-be initiate must come into contact with certain things and facts belonging to the higher worlds, but he can only see and hear them if his feeling is ripe for the perception of the spiritual forms, colors and tones described in the chapters on Preparation and Enlightenment.

The first trial consists in obtaining a truer vision than the average man has of the corporeal attributes of lifeless things, and later of plants, animals and human beings. This does not mean what at present is called scientific knowledge, for it is a question not of science but of vision. As a rule, the would-be initiate proceeds to learn how the objects of nature and the beings gifted with life manifest themselves to the spiritual ear and the spiritual eye. In a certain way these things then lie stripped — naked — before the beholder. The qualities which can then be seen and heard are hidden from the physical eyes and ears. For physical perception they are concealed as if by a veil, and the falling away of this veil for the would-be initiate consists in a process designated as the process of Purification by Fire. The first trial is therefore known as the Fire-Trial.

For many people, ordinary life is itself a more or less unconscious process of initiation through the Fire-Trial. Such people have passed through a wealth of experience, so that their self-confidence, courage and fortitude have been greatly strengthened in a normal manner while learning to bear sorrow, disappointment and failure in their undertakings with greatness of soul, and especially with equanimity and unbroken strength. Thus they are often initiates without knowing it, and it then needs but little to unseal their spiritual hearing and sight so that they become clairvoyant. For it must be noted that a genuine fire-trial is not intended to satisfy the curiosity of the candidate. It is true that he learns many uncommon things of which others can have no inkling, but this acquisition of knowledge is not the end, but the means to the end; the end consists in the attainment, thanks to this knowledge of the higher worlds, of greater and truer self-confidence, a higher degree of courage, and a magnanimity and perseverance such as cannot, as a rule, be acquired in the lower world.

The candidate may always turn back after the fire-trial. He will then resume his life, strengthened in body and soul, and wait for a future incarnation to continue his initiation. In his present incarnation he will prove himself a more useful member of society and of humanity than he was before. In whatever position he may find himself, his firmness, prudence, resoluteness, and his beneficent influence over his fellows will have greatly increased.

But if, after completing the fire-trial, he should wish to continue the path, a certain writing-system generally adopted in esoteric training must now be revealed to him. The actual teachings manifest themselves in this writing, because the hidden (occult) qualities of things cannot be directly expressed in the words of ordinary writing. The pupils of the initiates translate the teachings into ordinary language as best they can. The occult script reveals itself to the soul when the latter has attained spiritual perception, for it is traced in the spiritual world and remains there for all time. It cannot be learned as an artificial writing is learned and read. The candidate grows into clairvoyant knowledge in an appropriate way, and during this growth a new strength is developed in his soul, as a new faculty, through which he feels himself impelled to decipher the occurrences and the beings of the spiritual world like the characters of a writing. This strength, with the experience it brings of the corresponding trial, might possibly awaken in the soul as though of its own accord, as the soul continually develops, but it will be found safer to follow the instructions of those who are spiritually experienced, and who have some proficiency in deciphering the occult script.

The signs of the occult script are not arbitrarily invented; they correspond to the forces actively engaged in the world. They teach us the language of things. It becomes immediately apparent to the candidate that the signs he is now learning correspond to the forms, colors, and tones which he learned to perceive during his preparation and enlightenment. He realizes that all he learned previously was only like learning to spell, and that he is only now beginning to read in the higher worlds. All the isolated figures, tones, and colors reveal themselves to him now in one great connected whole. Now for the first time he attains complete certainty in observing the higher worlds. Hitherto he could never know positively whether the things he saw were rightly seen. A regular understanding, too, is now at last possible between the candidate and the initiate in the spheres of higher knowledge. For whatever form the intercourse between an initiate and another person may take in ordinary life, the higher knowledge in its immediate form can only be imparted by the initiate in the above-mentioned sign-language.

Thanks to this language the student also learns certain rules of conduct and certain duties of which he formerly knew nothing. Having learned these he is able to perform actions endowed with a significance and a meaning such as the actions of one not initiated can never possess. He acts out of the higher worlds. Instructions concerning such action can only be read and understood in the writing in question.

Yet it must be emphasized that there are people unconsciously gifted with the ability and faculty of performing such actions, though they have never undergone an esoteric training. Such helpers of the world and of humanity pass through life bestowing blessings and performing good deeds. For reasons here not to be discussed, gifts have been bestowed on them which appear supernatural. What distinguishes them from the candidate for initiation is only that the latter acts consciously and with full insight into the entire situation. He acquires by training the gifts bestowed on others by higher powers for the good of humanity. We can sincerely revere these favored of God; but we should not for this reason regard the work of esoteric training as superfluous.

Once the student has learned the sign-language there awaits him yet another trial, to prove whether he can move with freedom and assurance in the higher worlds. In ordinary life he is impelled to action by exterior motives. He works at one occupation or another because one duty or another is imposed on him by outward circumstances. It need hardly be mentioned that the student must in no way neglect any of his duties in ordinary life because he is living and working in higher worlds. There is no duty in a higher world that can force a person to neglect any single one of his duties in the ordinary world. The father will remain just as good a father to his family, the mother just as good a mother, and neither the official nor the soldier, nor anyone else will be diverted from his work by becoming an esoteric student. On the contrary, all the qualities which make a human being capable and efficient are enhanced in the student to a degree incomprehensible to the uninitiated. If, in the eyes of the uninitiated, this does not always appear to be the case, it is simply because he often lacks the ability to judge the initiate correctly. The deeds of the latter are not always intelligible to the former. But this only happens in special cases.

At this stage of initiation there are duties to be performed for which no outward stimulus is given. The candidate will not be moved to action by external pressure, but only through adherence to the rules of conduct revealed to him in the occult script. He must now show in this second trial that, led by such rules, he can act with the same firmness and precision with which, for instance, an official performs the duties that belong to him. For this purpose, and in the course of his further training, he will find himself faced by a certain definite task. He must perform some action in consequence of observations made on the basis of what he has learned during preparation and enlightenment. The nature of this action can be understood by means of the occult script with which he is now familiar. If he recognizes his duty and acts rightly, his trial has been successful. The success can be recognized in the alteration produced by his action in the figures, colors, and tones apprehended by his spiritual eyes and ears. Exact indications are given, as the training progresses, showing how these figures appear and are experienced after the action has been performed, and the candidate must know how to produce this change. This trial is known as the Water-Trial, because in his activity in these higher worlds the candidate is deprived of the support derived from outward circumstances, as a swimmer is without support when swimming in water that is beyond his depth. This activity must be repeated until the candidate attains absolute poise and assurance.

The importance of this trial lies again in the acquisition of a quality. Through his experiences in the higher worlds, the candidate develops this quality in a short time to such a high degree that he would otherwise have to go through many incarnations, in the ordinary course of his development, before he could acquire it to the same extent. It all centers around the fact that he must be guided only by the results of his higher perception and reading of the occult script, in order to produce the changes in question in these higher regions of existence. Should he, in the course of his activity, introduce any of his own opinions and desires, or should he diverge for one moment from the laws which he has recognized to be right, in order to follow his own willful inclination, then the result produced would differ entirely from what was intended. He would lose sight of the goal to which his action tended, and confusion would result. Hence ample opportunity is given him in the course of this trial to develop self-control. This is the object in view.

Here again, this trial can be more easily passed by those whose life, before initiation, has led them to acquire self-control. Anyone having acquired the faculty of following high principles and ideals, while putting into the background all personal predilection; anyone capable of always performing his duty, even though inclinations and sympathies would like to seduce him from this duty — such a person is unconsciously an initiate in the midst of ordinary life. He will need but little to succeed in this particular trial. Indeed, a certain measure of initiation thus unconsciously acquired in life will, as a rule, be indispensable for success in this second trial. For even as it is difficult for those who have not learned to spell correctly in their childhood to make good this deficiency when fully grown up, so too it is difficult to develop the necessary degree of self-control at the moment of looking into the higher worlds, if this ability has not been acquired to a certain degree in ordinary life. The objects of the physical world do not alter, whatever the nature of our wishes, desires, and inclinations. In the higher worlds, however, our wishes, desires, and inclinations are causes that produce effects. If we wish to produce a particular effect in these worlds, we must strictly follow the right rules and subdue every arbitrary impulse.

One human quality is of very special importance at this stage of initiation, namely, an unquestionably sound judgment. Attention should be paid to the training of this faculty during all the previous stages; for it now remains to be proved whether the candidate is shaping in a way that shows him to be fit for the truth path of knowledge. Further progress is now only possible if he is able to distinguish illusion, superstition, and everything fantastic, from true reality. This is, at first, more difficult to accomplish in the higher stages of existence than in the lower. Every prejudice, every cherished opinion with regard to the things in question, must vanish; truth alone must guide. There must be perfect readiness to abandon at once any idea, opinion, or inclination when logical thought demands it. Certainty in higher worlds is only likely to be attained when personal opinion is never considered.

People whose mode of thought tends to fancifulness and superstition can never make progress on the path to higher knowledge. It is indeed a precious treasure that the student is to acquire. All doubt regarding the higher worlds is removed from him. With all their laws they reveal themselves to his gaze. But he cannot acquire this treasure so long as he is the prey of fancies and illusions. It would indeed be fatal if his imagination and his prejudices ran away with his intellect. Dreamers and fantastical people are as unfit for the path to higher knowledge as superstitious people. This cannot be over-emphasized. For the most dangerous enemies on the way to knowledge of the higher worlds lurk in such fantastical reveries and superstitions. Yet no one need to believe that the student loses all sense of poetry in life, all power of enthusiasm because the words: You must be rid of all prejudice, are written over the portal leading to the second trial of initiation, and because over the portal at the entrance to the first trial he read: Without normal common sense all thine efforts are in vain.

If the candidate is in this way sufficiently advanced, a third trial awaits him. He finds here no definite goal to be reached. All is left in his own hands. He finds himself in a situation where nothing impels him to act. He must find his way all alone and out of himself. Things or people to stimulate him to action are non-existent. Nothing and nobody can give him the strength he needs but he himself alone. Failure to find this inner strength will leave him standing where he was. Few of those, however, who have successfully passed the previous trials will fail to find the necessary strength at this point. Either they will have turned back already or they succeed at this point also. All that the candidate requires is the ability to come quickly to terms with himself, for he must here find his higher self in the truest sense of the word. He must rapidly decide in all things to listen to the inspiration of the spirit. There is no time for doubt or hesitation. Every moment of hesitation would prove that he was still unfit. Whatever prevents him from listening to the voice of the spirit must be courageously overcome. It is a question of showing presence of mind in this situation, and the training at this stage is concerned with the perfect development of this quality. All the accustomed inducements to act or even to think now cease. In order not to remain inactive he must not lose himself, for only within himself can he find the one central point of vantage where he can gain a firm hold. No one on reading this, without further acquaintance with these matters, should feel an antipathy for this principle of being thrown back on oneself, for success in this trial brings with it a moment of supreme happiness.

At this stage, no less than at the others, ordinary life is itself an esoteric training for many. For anyone having reached the point of being able, when suddenly confronted with some task or problem in life, to come to a swift decision without hesitation or delay, for him life itself has been a training in this sense. Such situations are here meant in which success is instantly lost if action is not rapid. A person who is quick to act when a misfortune is imminent, whereas a few moments of hesitation would have seen the misfortune an accomplished fact, and who has turned this ability into a permanent personal quality, has unconsciously acquired the degree of maturity necessary for the third trial. For at this stage everything centers round the development of absolute presence of mind. This trial is known as the Air-Trial, because while undergoing it the candidate can support himself neither upon the firm basis of external incentive nor upon the figures, tones, and colors which he has learned at the stages of preparation and enlightenment, but exclusively upon himself.

Upon successfully passing this trial the student is permitted to enter the temple of higher wisdom. All that is here said on this subject can only be the slenderest allusion. The task now to be performed is often expressed in the statement that the student must take an oath never to betray anything he has learned. These expressions, however, "oath" and "betray", are inappropriate and actually misleading. There is no question of an oath in the ordinary sense of the word, but rather of an experience that comes at this stage of development. The candidate learns how to apply the higher knowledge, how to place it at the service of humanity. He then begins really and truly to understand the world. It is not so much a question of withholding the higher truths, but far more of serving them in the right way and with the necessary tact. The silence he is to keep refers to something quite different. He acquires this fine quality with regard to things he had previously spoken, and especially with regard to the manner in which they were spoken. He would be a poor initiate who did not place all the higher knowledge he had acquired at the service of humanity, as well and as far as this is possible. The only obstacle to giving information in these matters is the lack of understanding on the part of the recipients. It is true, of course, that the higher knowledge does not lend itself to promiscuous talk; but no one having reached the stage of development described above is actually forbidden to say anything. No other person, no being exacts an oath from him with this intent. Everything is left to his own responsibility, and he learns in every situation to discover within himself what he has to do, and an oath means nothing more than that he has been found qualified to be entrusted with such a responsibility.

If the candidate is found fit for the foregoing experiences, he is then given what is called symbolically the draught of forgetfulness. This means that he is initiated into the secret knowledge that enables him to act without being continually disturbed by the lower memory. This is necessary for the initiate, for he must have full faith in the immediate present. He must be able to destroy the veil of memory which envelops man every moment of his life. If we judge something that happens to us today according to the experience of yesterday, we are exposed to a multitude of errors. Of course this does not mean that experience gained in life should be renounced. It should always be kept in mind as clearly as possible. But the initiate must have the ability to judge every new experience wholly according to what is inherent in it, and let it react upon him, unobscured by the past. We must be prepared at every moment that every object and every being can bring to us some new revelation. If we judge the new by the standard of the old we are liable to error. The memory of past experiences will be of greatest use for the very reason that it enables us to perceive the new. Had we not gone through a definite experience we should perhaps be blind to the qualities of the object or being that comes before us. Thus experience should serve the purpose of perceiving the new and not of judging it by the standard of the old. In this respect the initiate acquires certain definite qualities, and thereby many things are revealed to him which remain concealed from the uninitiated.

The second draught presented to the initiate is the draught of remembrance. Through its agency he acquires the faculty of retaining the knowledge of the higher truths ever present in his soul. Ordinary memory would be unequal to this task. We must unite ourselves and become as one with the higher truths.

We must not only know them, but be able, quite as a matter of course, to manifest and administer them in living actions, even as we ordinarily eat and drink. They must become our practice, our habit, our inclination. There must be no need to keep thinking about them in the ordinary sense; they must come to living expression through man himself; they must flow through him as the functions of life through his organism. Thus doth man ever raise himself, in a spiritual sense, to that same stature to which nature raised him in a physical sense.

Some Practical Aspects

The training of thoughts and feelings, pursued in the way described in the chapters on Preparation, Enlightenment, and Initiation, introduces into the soul and spirit the same organic symmetry with which nature has constructed the physical body. Before this development, soul and spirit are undifferentiated masses. The clairvoyant perceives them as interlacing, rotating, cloud-like spirals, dully glimmering in reddish, reddish-brown, or reddish-yellow tones. After this training they begin to assume a brilliant yellowish-green, or greenish-blue color, and show a regular structure. This inner regularity leading to higher knowledge, is attained when the student introduces into his thoughts and feelings the same orderly system with which nature has endowed his bodily organs that enable him to see, hear, digest, breath, speak. Gradually he learns to breath and see with this soul, to speak and hear with the spirit.

In the following pages some practical aspects of the higher education of soul and spirit will be treated in greater detail. They are such that anyone can put them into practice regardless of other rules, and thereby be led some distance further into spiritual science.

A particular effort must be made to cultivate the quality of patience. Every symptom of impatience produces a paralyzing, even a destructive effect on the higher faculties that slumber in us. We must not expect an immeasurable view into the higher worlds from one day to the next, for we should assuredly be disappointed. Contentment with the smallest fragment attained, repose and tranquility, must more and more take possession of the soul. It is quite understandable that the student should await results with impatience; but he will achieve nothing so long as he fails to master this impatience. Nor is it of any use to combat this impatience merely in the ordinary sense, for it will become only that much stronger. We over-look it in self-deception while it plants itself all the more firmly in the depths of the soul. It is only when we ever and again surrender ourselves to a certain definite thought, making it absolutely our own, that any results can be attained. This thought is as follows: I must certainly do everything I can for the training and development of my soul and spirit; but I shall wait patiently until higher powers shall have found me worthy of definite enlightenment. If this thought becomes so powerful in the student that it grows into an actual feature of his character, he is treading the right path. This feature soon sets its mark on his exterior. The gaze of his eye becomes steady, the movement of his body becomes sure, his decisions definite, and all that goes under the name of nervousness gradually disappears. Rules that appear trifling and insignificant must be taken into account. For example, supposing someone affronts us. Before our training we should have directed our resentment against the offender; a wave of anger would have surged up within us. In a similar case, however, the thought is immediately present in the mind of the student that such an affront makes no difference to his intrinsic worth. And he does whatever must be done to meet the affront with calm and composure, and not in a spirit of anger. Of course it is not a case of simply accepting every affront, but of acting with the same calm composure when dealing with an affront against our own person as we would if the affront were directed against another person, in whose favor we had the right to intervene. It must always be remembered that this training is not carried out in crude outward processes, but in subtle, silent alterations in the life of thought and feeling.

Patience has the effect of attraction, impatience the effect of repulsion on the treasures of higher knowledge. In the higher regions of existence nothing can be attained by haste and unrest. Above all things, desire and craving must be silenced, for these are qualities of the soul before which all higher knowledge shyly withdraws. However precious this knowledge is accounted, the student must not crave it if he wishes to attain it. If he wishes to have it for his own sake, he will never attain it. This requires him to be honest with himself in his innermost soul. He must in no case be under any illusion concerning his own self. With a feeling of inner truth he must look his own faults, weaknesses, and unfitness full in the face. The moment he tries to excuse to himself any of his weaknesses, he has placed a stone in his way on the path which is to lead him upward. Such obstacles can only be removed by self-enlightenment. There is only one way to get rid of faults and failings, and that is by a clear recognition of them. Everything slumbers in the human soul and can be awakened. A person can even improve his intellect and reason, if he quietly and calmly makes it clear to himself why he is weak in this respect. Such self- knowledge is, of course, difficult, for the temptation to self-deception is immeasurably great. Anyone making a habit of being truthful with himself opens the portal leading to a deeper insight.

All curiosity must fall away from the student. He must rid himself as much as possible of the habit of asking questions merely for the sake of gratifying a selfish thirst for knowledge. He must only ask when knowledge can serve to perfect his own being in the service of evolution. Nevertheless, his delight in knowledge and his devotion to it should in no way be hampered. He should listen devoutly to all that contributes to such an end, and should seek every opportunity for such devotional attention.

Special attention must be paid in esoteric training to the education of the life of desires. This does not mean that we are to become free of desire, for if we are to attain something we must also desire it, and desire will always tend to fulfillment if backed by a particular force. This force is derived from a right knowledge. Do not desire at all until you know what is right in any one sphere. That is one of the golden rules for the student. The wise man first ascertains the laws of the world, and then his desires become powers which realize themselves. The following example brings this out clearly. There are certainly many people who would like to learn from their own observation something about their life before birth. Such a desire is altogether useless and leads to no result so long as the person in question has not acquired a knowledge of the laws that govern the nature of the eternal, a knowledge of these laws in their subtlest and most intimate character, through the study of spiritual science. But if, having really acquired this knowledge, he wishes to proceed further, his desire, now ennobled and purified, will enable him to do so.

It is also no use saying: I particularly wish to examine my previous life, and shall study only for this purpose. We must rather be capable of abandoning this desire, of eliminating it altogether, and of studying, at first, with no such intention. We should cultivate a feeling of joy and devotion for what we learn, with no thought of the above end in view. We should learn to cherish and foster a particular desire in such a way that it brings with it its own fulfillment.

If we become angered, vexed or annoyed, we erect a wall around ourselves in the soul-world, and the forces which are to develop the eyes of the soul cannot approach. For instance, if a person angers me he sends forth a psychic current into the soul-world. I cannot see this current as long as I am myself capable of anger. My own anger conceals it from me. We must not, however, suppose that when we are free from anger we shall immediately have a psychic (astral) vision. For this purpose an organ of vision must have been developed in the soul. The beginnings of such an organ are latent in every human being, but remain ineffective as long as he is capable of anger. Yet this organ is not immediately present the moment anger has been combated to a small extent. We must rather persevere in this combating of anger and proceed patiently on our way; then some day we shall find that this eye of the soul has become developed. Of course, anger is not the only failing to be combated for the attainment of this end. Many grow impatient or skeptical, because they have for years combated certain qualities, and yet clairvoyance has not ensued. In that case they have just trained some qualities and allowed others to run riot. The gift of clairvoyance only manifests itself when all those qualities which stunt the growth of the latent faculties are suppressed. Undoubtedly, the beginnings of such seeing and hearing may appear at an earlier period, but these are only young and tender shoots which are subjected to all possible error, and which, if not carefully tended and guarded, may quickly die.

Other qualities which, like anger and vexation, have to be combated, are timidity, superstition, prejudice, vanity and ambition, curiosity, the mania for imparting information, and the making of distinctions in human beings according to the outward characteristics of rank, sex, race, and so forth. In our time it is difficult for people to understand how the combating of such qualities can have anything to do with the heightening of the faculty of cognition. But every spiritual scientist knows that much more depends upon such matters than upon the increase of intelligence and employment of artificial exercises. Especially can misunderstanding arise if we believe that we must become foolhardy in order to be fearless; that we must close our eyes to the differences between people, because we must combat the prejudices of rank, race, and so forth. Rather is it true that a correct estimate of all things is to be attained only when we are no longer entangled in prejudice. Even in the ordinary sense it is true that the fear of some phenomenon prevents us from estimating it rightly; that a racial prejudice prevents us from seeing into a man's soul. It is this ordinary sense that the student must develop in all its delicacy and subtlety.

Every word spoken without having been thoroughly purged in thought is a stone thrown in the way of esoteric training. And here something must be considered which can only be explained by giving an example. If anything be said to which we must reply, we must be careful to consider the speaker's opinion, feeling, and even his prejudice, rather than what we ourselves have to say at the moment on the subject under discussion. In this example a refined quality of tact is indicated, to the cultivation of which the student must devote his care. He must learn to judge what importance it may have for the other person if he opposes the latter's opinion with his own. This does not mean that he must withhold his opinion. There can be no question of that. But he must listen to the speaker as carefully and as attentively as he possibly can and let his reply derive its form from what he has just heard. In such cases one particular thought recurs ever and again to the student, and he is treading the right path if this thought lives with him to the extent of becoming a trait of his character. This thought is as follows: The importance lies not in the difference of our opinions but in his discovering through his own effort what is right if I contribute something toward it. Thoughts of this and of a similar nature cause the character and the behavior of the student to be permeated with a quality of gentleness, which is one of the chief means used in all esoteric training. Harshness scares away the soul-pictures that should open the eye of the soul; gentleness clears the obstacles away and unseals the inner organs.

Along with gentleness, another quality will presently be developed in the soul of the student: that of quietly paying attention to all the subtleties in the soul-life of his environment, while reducing to absolute silence any activity within his own soul. The soul-life of his environment will impress itself on him in such a way that his own soul will grow, and as it grows, become regular in its structure, as a plant expanding in the sunlight. Gentleness and patient reserve open the soul to the soul-world and the spirit to the spirit-world. Persevere in silent inner seclusion; close the senses to all that they brought you before your training; reduce to absolute immobility all the thoughts which, according to your previous habits, surged within you; become quite still and silent within, wait in patience, and then the higher worlds will begin to fashion and perfect the organs of sights and hearing in your soul and spirit. Do not expect immediately to see and hear in the world of soul and spirit, for all that you are doing does but contribute to the development of your higher senses, and you will only be able to hear with soul and spirit when you possess these higher senses. Having persevered for a time in silent inner seclusion, go about your customary daily affairs, imprinting deeply upon your mind this thought: "Some day, when I have grown sufficiently, I shall attain that which I am destined to attain," and make no attempt to attract forcefully any of these higher powers to yourself. Every student receives these instructions at the outset. By observing them he perfects himself. If he neglects them, all his labor is in vain. But they are only difficult of achievement for the impatient and the unpersevering. No other obstacles exist save those which we ourselves place in our own path, and which can be avoided by all who really will. This point must be continually emphasized, because many people form an altogether wrong conception of the difficulties that beset the path to higher knowledge. It is easier, in a certain sense, to accomplish the first steps along this path than to get the better of the commonest every-day difficulties without this training. Apart from this, only such things are here imparted as are attended by no danger whatsoever to the health of soul and body. There are other ways which lead more quickly to the goal, but what is here explained has nothing to do with them, because they have certain effects which no experienced spiritual scientist considers desirable. Since fragmentary information concerning these ways is continually finding its way into publicity, express warning must be given against entering upon them. For reasons which only the initiated can understand, these ways can never be made public in their true form. The fragments appearing here and there can never lead to profitable results, but may easily undermine health, happiness, and peace of mind. It would be far better for people to avoid having anything to do with such things than to risk entrusting themselves to wholly dark forces, of whose nature and origin they can know nothing.

Something may here be said concerning the environment in which this training should be undertaken, for this is not without some importance. And yet the case differs for almost every person. Anyone practicing in an environment filled only with self-seeking interests, as for example, the modern struggle for existence, must be conscious of the fact that these interests are not without their effect on the development of his spiritual organs. It is true that the inner laws of these organs are so powerful that this influence cannot be fatally injurious. Just as a lily can never grow into a thistle, however inappropriate its environment, so, too, the eye of the soul can never grow to anything but its destined shape even though it be subjected to the self-seeking interests of modern cities. But under all circumstances it is well if the student seeks, now and again, his environment in the restful peace, the inner dignity and sweetness of nature. Especially fortunate is the student who can carry out his esoteric training surrounded by the green world of plants, or among the sunny hills, where nature weaves her web of sweet simplicity. This environment develops the inner organs in a harmony which can never ensue in a modern city. More favorably situated than the townsman is the person who, during his childhood at least, had been able to breathe the fragrance of pines, to gaze on snowy peaks, and observe the silent activity of woodland creatures and insects. Yet no city-dweller should fail to give to the organs of his soul and spirit, as they develop, the nurture that comes from the inspired teachings of spiritual research. If our eyes cannot follow the woods in their mantel of green every spring, day by day, we should instead open our soul to the glorious teachings of the Bhagavad Gita, or of St. John's Gospel, or of St. Thomas à Kempis, and to the descriptions resulting from spiritual science. There are many ways to the summit of insight, but much depends on the right choice. The spiritually experienced could say much concerning these paths, much that might seem strange to the uninitiated. Someone, for instance, might be very far advanced on the path; he might be standing, so to speak, at the very entrance of sight and hearing with soul and spirit; he is then fortunate enough to make a journey over the calm or maybe tempestuous ocean, and a veil falls away from the eyes of his soul; suddenly he becomes a seer. Another is also so far advanced that this veil only needs to be loosened; this occurs through some stroke of destiny. On another this stroke might well have had the effect of paralyzing his powers and undermining his energy; for the esoteric student it becomes the occasion of his enlightenment. A third perseveres patiently for years without any marked result. Suddenly, while silently seated in his quiet chamber, spiritual light envelops him; the walls disappear, become transparent for his soul, and a new world expands before his eyes that have become seeing, or resounds in his ears that have become spiritually hearing.

The Conditions of Esoteric Training

The conditions attached to esoteric training are not arbitrary. They are the natural outcome of esoteric knowledge. Just as no one can become a painter who refuses to handle a paint-brush, so, too, no one can receive esoteric training who is unwilling to meet the demands considered necessary by the teacher. In the main, the latter can give nothing but advice, and everything he says should be accepted in this sense. He has already passed through the preparatory stages leading to a knowledge of the higher worlds, and knows from experience what is necessary. It depends entirely upon the free-will of each individual human being whether or not he choose to tread the same path. To insist on being admitted to esoteric training without fulfilling the conditions would be equivalent to saying: "Teach me how to paint, but do not ask me to handle a paint-brush." The teacher can never offer anything unless the recipient comes forward to meet him of his own free-will. But it must be emphasized that a general desire for higher knowledge is not sufficient. This desire will, of course, be felt by many, but nothing can be achieved by it alone so long as the special conditions attached to esoteric training are not accepted. This point should be considered by those who complain that the training is difficult. Failure or unwillingness to fulfill these strict conditions must entail the abandonment of esoteric training, for the time being. It is true, the conditions are strict, yet they are not harsh, since their fulfillment not only should be, but indeed must be a voluntary action.

If this fact be overlooked, esoteric training can easily appear in the light of a coercion of the soul or the conscience; for the training is based on the development of the inner life, and the teacher must necessarily give advice concerning this inner life. But there is no question of compulsion when a demand is met out of free choice. To ask of the teacher: "Give me your higher knowledge, but leave me my customary emotions, feelings, and thoughts," would be an impossible demand. In this case the gratification of curiosity and desire for knowledge would be the only motive. When pursued in such a spirit, however, higher knowledge can never be attained.

Let us now consider in turn the conditions imposed on the student. It should be emphasized that the complete fulfillment of any one of these conditions is not insisted upon, but only the corresponding effort. No one can wholly fulfill them, but everyone can start on the path toward them. It is the effort of will that matters, and the ready disposition to enter upon this path.

1. The first condition is that the student should pay heed to the advancement of bodily and spiritual health. Of course, health does not depend, in the first instance, upon the individual; but the effort to improve in this respect lies within the scope of all. Sound knowledge can alone proceed from sound human beings. The unhealthy are not rejected, but it is demanded of the student that he should have the will to lead a healthy life. In this respect he must attain the greatest possible independence. The good counsels of others, freely bestowed though generally unsought, are as a rule superfluous. Each must endeavor to take care of himself. From the physical aspect it will be more a question of warding off harmful influences than of anything else. In fulfilling our duties we must often do things that are detrimental to our health. We must decide at the right moment to place duty higher than the care of our health. But just think how much can be avoided with a little good will. Duty must in many cases stand higher than health, often, even, than life itself; but pleasure must never stand higher, as far as the student is concerned. For him pleasure can only be a means to health and to life, and in this connection we must, above all, be honest and truthful with ourselves. There is no use in leading an ascetic life when the underlying motive is the same in this case as in other enjoyments. Some may derive satisfaction from asceticism just as others can from wine-bibbing, but they must not imagine that this sort of asceticism will assist them in attaining higher knowledge. Many ascribe to their circumstances everything which apparently prevents them from making progress. They say they cannot develop themselves under their conditions of life. Now, many may find it desirable for other reasons to change their conditions of life, but no one need do so for the purpose of esoteric training. For the latter, a person need only do as much as possible, whatever his position, to further the health of body and soul. Every kind of work can serve the whole of humanity; and it is a surer sign of greatness of soul to perceive clearly how necessary for this whole is a petty, perhaps even an offensive employment than to think: "This work is not good enough for me; I am destined for something better." Of special importance for the student is the striving for complete health of mind. An unhealthy life of thought and feeling will not fail to obstruct the path to higher knowledge. Clear, calm thinking, with stability of feeling and emotion, form here the basis of all work. Nothing should be further removed from the student than an inclination toward a fantastical, excitable life, toward nervousness, exaggeration, and fanaticism. He should acquire a healthy outlook on all circumstances of life; he should meet the demands of life with steady assurance, quietly letting all things make their impression on him and reveal their message. He should be at pains to do justice to life on every occasion. All one-sided and extravagant tendencies in his sentiments and criticisms should be avoided. Failing this, he would find his

way merely into worlds of his own imagination, instead of higher worlds; in place of truth, his own pet opinions would assert themselves. It is better for the student to be matter-of-fact, than excitable and fantastic.

2. The second condition is that the student should feel himself co-ordinated as a link in the whole of life. Much is included in the fulfillment of this condition, but each can only fulfill it in his own manner. If I am a teacher, and my pupil does not fulfill my expectations, I must not divert my resentment against him but against myself. I must feel myself as one with my pupil, to the extent of asking myself: "Is my pupil's deficiency not the result of my own action?" Instead of directing my feelings against him I shall rather reflect on my own attitude, so that the pupil may in the future be better able to satisfy my demands. Proceeding from such an attitude, a change will come over the student's whole way of thinking. This holds good in all things, great or small. Such an attitude of mind, for instance, alters the way I regard a criminal. I suspend my judgment and say to myself: "I am, like him, only a human being. Through favorable circumstances I received an education which perhaps alone saved me from a similar fate." I may then also come to the conclusion that this human brother of mine would have become a different man had my teachers taken the same pains with him they took with me. I shall reflect on the fact that something was given to me which was withheld from him, that I enjoy my fortune precisely because it was denied him. And then I shall naturally come to think of myself as a link in the whole of humanity and a sharer in the responsibility for everything that occurs. This does not imply that such a thought should be immediately translated into external acts of agitation. It should be cherished in stillness within the soul. Then quite gradually it will set its mark on the outward demeanor of the student. In such matters each can only begin by reforming himself. It is of no avail, in the sense of the foregoing thoughts, to make general demands on the whole of humanity. It is easy to decide what men ought to be; but the student works in the depths, not on the surface. If would therefore be quite wrong to relate the demand here indicated with an external, least of all political, demands; with such matters this training can have nothing to do. Political agitators know, as a rule, what to demand of other people; but they say little of demands on themselves.

3. This brings us to the third condition. The student must work his way upward to the realization that his thoughts and feelings are as important for the world as his actions. It must be realized that it is equally injurious to hate a fellow-being as to strike him. The realization will then follow that by perfecting ourselves we accomplish something not only for ourselves, but for the whole world. The world derives equal benefit from our untainted feelings and thoughts as from our good demeanor, and as long as we cannot believe in this cosmic importance of our inner life, we are unfit for the path that is here described. We are only filled with the right faith in the significance of our inner self, of our soul, when we work at

it s though it were at least as real as all external things. We must admit that our every feeling produces an effect, just as does every action of our hand.

4. These words already express the fourth condition: to acquire the conviction that the real being of man does not lie in his exterior but in his interior. Anyone regarding himself as a product of the outer world, as a result of the physical world, cannot succeed in this esoteric training, for the feeling that we are beings of soul and spirit forms its very basis. The acquisition of this feeling renders the student fit to distinguish between inner duty and outward success. He learns that the one cannot be directly measured by the other. He must find the proper mean between what is indicated by external conditions and what he recognizes as the right conduct for himself. He should not force upon his environment anything for which it can have no understanding, but also he must be quite free from the desire to do only what can be appreciated by those around him. The voice of his own soul struggling honestly toward knowledge must bring him the one and only recognition of the truths for which he stands. But he must learn as much as he possibly can from his environment so as to discover what those around him need, and what is good for them. In this way he will develop within himself what is known in spiritual science as the "spiritual balance." An open heart for the needs of the outer world lies on one of the scales, and inner fortitude and unfaltering endurance on the other.

5. This brings us to the fifth condition: steadfastness in carrying out a resolution. Nothing should induce the student to deviate from a resolution he may have taken, save only the perception that he was in error. Every resolution is a force, and if this force does not produce an immediate effect at the point to which it was applied, it works nevertheless on in its own way. Success is only decisive when an action arises from desire. But all actions arising from desire are worthless in relation to the higher worlds. There, love for an action is alone the decisive factor. In this love, every impulse that impels the student to action should fulfill itself. Undismayed by failure, he will never grow weary of endeavoring repeatedly to translate some resolution into action. And in this way he reaches the stage of not waiting to see the outward effect of his actions, but of contenting himself with performing them. He will learn to sacrifice his actions, even his whole being, to the world, however the world may receive his sacrifice. Readiness for a sacrifice, for an offering such as this, must be shown by all who would pursue the path of esoteric training.

6. A sixth condition is the development of a feeling of thankfulness for everything with which man is favored. We must realize that our existence is a gift from the entire universe. How much is needed to enable each one of us to receive and maintain his existence! How much to we not owe to nature and to our fellow human beings! Thoughts such as these must come naturally to all who seek esoteric training, for if the latter do not feel inclined to entertain them, they will

be incapable of developing within themselves that all-embracing love which is necessary for the attainment of higher knowledge. Nothing can reveal itself to us which we do not love. And every revelation must fill us with thankfulness, for we ourselves are the richer for it.

7. All these conditions must be united in a seventh: to regard life unceasingly in the manner demanded by these conditions. The student thus makes it possible to give his life the stamp of uniformity. All his modes of expression will, in this way, be brought into harmony, and no longer contradict each other. And thus he will prepare himself for the inner tranquillity he must attain during the preliminary steps of his training.

Anyone sincerely showing the good will to fulfill these conditions may decide to seek esoteric training. He will then be ready to follow the advice given above. Much of his advice may appear to be merely on the surface, and many will perhaps say that they did not expect the training to proceed in such strict forms. But everything interior must manifest itself in an exterior way, and just as a picture is not evident when it exists only in the mind of the painter, so, too, there can be no esoteric training without outward expression. Disregard for strict forms is only shown by those who do not know that the exterior is the avenue of expression for the interior. No doubt it is the spirit that really matters, and not the form; but just as form without spirit is null and void, so also would spirit remain inactive if it did not create for itself a form.

The above conditions are calculated to render the student strong enough to fulfill the further demands made on him during this training. If he fail in these conditions he will hesitate before each new demand, and without them he will lack that faith in man which he must possess. For all striving for truth must be founded on faith in and true love for man. But though this is the foundation it is not the source of all striving for truth, for such striving can only flow from the soul's own fountain-head of strength. And the love of man must gradually widen to a love for all living creatures, yes, for all existence. Through failure to fulfill the condition here given, the student will lack the perfect love for everything that fashions and creates, and the inclination to refrain from all destruction as such. He must so train himself that not only in his actions but also in his words, feelings, and thoughts he will never destroy anything for the sake of destruction. His joy must be in growth and life, and he must only lend his hand to destruction, when he is also able, through and by means of destruction, to promote new life. This does not mean that the student must simply look on while evil runs riot, but rather that he must seek even in evil that side through which he may transform it into good. He will then see more and more clearly that evil and imperfection may best be combated by the creation of the good and the perfect. The student knows that out of nothing, nothing can be created, but also that the imperfect can be transformed into the perfect. Anyone developing within himself the disposition to create, will soon find himself capable of facing evil in the right way.

It must be clearly realized that the purpose of this training is to build and not to destroy. The student should therefore bring with him the good will for sincere and devoted work, and not the intention to criticize and destroy. He should be capable of devotion, for he must learn what he does not yet know; he should look reverently on that which discloses itself. Work and devotion, these are the fundamental qualities which must be demanded of the student. Some come to realize that they are making no progress, though in their own opinion they are untiringly active. The reason is that they have not grasped the meaning of work and devotion in the right way. Work done for the sake of success will be the least successful, and learning pursued without devotion will be the least conducive to progress. Only the love of work, and not of success, leads to progress. And if in learning the student seeks straight thinking and sound judgment, he need not stunt his devotion by doubts and suspicions.

We are not reduced to service subjection in listening to some information with quiet devotion and because we do not at once oppose it with our own opinion. Anyone having advanced some way in the attainment of higher knowledge knows that he owes everything to quiet attention and active reflection, and not to willful personal judgment. We should always bear in mind that we do not need to learn what we are already able to judge. Therefore if our sole intention is to judge, we can learn nothing more. Esoteric training, however, center in learning; we must have absolutely the good will to be learners. If we cannot understand something, it is far better not to judge than to judge adversely. We can wait until later for a true understanding. The higher we climb the ladder of knowledge, the more do we require the faculty of listening with quiet devotion. All perception of truth, all life and activity in the world of the spirit, become subtle and delicate in comparison with the processes of the ordinary intellect and of life in the physical world. The more the sphere of our activity widens out before us, the more delicate are the processes in which we are engaged. It is for this reason that men arrive at such different opinions and points of view regarding the higher regions. But there is one and only one opinion regarding higher truths and this one opinion is within reach of all who, through work and devotion, have so risen that they can really behold truth and contemplate it. Opinions differing from the one true opinion can only be arrived at when people, insufficiently prepared, judge in accordance with their pet theories, their habitual ways of thought, and so forth. Just as there is only one correct opinion concerning a mathematical problem, so also is this true with regard to the higher worlds. But before such an opinion can be reached, due preparation must first be undergone. If this were only considered, the conditions attached to esoteric training would be surprising to none. It is indeed true that truth and the higher life abide in every soul, and that each can and must find them for himself But they lie deeply buried, and can only be brought up from their deep shafts after all obstacles have been cleared away. Only the experienced can advise how this may be done. Such advice is found in spiritual science. No truth is forced on anyone; no dogma is proclaimed; a way only is pointed out. It is true that everyone could find this way unaided, but only perhaps after many incarnations. By esoteric training this way is shortened. We thus reach more quickly a point from which we can cooperate in those worlds where the salvation and evolution of man are furthered by spiritual work.

This brings to an end the indications to be given in connection with the attainment of knowledge of higher worlds. In the following chapter, and in further connection with the above, it will be shown how this development affects the higher elements of the human organism (the soul-organism or astral body, and the spirit or thought-body.) In this way the indications here given will be placed in a new light, and it will be possible to penetrate them in a deeper sense.

Some Results of Initiation

One of the fundamental principles of true spiritual science is that the one who devotes himself to its study should do so with full consciousness; he should attempt nothing and practice nothing without knowledge of the effect produced. A teacher of spiritual science who gives advice or instruction will, at the same time, always explain to those striving for higher knowledge the effects produced on body, soul and spirit, if his advice and instructions be followed.

Some effects produced upon the soul of the student will here be indicated. For only those who know such things as they are here communicated can undertake in full consciousness the exercises that lead to knowledge of the higher worlds. Without the latter no genuine esoteric training is possible, for it must be understood that all groping in the dark is discouraged, and that failure to pursue this training with open eyes may lead to mediumship, but not to exact clairvoyance in the sense of spiritual science.

The exercises described in the preceding chapters, if practiced in the right way, involve certain changes in the organism of the soul (astral body). The latter is only perceptible to the clairvoyant, and may be compared to a cloud, psycho-spiritually luminous to a certain degree, in the center of which the physical body is discernible. (A description will be found in the author's book, Theosophy.) In this astral body desires, lusts, passions, and ideas become visible in a spiritual way. Sensual appetites, for instance, create the impression of a dark red radiance with a definite shape; a pure and noble thought finds its expression in a reddish-violet radiance; the clear-cut concept of the logical thinker is experienced as a yellowish figure with sharply defined outline; the confused thought of the muddled head appears as a figure with vague outline. The thoughts of a person with one-sided, queer views appear sharply outlined but immobile, while the thoughts of people accessible to the points of view of others are seen to have mobile, changeable outlines. (In all these and the following descriptions it must be noted that by seeing a color, spiritual seeing is meant. When the clairvoyant speaks of "seeing red," he means: "I have an experience, in a psycho-spiritual way, which is equivalent to the physical experience when an impression of red is received." This mode of expression is here used because it is perfectly natural to the clairvoyant. If this point is over-looked, a mere color-vision may easily be mistaken for a genuine clairvoyant experience.)

The further the student advances in his inner development, the more regular will be the differentiation within his astral body. The latter is confused and undifferentiated in the case of a person of undeveloped inner life; yet the clairvoyant can perceive even the unorganized astral body as a figure standing out distinctly from its environment. It extends from the center of the head to the middle of the physical body, and appears like an independent body possessing certain organs. The organs now to be considered are perceptible to the clairvoyant near the following part of the physical body: the first between the eyes; the second near the larynx; the third in the region of the heart; the fourth in the so-called pit of the stomach; the fifth and sixth are situated in the abdomen. These organs are technically known as wheels, chakrams, or lotus flowers. They are so called on account of their likeness to wheels or flowers, but of course it should be clearly understood that such an expression is not to be applied more literally than is the term "wings" when referring to the two halves of the lungs. Just as there is no question of wings in the case of the lungs, so, too, in the case of the lotus flowers the expression must be taken figuratively. In undeveloped persons these lotus flowers are dark in color, motionless and inert. In the clairvoyant, however, they are luminous, mobile, and of variegated color. Something of this kind applies to the medium, though in a different way; this question, however, need not be pursued here any further.

Now, when the student begins his exercises, the lotus flowers become more luminous; later on they begin to revolve. When this occurs, clairvoyance begins. For these flowers are the sense-organs of the soul, and their revolutions express the fact that the clairvoyant perceives supersensibly. What was said previously concerning spiritual seeing applies equally to these revolutions and even to the lotus flowers themselves. No one can perceive the supersensible until he has developed his astral senses in this way. Thanks to the spiritual organ situated in the vicinity of the larynx, it becomes possible to survey clairvoyantly the thoughts and mentality of other beings, and to obtain a deeper insight into the true laws of natural phenomena. The organ situated near the heart permits of clairvoyant knowledge of the sentiments and disposition of other souls. When developed, this organ also makes it possible to observe certain deeper forces in animals and plants. By means of the organ in the so-called pit of the stomach, knowledge is acquired of the talents and capacities of souls; by its means, too, the part played by animals, plants, stones, metals, atmospheric phenomena and so on in the household of nature becomes apparent.

The organ in the vicinity of the larynx has sixteen petals or spokes; the one in the region of the heart twelve, and the one in the pit of the stomach ten.

Now certain activities of the soul are connected with the development of these organs, and anyone devoting himself to them in a certain definite way contributes something to the development of the corresponding organs. In the sixteen-petalled lotus, eight of its sixteen petals were developed in the remote past during an earlier stage of human evolution. Man himself contributed nothing to this development; he received them as a gift from nature, at a time when his consciousness was in a dull, dreamy condition. At that stage of human evolution they were in active use, but the manner of their activity was only compatible with that dull state of consciousness. As consciousness became clearer and brighter, the petals became obscured and ceased their activity. Man himself can now develop the remaining eight petals by means of conscious exercises, and thereby the whole lotus flower becomes luminous and mobile. The acquisition of certain faculties depends on the development of each one of the sixteen petals. Yet, as already shown, only eight can be consciously developed; the remainder then appear of their own accord.

The development proceeds in the following manner. The student must first apply himself with care and attention to certain functions of the soul hitherto exercised by him in a careless and inattentive manner. There are eight such functions. The first is the way in which ideas and conceptions are acquired. In this respect people usually allow themselves to be led by chance alone. They see or hear one thing or another and form their ideas accordingly. As long as this is the case the sixteen petals of the lotus flower remain ineffective. It is only when the student begins to take his self-education in hand, in this respect, that the petals become effective. His ideas and conceptions must be guarded; each single idea should acquire significance fore him; he should see it in a definite message instructing him concerning the things of the outer world, and he should derive no satisfaction from ideas devoid of such significance. He must govern his mental life so that it becomes a true mirror of the outer world, and direct his effort to the exclusion of incorrect ideas from his soul.

The second of these functions is concerned with the control of resolutions. The student must not resolve upon even the most trifling act without well-founded and thorough consideration. Thoughtless and meaningless actions should be foreign to his nature. He should have well-considered grounds for everything he does, and abstain from everything to which no significant motive urges him.

The third function concerns speech. The student should utter no word that is devoid of sense and meaning; all talking for the sake of talking draws him away from his path. He must avoid the usual kind of conversation, with its promiscuous discussion of indiscriminately varied topics. This does not imply his preclusion from intercourse with his fellows. It is precisely in such intercourse that his conversation should develop to significance. He is ready to converse with everyone, but he does so thoughtfully and with thorough deliberation. He never speaks without grounds for what he says. He seeks to use neither too many nor too few words.

The fourth is the regulation of outward action. The student tries to adjust his actions in such a way that they harmonize with the actions of his fellow-men and with the events in his environment. He refrains from actions which are disturbing to others and in conflict with his surroundings. He seeks to adjust his actions so that they combine harmoniously with his surroundings and with his position in life. When an external motive causes him to act he considers how he can best respond. When the impulse proceeds from himself he weighs with minute care the effects of his activity.

The fifth function includes the management of the whole of life. The student endeavors to live in conformity with both nature and spirit. Never overhasty, he is also never indolent. Excessive activity and laziness are equally alien to him. He looks upon life as a means for work and disposes it accordingly. He regulates his habits and the care of his health in such a way that a harmonious whole is the outcome.

The sixth is concerned with human endeavor. The student tests his capacities and proficiency, and conducts himself in the light of such self- knowledge. He attempts nothing beyond his powers, yet seems to omit nothing within their scope. On the other hand, he sets himself aims that have to do with the ideals and the great duties of a human being. He does not mechanically regard himself as a wheel in the vast machinery of mankind but seeks to comprehend the tasks of his life, and to look out beyond the limit of the daily and trivial. He endeavors to fulfill his obligations ever better and more perfectly.

The seventh deals with the effort to learn as much from life as possible. Nothing passes before the student without giving him occasion to accumulate experience which is of value to him for life. If he has performed anything wrongly or imperfectly, he lets this be an incentive for meeting the same contingency later on rightly and perfectly. When others act he observes them with the same end in view. He tries to gather a rich store of experience, ever returning to it for counsel; nor indeed will he ever do anything without looking back on experiences from which he can derive help in his decisions and affairs.

Finally, the eighth is as follows: The student must, from time to time, glance introspectively into himself, sink back into himself, take counsel with himself, form and test the fundamental principles of his life, run over in his thoughts the sum total of his knowledge, weigh his duties, and reflect upon the content and aim of life. All these things have been mentioned in the preceding chapters; here they are merely recapitulated in connection with the development of the sixteen-petalled lotus. By means of these exercises the latter will become ever more and more perfect, for it is upon such exercises that the development of clairvoyance depends. The better the student's thoughts and speech harmonize with the processes in the outer world, the more quickly will he develop this faculty. Whoever thinks and speaks what is contrary to truth destroys something in the germ of his sixteen-petalled lotus. Truthfulness, uprightness, and honesty are in this connection creative forces, while mendacity, deceitfulness, and dishonesty are destructive forces. The student must realize, however, that actual deeds are needed, and not merely good intentions. If I think or say anything that does not conform with reality, I kill something in my spiritual organs, even though I believe my intentions to be ever so good. It is here as with the child which needs must burn itself when it touches fire, even though it did so out of ignorance. The regulation of the above activities of the soul in the manner described causes the sixteen-petalled lotus to shine in glorious hues, and imparts to it a definite movement. Yet it must be noted that the faculty of clairvoyance cannot make its appearance before a definite degree of development of the soul has been reached. It cannot appear as long as it is irksome for the student to regulate his life in this manner. He is still unfit as long as the activities described above are a matter of special pre-occupation for him The first traces of clairvoyance only appear when he has reached the point of being able to live in the specified way, as a person habitually lives. These things must then no longer be laborious, but must have become a matter of course. There must be no need for him to be continually watching himself and urging himself on to live in this way. It must all have become a matter of habit.

Now this lotus flower may be made to develop in another way by following certain other instructions. But all such methods are rejected by true spiritual science, for they lead to the destruction of physical health and to moral ruin. They are easier to follow than those here described. The latter, though protracted and difficult, lead to the true goal and cannot but strengthen morally.

The distorted development of a lotus flower results not only in illusions and fantastic conceptions, should a certain degree of clairvoyance be acquired, but also in errors and instability in ordinary life. Such a development may be the cause of timidity, envy, vanity, haughtiness, willfulness and so on in a person who hitherto was free from these defects. It has already been explained that eight of the sixteen petals of this lotus flower were developed in a remote past, and that these will re-appear of themselves in the course of esoteric development. All the effort and attention of the student must be devoted to the remaining eight. Faulty training may easily result in the re-appearance of the earlier petals alone, while the new petals remain stunted. This will ensue especially if too little logical, rational thinking is employed in the training. It is of supreme importance that the student should be a rational and clear-thinking person, and of further importance that he should practice the greatest clarity of speech. People who begin to have some presentiment of supersensible things are apt to wax talkative on this subject, thereby retarding their normal development. The less one talks about these matters the better. Only someone who has achieved a certain degree of clarity should speak about them. At the beginning of their instruction, students are as a rule astonishes at the teacher's lack of curiosity concerning their own experiences. It would be much better for them to remain entirely silent on this subject, and to content themselves with mentioning only whether they have been successful or unsuccessful in performing the exercises and observing the instructions given them. For the teacher has quite other means of estimating their progress than the students' own statements. The eight petals now under consideration always become a little hardened through such statements, whereas they should be kept soft and supple. The following example taken, for the sake of clarity, not from the supersensible world but from ordinary life, will illustrate this point. Suppose I hear a piece of news and thereupon immediately form an opinion. Shortly afterwards I receive some further news which does not tally with the previous information. I am thereby obliged to reverse my previous judgment. The result is an unfavorable influence upon my sixteen-petalled lotus. Quite the contrary would have been the case had I, in the first place, suspended judgment, and remained silent both inwardly in thought and outwardly in word concerning the whole affair, until I had acquired reliable grounds for forming my judgment. Caution in the formation and pronouncement of judgments becomes, by degrees, the special characteristic of the student. On the other hand his receptivity for impressions and experiences increases; he lets them pass over him silently, so as to collect and have the largest possible number of facts at his disposal when the time comes to form his opinions. Bluish-red and reddish-pink shades color the lotus flower as the result of such circumspection, whereas in the opposite case dark red and orange shades appear. (Students will recognize in the conditions attached to the development of the sixteen-petalled lotus the instructions given by the Buddha to his disciples for the Path. Yet there is no question here of teaching Buddhism, but of describing conditions governing development which are the natural outcome of spiritual science. The fact that these conditions correspond with certain teachings of the Buddha is no reason for not finding them true in themselves.)

The twelve-petalled lotus situated in the region of the heart is developed in a similar way. Half its petals, too, were already existent and in active use in a remote stage of human evolution. Hence these six petals need not now be especially developed in esoteric training; they appear of themselves and begin to revolve when the student sets to work on the other six. Here again he learns to promote this development by consciously controlling and directing certain inner activities in a special way.

It must be clearly understood that the perceptions of each single organ of soul or sprit bear a different character. The twelve and sixteen-petalled lotus flowers transmit quite different perceptions. The latter perceives forms. The thoughts and mentality of other beings and the laws governing natural phenomena become manifest, through the sixteen-petalled lotus, as figures, not rigid motionless figures but mobile forms filled with life. The clairvoyant in whom this sense is developed can describe, for every mode of thought and for every law of nature, a form which expresses them. A revengeful thought, for example, assumes an arrow-like, pronged form, while a kindly thought is often formed like an opening flower, and so on. Clear-cut, significant thoughts are regular and symmetrical in form, while confused thoughts have wavy outlines. Quite different perceptions are received through the twelve-petalled lotus. These perceptions may, in a sense, be likened to warmth and cold, as applied to the soul. A clairvoyant equipped with this faculty feels this warmth and cold streaming out from the forms discerned by the sixteen-petalled lotus. Had he developed the sixteen and not the twelve-petalled lotus he would only perceive, in the kindly thought, for instance, the figure described above, while a clairvoyant in whom both senses were developed would also notice what can only be described as soul-warmth, flowing from the thought. It would be noted in passing that esoteric training never develops one organ without the other, so that the above-mentioned example may be regarded as a hypothetical case in behalf of clarity. The twelve-petalled lotus, when developed, reveals to the clairvoyant a deep understanding of the processes of nature. Rays of soul-warmth issue from every manifestation of growth and development, while everything in the process of decay, destruction, ruin, gives an impression of cold.

The development of this sense may be furthered in the following manner. To begin with, the student endeavors to regulate his sequence of thought (control of thought). Just as the sixteen-petalled lotus is developed by cultivating thoughts that conform with truth and are significant, so, too, the twelve-petalled lotus is developed by inwardly controlling the trains of thought. Thoughts that dart to and fro like will-o'-the-wisps and follow each other in no logical or rational sequence, but merely by pure chance, destroy its form. The closer thought is made to follow upon thought, and the more strictly everything of illogical nature is avoided, the more suitable will be the form this sense organ develops. If the student hears illogical thoughts he immediately lets the right thoughts pass through his mind. He should not, however, withdraw in a loveless way from what is perhaps an illogical environment in order to further his own development. Neither should he feel himself impelled to correct all the illogical thoughts expressed around him. He should rather silently co-ordinate the thoughts as they pour in upon him, and make them conform to logic and sense, and at the same time endeavor in every case to retain this same method in his own thinking.

An equal consistency in his actions forms the second requirement (control of actions). All inconstancy, all disharmony of action, is baneful for the lotus here in question. When the student performs some action he must see to it that his succeeding action follows in logical sequence, for if he acts from day to day with variable intent he will never develop the faculty here considered.

The third requirement is the cultivation of endurance (perseverance). The student is impervious to all influences which would divert him from the goal he has set himself, as long as he can regard it as the right goal. For him, obstacles contain a challenge that impels him to surmount them, but never a reason for giving up.

The fourth requirement is forbearance (tolerance) toward persons, creatures, and also circumstances. The student suppresses all superfluous criticism of everything that is imperfect, evil and bad, and seeks rather to understand everything that comes under his notice. Even as the sun does not withdraw its light from the bad and the evil, so he, too, does not refuse them an intelligent sympathy. Should some trouble befall him he does not proceed to condemn and criticize, but accepts the inevitable, and endeavors to the best of his ability to give the matter a turn for the best. He does not consider the opinions of others merely from his own standpoint, but seeks to put himself into the other's position.

The fifth requirement is impartiality toward everything that life brings. In this connection we speak of faith and trust. The student meets every human being and every creature with this trust, and lets it inspire his every action. Upon hearing some information, he never says to himself: "I don't believe it; it contradicts my present opinions." He is far rather ready to test and rectify his views and opinions. He ever remains receptive for everything that confronts him, and he trusts in the efficacy of his undertakings. Timidity and skepticism are banished from his being. He harbors a faith in the power of his intentions. A hundred failures cannot rob him of this faith. This is the "faith which can move mountains."

The sixth requirement is the cultivation of a certain inner balance (equanimity). The student endeavors to retain his composure in the face of joy and sorrow, and eradicates the tendency to fluctuate between the seventh heaven of joy and the depths of despair. Misfortune and danger, fortune and advancement alike find him ready armed.

The reader will recognize in the qualities here described the six attributes which the candidate for initiation strives to acquire. The intention has been to show their connection with the spiritual organ known as the twelve-petalled lotus flower. As before, special instructions can be given to bring this lotus flower to fruition, but here again the perfect symmetry of its form depends on the development of the qualities mentioned, the neglect of which results in this organ being formed into a caricature of its proper shape. In this case, should a certain clairvoyance be attained, the qualities in question may take an evil instead of a good direction. A person may become intolerant, timid, or contentious toward his environment; may, for instance, acquire some feeling for the sentiments of others, and for this reason shun them or hate them. This may even reach the point where, by reason of the inner coldness that overwhelms him when he hears repugnant opinions, he is unable to listen, or he may behave in an objectionable manner.

The development of this organ may be accelerated if, in addition to all that has been stated, certain other injunctions are observed which can only be imparted to the student by word of mouth. Yet the instructions given above do actually lead to genuine esoteric training, and more-over, the regulation of life in the way described can be advantageous to all who cannot or will not undergo esoteric training. For it does not fail to produce an effect upon the organism of the soul, even though slowly. As regards the esoteric student, the observance of these principles is indispensable. Should he attempt esoteric training without conforming to them, this could only result in his entering the higher worlds with inadequate organs, and instead of perceiving the truth he would be subject to deceptions and illusions. He would attain a certain clairvoyance, but for the most part, be the victim of greater blindness than before. Formerly he at least stood firmly within the physical world; now he looks beyond this physical world and grows confused about it before acquiring a firm footing in a higher world. All power of distinguishing truth from error would then perhaps fail him, and he would entirely lose his way in life. It is just for this reason that patience is so necessary in these matters. It must ever be borne in mind that the instructions given in esoteric training may go no further than is compatible with the willing readiness shown to develop the lotus flowers to their regular shape. Should these flowers be brought to fruition before they have quietly attained their correct form, mere caricatures would be the result. Their maturity can be brought about by the special instructions given in esoteric training, but their form is dependent on the method of life described above.

An inner training of a particularly intimate character is necessary for the development of the ten-petalled lotus flower, for it is now a question of learning consciously to control and dominate the sense-impressions themselves. This is of particular importance in the initial stages of clairvoyance, for it is only by this means that a source of countless illusions and fancies is avoided. People as a rule do not realize by what factors their sudden ideas and memories are dominated, and how they are produced. Consider the following case. Someone is traveling by railway; his mind is busy with one thought; suddenly is thought diverges; he recollects an experience that befell him years ago and interweaves it with his present thought. He did not notice that in looking through the window he had caught sight of a person who resembled another intimately connected with the recollected experience. He remains conscious, not of what he saw, but of the effect it produced, and thus believes that it all came to him of its own accords. How much in life occurs in such a way! How great is the part played in our life by things we hear and learn, without our consciously realizing the connection! Someone, for instance, cannot bear a certain color, but does not realize that this is due to the fact that the schoolmaster who used to worry him many years ago wore a coat of that color. Innumerable illusions are based upon such associations.

Many things leave their mark upon the soul while remaining outside the pale of consciousness. The following may occur. Someone reads in the paper about the death of a well-known person, and forthwith claims to have had a presentiment of it yesterday, although he had neither heard nor seen anything that might have given rise to such a thought. And indeed it is quite true that the thought occurred to him yesterday, as though of its own accord, that this particular person would die; only one thing escaped his attention: two or three hours before this thought occurred to him yesterday, he went to visit an acquaintance; a newspaper lay on the table; he did not actually read it, but his eyes unconsciously fell on the announcement of the dangerous illness of the person in question. He remained unconscious of the impression he had received, and yet this impression resulted in his presentiment.

Reflection upon these matters will show how great is the source of illusion and fantasy contained in such associations. It is just this source which must be dammed up by all who seek to develop their ten-petalled lotus flower. Deeply hidden characteristics in other souls can be perceived by this organ, but their truth depends on the attainment of immunity from the above-mentioned illusions. For this purpose it is necessary that the student should control and dominate everything that seeks to influence him from outside. He should reach the point of really receiving no impressions beyond those he wishes to receive. This can only be achieved by the development of a powerful inner life; by an effort of the will he only allows such things to impress him to which his attention is directed, and he actually evades all impressions to which he does not voluntarily respond. If he sees something it is because he wills to see it, and if he does not voluntarily take notice of something it is actually non-existent for him. The greater the energy and inner activity devoted to this work, the more extensively will this faculty be attained. The student must avoid all vacuous gazing and mechanical listening. For him only those things exist to which he turns his eye or his ear. He must practice the power of hearing nothing, even in the greatest disturbance, if he does not will to hear; and he must make his eyes unimpressionable to things of which he does not particularly take notice. He must be shielded as by an inner armor against all unconscious impressions. In this connection the student must devote special care to his thought-life. He singles out a particular thought and endeavors to link with it only such other thoughts as he can himself consciously and voluntarily produce. He rejects all casual ideas and does not connect this thought with another until he has investigated the origin of the latter. He goes still further. If, for instance, he feels a particular antipathy for something, he will combat it and endeavor to establish a conscious relation between himself and the thing in question. In this way the unconscious elements that intrude into his soul will become fewer and fewer. Only by such severe self-discipline can the ten-petalled lotus flower attain its proper form. The student's inner life must become a life of attention, and he must learn really to hold at a distance everything to which he should not or does not wish to direct his attention.

If this strict self-discipline be accompanied by meditation as prescribed in esoteric training, the lotus flower in the region of the pit of the stomach comes to maturity in the right way, and light and color of a spiritual kind are now added to the form and warmth perceptible to the organs described above. The talents and faculties of other beings are thereby revealed, also the forces and the hidden attributes of nature. The colored aura of living creatures then becomes visible; all that is around us manifests its spiritual attributes. It must be understood that the very greatest care is necessary at this stage of development, for the play of unconscious memories is here exceedingly active. If this were not the case, many people would possess this inner sense, for it comes almost immediately into evidence when the impressions delivered by the outer senses are held so completely under control that they become dependent on nothing save attention or inattention. This inner sense remains ineffective as long as the powerful outer sense smother and benumb it.

Still greater difficulty attends the development of the six-petalled lotus flower situated in the center of the body, for it can only be achieved as the result of complete mastery and control of the whole personality through consciousness of self, so that body, soul and spirit form one harmonious whole. The functions of the body, the inclinations and passions of the soul, the thoughts and ideas of the spirit must be tuned to perfect unison. The body must be so ennobled and purified that its organs incite to nothing that is not in the service of soul and spirit. The soul must not be impelled through the body to lusts and passions which are antagonistic to pure and noble thought. Yet the spirit must not stand like a slave-driver over the soul, dominating it with laws and commandments; the soul must rather learn to obey these laws and duties out of its own free inclination. The student must not feel duty to be an oppressive power to which he unwillingly submits, but rather something which he performs out of love. His task is to develop a free soul that maintains equilibrium between body and spirit, and he must perfect himself in this way to the extent of being free to abandon himself to the functions of the senses, for these should be so purified that they lose the power to drag him down to their level. He must no longer require to curb his passions, in as much as they of their own accord follow the good. So long as self-chastisement is necessary, no one can pass a certain stage of esoteric development; for a virtue practiced under constraint if futile. If there is any lust remaining, it interferes with esoteric development, however great the effort made not to humor it. Nor does it matter whether this desire proceeds from the soul or the body. For example, if a certain stimulant be avoided for the purpose of self-purification, this deprivation will only prove helpful if the body suffers no harm from it. Should the contrary to be the case, this proves that the body craves the stimulant, and that abstinence from it is of no value. In this case it may actually be a question of renouncing the ideal to be attained, until more favorable physical conditions, perhaps in another life, shall be forthcoming. A wise renunciation may be a far greater achievement than the struggle for something which, under given conditions, remains unattainable. Indeed, a renunciation of this kind contributes more toward development than the opposite course.

The six-petalled lotus flower, when developed, permits intercourse with beings of higher worlds, though only when their existence is manifested in the astral or soul-world. The development of this lotus flower, however, is not advisable unless the student has made great progress on that path of esoteric development which enables him to raise his spirit into a still higher world. This entry into the spiritual world proper must always run parallel with the development of the lotus flowers, otherwise the student will fall into error and confusion. He would undoubtedly be able to see, but he would remain incapable of forming a correct estimate of what he saw. Now, the development of the six-petalled lotus flower itself provides a certain security against confusion and instability, for no one can be easily confused who has attained perfect equilibrium between sense (or body), passion (or soul), and idea (or spirit). And yet, something more than this security is required when, through the development of the six-petalled lotus flower, living beings of independent existence are revealed to his spirit, beings belonging to a world so completely different from the world known to his physical senses. The development of the lotus flowers alone does not assure sufficient security in these higher worlds; still higher organs are necessary. The latter will now be described before the remaining lotus flowers and the further organization of the soul-body are discussed. (This expression — soul-body — although obviously contradictory when taken literally, is used because to clairvoyant perception the impression received spiritually corresponds to the impression received physically when the physical body is perceived.)

The development of the soul-body in the manner described above permits perception in a supersensible world, but anyone wishing to find his way in this world must not remain stationary at this stage of development. The mere mobility of the lotus flowers is not sufficient. The student must acquire the power of regulating and controlling the movement of his spiritual organs independently and with complete consciousness; otherwise he would become a plaything for external forces and powers. To avoid this he must acquire the faculty of hearing what is called the inner world, and this involves the development not only of the soul-body but also of the etheric body. The latter is that tenuous body revealed to the clairvoyant as a kind of double of the physical body, and forms to a certain extent an intermediate step between the soul nature and the physical body. (See the description on the author's book Theosophy.) It is possible for one equipped with clairvoyant powers consciously to suggest away the physical body of a person.

This corresponds on a higher plane to an exercise in attentiveness on a lower plane. Just as a person can divert his attention from something in front of him so that it becomes non-existent for him, the clairvoyant can extinguish a physical body from his field of observation so that it becomes physically transparent to him. If he exerts this faculty in the case of some person standing before him, there remains visible to his clairvoyant sight only the etheric body, besides the soul-body which is larger than the other two — etheric and physical bodies — and interpenetrates them both. The etheric body has approximately the size and form of the physical body, so that it practically fills the same space. It is an extremely delicate and finely organized structure. (I beg the physicist not to be disturbed at the expression "etheric body". The word ether here is merely used to suggest the fineness of the body in question, and need not in any way be connected with the hypothetical ether of physics.)

Its ground-color is different from any of the seven colors contained in the rainbow. Anyone capable of observing it will find a color which is actually non-existent for sense perception but to which the color of the young peach-blossom may be comparable. If desired, the etheric body can be examined alone; for this purpose the soul-body must be extinguished by an effort of attentiveness in the manner described above. Otherwise the etheric body will present an ever changing picture owing to its interpenetration by the soul-body.

Now, the particles of the etheric body are in continual motion. Countless currents stream through it in every direction. By these currents, life itself is maintained and regulated. Every body that has life, including animals and plants, possesses an etheric body. Even in minerals traces of it can be observed. These currents and movements are, to begin with, independent of human will and consciousness, just as the action of the heart or stomach is beyond our jurisdiction, and this independence remains unaltered so long as we do not take our development in hand in the sense of acquiring supersensible faculties. For, at a certain stage, development consists precisely in adding to the unconscious currents and movements of the etheric body others that are consciously produced and controlled.

When esoteric development has progressed so far that the lotus flowers begin to stir, much has already been achieved by the student which can result in the formation of certain quite definite currents and movements in his etheric body. The object of this development is the formation of a kind of center in the region of the physical heart, from which radiate currents and movements in the greatest possible variety of colors and forms. The center is in reality not a mere point, but a most complicated structure, a most wonderful organ. It glows and shimmers with every shade of color and displays forms of great symmetry, capable of rapid transformation. Other forms and streams of color radiate from this organ to the other parts of the body, and beyond it to the astral body, completely penetrating and illuminating it. The most important of these currents flow to the lotus flowers. They permeate each petal and regulate its revolutions; then streaming out at the points of the petals, they lose themselves in outer space. The higher the development of a person, the greater the circumference to which these rays extend.

The twelve-petalled lotus flower has a particularly close connection with this central organ. The currents flow directly into it and through it, proceeding on the one side to the sixteen and the two-petalled lotus flowers, and on the other, the lower side, to the flowers of eight, six and four petals. It is for this reason that the very greatest care must be devoted to the development of the twelve-petalled lotus, for an imperfection in the latter would result in irregular formation of the whole structure. The above will give an idea of the delicate and intimate nature of esoteric training, and of the accuracy needed if the development is to be regular and correct. It will also be evident beyond doubt that directions for the development of supersensible faculties can only be the concern of those who have themselves experienced everything which they propose to awaken in others, and who are unquestionably in a position to know whether the directions they give lead to the exact results desired. If the student follows the directions that have been given him, he introduces into his etheric body currents and movements which are in harmony with the laws and the evolution of the world to which he belongs. Consequently these instructions are reflections of the great laws of cosmic evolution. They consist of the above-mentioned and similar exercises in meditation and concentration which, if correctly practiced, produce the results described. The student must at certain times let these instructions permeate his soul with their content, so that he is inwardly entirely filled with it. A simple start is made with a view to the deepening of the logical activity of the mind and the producing of an inward intensification of thought. Thought it thereby made free and independent of all sense impressions and experiences; it is concentrated in one point which is held entirely under control. Thus a preliminary center is formed for the currents of the etheric body. This center is not yet in the region of the heart but in the head, and it appears to the clairvoyant as the point of departure for movements and currents. No esoteric training can be successful which does not first create this center. If the latter were first formed in the region of the heart the aspiring clairvoyant would doubtless obtain glimpses of the higher worlds, but would lack all true insight into the connection between these higher worlds and the world of our senses. This, however, is an unconditional necessity for man at the present stage of evolution. The clairvoyant must not become a visionary; he must retain a firm footing upon the earth.

The center in the head, once duly fixed, is then moved lower down, to the region of the larynx. This is effected by further exercises in concentration. Then the currents of the etheric body radiate from this point and illumine the astral space surrounding the individual.

Continued practice enables the student to determine for himself the position of this etheric body. Hitherto this position depended upon external forces proceeding from the physical body. Through further development the student is able to turn his etheric body to all sides. This faculty is effected by currents moving approximately along both hands and centered in the two-petalled lotus in the region of the eyes. All this is made possible through the radiations from the larynx assuming round forms, of which a number flow to the two-petalled lotus and thence form undulating currents along the hands. As a further development, these currents branch out and ramify in the most delicate manner and become, as it were, a kind of web which then encompasses the entire etheric body as though with a network. Whereas hitherto the etheric body was not closed to the outer world, so that the life currents from the universal ocean of life flowed freely in and out, these currents now have to pass through this membrane. Thus the individual becomes sensitive to these external streams; they become perceptible to him.

And now the time has come to give the complete system of currents and movements its center situated in the region of the heart. This again is effected by persevering with the exercises in concentration and meditation; and at this point also the stage is reached when the student becomes gifted with the inner word. All things now acquire a new significance for him. They become as it were spiritually audible in their innermost self, and speak to him of their essential being. The currents described above place him in touch with the inner being of the world to which he belongs. He begins to mingle his life with the life of his environment and can let it reverberate in the movements of his lotus flowers.

At this point the spiritual world is entered. If the student has advanced so far, he acquires a new understanding for all that the great teachers of humanity have uttered. The sayings of the Buddha and the Gospels, for instance, produce a new effect on him. They pervade him with a rapture of which he had not dreamed before. For the tone of their words follows the movements and rhythms which he has himself formed within himself. He can now have positive knowledge that a Buddha or the Evangelists did not utter their own revelations but those which flowed into them from the inmost being of all things. A fact must here be pointed out which can only be understood in the light of what has been said above. The many repetitions in the sayings of the Buddha are not comprehensible to people of our present evolutionary stage. For the esoteric student, however, they become a force on which he gladly lets his inner senses rest, for they correspond with certain movements in the etheric body. Devotional surrender to them, with perfect inner peace, creates an inner harmony with these movements; and because the latter are an image of certain cosmic rhythms which also at certain points repeat themselves and revert to former modes, the student listening to the wisdom of the Buddha unites his life with that of the cosmic mysteries.

In esoteric training there is question of four attributes which must be acquired on the so-called preparatory path for the attainment of higher knowledge. The first is the faculty of discriminating in thoughts between truth and appearance or mere opinion. The second attribute is the correct estimation of what is inwardly true and real, as against what is merely apparent. The third rests in the practice of the six qualities already mentioned in the preceding pages: thought-control, control of actions, perseverance, tolerance, faith and equanimity. The fourth attribute is the love of inner freedom.

A mere intellectual understanding of what is included in these attributes is of no value. They must be so incorporated into the soul that they form the basis of inner habits. Consider, for instance, the first of these attributes: The discrimination between truth and appearance. The student must so train himself that, as a matter of course, he distinguishes in everything that confronts him between the non-essential elements and those that are significant and essential. He will only succeed in this if, in his observation of the outer world, he quietly and patiently ever and again repeats the attempt. And at the end he will naturally single out the essential and the true at a glance, whereas formerly the non-essential, the transient, too, could content him. "All that is transient is but a seeming" ("Alles Vergänglich ist nur ein Gleichnis," Goethe, Faust II.) is a truth which becomes an unquestionable conviction of the soul. The same applies to the remaining three of the four attributes mentioned.

Now these four inner habits do actually produce a transformation of the delicate human etheric body. By the first, discrimination between truth and appearance, the center in the head already described is formed and the center in the region of the larynx prepared. The actual development of these centers is of course dependent on the exercises in concentration described above; the latter make for development and the four attributes bring to fruition. Once the center in the larynx has been prepared, the free control of the etheric body and its enclosure within a network covering, as explained above, results from the correct estimation of what is true as against what is apparent and non-essential. If the student acquires this faculty of estimation, the facts of the higher worlds will gradually become perceptible to him. But he must not think that he has to perform only such actions which appear significant when judged by the standard of a mere intellectual estimate. The most trifling action, every little thing accomplished, has something of importance in the great cosmic household, and it is merely a question of being aware of this importance. A correct estimation of the affairs of daily life is required, not an underestimation of them. The six virtues of which the third attribute consists have already been dealt with; they are connected with the development of the twelve-petalled lotus in the region of the heart, and, as already indicated, it is to this center that the life-currents of the etheric body must be directed. The fourth attribute, the longing for liberation, serves to bring to fruition the etheric organ in the heart region. Once this attribute becomes an inner habit, the individual frees himself from everything which depends only upon the faculties of his own personal nature. He ceases to view things from his own separate standpoint, and the boundaries of his own narrow self fettering him to this point of view disappear. The secrets of the spiritual world gain access to his inner self. This is liberation. For those fetters constrain the individual to regard tings and beings in a manner corresponding to his own personal traits. It is from this personal manner of regarding things that the student must become liberated and free.

It will be clear from the above that the instructions given in esoteric training exert a determining influence reaching the innermost depths of human nature. Such are the instructions regarding the four qualities mentioned above. They can be found in one form or another in all the great cosmogonies that take account of the spiritual world. The founders of the great cosmogonies did not give mankind these teachings from some vague feeling. They gave them for the good reason that they were great initiates. Out of their knowledge did they shape their moral teachings. They knew how these would act upon the finer nature of man, and desired that their followers should gradually achieve the development of this finer nature. To live in the sense of these great cosmogonies means to work for the attainment of personal spiritual perfection. Only by so doing can man become a servant of the world and of humanity. Self-perfection is by no means self-seeking, for the imperfect man is an imperfect servant of the world and of humanity. The more perfect a man is, the better does he serve the world. "If the rose adorns itself, it adorns the garden."

The founders of the great cosmogonies are therefore the great initiates. Their teaching flows into the soul of men, and thus, with humanity, the whole world moves forward. Quite consciously did they work to further this evolutionary process of humanity. Their teachings can only be understood if it be remembered that they are the product of knowledge of the innermost depths of human nature. The great initiates knew, and it is out of their knowledge that they shaped the ideals of humanity. And man approaches these great leaders when he uplifts himself, in his own development, to their heights.

A completely new life opens out before the student when the development of his etheric body begins in the way described above, and at the proper time, in the course of his training, he must receive that enlightenment which enables him to adapt himself to this new existence. The sixteen-petalled lotus, for instance, enables him to perceive spiritual figures of a higher world. He must learn now how different these figures can be when caused by different objects or beings. In the first place, he must notice that his own thoughts and feelings exert a powerful influence on certain of these figures, on others little or no influence. One kind of figure alters immediately if the observer, upon seeing it, says to himself: "that is beautiful," and then in the course of his observation changes this thought to: "that is useful." It is characteristic of the forms proceeding from minerals or from artificial objects that they change under the influence of every thought and every feeling directed upon them by the observer. This applies in a lesser degree to the forms belonging to plants, and still less to those corresponding to animals. These figures, too, are full of life and motion, but this motion is only partially due to the influence of human thoughts and feelings; in other respects it is produced by causes which are beyond human influence. Now, there appears within this whole world a species of form which remains almost entirely unaffected by human influence. The student can convince himself that these forms proceed neither from minerals nor from artificial objects, nor, again, from plants or animals. To gain complete understanding, he must study those forms which he can realize to have proceeded from the feelings, instincts, and passions of human beings. Yet he can find that these forms too are influenced by his own thoughts and feelings, if only to a relatively small extent. But there always remains a residuum of forms in this world upon which such influences are negligible. Indeed, at the outset of this career the student can perceive little beyond this residuum. He can only discover its nature by observing himself. He then learns what forms he himself produces, for his will, his wishes, and so on, are expressed in these forms. An instinct that dwells in him, a desire that fills him, an intention that he harbors, and so forth, are all manifested in these forms: his whole character displays itself in this world of forms. Thus by his conscious thoughts and feelings a person can exercise an influence on all forms which do not proceed from himself; but over those which he brings about in the higher world, once he has created them. Now, it follows from what has been said that on this higher plan man's inner life of instincts, desires, ideas displays itself outwardly in definite forms, just like all the other beings and objects. To higher knowledge, the inner world appears as part of the outer world. In a higher world man's inner being confronts him as a reflected image, just as though in the physical world he were surrounded by mirrors and could observe his physical body in that way.

At this stage of development the student has reached the point where he can free himself from the illusion resulting from the initiation of his personal self. He can now observe that inner self as outer world, just as he hitherto regarded as outer world everything that affected his senses. Thus he learns by gradual experience to deal with himself as hitherto he dealt with the beings around him.

Were the student to obtain an insight into these spiritual worlds without sufficient preparation regarding their nature, he would find himself confronted by the picture of his own soul as though by an enigma. There his own desires and passions confront him in animal or, more rarely, in human forms. It is true that animal forms of this world are never quite similar to those of the physical world, yet they possess a remote resemblance: inexpert observers often take them to be identical. Now, upon entering this world, an entirely new method of judgment must be acquired; for apart from the fact that things actually pertaining to inner nature appear as outer world, they also bear the character of mirrored reflections of what they really are. When, for instance, a number is perceived, it must be read in reverse, as a picture in a mirror: 265 would mean here in reality, 562. A sphere is perceived as thought from its center. This inner perception must then be translated in the right way. The qualities of the soul appear likewise as in a mirror. A wish directed toward an outer object appears as a form moving toward the person wishing. Passions residing in the lower part of human nature can assume animal forms or similar shapes that hurl themselves against the individual. In reality, these passions are headed outward; they seek satisfaction in the outer world, but this striving outward appears in the mirrored reflection as an attack on the individual from whom they proceed.

If the student, before attaining insight into higher worlds, has learned by quiet and sincere self-observation to realized the qualities and the defects of his own character, he will then, at the moment when his own inner self confronts him as a mirrored image, find strength and courage to conduct himself in the right way. People who have failed to test themselves in this way, and are insufficiently acquainted with their own inner self, will not recognize themselves in their own mirrored image and will mistake it for an alien reality. Or they may become alarmed at the vision and, because they cannot endure the sight, deceive themselves into believing the whole thing is nothing but an illusion which cannot lead them anywhere. In either case the person in question, through prematurely attaining a certain stage of inner development, would fatally obstruct his own progress.

It is absolutely necessary that the student should experience this spiritual aspect of his own inner self before progressing to higher spheres; for his own self constitutes that psycho-spiritual element of which he is the best judge. If he has thoroughly realized the nature of his own personality in the physical world, and if the image of his personality first appears to him in a higher world, he is then able to compare the one with the other. He can refer the higher to something already known to him, so that his point of departure is on firm ground. Whereas, no matter how many other spiritual beings appeared to him, he would find himself unable to discover their nature and qualities, and would soon feel the ground giving way beneath him. Thus is cannot be too often repeated that the only safe entrance into the higher worlds is at the end of a path leading through a genuine knowledge and estimate of one's own nature.

Pictures, then, of a spiritual kind are first encountered by the student on his progress into higher worlds; and the reality to which these pictures correspond is actually within himself. He should be far enough advanced to refrain from desiring reality of a more robust kind at this initial stage, and to regard these pictures as timely. He will soon meet something quite new within this world of pictures. His lower self is before him as a mirrored image; but from within this image there appears the true reality of his higher self. Out of the picture of his lower personality the form of the spiritual ego becomes visible. Then threads are spun from the latter to other and higher spiritual realities.

This is the moment when the two-petalled lotus in the region of the eyes is required. If it now begins to stir, the student finds it possible to bring his higher ego in contact with higher spiritual beings. The currents form this lotus flower flow toward the higher realities in such a way that the movements in question are fully apparent to the individual. Just as the light renders the physical objects visible, so, too, these currents disclose spiritual beings of higher worlds.

Through inward application to the fundamental truths derived from spiritual science the student learns to set in motion and then to direct the currents proceeding form the lotus flower between the eyes.

It is at this stage of development especially that the value of sound judgment and a training in clear and logical thought come to the fore. The higher self, which hitherto slumbered unconsciously in an embryonic state, is now born into conscious existence. This is not a figurative but a positive birth in the spiritual world, and the being now born, the higher self, must enter that world with all the necessary organs and aptitudes if it is to be capable of life. Just as nature must provide for a child being born into the world with suitable eyes and ears, to too, the laws of self-development must provide for the necessary capacities with which the higher self can enter existence. These laws governing the development of the higher spiritual organs are none other than the laws of sound reason and morality of the physical world. The spiritual self matures in the physical self as a child in the mother's womb. The child's health depends upon the normal functioning of natural laws in the maternal womb. The constitution of the spiritual self is similarly conditioned by the laws of common intelligence and reason that govern physical life. No one can give birth to a soundly constituted higher self whose life in thought and feeling, in the physical world, is not sound and healthy. Natural, rational life is the basis of all genuine spiritual development. Just as the child when still in the maternal womb lives in accordance with the natural forces to which it has access, after its birth, through its organs of sense, so, too, the human higher self lives in accordance with the laws of the spiritual world, even during physical existence. And even as the child, out of a dim life instinct, acquired the requisite forces, so, too, can man acquire the powers of the spiritual world before his higher self is born. Indeed, he must do this if the latter is to enter the world as a fully developed being. It would be quite wrong for anyone to say: "I cannot accept the teachings of spiritual science until I myself become a seer," for without inward application to the results of spiritual research there is no chance whatever of attaining genuine higher knowledge. It would be as though a child, during gestation, were to refuse the forces coming to it through its mother, and proposed to wait until it could procure them for itself. Just as the embryonic child in its incipient feeling for life learns to appreciate what is offered to it, so can the non-seer appreciate the truth of the teachings of spiritual science. An insight into these teachings based on a deeply rooted feeling for truth, and a clear, sound, all-around critical and reasoning faculty are possible even before spiritual things are actually perceived. The esoteric knowledge must first be studied, so that this study becomes a preparation for clairvoyance. A person attaining clairvoyance without such preparation would resemble a child born with eyes and ears but without a brain. The entire world of sound and color would display itself before him, but he would be helpless in it.

At this stage of his esoteric development the student realizes, through personal inward experience, all that had previously appealed to his sense of truth, to his intellect and reason. He has now direct knowledge of his higher self. He learns how his higher self is connected with exalted spiritual beings and forms with them a united whole. He sees how the lower self originates in a higher world, and it is revealed to him how his higher nature outlasts his lower. He can now distinguish the imperishable in himself from the perishable; that is, he learns through personal insight to understand the doctrine of the incarnation of the higher self in the lower. It will become plain to him that he is part of a great spiritual complex and that his qualities and destiny are due to this connection. He learns to recognize the law of his life, his karma. He realizes that his lower self, constituting his present existence, is only one of the forms which his higher being can adopt. He discerns the possibility of working down from his higher self in his lower self, so that he may perfect himself ever more and more. Now, too, he can comprehend the great differences between human beings in regard to their level of perfection. He becomes aware that there are others above him who have already traversed the stages which still lie before him, and he realizes that the teachings and deeds of such men proceed from the inspiration of a higher world. He owes this knowledge to his first personal glimpse into this higher world. The so-called initiates of humanity now become vested with reality for him.

These, then, are the gifts which the student owes to his development at this stage: insight into his higher self; insight into the doctrine of the incarnation of this higher being in a lower; insight into the laws by which life in the physical world is regulated according to its spiritual connections, that is, the law of karma; and finally, insight into the existence of the great initiates.

Thus it is said of a student who has reached this stage, that all doubt has vanished from him. His former faith, based on reason and sound thoughts, is now replaced by knowledge and insight which nothing can undermine. The various religions have presented, in their ceremonies, sacraments, and rites, externally visible patterns of the higher spiritual beings and events. None but those who have not penetrated to the depths of the great religions can fail to recognize this fact. Personal insight into spiritual reality explains the great significance of these externally visible cults. Religious service, then, becomes for the seer an image of his own communion with the higher, spiritual world.

It has been shown how the student, by attaining this stage, becomes in truth a new being. He can now mature to still higher faculties and, by means of the life-currents of his etheric body, control the higher and actual life-element, thus attaining a high degree of independence from the restrictions of the physical body.

The Transformation of Dream Life

An intimation that the student has reached or will soon reach the stage of development described in the preceding chapter will be found in the change which comes over his dream life. His dreams, hitherto confused and haphazard, now begin to assume a more regular character. Their pictures begin to succeed each other in sensible connection, like the thoughts and ideas of daily life. He can discern in them law, cause, and effect. The content, too, of his dreams is changed. While hitherto he discerned only reminiscences of daily life and transformed impressions of his surroundings or of his physical condition, there now appear before him pictures of a world he has hitherto not known. At first the general character of his dream life remains unchanged, in as far as dreams are distinguished from waking mental activity by the symbolical presentation of what they wish to express. No attentive observer of dream life can fail to detect this characteristic. For instance, a person may dream that he has caught some horrible creature, and he feels an unpleasant sensation in his hand. He wakes to discover that he is tightly grasping a corner of the blanket. The truth is not presented to the mind, except through the medium of a symbolical image. A man may dream that he is flying from some pursuer and is stricken with fear. On waking, he finds that he has been suffering, during sleep, from palpitations of the heart. Disquieting dreams can also be traced to indigestible food. Occurrences in the immediate vicinity may also reflect themselves symbolically in dreams. The striking of a clock may evoke the picture of a troop of soldiers marching by to the beat of drums. A falling chair may be the occasion of a whole dream drama in which the sound of the fall is reproduced as the report of a gun, and so forth. The more regulated dreams of esoteric students whose etheric body has begun its development retain this symbolical method of expression, but they will cease merely to reflect reality connected with the physical body and physical environment. As the dreams due to the latter causes become more connected, they are mingled with similar pictures expressing things and events of another world. These are the first experiences lying beyond the range of waking consciousness.

Yet no true mystic will ever make his experiences in dreams the basis of any authoritative account of the higher world. Such dreams must be merely considered as providing the first hint of a higher development. Very soon and as a further result, the student's dreams will no longer remain beyond the reach of intellectual guidance as heretofore, but on the contrary, will be mentally controlled and supervised like the impressions and conceptions of waking consciousness. The difference between dream and waking consciousness grows ever smaller. The dreamer remains awake in the fullest sense of the word during his dream life; that is, he is aware of his mastery and control over his own vivid mental activity.

During our dreams we are actually in a world other than that of our senses; but with undeveloped spiritual organs we can form none other than the confused conceptions of it described above. It is only in so far present for us as, for instance, the world of sense could be for a being equipped with no more than rudimentary eyes. That is why we can see nothing in this world but counterfeits and reflections of daily life. The latter are perceptible to us because our own soul paints its daily experiences in pictorial form into the substance of which that other world consists. It must be clearly understood that in addition to our ordinary conscious work-a-day life we lead a second, unconscious life in that other world. We engrave in it all our thoughts and perceptions. These tracings only become visible when the lotus flowers are developed. Now, in every human being there are slender rudiments of these lotus flowers. We cannot perceive by means of them during waking consciousness because the impressions made on them are very faint. We cannot see the stars during the daytime for a similar reason: their visibility is extinguished by the mighty glare of the sun. Thus, too, the faint spiritual impressions cannot make themselves felt in the face of the powerful impressions received through the senses.

Now, when the gate of the senses is closed during sleep, these other impressions begin to emerge confusedly, and the dreamer becomes aware of experiences in another world. But as already explained, these experiences consist at first merely of pictures engraved in the spiritual world by our mental activity attached to the physical senses. Only developed lotus flowers make it possible for manifestations not derived from the physical world to be imprinted in the same way. And then the etheric body, when developed, brings full knowledge concerning these engraved impressions derived from other worlds.

This is the beginning of life and activity in a new world, and at this point esoteric training must set the student a twofold task. To begin with, he must learn to take stock of everything he observes in his dreams, exactly as though he were awake. Then, if successful in this, he is led to make the same observations during ordinary waking consciousness. He will so train his attention and receptivity for these spiritual impressions that they need no longer vanish in the face of the physical impressions, but will always be at hand for him and reach him in addition to the others.

When the student has acquired this faculty there arises before his spiritual eyes something of the picture described in the preceding chapter, and he can henceforth discern all that the spiritual world contains as the cause of the physical world. Above all things he can perceive and gain knowledge of his own higher self in this world. The next task now confronting him is to grow, as it were, into this higher self, that is, really to regard it as his own true self and to act accordingly. He realizes ever more clearly and intensely that his physical body and what he hitherto called his "I" are merely the instruments of his higher self. He adopts an attitude toward his lower self such as a person limited to the world of the senses adopts toward some instrument or vehicle that serves him. No one includes as part of himself the vehicle in which he is traveling, even though he says: "I travel"; so, too, when an inwardly developed person says: "I go through the door," his actual conception is: "I carry my body through the door." Only this must become a natural concept for him, so that he never for a moment loses his firm footing in the physical world, or feels estranged from it. If the student is to avoid becoming a fantastic visionary he must not impoverish his life through his higher consciousness, but on the contrary, enrich it, as a person enriches his life by using the railway and not merely his legs to cover a certain distance.

When the student has thus raised himself to a life in the higher ego, or rather during his acquisition of the higher consciousness, he will learn how to stir to life the spiritual perceptive force in the organ of the heart and control it through the currents described in the foregoing chapter. This perceptive force is an element of higher sustainability, which proceeds from the organ in question and flows with beautiful radiance through the moving lotus flowers and the other channels of the developed etheric body. Thence it radiates outward into the surrounding spiritual world rendering it spiritually visible, just as the sunlight falling on the objects of the physical world renders them visible.

How this perceptive force in the heart organ is created can only be gradually understood in the course of actual development.

It is only when this organ of perception can be sent through the etheric body and into the outer world, to illumine the objects there, that the actual spiritual world, as composed of objects and beings, can be clearly perceived. Thus it will be seen that complete consciousness of an object in the spiritual world is only possible when man himself casts upon it the spiritual light. Now, the ego which creates this organ of perception does not dwell within, but outside the physical body, as already shown. The heart organ is only the spot where the individual man kindles, from without, this spiritual light organ. Were the latter kindled elsewhere, the spiritual perceptions produced by it would have no connection with the physical world. But all higher spiritual realities must be related to the physical world, and man himself must act as a channel through which they flow into it. It is precisely through the heart organ that the higher ego governs the physical self, making it into its instrument.

Now, the feelings of an esoterically developed person toward the things of the spiritual world are very different from the feelings of the undeveloped person toward the things of the physical world. The latter feels himself to be at a particular place in the world of sense, and the surrounding objects to be external to him. The spiritually developed person feels himself to be united with, and as though in the interior of, the spiritual objects he perceives. He wanders, in fact, from place to place in spiritual space, and is therefore called the wanderer in the language of occult science. He has no home at first. Should he, however, remain a mere wanderer he would be unable to define any object in spiritual space. Just as objects and places in physical space are defined from a fixed point of departure, this, too, must be the case in the other world. He must seek out some place, thoroughly investigate it, and take spiritual possession of it. In this place he must establish his spiritual home and relate everything else to it. In physical life, too, a person sees everything in terms of his physical home. Natives of Berlin and Paris will involuntarily describe London in a different way. And yet there is a difference between the spiritual and the physical home. We are born into the latter without our co-operation and instinctively absorb, during our childhood, a number of ideas by which everything is henceforth involuntarily colored. The student, however, himself founds his own spiritual home in full consciousness. His judgment, therefore, based on this spiritual home, is formed in the light of freedom. This founding of a spiritual home is called in the language of occult science the building of the hut.

Spiritual vision at this stage extends to the spiritual counterparts of the physical world, so far as these exist in the so-called astral world. There everything is found which in its nature is similar to human instincts, feelings, desires, and passions. For powers related to all these human characteristics are associated with all physical objects. A crystal, for instance, is cast in its form by powers which, seen from a higher standpoint, appear as an active human impulse. Similar forces drive the sap through the capillaries of the plant, cause the blossoms to unfold and the seed vessels to burst. To developed spiritual organs of perception all these forces appear gifted with form and color, just as the objects of the physical world have form and color for physical eyes. At this stage in his development the student sees not only the crystal and the plant, but also the spiritual forces mentioned above. Animal and human impulses are perceptible to him not only through their physical manifestation in the individual, but directly as objects; he perceives them just as he perceives tables and chairs in the physical world. The whole range of instincts, impulses, desires and passions, both of an animal and of a human being, constitute the astral cloud or aura in which the being is enveloped.

Furthermore, the clairvoyant can at this stage perceive things which are almost or entirely withheld from the senses. He can, for instance, tell the astral difference between a room full of low or of high-minded people. Not only the physical but also the spiritual atmosphere of a hospital differs from that of a ballroom. A commercial town has a different astral air from that of a university town. In the initial stages of clairvoyance this perceptive faculty is but slightly developed; its relation to the objects in question is similar to the relation of dream consciousness to waking consciousness in ordinary life; it will, however, become fully awakened at this stage as well.

The highest achievement of a clairvoyant who has attained the degree of vision described above is that in which the astral counter-effects of animal and human impulses and passions are revealed to him. A loving action is accompanied by quite a different astral concomitant from one inspired by hate. Senseless desire gives rise to an ugly astral counterpart, while a feeling evoked by a high ideal creates one that is beautiful. These astral images are but faintly perceptible during physical life, for their strength is diminished by life in the physical world. The desire for an object, for example, produces a counterpart of this sort in addition to the semblance of the desire itself in the astral world. If, however, the object be attained and the desire satisfied, or if, at any rate, the possibility of satisfaction is forthcoming, the corresponding image will show but faintly. It only attains its full force after the death of the individual human being, when the soul in accordance with her nature still harbors such desires, but can no longer satisfy them, because the object and the physical organ are both lacking. The gourmand, for instance, will still retain, after death, the desire to please his palate; but there is no possibility of satisfying this desire because he no longer has a palate. As a result, the desire produces an especially powerful counterpart, by which the soul is tormented. These experiences evoked by the counterparts of the lower soul-nature after death are called the experiences in the soul-world, especially in the region of desires. They only vanish when the soul has purified herself from all desires inclining toward the physical world. Then only does the soul mount to the higher regions, to the world of spirit. Even though these images are faint during life in the physical world, they are none the less present, following man as his world of desire, in the way a comet is followed by its tail. They can be seen by a clairvoyant at the requisite stage of development.

Such and similar experiences fill the life of the student during the period described above. He cannot attain higher spiritual experience at this stage of development, but must climb still higher from this point.

The Continuity of Consciousness

Human life runs its course in three alternating states or conditions, namely, waking, dreaming sleep, and dreamless sleep. The attainment of the higher knowledge of spiritual worlds can be readily understood if a conception be formed of the changes occurring in these three conditions, as experienced by one seeking such higher knowledge. When no training has been undertaken to attain this knowledge, human consciousness is continually interrupted by the restful interval of sleep. During these intervals the soul knows nothing of the outer world, and equally little of itself. Only at certain periods dreams emerge from the deep ocean of insensibility, dreams linked to the occurrences of the outer world or the conditions of the physical body. At first, dreams are only regarded as a particular manifestation of sleep-life, and thus only two states are generally spoken of, namely, sleeping and waking. For spiritual science, however, dreams have an independent significance apart from the other two conditions. In the foregoing chapter a description was given of the alteration ensuing in the dream-life of the person undertaking the ascent to higher knowledge. His dreams lose their meaningless, irregular and disconnected character and form themselves more and more into a world of law and order. With continued development, not only does this new world born out of the dream world come to be in no way inferior to outer physical reality as regards its inner truth, but facts reveal themselves in it representing a higher reality in the fullest sense of the word. Secrets and riddles lie concealed everywhere in the physical world. In the latter, the effects are seen of certain higher facts, but no one can penetrate to the causes whose perception is confined merely to his senses. These causes are partly revealed to the student in the condition described above and developed out of dream life, a condition, however, in which he by no means remains stationary. True, he must not regard these revelations as actual knowledge so long as the same things do not also reveal themselves during ordinary waking life. But in time he achieves this as well: he develops this faculty of carrying over into waking consciousness the condition he created for himself out of dream life. Thus something new is introduced into the world of his senses that enriches it. Just as a person born blind and successfully operated upon will recognize the surrounding objects as enriched by all that the eye perceives, to, too, will anyone having become clairvoyant in the above manner perceive the whole world surrounding him peopled with new qualities, things, beings, and so forth. He now need no longer wait for his dreams to live in another world, but he can at any suitable moment put himself into the above condition for the purpose of higher perception. This condition then acquires a significance for him similar to the perception, in ordinary life, of things with active senses as opposed to inactive senses. It can truly be said that the student opens the eyes of his soul and beholds things which necessarily remain concealed form the bodily senses.

Now this condition is only transitional to still higher stages of knowledge. If the student continues his esoteric exercises he will find, in due time, that the radical change, as described above, does not confine itself to his dream life, but that this transformation also extends to what was previously a condition of deep dreamless sleep. Isolated conscious experiences begin to interrupt the complete insensibility of this deep sleep. Perceptions previously unknown to him emerge from the pervading unknown to him emerge from the pervading darkness of sleep. It is, of course, not easy to describe these perceptions, for our language is only adapted to the physical world, and therefore only approximate terms can be found to express what does not at all belong to that world. Still, such terms must be used to describe the higher worlds, and this is only possible by the free use of simile; yet seeing that everything in the world is interrelated, the attempt may be made. The things and beings of the higher worlds are closely enough related to those of the physical world to enable, with a little good will, some sort of conception of these higher worlds to be formed, even though words suitable for the physical world are used. Only the reader must always bear in mind that such descriptions of supersensible worlds must, to a large extent, be in the nature of simile and symbol. The words of ordinary language are only partially adopted in the course of esoteric training; for the rest, the student learns another symbolical language, as a natural outcome of his ascent to higher worlds. The knowledge of this language is acquired during esoteric training itself, but that does not preclude the possibility of learning something concerning the higher worlds even fro such ordinary descriptions as those here given.

Some idea can be given of those experiences which emerge from the insensibility of deep sleep if they be compared to a kind of hearing. We may speak of perceptible tones and words. While the experiences during dreaming sleep may fitly be designated as a kind of vision, the facts observed during deep sleep may be compared to auricular impressions. (It should be remarked in passing that for the spiritual world, too, the faculty of sight remains the higher. There, too, colors are higher than sounds and words. The student's first perceptions in this world do not yet extend to the higher colors, but only to the lower tones. Only because man, according to his general development, is already more qualified for the world revealing itself in dreaming sleep does he at once perceive colors there. He is less qualified for the higher world unveiling itself in deep sleep; therefore the first revelations of it he receives are in tones and words; later on, he can here, too, ascend to colors and forms.)

Now, when these experiences during deep sleep first come to the notice of the student, his next task must be to sense them as clearly and vividly as possible. At first this presents great difficulty, the perception of these experiences being exceedingly slight. The student knows very well, on waking, that he has had an experience, but is completely in the dark as regards its nature. The most important thing during this initial stage is to remain quiet and composed, and not for a moment lapse into any unrest or impatience. The latter is under all circumstances detrimental; it can never accelerate development, but only delays it. The student must cultivate a quiet and yielding receptivity for the gift that is presented to him; all violence must be repressed. Should he at any period not become aware of experiences during sleep he must wait patiently until this is possible. Some day this moment will assuredly arrive. And this perceptive faculty, if awaited with patience and composure, remains a secure possession; while should it appear momentarily in answer to forcible methods, it may be completely lost for a long time.

Once this perceptive faculty is acquired and the experiences during sleep are present to the student's consciousness in complete lucidity and clarity, his attention should be directed to the following point. All these experiences are seen to consist of two kinds, which can be clearly distinguished. The first kind will be totally different from anything that he has ever experienced. These experiences may be a source of joy and edification, but otherwise they should be left to themselves for the time being. They are the first harbinger of higher spiritual worlds in which the student will find his way later on. In the other kind of experiences the attentive observer will discover a certain relationship with the ordinary world in which he lives. The subjects of his reflections during life, what he would like to understand in these things around him but cannot understand with the ordinary intellect, these are the things concerning which the experiences during sleep give him information. During every-day life man reflects on his environment; his mind tries to conceive and understand the connection existing between things; he seeks to grasp in thought and idea what his senses perceive. It is to these ideas and concepts that the experiences during sleep refer. Obscure, shadowy concepts become sonorous and living in a way comparable only to the tones and the words of the physical world. It seems to the student ever more and more as though the solution of the riddles over which he ponders is whispered to him in tones and words out of a higher world. And he is able to connect with ordinary life whatever comes to him from a higher world. What was formerly only accessible to his thought now becomes actual experience, just as living and substantial as an experience in this physical world can be. The things and beings of this physical world are by no means only what they appear to be for physical perception. They are the expression and effluence of a spiritual world. This spiritual world, hitherto concealed from the student, now resounds for him out of his whole environment.

It is easy to see that this higher perceptive faculty can prove a blessing only if the opened soul-senses are in perfect order, just as the ordinary senses can only be used for a true observation of the world if their equipment is regular and normal. Now man himself forms these higher senses through the exercises indicated by spiritual science. The latter include concentration, in which the attention is directed to certain definite ideas and concepts connected with the secrets of the universe; and meditation, which is a life in such ideas, a complete submersion in them, in the right way. By concentration and meditation the student works upon his soul and develops within it the soul-organs of perception. While thus applying himself to the task of concentration and meditation his soul grows within his body, just as the embryo child grows in the body of the mother. When the isolated experiences during sleep begin, as described, the moment of birth is approaching for the liberated soul; for she has literally become a new being, developed by the individual within himself, from seed to fruit. The effort required for concentration and meditation must therefore be carefully and accurately maintained, for it contains the laws governing the germination and fruition of the higher human soul-being. The latter must appear at its birth as a harmonious, well-proportioned organism. Through an error in following the instructions, no such normal being will come to existence in the spiritual spheres, but a miscarriage incapable of life.

That this higher soul-being should be born during deep sleep will be easily grasped, for if that delicate organism lacking all power of resistance chanced to appear during physical every-day life it could not prevail against the harsh and powerful processes of this life. Its activity would be of no account against that of the body. During sleep, however, when the body rests in as far as its activity is dependent on sense perception, the activity of the higher soul, at first so delicate and inconspicuous, can come into evidence. Here again the student must bear in mind that these experiences during sleep may not be regarded as fully valid knowledge, so long as he is not in a position to carry over his awakened higher soul into waking consciousness as well. The acquisition of this faculty will enable him to perceive the spiritual world in its own character, among and within the experiences of the day; that is, the hidden secrets of his environment will be conveyed to his soul as tones and words.

Now, the student must realize at this stage of development that he is dealing with separate and more or less isolated spiritual experiences. He should therefore beware of constructing out of them a complete whole or even a connected system of knowledge. In this case, all manner of fantastic ideas and conceptions would be mixed into the soul-world, and a world might thus easily be constructed which had nothing to do with the real spiritual world. The student must continually practice self-control. The right thing to do is to strive for an ever clearer conception of the isolated real experiences, and to await the spontaneous arrival of new experiences which will connect themselves, as though of their own accord, with those already recorded. By virtue of the power of the spiritual world into which he has now found his way, and through continued application to his prescribed exercises, the student experiences an ever increasing extension and expansion of consciousness during sleep. The unconscious intervals during sleep-life grow ever smaller, while more and more experiences emerge from erstwhile unconsciousness. These experiences thus link themselves together increasingly of their own accord, without this true unity being disturbed by all manner of combinations and inferences, which in any case would only originate in an intellect accustomed to the physical world. Yet the less the habits of thought acquired in the physical world are allowed to play into these higher experiences, the better it is.

By thus conducting himself the student approaches ever nearer to the attainment of that condition, on his path to higher knowledge, in which the unconsciousness of sleep-life is transformed into complete consciousness. When his body rests, man lives in surroundings which are just as real as those of his waking daily life. It is needless to say that the reality during sleep is different from physical reality surrounding the physical body. The student learns — indeed he must learn if he is to retain a firm footing in the physical world and not become a visionary — to connect the higher experiences of sleep with his physical environment. At first, however, the world entered during sleep is a completely new revelation. This important stage of development, at which consciousness is retained in the life during sleep, is known in spiritual science as the continuity of consciousness. The condition here indicated is regarded, at a certain stage of development, as a kind of ideal, attainable at the end of a long path. What the student first learns is the extension of consciousness into two soul-states, in the first of which only disordered dreams were previously possible, and in the second only unconscious dreamless sleep. Anyone having reached this stage of development does not cease experiencing and learning during those intervals when the physical body rests, and when the soul receives no impressions through the instrumentality of senses.

The Splitting of the Human Personality During Spiritual Training

During sleep no impressions are conveyed to the human soul through the instrumentality of the physical sense-organs. The impressions from the ordinary outer world do not find their way to the soul when in that condition. In certain respects the soul is actually outside the part of the human being — the so-called physical body — which in waking life is the medium for sense perceptions and thought. The soul is then only connected with the finer bodies (the etheric body and the astral body), which are beyond the scope of physical sense observation. But the activity of these finer bodies does not cease during sleep. Just as the physical body is connected and lives with the things and beings of the physical world, affecting them and being affected by them, so, too, does the soul live in a higher world; only, this life of the soul continues also during sleep. The soul is in full activity during sleep, but we can know nothing of this activity so long as we have no spiritual organs of perception through which to observe what is going on around us and see what we ourselves are doing during sleep, as we observe our daily physical environment with our ordinary senses. The preceding chapters have shown that esoteric training consists in the development of such spiritual sense organs. Now if, as a result of esoteric training, the student's life during sleep is transformed in the manner described in the foregoing chapter, he will, when in that condition, be able to follow consciously everything going on around him. He can at will find his way in his environment as he could, when awake, with his ordinary senses. It should here be noted that a higher degree of clairvoyance is required for the higher perception of ordinary physical environment. This was indicated in the last chapter. In the initial stages of his development the student perceives things pertaining to another world without being able to discern their connection with the objects of his daily physical environment.

These characteristics of life during sleep or in dreams illustrate what is continually taking place in the human being. The soul lives in uninterrupted activity in the higher worlds, even gathering from them the impulse to act upon the physical body. Ordinarily unconscious of his higher life, the esoteric student renders himself conscious of it, and thereby his whole life becomes transformed. As long as the soul remains unseeing in the higher sense it is guided by superior cosmic beings. And just as the life of a person born blind is changed, through a successful operation, from its previous dependence on a guide, so too is the life of a person changed through esoteric training. He outgrows the principle of being guided by a master and must henceforward undertake to be his own guide. The moment this occurs he is, of course, liable to commit errors totally unknown to ordinary consciousness. He acts now from a world from which, formerly, higher powers unknown to him influenced him. These higher powers are directed by the universal cosmic harmony. The student withdraws from this cosmic harmony, and must now himself accomplish things which were hitherto done for him without his co-operation.

It is for this reason that so much is found in books dealing with these matters concerning the dangers connected with the ascent into higher worlds. The descriptions sometimes given of these dangers may well make timid souls shudder at the prospect of this higher life. Yet the fact is that dangers only arise when the necessary precautions are neglected. If all the measures counseled by true esoteric science are adopted, the ascent will indeed ensue through experiences surpassing in power and magnitude everything the boldest flights of sense-bound fantasy can picture; and yet there can be no question of injury to health or life. The student meets with horrible powers threatening life at every turn and from every side. It will even be possible for him to make use of certain forces and beings existing beyond physical perception, and the temptation is great to control these forces for the furtherance of personal and forbidden interests, or to employ them wrongly out of a deficient knowledge of the higher worlds. Some of these especially important experiences, for instance, the meeting with Guardian of the Threshold, will be described in the following chapters. Yet we must realize that the hostile powers are none the less present, even though we know nothing of them. It is true that in this case their relation to man is ordained by higher power, and that this relation alters when the human being consciously enters this world hitherto concealed from him. But at the same time his own existence is enhanced and the circle of his life enriched by a great and new field of experience. A real danger can only arise if the student, through impatience or arrogance, assumes too early a certain independence with regard to the experiences of the higher worlds; if he cannot wait to gain really sufficient insight into the supersensible laws. In these spheres, modesty and humility are far less empty words than in ordinary life. If the student possesses these qualities in the very best sense he may be certain that his ascent into the higher life will be achieved without danger to all that is commonly called health and life. Above all things, no disharmony must ensue between the higher experiences and the events and demands of every-day life. Man's task must be entirely sought for on this earth, and anyone desiring to shirk his earthly task and to escape into another world may be certain he will never reach his goal. Yet what the senses perceive is only part of the world, and it is in the spirit world that the beings dwell who express themselves in the facts of the physical world. Man must become a partaker of the spirit in order to carry its revelations into the physical world. He transforms the earth by implanting in it what he has ascertained in the spiritual world. That is his task. It is only because the physical world is dependent upon the spiritual, and because man can work upon earth, in a true sense, only if he is a participator in those worlds in which the creative forces lie concealed — only for these reasons should he have the desire to ascend to the higher worlds. No one approaching esoteric training with these sentiments, and resolved not to deviate for a moment from these prescribed directions, need fear the slightest danger. No one should allow the prospect of these dangers to deter him from esoteric training; it should rather act as a strong challenge to one and all to acquire those faculties which every true esoteric student must possess.

After these preliminary observations that should dispel any element of terror, a description of some of the so-called dangers will be given. It is true that great changes take place in the student's finer bodies, as described above. These changes are connected with certain processes in the development of the three fundamental forces of the soul, with willing, feeling, and thinking. Before esoteric training, these forces are subject to a connection ordained by higher cosmic laws. Man's willing, feeling and thinking are not arbitrary. A particular idea arising in the mind is attended by a particular feeling, according to natural laws; or it is followed by a resolution of the will in equally natural sequence. We enter a room, find it stuffy, and open the window. We hear our name called and follow the call. We are questioned and we answer. We perceive an ill-smelling object and experience a feeling of disgust. These are simple connections between thinking, feeling, and willing. When we survey human life we find that everything is built up on such connections. Indeed, life is not termed normal unless such a connection, founded on the laws of human nature, is observed between thinking, feeling and willing. It would be found contrary to these laws if the sight of an ill-smelling object gave anyone pleasure, or if anyone, on being questioned, did not answer. The success anticipated from a right education or fitting instruction is based upon the presumption that a connection between thinking, feeling, and willing, corresponding to human nature, can be established in the pupil. Certain ideas are conveyed to him on the assumption that they will be associated, in regular fashion, with his feelings and volitions.

All this arises from the fact that in the finer soul-vehicles of man the central points of the three forces — thinking, feeling and willing — are connected with each other according to laws. This connection in the finer soul organism has its counterpart in the coarser physical body. In the latter, too, the organs of will are connected according to laws with those of thinking and feeling. A particular thought, therefore, inevitably evokes a feeling or an activity of will. In the course of higher development, the threads interconnecting the three fundamental forces are severed. At first this severance occurs only within the finer soul organism, but at a still higher stage the separation extends also to the physical body. It is a fact that in higher spiritual development the brain divides into three separate parts. This separation is not physically perceptible in the ordinary way, nor can it be demonstrated by the keenest instruments. Yet it occurs, and the clairvoyant has means of observing it. The brain of the higher clairvoyant divides into three independently active entities: The thought-brain, the feeling-brain, and the will-brain.

Thus the organs of thinking, feeling, and willing become individualized; their connection henceforth is not maintained by laws inherent in themselves, but must be managed by the awakened higher consciousness of the individual. This, then, is the change which the student observes coming over him: that no connection arises of itself between an idea and a feeling or a will-impulse, unless he himself provides one. No impulse urges him from thought to action unless he himself in freedom give rise to this impulse. He can henceforth confront, devoid of feeling, a fact which before his training would have filled him with glowing love or bitter hatred; and he can remain impassive at the thought which formerly would have spurred him on to action, as though of its own accord. He can perform actions through resolutions of the will for which there is not the slightest reason for anyone not having undergone esoteric training. The student's great achievement is the attainment of complete mastery over the combined activity of the three soul forces; but at the same time the responsibility for this activity is placed entirely in his own hands.

It is only through this transformation of his being that the student can enter consciously into relation with certain supersensible forces and beings, for his own soul forces are related to certain fundamental forces of the world. The force, for instance, inherent in the will can affect definite things and the beings of the higher worlds, and also perceive them; but it can only do so when liberated from its connection with thinking and feeling within the soul. The moment this connection is severed, the activity of the will can be exteriorized. The same applies to the forces of thinking and feeling. A feeling of hatred sent out by a person is visible to the clairvoyant as a fine luminous cloud of special coloring; and the clairvoyant can ward off this feeling of hatred, just as an ordinary person wards off a physical blow that is aimed at him. In the supersensible world, hatred becomes a visible phenomenon, but the clairvoyant can only perceive it in so far as he is able to project outwards the force lying in his feeling, just as the ordinary person directs outwards the receptive faculty of his eye. And what is said of hatred applies also to far more important phenomena of the physical world. The student can enter into conscious intercourse with them, thanks to the liberation of the fundamental forces of his soul.

Through the separation of the forces of thinking, feeling, and willing, the possibility of a three-fold aberration arises for anyone neglecting the injunctions given by esoteric science. Such an aberration can occur if the connecting threads are severed before the higher consciousness is sufficiently advanced to hold the reins and guide properly the separated forces into free and harmoniously combined activity. For as a rule, the three human soul-forces are not equally advanced in their development at any given period of life. In one person, thinking is ahead of feeling and willing; in a second, another soul-force has the upper hand over its companions. As long as the connection between the soul-forces is maintained as established by higher cosmic laws, no injurious irregularity, in a higher sense, can occur through the predominance of one force or another. Predominating will, for instance, is prevented by the leveling influence of thinking and feeling from lapsing into any particular excesses. When, however, a person of such predominating will undertakes esoteric training, feeling and thinking cease to exert their regular influence on the will when the latter constantly presses on to great exertions of power If, then, such a person is not sufficiently advanced to control completely the higher consciousness and himself restore harmony, the will pursues its own unbridled way, continually overpowering its possessor. Feeling and thought lapse into complete impotence; the individual is scourged by his over-mastering will. A violent nature is the result, rushing from one unbridled action to another.

A second deviation occurs when feeling unduly shakes off its proper control. A person inclined to the revering of others may then diverge into unlimited dependence, to the extent of losing all personal will and thoughts. Instead of higher knowledge, the most pitiful vacuity and feebleness would become such a person's lot. Or, in the case of such inordinate predominance of the feeling life, a person with an inclination toward religious devotion can sink into the most degenerate welter.

The third evil is found when thought predominates, resulting in a contemplative nature, hostile to life and locked up within itself. The world, for such people, has no further importance save that it provides them with objects for satisfying their boundless thirst for wisdom. No thought ever moves them to an action or a feeling. They appear everywhere as cold and unfeeling creatures. They flee from every contact with the things of ordinary life as though from something exciting their aversion, or which, at any rate, had lost all meaning for them.

These are the three ways of error into which the student can stray: (1) exuberant violence of will, (2) sentimental emotionalism, and (3) cold, loveless striving for wisdom. For outward observation, and also from the ordinary (materialistic) medical standpoint, anyone thus gone astray is hardly distinguishable (especially in degree) from an insane or, at least, a highly neurasthenic person. Of course, the student must not resemble these. It is essential for him that the three fundamental soul-forces, thinking, feeling, and willing, should have undergone harmonious development before being released from their inherent connection and subordinated to the awakened higher consciousness. For once a mistake is made and one of the soul-forces falls a prey to unbridled excess, the higher soul comes into existence as a miscarriage. The unrestrained force pervades the individual's entire personality, and for a long time there can be no question of the balance being restored. What appears to be a harmless characteristic as long as its possessor is without esoteric training, namely, a predominance of thinking or feeling or willing, is so intensified in an esoteric student that the universally human element, indispensable for life, becomes obscured.

Yet a really serious danger cannot threaten the student until he has acquired the ability to include in his waking consciousness the experiences forthcoming during sleep. As long as there is only the question of illumination of the intervals of sleep, the life of the senses, regulated by universal cosmic laws, reacts during the waking hours on the disturbed equilibrium of the soul, tending to restore the balance. That is why it is so essential that the waking life of the student should be in every respect regular and healthy. The more capable he is of meeting the demands made by the outer world upon a healthy, sound constitution of body, soul, and spirit, the better it is for him. On the other hand, it may be very bad for him if his ordinary waking life affects him in an exciting or irritating way, that is, if destructive or hampering influences of outer life affect him in addition to the great changes taking place in his inner self. He must seek to find everything corresponding to his powers and faculties which can lead him into undisturbed, harmonious communion with his surroundings, while avoiding everything detrimental to this harmony — everything that brings unrest and feverish haste into his life. And here it is not so much a question of casting off this unrest and haste in an external sense, but much more of taking care that thoughts, feelings, intentions, and bodily health are not thereby exposed to continual fluctuation. All this is not so easy for the student to accomplish as it was before esoteric training, for the higher experiences now playing into his life act upon his entire existence. Should anything within these higher experiences not be as it should, the irregularity continues lying in wait for him and may at every turn throw him off the right path. For this reason the student should omit nothing which can secure for him unfailing mastery over his whole being. He should never be found wanting in presence of mind or in calm penetration of all situations of life. In the main, a genuine esoteric training gives rise of itself to all these qualities, and as it progresses the student only becomes acquainted with the dangers while simultaneously and at the right moment acquiring the full power to rout them from the field.

The Guardian of the Threshold

The important experiences marking the student's ascent into the higher worlds include his meeting with the Guardian of the Threshold. Strictly speaking, there are two Guardians: a lesser and a greater. The student meets the lesser Guardian when the threads connecting willing, feeling, and thinking within the finer astral and etheric bodies begin to loosen, in the way described in the foregoing chapter. The greater Guardian is encountered when this sundering of the connections extends to the physical parts of the body, that is, at first to the brain. The lesser Guardian is a sovereign being. He does not come into existence, as far as the student is concerned, until the latter has reached the requisite stage of development. Only some of his most important characteristics can here be indicated.

The attempt will now be made to describe in narrative form this meeting with the lesser Guardian of the Threshold, as a result of which the student learns that his thinking, feeling, and willing have become released within him from their inherent connection.

A truly terrible spectral being confronts him, and he will need all the presence of mind and faith in the security of his path which he has had ample opportunity to acquire in the course of his previous training.

The Guardian proclaims his signification somewhat in the following words: "Hitherto, powers invisible to thyself watched over thee. They saw to it that in the course of thy lives each of thy good deeds brought its reward, and each of thine evil deeds was attended by its evil results. Thanks to their influence thy character formed itself out of thy life-experiences and thy thoughts. They were the instruments of thy destiny. They ordained that measure of joy and pain allotted to thee in thine incarnations, according to thy conduct in lives gone by. They ruled over thee as the all-embracing law of karma. These powers will now partly release thee from their constraining influence; and henceforth must thou accomplish for thyself a part of the work which hitherto they performed for thee. Destiny struck thee many a hard blow in the past. Thou knewest not why. Each blow was the consequence of a harmful deed in a bygone lie. Thou foundest joy and gladness, and thou didst take them as they came. They, too, were the fruits of former deeds. Thy character shows many a beautiful side, and many an ugly flaw. Thou hast thyself to thank for both, for they are the result of thy previous experiences and thoughts. These were till now unknown to thee; their effects alone were made manifest. The karmic powers, however, beheld all thy deeds in former lives, and all thy most secret thoughts and feelings, and determined accordingly thy present self and thy present mode of life. But now all the good and evil sides of thy bygone lives shall be revealed to thee. Hitherto they were interwoven with thine own being; they were in thee and thou couldst not see them, even as thou canst not behold thine own brain with physical eyes. But now they become released from thee; they detach themselves from thy personality. They assume an independent form which thou canst see even as thou beholdest the stones and plants of the outer world. And . . . I am that very being who shaped my body out of thy good and evil achievements. My spectral form is woven out of thine own life's record. Till now thou hast borne me invisibly within thee, and it was well that this was so; for the wisdom of thy destiny, though concealed from thee, could thus work within thee, so that the hideous stains on my form should be blotted out. Now that I have come forth from within thee, that concealed wisdom, too, has departed from thee. It will pay no further heed to thee; it will leave the work in thy hands alone. I must become a perfect and glorious being, or fall a prey to corruption; and should this occur, I would drag thee also down with me into a dark and corrupt world. If thou wouldst avoid this, then thine own wisdom must become great enough to undertake the task of that other, concealed wisdom, which has departed from thee. As a form visible to thyself I will never for an instant leave thy side, once thou hast crossed my Threshold. And in future, whenever thou dost act or think wrongly thou wilt straightway perceive thy guilt as a hideous, demoniacal distortion of my form. Only when thou hast made good all thy bygone wrongs and hast so purified thyself that all further evil is, for thee, a thing impossible, only then will my being have become transformed into radiant beauty. Then, too, shall I again become united with thee for the welfare of thy future activity.

"Yet my Threshold is fashioned out of all the timidity that remains in thee, out of all the dread of the strength needed to take full responsibility for all thy thoughts and actions. As long as there remains in thee a trace of fear of becoming thyself the guide of thine own destiny, just so long will this Threshold lack what still remains to be built into it. And as long as a single stone is found missing, just so long must thou remain standing as though transfixed; or else stumble. Seek not, then, to cross this Threshold until thou dost feel thyself entirely free from fear and ready for the highest responsibility. Hitherto I only emerged from thy personality when death recalled thee from an earthly life; but even then my form was veiled from thee. Only the powers of destiny who watched over thee beheld me and could thus, in the intervals between death and a new birth, build in thee, in accordance with my appearance, that power and capacity thanks to which thou couldst labor in a new earth life at the beautifying of my form, for thy welfare and progress. It was I, too, whose imperfection ever and again constrained the powers of destiny to lead thee back to a new incarnation upon earth. I was present at the hour of thy death, and it was on my account that the Lords of Karma ordained thy reincarnation. And it is only by thus unconsciously transforming me to complete perfection in ever recurring earthly lives that thou couldst have escaped the powers of death and passed over into immortality united with me.

"Visible do I thus stand before thee today, just as I shave ever stood invisible beside thee in the hour of death. When thou shalt have crossed my Threshold, thou wilt enter those realms to which thou hast hitherto only had access after physical death. Thou dost now enter them with full knowledge, and henceforth as thou wanderest outwardly visible upon the earth thou wilt at the same time wander in the kingdom of death, that is, in the kingdom of life eternal. I am indeed the Angel of Death; but I am at the same time the bearer of a higher life without end. Through me thou wilt die with thy body still living, to be reborn into an imperishable existence.

"Into this kingdom thou art now entering; thou wilt meet beings that are supersensible, and happiness will be thy lot. But I myself must provide thy first acquaintance with that world, and I am thine own creation. Formerly I drew my life from thine; but now thou hast awakened me to a separate existence so that I stand before thee as the visible gauge of thy future deeds — perhaps, too, as thy constant reproach. Thou hast formed me, but by so doing thou hast undertaken, as thy duty, to transform me."

(It will be gathered from the above that the Guardian of the Threshold is an (astral) figure, revealing itself to the student's awakened higher sight; and it is to this supersensible encounter that spiritual science conducts him. It is a lower magical process to make the Guardian of the Threshold physically visible also. That was attained by producing a cloud of fine substance, a kind of frankincense resulting from a particular mixture of a number of substances. The developed power of the magician is then able to mould the frankincense into shape, animating it with the still unredeemed karma of the individual. Such physical phenomena are no longer necessary for those sufficiently prepared for the higher sight; and besides this, anyone who sees, without adequate preparation, his unredeemed karma appear before his eyes as a living creature would run the risk of straying into evil byways. Bulwer Lytton's Zanoni contains in novel form a description of the Guardian of the Threshold.)

What is here indicated in narrative form must not be understood in the sense of an allegory, but as an experience of the highest possible reality befalling the esoteric student.

The Guardian must warn him not to go a step further unless he feels in himself the strength to fulfill the demands made in the above speech. However horrible the form assumed by the Guardian, it is only the effect of the student's own past life, his own character risen out of him into independent existence. This awakening is brought about by the separation of will, thought, and feeling. To feel for the first time that one has oneself called a spiritual being into existence is in itself an experience of deepest significance. The student's preparation must aim at enabling him to endure the terrible sight without a trace of timidity and, at the moment of the meeting, to feel his strength so increased that he can undertake fully conscious the responsibility for transforming and beautifying the Guardian.

If successful, this meeting with the Guardian results in the student's next physical death being an entirely different event from the death as he knew it formerly. He experiences death consciously by laying aside the physical body as one discards a garment that is worn out or perhaps rendered useless through a sudden rent. Thus his physical death is of special importance only for those living with him, whose perception is still restricted to the world of the senses. For them the student dies; but for himself nothing of importance is changed in his whole environment. The entire supersensible world stood open to him before his death, and it is this same world that now confronts him after death.

The Guardian of the Threshold is also connected with other matters. The person belongs to a family, a nation, a race; his activity in this world depends upon his belonging to some such community. His individual character is also connected with it. The conscious activity of individual persons by no means exhausts everything to be reckoned with in a family, a nation, or a race. Besides their character, families, nations, and races have also their destiny. For persons restricted to their senses these things remain mere general ideas; and the materialistic thinker, in his prejudice, will look down with contempt on the spiritual scientist when he hears that for him, family and national character, lineal or racial destiny, are vested in beings just as real as the personality in which the character and destiny of the individual man are vested. The spiritual scientist becomes acquainted with higher worlds of which the separate personalities are members, just as arms and legs are members of the human being. Besides the separate individuals, a very real family and national group soul and racial spirit is at work in the life of a family, a people, or a race. Indeed, in a certain sense the separate individuals are merely the executive organs of these family group souls, racial spirits, and so on. It is nothing but the truth to say, for instance, that a national group soul makes use of each individual man belonging to that nation for the execution of some work. The group soul of a people does not descend into physical reality but dwells in the higher worlds and, in order to work in the physical world, makes use of the physical organs of each individual human being. In a higher sense, it is like an architect making use of workmen for executing the details of a building. In the truest sense, everyone receives his allotted task from his family, national, or racial group soul. Now, the ordinary person is by no means initiated into the higher design of his work. He joins unconsciously in the tasks of his people and of his race. From the moment the student meets the Guardian, he must not only know his own tasks, but must knowingly collaborate in those of his folk, his race. Every extension of his horizon necessarily enlarges the scope of his duties. What actually happens is that the student adds a new body to his finer soul-body. He puts on a second garment. Hitherto he found his way through the world with the coverings enveloping his personality; and what he had to accomplish for his community, his nation, his race, was directed by higher spirits who made use of his personality.

And now, a further revelation made to him by the Guardian of the Threshold is that henceforth these spirits will withdraw their guiding hand from him. He must step out of the circle of his community. Yet as an isolated personality he would become hardened in himself and decline into ruin, did he not, himself, acquire those powers which are vested in the national and racial spirits. Many, no doubt, will say: "Oh, I have entirely freed myself from all lineal and racial connections; I only want to be a human being and nothing but a human being." To these one must reply: "Who, then, brought you to this freedom? Was it not your family who placed you in the world where you now stand? Have you not your lineage, your nation, your race to thank for being what you are? They have brought you up. And if now, exalted above all prejudices, you are one of the light-bringers and benefactors of your stock and even of your race, it is to their up-bringing that you owe it. Yes, even when you say you are `nothing but a human being,' even the fact that you have become such a personality you owe to the spirits of your communities." Only the esoteric student learns what it means to be entirely cut off from his family, national, or racial spirit. He alone realizes, through personal experience, the insignificance of all such education in respect of the life now confronting him. For everything inculcated by education completely melts away when the threads binding will, thought, and feeling are severed. He looks back on the result of all his previous education as he might on a house crumbling away brick by brick, which he must now rebuild in a new form. And again, it is more than a mere symbolical expression to say that when the Guardian has enunciated his first statement, there arises from the spot where he stands a whirlwind which extinguishes all those spiritual lights that have hitherto illumined the pathway of his life. Utter darkness, relieved only by the rays issuing from the Guardian himself, unfolds before the student. And out of this darkness resounds the Guardian's further admonition: "Step not across my Threshold until thou dost clearly realize that thou wilt thyself illumine the darkness ahead of thee; take not a single step forward until thou art positive that thou hast sufficient oil in thine own lamp. The lamps of the guides whom thou hast hitherto followed will now no longer be available to thee." At these words, the student must turn and glance backward. The Guardian of the Threshold now draws aside a veil which till now had concealed deep life-mysteries. The family, national, and racial spirits are revealed to the student in their full activity, so that he perceives clearly on the one hand, how he has hitherto been led, and no less clearly on the other hand, that he will henceforward no longer enjoy this guidance. That is the second warning received at the Threshold from its Guardian.

Without preparation, no one could endure the sight of what has here been indicated. But the higher training which makes it possible at all for the student to advance up to the Threshold simultaneously puts him in a position to find the necessary strength at the right moment. Indeed, the training can be so harmonious in its nature that the entry into the higher life is relieved of everything of an agitating or tumultuous character. His experience at the Threshold will then be attended by a premonition of that felicity which is to provide the keynote of his newly awakened life. The feeling of a new freedom will outweigh all other feelings; and attended by this feeling, his new duties and responsibilities will appear as something which man, at a particular stage of life, must needs take upon himself.

Life and Death: The Greater Guardian of the Threshold

It has been described in the foregoing chapter how significant for the human being is his meeting with the so-called lesser Guardian of the Threshold by virtue of the fact that he becomes aware of confronting a supersensible being whom he has himself brought into existence, and whose body consists of the hitherto invisible results of the student's own actions, feelings, and thoughts. These unseen forces have become the cause of his destiny and his character, and he realizes how he himself founded the present in the past. He can understand why his inner self, now standing to a certain extent revealed before him, includes particular inclinations and habits, and he can also recognize the origin of certain blows of fate that have befallen him. He perceives why he loves one thing and hates another; why one thing makes him happy and another unhappy. Visible life is explained by the invisible causes. The essential facts of life, too — health and illness, birth and death — unveil themselves before his gaze. He observes how before his birth he wove the causes which necessarily led to his return into life. Henceforth he knows that being within himself which is fashioned with all its imperfections in the visible world, and which can only be brought to its final perfection in this same visible world. For in no other world is an opportunity given to build up and complete this being. Moreover, he recognizes that death cannot sever him forever from this world; for he says to himself: "Once I came into this world because, being what I was, I needed the life it provided to acquire qualities unattainable in any other world. And I must remain bound to this world until I have developed within myself everything that can here be gained. I shall some day become a useful collaborator in another world only by acquiring all the requisite faculties in this physical world."

Thanks to his insight into the supersensible world, the initiate gains a better knowledge and appreciation of the true value of visible nature than was possible before his higher training; and this may be counted among his most important experiences. Anyone not possessing this insight and perhaps therefore imagining the supersensible regions to be infinitely more valuable, is likely to underestimate the physical world. Yet the possessor of this insight knows that without experience in visible reality he would be totally powerless in that other invisible reality. Before he can live in the latter he must have the requisite faculties and instruments which can only be acquired in the visible world. Consciousness in the invisible world is not possible without spiritual sight, but this power of vision in the higher world is gradually developed through experience in the lower. No one can be born in the spiritual world with spiritual eyes without having first developed them in the physical world, any more than a child could be born with physical eyes, had they not already been formed within the mother's womb.

From this standpoint it will also be readily understood why the Threshold to the supersensible world is watched over by a Guardian. In no case may real insight into those regions be permitted to anyone lacking the requisite faculties; therefore, when at the hour of death anyone enters the other world while still incompetent to work in it, the higher experiences are shrouded from him until he is fit to behold them.

When the student enters the supersensible world, life acquires quite a new meaning for him; he discerns in the physical world the seed-ground of a higher world, so that in a certain sense the higher will appear defective without the lower. Two outlooks are opened before him; the first into the past and the second into the future. His vision extends to a past in which this physical world was not yet existent; for he has long since discarded the prejudice that the supersensible world was developed out of the sense-world. He knows that the former existed first, and that out of it everything physical was evolved. He sees that he himself belonged to a supersensible world before coming for the first time into this sense-world. But this pristine supersensible world needed to pass through the sense-world, for without this passage its further evolution would not have been possible. It can only pursue its course when certain things will have developed requisite faculties within the realm of the senses. These beings are none other than human beings. They owe their present life to an imperfect stage of spiritual existence and are being led, even within this stage, to that perfection which will make them fit for further work in the higher world. At this point the outlook is directed into the future. A higher stage of the supersensible world is discerned which will contain the fruits matured in the sense-world. The sense-world as such will be overcome, but its results will be embodied in a higher world.

The existence of disease and death in the sense-world is thus explained. Death merely expresses the fact that the original supersensible world reached a point beyond which it could not progress by itself. Universal death must needs have overtaken it, had it not received a fresh life-impulse. Thus this new life has evolved into a battle with universal death. From the remnants of a dying, rigid world there sprouted the seeds of a new one. That is why we have death and life in the world. The decaying portion of the old world adheres to the new life blossoming from it, and the process of evolution moves slowly. This comes to expression most clearly in man himself. The sheath he bears is gathered from the preserved remnants of the old world, and within this sheath the germ of that being is matured which will live in the future.

Thus man is twofold: mortal and immortal. The mortal is in its last, the immortal in its first stage. But it is only within this twofold world, which finds its expression in the sense-world, that he can acquire the requisite faculties to lead the world to immortality. Indeed, this task is precisely to gather the fruits of the mortal for the immortal. And as he glances at himself as the result of his own work in the past he cannot but say: "I have in me the elements of a decaying world. They are at work in me, and I can only break their power little by little, thanks to the new immortal elements coming to life within me." This is the path leading man from death to life. Could he but speak to himself with full consciousness at the hour of his death, he would say: "The perishing world was my task-master. I am now dying as the result of the entire past in which I am enmeshed. Yet the soil of mortal life has matured the seeds of immortal life. I carry them with me into another world. If it had merely depended on the past, I could never have been born. The life of the past came to an end with birth. Life in the sense-world is wrested from universal death by the newly formed life-germ. The time between birth and death is merely an expression for the sum of values wrested from the dying past by the new life; and illness is nothing but the continued effect of the dying portions of the past."

In the above the answer will be found to the question why man works his way only gradually through error and imperfection to the good and true. His actions, feelings, and thoughts are at first dominated by the perishing and the mortal. The latter gave rise to his sense-organs. For this reason, these organs and all things activating them are doomed to perish The imperishable will not be found in the instincts, impulses, and passions, or in the organs belonging to them, but only in the work produced by these organs. Man must extract from the perishable everything that can be extracted, and this work alone will enable him to discard the background out of which he has grown, and which finds its expression in the physical sense-world.

Thus the first Guardian confronts man as the counterpart of his two-fold nature in which perishable and imperishable are blended; and it stands clearly proved how far removed he still is from attaining that sublime luminous figure which may again dwell in the pure, spiritual world. The extent to which he is entangled in the physical sense-world is exposed to the student's view. The presence of instincts, impulses, desires, egotistical wishes and all forms of selfishness, and so forth, expresses itself in this entanglement, as it does further in his membership in a race, a nation, and so forth; for peoples and races are but steps leading to pure humanity. A race or a nation stands so much the higher, the more perfectly its members express the pure, ideal human type, the further they have worked their way from the physical and perishable to the supersensible and imperishable. The evolution of man through the incarnations in ever higher national and racial forms is thus a process of liberation. Man must finally appear in harmonious perfection. In a similar way, the pilgrimage through ever purer forms of morality and religion is a perfecting process; for every moral stage retains the passion for the perishable beside the seeds of an ideal future.

Now in the Guardian of the Threshold as described above, the product of the past is manifest, containing only so many seeds of the future as could be planted in the course of time. Yet everything that can be extracted from the sense-world must be carried into the supersensible world. Were man to bring with him only what had been woven into his counterpart out of the past, his earthly task would remain but partially accomplished. For this reason the lesser Guardian of the Threshold is joined, after a time, by the greater Guardian. The meeting with the second Guardian will again be described in narrative form.

When the student has recognized all the elements from which he must liberate himself, his way is barred by a sublime luminous being whose beauty is difficult to describe in the words of human language. This encounter takes place when the sundering of the organs of thinking, feeling, and willing extends to the physical body, so that their reciprocal connection is no longer regulated by themselves but by the higher consciousness, which has now entirely liberated itself from physical conditions. The organs of thinking, feeling and willing will then be controlled from supersensible regions as instruments in the power of the human soul. The latter, thus liberated from all physical bonds, is now confronted by the second Guardian of the Threshold who speaks as follows:

"Thou hast released thyself from the world of the senses. Thou hast won the right to become a citizen of the supersensible world, whence thine activity can now be directed. For thine own sake, thou dost no longer require thy physical body in its present form. If thine intention were merely to acquire the faculties necessary for life in the supersensible world, thou needest no longer return to the sense-world. But now behold me. See how sublimely I tower above all that thou hast made of thyself thus far. Thou hast attained thy present degree of perfection thanks to the faculties thou wert able to develop in the sense-world as long as thou wert still confined to it. But now a new era is to begin, in which thy liberated powers must be applied to further work in the world of the senses. Hitherto thou hast sought only thine own release, but now, having thyself become free, thou canst go forth as a liberator of thy fellows. Until today thou hast striven as an individual, but now seek to coordinate thyself with the whole, so that thou mayst bring into the supersensible world not thyself alone, but all things else existing in the world of the senses. Thou wilt some day be able to unite with me, but I cannot be blessed so long as others remain unredeemed. As a separate freed being, thou wouldst fain enter at once the kingdom of the supersensible; yet thou wouldst be forced to look down on the still unredeemed beings in the physical world, having sundered thy destiny from theirs, although thou and they are inseparably united. Ye all did perforce descend into the sense-world to gather powers needed for a higher world. To separate thyself from thy fellows would mean to abuse those very powers which thou couldst not have developed save in their company. Thou couldst not have descended had they not done so; and without them the powers needed for supersensible existence would fail thee. Thou must now share with thy fellows the powers which, together with them, thou didst acquire. I shall therefore bar thine entry into the higher regions of the supersensible world so long as thou hast not applied all the powers thou hast acquired to the liberation of thy companions. With the powers already at thy disposal thou mayst sojourn in the lower regions of the supersensible world; but I stand before the portal of the higher regions as the Cherub with the fiery sword before Paradise, and I bar thine entrance as long as powers unused in the sense-world still remain in thee. And if thou dost refuse to apply thy powers in this world, others will come who will not refuse; and a higher supersensible world will receive all the fruits of the sense-world, while thou wilt lose from under thy feet the very ground in which thou wert rooted. The purified world will develop above and beyond thee, and thou shalt be excluded from it. Thus thou wouldst tread the black path, while the others from whom thou didst sever thyself tread the white path."

With these words the greater Guardian makes his presence known soon after the meeting with the first Guardian has taken place. The initiate knows full well what is in store for him if he yields to the temptation of a premature abode in the supersensible world. An indescribable splendor shines forth from the second Guardian of the Threshold; union with him looms as a far distant ideal before the soul's vision. Yet there is also the certitude that this union will not be possible until all the powers afforded by this world are applied to the task of its liberation and redemption. By fulfilling the demands of the higher light-being the initiate will contribute to the liberation of the human race. He lays his gifts on the sacrificial altar of humanity. Should he prefer his own premature elevation into the supersensible world, the stream of human evolution will flow over and past him. After his liberation he can gain no new powers from the world of the senses; and if he places his work at the world's disposal it will entail his renouncement of any further benefit for himself.

It does not follow that, when called upon to decide, anyone will naturally follow the white path. That depends entirely upon whether he is so far purified at the time of his decision that no trace of self-seeking makes this prospect of felicity appear desirable. For the allurements here are the strongest possible; whereas on the other side no special allurements are evident. Here nothing appeals to his egotism. The gift he receives in the higher regions of the supersensible world is nothing that comes to him, but only something that flows from him, that is, love for the world and for his fellows. Nothing that egotism desires is denied upon the black path, for the latter provides, on the contrary, for the complete gratification of egotism, and will not fail to attract those desiring merely their own felicity, for it is indeed the appropriate path for them. No one therefore should expect the occultists of the white path to give him instruction for the development of his own egotistical self. They do not take the slightest interest in the felicity of the individual man. Each can attain that for himself, and it is not the task of the white occultists to shorten the way; for they are only concerned with the development and liberation of all human beings and all creatures. Their instructions therefore deal only with the development of powers for collaboration in this work. Thus they place selfless devotion and self-sacrifice before all other qualities. They never actually refuse anyone, for even the greatest egotist can purify himself; but no one merely seeking an advantage for himself will ever obtain assistance from the white occultists. Even when they do not refuse their help, he, the seeker, deprives himself on the advantage resulting from their assistance. Anyone, therefore, really following the instructions of the good occultists will, upon crossing the Threshold, understand the demands of the greater Guardian; anyone, however, not following their instructions can never hope to reach the Threshold. Their instructions, if followed, produce good results or no results; for it is no part of their task to lead to egotistical felicity and a mere existence in the supersensible worlds. In fact, it becomes their duty to keep the student away from the supersensible world until he can enter it with the will for selfless collaboration.